CONTENTS

KU-646-891

PART 1: INTRODUCTION

PART 2: COUNTRY BY COUNTRY GUIDE

Teaching English Abroad

A fresh and fully up-to-date guide to teaching English around the world

Susan Griffith

VACATION WORK
PUBLICATIONS

This edition first published in Great Britain 2009 by
Crimson Publishing, a division of Crimson Business Ltd
Westminster House
Kew Road
Richmond
Surrey
TW9 2ND

First published 1991
Ninth edition 2009

© Susan Griffith
Revised by Hannah Adcock
The right of Susan Griffith to be identified as the author of this work has been asserted by her in
accordance with the Copyright, Designs and Patents Act, 1988.

A catalogue record for this book is available from the British Library.

ISBN 978 1 85458 440 3

Colour section photos 1, 3 and 4 and photos on p. 115 and p. 523 © Tom Grundy
(www.globalcitizen.co.uk).
Colour section photo 2 and photo on p.1 © Scott Banks, Granada English College, Nicaragua.

Printed and bound by Mega Printing, Turkey

PREFACE

Those of us who speak English as a first language tend to take for granted how universally dominant it has become. For several years in the run-up to the Beijing Games, masses of Olympics-related *Conversational English Readers* were distributed in China and Hong Kong. To take just one example, many young Slovaks work for international companies in which all communication is in English, so for them a facility for speaking English is even more important now than it was even a couple of years ago. English is the global language of pop songs, air traffic control, computer games and most of facebook.

An ability to teach the English language is the most globally mobile skill there is. Language institutes have opened in areas of the world once closed to EFL teachers from Ulaan Baatar in Mongolia to Nouakchott, capital of Mauritania, and in a thousand more familiar places from Crete to Caracas. On the one hand *Teaching English Abroad* is not aimed primarily at the professional teacher who already has access to a wide range of information on working abroad. Neither is it intended to encourage people to bluster their way into jobs abroad on the insufficient grounds that they are native speakers of the language. Between these two extremes, countless ordinary people have the appropriate backgrounds and personalities to become successful teachers of their native language. The beauty of English teaching is that it is accessible to so many.

No average profile of the travelling teacher can be identified. For this ninth edition, my excellent revisions editor Hannah and I have received enthusiastic feedback from many interesting world-roaming teachers, including one of the co-founders of a quirky English language bookshop on the Greek island of Santorini who did occasional teaching; an American entrepreneur who set up a language school in a small city in Nicaragua because of his devotion to re-building the country; a 60-something woman who in anticipation of being laid off from her job in computer programming decided to move to Vietnam to teach and learn the language; a widow who built up a client base of private students in Berlin; a young woman who found herself involved with a play called *The Superlative Vacuum Cleaner* while employed by a company in Tokyo that uses drama to teach kids; a man who got a job teaching in Israel after doing a Naomi Campbell impression at his interview; a teacher who was teaching in a fourth floor classroom in Chengdu when the big earthquake struck in May 2008 and survived along with all her students; an American who found a loophole for teaching legally in Portugal; and a former flight attendant from Manchester who decided to change direction by obtaining a TEFL certificate and teaching in the country that took her fancy, which turned out to be Latvia.

Note that the hundreds of language schools and teaching organisations around the world that submitted details of their teaching vacancies for 2009/10 have not paid to be included in this book. It is beyond the scope of the author and her team to investigate every school included so it is up to the readers to carry out their own checks on prospective employers.

In addition to all the hard information and listings of actual vacancies, this book tries to convey a flavour of life as a teacher abroad, by including first-hand descriptions of everything from banquet-induced hangovers in China to tips for renting accommodation in Buenos Aires. My aim from the first edition has been to make the information as concrete as possible, to cut the waffle. This book can be the stepping stone to a brilliant year or two of adventure abroad.

Susan Griffith
Cambridge
February 2009

ACKNOWLEDGMENTS

The new revised edition of *Teaching English Abroad* would not have been possible without the help of scores of English teachers and the people who employ them. They have generously shared their wealth of information, insights and anecdotes. As well as all the people who helped with the eight previous editions, the following should be thanked for their contributions, some of them substantial, to the research for this updated edition:

Kerstin Lindh Adcock, Jason Alavi, Jonathan Alderman, Anxela Fernandez Alonso, Dagmar Andrade, Tom Balfour, Scott Banks, Rachel Beebe, Peter Beech, Shelley Beyak, Will Brady, Nick Britton, Beth Buffam, Doug Burgess, Michael Buxton, Jain Cook, Kathy Cooper, Jessie Cox, Yvonne Dalhuijsen, Tristan Edmondson, Richard Ferguson, Cassandra Filio, Louise FitzGerald, Tom Grundy, Martin Haigh, Johanna Hannerfeldt Hoffert, Bradwell Jackson, Robert Jensky, Susannah Kerr, Jessie Levene, Gareth Lewis, Cathryn Lock, Ross McKay, Sam Meekings, Alicia Meta, Amanda Moody, Laetitia Mouillet, Steve Oakes, Barry O'Leary, Stelios Papantoniou, Ellen Parham, Fiona Passey, Yasmin Peiris, Genevieve Pierce, Dana Piffkova, Nina Purdey, Simon Redman, Ed Reinert, Heidi Resetarits, Laura Rich, Mary Rose, Penny Salter, Joe Scarangella, Evis Sferdelli, Kevin Sissons, Emily Sloane, Fatma Stanners, John Sydes, Rachid Taouil, Hajni Vancsik, Carlos Vega, Zayra Vogensen, Jimmy Warblegoose, Sylvia Weismiller, Stefan Wheaton, Andrew Whitmarsh, Vicky Williams.

With special thanks to Kayleigh Bohan

NOTE: While every effort has been made to ensure that the information contained in this book was correct at the time of going to press, details are bound to change, especially those pertaining to visa requirements for teachers, exchange rates and the conditions offered by the schools listed in the country directories. Readers are invited to write to Susan Griffith (Crimson Publishing, Westminster House, Kew Road, Richmond, Surrey TW9 2ND; s.griffith@ntlworld.com) with any comments or corrections. The best contributions will be rewarded with a free copy of the next edition or any other Crimson title of their choice.

PART 1
INTRODUCTION

INTRODUCTION
TRAINING
FINDING A JOB
PREPARATION
PROBLEMS

INTRODUCTION

One billion people speak or are trying to speak English, according to an estimate published by the British Council. It isn't clear who has counted them all, but it has been said that 300 million people are learning English at the present time. Nine-tenths of the world's electronically stored information is in English and a majority of the 50 million internet users communicate in the language you are reading at this moment. Mind-boggling statistics aside, the demand for instruction at all levels by people who speak English as their first language is enormous and set to continue increasing for the foreseeable future.

For whatever historical and economic reasons, English has come to dominate the world, the 21st-century sequel to colonialism. When the newly liberated nations of Eastern Europe sloughed off Russian, they turned in very large measure to English rather than to the other main European languages. Countries as far-flung as Cambodia, Namibia and Turkmenistan are busy making English one of the keystones of their educational systems. In German-speaking Switzerland, there are signs that English is replacing French as the preferred second language at school. English is the international language of science, of air traffic control and to a very large extent of trade and export. This is bad news for all those Germans, Swedes and French Canadians who would like to market their language skills to fund a short or long stay abroad. But it is English speakers, mainly from Britain, Ireland, North America and Australia/New Zealand who accidentally find themselves in possession of such a sought-after commodity.

SOME DEFINITIONS

The commonly used acronyms ELT, TEFL, TESL and TESOL can be confusing, especially since they are often used interchangeably. ELT, which stands for English Language Teaching, has come to be the mainstream expression in the UK (preferred by such august bodies as the University of Cambridge and by the publishers of the main journal in the field). But most people still refer to TEFL (pronounced 'teffle') – Teaching English as a Foreign Language. TESL stands for Teaching English as a Second Language, and TESOL stands for Teaching English to Speakers of Other Languages. English is learned as a foreign language by people who may need the language for certain purposes such as business or tourism but who live in countries where English has no official status. English is learned as a second language when it will have to be used for day-to-day life, for example by emigrants to the UK and the USA or by inhabitants of ex-colonies where English retains official status and may well be the medium of instruction in schools. (English is the official or joint-official language in 75 countries.)

As this book is for people who want to travel abroad to teach, the term TEFL is mainly used, along with ELT. Teachers of ESL are usually involved with multicultural education. In the USA, the vast majority of English language teaching is ESL because of the huge demand for English among those people who have emigrated to the USA and whose first language isn't English. Therefore the term ESL dominates in American contexts, even when (technically) EFL is meant.

The acronym TESOL covers both situations, yet it is not widely used apart from in institutions which favour the Trinity College London qualifications known as the Certificate and Licentiate Diploma in TESOL (see Training section later) and also in the context of the American organisation TESOL, which is the largest English teachers' organisation in the world – it claims to have more than 15,000 members.

There is no shortage of other acronyms in the world of TEFL. One of the main ones is ESP, which means English for Specific Purposes. ESP aims to match language teaching with the needs of various professions such as business, banking, tourism, medicine, science and technology, secretaries, etc. Business English is probably the most important in this category (and 'English for Shopping' as sometimes offered in Japan is the least important). Because a great many learners are motivated by a desire to use English at work, they want their teachers to adopt a functional rather than a structural approach. In other words they want to have lessons in which they can pretend to be telephoning a client, recommending, advising, agreeing, complaining and so on. They are certainly not interested in the subjunctive.

EAP stands for English for Academic Purposes, ie English at an advanced level taught to people who are planning to study at foreign universities. EAP is largely in the hands of government-funded programmes, such as those run by the British Council.

Note that the acronym TOEFL can cause confusion. The Test of English as a Foreign Language is a US-based standardised test administered to language learners. Passing a TOEFL exam is widely held to be a reliable indicator of how well an individual can communicate in English. The focus of many language schools abroad is to prepare candidates for the exam, and so may advertise for teachers with 'TOEFL' experience.

SCOPE OF OPPORTUNITIES

The range of locations and situations in which English is in demand covers an enormous spectrum. With TEFL booming in Laos and Kazakhstan, there can be few corners of the world which English has not penetrated. English has been called a 'barometer of Western influence' and there is only a handful of countries in the world which have rejected Western influence outright (eg Bhutan and North Korea) and which therefore have no call for EFL teachers. More important nations with their own native English-speaking population (such as India) are also not promising destinations for the aspiring teacher.

Many years have passed since the arrival of the single European market, which precipitated the greatest expansion of the English language that has ever been seen in Europe's history. There has been an enormous increase in demand – especially from companies and professionals eager to participate in an integrated Europe. One German-based multinational has gone so far as to decree that all operations will be conducted in English. The field of teaching English to young children is especially flourishing in Mediterranean and Pacific Rim countries. The attraction of European Union (EU) countries for British and Irish teachers is enhanced by the fact that they have the legal right to work there.

The kinds of people who want to learn English are as numerous as the places in which they live. The Asian economic crisis a few years ago prompted a decline in the number of 'leisure students', people attending English classes simply for pleasure; yet the market has recovered amazingly quickly. The area of the industry which seems to be booming almost everywhere is the teaching of children (known as Young Learners in the trade). Kids as young as 3 years are being sent to private English classes to improve their career prospects.

There are dozens of reasons why people around the world sign up for private English lessons:

- A Taiwanese student dreams of studying at UCLA
- A Polish bus driver, proud to be from a member state of the EU, wants to work in Denmark where he will be able to communicate in English

- The wife of the Peruvian ambassador in Islamabad wants to be able to speak English at official functions
- A Greek secondary school student has to pass her English exams in order to proceed to the next year and, like most of her classmates, attends a private tutorial college for English lessons
- A Siberian worker associates English with the language of freedom and liberalism
- A Turkish youth wants to be able to flirt with tourists from northern Europe
- A Mexican waiter wants to get a job in the Acapulco Hilton
- A Saudi engineer has to be able to read reports and manuals in English for his job.

The list is open-ended, and prospects for hopeful teachers are therefore excellent. There are also hundreds of international schools throughout the world where English is the medium of instruction

for all subjects and there may be specific EFL vacancies. These will be of most interest to certified teachers who wish to work abroad.

However, the situation isn't all rosy for the prospective teacher. As the profile of the English language has risen, so has the profile of the profession which teaches it, and the number of qualified and experienced English teachers has increased along with the rise in demand. The phenomenal explosion in the availability of training courses means that a much higher proportion of job-seekers has a TEFL certificate than was the case a decade ago, and (quite rightly) foreign language schools are becoming more selective when hiring staff.

People who cruise into a country expecting to be hired as an EFL teacher simply on the basis of being a native English speaker are in most cases (though not quite all) in for a nasty shock. Employers at all levels will ask for evidence of the ability to teach their language or at least a university degree as proof of a sound educational background. Certainly without a degree, a TEFL qualification or any relevant experience, the scope of opportunities shrinks drastically.

WHO IS ELIGIBLE TO TEACH?

Anyone who can speak English fluently and has a lively positive personality has a fighting chance of finding an opening as a teacher somewhere. Geordies, Tasmanians and Alabamans have all been known to be hired as English teachers (not to mention Norwegians and North Africans), though most employers favour native speakers of English without a heavy regional accent. Depending on the economic and cultural orientation of a country, schools will prefer British English (what the Director-General of the British Council likes to call 'standard English') or North American English. For obvious geopolitical reasons Europe and Africa prefer Britain while Latin America and the Far East prefer the USA. However, many countries don't have a preference, for example Indonesia and Turkey. Clear diction is usually more important than accent.

English language teaching is an industry which is seldom regulated, giving rise to a host of cowboy schools, which are mentioned (usually disparagingly) throughout this book. The other side of the coin is the proliferation of cowboy teachers, who have no feel for language, no interest in their pupils and no qualms about ripping them off. The issue of qualifications must be considered carefully. It is obviously unwise to assume that fluency in English is a sufficient qualification to turn someone into an EFL teacher. Many experienced teachers of English strongly feel that untrained teachers do a disservice both to their pupils and to their language, and most books and journals about language teaching are unanimous in their condemnation of such amateurs. Yet there are some excellent teachers who have learned how to teach by practising rather than by studying. Certainly anyone who is serious about travelling and teaching English should turn to the relevant chapter to consider the training options.

For certain kinds of teaching jobs, a background in business and commerce might be far more useful than any paper qualifications in teaching. Therefore we have not excluded the unqualified teacher-traveller from our account. As long as they take their responsibilities seriously and bear in mind that their pupils have entrusted them with significant quantities of time and money to help them learn, they need not bring the EFL profession into disrepute. Some untrained teachers we talked to during the research for this book found the responsibility so unnerving that they promptly enrolled in a TEFL course before unleashing themselves on an unsuspecting language-learning public.

Non-native speakers should not assume that their services will not be in demand outside their home countries. **Richard Ridha Guellala** was born in the Netherlands, raised in Tunisia and partly educated in England, and now has one of the most highly respected qualifications in TEFL, the Cambridge Diploma. While teaching in Thailand, he wrote:

Most non-native speakers think that a position as an EFL teacher is impossible for them. However I came to the conclusion that even unqualified non-native speakers are often hired by Asian schools, as long as they project a professional image during the interview, speak clearly, are well groomed, know the basics of English grammar and are fluent in the language. Scandinavians and Dutch are sometimes even more successful in finding teaching jobs at top schools than native speakers. True, we non-native speakers possess a rather 'heavy' or 'funny' accent but, believe it or not, some Asian employers favour our accents to the native speaker's because we speak more slowly and use very simple basic vocabulary.

At an extreme opposite from the casual teacher-traveller is the teacher who makes ELT a career. Only a minority of people teaching English abroad are professional teachers. Career prospects in ELT are in fact not very bright. After teachers have achieved a certain level of training and experience, they can aspire to work for International House and then for the British Council. From there, they might become a director of studies at a private language institute, though are unlikely to become a director unless their primary interest is business and administration.

An increasing number of early-retired and other mature people are becoming interested in teaching English abroad for a year or two. Although it may be true that in certain contexts, language institutes are more inclined to employ a bright young graduate, if only for reasons of image, there are plenty of others who will value maturity, especially the growing number of establishments that specialise in teaching young children. Another area in which work experience and specific skills are valued is in the teaching of business English or English for Special Purposes. Unfortunately, the cult of youth holds sway over much of the world, especially in the Far East. Language school owners often try to match their teachers with their clientele, the majority of whom are adolescents and people in their 20s and 30s. Whereas few companies openly impose an upper age limit, some age discrimination does regrettably take place. For older job-seekers it will be a matter of spreading their net as widely as possible by contacting as many relevant organisations, including voluntary ones, as possible. Older applicants may have to work harder to demonstrate enthusiasm, energy and adaptability to prospective employers – but this should be no bar to someone committed to creating adventures later in life.

WHAT EMPLOYERS ARE LOOKING FOR

Between the British Council and the dodgy operators is a vast middle ground of respectable English teaching establishments. Many would prefer to hire only qualified staff, yet they are not always available. On the whole these schools are looking for teachers with a good educational background, clear correct speech, familiarity with the main issues and approaches to TEFL and an outgoing personality.

A BA AND/OR TEFL CERTIFICATE IS NO GUARANTEE OF ABILITY AS MARTA ELENIAK OBSERVED IN SPAIN WHERE SHE TAUGHT DURING HER GAP YEAR (AFTER DOING A ONE-WEEK INTRODUCTORY TEFL COURSE):
I've seen graduate teachers make such a mockery of the enterprise that it's almost criminal. TEFL is creative teaching. Forget about your educational experiences. In TEFL you have got to be able to do an impression of a chicken, you've got to be a performer. And you have to be flexible. If the pupils are falling asleep, conduct a short aerobics class and change tack to something more interesting. A good teacher builds a rapport with the class, and is enthusiastic, patient, imaginative and genuinely interested in the welfare of the pupils.

A sophisticated knowledge of English grammar isn't needed, since in most cases, native speakers are hired to encourage conversation and practise pronunciation, leaving the grammar lessons to local teachers. On the other hand, a basic grasp is necessary, if only to keep up with your pupils.

MOTIVES FOR TEACHING ENGLISH

There are perhaps five main types of individual to be found teaching English from Tarragona to Taipei:

- The serious career teacher
- The student of the prevailing language and culture who teaches in order to fund a longer stay
- The long-term traveller who wants to prolong and fund his or her travels
- The philanthropic or religious person sponsored by an aid organisation, charity or mission society
- The misfit or oddball, perhaps fleeing unhappiness at home

In many countries, English teaching is the most easily attainable employment, in fact the only available employment for foreigners. Anyone who wants to transcend the status of mere tourist in a country such as Thailand, Bolivia or Japan will probably be attracted to the idea of teaching English. The assumption behind some thinking at the snobbish end of the EFL spectrum is that people who do it for only a year or two as a means to an end (eg learning Chinese, studying Italian art, eating French food) are necessarily inadequate teachers.

There are small pockets of people (mainly in the Far East) whose sole ambition is to earn as much money as possible to pay off debts or fund further world travels. These are seldom good teachers if only because they take on so many hours of teaching that they can't possibly prepare properly for their lessons. But for most teachers, making a lot of money isn't a priority or, if it was at the outset, they are soon disillusioned.

Salaries in popular tourist destinations (such as Paris, Barcelona, Chiang Mai) may actually be lower than in less appealing neighbouring towns, even though the cost of living is higher. Pay scales are relatively meaningless out of context. For example the high salaries paid in Japan are usually eaten up (at least in the first year) by the high rents and other expenses. When converted into sterling a salary in Venezuela might sound reasonable, but chronic inflation and currency devaluations could soon alter the picture. In some countries such as the Ukraine and Kenya, a TEFL salary may not be enough to fund anything beyond a spartan lifestyle, and savings from home are essential to fund any travelling. Yet the majority of people who spend time abroad teaching English are able to afford to live comfortably and have an enjoyable time without feeling pinched, although they end up saving little.

RED TAPE

The EU now consists of the UK, Ireland, the Netherlands, Belgium, Luxembourg, Denmark, Sweden, Finland, Austria, Estonia, Latvia, Lithuania, Poland, Czech Republic, Slovakia, Hungary, Slovenia, Malta, Bulgaria, Romania, the Greek populated area of Cyprus, France, Germany, Italy, Greece, Spain and Portugal, the latter six of which have enormous EFL markets. Within the EU, red tape should be minimal for all nationals of member states who wish to work in any capacity (though the relevant sections of the country chapters make it clear that this isn't always the case). Note that EU nationals who intend to stay for more than three months no longer require a residence permit.

Outside the EU, legislation varies from country to country. In theory there is also 'free reciprocity of labour' within the European Economic Area (EEA). The EEA includes those western European countries which have decided to stay outside the EU, viz. Iceland, Liechtenstein, Norway and Switzerland.

All of this means that British and Irish nationals have a significant advantage over Americans, Canadians, Australians and New Zealanders when job-hunting in Europe. Although not impossible for other nationalities, it is difficult for them to find an employer willing to undertake the task of proving to the authorities that no EU national is available or able to do the job. **Brian Komyathy** from Long Island, New York, was pleasantly surprised at how easy it was to arrange a job in Hungary (then not part of the EU), but then correspondingly disappointed when he made enquiries about moving to an EU country the following year:

> *European walls of regulations do not exactly bespeak 'Americans welcome aboard'. I'm technically eligible to acquire Irish and hence EU citizenship through my grandparents, so as soon as various documentary records are located and processed I'll not have the problems I do now. A slew of phone calls convinced me of the necessity of taking this course. Greece will be my last resort since it was the only place which didn't (figuratively) hang up on me when they recognised the origin of my accent.*

Other Americans find ingenious ways to stay just about legal. **Rachel Beebe** worked in Portugal using *recibos verdes* (green receipts), which are intended for use by temporary workers in the country. She found it impossible to get a work visa (and therefore a contract from her school).

International exchange organisations may be able to assist. Other US-based organisations cooperate with partner organisations in various countries, especially China, to place native speaker teachers in schools or institutes, often as volunteers. For particulars, see the section Opportunities for North Americans in the chapter Finding a Job.

The immigration authorities of many countries accord English teachers special status, recognising that their own nationals cannot compete as they can for other jobs. Other countries may lack the mechanism for granting work visas to English teachers and so will often turn a blind eye to those teaching on tourist visas, since everyone knows that locals are not being deprived of jobs; rather they're being given an advantage by having the chance to learn English.

Some organisations have developed a study-and-teach solution. While you are learning Russian in Moscow or Spanish in Caracas, you do some English tutoring on the side. Since your status is primarily as a student, it is unnecessary to obtain a full work authorisation.

If you fix up a teaching job before leaving home you can usually sort out your visa or at least set the wheels in motion before arrival, which greatly simplifies matters. You can only start the process after finding an employer willing to sponsor your application, preferably one who is familiar with the processes. There is no point applying to the embassy or consulate until you have found an employer. The majority of countries will process visas only when they are applied for from outside the country. So if you have to visit your chosen country on a tourist visa in order to find a job (which is the usual process), you will have to leave the country to apply for the work visa, though often this can be done from a neighbouring country rather than your country of residence. The restrictions and procedures for obtaining the appropriate documentation to teach legally are set out country by country in Part II of this book. Prospective teachers should contact the relevant Consulate for the official line (addresses in Appendix 2). If you do get tangled up in red tape, always remain patient with consular officials. If things seem to be grinding to a halt, it may be helpful to pester them, provided this is done courteously.

REWARDS AND RISKS

The rewards of teaching abroad are mostly self-evident:

- The chance to become integrated in a foreign culture
- The pleasure of making communication possible for your students
- The interesting characters and lifestyles you will encounter
- A feeling of increased self-reliance
- A better perspective on your own culture and your own habits
- A base for foreign travel
- Or even a good suntan ... and so on.

YASMIN PEIRIS, AWAY FROM HOME FOR THE FIRST TIME AND TEACHING IN CHINA, SUMS UP THE HIGHS AND LOWS:
Looking back on the last 12 months, some experiences stand out very clearly. Unfortunately, that includes times when you fall ill or feel homesick, or even feel lonely. Homesickness is natural and is a phase that passes very quickly. This is my first time away from home and I feel like the past year has been a massive achievement personally and professionally. It's been great having my own apartment, making friends from all over the world, learning Chinese, and more importantly, realising my own strengths, limits and skills through my time here. The work experience gained and the friendships made will be the most precious souvenir – that I know won't get lost or confiscated by customs. I already knew that I had to come into this experience with an open mind, and I'm glad I did because China surprised me at every turn, constantly giving me something weird or wonderful to write home.

Good teachers often find their classes positively fun and place a high value on the relationships they form with their students. Teaching is a lot of fun when it's done right. One-to-one teaching can also be enjoyable since you have a better chance to get to know your students or clients. (By the same token, it can be miserable if you don't get on, since there is no escape from the intimacy of the arrangement.) Off-site teaching provides glimpses into a variety of workplaces and private homes, perhaps even resulting in hospitality and friendship with your students.

As competition for jobs has increased, working conditions have not improved. There is a growing tendency for EFL teachers to be offered non-contract freelance work, with no guarantee of hours, making it necessary for them to work for more than one employer in order to make a living. Job security is a scarce commodity. Part-time workers of course miss out on all the benefits of full-time work such as bonuses, holiday pay, help with accommodation in some cases and so on.

Uninitiated teachers run the risk of finding themselves working for a shark or a cowboy who doesn't care a fig about the quality of teaching or the satisfaction of the teachers, as long as pupils keep signing up and paying their fees. 'Client satisfaction' is their only criterion of success; business takes complete precedence over education. Exploitation of teachers isn't uncommon since the profession is hampered by a lack of both regulation and unionisation.

The job of teaching English is demanding: it demands energy, enthusiasm and imagination, which are not always easy to produce when confronted with a room full of stonily silent faces. Instead of the thrill of communication, the drudgery of language drills begins to dominate. Instead of the pleasure of exchanging views with people of a different culture, teachers become weighed down by sheafs of photocopies and visual aids. Like most jobs when done right, teaching English is no piece of cake and is at times discouraging, but invariably it has its golden moments. It offers opportunities for creativity, learning about other cultures and attitudes, making friends and of course travelling. Not a bad job in many ways.

ROBERTA WEDGE WRITES AMUSINGLY ON A POSSIBLE SPIN-OFF FROM A TEACHING CONTRACT ABROAD:

TEFL is one of the most sex-balanced job fields I know (though the Director of Studies is usually a man) and, for those who are interested, the possibilities of finding your one true love appear to be high. Thrown together in an isolated Spanish village, eating tapas in the bar, hammering out lesson plans together – we found we have so much in common.

And a year later they were married. (A true story.)

On a more serious note, teachers should inform themselves about the political situation before offering their EFL services and take stock of their particular sensitivities concerning issues such as political freedom, democracy, human rights, religion, and so on. To take a couple of examples, teachers in China have been shocked by the overt racism. A Ghanaian teacher working in a small city not that far from Beijing had got used to the local people coming up to him to rub his skin to see if the black would come off. In the Central Asian Republics, home to ethnically diverse populations, certain groups are treated shamefully. If you are concerned by these matters, check the Freedom House website (www.freedomhouse.org) for updates. Additional insight can be gained from Reporters Sans Frontieres (Reporters without Borders; www.rsf.org). With regard to 'press freedom' the Worldwide Press Freedom Index rates countries according to the liberality of their press.

TRAINING

THE VALUE OF ELT QUALIFICATIONS

Training in teaching English as a foreign language isn't absolutely essential for successful job-hunting; but it makes the task easier by an order of magnitude. Anyone with the Cambridge Certificate (CELTA) or the Trinity Certificate in TESOL (both discussed in detail below) is in a much stronger position to get a job in any country where English is widely taught. These certificate courses provide a rigorous introduction to teaching English in just one month full-time (admittedly at considerable expense) or part-time over a period of months. So anyone interested in spending some time teaching abroad should seriously consider enrolling on a certificate course. Numerous other qualifications are also available, some obtainable after a weekend course and others after years of university study; many are listed briefly in the Directory of Training Courses below.

However, the Cambridge and Trinity Certificates should not be thought of as a magical passport to work. Increasingly, even certificate-holders are having to struggle to find a decent job, mainly because so many more people now have the qualification than 5 or 10 years ago. Many language schools, especially in France and Germany, will not want to hire a novice teacher and are unlikely to be tempted to take on anyone who does not present a dynamic and energetic image. Still, the certificate training continues to give applicants an important edge over the competition.

Increasing your marketability is not the only reason to get some training. The assumption that just because you can speak a language you can teach is simply false. There may be plenty of people who have a natural flair for teaching and who can do an excellent job without the benefit of a Certificate or any other English Language Teaching (ELT) qualification. (As mentioned in the previous chapter, the term ELT has come to be preferred to TEFL in many contexts.) There are, however, many other people who, when faced with a class full of eager adolescents, would not have a clue where to begin. Doing a TEFL course cannot fail to increase your confidence and provide you with a range of ideas on how to teach and (just as important) how not to teach. Even a short introductory course can usually illustrate methods of making lessons interesting and of introducing the range of teaching materials and approaches available to the novice teacher. What is needed more than theory or academic attainment, is an ability to entertain and to dramatise, but not without a framework into which your classroom efforts can be placed.

A perpetual problem which a TEFL course solves is the general level of ignorance of grammar among native speakers. Native-speaker teachers often find that their pupils, who are much better

informed on English grammar than they are, can easily catch them out with questions about verb tenses and subjunctives, causing embarrassment all round. Some training courses can also introduce you to the cultural barriers you can expect to encounter and the specific language-learning difficulties experienced by various nationalities (many of which will be touched on in the country chapters).

Some go so far as to see training almost as a moral obligation. Completely untrained teachers may end up being responsible for teaching people who have paid a great deal of money for expert instruction. This is of special concern in countries which have been inundated with 'tourist-teachers', while the Ministries of Education may be struggling to create all-graduate teaching professions. If you happen not to be a natural in the classroom, you may well fail to teach anything much to your pupils, whether they be young children in Hong Kong or businessmen in Portugal.

One of the practical advantages of joining a TEFL course is that many training centres have contacts with recruitment agencies or language schools abroad and can advise on, if not fix up, a job for you at the end of the course. Training centres differ enormously on how much help they can offer. If the 'after-sales service' is important to you, shop around before deciding which training course to do.

Even in countries where it may be commonplace to work without a formal TEFL qualification (for example Thailand and Japan), teachers who lack a specific grounding in TEFL will often be at a disadvantage. In some cases, the jobs available to the unqualified tend to be at the cowboy end of the market and may therefore offer exploitative conditions. In some countries (such as Turkey) a TEFL certificate is a prerequisite for a work visa, which is yet another justification for doing some formal training before setting off.

NOT SATISFIED THAT A ONE-WEEK COURSE WAS ENOUGH TO QUALIFY HIM AS A TEACHER, IAN ABBOTT WENT ON TO DO THE CAMBRIDGE CERTIFICATE AT INTERNATIONAL HOUSE IN ROME AND SUMMARISES HIS VIEW OF TEFL TRAINING:

I wouldn't recommend teaching English as a foreign language without investing in a course first. You've got to remember that the people coming along to your lessons are desperate to learn your language and it is costing them a small fortune. It is only fair that you know what you are doing and can in the end take that money without guilt, knowing you haven't ripped them off to increase your travel funds.

TEFL International
'Where the world is your classroom'
Argentina - France - Canada - China - Colombia - Costa Rica - Cyprus
Czech Republic - Dubai - India - Italy - Nepal - Philippines
Poland - South Africa - Spain - UK - USA - Korea - Thailand - Vietnam

__INTERNATIONALLY RECOGNISED TESOL CERTIFICATE__

Learn and then earn in the country of your choice.
Life time job finding assistance. Gap, internship and community projects.

www.teflinternational.org.uk   UK Helpline 0800 652 1724

RANGE OF COURSES

There is a bewildering array of courses available, at vastly different levels and costs, so it is wise to carry out some careful research before choosing. The British Council Information Centre (Bridgewater House, 58 Whitworth St, Manchester M1 6BB; © 0161 957 7755; general.enquiries@britishcouncil. org) publishes a free information leaflet *How to Become a Teacher of English as a Foreign Language* and distributes lists of Academic Courses in TEFL, Cambridge Certificate and Diploma courses and Trinity College London Certificate and Licentiate Diploma courses, all described below.

PAYING FOR THE COURSE

If you need help funding a training course, you may be eligible for a Career Development Loan (CDL). CDLs are bank loans covering up to 80% of the cost of a vocational course lasting less than two years followed by up to a year's practical experience. The Learning & Skills Council pays the interest until a month after the course finishes whereupon you must begin repayments at a favourable rate of interest. Write for details to Freepost, Career Development Loans (0800 585505; www.direct.gov.uk/cdl). Note that long-term unemployed people over 25 may be eligible for Job Seeker's Allowance even though they are doing a full-time training course (www.jobcentreplus. gov.uk). Some colleges are entitled to offer special dispensation to mature students. For example people over the age of 30 may be given tax relief by some UK colleges. Learner Support Funds (www.support4learning.org.uk) may help with part of the fees and for books and travel.

KEY ISSUES TO CONSIDER WHEN CHOOSING A COURSE

When choosing a course, it is worth asking certain questions which will indicate how useful the qualification will be at the end of it, such as, is there any external validation of the course and how much opportunity is there for teaching practice? Also find out what size a class you will be in (10–12 is much better than 15–20) and what qualifications and experience the tutors have. Cactus TEFL (www.cactustefl.com) is a huge mine of information about all things related to TEFL. It offers a useful advice, orientation and admissions service for prospective TEFL teachers. The online and telephone support offers personal guidance on courses, and allows you to apply directly to a wide range of TEFL course providers worldwide. Cactus also has a jobs website (www.cactustefl.com/jobs/index. php).The Directory of Training Courses in this chapter organises the courses available under various headings: the 100+ hour Certificate courses externally validated by the University of Cambridge and Trinity College London, 'Academic and Other Recognised Courses' which are primarily full academic courses offered at universities (this list is far from comprehensive), a few 'Distance Learning' courses, 'Short introductory courses in the UK' and, finally, a selection of courses offered worldwide ('Training Courses in North America' and 'Training Courses Abroad').

CERTIFICATE COURSES

The most useful qualification for anyone intending to spend a year or more abroad as an English teacher is a Certificate in English Language Teaching validated by one of the two examination bodies active in the field of ELT, University of Cambridge ESOL Examinations and Trinity College London. The Certificate qualification is acquired after an intensive 120–130 hour course offered full-time over one month or (increasingly) part-time over several months.

Most centres expect applicants to have the equivalent of university entrance qualifications, ie three GCSEs and two A levels and some require a degree. Admission to the course is at the discretion of the course organiser after a sometimes lengthy selection process. Places on courses at the well-established centres may be difficult to get because of high demand, especially in summer, so early application is advised.

Applicants must be able to demonstrate a suitable level of language awareness and convince the interviewer that they have potential to develop as a teacher. Past academic achievement is less important than aptitude; even a PhD does not guarantee acceptance. Most schools will send you a task sheet or grammar research activity as part of the application. Sample questions might be 'How would you convey the idea of regret to a language learner?' or 'Describe the difference in meaning between 'I don't really like beetroot' and 'I really don't like beetroot'?'

Courses are not cheap but should be viewed as an investment and a potential passport to a worthwhile profession in many different countries. In fact, prices have not risen much over the past two years, with many centres trying to survive amid keen competition. The range is about £700–£1,000 for a full-time course with an average halfway between those two figures. Most centres include the validation body's fee, variously called assessment, moderation or examination fee, which in 2008 was about £100 in most centres. Many colleges of further education offer the Trinity or Cambridge Certificate part-time and these are usually less expensive, as low as £350–£400. These courses enable you to work in general English language teaching in schools both within and outside the UK. Timetables for part-time courses vary, but the norm is to attend classes one or two evenings a week for one or two terms of the academic year plus occasional full days for teaching observation and practice. Some universities and colleges have language institutes which run intensive ELT/ESOL courses at various levels on a commercial basis, and fees at these institutions are often equivalent to private training courses.

Once accepted onto a Certificate course, you will usually be given a pre-course task to familiarise yourself with some key concepts and issues before the course begins. Full-time courses are very intensive and 100% attendance is expected, so you need to be in a position to dedicate yourself completely to the task in hand for four weeks. The standard of teaching is high, the course rigorous and demanding and the emphasis is on the practice of any theory taught. One of the requirements is that participants teach a minimum of six hours of observed lessons to authentic English language students.

CAMBRIDGE CELTA

Cambridge CELTA (Certificate in English Language Teaching to Adults) has established itself as the passport to teaching opportunities overseas. It has a rock-solid reputation in the international teaching community and high levels of recognition among employers around the world. CELTA is administered and regulated by University of Cambridge ESOL Examinations (Cambridge ESOL, 1 Hills Road, Cambridge CB1 2EU; ✆ 01223 553355; ESOLHelpdesk@CambridgeESOL.org; www. cambridgeESOL.org) and is sometimes referred to simply as the Cambridge Certificate. Many believe that CELTA is the most reliable route to jobs with better rates of pay, and with employers who are willing to give more support to novice teachers.

You don't have to stay in the UK to take CELTA training. Administered and regulated by University of Cambridge ESOL Examinations, CELTA courses are offered at more than 280 centres worldwide. For example, the British Council runs courses in Milan, Naples, Istanbul, Dhaka, Mumbai, Tokyo and Casablanca. CELTA courses are offered by 20 centres in Australia, eight in New Zealand and holding steady in North America so that there are now seven CELTA course providers in the USA and the same number in Canada. A full list is available at the Cambridge ESOL website (www.CambridgeESOL. org/teaching).

Securing a place on a CELTA course isn't automatic. Course providers are selective in order to ensure standards are kept high – and as a result, the pass rate is usually at least 90%. Grades available are Pass, Pass 'B' and Pass 'A', giving candidates the chance to distinguish themselves. CELTA provides a foundation of theory but focuses on effective teaching skills and practical tools for teaching English to adult learners. You'll gain hands-on teaching practice and the experience and support to build confidence in the classroom.

> **DOUG BURGESS, WHO TEACHES IN CHILE, BELIEVES THAT A CELTA PLUS SOME TEACHING EXPERIENCE IS THE PERFECT RECIPE FOR SECURING A GOOD TEACHING JOB:**
> *If you are interested in job security and acquiring a work visa, it is highly advisable that you complete the CELTA and try to get some experience as it will give you flexibility and options when you are here so that you can have the most comfortable and enjoyable time possible.*

Cambridge ESOL also offers an equivalent course for people who want to teach young learners – CELTYL (Certificate in English Language Teaching to Young Learners) at a selected number of centres in the UK and abroad.

TRINITY COLLEGE LONDON

The other principal initial Certificate in TESOL is awarded by Trinity College London, (89 Albert Embankment, London SE1 7TP; ✆ 020 7820 6100; fax 020 7820 6161; email tesol@trinitycollege.co.uk; www.trinitycollege.co.uk/CertTESOL). Job details in this book refer to Cambridge CELTA

TRINITY
COLLEGE LONDON

Qualify with Trinity

CertTESOL
an initial Level 4 TESOL/TEFL qualification

DipTESOL
an advanced Level 7 TESOL/TEFL qualification

Fellowship Diploma in TESOL Education Studies (FTCL)
an advanced Level 7 TESOL/TEFL qualification

Diploma in Teaching in the Lifelong Learning Sector ESOL (DTLLS)
a Level 5 TESOL qualification available in the UK

Trinity's TESOL qualifications are among the most widely recognised in
their field and are highly regarded by employers worldwide, including
the British Council. Whether you are starting out on an English teaching
career or stepping up to more senior posts, a Trinity TESOL qualification
will help you achieve your goal

Find out more www.trinitycollege.co.uk/tesol

and Trinity CertTESOL which are regarded as having equal academic standing. Elsewhere you may find 'Cambridge or equivalent', which is referring primarily to the Trinity qualifications. The Trinity Certificate TESOL (CertTESOL) has international recognition and is highly regarded by employers in the UK and around the world. There are currently more than 100 centres worldwide offering CertTESOL training full – or part-time. Nearly a third are outside the UK, with six centres in Spain, eight in New Zealand and one or two in the USA, Argentina, Bali, Canada, Germany, Spain, Greece, Hungary, Hong Kong, Czech Republic, Ireland, Italy, Japan, United Arab Emirates, Malta, Paraguay and Uruguay.

Trinity stipulates a minimum of 130 hours offered intensively over a minimum of four weeks or part-time over a longer period. All intensive courses must have a pre-course learning component in addition to the minimum hours. The course content includes grammar and phonology, a range of teaching approaches and methodologies, classroom management and motivation, hands-on experience of teaching aids (from blackboards to computers), introduction to the learning of an unknown language (in which trainees receive four hours' instruction and lesson planning). In addition, they must complete a minimum of six hours of observed and assessed teaching practice and at least four further hours observing experienced teachers of English.

Trinity's CertTESOL is accredited by the UK Qualifications and Curriculum Authority, the national body for the regulation of vocational qualifications outside the higher education sector, at Level 4 of the UK National Qualifications Framework. In addition, its CertTESOL is accepted by the British Council as an appropriate initial TESOL qualification in its accredited English language teaching organisations in the UK and its own teaching centres in 100+ countries around the world. All courses meet the core Trinity requirements but there are variations in course delivery across the different providers to reflect the best of their in-house practice and philosophy. Trinity also works closely with QuiTE – Quality in TESOL Education (www.quality-tesol-ed.org.uk) to ensure that its qualifications are in line with those of other comparable awarding bodies – principally Cambridge ESOL. The Trinity CertTESOL can also be taken as an integral module within a BA programme at the universities of Central Lancashire (Preston), Keele, Portsmouth, Sheffield Hallam, Sussex and Wolverhampton.

CHOOSING A COURSE

It is up to prospective trainees to weigh up the pros and cons of the courses available to them and to establish how rigorously the course he or she is considering is monitored. One reservation that a few employers abroad have expressed is that the proliferation of providers of certificate courses whether on behalf of Cambridge, Trinity or independents, has made it more difficult to maintain a uniform standard, especially since so much of the assessment of candidates is subjective. The general decline in standards of literacy in Britain and North America has also prompted some to complain of a decline.

When it comes to work load, trainees in both CELTA and Trinity TESOL courses complain of a punishing schedule. But most come away claiming that the course elements are superb. At the time, participants sometimes feel as though they are drowning in information, but realise that the course has to pack a great deal of material into four brief weeks. The majority who go on to teach abroad are very grateful for the training it gave them, as in the case of **Andrew Sykes** teaching in Bordeaux:

> *As for the Certificate course that I did at Leeds Metropolitan University, it was certainly one of the most stimulating, challenging and interesting things I have ever studied for. Initially I felt a bit out of place – I had a background of science A levels, a maths degree and two years as a (failed) accountant. The course was professionally run and there were good teacher–student relations. Most people had never taught anybody anything before in their life, but we were gradually eased into teaching by the supportive teaching staff who were refreshingly (and diplomatically) critical when required to be. A criticism which some students had was that there wasn't enough feedback about what was expected to gain a pass, let alone achieve an A or B. The best recommendation for the course is perhaps that I would never have felt comfortable teaching without it.*

So even if your social life disappears for a month and all you can talk about at weekends is gerunds and infinitives, the consensus is that it is worthwhile.

For many, one of the key factors will be cost. Generic certificate courses are available in dozens of countries and the cheapest ones are offered in the cheapest countries. When **James Clarke** and his girlfriend Sally were looking for a course for under $1,000 inclusive in South America they ended up at Vive Peru in Trujillo, Peru, but that training course has not survived.

Cactus TEFL (www.cactustefl.com) works with a large number of course providers worldwide and has an efficient search engine to find the training course suited to your requirements. Cactus TEFL also publishes the *Little Book of TEFL*, available free from Cactus (info@cactustefl.com).

Possible advantages of doing a TEFL training course abroad are:

■ You may already be teaching or living in that country and want to upgrade your qualifications locally
■ The course and cost of living may be cheaper than in your home country
■ Successful course participants will almost certainly be put in touch with local employers, making it much easier to land a job

Teaching practice is key. Further Education Colleges like Ealing, Hammersmith and West London College offer an insight into the diversity of ELT work because they teach such a wide range of students, to whom their CELTA trainees are exposed during teaching practice sessions.

OTHER RECOGNISED QUALIFICATIONS

In 2005, Cambridge ESOL introduced the Teaching Knowledge Test (TKT), a new accessible test about teaching English to speakers of other languages, delivered to international standards. The test, which can be taken by both practising and aspiring teachers, involves three modules that cover the background to language learning and teaching, planning lesson/using resources and managing the teaching and learning process. TEFL training centres worldwide are offering short courses to candidates who want to prepare for TKT, which is more accessible than CELTA and does not include teaching practice as part of the assessment. For further information visit www.cambridgeesol.org/ TKT. International House in London (see entry below) offers a two-week preparatory course costing £525; courses abroad tend to cost less.

Beyond CELTA is the Diploma. Whereas CELTA is considered an initial qualification, the Diploma (as distinct from any old diploma with a lower case) is an in-service course for experienced English language teachers. The Cambridge Diploma in English Language Teaching to Adults (DELTA) and the Trinity Licentiate Diploma (LTCT TESOL) are high-level qualifications usually open to graduates who have at least two years of recent ELT classroom experience. The Diploma course is available intensively over a minimum of eight weeks but more usually part-time over several months or a year. A Distance DELTA option is also available (www.thedistancedelta.com). The fees of more than £1,000 are sometimes subsidised by employers.

Universities (especially the former polytechnics) from Brighton to Belfast offer their own certificate or diploma in TEFL. Most are one or two-year courses, full or part-time, and tend to be more theoretical than Cambridge and Trinity courses. It is important to do some research before committing yourself to a course so that you are sure that the qualification you obtain will be recognised by employers both in the UK and overseas. Once again find out if there is some form of external assessment and whether the course includes a reasonable amount of teaching practice.

A number of undergraduate institutions offer TESL as part of an undergraduate course; the weighty *UCAS Handbook* lists all university courses in the UK and can be consulted in any careers or general library. MA courses in ELT and applied linguistics are offered at dozens of universities and colleges.

STEPHEN CURRY FELT LET DOWN BY THE COURSE HE CHOSE:
I called my local university to see what courses were available and was advised that they could provide a course consisting of two modules, one from the PGCE and one from the MEd programme which would be

> *equivalent in status to a one-month Certificate and would be 'recognised'. The course of study took from May to February to complete. It was a lot of hard work, research based and absolutely no fun whatsoever. I did the course on the understanding that it would lead to a stand-alone TEFL certificate. I have since tried to get the university to confirm in writing that this module carries the recognition they claimed it would but they now say that they cannot do this. Unfortunately it was not until the latter stages of the course that I (and others) began to see that the eventual outcome would be a qualification that was unlikely to be recognised in the eyes of anyone outside the university, let alone as being equivalent to the Cambridge/Trinity certificate.*

Some offer a master's by distance learning aimed at practising ELT teachers worldwide. Arguably, there is a world oversupply of MAs, since there is a relative scarcity of high level posts which require an MA; for example the British Council has only ten or so positions a year. On the other hand, an MA is a pre-requisite for many posts in some countries, especially in the Middle East.

INTRODUCTORY COURSES

Although the Cambridge and Trinity Certificates are sometimes referred to as 'introductory courses', there are many cheaper, shorter and less rigorous introductions to the subject. With the rise in the popularity of Certificate courses there has been a decline in what might be considered as more amateurish courses, though these do have a role to play, for example for school leavers who would not be accepted onto a Certificate course or for the curious who do not want to commit themselves to a month-long course or pay £800+.

As there are some commercial enterprises and 'cowboy' operators cashing in on the present EFL boom, standards vary and course literature should be studied carefully before choosing. Most people who have done a TEFL training course claim that the most worthwhile part is the actual teaching practice, preferably to real students rather than in mock lessons to fellow participants. The fact is that most short introductory courses do not allow for much chance to do teaching practice. Many schools looking for teachers have expressed the view that peer-teaching is of little value.

The more upmarket introductory courses often present themselves as an opportunity to sample the field to see whether you want to go on to do a Certificate at a later stage. Others make their course sound as if it alone will be sufficient to open doors worldwide. It would be unreasonable to expect a weekend or five-day course to equip anyone to teach, but most participants do find them helpful. After seeing an advertisement in the New York subway advertising for English teachers, **Roger Blake** was prompted to seek out some training. Back in England, Roger, who admits to being a not particularly academic type, enjoyed the 'crash' weekend training he did with i-to-i so much that he enrolled in a home-study module of a further 20 hours. Later when he was asking about local teaching possibilities at the British Council in Addis Ababa, he felt more confident being able to show two course certificates.

The majority of residential courses last a weekend or for four to five days and cost between £180 and £450, not counting accommodation. Almost all will issue some kind of certificate which can sometimes be used to impress prospective employers. Anyone who wants a job after doing a short course should aim to do it in the spring when the majority of jobs are advertised for the following academic year. Many people who complete an introductory or 'taster' course go on to do an intensive certificate, often at the same centre.

A number of private language centres offer their own short courses in TEFL which may focus on their own method, developed specifically with the chain of schools in mind (for example Berlitz) or may offer a more general introduction. Anyone who wishes to specialise in the highly marketable field of business English should enquire about specialist courses such as the Foundation Certificate for Teachers of Business English validated by the London Chamber of Commerce & Industry (LCCI) and offered by a number of companies involved in this market, such as Inlingua Teacher Training.

DISTANCE LEARNING

Some practising teachers of English who want to obtain a qualification are attracted to the idea of self-study by distance learning, partly because it will be cheaper than a conventional course and because it can be done in the candidate's own time and/or in any part of the world. Course providers are making increased use of electronic communications, doing away not only with the necessity of having physical access to a training course but of being dependent on the post, often unreliable in distant parts of the world. Some companies are delivering complete courses online, for example i-to-i, which for some years has been offering intensive weekend courses around the UK (www.onlinetefl.com).

As a part of the general move within the profession to monitor standards and offer assurances of quality, the College of Teachers (Institute of Education, University of London, 57 Gordon Square, London WC1H 0NU; ✆ 020 7911 5536; fax 020 7612 6482; info@cot.ac.uk; www.collegeofteachers.ac.uk) is the main awarding body. It has accorded recognition to a few distance learning course providers.

ACTDEC (Accreditation Council for TESOL Distance Education Courses) is a non-profit making independent body governed by officers. Established in 1993, the Council aims to advance professionalism by maintaining and improving on standards of distance TESOL/TEFL programmes. ACTDEC is for the benefit of the public and aimed at helping TESOL course applicants locate suitably accredited institutions offering distance teacher training courses. The new entrant to the profession is faced with a bewildering array of distance courses to choose from but does not always possess the knowledge or experience to judge between them. A copy of the ACTDEC code of practice and other details, including a list of accredited members can be viewed online at www.ACTDEC.org.uk or requested from the Admin Officer, 21 Wessex Gardens, Dore, Sheffield S17 3PQ (✆ 0114 235 7836; fax 0114 236 0774; info@ACTDEC.org.uk; www.ACTDEC.org.uk).

The International Accreditation of TESOL Qualifying Organisations (IATQuO) is another monitoring organisation which was initially set up in conjunction with the commercial company TEFL International but is gradually expanding its inspection role; for details contact IATQuO (Park View, Alveston Road, Bristol BS32 4PH; www.iatquo.org).

Typically, distance courses at the professional end of the spectrum involve at least 150 hours of home study. Some offer distance learning in combination with a residential element sometimes referred to as a hybrid course. It is strongly recommended by Intesol (4 Higher Downs, Knutsford, Cheshire WA16 8AW; ✆ 01565 631743; enquiries@intesoltesoltraining.com; www.intesoltesol-training.com) that you ensure that the certificate course for which you are applying is accredited and that the provider also offers a real teaching practice option.

Various accrediting bodies boldly display their logos on the websites of various course providers. It is always a wise precaution to investigate as deeply as possible. In some cases providers of distance learning courses club together to set up their own agency to accredit their own courses. In other cases, providers need only pay a subscription fee to be 'accredited' without any process of impartial inspection. Another trick is that some dodgy schools falsely claim to be accredited by a certain body. For example IATQuO publishes a list of companies making fraudulent claims (www.iatquo.org/LIST.htm). So it is prudent to be sceptical.

People considering this route to TEFL training should be cautious. The most obvious disadvantage is the lack of face-to-face teaching practice, though some do provide opportunities for blocks of teaching practice and others provide plenty of tutor feedback. If you are not satisfied with the course but have paid your money (typically £400+ for a certificate course), you have little recourse. One way of ascertaining the worth of a distance learning course you may be considering is to ask to be put in touch with past students. For example Global English asks its students to complete appraisal forms, many of which are very positive. **Glyn Askey** from Yorkshire gave positive feedback:

> *Having had an interest in TEFL for some time, I required a course which would give me an insight into TEFL at an affordable cost. I found that the Global English course made you think from the outset about your students, your lesson planning and the methods of teaching . . . A well put together course and positive friendly feedback.*

Of the range of distance courses and qualifications on offer, most offer professional courses of quality. One or two are sound but provide relatively short basic programmes, yet frequently lead to a so-called Diploma. A few however have a definite credibility gap; even their course information and covering letters are riddled with spelling and grammatical mistakes. Be especially cautious if the organisation operates from a PO box and/or provides no telephone number. Scrutinise the claims it makes in its literature. One organisation trumpets the fact that it is 'validated by Trinity University and College' which sounds reassuringly like the mainstream Trinity College London. However this Trinity has its headquarters in Kuala Lumpur with branches in Delaware (USA) and Dhaka (Bangladesh).

Details of introductory, internet and distance training courses both in Britain and abroad are provided in the Directory of Training Courses.

TRAINING IN THE USA

Most TESL training in the USA is integrated into university degree courses in applied linguistics at both the undergraduate and graduate levels. Until the beginning of the 1990s, there were virtually no short intensive courses in TEFL available in North America. That has now changed. In addition to the Cambridge centres in the USA, several independent TEFL training organisations offer four-week intensive courses (see Directory of Training Courses below). The major providers such as Transworld and Worldwide Teachers are well connected with language schools abroad (particularly in Latin America and the Far East). Competition is keen among the schools, and prices fairly consistent at about US$2,000 for a four-week course.

The American Language Institute in San Diego has received high praise from a number of graduates particularly for its job placement service, as described here by **Bryson Patterson** writing from Costa Rica:

> *The amTEFL course at the American Language Institute (ALI) at San Diego State University is a solid teacher training programme encompassing methodology, live classroom practice, grammar and job placement. A day at the amTEFL begins with four hours of methodology (the theory and practice of second language acquisition). Trainees are then instructed in the ins and outs of lesson planning, and annual planning. Mock classes are video taped, helping students to evaluate their own performance. Afternoons are spent working as assistants for mentor teachers in live EFL classrooms and rotating through all the levels of EFL classes at the ALI. The video tape is later used to help amTEFLers land a job. What sets the ALI apart is that it not only promises but delivers lifetime job placement assistance to its alums. Rob Shaffer is the Job Placement Coordinator at the ALI. His office has a large, full-colour world map above the desk, perforated with over 100 pins. Each pin on the map represents a former amTEFLer, who is currently teaching EFL somewhere in the world. Rob maintains regular contact with ALI alums in dozens of countries, and he makes it*

his personal mission to find each amTEFLer a job. The amTEFL job search puts the alumni network to work for current students providing reliable information about schools, living and working conditions, wages and everything else.

Increasingly American universities and colleges are offering intensive TESL training including one-semester courses. If you can't afford to do a course but want to learn about TEFL, it may be possible to audit such a course. One resource for finding a programme of study in the field of TESOL within North America is the *Directory of Teacher Education Programs in TESOL in the United States and Canada*. This is the most comprehensive listing available, containing information about graduate, PhD and certificate programmes. Each entry lists contact information, course descriptions, faculty information and tuition costs. The 2005–2007 edition costs US$39.95 plus postage (or US$19.95 plus postage for TESOL members; see Finding a Job). The 2008–2010 Directory of Teacher Education Programs in TESOL (DTEP) is being revised and will become a searchable database on the TESOL website (for members only). Its publications are available from TESOL (Teachers of English to Speakers of Other Languages, Inc.), 700 South Washington Street, Suite 200, Alexandria, Virginia 22314 4287 (✆ 703 836 0774; fax 703 836 6447; tesolpubs@tasco1.com; www.tesol.org).

It is easier to get practical experience of teaching English (without a qualification) by joining one of the many voluntary ESL programmes found in almost every American city, run by community colleges, civic organisations and literacy groups. ProLiteracy Worldwide (the result of the merger of Literacy Volunteers of America and Laubauch Literacy in 2002; 1320 Jamesville Ave, Syracuse, New York 13210; ✆ 315 422 9121; fax 315 422 6369; info@proliteracy.org; www.proliteracy.org) operates in most states and offers volunteer tutors a free 18-hour pre-service training programme but you have to buy its materials (about US$35). It also offers a 12-hour tutor training workshop for volunteers and oversees literacy projects in dozens of countries overseas.

DIRECTORY OF TRAINING COURSES

CAMBRIDGE CERTIFICATE (CELTA) COURSES IN THE UK

Action English Language Training LLP: Leeds; ✆ 0113 242 4468; www.aelt.co.uk; Full-time; Rough frequency 12 per year.

Anglo-Continental Teacher Training Centre: Bournemouth; ✆ 01202 557414; www.anglo-continental.com; Full and part-time; Rough frequency 5 per year.

Basil Paterson College: Edinburgh; ✆ 0131 225 3802; www.basilpaterson.co.uk; Full-time; Rough frequency 10 per year.

Bath Spa University: Bath; ✆ 01225 875884; www.bathspa.ac.uk; Full-time; Rough frequency 1 per year.

Belfast Institute of Further & Higher Education: Belfast; ✆ 028 90265184; www.belfast institute.ac.uk; Part-time; Rough frequency 2 per year.

Bell International: Cambridge; ✆ 01223 212333; www.bell-centres.com/celta; Full and part-time; Rough frequency 5 per year.

Blackburn College: Blackburn; ✆ 01254 292904; www.blackburn.ac.uk; Part-time.

Bolton Community College: Bolton; ✆ 01204 907333; www.bolton-community-college. ac.uk; Part-time.

Brasshouse Language Centre: Birmingham; ✆ 0121 3030114; www.birmingham.gov.uk/brasshouse; Full and part-time; Rough frequency 1 per year.

British Study Centre: Oxford; ✆ 01865 246620; www.british-study.com/teachertraining; Full-time; Rough frequency once a month.

Bromley College of Further & Higher Education: Bromley (Kent); ✆ 020 8295 7000; www.Bromley.ac.uk; Part-time.

Brooklands College: Weybridge (Surrey); ✆ 01932 797700; www.brooklands.ac.uk; Full and part-time; Rough frequency 1 per year.

Canterbury Christ Church University: Canterbury; ✆ 01227 767700; www.cant.ac.uk; Full and part-time; Rough frequency 1 per year.

CILC (Cheltenham International Language Centre): Cheltenham (Gloucestershire); ✆ 01242 714092; www.glos.ac.uk/cilc; Full-time; Rough frequency 3 per year.

City College Handsworth: Birmingham; ✆ 0121 2561099; www.citycol.ac.uk; Part-time.

City of Bath College: Bath; ✆ 01225 312191; www.citybathcoll.ac.uk; Full and part-time; Rough frequency 1 per year.

City of Bristol College: Bristol; ✆ 0117 904 5163; www.cityofbristol.ac.uk; Part-time.

Concorde International Study Centre: Canterbury; ✆ 01227 451035; www.concorde-international.com; Full-time; Rough frequency 3 per year.

Croydon Continuing Education & Training Service (CETS): London; ✆ 020 8656 6620; Part-time.

Dundee College: Dundee; ✆ 01383 834898; www.dundeecoll.ac.uk; Full and part-time; Rough frequency 1 per year.

Durham University Language Centre: Durham; ✆ 0191 334 2230; www.durham.ac.uk/language.centre; Full-time; Rough frequency 1 per year.

Ealing, Hammersmith & West London College: London; ✆ 0800 034 0384; www.wlc.ac.uk; Full and part-time, both 4 times a year.

Embassy CES Hastings: St Leonards on Sea; ✆ 01424 464820; www.embassyces.com; Full-time; Rough frequency 4 per year.

Embassy CES Newnham: Cambridge; ✆ 01223 311344; www.embassyces.com; Full-time; Rough frequency 4 per year.

English Language & Teacher Training Centre: Reading (Berkshire); ✆ 0118 939 1833; www.efl-reading.co.uk; Semi-intensive; 3 per year.

English Language House: Milton Keynes; ✆ 01908 694357; www.englishlanguagehouse.co.uk; Full and part-time; Rough frequency 5 per year.

TRAINING

DIRECTORY OF TRAINING COURSES

GEOS English Academy: Hove (East Sussex); ✆ 01273 735975; www.geos-brighton.com; Full-time; Rough frequency 5 per year.

GLOSCAT (Gloucester College of Arts & Technology): Cheltenham; ✆ 01273 735975; www.gloscat.ac.uk; Full and part-time; Rough frequency 2 per year.

Greenwich Community College: London; ✆ 020 8355 3923; www.gcc.ac.uk; Full and part-time; Rough frequency 1 per year.

Intensive School of English & Business Communication: Brighton; ✆ 01273 384800; www.ise.uk.com; Full and part-time; Rough frequency 2 per year.

International House London: London; ✆ 020 7611 2414; www.ihlondon.com; Full and part-time; offered monthly.

International House Newcastle Upon Tyne: Newcastle; ✆ 0191 232 9551; www.ihnewcastle.com; Full-time; Rough frequency 2 per year.

ITTC: Bournemouth; ✆ 01202 397721; www.ittc.co.uk; Full-time; Rough frequency 12 per year.

Kingston Adult Education: Surbiton (Surrey); ✆ 020 854 76875; www.kingston.gov.uk/learning/adulteducation; Part-time.

R *andolph*

School of English
SCOTLAND

63 Frederick Street
Edinburgh EH2 1LH
Tel +44 (0)131 226 5004
Tel +44 (0)131 226 5003
RandolphSE@aol.com

www.randolph.org.uk

- Full and part time CELTA courses throughout the year
- Accommodation arranged
- Small school with personal attention
- Scotland's most experienced teacher trainers

Language Link Training: London; ✆ 020 737 04755; www.languagelink.co.uk; Full and part-time; Rough frequency 10 per year.

Manchester Academy Teacher Training (UK) Ltd: Manchester; ✆ 0161 237 5619; www.manacad.co.uk; Full and part-time; Rough frequency 8 per year.

Newcastle College: Newcastle; ✆ 0191 200 4467; www.ncl-coll.ac.uk; Part-time.

New College Nottingham: Nottingham; ✆ 0115 9100 100; www.ncn.ac.uk; Part-time.

NILE: Norwich; ✆ 01603 664473; www.nile-elt.com; Full-time; Rough frequency 8 per year.

Oxford and Cherwell Valley College: Oxford; ✆ 01865 551828; www.ocvc.ac.uk/about-teacher-training; Full and part-time; Rough frequency 4 per year.

Oxford House College: London; ✆ 020 7580 9785; www.oxfordhousecollege.co.uk; Full and part-time; Rough frequency 12 per year.

Randolph School of English: Edinburgh; ✆ 0131 226 5004; www.randolph.org.uk; Full and part-time; Rough frequency 9 per year.

Regent London: London; ✆ 020 7872 6620; www.regent.org.uk; Full and part-time; Rough frequency 10 per year.

Regent Oxford: Oxford; ✆ 01865 515566; www.regent.org.uk; Full-time; Rough frequency 10 per year.

St Giles International London Highgate: London; ✆ 020 8340 0828; londonhighgate@stgiles.co.uk www.stgiles-international.com; Full and part-time; Rough frequency 10 per year.

St Giles International Brighton: Brighton; ✆ 01273-682747; brighton@stgiles.co.uk; www.stgiles-international.com; Four week full time courses; Held 10 times around the year.

Saxoncourt Teacher Training: London; ✆ 020 7499 8533; www.saxoncourt.com; Full and part-time; Rough frequency 12 per year.

Skola Teacher Training: London; ✆ 020 7287 3126; www.skola.co.uk; Full and part-time; Rough frequency 1 per year.

Solihull College: Solihull; ✆ 0121 6787173; www.solihull.ac.uk; Part-time.

South Leicestershire College: Leicester; ✆ 0116 288 5051; www.slcollege.ac.uk; Part-time.

South Thames College: London; ✆ 020 8918 7777; www.south-thames.ac.uk; Part-time.

Stanton Teacher Training: London; ✆ 020 7221 7259; www.stanton-school.co.uk; Full-time; Rough frequency 9 per year.

Stevenson College: Edinburgh; ✆ 0131 535 4700; www.stevenson.ac.uk; Part-time.

Stoke-On-Trent College: Stoke-On-Trent; ✆ 01782 208208; www.stokecoll.ac.uk; Full-time; Rough frequency 1 per year.

Studio School: Cambridge; ✆ 01223 369701; www.studiocambridge.co.uk; Full-time; Rough frequency 2 per year.

Sussex Downs College: Eastbourne; ✆ 01323 637232; www.sussexdowns.ac.uk; Full and part-time; Rough frequency 4 per year.

Torbay Language Centre: Devon; ✆ 01803 558555; www.lalgroup.com/torbay; Full-time; Rough frequency 4 per year.

Waltham Forest College: London; ✆ 020 8501 8501; www.waltham.ac.uk; Full and part-time; Rough frequency 1 per year.

Westminster Kingsway College: London; ✆ 0870 060 9800; www.westking.ac.uk; Full-time; Rough frequency 1 per year.

CAMBRIDGE CERTIFICATE (CELTA) COURSES ABROAD

The following centres, listed alphabetically by country, offer the Cambridge Certificate course.

Australia

Australian TESOL Training Centre (ATTC): Sydney; ✆ +6 12 9389 0249; www.attc.edu.au; Full and part-time; Rough frequency 12 per year.

Curtin University: Perth; ✆ +8 9266 4224; www.celta.curtin.edu.au; Full-time; Rough frequency 2 per year.

Holmesglen Language Centre: Chadstone (Victoria); ✆ +3 9564 1820; www.holmesglen. vic.edu.au; Full and part-time; Rough frequency 4 per year.

Holmes Institute Teacher Training: Melbourne; ✆ +3 9662 2055; www.holmesinstitute. edu.au; Full-time; Rough frequency 6 per year.

Insearch University of Technology, Sydney (UTS): Sydney; ✆ +2 9218 8666; www.insearch. edu.au; Full and part-time; Rough frequency 4 per year.

Institute of Continuing & TESOL Education (ICTE): Brisbane; ✆ +7 3365 6565; www.icte. uq.edu.au; Full and part-time; Rough frequency 4 per year.

International House Queensland: Cairns/Brisbane; ✆ +7 4031 3466/7 3220 1011; www. ihqld.com; Full and part-time; Rough frequency 5 per year.

International House Sydney: Sydney; ✆ +2 9279 0733; www.training.ihsydney.com; Full and part-time; Rough frequency 10 per year.

La Trobe University Language Centre: Melbourne; ✆ +3 9479 2417; www.latrobe.edu.au; Full-time; Rough frequency 5 per year.

Milner International College of English: Perth; ✆ +8 9325 5444; www.celta.milner.com.au; Full-time; Rough frequency 6 per year.

Monash University English Language Centre: Clayton (Victoria); ✆ +3 9905 5270; www. monash.edu.au; Full-time; Rough frequency 1 per year.

Phoenix English Language Academy: Perth; ✆ +8 9227 5538; www.phoenixela.com.au; Full-time; Rough frequency 2 per year.

RMIT English Worldwide: Melbourne; ✆ +3 9657 5800; www.rmitenglishworldwide.com; Full and part-time; Rough frequency 2 per year.

South Australian College of English (SACE Adelaide): Adelaide; ✆ +8 8232 0335; www.sacecoll.sa.edu.au; Full-time; Rough frequency 4 per year.

Tasmanian College of English (SACE Hobart): Tasmania; ✆ +3 6231 9911; www.tas.sace.com.au; Full-time; Rough frequency 4 per year.

Austria

BFI Vienna: Vienna; ✆ +1 811 78 10100; www.bfi-wien.at; Full-time; Rough frequency 2 per year.

Bangladesh

British Council Bangladesh: Dhaka; ✆ +2 911 6171/6545; www.britishcouncil.org/bangladesh; Full-time; Rough frequency 1 per year.

Brazil

Britannia International English: Rio de Janeiro; ✆ +21 2511 0143; www.britannia.com.br; Part-time.

Sociedade Brasileira De Cultura Inglesa: Recife; ✆ +81 3228 6649; www.culturainglesa.com.br; Full-time; Rough frequency 1 per year.

SBCI Rio De Janeiro: Rio de Janeiro; ✆ +21 2528 1104; www.culturainglesa.net; Full-time.

Up Language Consultants: Sao Paulo; ✆ +11 5105 0200; www.uplanguage.com.br; Full-time.

Bulgaria

Avo-3 School of English: Sofia; ✆ +2 944 3032/943 3943; www.avo-3.com; Full-time; Rough frequency 4 per year.

Canada

English Canada World Organization: Halifax (Nova Scotia); ✆ +902 429 3636; www.celta.ca; Full-time; Rough frequency 6 per year.

International Language Schools of Canada - Montreal: Montreal; ✆ +514 876 4572; www. ilsc.ca; Full-time; Rough frequency 6 per year.

Kwantlen University College: Richmond (Br Columbia); ✆ +604 599 2693; www.kwantlen. ca/esl/celta; Part-time.

Language Studies Canada: Toronto; ✆ +416 488 2200; www.lsc-canada.com; Full-time; Rough frequency 7 per year.

Language Studies International: Toronto; ✆ +416 928 6888; www.lsi-canada.com; Part-time.

Global Village: Vancouver; ✆ +403 543 7300; www.gvenglish.com; Full and part-time; Rough frequency 6 per year.

China

Language Link China Trade Center: Beijing; ✆ +10 5169 5591/ 92/ 93; www.languagelink. com.cn; Full-time; Rough frequency 5 per year.

Sydney Institute of Language and Commerce (SILC): Shanghai; ✆ +021 5633 3082; Full-time; Rough frequency 1 per year.

Colombia

British Council Bogotá: Bogotá; ✆ +571 325 9090; www.britishcouncil.org/colombia; Full-time; Rough frequency 2 per year.

Costa Rica

Instituto Britanico: San José; ✆ +506 225 0256; www.institutobritanico.co.cr; Full-time; Rough frequency 3 per year.

Czech Republic

Akcent International House: Prague; ✆ +2 61 109 249; www.akcent.cz; Full and part-time; Rough frequency 10 per year.

Masaryk University: Brno; ✆ +549 498 403; Part-time.

Egypt

British Council: Cairo; ✆ +2 300 1666; www.britishcouncil.org/egypt; Full-time; Rough frequency 2 per year.

France

ILC France (International Language Centre): Paris; ✆ +1 44 41 80 20; www.ilcfrance.com; Full-time; Rough frequency 6 per year.

Transfer: Paris; ✆ +1 42 66 14 11; www.transfer.fr; Full-time; Rough frequency 4 per year.

Germany

Berlin School of English: Berlin; ✆ +30 229 0456; www.berlin.school-of-english.de; Full and part-time; Rough frequency 8 per year.

Hamburg School of English: Hamburg; ✆ +40 480 21 19; www.hamburg.school-of-english. de; Full and part-time; Rough frequency 5 per year.

Munchner Volkshochschule: Munich; ✆ +8106 300631; www.munichcelta.co.uk; Full and part-time; Rough frequency 2 per year.

Hungary

International House: Budapest; ✆ +1 212 4010; www.ih.hu; Full and part-time; Rough frequency 12 per year.

India

The British Council English Language Teaching Centre: New Delhi/Mumbai; ✆ +40 3980 2740; www.britishcouncil.org.in; Full-time; Rough frequency 4 per year.

Indonesia

The British Institute (TBI): Jakarta; ✆ +21 525 6750; www.tbi.co.id; Full and part-time; Rough frequency 2 per year.

Ireland

International House: Dublin; ✆ +1 4759011/1 4759013; www.ihdublin.com; Full and part-time; Rough frequency 9 per year.

Language Centre of Ireland: Dublin; ✆ +1 671 6266; www.lci.ie; Full-time; Rough frequency 3 per year.

Language Centre: Cork; ✆ +21 490 2043/ 490 2898; www.ucc.ie/en; Part-time.

Italy

British Council: Naples; ✆ +81 578 82 47; www.britishcouncil.it; Full-time; Rough frequency 1 per year.

The Cambridge School: Verona; ✆ +45 800 3154; www.cambridgeschool.it; Full and part-time; Rough frequency 2 per year.

International House Milan: Milan; ✆ +2867903; www.ihmilano.it; Full and part-time; Rough frequency 2 per year.

International House Rome/Accademia Britannica: Rome; ✆ +6 704 76 894; www.ihro-mamz.it; Full-time and semi-intensive; 6 per year.

International House Palermo: Palermo; ✆ +91 584954; www.ihpalermo.it; Full-time; Rough frequency 1 per year.

Teachertraining: Milan; ✆ +328 887 3365; www.teachertraining.it; Full and part-time; Rough frequency 5 per year.

Japan
Language Resources: Kobe; ✆ +78 382 0394; www.languageresources.org; Part-time.

Korea
The British Council, Seoul: Seoul; ✆ +2 3702 0646; www.britishcouncil.org/korea.htm; Full-time; Rough frequency 1 per year.

Lebanon
ALLC International House Beirut: Beirut; ✆ +1 500 978; www.allcs.edu.lb; Full-time; Rough frequency 3 per year.

Malaysia
The British Council Language Centre: Kuala Lumpur; ✆ +3 2723 7900; www.britishcouncil.org/malaysia; Full and part-time; Rough frequency 2 per year.

Malta
NSTS English Language Institute: Gzira; ✆ +2558 8500; www.nsts.org; Full-time; Rough frequency 2 per year.

Morocco
British Council Casablanca: Casablanca; ✆ +022 520990; www.britishcouncil.org/morocco-english-teach-celta.htm; Full-time; Rough frequency 1 per year.

Netherlands
British Language Training Centre: Amsterdam; ✆ +20 622 3634; www.bltc.nl; Full and part-time; Rough frequency 1 per year.

New Zealand
Aspect Education: Christchurch; ✆ +3 379 5452; www.kaplanaspect.com; Full-time; Rough frequency 2 per year.

Auckland Language Centre: Auckland; ✆ +9 303 1962; www.geosalc.co.nz; Full and part-time; Rough frequency 4 per year.

Christchurch College of English: Christchurch; ✆ +3 343 3790; www.ccel.co.nz; Full-time; Rough frequency 3 per year.

Christchurch Polytechnic Institute of Technology: Christchurch; ✆ +3 940 8021; www.cpit.ac.nz; Part-time.

Languages International: Auckland; ✆ +9 309 0615; www.languages.ac.nz; Full-time; Rough frequency 4 per year.

Rotorua English Language Academy: Rotorua; ✆ +7 349 0473; www.rela.co.nz; Full-time; Rough frequency 2 per year.

University of Waikato Language Institute: Hamilton; ✆ +7 858 5600; www.waikato.ac.nz; Full-time; Rough frequency 4 per year.

Oman
Caledonian College of Engineering: Seeb; ✆ +24536165 ext 376; www.cce.edu.om; Full-time; Rough frequency 1 per year.

Poland

ELS-Bell School of English: Gdansk; ✆ +58 551 3298; www.bellschools.pl; Full and part-time; Rough frequency 3 per year.

International House Krakow: Krakow; ✆ +12 421 9440; www.ih.pl; Full-time; Rough frequency 12 per year.

International House Wroclaw: Wroclaw; ✆ +71 78 17 290; www.ttcentre.ih.com.pl; Full-time; Rough frequency 3 per year.

Portugal

International House Lisbon: Lisbon; ✆ +21 315 1493/4/6; www.international-house.com; Full and part-time; Rough frequency 10 per year.

Russia

BKC-International House Moscow: Moscow; ✆ +495 234 0314; www.bkc.ru/eng; Full-time; Rough frequency 7 per year.

Singapore

The British Council Singapore: Napier Road; ✆ +64721010; www.britishcouncil.org/singapore; Part-time.

South Africa

Good Hope Studies: Cape Town; ✆ +21 683 1399; www.ghs.co.za; Full-time; Rough frequency 3 per year.

International House Durban: Durban; ✆ +31 566 5356/7; www.ihdurban.co.za; Full-time; Rough frequency 6 per year.

International House Johannesburg: Johannesburg; ✆ +11 339 1051; www.ihjohannesburg.co.za; Full-time; Rough frequency 10 per year.

Shane Global Language Centres Cape Town: Cape Town; ✆ +21 419 8524; www.shaneglobal.co.za; Full-time; Rough frequency 6 per year.

Spain

The British Language Centre: Madrid; ✆ +91 733 0739; www.british-blc.com; Full and part-time; Rough frequency 6 per year.

Cambridge School: Barcelona; ✆ +93 870 2001; www.cambridgeschool.com; Full-time; Rough frequency 6 per year.

CLIC International House: Seville; ✆ +95 450 0316; www.tefl.es; Full-time; Rough frequency 12 per year.

Instituto De Idiomas: Santiago; ✆ +981 563 100; www.usc.es; Full-time; Rough frequency 2 per year.

International House Barcelona: Barcelona; ✆ +93 268 4511; www.ihes.com/bcn; Full and part-time; Rough frequency 10 per year, €1550.

International House Madrid: Madrid; ✆ +91 310 1314; www.ihmadridtraining.com/allaboutcelta; Full and part-time; Rough frequency 12 per year.

International House Palma: Palma; ✆ +971 726408; www.ihes.com/pal; Full-time; Rough frequency 7 per year.

Lewis School of Languages: Barcelona; ✆ +93 411 1333; www.lewis-school.com; Full-time; Rough frequency 8 per year.

Switzerland
Bell Switzerland: Geneva; ✆ +22 749 16 16; www.bell-school.ch; Full and part-time; Rough frequency 1 per year.
Flying Teachers: Zurich; ✆ +1 350 3344; www.flyingteachers.ch; Full-time; Rough frequency 5 per year.
TLC The Language Centre Baden: Baden; ✆ +56 205 51 78; www.tlcsprachschule.ch; Part-time.
Volkshochschule, Bern: Bern; ✆ +31 302 8209; www.up-vhs.ch; Full and part-time; Rough frequency 1 per year.

Thailand
ECC (Thailand): Bangkok; ✆ +2 655-1236; www.eccthai.com; Full-time; Rough frequency 8 per year.
ECC (Phuket): Phuket; ✆ +76 219906; www.eccthai.com; Full-time; Rough frequency 5 per year.
ECC (Chiang Mai): Chiang Mai; ✆ +53 224565; www.eccthai.com; Full-time; Rough frequency 4 per year.

Turkey

Bilkent University: Ankara; ✆ +312 290 1912; www.bilkent.edu.tr/~busel; Part-time.

International Training Institute: Istanbul; ✆ +212 245 99 91/2; www.iti-istanbul.com; Full and part-time; Rough frequency 5 per year.

Izmir University of Economics: Izmir; ✆ +232 279 2525; www.ieu.edu.tr; Full-time; Rough frequency 1 per year.

Ukraine

British Council Kiev: Kiev; ✆ +955746008; www.britishcouncil.org/ukraine; Full-time; Rough frequency 1 per year.

International House Kyiv: Kiev; ✆ +442389870; www.ih.kiev.ua; Full-time; Rough frequency 3 per year.

United Arab Emirates

The British Council, Abu Dhabi: Abu Dhabi; ✆ +2 6910600; www.britishcouncil.org/me; Full and part-time; Rough frequency 1 per year.

Higher Colleges of Technology CERT: Many locations; ✆ +2681 2070; www.hct.ac.ae.

University of Wollongong: Dubai; ✆ +4 367 2760; www.uowdubai.ac.ae; Full and part-time; Rough frequency 1 per year.

USA

Cy-Fair College: Cypress, Texas; ✆ 832 482 1024; www.cy-faircollege.com/goto/celta; Full and part-time; Rough frequency 3 per year.

Denver Bridge-Linguatec: Denver; ✆ 303 777-7783 ext. 853; www.bridgetefl.com; Full-time; Rough frequency 6 per year.

Intercultural Communications College: Honolulu; ✆ 808 946 2445; www.icchawaii.edu; Full-time; Rough frequency 3 per year.

International House San Diego: San Diego; ✆ 619 299 2339; www.ih-sandiego.com; Full-time; Rough frequency 2 per year.

North Harris College: Houston; ✆ 281 618 5606; http://celta.nhceducatesu.com; Full-time; Rough frequency 2 per year.

St Giles International: San Francisco; ✆ 415 788 3552; email english@stgiles-usce.com; www.stgiles-usa.com; Full and part-time; Rough frequency 6 per year.

Teaching House, New York: New York; ✆ 212 732 0277; email info@teachinghouse.com; www.teachinghouse.com; Full-time CELTA courses are run monthly, as well as 3 part-time courses per year.

Vietnam

Language Link Vietnam: Hanoi; ✆ +4 9744 999; www.languagelink.edu.vn; Full-time; Rough frequency 3 per year.

International Language Academy (ILA): Ho Chi Minh City; ✆ +8 929 0100 Ext 149; www. ilavietnam.com; Full-time; Rough frequency 9 per year.

TRINITY COLLEGE LONDON CERTIFICATE (TESOL) COURSES

UK

Aberdeen College: Aberdeen; ✆ 01224 612000; www.abcol.ac.uk; Part-time.

Aberystwyth University: Aberystwyth, Wales; ✆ 01970 622545/622547; www.aber.ac.uk/tesol; Full-time; Rough frequency 2 per year.

Anglolang Academy: Scarborough, North Yorkshire; ✆ 01723 501 991 or 367 141; www.anglolang.com; Full-time.

Basingstoke College of Technology: Basingstoke, Hants; ✆ 01256 354141; www.bcot.ac.uk; Full and part-time; Rough frequency 1 per year.

Blackpool and the Fylde College: Blackpool; ✆ 01253 504343; www.blackpool.ac.uk; Course not run annually.

Bracknell & Wokingham College: Bracknell, Berkshire; ✆ 0845 330 3343; www.bracknell.ac.uk; Full and part-time; Rough frequency 1 per year.

Bury College: Bury, Lancashire; ✆ 0161 280 8280; www.burycollege.ac.uk; Part-time.

City College Manchester: Manchester; ✆ 0800 013 0123; www.ccm.ac.uk; Full and part-time; Rough frequency 1 per year.

Colchester Institute: Colchester; ✆ 01206 518777; www.colchester.ac.uk; Part-time; Rough frequency 3 per year of 8 weeks.

Crawley College: Crawley, West Sussex; ✆ 0845 1550043; www.centralsussex.ac.uk.

Darlington College of Technology: Co. Durham; ✆ 01325 503050; www.darlington.ac.uk; Part-time.

East Berkshire College: Slough, Berkshire; ✆ 0845 373 2500; www.eastberks.ac.uk; Part-time.

EF English First: Manchaster; ✆ 0161 256 1400; www.englishfirst.com; Full-time; Rough frequency 7 per year.

Gateshead College: Gateshead, Tyne and Wear; ✆ 0191 490 0300; www.gateshead.ac.uk; Part-time.

Golders Green Teacher Training Centre: London; ✆ 0208 905 5467; www.goldersgreen-college.co.uk; Full and part-time; Rough frequency 8 per year.

Guildford College: Guildford, Surrey; ✆ 01483 448500; www.guildford.ac.uk/international; Part-time.

Inlingua Cheltenham: Cheltenham, Gloucester; ✆ 01242 250493; www.inlingua-cheltenham.co.uk; Full and part-time; Rough frequency 7 per year.

International Training Network: Christchurch, Dorset; ✆ 01202 475956; www.itnuk.com; Full and part-time; Rough frequency 3 per year.

Isis Greenwich School of English: London; ✆ 0208 293 1444; www.isisgroup.co.uk; Full-time; Rough frequency 10 per year.

Keele University: Keele, Staffordshire; ✆ 01782 621111; www.keele.ac.uk; Part-time.

Kent School of English: Broadstairs, Kent; ✆ 01843 874 870; www.kentschoolofenglish.com; Full-time.

Kingston College: Kingston Upon Thames, Surrey; ✆ 020 8546 2151; www.kingston-college.ac.uk; Full and part-time; Rough frequency 1 per year.

Langside College Glasgow: Glasgow; ✆ 0141 272 3600; www.langside.ac.uk; Full and part-time; Rough frequency 3 per year.

Languages Training & Development: Witney, Oxfordshire; ✆ 01993 708637; www.ltdoxford.com; Full-time; Rough frequency 6 per year.

London Study Centre: London; ✆ 0207 731 3549; www.londonstudycentre.co.uk.

Manchester College of Arts and Technology: Manchester; ✆ 0800 068 8585; www.mancat.ac.uk; Full and part-time; Rough frequency 1 per year.

Medway Adult & Community Learning Service: Eastgate, Rochester; ✆ 01634 338400; www.medway.gov.uk/index/learning/adults-2/adultlearning.htm; May offer course in future.

Northampton College: Northampton; ✆ 01604 734567; www.northamptoncollege.ac.uk; Part-time.

Northbrook College: Northbrook, Sussex; ✆ 0845 155 60 60; www.northbrook.ac.uk; Full and part-time; Rough frequency 4 per year.

Oaklands College: St Albans, Hertfordshire; ✆ 01727 737000; www.oaklands.ac.uk

Oxford TEFL Londan: ✆ +93 458 0111; www.oxfordtefl.com; Part-time and full-time courses; Rough frequency 8 per year.

Peterborough Regional College: Peterborough, Cambridgeshire; ✆ 0845 872 8722; www.peterborough.ac.uk

Plymouth College of Further Education: Plymouth; ✆ 01752 305300; www.cityplym.ac.uk; Part-time.

Saint George International: London; ✆ 020 72991711; www.tesoltraining.co.uk; Full and part-time; Rough frequency 7 per year.

St Brelade's College: St Aubin, Jersey; ✆ 01534 741305; www.st-brelades-college.co.uk; Full-time; Rough frequency 2 per year.

St Giles London Central: London; ✆ 020 7837 0404; email londoncentral@stgiles.co.uk. www.stgiles-international.com; Full-time; Rough frequency 9 per year.

Sheffield Hallam University Tesol Centre: Sheffield; ✆ 0114 225 5515; www.shu.ac.uk/tesol/teaching; Full and part-time; Rough frequency 5 per year.

Sidmouth International School: Sidmouth, Devon; ✆ 01395 516754; www.sidmouth-int.co.uk; Full-time; Rough frequency 3 per year.

South East Essex College: Southend-on-Sea, Essex; ✆ 01702 220400; www.southend.ac.uk/index.html; Part-time.

St Giles International Eastbourne: Eastbourne; ✆ 01323-729167; email english@stgiles-eastbourne.co.uk; www.stgiles-international.com; Four week full time courses; Held 3 times around the year.

Students International Ltd: Melton Mowbray, Leicestershire; ✆ 01664 481997; www.studentsint.com; Full-time; Rough frequency 4 per year.

Sussex Language Institute: Brighton, East Sussex; ✆ 01273 873234; www.sussexdowns.ac.uk; Full-time; Rough frequency 3 per year.

Sutton College of Learning For Adults: Sutton, Surrey; ✆ 020 8770 6901; www.scola.ac.uk; Part-time.

The Language Institute/TLI English Language Training: Edinburgh; ✆ 0131 226 6975; www.tlieurope.com; Full-time; Rough frequency 4 per year.

The Language Project: Bristol; ✆ 0117 9090 911; www.languageproject.co.uk; Full-time, 5 week courses; Rough frequency 6 per year.

The Regency School of English: Ramsgate, Kent; ✆ 01303 252 717; www.regencyschool.co.uk.

Universal Language Training (ULT): Woking, Surrey; ✆ 01483 770911; www.universal-language.co.uk; Full and part-time; Rough frequency 4 per year.

University College Chichester: Chichester, West Sussex; ✆ 01243 816000; www.chiuni.ac.uk; Full and part-time; Rough frequency 1 per year.

University of Bedfordshire: Luton Campus, Park Square, Luton, Bedfordshire, LU1 3JU; ✆ 01234 400 400; www.beds.ac.uk; Full and part-time; Rough frequency 1 per year.

University of the West of England: Bristol; ✆ 0117 32 83813; www.uwe.ac.uk; Full-time; Rough frequency 1 per year.

University of Wolverhampton: Wolverhampton; ✆ 01902 322222; www.wlv.ac.uk; Full-time combined degree; 3 year course.

Argentina

Casa De Ingles: Chaco; ✆ +3722 443443; Part-time.

Centum, Servicios De Idiomas: Buenos Aires; ✆ +011 4328-2385; http://centumidiomas.homestead.com; Part-time.

Canada

Coventry House International: Toronto, Ontario; ✆ +416 929 0227; www.study-at-coventry.com; Full-time; Rough frequency 9 per year.

Czech Republic

Academy of Prague Schools: Prague; ✆ +2333 227 42; www.tefl.cz; Full-time; Rough frequency 13 per year.

Oxford TEFL: Prague; ✆ 226 211 900; www.teflprague.com; Full-time; Rough frequency 10 per year.

Hong Kong

English For Asia Ltd: Sheung Wan, Hong Kong; ✆ +2366 3792; www.englishforasia.com; Full-time; Rough frequency 4 per year.

Ireland

Atlantic School of English and Active Leisure: Schull, Co.Cork; ✆ +028 28943; www.atlantic-english.com; Full-time; Rough frequency 3 per year.

Indonesia

IALF Bali (Indonesia Australia Language Foundation): Bali; ✆ +361 225243; www.tesolbali.com; Full-time; Rough frequency 2 per year.

Italy

The Learning Center of Tuscany: Firenze; ✆ +55 051 5035; www.learningcentertuscany.com; Full-time; Rough frequency 11 per year.

New Zealand

Alpha Educational Institute: Christchurch City; ✆ +3 359 1525; www.alpha.school.nz; Full-time; Rough frequency 1 per year.

Edenz Colleges: Auckland; ✆ +9 920 5920; www.teachertraining.co.nz; Full and part-time; Rough frequency 5 per year.

English Language Academy: Auckland; ✆ +9 919 7695; www.ela.auckland.ac.nz; Full and part-time; Rough frequency 1 per year.

International Pacific College: Queenstown; ✆ +6 354 0922; www.ipc.ac.nz/index.php; Full-time; Rough frequency 1 per year.

Paraguay

Stael Ruffinelli De Ortiz – English: Asuncion; ✆ +21 226062/207017; Part-time.

Spain

Chester School of English: Madrid; ✆ +91 401 97 29; www.chester.es; Full-time; Rough frequency 5 per year.

The Language Institute: Pontevedra; ✆ +986 104763/862461; www.tlieurope.com; Full-time; Rough frequency 4 per year.

Oxford TEFL: Barcelona; ✆ +93 458 0111; www.oxfordtefl.com; Full-time; Rough frequency 12 per year.

Universal Language Training (ULT): Zamora; ✆ +01483 770911; www.universal-language.co.uk; Full and part-time.

United Arab Emirates

Woods James Consultants: Dubai; ✆ +4 2868629; www.wjconsultants.com; Full and part-time; Rough frequency 5 per year.

Uruguay

Dickens Institute: Montevideo; ✆ +2 710 7555; www.dickens.edu.uy; Part-time.

SHORT INTRODUCTORY COURSES

Berlitz (UK) Ltd: London; ✆ 020 7611 9640; www.berlitz.co.uk; Free in-house training for new teacher recruits.

EF English First Teacher Training: Manchester; ✆ 0161 256 1400; www.ef.com/master/tl/professional-development/prices-dates.asp; Approx. £450 for 1 week, £850 for 2 weeks; Cost is variable upon location.

Embassy CES Hastings: St Leonards on Sea, UK; ✆ 01273 339400; www.embassyces.com.

Embassy CES Newnham: Cambridge, England; ✆ 01223 311344; www.embassyces.com.

Intensive School of English & Business Communication: Brighton, UK; ✆ 01273 384800; www.ise.uk.com; £175; Frequency 1 per year.

Intensive Training Courses (ITC): Darlington, Co. Durham, UK; ✆ 0845 644 5464; www.tefl.co.uk; £210; Various locations, Frequency most weekends all year.

International English: West Sussex, UK; ✆ 01903 889797; www.internationalenglish.co.uk; From £245; Frequency 10 per year.

Intesol: see listing in next section.

i-to-i: Leeds, UK; ✆ 0871 423 9942; www.i-to-i.com, www.teflcourses.com; From £215; Various locations, Frequency most weekends all year.

ITTC: Bournemouth, UK; ✆ 01202 397721; www.ittc.co.uk; £50; Frequency 10 per year.

Northampton College: Northampton, UK; ✆ 01604 734567; www.northamptoncollege.ac.uk; £50; Frequency 1 per year.

Northbrook College Sussex: Sussex, UK; ✆ 0845 155 60 60; www.northbrook.ac.uk; £210 with concessions; Frequency 4 per year.

Projects Abroad: Sussex, UK; ✆ 01903 708300; www.projects-abroad.co.uk, www.internatio-nalenglish.co.uk; From £245 for 2-day course; Frequency 10 per year.

Saxoncourt Teacher Training: London; ✆ 020 7491 1911; www.saxoncourt.com; £250; Frequency 6 per year.

Sussex Downs College: Sussex, UK; ✆ 01273 483188; www.sussexdowns.ac.uk; £15; Frequency 1 per year.

Sussex Language Institute: Sussex, UK; ✆ 01273 873234; www.sussex.ac.uk; £200; Frequency 1 per year.

TEFL Time: Sussex, UK; ✆ 01903 708178; www.tefltime.com; £189; Frequency 9 per year.

TEFL Training: Oxon, UK; ✆ 01993 891996; www.tefltraining.co.uk; From £210; Various locations, Frequency most weekends all year.

DISTANCE LEARNING COURSES

Eurolink Courses: Sheffield, UK; ✆ 0114 262 1522; www.eurolinkcourses.co.uk; £600 in instalments/£540 if paid in full; Offers optional practical teaching placement; Cost with practical teaching placement is £1,095 in instalments/£1,020 if paid in full.

Global English: Exeter, Devon, UK; ✆ 01392 411999; www.global-english.com; £185; Offers specialist components in Young Learners, Business English, etc. Teaching practice can be arranged in Portugal.

ICAL: London, UK; ✆ 0845 310 4104; www.teacher-training.net; £135; Offers practical teaching placement; Cost is £395.

i-to-i: Leeds, UK; ✆ 0871 702 4437; www.i-to-i.com, www.onlinetefl.com; £156; Does not offer practical teaching placement.

INTESOL WORLDWIDE LTD: 4 Higher Downs, Knutsford, Cheshire WA16 8AW, UK; ✆ 0800 567 7189; www.intesoltesoltraining.com. Accredited by the College of Teachers. Online

and offsite courses from £395 to £895. Offers teaching practice in accredited schools. Accredited for quality of service with a money back guarantee by ODLQC. INTESOL works in partnership with English First (EF) to provide teaching positions.

Languages Training & Development (Ltd): Witney, Oxfordshire, England; ✆ 01993 708637; www.ltdoxford.com; £350; Does not offer practical teaching placement.

London Teacher Training College: London; ✆ 0208 133 2027; www.teachenglish.co.uk; £175; Offers practical teaching placement; Cost with practical teaching placement is £255.

Net Learn Languages: Middlesex, England; ✆ 07092 351821; www.netlearnlanguages.com; Does not offer practical teaching placement.

Norwood English: Laois, Eire; ✆ 57 8756325; www.norwoodenglish.com; From £160; Does not offer practical teaching placement.

Passport TEFL: San Francisco, Prague, Madrid, Barcelona; www.passporttefl.com; US$735; Does not provide practical teaching placement but will help arrange it.

TEFL Training: Oxon, UK; ✆ 01993 891121; www.tefltraining.co.uk; £395 if paid in full/£420 in instalments; Offers practical teaching placement; Cost is £250 for additional course.

Training Link Online: Sheffield, UK; ✆ 0114 262 1522; www.traininglinkonline.co.uk; £755 if paid in full/£810 in instalments; Offers practical teaching placement; Cost with practical teaching placement is £1,000 if paid in full/£1,080 in instalments.

University of Birmingham: Birmingham, UK; ✆ 0121 414 5695/6; www.cels.bham.ac.uk; Does not offer practical teaching placement.

University of Manchester: Manchester, UK; ✆ 0161 275 4740; www.manchester.ac.uk; £1,660 per year; in-service teachers development.

Words Language Services: Dublin, Ireland; ✆ 353 1 6610240; www.wls.ie; £325; Does not offer practical teaching placement.

ACADEMIC COURSES

This represents a small selection of university courses in TEFL/TESL in the UK. On the UCAS.com website, you can search by subject and find courses in TEFL/TESOL usually offered in combination with another subject such as a modern language or tourism.

Anglia Ruskin University: East Road, Cambridge CB1 1PT; ✆ 01223 363271; answers @anglia.ac.uk; www.anglia.ac.uk. Offers a BA in English Language teaching and an MA in Applied Linguistics and TESOL.

Aston University: School of Languages & Social Sciences, Aston Triangle, Birmingham B4 7ET; ✆ 0121 204 3762; lss_pgadmissions@aston.ac.uk; www.aston.ac.uk. MSc in Teaching English to Speakers of Other Languages (TESOL); with options to specialise in ESP, TEYL and EMT. Also Certificate in Advanced Studies in ELT, Diploma in Professional TESOL Studies, and Distance Learning Courses for practising and experienced teachers.

Canterbury Christ Church University: North Holmes Road, Canterbury CT1 1QU; ✆ 01227 767700 (Department of English and Language Studies); languagestudies@ canterbury.ac.uk; www.canterbury.ac.uk (Faculty of Arts & Humanities/Department of English and Language Studies). Offers Diploma/MA in TESOL, full (12 months), part-time or as a distance course. Also offers the CELTA (see entry).

Leeds Metropolitan University: School of Languages, Headingley Campus, Beckett Park, Leeds LS6 3QS; ✆ 0113 812 3113; course-enquiries@leedsmet.ac.uk. MA Materials Development for Language Teaching, and MA Professional Development for Language Education. 1-year full-time.

London Metropolitan University: 166–220 Holloway Road, London N7 8DB; ✆ 020 7133 4202; admissions@londonmet.ac.uk; www.londonmet.ac.uk. MA in International ELT & Applied Language Studies (for experienced teachers); MA TEFL (for newly qualified teachers). Full-time 1-year course. Fees £4,050 for EU students or £6,930 for non-EU students.

Middlesex University: The Burroughs, London NW4 4BT; ✆ 020 8411 5555; www.mdx.ac.uk. One of the few undergraduate degree courses in TEFL in the UK.

University of Bedford: Park Square, Luton, Bedfordshire LU1 3JU; ✆ 01234 400400; www.beds.ac.uk. English Language Studies with Teaching English as a Foreign Language (TEFL) BA Hons, Applied Linguistics (TEFL) MA, English as a Foreign Language (EFL) Credit, Teaching English as a Foreign Language TEFL Certificate (summer school) and teaching English as a Foreign Language TEFL Certificate (part-time evening).

University of Birmingham: Centre for English Language Studies, Westmere, Edgbaston Park Road, Edgbaston, Birmingham B15 2TT; ✆ 0121 414 3239/5696; fax 0121 414 3298; cels@bham.ac.uk; www.cels.bham.ac.uk. The Centre for English Language Studies specialises in language research, training and consultancy. CELS is part of the Department of English at the University of Birmingham. The department holds the highest possible ratings for both research and teaching. Offers full-time or part-time courses on campus in TEFL/TESL, Applied Linguistics, English for Specific Purposes, Language and Lexicography, Special Applications of Linguistics, Translation Studies, Applied Corpus Linguistics, Critical Discourse, Culture and Communication. Also offers distance learning courses in TEFL/TESL, Translation Studies and Applied Linguistics in addition to Postgraduate Research Degrees by distance learning. All campus-based courses last for 1 year and begin in October. Distance-learning MA courses begin in April and October and typically take 30 months. Possibility to study part-time, one term per year. Accommodation available on campus. Contact CELS administrator via www.cels.bham.ac.uk.

University of Brighton: School of Languages, Falmer, Brighton, East Sussex BN1 9PH; ✆ 01273 643336; a.pickering@brighton.ac.uk; www.bton.ac.uk. Offers Diploma and MA in TESOL; 1-year full-time or part-time. These are both post-graduate courses; applicants must have some English teaching experience for the MA and 2 years for the Diploma. Also offers an MA in English Language Teaching, 1-year full-time or part-time, for teachers with a limited amount of experience.

University of Central Lancashire: Department of Languages and International Studies, Preston, PR1 2HE; ✆ 01772 893136; ccerttefl@uclan.ac.uk; www.uclan.ac.uk. Certificate in TESOL. Intensive summer course. Accommodation is available in halls of residence if required.

University of Edinburgh: Institute for Applied Language Studies, 21 Hill Place, Edinburgh EH8 9DP; ✆ 0131 650 6200; fax 0131 667 5927; ials.enquiries@ed.ac.uk; www.ials.ed.ac.uk. Offer Cambridge DELTA, a 3-stage course comprising 11 weeks' intensive coursework, 6 weeks' teaching and a revision phase, with a written exam. Starts in April. The structure may be changed to make it more appropriate for the new modularised DELTA course. Fees £2,088 (2009) including exam fee.

University of Essex: International Academy, Wivenhoe Park, Colchester, Essex CO4 3SQ; ✆ 01206 872217; fax 01206 873107; dilly@essex.ac.uk; www.essex.ac.uk/eltc. One of only three BA degrees offered in TEFL. Also MA TESOL/Diploma TESOL/Certificate TESOL.

MANCHESTER 1824

The University of Manchester

MA TESOL/ MA Educational Technology & TESOL

These two MA programmes aim to develop the professional practice and career opportunities of experienced TESOL professionals (both native and non-native speakers). Particular strengths of the two MA programmes include: *Intercultural Communication; Language Teacher Education; Materials and Methods for Language Teaching*. There is an emphasis on technology and research methods in both MA programmes. In addition, the specialist MA in Educational Technology and TESOL has the following key elements: *ICT in Language Teaching and Learning; Multimedia Materials Design; Online Education and Courseware Development.*

These MA programmes can be taken as full or part-time courses in Manchester, or by distance learning from anywhere in the world.

PhD Studies

We offer doctoral research in any of our areas of expertise. Doctoral programmes include comprehensive training in research methods. See our websites for further details on all our MA and PhD programmes. **www.education.manchester.ac.uk or edtechandtesol.info**

Postgraduate Admissions Office
School of Education, Faculty of Humanities, The University of Manchester Oxford Road, Manchester, M13 9PL

Tel: +44 (0)161 275 3463
E-mail: education.enquiries@manchester.ac.uk

The modular MA TESOL (180 credits) can be taken either within 1 year or over a period of 4 years with exit points at Diploma (120 credits) or Certificate (60 credits).

University of Exeter: School of Education and Lifelong Learning, St Luke's Campus, Heavitree Road, Exeter EX1 2LU; ℂ 01392 264837; ed-student@exeter.ac.uk. Offer EdD/PhD/MPhil/ MEd/PgDip/PgCert TESOL by full-time, part-time and intensive summer study.

University of Manchester: Postgraduate Admissions Office, School of Education, Faculty of Humanities, Oxford Road, Manchester M13 9PL; ℂ 0161 275 3463; pg-education@ manchester.ac.uk; www.education.manchester.ac.uk. Offers MA TESOL or MA Educational Technology and TESOL in 3 modes of study: 1 year full-time (on-site), UK/EU £3,300 and overseas £10,500; 27 or 36 months part-time (on-site), EU/UK £1,650; and 3 years' distance, £1,660 a year. Entry requirements include 3 years' teaching experience. The university also offers an introduction to TESOL as part of an undergraduate degree (one term).

University of Reading: Department of Applied Linguistics, School of Languages and European Studies, Whiteknights, PO Box 218, Reading RG6 6AA; ℂ 0118 378 8123; languages@ reading.ac.uk; www.rdg.ac.uk/app_ling. MA ELT in both campus-based and distance-study modes, with an additional study track for novice teachers. Also, MA Applied Linguistics, BA Applied English Language Studies.

University of Stirling/CELT: Institute of Education (CELT), Stirling FK9 4LA; ℂ 01786 467937; fax 01786 466131; celt@stir.ac.uk; www.celt.stir.ac.uk. MSc in TESOL (Teaching English to Speakers of Other Languages) and undergraduate degrees in EFL/ELT available. General English, IELTS Preparation, Short Courses for Teachers and a Summer School in August are also offered.

University of Sussex: Admissions, Sussex House, Falmer, Brighton, East Sussex BN1 9RH; © 01273 678416; fax 01273 678545; UG.Admissions@sussex.ac.uk (for BA programme) or PG.Admissions@sussex.ac.uk (for MA programmes); www.sussex.ac.uk. BA English Language Teaching. 3- or 4-year joint major in ELT with English, English Language, Language(s) or Linguistics. Includes opportunity to take Trinity TESOL Certificate as part of degree. MA in English Language Teaching; MA in International English Language Teaching and a Postgraduate Diploma in ELT (full-time 1 year, part-time 2 years).

University of Warwick: Centre for Applied Linguistics, Coventry CV4 7AL; © 024 7652 3200; fax 024 7652 4318; appling@warwick.ac.uk; www2.warwick.ac.uk/fac/soc/al/. MA in ELT/ ESP/English for Young Learners (all post-experience), English Language Studies and Methods (less than two years' experience), ELT and Multimedia/British Cultural Studies and ELT (both either pre- or post-experience). One-term PG Certificates in any of the MA specialisms (January to March), two terms for a postgrad diploma.

TRAINING COURSES IN NORTH AMERICA

USA

American Language Institute: San Diego State University, 5250 Campanile Drive, San Diego, CA 92115 1914; © 619 594–8740; fax 619 287 8735; ali@mail.sdsu.edu; www.americanlanguage.com/home.html. Well-known amTEFL Certificate validated by SDSU Department of Education (3 graduate credits). 4 weeks, 130 hours, offered four times a year. $2,650. Dormitory/homestay/apartment accommodation can be arranged through the ALI housing office. Each participant has a mentor, and each participant teaches real, tuition-paying students supervised by a master teacher. Coordinator Rob Shaffer offers extensive job assistance; 160 ALI graduates have taught in 38 countries.

Boston Academy of English: 59 Temple Place, 2nd Floor, Boston, MA 02111; © 617 338 6243; fax 617 695 9349; info@bostonacademyofenglish.com; www.bostonacademyofenglish.com. 4 weeks' intensive 120-hour CTEFL course, US$2,300, part-time US$2,150.

Boston Language Institute: 648 Beacon St, Boston, MA 02215; © 617 262 3500 fax 617 262 3595; info@teflcertificate.com; www.teflcertificate.com. Intensive 4-week TEFL Certificate course (120 hours) offered monthly. 12-week Saturday programmes also offered three times a year. Teacher-trainer programme is based on giving TEFL students extensive opportunities to practise what they learn and to lead their own classes of ESL students with guidance and feedback from experienced ESL teachers. Special TEFL Certificate Programme for Non-Native Speakers of English also offered: course includes additional training on pronunciation, American culture and other relevant topics. Tuition of $2,645 includes fees, all study materials and lifetime job assistance.

Global TEFL: © 312 209 3660; mail@globaltefl.org; www.globaltefl.org. Full-time School for International Training (SIT) TESOL Certificate courses offered by freelance certified trainers Ron and Ellen Bradley and other SIT certified trainers in Chicago, California, Grand Junction, CO and Boston. Part-time courses offered at some locations. $2,295 inclusive. (For further details of course see website.)

Hamline University, TEFL Certificate Program: Graduate School of Education, 1536 Hewitt Avenue, St Paul, MN 55104; © 651 523 2600; gse@hamline.edu; www.hamline.edu. Intensive 1-month courses and one evening extensive (September–February). Current tuition

$3,120. Focus is on developing communicative language teaching strategies. Ongoing career counselling provided. Graduate credit granted. Course can be used towards Hamline's MA in ESL. Advanced TEFL option offered.

Midwest Teacher Training Program: 19 N. Pinckney Street, Madison, WI 53703; ✆ 800 765 8577 or 608 257 8476; fax 608 257 4346; info@mttp.com; www.mttp.com. Practical, hands-on 5-week TEFL Certificate Course (130 hours including 10 hours of teaching practice) in a progressive university city. Housing arranged if needed. Integrated with an ESL school providing an international environment. Job placement assistance including resource library, job search workshop and personal résumé editing. Graduates have found jobs in 45+ countries.

School for International Training (SIT): Kipling Road, PO Box 676, Brattleboro, VT 05302 0676; ✆ 800.257.7751; tesolcert@sit.edu; www.sit.edu/tesolcert. Full-time 130-hour SIT TESOL Certificate course offered in various locations including New York, NY; Chicago, IL; Rohnert Park, CA; Northampton, MA; Grand Junction, CO; and Mexico, Ecuador, Thailand, Bulgaria, Chile and Brazil.

School of Teaching English as a Second Language (Affiliate Programme with Seattle University College of Education): 9620 Stone Avenue. N., Suite 101, Seattle, WA 98103; ✆ 206 781 8607; fax 206 781 8922; STESLinfo@seattleu.edu; www.schooloftesl.com/. 12-credit, 4-week intensive courses (monthly), non-intensive evening classes (quarterly), and online classes (quarterly). US$233 per credit, 2008/09 academic year. Accommodation available on request. Classes carry college credit and can be used as a portion of Master's degrees at Seattle University (except online classes) and for a Washington State approved ELL Endorsement. Post-Baccalaureate Certificate in TESOL issued by Seattle University to qualifying students. Counselling, monthly employment seminars, graduates' networking services and an on-site ESOL class.

Transworld Schools, CTESOL (Certificate in Teaching English to Speakers of Other Languages) Teacher Training at Transworld Schools: 701 Sutter Street, 6th Floor, San Francisco, CA 94109; ✆ 1 888 588 8335/415 928 2835; fax 415 928 0261; transwd@aol.com; www.transworldschools.com. Comprehensive CTESOL (4 weeks full-time, 14 weeks part-time, US$2,000); CTESOL (3 weeks full-time, 10 weeks part-time US$1,800); Intensive CTESOL (for working teachers – 2 weeks full-time; 7 weeks part-time, US$1,600); Advanced CTESOL (for working teachers – 1 week full-time; 4 weeks part-time, $900); Online CTESOL with 1 week on-site residency US$1,200. All courses internationally recognised. Approved by State of California, BPPVE and accredited by ACCET. High-quality training at low tuition. Job placement worldwide and lifetime job assistance. Accommodation (US$130–US$250 per week) within 5 minutes walk in downtown San Francisco. Courses include evaluated Teaching Practice, teaching children and adults, grammar, business English, TOEFL and syllabus design. Facilities include multi-media lab, video and internet.

Washington Academy of Languages, TESL Graduate Certificate/Endorsement Program: 2 Nickerson St., Suite 201, Seattle, WA 98109; ✆ 206 682 4463 or toll-free 888 682 4463; fax 206 224 7927; info@wal.org; www.wal.org. Graduate TEFL Certificate offered in conjunction with Seattle Pacific University. Eight courses for total of 24 quarter credits. Offered intensively as 8-week summer course, online or in evening classes over academic year.

Western Washington University TESOL Program: Bellingham, WA 98225 9091; ✆ 360 650 4949; Trish.Skillman@wwu.edu; www.wce.wwu.edu/Resources/TESOL/. Full-time and part-time university courses starting in September, with a summer intensive option. Interdisciplinary course work and practical experience lead to a certificate of achievement and a supporting endorsement in Teaching ESL. Distance education and Overseas practicum experiences available.

Worldwide Teachers Development Institute: 29 Walton St, Boston, MA 02124; ✆ 617 262 5722; admin@bostontefl.com; www.bostontefl.com. Intensive American TEFL and Cert. TBE (Business English) certificate programmes offered in Boston. Also via distance learning or a mixture of online and residency courses.

TRAINING COURSES IN CANADA

The website of TESL Canada (www.tesl.ca) has links to a large number of approved teacher training programmes across Canada.

Archer College Toronto (formerly Languages International): 330 Bay Street, Suite 910, Toronto, Ontario M5H 2S8; ✆ 416 361 2411; fax 416 361 2403; info@litoronto.com; www.litoronto.com. 4-week Introductory TESL Certificate course several times a year, $995. Also offers 12-week advanced TEFL certificate, $2,940. Homestay and reasonably priced accommodation arranged near school. Refers graduates to recruiters and potential employers and maintains current job listings. Valuable practice teaching period included in programme.

Archer College Vancouver: Main Floor, 788 Beatty Street, Vancouver, BC V6B 2M1; ✆ 604 608 0538; Info@ArcherEducation.com; www.archereducation.com. 150-hour TESL Canada recognised courses offered full-time for 1 month, or part-time over 14 weeks. Other training courses include a 100-hour distance education course. All courses include practicum and are offered year-round. Prices about US$1,045 depending on course. Recommendations are given on local accommodation. Archer is recognised by federal Human Resources Canada and is a member of the Canadian Association of Private Language Schools and the Better Business Bureau.

College of Applied Linguistics: 90 University Ave, Stanton 102, Ottawa, Ontario K1N 1H3; toll free ✆ 1 888 246 6512; www.intlcollegeoflinguistics.com. TEFL and TESL certificate courses. Courses are held on various campuses. Job placement assistance given.

GLOBAL TESOL COLLEGE, TESOL Certification & Learn English in Canada. Travel and Teach English Center, 10037 B -82 Avenue, Edmonton, Alberta T6E 1Z2; Toll-free in North

America: 1-888-270 2941; 780-438-5704; fax 780-665-6141; e-mail info@globaltesol.com; www.globaltesol.com. Office/training centres across Canada, and in many other countries worldwide. World's largest TESOL Certificate and Diploma granting programme as described in a free Travel-and-Teach information package. 40,000 graduates teaching English in 85 countries. Range of Canada Government certified TESOL Certificate and Diploma courses held regularly in cities throughout Canada and other countries. 5-Day intensive format, or online and correspondence study options available worldwide. Overseas job guaranteed. Prices range from $695 to $3,495. Famous for its 16 Specialization course options. 120-hour to 600-hour programme available. Other courses offered online or by correspondence include Teaching Business English, Teaching TOEFL Preparation, Teaching Grammar, Teaching Children, Teaching Adults, Tourism English, Teaching CALL Computer English and more. Accommodation can be arranged. Franchises available, e-mail for details.

Global Village English Centres: 180 Bloor Street W, Suite 202, Toronto, Ontario M5S 2V6; ✆ 416 968 1405; fax 416 968 6667; toronto@gvenglish.com; www.gvenglish.com. Full-time TESL course recognised by TESL Canada, 8 weeks in length. Courses offered four times a year. Fees $2,500 plus $100 materials fee and $100 registration fee. Homestay or on-site accommodation available. TESOL Diploma is also available at the Career Training Centre in Vancouver and Global Village in Calgary.

Oxford Seminars: 131 Bloor St. West, Suite 200–390, Toronto, ON M5S 1R8 and office also in Vancouver ✆ 1 800 269 6719; info@oxfordseminars.com; www.oxfordseminars.com. TESOL/TESL weekend courses held in hundreds of cities around the USA and Canada, usually on university/college campuses. CAN$1,045/US$995.

Peak TESOL: Rocky Mountain School District 6, ✆ 1 877 427 5114 or 250 427 5114; peak.tesol@gmail.com; www.peaktesol.ca.

TRAINING COURSES ABROAD

Worldwide

Bridge-Linguatec: Head office: 915 S. Colorado Blvd., Denver, Colorado 80246; ✆ 303 785–8864; Toll free (USA and Canada) ✆ 1 888 827 -4757; ✆ 0800 028 8051 (UK); www.bridgetefl.com. Intensive 140-hour TEFL courses offered in centres in Argentina, Brazil, Chile, Peru, China, Costa Rica, Czech Republic, Greece, Italy, Mexico, Spain, Thailand, Turkey and Vietnam. All courses cost US$1,995 including registration fee, tuition and books. Also offers 2-week residential plus 80 hours online course (US$1,495).

Global TESOL: 10037 B-82 Avenue, Edmonton, Alberta T6E 1Z2, Canada; & 1 888 270 2941 or 780 438 5704; info@globaltesol.com; www.globaltesol.com. Range of Canada Government certified TESOL Certificate and Diploma courses held regularly in cities throughout Canada and other countries. Online and correspondence study options available worldwide. Overseas job guaranteed. Prices range from $695 to $3,495. For online or correspondence TESOL Certification Course information from anywhere in the world, email info@globaltesol.com For information on in-class TESOL Certification Course locations near you, email info@globaltesol.com For Global TESOL College Franchise information to offer our in-class TESOL Certification Courses in your area, email franchise@globaltesol.com

TEFL International: admin@teflinternational.org.uk; www.teflinternational.org.uk. USA Head office: 1200 Belle Passi Rd, Woodburn, OR 97071. TEFL International TESOL Certificate, 120-hour PELT (Practical English Language Teaching) certificate courses and TEFL taster courses offered at centres around the world. Special Projects with guaranteed work or

internship (including volunteer projects). Cities where it is currently possible to take the TEFL International course are: London, Beijing, Buenos Aires, Zhuhai, Manual Antonio (Costa Rica), Prague, Alexandria, Brittany, Ios (Greece), Calcutta, Florence, Rome, Kathmandu, Cebu (Philippines), Lubin (Poland), Seoul, Barcelona, Seville, Bah Phe, Chiang Mai and Phuket (Thailand) and Ho Chi Minh City. Most centres offer the course every month. Prices vary slightly but are usually £820 without accommodation and £875 with accommodation, but with regular specials and discount programmes available.

TEFL International UK: admin@teflinternational.org.uk; www.teflinternational.org.uk. UK address: Inforteach Limited, Redwood Centre, St Michaels, Tenbury Wells, Worcestershire WR15 8TL; tel 01568-750353. The marketing agents in the UK for the major international organisation TEFL International (listing above).

The World TEFL School: Endeavour House, Coopers End Road, Stansted, Essex CM24 1SJ, ✆ +0207 193 1541 (UK), 508 471 3662 (US); www.worldteflschool.com. 4-week Advanced TEFL courses can be taken in the UK, France, Spain, Italy, Greece, Czech Republic, Russia, Cambodia, Vietnam, Thailand, Argentina, Mexico, China or Costa Rica. Cost of advanced 120-hour course varies among locations but mostly £800–£1,000. No experience or qualifications required to enrol. Volunteer teaching programmes available in Vietnam, Cambodia and Costa Rica.

Argentina

EBC Servicios Lingüísticos: Anchorena 1676, 1425 Capital Federal, Buenos Aires; ✆ +0800 845 6719 (UK, free); 1 888 393 4015 (US free); info@ebc-tefl-course.com; www.ebc-tefl-course.com. US$1,559.

Íbero Spanish School: 150 Uruguay Street, Buenos Aires; ✆ +54 11 5218 0240; florencia@ iberospanish.com; www.iberospanish.com. Intensive 4-week TEFL certificate courses offered monthly; from $950. Can be combined with 3 weeks Spanish tuition for $1,410. Followed by optional 4-day trip to Iguazu Falls.

TEFLocal: 1472 Junin, Buenos Aires, Capital Federal, 11113 – Argentina; ✆ +11 54 4807 4360; in USA: ✆ +312 602 3349; fax 312 276-TEFL (8335); info@TEFLocal.org; www. TEFLocal.com. TEFL and TESOL certificate courses, $1,399 plus for four weeks.

Australia

Australian TESOL Training Centre (ATTC): Sydney: Level 1, 31 Market Street, Sydney, NSW 2000; ✆ +61 2 9389 0249; fax +61 2 9389 7788: Brisbane: Level 1, 295 Ann Street, Brisbane, QLD 4001; 61 7 3229 0350; fax 61 2 9389 7788: train@attc.edu.au; www.attc.edu.au. CELTA centres that offer full- and part-time courses throughout the year. Accommodation service available. Internet enrolment.

English Language Services: Adelaide Institute of Technical and Further Education (part of the Government Department of Education, Training and Employment), 5th Floor, Renaissance Centre, 127 Rundle Mall, Adelaide, South Australia 5000; ✆ +8 8207 8805; els.tesol@ tafesa.edu.au; http://els.sa.edu.au. Certificate IV in TESOL, TESOL for overseas teachers and TESOL online.

Global TESOL Australia: Sarina Russo Centre, 82 Ann Street, Brisbane, Queensland 4000. ✆ +61 7 3221 5100; fax +61 7 3221 5161; teachenglish@sarinarusso.com.au; www.globaltesol.com; 120-hour to 600-hour programmes available; tuition fees AUS$995– AUS$2,300. All courses can be completed in-class, online or by correspondence. Job overseas guaranteed.

Teach International: Head Office, Level 2, 370 George Street, Brisbane, Queensland 4000; ✆ +7 3211 4633 (ext 4); fax 7 3211 4644; www.teachinternational.com. Foundation in TESOL, 100 hours, $1,695; Certificate III in TESOL, 110 hours, $1,995, and Certificate IV in TESOL, 220 hours, $2,495, accredited by Australian government. Offered throughout the year.

Chile

The TEFL Academy: Av. Hernando de Aguirre 129, Providencia, Santiago; ✆ +8 791 0828; fax 2 233 3218; info@tefl-academy.com; www.tefl-academy.com. 120-hour certificate course. Offered monthly. $1,499. Lifelong job assistance.

China

The Boland School T.E.F.L. Training Centre: Su Zhou City, Jiangsu Province, No. 10–1 Fengmen Rd. 6th fl. Suzhou, Jiangsu Province, China; ✆ +512 6741 3422, fax 512 6750 6042; info@boland-china.com; www.boland-china.com. The Boland School was founded in 1992 and has TEFL teacher training centres in both Europe and Asia. Offers International TEFL Diploma, a 4-week residential programme. Courses are held monthly, all year round. 25-hour mini-preparation course (online) prior to course commencement, followed by 148 class hours on site, including 12 hours of peer teaching practice, and 8 hours of observed teaching of EFL students. There is full trainer support and feedback for every trainee for both teaching practice types. Programme participants train in small groups with two qualified native-speaker trainers working with each group of eight students. Course fees €1,000, plus €250 EU registration fee. 90-hour TEFL Language Awarness Online Preparation Programme (€480 including certificate). TEFL-China Certificate also offered (20-hour additional elective course including survival Chinese, traditions, education system, culture and etiquette). Optional paid internship programme at Chinese school for all graduates. Monthly job fairs for programme participants and graduates. Job guarantee for native English speakers and tuition reimbursement options offered by partner schools. Single-room accommodation available for the duration of the course for €300 for furnished apartment or hotel for five weeks. The Boland school also offers a full range of cultural electives, such as Mandarin Chinese lessons, Kungfu and China Business seminars. Contact Sinead Ievers, Programme Director.

Business English Solutions International: LLC: Zhejiang China and 510 West Deming Place, Chicago IL 60614; ✆ +773 572 2473 (Chicago); ✆ 86 13757252787 (China); fax 858 300 5465; Info@journeyeast.org; www.Journeyeast.org. TEFL Certification and iTEFL (Intensive TEFL China Certification). US$1,800–US$2,800 including accommodation. ESL Job Placement Service.

TEFL International: At Gateway Language Village, Xiangzhou Culture Plaza, Ningxi Road, Zhuhai; ✆ +756 229 8967; admin@teflinternational.org.uk; www.teflinternational.org.uk. 120-hour proprietary PELT certificate course. £875 including private accommodation, £765 without.

Costa Rica

Centro Espiral Mana/TESOL Training Costa Rica: El INVU de Peñas Blancas, Via San Carlos, Alajuela; ✆ fax 506 468 0020 or in USA: 585 200 3091; tesoltrainingcostarica@hotmail.com; www.tesoltrainingcostarica.org. School for International Training's TESOL Certificate Course. 1 month intensive, 3 month extensive. $1,950 tuition, $600 room and board in local homes or rented houses plus materials.

Costa Rica TEFL: Heredia and Playa Samara; info@costaricatefl.com; www.costaricatefl.com. Offers 10 TEFL Certification courses per year, 160 hours contact time. Costs $1,215, including job placement assistance, free Latin dance classes etc. The core instructors all have masters degrees and/or higher education and in teaching English as a second or foreign language with more than 22 years of professional teaching experience. Heredia course affiliated to Intercultura Costa Rica (www.interculturacostarica.com; see entry in Central America chapter).

Cyprus

Papantoniou Institute: 30a Ippocratous, Nicosia 2122; 00357–22455724; ✆ 00357 99957727; fax 00357 22334107; papantoniouinstitute@yahoo.co.uk; www.papantoniou-institute.com. 6-week teaching refresher courses and 8-week TEFL courses, with monthly start dates. Validated by IATQI and ASET/CIACQ. Full range of LTTC and LCCI courses.

Czech Republic

The Boland School TEFL Training Centre: Krenova 66, 60200 Brno; ✆ /fax: 420 541 241 674; info@boland-czech.com; www.boland-czech.com. The Boland School was founded in 1992 and has TEFL teacher training centres in both Europe and Asia. Offers International TEFL Diploma, a 148-hour, 4-week residential programme. Courses are held monthly, all year round. 25-hour mini-preparation course (online) prior to course commencement, followed by 148 class hours on-site, including 12 hours of peer teaching practice with trainer feedback and 8 hours of observed teaching of EFL students. Course fees €1,050 plus €250 EU registration fee. Additional TEFL-Czech Certificate (20-hour elective course including survival Czech, traditions, education system, culture and etiquette) costs € 75. 90-hour TEFL

Language Awarness Online Programme also offered (€480 including certificate). Optional mini-internship programme at local secondary school free of charge for all graduates. Comprehensive job placement with guarantee for native English speakers. Single-room accommodation available for the duration of the course for €350. Contact Kathryn Boland, General Director.

The Caledonian School: Vitavská 24, 150 00 Prague 5; ✆ 2 5731 3650; fax 2 5151 2528; jobs@caledonianschool.com; www.caledonianschool.com. 4-week intensive TEFL course in Prague, successful trainees are guaranteed position at the school. Full-time jobs year round.

ITC International TEFL Certificate: Kaprova 12, 110 00 Prague 1; ✆ /fax 224817530; info@itc-training.com. ITC trains English speakers during a 4-week intensive course offered monthly in Prague and also offered regularly in other destinations around the world, from India to Costa Rica. Upon completion of the course successful graduates are guaranteed to find jobs in the EU and Asia. Lifetime TEFL career assistance is offered to all graduates as well as travel, housing and visa help. Tuition is €1,900 (Prague only) which includes registration, lifetime job guidance, course manual, all materials, foreign language lessons and more. ITC is a member of IATEFL, College of Teachers (UK), and TESOL. Interested applicants should contact info@itc-training.com or apply online at www.itc-training.com.

TEFL Worldwide Prague: Freyova ul. 12/1, 190 00 Prague; ✆ 603 486 830; fax 283 892 440; info@teflworldwideprague.com; www.teflworldwideprague.com. 4-week courses offered monthly. €1,300 plus 8,000–10,000 Cz crowns for 30 nights of accommodation. Courses include 8–10 hours of practice in real classroom. Job assistance worldwide. Member of the Czech American Chamber of Commerce and IATEFL (International Association of Teachers of English as a Foreign Language). Accredited by the Czech Ministry of Education.

Ecuador

Centro De Estudios Interamericanos/Cedei: Casilla 597, Cuenca; ✆ +7 283 9003; fax 7 283 3593; info@cedei.org; www.cedei.org. Summer TEFL programme, $3,225 including accommodation.

Egypt

American University in Cairo: PO Box 2511, Cairo 11511; ✆ +2 2797 5081/2 27975095; teflinfo@aucegypt.edu; www.aucegypt.edu. US enquiries to 420 Fifth Avenue, 3rd Floor, New York, NY 10018 2729 (✆ +212 730 8800; fax 212 730 1600). Offers MA in Teaching English as a Foreign Language (MA/TEFL). American-style education in an overseas setting.

France

WICE: 20 boulevard du Montparnasse, 75015 Paris; ✆ +1 45 66 75 50; fax 1 40 65 96 53; wice@wice-paris.org; www.wice-paris.org. Internationally recognised WICE TEFL Certificate programme in conjunction with Rutgers the State University of New Jersey (USA), Graduate School, Newark (USA). Two courses are offered, an 8-month, part-time extensive course and a 4-week, full-time accelerated course (€1,655).

Germany

Language Specialists International: Pfalzburger Strasse 83, 10719 Berlin; ✆ +30 3450 2180; fax 30 3450 2181; info@lsi-berlin.de; www.tefl-germany.com. 4-week TESOL courses run every month. Fees €1,375.

Greece

Anglo-Hellenic Teacher Training: PO Box 263, Corinth 20100; ✆ +27410 53511; fax 27410 85579; info@teflcorinth.com; www.teflcorinth.com. Via Lingua TEFL certificate offered every month. 120 hours full-time over 4 weeks, 10 hours observed teaching practice. Moderated by the University of Birmingham. All tutors are Britons or Americans resident in Greece and experienced teachers with MAs in ELT. Cost €1,325. Accommodation in furnished apartment €350 single, €250 shared. Extensive optional social programme. Help with job placement via Anglo-Hellenic Teacher Recruitment (see Greece chapter). Range of short teacher development courses including preparation course for the Cambridge ESOL TKT. 30 hours full-time over 1 week, or weekend options (see www.tkt.gr). Cost €275.

Celt Athens: 77 Academias Street, 10678 Athens; ✆ +210 330 2406; fax 210 330 1202; info@celt.edu.gr; www.celt.edu.gr. Offers full-time (4 weeks) or part-time (12 weeks) Certificate in TEFL regularly throughout the year, €1,450. Other courses on offer include Cambridge CELTA (€1,850); Language Awareness for Teachers of English (€1,300); Cambridge DELTA, part-time (8 months) or 10 intensive weekends (€3,750); Short Courses on Teaching Adults, Young Learners, Exam Classes, Business English, CALL (€300 450); TKT Preparation (€450); and Translation Diplomas (€3,200–3,600). Help with accommodation for overseas students. Job placement assistance.

Hong Kong

The Chinese University of Hong Kong: 23/F, Tower, B School of Continuing and Professional Studies, The Chinese University of Hong Kong, Mongkok Town Centre, 90 Shantung Street, Mongkok, Kowloon; ✆ +825 27810510; http://english.scs.cuhk.edu.hk. Two courses on offer: Diploma Programme in Teaching English as a Second Language, 10 months, tuition fee HK$13,950; Master of Arts Programme in Teaching English to Speakers of Other Languages (jointly organised by School of Continuing and Professional Studies, The Chinese University of Hong Kong and Lancaster University), 2 years, tuition fee HK$ 91,600. Contact Carol To, Programme Coordinator.

Hungary

Via Lingua Budapest: Tavasz u. 3, 1033 Budapest; ✆ fax 1 368 11 56; info@via-lingua. hu; www.via-lingua.hu. 4-week intensive Certificate in TEFL course. Affiliated to Tudomany Nyelviskola (see entry in Hungary chapter).

Ireland

The Advisory Council for English Language Schools (ACELS) is the quality assurance body for English language teaching in Ireland, operating under the Department of Education and Science. As part of its quality assurance remit, a project, developed with the Irish ELT sector, was implemented as of 1 January 2005 with regard to pre-service TEFL certificates. This means that there is now a recognition scheme for TEFL certificate courses provided in Ireland which meet the standards specified by ACELS. All information on the scheme can be found on the ACELS website (www.acels.ie/acelselt.html).

Two types of recognised TEFL certificate course are available in Ireland. Firstly, there is the Initial TEFL Certificate. The key standards for this course specify five key areas which all the recognised courses need to comply with in order to receive recognition: trainee entry specifications; course duration; course programme; assessment; quality assurance (covering such issues as profile of the training team, resources, etc.). All courses have a requisite amount of teaching practice with real students with support from a trainer as well as input on such core issues as language awareness, teaching methodologies, learner issues related to motivation, affect, the fostering of independence, etc. Many of the recognised course providers are ex-providers of the Irish RELSA TEFL certificate, which is no longer on offer.

The following are recognised course providers of the ACELS Initial TEFL Certificate:

Abbey College: 33–34, Dame Street, Dublin 2; ✆ 1 679 13 52; fax 1 679 25 19; reception@ abbeycollege.ie; www.abbeycollege.ie.

Alpha College of English: 4, North Great George's Street, Dublin 1; ✆ 1 8747024; fax 1 8747031; admin@alphacollege.com; www.alphacollege.com.

Centre of English Studies: 31, Dame Street, Dublin 2; ✆ 1 6714233; fax 1 6714425; info@ cesireland.ie; www.cesireland.ie.

Clare Language Centre: Erasmus Smith Building, College Road, Ennis, Co Clare; ✆ 65 6841681; fax 65 6841683; clarelc@iol.ie; www.clarelc.ie.

Cork Language Centre International: Wellington House, 16, St Patrick's Place, Wellington Road, Cork; ✆ +21 4551661; fax 21 455 1662; info@corklanguagecentre.ie; www. corklanguagecentre.ie.

Dorset College: 66 Lower Dorset St, Dublin 1; ✆ +1 8309677; fax 1 8828934; info@dorset-college.ie; www.dorset-college.ie.

Dublin School of English: Dollard House, 2–5 Wellington Quay, Temple Bar, Dublin 2; ✆ +1 6773322; fax 1 6795454; admin@dse.ie; www.dse.ie.

Galway Language Centre: The Bridge Mills, Galway; ✆ +91 566468; fax 91 564122; info@ galwaylanguage.com; www.galwaylanguage.com.

International House Dublin: 66, Lower Camden Street, Dublin 2; ✆ +1 4759011/3; fax 1 4759799; info@ihdublin.com; www.ihdublin.com.

The Language Centre of Ireland: 45 Kildare Street, Dublin 2; ✆ +1 6716266; fax 1 6716430; info@lci.ie; www.lci.ie.

North Mon Language Institute: North Monastery Road, Cork; ✆ +21 4394458; fax 21 4395503; info@nmli.ie; www.nmli.ie.

U-Learn: 205, New Street Mall, Malahide, Co Dublin; ✆ +1 8451619; fax 1 8452858; ulearn@ eircom.net; www.u-learn.ie.

The second TEFL certificate course – the Preparatory TEFL Certificate – is open exclusively to state-qualified teachers and equips the trainee only for the teaching of English as a Foreign Language to juniors (teenagers). This again has a set of key standards that all course providers have to comply with in order to receive recognition. This is a new type of TEFL certificate to be offered in Ireland and is aimed particularly at teachers wanting to work in the junior summer school sector. Irish university TEFL certificate courses are recognised through their own quality assurance systems.

MEI-RELSA: 1 Lower Pembroke Street, Dublin 2; ✆ +1 618 0910; 1 618 0909; brian.burns@ mei.ie; www.mei.ie) is an association of recognised schools and a representative body (similar to English UK). Many MEI-RELSA schools provide teacher training courses (TEFL) and ACELS-accredited courses.

Other course providers in the Republic of Ireland are:

International TEFL College of Ireland: 29 Northumberland Avenue, Dun Laoghaire, Co. Dublin; ✆ fax 1 280 7001; info@itci.ie; www.itci.ie. 100-hour TEFL training courses, four full weekends in the autumn. Fee €500. Teaching practice with foreign students free of charge.

Words Language Services (WLS) TEFL Courses: 44 Northumberland Road, Dublin 4; ✆ +1 661 0240; fax 1 285 7705; tefl@wls.ie; www.wls.ie/tefl.htm. 100-hour course delivered via email. £230/€325.

Italy

ACLE (Associazione Culturale Linguistica Educational): Via Roma, 54, 18038 Sanremo; ✆ +0184 506070; fax 0184 509996; info@acle.org; www.acle.org. 4–5 day intensive TEFL-TP (Through Theatre and Play) introductory course with full board and lodging included. €150 course fee is deducted from final wages. Successful students work as paid tutors, teaching English at camps throughout Italy (see Italy chapter). This project offers a combination of theory plus invaluable practical experience with emphasis on drama and child-centred learning activities. Tutors receive an introductory TEFL Certificate at the end of the working period.

Interlingue Language System: Via Ennio Quirino Visconti 20, 00193 Rome; ✆ +06 321 5740/321 0317; fax 06 323 5709; info@interlingue-it.com; www.interlingue-it.com. TEFL International PELT Certificate courses run monthly (tefl.rome@interlingue-it.com; www. teflinternationalrome.it). €1,300 without accommodation; accommodation from €400. Jobs often available for the best students on the courses.

The Learning Center of Tuscany, LLC: Viale Corsica, 15c/17a, Florence 50134; ✆ + 055 051 5035; Cell USA 1 831 917–4752; www.learningcentertuscany.com. CTEFL school affiliated with TEFL International, offering a 4-week course in the basic methods of English language teaching, mainly for native English speakers. Offered monthly. Deposit of $500 plus €960.

Via Lingua Florence: Via Brunelleschi 1, 50123 Florence; ✆ +055 283161; florence@vialingua.org; www.cteflflorence.com. TEFL Certificate moderated by ELT Institute, Hunter College, City University of New York. 1-month intensive, 10 a year. Course fee €1,175.

Mexico

Dunham Institute: Avenida Zaragoza 23, Chiapa de Corzo, Chiapas; ✆ +961 61 61498; academic-coordinator@dunhaminstitute.com; www.dunhaminstitute.com. 4-week TEFL course in conjunction with Spanish courses and language exchange and tutoring of local students. Minimum commitment 8 weeks if tutoring local students or 5 months if teaching in schools. $1,500 includes free homestay with local family.

International Teacher Training Organization: Madero No.469, Guadalajara, Jalisco 44100; ✆ +52 33–3658 3224/3614 3800; toll-free from UK: ✆ +0 800 404 9800, and from USA: ✆ +1 866 514 7479; info@teflcertificatecourses.com; www.teflcertificate courses.com/guadalajara.html. Offered monthly. $1,400.

Teachers Latin America: Alvaro Obregon 153, Suite 305, Colonia Roma Mexico, DF, CP, 06700; ✆ +55 55 11 8149 teachers@innovative-english.com; www.innovative-english.com. 75-hour plus TEFL Certificate Programme. 40 hours in-class study, 10–20 hours of instructor-assessed student teaching and at least 25 additional hours of self-study on grammar, lesson planning, etc. $1,190 including accommodation. $200 fee for Job Assistance for up to 2 years. TEFL online certificate course $350.

Peru

Máximo Nivel Executive Language Center: Avenida El Sol 612, Cusco (Peru) and Antiguo Higueron 100 metros sur 50 metros este, San Pedro, San Jose (Costa Rica); ✆ +51 84 25 7200; info@maximonivel.net; www.maximonivel.net. 150-hour TEFL/TESOL Certificate (over 4-weeks) for $1,600 offered monthly except December; 50-hour TEIB (Teaching English for International Business) Certificate and TIEEP (Teaching International English Exam Preparation) Certificate (over 6 days), $400 each, offered 4 times a year. Housing arranged with families, in shared apartments, hostels, etc. from $225 for 4 weeks. Lifetime job-finding assistance, and an average of five graduates are employed by Máximo Nivel each month.

Sepa del Peru (Servicios Educativos Peruanos Americanos del Peru): Puente Bolognesi 114–116, Arequipa; ✆ 54 222390; educationalexcellence@gmail.com or sepa@peru-pass.com; www.perupass.com (click on the logo of SEPA del Peru). 13-week TEFL training and volunteer teaching programme ('World's Toughest TEFL/TESOL Program'). Monthly start dates. $2,955. Possibility of extra Spanish classes ($75 for 10 hours per week). Homestay or alternative accommodation ($40–$65 a week).

Poland

ITC International TEFL Certificate: Wejherowo (www.itc-training.com). See description under heading Czech Republic above.

Portugal

International House Lisbon: Rua Marques Sá da Bandeira 16, 1050 148 Lisbon; ✆ +21 315 1493/4/6; fax 21 353 0081; ttraining@ihlisbon.com. CELTA courses 10 times a year (€1,280). Also part-time DELTA course (€2,100) and IH Younger Learners Certificate (€700).

South Africa

Teachers SA/One World Language School: 5th Floor, 50 Long Street, Cape Town 8001; ✆ +21 422 4493 info@teacherssa.co.za; www.teacherssa.co.za. Entry-level TEFL courses focusing on the fundamentals of communicative language teaching, run throughout the year. Courses run in Cape Town and Pretoria.

Spain

EBC Servicios Lingüísticos: Orense 16, 2E, 28020 Madrid; ✆ 1 631 912 7495; info@ebc-tefl-course.com; www. ebc-tefl-course.com. Offered monthly. Approx. £915/€1,175.

Europe TEFL Teacher Training: Salvador Espriu 91, 08005 Barcelona, Spain; ✆ +932 215 515; info@europetefl.com; www.europetefl.com. 4-week intensive full-time TEFL courses run throughout the year in Barcelona, Seville, and many other locations in Europe and Latin America. Cost €1,300, including all course materials, expert job guidance, alumni network and more. Accommodation in the city centre and close to the schools can be arranged, €400–€500 a month. Contact: Kevin Cline.

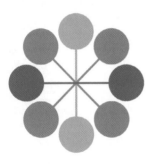
International House Barcelona: Calle Trafalgar 14, 08010 Barcelona, ☎ +93 268 4511; fax 93 268 0239; training@bcn.ihes.com; www.ihes.com/bcn. Business English Teachers course. 30 hours over 1 week. July only, €450. Also, Director of Studies Training Course and Trainer Training Course, both 1 week July, €450. And the International Diploma in Language Teaching Management (IDLTM) 2-week face-to-face course in July followed by 8 months of online assignments. Help given with finding accommodation. 3,500 Very Young Learner's course 17.5 hours over 1 week in September €180.

ITC International TEFL Certificate Barcelona/Madrid: See entry under heading Czech Republic above.

TEFL International has centres in Madrid, Barcelona and Seville; admin@teflinternational. org.uk; www.teflinternational.org.uk. TEFL TESOL course. £875 without accommodation.

TtMadrid: Calle General Yague 70, 1º, 28020 Madrid. ☎ +34 91 572 1999; info@ttmadrid .com; www.ttmadrid.com). 4-week intensive courses accredited by IATQUO. Courses run monthly. Course fee €1,250. Participants must be at least 21 and have a degree or equivalent work experience. Assistance with accommodation. Interviews with top teaching agencies arranged for you on graduation with members of their agency group. Course emphasis on teaching business English. Real teaching experience with adults and elective inputs on how to teach children. Small, intimate groups with complete support during and after the course.

Thailand

Chichester College, Thailand: 1st Fl., Muangthai Phatra Complex, 252/193 Rachadapisek Rd., Bangkok 10310; MRT Station: Sutthisan; +66 2-693 2901; fax +66 2-693 2599; www. chichester.ac.th. TESOL (TEFL/ESL) certificate and diploma courses in co-operation with Chichester College UK. Full time certificate course (4 weeks) runs monthly; part time (10 week) course runs 3 times per year; diploma course runs over 6 months beginning in April and October. $1,595 for full-time Cert; $995 for part-time Cert; $1,995 for Diploma. Accommodation offered at a private lodge near the Chichester training centre in Bangkok, and provided at a special subsidised rate of US$1000 for the entire duration of the full time course only. Graduates are provided teaching placements in Thailand or neighouring countries.

Paradise TEFL Thailand: ☎ +66 846 161609; info@teachinparadise.com; www.teachinparadise.com. 4-week courses in Chiang Mai in Northern Thailand. 4-week Certificate course (120 hours) plus 2-week and weekend intro course. 4-week course costs 40,000 baht including guaranteed job placement.

The TEFL Institute: United Educational Consultants Co. Ltd, 4th Floor, Silom Plaza, Silom Road corner Narathiwat Road, Bangkok 10500; ✆ +2 233 2388; fax 2 233 2387; info@teflthai.com; www.teflthai.com. 120 hours over 5 weeks with more than 20 start dates throughout the year. 44,500 Baht. Course earns eligible graduates 9 US graduate credits in education, US Master degree can be completed in 1 year while teaching in Thailand, also offered graduate diploma in teaching, 3.5 year part-time bachelor's degree in education, and weekend study 1.5-year dual US- and Thai-accredited master's degree (www.uecthai.com), including required Thai teaching licence.

TEFL International: 38/53–55 Moo 1, Klaeng, Muang Rayong 21160; ✆ +38 652 280; admin@teflinternational.org.uk; www.teflinternational.org.uk. 120-hour TESOL certificate course at Ban Phe, Chiang Mai and Phuket. £875 (includes accommodation).

Text and Talk Academy: 1960 Phaholyothin Road (opposite Mayo Hospital), Lardyao, Chatuchak, Bangkok 10900; ✆ +2 561 3443; info@TEFLTeachThai.com www.tefl-teach-thai.com. 4- and 6-week certificate courses (about £650), upgrade and refresher course, 16-week diploma course, 8-week TEYL course, 8-week advanced skills course and home study course.

FINDING A JOB

You can fix a teaching job either from home or look for one on location. Having a job arranged before departure obviously removes much of the uncertainty and anxiety of leaving home for an extended period. It also allows the possibility of preparing in appropriate ways: sorting out the right visa, researching the course books in use, etc. However, some people prefer to meet their employer and inspect the school before signing a contract. It is always an advantage to meet other teachers and learn about the TEFL scene in that particular place firsthand before committing yourself, rather than accepting a job in complete ignorance of the prevailing conditions. But of course this isn't always feasible.

Employers usually choose their staff several months before they are needed, so most schools advertise between April and July for jobs starting in September. If you want to fix up a job in person, you will either have to go on a reconnaissance mission well in advance of your proposed starting date or take your chances of finding a last-minute vacancy.

There are three ways of fixing up a teaching job in advance:

- Answering an online advertisement
- Using a recruitment agency (which includes the large international English teaching organisations like International House)
- Conducting a speculative job search, ie making contact by email or letter with all the schools whose addresses you can find in books, lists or on the internet.

ADVERTISEMENTS

Far fewer print advertisements appear than was the case before the rise of the internet. But it is still worth buying the *Guardian* on Tuesdays to check the TEFL classifieds in the Education section. You might also check out the *Independent* on Thursdays and *The Times Educational Supplement* (TES) on Fridays, though don't expect more than a sprinkling of international job advertisements. Internet users can save themselves £1.20 (and at least two trees) by checking the TES classifieds online which are posted at 7.30am every Friday (www.jobs.tes.co.uk).

The monthly *EL Gazette* is a good source of news and developments in the ELT industry for all interested individuals, though it is pitched at the professional end of the market. An annual subscription costs £33 in the UK, and £55 worldwide. Contact *EL Gazette*, Unit 3, Constantine Court, 6 Fairclough St, London E1 1PW (✆ 020 7481 6700; www.elgazette.com). *EL Prospects* is the employment supplement which comes free with the *EL Gazette* and is now available online.

One of the best sources of job advertisements for qualified TEFL teachers is TESOL Inc's *Placement Bulletin*. The electronic newsletter includes ESL/EFL job listings and articles about employment in ESOL. An email subscription is free with membership in TESOL (Teachers of English to Speakers of Other Languages, Inc.), 700 S Washington Street, Suite 200, Alexandria, VA 22314 (✆ +703 836 0774; fax 703 836 6447; careers@tesol.org; www.tesol.org).

Another American publication in the field of overseas education is *The International Educator* (PO Box 513, Cummaquid, MA 02637, USA; and 102A Pope's Lane, London W5 4NS; ✆ /fax 020 8840 2587; tie@tieonline.com; www.tieonline.com). It concentrates on jobs in international English-medium schools, most of which follow an American curriculum, British curriculum or the International Baccalaureate (IB). The schools which advertise in TIE mainly employ qualified primary and secondary teachers of all subjects. The EFL/ESL jobs that are advertised are usually open to EFL teachers with experience of teaching children and not just adults. The journal is published five times a year plus there is a jobs-only supplement in the late spring. An annual subscription costs US$47 for US/Canada subscribers and US$57 for the rest of the world though most people now opt for an online subscription for US$36. For an extra US$29 you can be notified by email of suitable job vacancies.

Job-seekers without a computer can still turn to print. *ESL Magazine* (Modern English Publishing, 211 E. Ontario Street, Suite 1800, Chicago, IL 60611; © 312 283 3756 or 32–34 Great Peter Street, London SW1P 2DB; © 020 7222 1155; info@eslmag.com; www.eslmag.com) lists TEFL job vacancies and includes articles not posted on the internet. An annual subscription of six issues costs US$24.95 including postage. Various newsletters and publications contain lists of international schools which usually do not relate to actual vacancies. Given that any good library (public or careers) should have a copy of one of the directories of international schools (like the ones available from ECIS in the UK or ISIS in Princeton), it may be superfluous to purchase separate lists.

The internet offers an increasingly useful medium for ELT recruiters and teachers alike. See section at the end of this chapter.

INTERPRETING ADVERTISEMENTS

Jobs are listed year round, though schools which advertise in February or October are often advertising a very urgent vacancy, eg 'to start immediately, good salary, air fares, accommodation' – but these are exceptional.

Almost all advertisements specify TEFL training/experience as a minimum requirement. But there is always a chance that this is merely rhetorical. Those who lack such a background should not feel defeated before they begin, since a TEFL background may turn out not to be essential. A carefully crafted CV and enthusiastic personality (not to mention a shortage of suitable applicants) could well persuade a school that it doesn't really have to insist on a Cambridge or Trinity Certificate with 2 years' experience after all.

TES includes two relevant headings. 'Overseas Appointments' primarily (but not exclusively) lists jobs in English-medium schools, while 'English as a Foreign Language' is for TEFL jobs outside Britain. Although there is no guarantee that schools which use the British educational press for their advertisements of employment will be reasonable employers, most are established schools which go to the trouble and expense of recruiting abroad.

Advertisements will sometimes include a contact name or company in the UK to which enquiries should be addressed for posts abroad. This may be a recruiting agency, TEFL training centre or a language school in the UK which is in contact with language schools abroad or it may just be an ex-employee who has agreed to do some recruitment for a commission fee. Note that none of these middle men is allowed to charge the job-seeker any fee. When discussing terms and conditions with an agent, bear in mind that the agent may be more interested in collecting a commission for finding someone to fill the vacancy than in conveying all the seamy facts.

Occasionally cases crop up of misleading or even fraudulent advertisements. A case a few years ago resulted in a headline in the TES: 'Thousands conned by Botswana job hoax.' A conman placed advertisements for teaching jobs in a fictitious school in Botswana, sent a letter of acceptance to all who applied and a request for $100 as a visa-processing fee. Even if this sort of bare-faced fraud is rare, it is best to be sceptical when interpreting advertisements, including on the internet where promises of earning huge salaries, particularly in less than affluent countries, are usually pie-in-the-sky.

> **BASED ON HIS EXPERIENCE OF ANSWERING ADVERTISEMENTS PLACED BY TURKISH LANGUAGE SCHOOLS, ONE EXPERIENCED JOB-HUNTER HAS DRAWN UP A GLOSSARY OF TERMS, HELPING NEW APPLICANTS TO 'READ BETWEEN THE LINES':**
>
> - *'Dollar Linked Salary' – paid in the local currency and only linked to the dollar every three or six months*
> - *'Free Accommodation' – no way can you afford to rent a place of your own. You have no say in who your flatmates are.*
> - *'Paid Flight' – this is usually for a one-way flight*
> - *'Leading School' – all the schools say this about themselves*
> - *'Provides In-Service Training' – weekly, monthly or annually*
> - *'Degree and Cert essential' – that's what the Ministry of Education wants. Will recruit anybody if desperate (good schools) or anybody at all (cowboys)*
> - *'Central Location' – near all the good pubs*
> - *'Young and Dynamic Team' – be like a student again*
> - *'Teachers are encouraged to use their own materials and be creative' – there isn't much in the way of resources.*

Apart from newspapers, there are a few other places where vacancies abroad might be mentioned. ELT training centres often have numerous links with foreign schools and may have a notice board with posted vacancies (as in the case of International House London). Unless you are a trainee at the relevant centre, it will probably be tricky consulting such a notice board, but a cooperative secretary might not mind a potential trainee consulting the board. University careers offices may also have contacts with schools abroad to which their graduates have gone in the past, so if you have a university connection, it is worth making enquiries.

THE BRITISH COUNCIL

The British Council (www.britishcouncil.org) is the largest ELT (English language teaching) employer in the world. The Council represents the elite end of the English language teaching industry. At its own teaching centres in 50 countries, it offers the highest quality language teaching available in those countries and employs the best qualified teachers, so it is important to understand that the British Council will not welcome applications from very inexperienced or unqualified teachers. The British Council is a very professional organisation and jobs tend to come with attractive terms and conditions.

Council offices abroad are usually well informed about opportunities for English language teaching locally. Most maintain a list of private language schools (while making it clear that inclusion does not confer recognition), which is often a useful starting point for a job search.

The Council publishes an Address Book of its offices worldwide which is updated quarterly. It is available online at www.britishcouncil.org/home-contact-worldwide.htm or a copy can be requested from the Council's Information Centre (Bridgewater House, 58 Whitworth St, Manchester M1 6BB; ✆ 0161 957 7755).

The charter of the British Council defines its aims as '*to promote Britain abroad, providing access to British ideas, talents and experience in education and training, books and periodicals, the English language, the arts, the sciences and technology*'. It is non-profit-making and works non-politically in more than 100 countries (although recently that didn't stop President Putin putting pressure on it to suspend operations in Russia). It employs about 7,500 staff in all, divided between Britain and abroad, a good percentage of whom are involved with the teaching of the English language in some capacity. In some countries such as Hungary the British Council has closed its teaching centre and prefers to work with local organisations to promote the teaching of English. In the past two years the British Council has closed close to 30 teaching centres. Other work which the Council carries out includes the running of libraries, the organisation of cultural tours and exchanges, etc. But language teaching and teacher recruitment remain one of its central concerns.

A useful starting place for qualified EL teachers is to review the information published on-line at www.britishcouncil.org/teacherrecruitment where current vacancies are also published. Further information is available by email; teacher.vacancies@britishcouncil.org or telephone 020 7389 4931.

In conjunction with the BBC, the British Council also maintains a website called Teaching English (www.teachingenglish.org.uk), which is a free resource for teachers and includes lesson plans, work sheets, teaching tips, etc.

The British Council is a large and complex institution with two headquarters: one at 10 Spring Gardens, London SW1A 2BN (✆ 020 7930 8466), and the other at Bridgewater House, 58 Whitworth St, Manchester M1 6BB (✆ 0161 957 7000). Those who do not know exactly which department they need should contact the Council's Information Unit in Manchester (✆ 0161 957 7755).

Here is a layman's guide to the sections and departments of possible interest to prospective teachers:

Teacher Recruitment: 10 Spring Gardens, London SW1A 2BN; ✆ 020 7389 4931; fax 020 7389 4754; teacher.vacancies@britishcouncil.org; www.britishcouncil.org/teacher recruitment.

The department oversees recruitment for the Council's 90 or so teaching outlets around the world and is responsible for the bulk of the hiring of contract teachers. Each teaching centre employs between 3 and 200 teachers, many of whom are qualified to diploma level, though most teachers are hired initially with a certificate level qualification and two years experience.

Teaching centres recruit both through London and locally. Qualified teachers who are planning to move to a location where there is a British Council Teaching Centre would be welcome to apply direct to the Teaching Centre Manager for information on opportunities for local contracts. At the time of writing, the Recruitment Service anticipated hiring several hundred teachers in the coming year, as well as about 25 middle managers and the same number of managers, many of whose posts are filled through internal transfer. The British Council regularly advertises in the national press and also links to current vacancies from its website. It especially welcomes applications from teachers with experience or an interest in specialist areas such as Young Learners, Business English, skills through English, IT/CALL, etc.

Contracts are usually for two years and renewable. Recruitment goes on year round though the majority of vacancies are still for September/October starts. Interviews for these posts are held between April and August. Although terms and conditions vary from centre to centre, the terms of employment with the British Council are generally favourable. Teachers recruited on UK contracts have their airfares paid, an allowance for shipping their belongings and an attractive salary package. Many teachers value all the intangible benefits such as the security of working for an established institution, and encouragement of professional development with possible perks such as receiving a subsidy to study for a diploma qualification or other training grants. Once you have secured one job with the Council, it is possible to move to other jobs in other places, since the Council regularly notifies its network of all vacancies.

Overseas Appointments Service/OAS: Bridgewater House, 58 Whitworth St, Manchester M1 6BB; ✆ 0161 957 7375.

The Overseas Appointments Service recruits personnel for posts abroad in universities, teacher training colleges, ministries of education, etc. The majority of educational vacancies are related to ELT but the Council is also asked to provide technical experts.

A substantial part of OAS's work is on behalf of the UK government's Department for International Development (Abercrombie House, Eaglesham Road, East Kilbride, Glasgow G75 8EA; www.dfid. gov.uk). Large display advertisements bearing both logos can occasionally be seen in the TES and the *Guardian*. Anyone who is sufficiently qualified to be eligible for these positions can submit an application which will be kept active for a calendar year. (Note that DfID supports national education systems rather than stand-alone ELT projects, so there are few straight ELT openings with the British government's main aid agency.)

Information Centre: Bridgewater House, 58 Whitworth St, Manchester M1 6BB; ✆ 0161 957 7755; fax 0161 957 7762.

The Information Centre distributes two information packs to members of the public: *How to Become a Teacher of English as a Foreign Language*, which includes lists of TEFL training courses, and a list of English language centres in the UK that have been accredited by the British Council under the English in Britain Accreditation Scheme. These are also listed online at www.britishcouncil. org/accreditation-az-list.htm.

RECRUITMENT ORGANISATIONS

Major providers of ELT and teacher placement organisations of various kinds may be able to assist prospective teachers in English-speaking countries to find teaching jobs. Some are international educational foundations; some are voluntary organisations such as Voluntary Service Overseas (VSO) or charities; some are major chains of commercial language schools; and others are small agencies which serve as intermediaries between independent language schools abroad and prospective teachers. The companies and organisations listed in this chapter have been assigned to the following categories (though there is some blurring of distinctions): International ELT organisations (including the major language school chains); commercial recruitment agencies; voluntary, gap year and religious organisations; North American organisations, which cater primarily (though not exclusively) to citizens of the USA and Canada; and, finally, placement services for British and American state-qualified teachers. Note that agencies and organisations that operate only in one country or one region are described in the country chapters in the second part of this book.

It is hardly worthwhile for a family-run language school in northern Greece or southern Brazil to pay the high costs which most agencies charge schools just to obtain one or two native speaker teachers. Vacancies that are filled with the help of agencies and recruitment consultants tend to be at the elite end of the ELT market. Jobs advertised by agencies are usually for specialised or high level positions, for example in corporations with in-house EFL programmes or foreign governments.

Agencies make their money by charging client employers; the service to teachers is usually free of charge. By law in the UK, no fee can be charged to job-seekers either before or after placement, except if a package of services is sold alongside (eg insurance, visas, travel, etc). Note that different rules apply in other countries, so that placement fees are the norm in the USA. Some of the best recruitment organisations to deal with are ones which specialise in a single country in situ, such as English Educational Services in Madrid or Cambridge Teachers Recruitment in Athens (see Spain and Greece chapters). They tend to have more first-hand knowledge of their client schools.

On the other hand, the use of an intermediary by foreign language institutes is no guarantee of anything. Particularly in the American context, small independent recruiters are sometimes trying to fill vacancies that no one in the country who is familiar with the employer would deign to fill. As the American Rusty Holmes said of his employer in Taiwan, 'The school was so bad it had to recruit from America.' If you are in any doubt about the reliability of an agency or the client he/she represents, it is a sensible precaution to ask for the name of one or more previous teachers whom you can ask for a first-hand account. It is a bad sign if the agency is unable or reluctant to oblige.

The hiring of teachers for chain schools abroad is done either at a local level (so direct applications are always worthwhile) or centrally, if the school has trouble filling vacancies.

One way in which recruitment agencies work is to create a database of teachers' CVs and to try to match these with suitable vacancies as they occur. In order to be registered with such an agency it is usually essential to have a relevant qualification, often at least the Cambridge or Trinity Certificate. When applicants outnumber vacancies, it isn't surprising to hear that most agencies are unwilling to register non-nationals without superior qualifications. Recruitment agencies in the UK may find it difficult to cope with applications from the USA since it is difficult to translate qualifications; one mentioned that because of anti-discrimination legislation, American applicants do not always mention their age or sex, which most language school directors want to know.

Smaller agencies may have fewer vacancies on their books but they can often offer a more personal service. It is a legal requirement for agencies to obtain references from any client to which it wants to send teachers. A good agency will provide a full briefing and information pack on the school in particular and the country in general, and will make sure that the contract offered is a reasonable one. If a job doesn't work out, the agency should provide a back-up service and be available to sort out misunderstandings and offer an alternative placement.

MARISA WHARTON DESCRIBES THE SUPPORT AN AGENCY SHOULD PROVIDE:
When our employers in the Czech Republic broke the contract and behaved like mafiosi, our agency was very helpful. They found my husband a different job in Poland, so at least one of us has been placed. At the moment they are trying to sort out some sort of compensation for us.

Volunteer English teachers are in demand by dozens of commercial sending agencies which routinely charge volunteers £500–£2,000 for placement and related services. Before her final year at univer-

Work with Bell and travel the world

Bell provides English language and educational services worldwide. Each year the organisation helps over 100,000 students, from more than 120 countries, through one of its 45 worldwide teaching centres and e-channels.

45 teaching centres in 18 countries

■ Centres providing English language teaching to international students

□ Centres/Projects providing language training to local students

Excellent professional development opportunities, including support to undertake the new modular **online Bell Delta**

For further information about these roles and other opportunities around the world visit **www.bell-worldwide.com/jobs** or email your CV to **recruitment@bell-centres.com** quoting your preferred location as a reference.

Vietnam

China

Bulgaria

Romania

Azerbaijan

Ukraine

Thailand

Qatar

Saudi Arabia

Jordan

Malta

Czech Republic

Poland

Libya

UK

Switzerland

Mexico

Chile

sity, **Susannah Kerr** took up one of these placements in Thailand which she found to be less structured than the agency literature had promised. She felt that the school to which she was assigned did not really need English-speaking volunteers and she suspected that they invited foreigners merely as status symbols. With hindsight she felt that she had been naïve to assume that the school would be grateful for her efforts. She was allowed to teach whatever she liked, so naturally she concentrated on spoken English and taught no grammar and only occasional writing exercises. She was given no lesson plans and was not required to prepare the students for exams. When the teachers saw that the volunteers were coping, they took a holiday.

INTERNATIONAL ELT ORGANISATIONS

The Bell Educational Trust: Bell recruits teachers for its projects and centres worldwide. Candidates are required to have a degree and a CELTA qualification. For further information contact The Bell Educational Trust, Recruitment Department, Hillscross, Red Cross Lane, Cambridge CB2 2QX; Tel 01223-275500; fax 01223-414080; e-mail recruitment@bell-centres.com; www.bell-centres.com.

Bénédict International Sarl: 3 Place Chauderon, PO Box 270, 1000 Lausanne 9, Switzerland; ✆ 21 312 4728; fax 21 323 6777; info@benedict-schools.com; www.benedict-international.com. Over 50 business and language schools in Europe (mostly in Germany, Switzerland and Italy), plus a couple in Russia and Ecuador.

Berlitz UK Ltd: 2nd Floor, Lincoln House, 296–302 High Holborn, London WC1V 7JH; 020 7611 9640; fax 020 7611 9656; www.berlitz.co.uk. Berlitz International, 400 Alexander Park, Princeton, NJ 08540 6306, USA; ✆ 609 514 9650; fax 609 514 9689. Global website: www.berlitz.com. Berlitz is one of the largest language training organisations in the world with about 450 centres in 60 countries. It is also one of the oldest, founded in 1878. The company's core business is language and cultural training, and teacher vacancies occur most often in Latin America, Spain, Italy, Germany, France and Korea. All Berlitz teachers are native-fluent speakers and university graduates trained in the 'Berlitz Method', a direct 'see-hear-speak' teaching approach that does not rely on translation. Berlitz is known for supervising its teachers' techniques very closely. When Berlitz has urgent vacancies to fill, usually in Spain and Italy, it places an advertisement in British newspapers inviting any interested university graduates to attend interviews in London, Manchester, Edinburgh or Dublin. Normally, however, Berlitz schools abroad employ teachers directly, usually on a part-time basis initially, after they have completed a two-week method course.

British Council, Assistants Team: 10 Spring Gardens, London SW1A 2BN; ✆ 020 7389 4596; fax 020 7389 4594; assistants@britishcouncil.org; www.britishcouncil.org/languageassistants. Also offices in Scotland (British Council Scotland, The Tun, 4 Jackson's Entry, Holyrood Road, Edinburgh EH8 8PJ; ✆ 0131 524 5735); and Northern Ireland (7 Fountain Street, Belfast BT1 5EG; ✆ 028 9024 8220). The Language Assistants Team administers exchange programmes with 19 countries worldwide. Applicants for assistant posts must be aged 20–30 and native speakers of English who have completed their secondary education and at least two years of degree-level study in the UK, usually but not necessarily in the language of the destination country. In some countries (especially China and countries in Latin America and Africa) posts are of particular interest to graduates interested in a career in TEFL. Application forms are available from October and the deadline for submission is

1 December (for a job starting the following autumn), although the deadlines may be extended for posts in China and Russia.

Cactus TEFL (www.cactustefl.com) publishes a guide to working in TEFL, *The Little Book of TEFL Jobs*, which is packed with advice for the teacher searching for a job in TEFL, and advertisements from schools which regularly employ teachers. The booklet is available free (while stocks last) and can be requested by email from info@cactustefl.com. See also the Jobs section of the website: www.cactustefl.com/jobs/index.php.

CfBT Education Trust: 60 Queens Road, Reading RG1 4BS; © 0118 902 1000; fax 0118 902 1739; www.cfbt.com. Has offices in Brunei, Malaysia and Oman which recruit for and manage EFL/EAP/ESP/Primary/Secondary teachers and instructors for various projects and contracts. The website contains contact details for each office and information on how to apply. CfBT's International and Consultancy Group (© 0118 902 1613; consultancydatabase@cfbt.com), at above address, with regional bases in Africa, South East Asia, and the Gulf recruits education consultants for donor-funded projects and programmes in developing countries.

EF English First Teacher Recruitment and Training: 26 Wilbraham Road, Fallowfield, Manchester M14 6JX; © 0161 256 1400; fax 0161 256 1936; recruitment@englishfirst.com; www.englishfirst.com. Recruitment of teachers for 200 EF schools in 16 countries primarily Russia, China and Indonesia. Subsidised training places available to those who sign a contract on completion of proprietary certificate course (www.efteflscholarships.com).

English Town Inc: www.englishtown.com. Branch of English First in which online English tutors are recruited worldwide. They are looking for native speakers with a degree and TEFL background who have a fast and reliable connection to the internet.

Geos: www.geoscareer.com. International group of schools mainly in Japan. Hiring campaigns held in Canada, etc.

ICC – The European Language Network: Berner Heerweg 183, D- 22159, Hamburg, Germany © 40 428 853 233; fax 40 428853 237; info@icc-languages.eu; www.icc-languages.eu. Umbrella organisation for adult education associations (eg Volkshochschulen, folk high schools or Universities of Applied Sciences) in 16 European countries cooperating in the learning and teaching of foreign languages in Europe. Can provide enquirers with a list of member organisations and contact names. The ICC runs specialist training courses for foreign language teachers in adult, continuing and vocational education. A teacher certification scheme (EUROLTA = European Language Teaching to Adults) is also in operation.

IH World Organisation: Unity Wharf, 13 Mill Street, London SE1 2BH. worldrecruit@ihworld. co.uk; ✆ 020 7394 2144. International House (IH) is one of the largest and oldest groups of language schools, teaching English as a foreign language (and 25 modern languages) in 145 schools in 50 countries worldwide. IHWO Recruitment Services is based in London at the International House World office, which is the coordinating body for all International House affiliated schools. They are responsible for managing the recruitment of teachers, trainers and senior staff for IH schools and annually expect to assist in the recruitment of between 350 and 400 teachers for International House schools worldwide. The minimum qualification requirement for teaching posts is the Cambridge CELTA, IH CTL or Trinity TESOL Certificate. All IH schools adhere to internal quality standards, which provide strict guidelines on terms and conditions, working hours and working environment. For further information on teaching and senior posts abroad visit www.ihworld.com/recruitment.

IST Plus: Rosedale House, Rosedale Road, Richmond, Surrey; ✆ 020 8939 9057; www.istplus. com. Formerly CIEE UK, Ist Plus administers the Teach in China and Teach in Thailand programmes (see respective chapters).

Language Link: 21 Harrington Road, London SW7 3EU; ✆ 020 7225 1065; fax 020 7584 3518; recruitment@languagelink.co.uk; www.languagelink.co.uk. Training and recruitment agency which places about 200 qualified (including newly qualified) teachers in its network of affiliated schools in Russia, China, Slovakia, Vietnam, Kazakhstan and Uzbekistan. Usually minimum qualifications are TEFL Certificate or PGCE or experience but visit the website of the country you wish to work in as the company may be running in-service training courses over the period of the contract. Employment contracts are from 36 weeks and can be extended. 24 contact hours per week. Local pay rates. Shared apartment accommodation is usually provided at no additional cost or deduction from the salary. Interested teachers should ring to arrange an interview (in the UK or in Russia etc.), and then send CV and photo. (See Training chapter for details of Language Link's CELTA courses.)

Linguarama, Group Personnel Department, Marcus Evans Linguarama: 1 Elm Court, Arden St, Stratford-upon-Avon CV37 6PA; ✆ 01789 203910; fax 01789 266462; personnel@ linguarama.com; www.linguarama.com. Linguarama specialises in providing language training for professionals. Applicants for jobs in Linguarama language schools abroad must have at least a degree and a Cambridge/Trinity Certificate (or equivalent). Linguarama finds placements for 50–100 teachers and has an office in London for teacher interviews as well as the above address which deals with vacancies at more than 20 European centres in Germany, France, Spain and Italy.

Richard Lewis Communications: Riversdown House, Warnford, Southampton, Hampshire SO32 3LH; ✆ 01962 771111; www.crossculture.com. RLC has a network of offices worldwide, especially in Finland, Sweden and Germany, specialising in cross-cultural training and language teaching.

Saxoncourt: 59 South Molton Street, London W1K 5SN; ✆ 020 7491 1911; recruit@saxoncourt.com; www.saxoncourt.com. One of the largest UK-based recruiters of EFL teachers, Saxoncourt places more than 600 teachers per year in schools in 20 countries. Currently, clients are based in Japan, Taiwan, Poland, China, Italy, Spain, Russia (including Siberia), Thailand, Vietnam, Peru, Brazil and elsewhere. Applications are welcome, particularly from candidates with a Cambridge CELTA, Trinity TESOL or equivalent qualifications. Interviews are held in London, New Zealand and South Africa. Interested candidates should register online at http://register.saxoncourt.com. The Saxoncourt website features a regularly up-

dated current vacancies page, online registration and individual country specific sections
with slideshows and downloadable information packs.

Shane Global Language Centres: www.shaneglobal.com. ELT centres in English-speaking
countries (UK, New Zealand and South Africa) but with links to international language
schools.

Wall Street Institute (WSI): www.wallstreetinstitute.com. Operates both company-owned and
franchised centres, and employs more than 2,000 teachers in nearly 400 centres in 26 countries and territories in Asia (China, Indonesia, Hong Kong, Singapore, South Korea, Taiwan,
Thailand), Europe (France, Germany, Italy, Portugal, Spain, Switzerland, Russia, Turkey), Latin

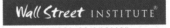

America (Argentina, Brazil, Chile, Colombia, Dominican Republic, Ecuador, Mexico, Peru, Venezuela) and the Middle East (Israel, Saudi Arabia). The company is projecting strong growth throughout the coming year, including developing centres in more countries, such as Morocco and the Czech Republic. Openings for qualified native English speaking ESL teachers exist throughout the network. Applicants should have at least a bachelor's degree and the appropriate professional qualifications of a CELTA or equivalent TEFL certificate. 1 year's teaching experience is an advantage. Due to restrictions on visa legislation in many countries within the network, WSI prefers teachers from the UK, Ireland, USA, Canada, Australia, New Zealand and South Africa. The interview process is as follows: a first round interview is a 'get to know you' interview. A second round interview will involve discussing a lesson plan created by the applicant and giving a brief teaching presentation of approximately 15 minutes. Both interviews will last approximately 45 minutes. Some countries will consider doing this via phone with off-shore applicants. In this case the applicant will discuss how they would deliver a particular language point. Qualified applicants can apply online at www.wallstreetinstitute.com/jobSeekers/teachingStaff/teachingStaff.aspx. All questions can be directed to the recruiting department at: teach@wallstreetinstitute.com.

COMMERCIAL AGENCIES

Anyone with a TEFL background should email or write to relevant agencies with a CV and covering letter, preferably enclosing a self-addressed envelope or (if overseas) international reply coupons. Agencies which specialise in a single country are not included in this chapter, but are mentioned in the country chapters.

Anglo-Pacific (Asia) Consultancy: Suite 32, Nevilles Court, Dollis Hill Lane, London NW2 6HG; ✆ 020 8452 7836. Educational consultancy which specialises in recruitment in Thailand, Taiwan, China, Japan and the rest of south-east Asia. Also offers careers counselling to TEFL teachers returning from overseas. It welcomes hearing from graduates (or people with HND/equivalent higher qualifications) who have a recognised TEFL Certificate. Places teachers at all levels in the public and private sectors. Aims to provide teachers with background information about their destination country including teaching tips and cultural information.

Avalon School Of English: 9 Great Newport Street, London WC2H 7JA; ✆ 020 7240 9321/020 7379 1998; jobs@avalonschool.co.uk or Andrew.Day@avalonschool.co.uk; www.avalonschool.co.uk. Candidates may be eligible for work in Avalon schools in China, France, Brazil, Poland or London. Candidates must have a degree and TEFL certificate for London. TEFL Certificate preferred for schools abroad.

Professional Language Solutions: 11 Coldbath Square, London EC1R 5HL; ✆ 020 7689 1900; fax 020 7689 1901; enq@langsols.com; www.langsols.com. Network of privately owned schools abroad which specialise in teaching working adults in the energy industry and to which qualified and experienced EFL teachers can apply: Milan, Madrid, Baku (Azerbaijan), Atyrau (Kazakhstan), Algeria and Jubail Industrial City, Saudi Arabia. Must have minimum CELTA to be considered.

Teacharound ESL Recruitment: 34 Hastings Road, Bolton, BL1 4NQ; 0800 1777 972; clairef@teacharound.co.uk; www.teacharound.co.uk. Recruit teachers for schools in Asia, mainly China, Taiwan and Japan. Degree and TEFL/CELTA/PGCE required but other experience not necessary. Presentations and face-to-face interviews in several UK cities. Also provides information about voluntary placements for qualified and unqualified teachers.

VOLUNTARY, GAP YEAR AND RELIGIOUS ORGANISATIONS

Christians Abroad: Room 233 Bon Marché Centre, 241–251 Ferndale Road, London SW9 8BJ; ✆ 0870 770 7990; fax 0870 770 7991; recruitment@cabroad.org.uk; www.cabroad.org. uk. Ecumenical charity which provides information and advice to people of any faith or none who are thinking of working overseas, whatever their circumstances, whether short- or long-term, voluntary or paid. Recruit teachers year-round for 3-month to 2-year assignments, most as volunteers but some paid posts. Countries include China (paid posts), Kenya, Tanzania (some local salary for longer-term teachers), Nigeria, Zambia and India. Occasional posts are advertised for Hong Kong and Japan. Other volunteer positions available. With sister agency World Service Enquiry, it publishes an annual *Guide to Volunteering*, which includes many agencies looking for teacher volunteers. *Opportunities Abroad* is a monthly listing of vacancies available on subscription. Face-to-face consultations and an email coaching course ('E>volve') are also available, as is a general booklet on *Working in Development* (see www.wse.org.uk).

The most important voluntary agency in the UK recruits EFL teachers as well as many other kinds of volunteer.

VSO (Voluntary Service Overseas), 317 Putney Bridge Road, London SW15 2PN; 020 8780 7500; fax 020 8780 7300; e-mail enquiry@vso.org.uk; www.vso.org.uk. Leading international development charity VSO works through volunteers to tackle poverty in 34 developing countries

worldwide. VSO recruits EFL teachers as well as other skilled professionals across Education, Health, Business and IT sectors. Its work in education focuses on improving the quality of, and access to education. The organisation receives requests for EFL volunteers from a number of countries including China, Ethiopia, Mongolia, Rwanda and Mozambique.

VSO offers different types of volunteering opportunities. The standard volunteering placement is 1–2 years' in duration. VSO is currently recruiting EFL teachers with a degree plus a PGCE or TEFL, Trinity TESOL or Cambridge CELTA qualification and three years' teaching experience (occasionally it may be able to consider with 2 years' experience). Specialist assignment placements vary from 4 weeks to 6 months in length and require professionals with extensive experience who can provide advice and work in a consultancy capacity. VSO also has two youth volunteering programmes for 18 – 25 year olds: Global Xchange (GX) and Youth for Development (YfD). More information on the different volunteering opportunities and requirements can be found at www.vso.org.uk/volunteering.

VSO provides a comprehensive package of financial, personal and professional support. This includes return flights, accommodation, a local living allowance, medical insurance and extensive pre-departure and in-country training. In addition to this, public service employees now receive pension payments for the entirety of their placement.

Several UK organisations make it possible for school-leavers in their gap year to work for six months abroad, and many of these placements are in schools where volunteers teach English. Most of the organisations listed here are founder members of the Year Out Group (Queensfield, 28 Kings Road, Easterton, Wiltshire SN10 4PX; 01380 816696; info@yearoutgroup.org; www.yearoutgroup.org), formed to promote well-structured gap year programmes:

Cross-Cultural Solutions: UK office: Tower Point, 44 North Road, Brighton BN1 1YR; ✆ 0845 458 2781; infouk@crossculturalsolutions.org; www.crossculturalsolutions.org. US address: 2 Clinton Place, New Rochelle, NY10801; ✆ 1 800 380 4777. International volunteer programme in 12 countries (Brazil, China, Costa Rica, Ghana, Guatemala, India, Morocco, Peru, Russia, South Africa, Tanzania and Thailand) lasting 1-12 weeks, some of which involve English teaching. Programme fees start at £1,448 ($2,588) for a 2-week programme.

Educators Abroad Ltd: 5 Talfourd Way, Royal Earlswood Park, Redhill, Surrey RH1 6GD; ✆ 01737 785468/768254; fax 01737 768254; craig@educatorsabroad.org; www.educatorsabroad.org. Company that manages and operates the English Language Teaching Assistant Program (ELTAP) for universities in the USA and participants from other countries (www.eltap.org). ELTAP is a volunteer/college-sponsored programme operating in 25 countries, open to adults as a non-credit certificate option as well as to students. Placements last 4 or 10 weeks throughout the year, and the programme fee is $2,300–$4,200, plus travel.

i-to-i: 261 Low Lane, Leeds, LS18 5NY; ✆ 0870 442 3043; fax 0113 205 4618; info@i-to-i.com; www.i-to-i.com. i-to-i offers TEFL/TESOL training, either weekend courses or distance learning, and many teaching placements worldwide for paying volunteers.

Lattitude Global Volunteering: 44 Queen's Road, Reading, Berkshire RG1 4BB; ✆ 0118 959 4914; fax 0118 957 6634; volunteer@lattitude.org.uk; www.lattitude.org.uk. Overseas volunteering opportunities for 17–25 year olds, including teaching, community, caring, medical and environment in Latin America (Argentina, Brazil, Ecuador, Mexico, Paraguay), North America, Asia (China, India including working with Tibetan refugees, Japan, Malaysia, Nepal, Thailand, Vietnam), Australasia (Australia, New Zealand, Fiji and Vanuatu), Africa (Ghana, Malawi, South Africa, Tanzania) and Europe (Germany). Posts are for between three and

Projects Abroad offers you the chance to take part in one of our tailor-made Teaching projects.
- 23 destinations
- The chance to make a difference in a developing country
- A new and exotic backdrop to develop your skills

TEACHING

→ www.projects-abroad.co.uk
Tel: +44 (0)1903 708300

12 months (six is average) and cost the volunteer £1,500 plus airfare, insurance and medical costs. Board, lodging and (sometimes) a living allowance are provided. A one-week teaching skills course is mandatory for those undertaking to teach English. Contact sales manager Hannah Jones on 0118 956 2932.

Project Trust: Hebridean Centre, Ballyhough, Isle of Coll, Argyll PA78 6TE; ✆ 01879 230444; fax 01879 230357; info@projecttrust.org.uk; www.projecttrust.org.uk. Sends school leavers (aged 17–19) to teach (often other subjects as well as English) in schools across South America, Africa and Asia including Namibia, Uganda, Botswana, Chile, Honduras, China, Japan and Thailand. Participants must fund-raise to cover part of the cost of their 12-month placement, at present £4,660.

Projects Abroad: Aldsworth Parade, Goring, Sussex BN12 4TX; ✆ 01903 708300; fax 01903 501026; info@projects-abroad.co.uk; www.projects-abroad.co.uk. Send about 4,000 people abroad annually on a variety of projects in developing countries, such as Argentina, Bolivia, Costa Rica, Mexico, Peru; Cambodia, China, India, Mongolia, Nepal, Sri Lanka and Thailand; Ghana, Senegal and South Africa; Moldova, Romania, Togo, Morocco and Ethiopia. Projects include teaching, care and community, conservation, medicine, veterinary medicine, physiotherapy, sport, journalism, archaeology, business, law, drama, arts and crafts and dissertation. Other projects are also available. Projects start from 2 weeks in length, with an average volunteer spending 3 or 4 months. Volunteers choose their own dates. Minimum age is 16. Projects start at £895. Price includes accommodation, food, insurance, placement, transfer to and from airport with a member of staff, and in-country support. Also offers a 2-week high school summer special for teens 16–19. Recruits through the internet, directories, careers fairs, open days, talks, advertising and word-of-mouth.

Travellers Worldwide: 2A Caravelle House, 17/19 Goring Road, Worthing, West Sussex, BN12 4AP; ✆ 01903 502595; fax 01903 708179; info@travellersworldwide.com; www.travellersworldwide.com. Provides teaching as well as many other work experience and volunteer placements worldwide. Sample prices for 2 weeks to 12 weeks of teaching are £675–£1,425, which covers food, accommodation, transport, airport pick-up and excellent support and backup throughout. External flights are not included. Travellers also runs a weekend TEFL course in the UK, check details at www.tefltime.com.

Charities and mission societies which occasionally require EFL teachers include:

Bosco Volunteer Action (BOVA): ✆ 01625 560724; bova@salesianyouthministry.com; www.salesianyouthministry.com. Offers opportunities to live and work alongside Catholic priests and brothers in their service to the young and the poor around the world. Some (but not all) of the volunteer opportunities involve teaching English.

Interserve: 5/6 Walker Avenue, Wolverton Mill, Milton Keynes, MK12 5TW; ✆ 01908 552700; enquiries@isewi.org; www.interserveonline.org.uk. Teaching posts in 19 countries.

OMS International: 1 Sandileigh Avenue, Manchester M20 3LN; ✆ 0161 283 7992; fax 0161 283 8981; info@omsinternational.co.uk; www.omsinternational.co.uk. US Headquarters: PO Box A, Greenwood, IN 46142 6599. An evangelical, independent, Christian mission organisation which provides English lessons/camps through OMS-affiliated national churches in countries worldwide.

World Exchange: St Colm's International House, 23 Inverleith Terrace, Edinburgh EH3 5NS; ✆ 0131 315 4444; fax 0131 315 2222; we@stcolms.org; www.worldexchange.org.uk. Concentrating on management, health and education in Malawi and India.

OPPORTUNITIES FOR NORTH AMERICANS

Although the companies, agencies and charities listed here are based in the USA and cater primarily to North Americans, some may be in a position to help overseas applicants. Recruitment agencies in the USA have stronger links with Latin America and the Far East than with Europe. As in Britain, some organisations are involved primarily with English-medium international schools following an American curriculum and are looking to recruit state-certified teachers; these are listed separately at the end of this section.

The most important organisations for Americans looking for employment opportunities in the field of TEFL are:

AIDE: 1221 S. Mopac Expressway, Suite 100, Austin, TX 78746; ✆ 1 512 457 8062; www.aideabroad.org. Operates programmes in Argentina, Chile, China and Spain.

English Language Fellow Program: Georgetown University, PO Box 579400, Washington, DC 20057 9400; http://elf.georgetown.edu/index.html. Administered by the Center for Intercultural Education and Development (CIED). The English Language Fellow Program is a 10-month fellowship sponsored and funded by the US Department of State. Participants must be US citizens and have an MA in TESOL or a related field. There are two different levels to the programme. Junior fellows are recent graduates of MA programmes in TESOL and they work mainly as classroom teachers. Senior fellows have more teaching experience and have extensive teacher training experience in addition to at least an MA in TESOL or related field. Participants receive a stipend, living allowance to cover food, housing, local transportation and utilities, plus an international travel pre-departure allowance and a shipping allowance. Pre-departure briefings take place in August.

The Fulbright Scholar Program administered by the US Department of State, provides grants for teaching English in over 30 countries. A doctorate is usually required, although a master's degree is sufficient in some countries. Applicants must be US citizens. Application information is available from the Council for International Exchange of Scholars (3007 Tilden St NW, Suite 5L, Washington, DC 20008 3009; ✆ 202 686 4000; scholars@cies.iie.org; www.cies.org).

Office of English Language Programs (OELP): US State Department, SA 44, Room 304, 301 4th Street, SW, Washington DC 20547; http://exchanges.state.gov/education/engteaching. OELP creates and implements high quality, English language programmes in specific regions and countries around the world. OELP's programmes promote understanding of

American language, society, culture, values and policies. In some embassies, the public affairs departments provide English language instruction as do binational centres, which work closely with American embassies. All of these are listed on the website. Most teachers for binational centres are hired directly by the centre in question; addresses are listed on the website above. Teachers with a masters degree in TESL/TEFL may apply for the English Language Fellow Program, a 10-month fellowship programme which provides American professional expertise in teaching English as a foreign language. Qualified candidates who want to teach in US Department of State Cultural Centers should go to the website and follow the link to 'Employment Outside the United States'. The English Language Specialist programme recruits US academics in the fields of TEFL/TESL and applied linguistics for short-term (2–4 weeks) assignments abroad.

Peace Corps: 1111 20th Street NW, Washington, DC 20526; ✆ 1 800 424 8580; www.peacecorps.gov. TEFL has historically been one of the major programme areas of the Peace Corps which has programmes in more than 70 countries. One-third of the nearly 8,000 volunteers who serve work in the education sector, with the majority of them in ELT. Volunteers, who must be US citizens, over age 18 and in good health, are sent on 27-month assignments. All expenses, including airfare and health insurance, are covered. Peace Corps volunteers teach at both secondary and university level while some become involved with teacher training and curriculum development. It can take up to a year between application and departure. Education volunteers must have a college degree (not necessarily in education) and a minimum of 3 months experience of ESL tutoring one-to-one or classroom teaching.

TESOL (Teachers of English to Speakers of Other Languages): 700 S Washington St, Suite 200, Alexandria, VA 22314; ✆ 703 836 0774; fax 703 836 6447; info@tesol.org; www.tesol.org. A key organisation for ESL/EFL teachers worldwide, TESOL is a non-profit, professional association which offers various publications and services to 14,000 members in 125 countries. Full individual membership is US$85 (US$33 for students) per year, there is also electronic membership. Members can receive a listing of job vacancies worldwide, or search jobs online. TESOL also organises the Job MarketPlace, an ESL/EFL job fair held during TESOL's annual convention. Job seekers can view job listings, submit résumés, and may be selected for interviews held on site.

WorldTeach Inc: Center for International Development, Harvard University, 79 John F Kennedy Street, Box 122, Cambridge, MA 02138; ✆ +1 617 495 5527/+1 800 4 TEACH 0; fax +1 617 495 1599; info@worldteach.org; www.worldteach.org. Private, non-profit organisation founded in 1986 which places several hundred volunteers as teachers of EFL or ESL in countries which request assistance. WorldTeach provides college graduates with one-year contracts to American Samoa, Bangladesh, Costa Rica, Ecuador, Namibia, Kenya, the Marshall Islands, China, Venezuela, Chile, Pohnpei, Mongolia, Rwanda, South Africa and Guyana. WorldTeach offers 8-week summer programmes in Bulgaria, China, Costa Rica, Ecuador, Poland, Namibia and South Africa. Many participants pay a volunteer contribution ranging from $500 to $7,990, but several new programmes are fully funded by the host country. The contributions cover training, airfares, orientation, insurance, room and board and in-country support. Volunteers are given a living allowance based on local rates of pay (roughly US$100–$300 per month). Programmes run year round. Participants do not have to be US citizens, but must be a native English speaker at least 18 years of age (year-long programmes require a BA). Contact Dahm Choi, Director of Admissions and Recruiting.

The following commercial language providers and volunteer recruitment agencies may be able to assist EFL job-seekers:

EF English First: recruitment@englishfirst.com; www.englishfirst.com. Schools in China, Indonesia, Russia, Saudi Arabia, Thailand, Malaysia, Vietnam, Azerbaijan, Kazakhstan, Poland, Lithuania, Morocco, Turkey, Mexico, Ecuador, Chile and more. All academic staff are recruited through EF's Online Recruitment Centre. Candidates are requested to register their details via www.englishfirst.com.

Global Routes: 1 Short Street, Northampton, MA 01060; ✆ 413 585 8895; fax 413 585 8810; mail@globalroutes.org; www.globalroutes.org. Summer Teen Community service programmes and gap year/college semester internships in Africa, Asia and Latin America. Programme fees from $6,250 to $6,750 (2009).

Global Service Corps: 300 Broadway, Suite 28, San Francisco, CA 94133; ✆ 415 788 3666 ext 128; fax 415 788 7324; gsc@globalservicecorps.org; www.globalservicecorps.org. Runs short-stay, long-term and internship volunteer programmes in Tanzania and Thailand. The English teaching programmes run year-round and attract volunteer participants worldwide. Education volunteers may work teaching English language skills and conversation to students (elementary to university level), community members, orphans, Buddhist monks, and government groups. Volunteers interested in health and HIV/Aids may work at hospitals and health clinics while also helping the doctors and medical staff with their English conversation skills.

Global Volunteers: 375 East Little Canada Road, St. Paul, MN 55117 1628; ✆ 651 407 6100; email@globalvolunteers.org; www.globalvolunteers.org. 1–3-week placements as English conversation assistants in southern Hungary, southern Italy, eastern Poland, Romania and Greece, as well as a range of developing countries.

Reach to Teach: 21 Everett Rd. Extension, Albany, NY 12205; ✆ 518 632 4506; info@reachtoteachrecruiting.com; www.reachtoteachrecruiting.com. Recruits 200+ English teachers per year to work in Taiwan, Korea, Japan and China.

The following consultancies and exchange organisations may be able to guide students towards a range of overseas options including teaching English:

CIEE: Council on International Educational Exchange: 300 Fore Street, Portland, ME 04101; ✆ 207 553 4000; fax 207 553 4299; teach@ciee.org; www.ciee.org/teach. Administers Teach in Chile, China, Spain and Thailand from the USA (see relevant chapters). Participants are placed in local schools where they teach English and are compensated with a local salary and temporary to permanent housing. CIEE provides guidelines for visas (and acquires them for programmes in Asia), insurance and support services. CIEE has partners in London (see IST Plus www.istplus.com), Canada (SWAP www.swap.ca) and Australia (Student Placement Australia, www.studentplacement.com.au) who also send candidates abroad on teaching opportunities. CIEE's website provides info on new teaching abroad programmes and other international opportunities.

Interexchange: 161 Sixth Avenue, New York, NY 10013; ✆ 212 924 0446; fax 212 924 0575; info@interexchange.org; www.interexchange.org. Teach English in Spain ($695 for 1–3 months) or Ghana ($1,595 for 3 months). Programme fees do not include airfare.

CERTIFIED TEACHERS

Certified primary and secondary teachers who want to work in mainstream international schools abroad should be aware of the following agencies and organisations which match up qualified candidates with vacancies. Most of the hiring for primary and secondary schools abroad (often referred to in the American context as K-12 – kindergarten to grade 12) is done at recruitment fairs included on the list below. The files of job-seekers are added to a database which can be consulted by recruiters who then choose whom they want to interview. Candidates who successfully land a job abroad with the help of a US agency may have to pay a placement fee of US$300–US$600, though in some cases the employer underwrites this expense.

Council of International Schools: 21a Lavant St, Petersfield, Hampshire GU32 3EL; ✆ 01730 268244; www.cois.org. Assists only teachers who have a BEd or PGCE with at least 2 years' teaching experience. It published a new edition of the *International Schools Directory* every year; the most recent edition costs £40. You can also carry out international school searches on their website.

Gabbitas Educational Consultants: 126–130 Regent Street, London W1B 5EE; ✆ 020 7734 0161; fax 020 7437 1764; admin@gabbitas.co.uk; www.teacher-recruitment.co.uk. Established for over 130 years, Gabbitas maintains a register of qualified and experienced teachers available for teaching posts in South America, the Middle East, Africa and many other parts of the world. Gabbitas generally recruits subject-specialist teachers for English-medium schools.

WES World-Wide Education Service of CfBT Education Trust: East Devon Business Centre, Heathpark Way, Heathpark, Honiton, Devon, EX14 1SF; ✆ 01404 47301; wes@cfbt.com; www.wesworldwide.com and www.cfbt.com. Educational consultancy which, as part of its work, recruits mostly fully qualified teachers for full-time posts with British and international schools worldwide. WES maintains a register of qualified mainstream teachers and consultants – the latter, to act as advisers/mentors on overseas projects. As part of the CfBT Education Trust, WES is also associated with major EFL projects in Brunei, Malaysia, Singapore, Oman, Abu Dhabi and other countries. (These are not vacation positions.)

International Schools Services: PO Box 5910, Princeton, NJ 08543, USA; ✆ 609 452 0990; fax 609 452 2690; edustaffing@iss.edu; www.iss.edu. Teaching opportunities for educators exist in private American and international schools around the world. ISS hosts three international recruitment centres (IRCs) annually, where interviews are conducted by international school administrators. Applicants must have a bachelor's degree and relevant K-12 experience. IRC registration materials are provided upon approval of application.

Queen's University: Placement Office, Faculty of Education, Kingston, Ontario K7L 3N6, Canada; ✆ 613 533 6222; fax 613 533 6691; http://educ.queensu.ca/placment. Host an annual recruiting fair in February for international schools. Registration costs CAN$100. Teacher certification required plus at least 2 years' K-12 teaching experience.

Search Associates: British branch: David Cope, Berry House, 41 High Street, Over, Cambridgeshire CB24 5NB, UK; ✆ 01954 231130; fax 01954 232145; dr.cope@virgin.net; www.search-associates.co.uk. These contact details should be used by fully qualified primary and secondary teachers with some experience either in the UK or in a British system international school overseas. Teachers preferring to work in International Baccalaureate schools overseas should contact Harry Deelman, Search Associates, PO Box 168, Chiang Mai 50000, Thailand; ✆ 53 244322; fax 53 260118; deelman@loxinfo.co.th; www.search-associates.com. Contact address for teachers resident in the USA: Search Associates, PO Box 636, Dallas, PA 18612, USA; ✆ 570 696 4600; fax 570 696 9500; searchcentralhq@cs.com. Contact address for teachers resident in Canada: Search Associates, 23 Edward Avenue, Westville, Nova Scotia B0K 2A0; ✆ 902 396 1817; fax 902 396 4224; raysparks@eastlink.ca. Search Associates isn't normally appropriate for TEFL teachers who have no school experience, but offers information and placement assistance for teachers with at least some mainstream school experience (with pupils aged 3–18). Long-term positions only (1–3 year contracts, renewable). Recruitment fairs for candidates seeking jobs in international schools are held annually in London, Dubai, Istanbul, Bangkok, Hong Kong, Sydney, Toronto, San Francisco, Cambridge (Massachusetts) and Bethesda (Maryland).

Teacher Recruitment International (Australia): PO Box A1317, Sydney South, New South Wales 1235, Australia; ✆ 2 9360 0458; fax 2 9360 0857; enquiries@triaust.com; www.triaust.com. Place teachers in primary and secondary school posts in international schools in Europe, Asia, the Middle East, and, to a lesser extent, South America. Initial small registration fee – no placement fee.

University of Northern Iowa (UNI): Overseas Placement Service for Educators, UNI, Cedar Falls, Iowa 50614 0390; ✆ 319 273 2083; fax 319 273 6998; overseas.placement@uni.edu; www.uni.edu/placement/overseas. UNI is a non-profit organisation and it does not charge any placement fees to schools or teaching candidates. Educators must hold current certification in elementary or secondary education. A comprehensive service includes the annual UNI Overseas Recruiting Fair in February attended by more than 120 American international schools. Interested educators should contact the UNI office for registration materials and deadlines.

SPECULATIVE JOB HUNT

Only a small percentage of language schools advertise in the foreign press or use an agency. The vast majority depend on local advertisements, word of mouth, personal contacts, the internet and direct approaches. Therefore a speculative job search probably has a better chance with TEFL jobs than in many other fields of employment. For a successful campaign, only two things are needed: a reasonable CV and a list of addresses of potential employers.

APPLYING IN ADVANCE

Entire books and consultancy companies are devoted to showing people how to draw up an impressive curriculum vitae (CV or résumé as it is called in the USA). But it is really just a matter of common sense:

- Any relevant training or experience should be highlighted
- Hobbies can be mentioned but in passing
- If you lack TEFL experience, try to bring out anything in your past which demonstrates your 'people skills', such as voluntary work, group counselling, one-to-one remedial tutoring, etc. and your interest in (and ability to adapt to) foreign countries
- If you are targeting one country, it would be worth drawing up a CV in the local language

Judith Twycross was convinced that her CV in Spanish was a great asset when looking for teaching work in Colombia. If you get the job, however, be prepared for your new employer to expect you to be able to speak the vernacular.

Attitudes and personality are probably just as important as educational achievements in TEFL, so anything which proves an aptitude for teaching and an extrovert personality will be relevant. Because this is difficult to do on paper, some eager job-hunters have gone so far as to send off a video/DVD of themselves, preferably a snippet of teaching. This isn't worth doing unless (a) a school has expressed some interest and (b) you can make a good impression on an amateur film. A cheaper alternative might be to send a photo and a cassette/CD of your speaking voice, again assuming this will be a help rather than a hindrance.

The other essential ingredient is a list of addresses. Each of the country chapters in this book provides such a list and recommends ways of obtaining other addresses, for example by contacting a federation of language schools (if there is one) or the British Council in your destination country. It is always worth writing to or even phoning the local British Council office, since they may be prepared to offer a general assessment of the local TEFL scene as well as provide a list of selected language schools in their region (for the benefit of enquiries from local language learners). The degree of their helpfulness will be at the discretion of the English Language Adviser or her/his secretary.

The book in your hand provides a good starting place for gathering a list of addresses, by including entries for about 600 institutes and organisations. Their teacher requirements were checked and updated at the time of writing.

Note that international telephone access codes are 00 from Britain, 011 from the USA. Individual country codes can be found listed at the front or back of telephone directories. The numbers quoted throughout this book give the area codes minus the prefix 0 (which should be used only when dialling within the country rather than from abroad).

The most comprehensive source of addresses of language schools is usually the *Yellow Pages*, which in many cases can now be consulted online. Just type *Yellow Pages* and your destination country into a search engine and then search for *scuoli di lingue* in Italy, *jazykova skola* in the Czech Republic and so on. Some countries are much better than others, for example the online Portuguese *Yellow Pages* is very helpful whereas the Turkish ones are not.

Of course it has to be stressed that it is difficult, and increasingly so, to set up a firm job offer simply by correspondence. A language school would have to be fairly desperate to hire a teacher they had never met for a vacancy that had never been advertised. It is a good idea to follow up any hint of interest with a phone call. The best time to phone language school directors is six or seven weeks before the beginning of term. Perhaps the school has a contact in your country who would be willing to conduct an informal interview on their behalf or perhaps the school will be content with a telephone interview.

If you haven't got enough experience to talk about, it might still be worth sending off a batch of warm-up letters, stating your intention to present yourself in person a couple of weeks or months hence. Even if you don't receive a reply, such a strategy may stick in the mind of employers, as an illustration of how organised and determined you are.

INTERVIEWS

Schools which advertise in foreign journals often arrange for candidates to be interviewed either by their own representative or by a proxy, such as a previous teacher or an appointed agent. Interviews can take place in strange and unlikely places including private homes. As a woman **Roberta Wedge** felt that she had to be cautious. Once she was stuck in a seedy pub at the end of a tube line at 9pm looking eagerly at every man who came through the door, and then the Director of Studies stood her up. Take along a friend if you are nervous.

Sometimes large organisations such as Berlitz arrange open days and invite anyone who wants to be interviewed to come along. Chances are that British job-seekers will have to travel to London for an interview. Whether you are interviewed at home or abroad, slightly different rules apply. For example smart casual dress, neither flashy nor scruffy, is appropriate in Britain, while something a little more formal might be called for in certain cultures. Even if all your friends laugh when you pack a suit before going abroad, you may find it a genuine asset when trying to outdo the competition. As **Steven Hendry**, who has taught English in both Japan and Thailand with none of the usual advantages apart from traveller's canniness, says: 'You may not need a tailor-made suit but you definitely need to be able to present a conservative and respectable image.'

As with the CV, so at interview. Highlight anything that is remotely connected with teaching even if it has nothing to do with the English language, and do it energetically and enthusiastically. Yet keenness will seldom be sufficient in itself. You do not have to be an intellectual to teach English; in fact the quiet bookish type is probably at a disadvantage. An amusing illustration of this is provided by **Robert Mizzi**'s description of his interview for the JET Programme in the Japan chapter.

Without a TEFL background you should do a certain amount of research, eg acquaint yourself with some of the jargon such as 'notional', 'communicative-based', etc. It isn't uncommon for an interviewer to ask a few basic grammar questions. To help you deal with this eventuality you might turn to the list of recommended reading in the chapter on Preparation. By visiting the ELT section of a bookshop, you can begin to familiarise yourself with the range of materials on offer. Always have some questions ready to ask the interviewer, such as 'Do you use Cambridge or Streamline?', 'What audio materials do you have?', 'Do you encourage the use of songs?' or 'Do you teach formal grammar structures?' If you are looking for an opening in a business context, you might pick up a few tips from the section on Interviews in the chapter on Germany.

You will certainly be asked how long you intend to stay and (depending on the time of year) nothing less than nine months will be considered. They will also want to know whether you have had any experience. With luck you will be able to say truthfully that you have (at least) taught at a summer school in Britain (again, see chapter on Preparation). Some applicants who are convinced that they can do a good job make a similar claim, untruthfully, knowing that at the lower end of the TEFL spectrum this will never be checked. Similarly some candidates claim to have done a TEFL course and pretend to have left the certificate at home. A certain amount of bluffing goes on in all interviews, so you'll just have to decide how far you are prepared to go. Bear in mind that the true depths of your ignorance could easily be plumbed ('Ah, so you've used Cambridge. Why do you prefer it to Streamline?').

Another of your skills you may be tempted to exaggerate is your knowledge of the local language. **Philip Dodd** was hired by a language teaching agency in Madrid on the understanding that he could speak fluent Spanish and was sent out on his first assignment, to give English lessons to a young child living in a wealthy suburb. He was greeted at the door by the mother who wished to make sure of a few things before she entrusted her precious offspring to this stranger. Not able to follow her voluble stream, Philip nodded affably and said 'si' whenever he guessed it was appropriate. After one of his affable 'si's', the woman's face turned grey and she ordered him out of her house. He still doesn't know what he said 'si' to that was so shocking. On the other hand, a certain inflation of your abilities may be expected, and will be met with distortions of the truth from the employer as you both decide whether you are going to hit it off.

Of course many applicants avoid potential embarrassment at interviews by having prepared themselves for a stint as a teacher. If you have done a TEFL course of any description, be sure to take along the certificate, however humble the qualification. Even schools in farflung places are becoming increasingly familiar with the distinctions between various qualifications and are unlikely to confuse a Cambridge Certificate with an anonymous correspondence 'certificate'. In Asia especially, nothing short of the original will do, since there are so many counterfeit copies around.

If you have a university degree, take the certificate along. Even if the interviewer is prepared to take your word for it, the school administration may need the document at a later stage either to give you a salary increment or to obtain a work permit. **Adam Hartley**, who taught English in China, hadn't realised that his masters would have earned him a higher salary; although he arranged for two separate copies to be sent from Britain, neither arrived and he had to be content with the basic salary. Americans should take along their university transcripts; any school accustomed to hiring Americans will be familiar with these. Also take along any references; something written on headed paper will always impress, even if your previous jobs were not in teaching.

Once the interviewer indicates that you are a strong contender, it is your turn to ask questions. Ask about the details of pay, hours and conditions and take notes (see the section on Contracts below). Often there are disappointing discrepancies between what is promised in the early stages and what is delivered; at least if these things have been discussed at interview, you will be in a stronger bargaining position if the conditions are not met.

Unrealistic expectations are a genuine hazard when contemplating an exciting stint of working abroad.

A RECRUITMENT CONSULTANT IN THE FIELD OFFERS THE FOLLOWING SENSIBLE ADVICE:

Teachers should be made aware that they are being employed to do a professional job and it is hard work and long hours. They should not underestimate the cultural differences even in countries they think they know. These often lead to misunderstandings and dissatisfied teachers. I am also constantly surprised by teachers who take jobs without knowing the first thing about the place, the job, the sort of classes they will have, etc. They should make a checklist of questions and if they are making applications on their own they should ask to speak to teachers who are there at the time or who have just left. Research is the key. You wouldn't apply for a job in the UK without knowing something about it so why do so when you're going to another country? If you are offered a job by an agent and are worried about what kind of employer the school will be, you could phone the local British Council office to find out whether the school enjoys a good local reputation. Occasionally an embassy or consulate will assist, as in the case of the US Embassy in Seoul which keeps a file of language schools about which they have received persistent complaints. More commonly, someone will have set up a web-page where this kind of inside information can be obtained (again, common in Korea).

Professional EL teachers often try to attend a regional conference sponsored by TESOL or IATEFL (mentioned below).

SANDEHA LYNCH DESCRIBES THE TESOL ARABIA CONFERENCE HE ATTENDED A COUPLE OF YEARS AGO IN AL-AIN:

These are serious ELT conferences not only as marketing fairs for publishers, booksellers and software companies, but they are an open job shop for the local employers. Teachers from all over the Gulf try to get there to socialise, look for a new job or just absorb enough academic wisdom to last them another year. If teachers are looking for a job then most of the time they'll be making appointments, checking off their interview score cards and watching the clock. All of the local colleges and recruiting agencies have stands there, and they are busy from morning to night giving interviews to anyone who knows the local scene and has the right qualifications.

ON THE SPOT

It is almost impossible to fix up a job in advance in some countries, due to the way the TEFL business operates. For example, written applications to the majority of language schools in Bangkok (assuming you could compile a list of addresses) are a waste of time since the pool of teacher-travellers on the spot is appropriate to the unpredictable needs of Thai schools. Even in countries such as Spain and Germany for which advertisements appear in the UK, the bulk of hiring happens on the spot.

When you arrive in a likely place, your initial steps might include some of the following: transcribing a list of schools from the *Yellow Pages,* reading the classified column of the local newspapers including the English language papers, checking notice boards in likely locations such as the British Council, US Embassy/cultural centres, universities, TEFL training centres, English language bookshops (where you should also notice which EFL materials are stocked), or hostels which teacher-travellers frequent.

Till Bruckner from Cornwall recommends preparing a CV before you leave home and emailing it to yourself as an attachment. That way you don't have to carry it around with you and you can easily modify it in any internet café.

> **A RECONNAISSANCE TRIP IS A GOOD IDEA IF POSSIBLE; ALTHOUGH ANDREW WHITMARSH DIDN'T EVEN REALISE HE WAS LOOKING FOR A NEW JOB, WHEN ONE FOUND HIM IN INDONESIA:**
> *As often happens, I didn't find my job, my job found me. I was standing on top of a volcano in Indonesia when a gentleman in my hiking group asked me what I did for a living. Upon my reply of 'English Teacher', he declared that this was wonderful news to hear and he had just the job for me. The gentleman just happened to be the President Director of Wall Street Institute – and he needed teachers.*

With a little more purpose and a little less serendipity, **Fiona Paton** found a job teaching English in France. On her way back from a summer holiday in Spain, she jumped off the train in Vichy for long enough to distribute her CV to several language schools. To her surprise, a letter arrived from one of them once she was at home offering her a job for the academic year, which she subsequently accepted and greatly enjoyed.

After obtaining a list of potential employers and before contacting them, get hold of a detailed map and guide to the public transport network so you can locate the schools. Phone the schools and try to arrange a meeting with the director or director of studies (DOS). Even if an initial chat does not result in a job offer, you may learn something about the local TEFL scene which will benefit you at the next interview, especially if you ask lots of questions. You might also be able to strike up a conversation with one of the foreign teachers who could turn out to be a valuable source of information about that school in particular and the situation generally. It is very common to have to begin with just a few hours a week. Make it clear that you are prepared to stand in at short notice for an absent teacher. The longer you stay in one place, the more hours will come your way and the better your chances of securing a stable contract.

This gradual approach also gives you a chance to discover which are the cowboy schools, something which is difficult to do before you are on the scene. The British Council has called for an EU-wide recognition scheme for language schools, to force rogue schools out of business. But this is a long way off, and in the meantime disreputable schools flourish in Europe just as they do in other parts of the world. It is not always easy to distinguish them, though if a school sports a sign 'Purrfect Anglish' you are probably not going to need an MA in Applied Linguistics to get a job there. Working for a cowboy outfit may not be the end of the world, though it often spells trouble, as the chapter Problems will reveal. But without many qualifications you may not have much choice.

FREELANCE TEACHING

Private English lessons are usually more lucrative than contract teaching simply because the middle man has been cut out. Learners may prefer them as well, not only because of the more personal attention they receive in a private lesson but because it costs them less. As a private tutor working from your own home or visiting pupils in theirs, you can undercut the big schools with their overheads. But at the same time you deprive yourself of the advantages of working for a decent school: access to resources and equipment, in-service training, social security schemes and holiday pay. The life of a freelance teacher can be quite a lonely one. Usually teachers working for a school take on a small amount of private teaching to supplement their income, provided this is allowed in their contracts. Most employers do not mind unless your private teaching is interfering with your school schedule or (obviously) if you are pinching potential clients from your employer.

In order to round up private pupils, you will have to sell yourself as energetically as any salesman. Turn to the section on Freelance Teaching in the Spain chapter for some ideas which have worked in Spain but could work anywhere. It might be possible to persuade companies to pay you to run English classes for employees during the lunch hour or siesta (if appropriate), though you would have to be a confident teacher and dynamic salesperson to succeed. You are far more likely to find one or two pupils by word of mouth and build from there.

Self-promotion is essential. Steven Hendry recommends plastering neatly printed bilingual notices all over town, as he did to good effect in Chiang Mai in northern Thailand. Meanwhile Ian McArthur in Cairo made a large number of posters (in Arabic and English) and painstakingly coloured in the Union Jack by hand in order to attract attention. (Unfortunately these were such a novelty that many posters were pinched.) Putting a notice on appropriate notice boards (in schools, universities, public libraries, popular supermarkets) and running an advertisement in the local paper are good ideas; you will need a reliable mobile phone and preferably frequent access to your email. These methods should put you in touch with a few hopeful language learners. If you are any good, word will spread and more paying pupils will come your way, though it can be a slow process.

To counterbalance the advantages of higher pay and a more flexible schedule, freelance teaching has many disadvantages. Everyone, from lazy Taiwanese teenagers to busy Barcelona businessmen, cancels or postpones one-to-one lessons with irritating frequency. People who have taught in Latin countries complain that the problem is chronic. Cancellations among school and university students especially escalate at exam time. It is important to agree on a procedure for cancellations which won't leave you out of pocket. Although it is virtually impossible to arrange to be paid in advance, you can request 24 hours notice of a cancellation and mention politely that if they fail to give due warning you will insist on being paid for the missed lesson. But you can't take too tough a line, since your clients are paying above the odds for your flexibility. Another consideration is the unpaid time spent travelling between clients' homes and workplaces.

Some people do their teaching without ever leaving the comfort of their own homes. Teaching by telephone is commonplace in Europe, especially in France, and the newest method is to teach by Skype as **Lyndon Owen** describes:

> *I teach Business English one to one in my home in England and one of my recent students, a French professor of law, asked me to provide him with four lessons a week on the telephone. We have not finalised the details yet but since I have recently acquired Skype I thought this might have been a cheaper medium for him once he has acquired the microphone and software.*

One company which uses this medium exclusively is www.telephonenglish.com, which is recruiting qualified native speakers to add to its team of Skype teachers (CVs to dos@telephoneenglish.com).

If you are less interested in making money than integrating with a culture, exchanging conversation for board and lodging may be an appealing possibility. This can be set up by answering (or placing) small advertisements in appropriate places (the American Church in Paris notice board is famous for this). **Hannah Start**, a school leaver in Merseyside, put up a notice at her local English language school indicating that she wanted to exchange English conversation for accommodation in Paris; a businesswoman on an intensive English course contacted her and invited her to stay with her.

TEFL WEBSITES

For schools, a website advertisement offers an easy and instantaneous means of publicising a vacancy to an international audience. It is far quicker and cheaper for schools in Thailand, Ecuador and Russia to post vacancy notices on the internet than it would be to place an advert in a foreign newspaper. Teachers looking for employment can use search engines to look for all pages with references to EFL, English language schools and recruitment. CVs can be emailed quickly and cheaply to advertising schools, who can then use email themselves to chase up references. This presupposes a degree of IT awareness which the majority of job-seekers in this field now have. The internet has very quickly taken over as the primary means of recruitment.

Arguably it has become a little too easy to advertise and answer job advertisements online. At the press of a button, your CV can be clogging up dozens, nay, hundreds of computers. It is interesting to remark that some of the schools that corresponded with this book for the current edition said that they seemed to get a more reliable brand of teacher from readers of this book and that they are more impressed with a job-seeker who goes to the trouble of assimilating the information in a book than the ones who spend their days skating over the internet. But basically, recruitment via the internet is here to stay.

While opening up an enormous range of possibilities, the internet can be a bewildering place to job-hunt. A host of websites promises to provide free online recruitment services for English teachers. Because many sites are in their infancy, they often seem to offer more than they can deliver and you may find that the number and range of jobs posted are disappointing. You would hope that a site with a name like 'eflteachingjobs.com' would have more choice of possibilities abroad than a handful of UK gap year placement organisations and some tips on preparing a CV.

But everywhere you look on the internet, potentially useful links can be found. More than 100 websites are devoted to EFL/ESL jobs, many in Asia. Most of them have links to Dave Sperling's ESL Café (www.eslcafe.com) which so expertly dominates the field that it is hard to see how others can compete (though dozens try). 'Dave' provides a mind-boggling but well-organised amount of material for the future or current teacher including accounts of people's experiences of teaching abroad (but bear in mind that these are the opinions of individuals). It also provides links to specific institutes and chains in each country.

IT IS POSSIBLE AT DAVE'S ESL CAFÉ TO POST A MESSAGE OFFERING YOUR SERVICES, BUT IT IS IMPORTANT TO BE FAIRLY SPECIFIC AS FERGUS COONEY DISCOVERED:
I posted a message simply stating 'Qualified teacher seeking job'. Within two days I was inundated with many dozens of replies requesting my CV and, more surprisingly, with job offers everywhere, although the

1   Tom Grundy with his English class in Hong Kong

2   An English class at the Granada English College, Nicaragua

The Ma Tau Chung Government Primary School in Hong Kong 3

Outside the St Anthony's Boys Primary School in Uganda 4

Teach
English Through Drama
in Japan

Are you interested in teaching English to young children in one of the most exciting countries in the world?
Does the idea of combining ENGLISH and DRAMA to teach fun-filled classes sound good to you?

applications to: careers@mls-etd.co.jp

mls-etd.co.jp

majority were from Korea, Taiwan and China. 'Jackpot' I thought (I have since realised that many schools/ agents must have an automatic reply system which emails those who advertise in the way I did). I quickly began sifting through them, but not as quickly as they kept arriving in my inbox. Before a few more days had passed, I had become utterly confused and had forgotten which school was which, so I deleted them all, got a new email address and posted a second, more specific message on Dave's.

Note that the website www.onestopenglish.com has a very good annotated links page to a range of ELT sites. Here is a brief survey of some of the key recruitment sites.

www.TEFL.com – popular vehicle for schools around the world to publicise vacancies. When subscribing (for free) to the TEFL Professional Network, you can specify whether you want to be notified of vacancies by email on a daily or weekly basis. At the time of writing the countries with the most vacancies listed were Italy (41), Spain (37), China (32) and Poland (16).

www.tefljobs.co.uk – part of the well-known www.seasonworkers.com site, www.tefljobs. co.uk aims to provide useful information both to those new to TEFL teaching and already qualified job-hunters. The site provides a comprehensive listing of TEFL courses and teaching vacancies worldwide, backed up by relevant and up-to-date information on living and working in the countries concerned. You can even use the 'reunion' service to track down old friends and teaching colleagues.

www.englishjobmaze.com – facilitates the job-search process for ESL/EFL teachers around the world and assists ESL/EFL institutions in their search for teachers.

www.free-esl.com – 1 or 2 very current jobs for most countries; some have complete contact details, others not.

www.cactusteachers.com – For TEFL articles, information and advice for all practising TEFL teachers, especially on admission to all post-initial training and teacher development courses.

www.cactustefl.com – for articles, information and advice relating to entry into the world of TEFL. Provides a TEFL courses admissions service.

www.cactustefl.com/jobs/index.php carries classified advertisements for TEFL jobs worldwide.

www.ihworld.com – International House World's website. IH is an established and expanding ELT organisation with 145 schools worldwide. The site has detailed information about recruitement and training as well as up-to-date details of ITI schools accessible to all.

www.jobs.edufind.com

www.tefllogue.com

http://jobs.guardian.co.uk/jobs/education/tefl – job vacancy listings on the Guardian Unlimited website; also check the Guardian's TEFL pages http://education.guardian.co. uk/tefl.

www.joyjobs.com – one of the few in the field which charge a subscription (US$39.95). You can check out the range of vacancies but will have to pay to access contact details. Some emphasis on 'K-12' schools.

www.tefl.net – more limited choice than some, but carries some up-to-date vacancies.

www.footprintsrecruiting.com – Vancouver-based service listing vacancies in Korea, Taiwan, China, Chile, etc.

Other websites which are country specific eg www.ohayosensei.com (jobs in Japan) or www.ajarn. com (teaching in Thailand) are listed in the relevant country chapters.

PREPARATION

The preceding chapters on ELT training and job-hunting set out ways in which you can make yourself more attractive to potential employers. One of the best ways in which to prepare for a stint of teaching abroad is to teach English locally. Relevant experience can usually be gained by volunteering to tutor immigrants in your home town; this is particularly feasible in the USA where literacy programmes take place on a massive scale. It might also be a good idea to contact the director of a local commercial language school and ask to sit in on some lessons to see what it's all about and to talk to teachers. A polite note expressing your interest in TEFL would probably meet with a positive response. EFL teachers are like everyone else; they are experts at what they do and don't mind sharing that knowledge with interested outsiders.

More prolonged exposure to TEFL can best be gained by working at a language summer school. This not only provides a chance to find out whether you will enjoy English teaching for a longer period, but may put you in touch with people who are well informed on overseas possibilities.

UK SUMMER SCHOOLS

Language summer courses take place throughout the British Isles, especially in tourist areas. The short-term nature of the teacher requirements means that schools sometimes have difficulties finding enough qualified staff, though with a recent decrease in the number of language learners coming to Britain, there are fewer jobs floating around. Wages are higher than for most seasonal summer jobs and as a result it is harder to get a job teaching English in Torquay than in Taipei. You may have to use the same wiles as described above in the section on interviews in order to be hired.

It is estimated that there are 600–800 English language schools in operation in Britain during July and August, mainly catering for foreign students, especially from France, Spain, Italy and other EU countries, but increasingly from further afield (eg eastern Europe and Turkey). Many of these schools advertise heavily in the spring, eg 'Teach English on the English Riviera'. Quality varies dramatically of course. The more established schools are usually members of English UK which has absorbed ARELS, the Association of Recognised English Language Services (www.englishuk.com), which is trying to raise standards and whose staff are less likely to be novice teachers. The organisation has 388 member schools. The counterpart in the state sector is BASELT (British Association of State English Language Teaching). The two organisations merged in May 2004 to create English UK, a comprehensive association for accredited English Language Centres (www.arels.org.uk).

> **WHILE WAITING FOR VSO TO FIND HIM A TEACHING PLACEMENT IN MONGOLIA, MR R ROY TAUGHT ENGLISH FOR PILGRIMS IN CANTERBURY WHICH GAVE HIM FURTHER EXPERIENCE AT THE SAME TIME AS EARNING HIM A TIDY SUM:**
> *I worked two three-week courses back to back which left me very little time to myself but also no time to spend any money and of course food and accommodation were included in the deal. It was really intense and tiring but good experience with all the visits and sports and performances and producing videos and magazines and reports. Pilgrims provided a good stock of books and equipment to help teachers prepare their lessons. I'm still in touch with them and would like to work another summer when I'm back in Britain.*

At the other end of the spectrum are the entrepreneurs who rent space (possibly ill-suited to teaching) and will take on almost anyone to teach. Teachers are thrown in at the deep end with little preparation and few materials. **Marta Eleniak** was not very happy with her employer:

> *I have got nothing good to say about my employer. We were expected to do nearly everything including perform miracles, with no support and pathetic facilities. I can only liken it to being asked to entertain 200 people for four hours with a plastic bowl. The pupils got a raw deal too because of false promises made to them.*

She does admit that it was on the basis of this three-week job that she got a job in a Madrid language school.

Schools at both extremes are listed in the *Yellow Pages* and advertise in the national press. They are located throughout the UK, but are concentrated in London and the South-East, Oxford, Cambridge and resorts such as Bournemouth and Blackpool. Recruitment of summer teachers gets underway in the new year and is usually well advanced by Easter. The average starting salary for teachers is £170–£200 per week, though Certificate-qualified teachers should earn £250–£300. Residential schools may pay less if they are providing board and lodging, though some pay the same because the hours are so much longer. Since most schools are located in popular tourist destinations, private accommodation can be prohibitively expensive and the residential option attractive. Without any TEFL background it is easier to get taken on as a non-teaching sports and activities supervisor which at least would introduce you to the world of TEFL. EFL teachers must expect a number of extracurricular activities such as chaperoning a group of over-excited adolescents to a West End theatre or on an art gallery visit.

Here is a short list of major language course organisations which usually offer a large number of summer vacancies.

Anglo Continental Educational Group: 29–35 Wimborne Road, Bournemouth BH2 6NA; ✆ 01202 557414; fax 01202 556156; english@anglo-continental.com; www.anglo-continental.com.

Ardmore Language Schools: Hall Place, Berkshire College, Burchetts Green, Maidenhead, Berkshire SL6 6QR; ✆ 01628 826699; fax 01628 829977; recruitment@theardmore group.com; www.theardmoregroup.com.

Concorde International Summer Schools: Arnett House, Hawks Lane, Canterbury, Kent CT1 2NU; ✆ 01227 451035; fax 01227 762760; info@concorde-int.com; www.concorde-international.com.

EF Language Travel: Cherwell House, 3rd Floor, 1 London Place, Oxford OX4 1BD; ✆ 01865 200720; fax 01865 243196; lt.oxford@ef.com; www.ef.com.

EJO: Eagle House, Lynchborough Rd, Passfield, Surrey GU30 7SB; ✆ 01428 751933; steve@ejo.co.uk; www.ejo.co.uk/employ.asp.

Embassy CES: Head Office: Brighton Study Centre,1 Billinton Way, Brighton, East Sussex BN1 4LF; ✆ 1273 339 400; vacjobsuk@embassyces.com; www.embassyces.com.

International Study Programmes: The Manor, Hazleton, Cheltenham, Gloucestershire GL54 4EB; ✆ 01451 860379; Discover@International-Study-Programmes.org.uk; www.international-study-programmes.org.uk.

Isis Education & Travel: 259 Greenwich High Road, London SE10 8NB; ✆ 020 8293 1188; info@isisgroup.co.uk.

Kent School of English: 10–12 Granville Road, Broadstairs, Kent CT10 1QD; ✆ 01843 874870; fax 01843 860418; enquiries@kentschool.co.uk; www.kentschoolofenglish.com.

Oise Youth Language Schools: OISE House, Binsey Lane, Oxford OX2 0EY; ✆ 01865 258300; fax 01865 244696; info@oise.com; www.oise.com.

Project International: 20 Fitzroy Square, London W1T 6EJ; ✆ 020 7916 2522; fax 020 7916 8586; info@projectinternational.uk.com; www.projectinternational.uk.com.

Quest for English: 7 Trinity, 161 Old Christchurch Road, Bournemouth, BH1 1JU; ✆ 01202 296868, fax 01202 298836; teaching@questforenglish.com; www.questforenglish.com. Division of International Quest, has hundreds of vacancies for qualified teachers and activity staff in residential centres throughout the UK from mid-June to end of August. Residential and non-residential posts available for native and non-native speakers for one to eight weeks.

Stafford House School of English: 19 New Dover Road, Canterbury, Kent CT1 3AH; ✆ 01227 452250; fax 01227 453579; recruitment@ceg-uk.com; www.staffordhouse.com. Part of Cambridge Education Group.

SUL Language Schools: 31 Southpark Road, Tywardreath, Par, Cornwall PL24 2PU; ✆ 01726 814227; fax 01726 813135; efl@sul-schools.com; www.sul-schools.com.

TASIS England American School: Coldharbour Lane, Thorpe, Surrey TW20 8TE; ✆ 01932 565252 ext 2313; jeffbarton@tasis.com (Summer programmes); www.tasis.com. Of special interest to American EFL teachers.

Thames Valley Cultural Centres: 13 Park St, Windsor, Berkshire SL4 1LU; ✆ 01753 852001; fax 01753 831165; recruit@thamesvalleysummer.co.uk; www.thamesvalleycultural.com.

Torbay Language Centre: Conway Road, Paignton, Devon TO4 5LH; ✆ 01803 558555; fax 01803 559606; mark.cook@lalgroup.com; www.lalgroup.com.

WHILE YOU'RE WAITING

After you have secured a job, there may be a considerable gap which will give you a chance to organise the practicalities of moving abroad and to prepare yourself in other ways. If you are going to
a country which requires immigration procedures (the majority of cases unless you're an EU national
planning to work in another member state) you can start the visa procedures. In addition to deciding
what to take and how to get to your destination, you should think about your tax position and health
insurance, plus find out as much as you can about the situation in which you will find yourself.

Many teachers take out a subscription to the *Guardian Weekly* (164 Deansgate, Manchester M3
3GG; ℂ 0870 066 0510; www.guardianweekly.com) to guarantee access to world news, though you
might prefer to wait until you arrive to see what newspapers are available. A one-year subscription
costs just under £100. Also contact BBC English, the English language teaching arm of BBC World
Service, Bush House, London WC2B 4PH (www.bbc.co.uk/worldservice/learningenglish), which also
publishes information sheets to go with its programmes and material on its websites. Further enquiries can be made to the BBC World Service (ℂ 020 7240 3456).

Alternative English language broadcasting organisations are Voice of America, Radio Canada International (PO Box 6000, Montreal, Canada H3C 3A8) and Swiss Radio International (SRI; SBC,
CH-3000 Bern 15, Switzerland; www.swissinfo.org; info@sri.ch), all of which will send information
about their services. SRI publishes a monthly magazine *Swiss World* in English and other languages
which would be useful to teachers in Germany and elsewhere in Europe.

A website called www.eltlinkup.org serves as a base for anyone with an EFL/ESOL link – but
mainly those with a more professional interest – for finding old contacts, jobs, EFL issues, conferences, etc. Joining is free and it has members in 92 countries.

ELT professionals should consider joining the International Association of Teachers of English as a
Foreign Language (IATEFL, Darwin College, University of Kent, Canterbury, Kent CT2 7NY; ℂ 01227
824430; fax 01227 824431; generalenquiries@iatefl.org; www.iatefl.org). Membership, which
costs £43 to individuals or £138 to institutions, entitles teachers to various services including six
newsletters annually and access to special interest groups, conferences, workshops and symposia.

> *job unless they are really confident that they'll be able to develop the framework themselves. I would look for a school that said something like, 'You'll guide the students through Hotline 1 textbook, and also give them extra vocabulary and speaking exercises to supplement the text. You'll also work with a phonics text for a few weeks, because these students have poor pronunciation. You'll probably find it useful to bring some old magazines but the school has several ESL textbooks already.' This would show that the school takes both curriculum and organisation seriously.*

An invaluable source of information is someone who has taught at the school before; ask your employer for a couple of addresses. Past teachers pass on priceless minutiae, not only recommending pubs, bakeries, etc. but (if the accommodation is tied to the job) to arrive early and avoid the back bedroom because of the noisy plumbing.

CONTRACTS

This is the point at which a formal contract or at least an informal agreement should be drawn up. Any employer who is reluctant to provide something in writing is definitely suspect. Horror stories abound of the young unsuspecting teacher who goes out to teach overseas and discovers no pay, no accommodation and maybe even no school. For this reason it is not only very important to sign a contract, but also to have a good idea as to what it is letting you in for.

The following items should be covered in a contract or at least given some consideration:

- Name and address of employer.
- Details of the duties and hours of the job. (A standard load might be 24 contact teaching hours a week, plus three hours on standby to fill in for an absent teacher, fill all the board markers in the staff room, etc.)
- The amount and currency of your pay. Is it adequate to live on? How often are you paid? Is any money held back? Can it be easily transferred into sterling or dollars? What arrangements are there if the exchange rate drops suddenly or the local currency is devalued?
- The length of the contract and whether it is renewable.
- Help with finding and paying for accommodation. If accommodation isn't provided free, is your salary adequate to cover this? If it is, are utilities included? Does the organisation pay for a stay in a hotel while you look for somewhere to live? How easy is it to find accommodation in the area? If it is unfurnished what help do you get in providing furniture? Can you get a salary advance to pay for this and for any rent deposits?
- Your tax liability.
- Provisions for healthcare and sick pay.
- Payment of pension or national insurance contributions.
- Bonuses, gratuities or perks.
- Days off, statutory holidays and vacation times.
- Paid flights home if the contract is outside Europe, and mid-term flights if you are teaching for two years.
- Luggage and surplus luggage allowance at the beginning and end of the contract.
- Any probationary period and the length of notice which you and the employer must give.
- Penalties for breaking the contract and circumstances under which the penalties would be waived (eg extreme family illness, etc.).

Obviously any contract should be carefully studied before signing. It is a wise precaution to make a photocopy of it before returning to avoid what happened to Belinda Michaels whose employer in Greece refused to give her a copy when she started to dispute some points. In some cases the only contract offered will be in a foreign language (eg Arabic) and you will either have to trust your contact at the school for a translation or consider obtaining an independent English translation. Amanda Moody signed documents that were only in Japanese and later found out that she'd been diddled out of her end-of-year bonus.

HEALTH AND INSURANCE

Increasingly, the immigration authorities abroad will not grant a teacher a work permit until they have provided a medical certificate. Many countries now insist on an HIV test and various other health checks including for syphilis and tuberculosis. GPs will charge for carrying out these tests, whether you do it before you leave home or after arrival.

Reputable schools will make the necessary contributions into the national health insurance and social security scheme. Even if you are covered by the national scheme, however, you may find that there are exclusion clauses such as dental treatment, non-emergency treatment, prescription drugs, etc. or you may find that you are covered only while at work. Private travel insurance can be very expensive. Most insurance companies offer a standard rate that covers medical emergencies and a premium rate that covers personal baggage, cancellation, etc. Expect to pay roughly £20–£25 per month for basic cover and £35–£40 for more extensive cover. Premiums vary depending on age and gender as Sylvia Weismiller, Director of Euro-Lingua, points out. As a 40-year-old woman she was paying €400 a month for official German health insurance (women pay double), which doesn't depend on your income.

Specialist expatriate policies might be worth investigating. Policies endorsed by American Citizens Abroad (5, rue Liotard, CH-1202 Geneva, Switzerland) are available from Abrams Insurance Agency (1051 North George Mason Drive, Arlington, VA 22205, USA). The following UK companies are familiar with insuring expats including EFL teachers:

Club Direct Travel Insurance: Southgate Place, 41/42 Southgate, Chichester, West Sussex, PO19 1ET; customer.services@clubdirect.com; www.clubdirect.com. Offers special backpacker policies (either basic or comprehensive) for long trips of 2 months to a year or more. A 1-year basic policy costs £179, a comprehensive policy costs £249.

KW Batten Insurance Consultants: The Chestnuts, 18 East Street, Farnham, GU9 7SD; ✆ 01252 710546; h.f.lavery.t21@btinternet.com. Specialist service for teachers abroad.

Options Insurance: Lumbry Park, Selborne Road, Alton, Hampshire GU34 3HF; ✆ 0870 876 7878; options@inter-group.co.uk; www.optionsinsurance.co.uk. Extended stay policy at competitive price for anyone under 40. £170 per year for standard cover, £250 for higher cover.

The European Health Insurance Card is valid throughout the European Economic Area and Switzerland: the E111 has now been phased out. You can apply online for a EHIC (www.dh.gov.uk/en/Health care/index.htm). Even if your employer will be paying into a health scheme, cover may not take effect immediately and it is as well to have the ordinary tourist cover for the first three months.

If your destination is tropical, consult an up-to-date book on health such as *Travellers' Health: How to Stay Healthy Abroad* by Richard Dawood (Oxford University Press, £15.99), the *Rough Guide* to Travel Health by Dr Nick Jones (Penguin, £9.99) or the definitive US state handbook called CDC Health Information for International Travel 2008 The Yellow Book. MASTA (see below) oversees a network of travel clinics throughout the UK which will give advice on specific destinations, administer jabs and prescribe the correct anti-malarials, etc. Telephone/internet advice on immunisations and malaria is available from MASTA (Medical Advisory Service for Travellers Abroad), Moorfield Road, Yeadon, Leeds LS19 7BN. The Travellers' Health Line operates on 0906 822 4100; after callers leave details of their itinerary, dates of arrival and expected living conditions, a basic MASTA Health Brief will be sent to them, though the call on this premium rate line will cost £2–£3 (£1 per minute). MASTA health briefs are also available online (www.masta.org) for £3.99. If you are heading off to central Africa or any other place where the incidence of HIV is high, you will be understandably worried about the standards of healthcare in general and the quality of blood and syringes in particular. Sterile medical packs containing hypodermic needles, intravenous drip needles, etc. are available from MASTA.

NATIONAL INSURANCE CONTRIBUTIONS, SOCIAL SECURITY AND PENSIONS

If you are a national of a European Economic Area country working in another member state, you will be covered by European Social Security regulations. Advice and the free information leaflet SA29 'Your Social Security Health Care and Pension Rights in the European Community plus Iceland, Liechtenstein and Norway' may be obtained from the NI Contributions Office International Services, Benton, Newcastle-upon-Tyne NE98 1ZZ (© 0845 915 4811, local rate call). The leaflet explains that payments made in any EEA country count towards benefit entitlement when you return home. The UK also has Social Security agreements with other countries including Croatia, Cyprus, Israel, Jamaica, Malta, Slovenia, Switzerland, Turkey, USA and republics of the former Yugoslavia. If you are going to teach in any of these countries, contact International Services for the appropriate leaflet.

The EUlisses website (pronounced Ulysses after the hero himself) http://ec.europa.eu/employment_social/social_security_schemes/eulisses/jetspeed explains national social security arrangements throughout Europe.

In countries where no Social Security agreement exists, the leaflet NI38 'Social Security Abroad' gives an outline of the arrangements and options open to you. If you don't make National Insurance contributions while you are out of the UK, you will forfeit entitlement to benefits on your return. You can decide to pay voluntary contributions at regular intervals or in a lump sum in order to retain your rights to certain benefits. Unfortunately this entitles you only to a retirement/widow's pension, not to sickness benefit or unemployment benefit.

The question of pensions may seem irrelevant if you are just taking off for a year or two to teach English abroad. However, anyone who remains in the job for more than a couple of years should give some thought to starting or maintaining a pension. Because most English language teachers move between countries, it makes sense to pay into a personal pension scheme in your home country and also to maintain your right to a state pension by keeping up voluntary contributions. The question becomes vexed in those countries where state pension contributions are compulsory, as in Germany (see country chapter). Regulations of course vary from country to country so that for instance you are entitled to receive a pension after paying into the German scheme for five or more years but in Portugal you have to contribute for 17 years. If you pay into a scheme and leave before you are entitled to claim a pension, you will have to try to reclaim some of the money you paid in. In Germany you won't get back more than half. If you work in a number of countries you may find that you spend your retirement corresponding with national pension authorities.

JOHN SYDES, AN EXPATRIATE TEACHER IN MUNICH, HAS LOOKED INTO THE QUESTION OF PENSIONS AND HAS BEEN LOBBYING THE EUROPEAN PARLIAMENT TO CONSIDER THE PREDICAMENT OF PERIPATETIC ENGLISH TEACHERS:

Social security regulations vary from country to country, so it is important to look into whether you will be entitled to a pension later if you intend spending any length of time in one place and have to pay pension contributions in a state scheme.

It's nice to hop around when you are young and full of energy and ideas. It's not so nice to find out that you have paid a lot of money into a scheme that won't pay you a pension later. English teachers are adventurers, but I'm afraid too many of us are forgetting a fundamental problem: How do we survive when we are old? We have managed to get the EU to realise that there is at least one group of professionals, ie TEFL teachers, who are living up to the European ideal of mobility of labour, may well find that they face a bureaucratic nightmare when they retire and apply for a state pension.

TAX

Calculating your liability to tax when working outside your home country is notoriously complicated so, if possible, check your position with an accountant. Everything depends on whether you fall into the category of 'resident', 'ordinarily resident' or 'domiciled'. Most EFL teachers count as domiciled in the UK since it is assumed that they will ultimately return. New legislation has removed the 'foreign earnings deduction' for UK nationals unless they are out of the country for a complete tax year. Since most teaching contracts operate from September, this means that the vast majority of EFL teachers, including teachers on high salaries in the Middle East or on the Japan Exchange and Teaching scheme which were formerly tax-free, will now be liable to UK tax. If you are out of the country for a tax year, you will be entitled to the exemption, provided no more than 62 days (ie one-sixth of the year) have been spent in the UK.

If the country in which you have been teaching has a double taxation agreement with Britain, you can offset tax paid abroad against your tax bill at home. But not all countries have such an agreement and it is not inconceivable that you will be taxed twice. Keep all receipts and financial documents in case you need to plead your case at a later date.

Inland Revenue leaflets which may be of assistance are IR20 'Residents and non-residents: Liability to tax in the UK' and IR139 'Income from Abroad? A guide to UK tax on overseas income'. The Inland Revenue also has a good website if you have the patience to look for the information you need (www.inlandrevenue.gov.uk); it lists the relevant contact offices that deal with specific issues. For enquiries about income tax for customers who are going to live or work abroad ring 0845 070 0400 (fax 0151 472 6067).

If US citizens can establish that they are resident abroad, the first US$80,000 of overseas earnings is tax-exempt in the USA.

TRAVEL

London is the cheap airfare capital of the world and the number of agencies offering discount flights to all corners of the world is seemingly endless. To narrow the choice you should find a travel agency which specialises in your destination. Those who know their way around the web can find lots of useful information. Start with www.cheapflights.co.uk which allows users to log onto a destination and see a list of prices offered by a variety of airlines and agents. It also has links to other travel-related topics (exchange rates, weather forecast, health advice). Compare the prices posted on www.travelocity.com, www.opodo.co.uk and other cheap travel websites including www.expedia. co.uk and www.lastminute.com.

Alternatively, consult specialist travel magazines such as *TNT* (which is free in London) plus *Time Out* and the Saturday edition of the *Independent* or other national papers. By ringing a few of the agencies with advertisements you will soon discover which airlines offer the cheapest service. STA, with branches in most university towns, can usually be relied on to come up with the best flight options to suit your needs. STA's telephone sales number is 0870 1 600 599 and website is www.statravel.co.uk.

Another recommended travel agent is Trailfinders (www.trailfinders.com) with offices in London, Birmingham, Manchester, Bristol, Cambridge, Glasgow, Dublin, Sydney and Brisbane (among others).

In North America, the best newspapers to scour for cheap flights are the *New York Times* (the Sunday edition has a section devoted to travel with cut-price flights advertised), the *LA Times*, *San Francisco Chronicle-Examiner*, *Miami Herald*, *Dallas Morning News*, *Chicago Sun Times*, the *Boston Globe* and the Canadian *Globe & Mail*. Recommended agencies include STA (www.statravel.com) with 100 offices worldwide including 15 in the USA. If your dates are flexible, contact Airtech, 584 Broadway, Suite 1007, New York, NY 10012; (℗ 212 219 7000; www.airtech.com) which advertises its fares by saying, '*if you can beat these prices, start your own damn airline*'. One-way transatlantic fares start at US$189 plus US$125 tax. Travel CUTS in Canada and now the USA sell discounted fares (www.travelcuts.com).

Within Europe, rail is often the preferred way of travelling, especially since the months of September and June when most teachers are travelling to and from their destinations are among the most enjoyable times to travel. Good discounts are available to travellers under 26; details are available from Rail Europe on 0870 584 8848 or www.raileurope.co.uk, which has schedules, fares etc. for European rail passes, Eurostar and for point-to-point tickets throughout Europe. You can also book online.

HOSPITALITY EXCHANGES

If you are planning to travel and conduct a speculative job hunt, you might want to take advantage of one of the hospitality exchanges that flourish over the internet.

Roving EL teacher **Bradwell Jackson** had been mulling over the possibility of travelling the world for about a decade before he finally gave up his drug misuse counselling job in the USA to take off. On his earlier travels he had discovered the benefits of joining Servas (www.usservas.org in the USA, www.servasbritain.u-net.com in the UK) and two other hospitality exchange programmes, Global Freeloaders (www.globalfreeloaders.com) and the Hospitality Club (www.hospitalityclub.org). His first destination was Mexico where to his amazement he found English teaching work at the first place he happened to enquire in Mexico City:

> *I really must say right away that Servas isn't simply for freeloading in people's homes. However, once you take the plunge and commit to wandering the earth, things just start to fall into place. If you belong to clubs such as Global Freeloaders, Hospitality Club, or any of the other homestay organisations, don't be surprised if the family you stay with invites you for an extended stay. The first such family I stayed with in Mexico invited me to stay for six months. All they asked is that I help with the costs of the food they prepared for me and hot water I used.*

Bradwell is continuing his couchsurfing travels in some unlikely locations. He left Mauritania at the beginning of 2008 and stayed with a host in Bamako, Mali who offered to let him stay for two months in exchange for two hours of English lessons a day. He was a wealthy man who gave Brad all his meals, internet access, laundry and so on. He commented that '*once one lands into a dream situation like this, you are apt to feel a bit guilty, and such hospitality takes time to get used to. Still, I am certainly not complaining*'. More recently, en route to his teaching job in China, he stayed with a host in Hong Kong.

MAPS & INFORMATION

Good maps and guide books always enhance one's anticipation and enjoyment of going abroad. If you are in London, visit the famous map shop Edward Stanford Ltd (12–14 Long Acre, Covent Garden, WC2E 9LP; ✆ 020 7836 1321) which also sends maps by post. The Map Shop (15 High St, Upton-on-Severn, Worcestershire WR8 0HJ; ✆ 01684 593146) does an extensive mail order business and will send you the relevant list of their holdings. Daunt Books for Travellers (83 Marylebone High Street, London W1M 4DE; ✆ 020 7224 2295; www.dauntbooks.co.uk) organises its holdings according to region, shelving practical guides next to relevant travel literature. The Travel Bookshop (13 Blenheim Crescent, London W11; ✆ 020 7229 5260) divides travel books by region and stocks literary titles connected with them.

Browsing in the travel section of any bookshop will introduce you to the range of travel guides. The Rough Guides series is generally excellent, and the very detailed books published by Lonely Planet are also popular. If you want a detailed historical and architectural guide, obtain a Blue Guide or a Michelin Green Guide. If you are heading for a remote or politically unstable part of the world, it would be worth obtaining up-to-date safety information from the Foreign & Commonwealth Office. You can ring their Travel Advice Unit on ✆ 0870 606 0290 or check www.fco.gov.uk/travel which carries up-to-date travel warnings and some visa information.

LEARNING THE LANGUAGE

Even if you will not need any knowledge of the local language in the classroom, the ability to communicate will increase your enjoyment many times over. After a long hard week of trying to din some English into your pupils' heads, you probably won't relish the prospect of struggling to convey your requests to uncomprehending shopkeepers, neighbours, etc. A refusal to try to learn some of the local language reflects badly on the teacher and reinforces the suspicion that English teachers are afflicted with cultural arrogance.

If there is time before you leave home, you might consider enrolling in a part-time or short intensive course of conversation classes at a local college of further education or using a self-study programme with books and tapes or an online course. This will have the salutary effect of reminding you how difficult it is to learn a language. Although many people have been turning to the web to teach them a language, many conventional teach-yourself courses are still on the market, for example Take Off In from Oxford University Press (www.oup.com/takeoffin), Berlitz (✆ +020 7518 8300), the BBC (✆ 08700 100222), Linguaphone (✆ +0800 282417; www.linguaphone.co.uk) and Audioforum (www.audioforum.com). All of them offer deluxe courses with refinements such as interactive videos and of course these cost more. Linguaphone recommends half an hour of study a day for three months to master the basics of a language.

Also, check out noticeboards in local cafés etc for advertisements from young foreigners who offer conversation classes (or will swap their expertise for yours). A great resource is www.gumtree.com, which has a skills/language swap section. If you're lucky, your conversation partner might also be able to help you with advice/contacts for your trip.

If you are heading for a remote place, take a language course with you, since tapes/CDs and books (including a good dictionary) may not be available locally and your enthusiasm to learn may be rekindled once you are on location. It is also popular to download language podcasts onto your iPod, although it's an expensive piece of equipment to keep safe. Of course it is much easier to learn the language once you are there. Some employers may even offer you the chance to join language classes free of charge; if you are particularly interested in this perk, ask about it in advance.

SIGNING UP FOR LANGUAGE CLASSES ON LOCATION IS A GOOD WAY OF FINDING OUT ABOUT LOCAL TEACHING OPENINGS AS TILL BRUCKNER FOUND:
The first thing I do when I arrive somewhere now is to get myself language lessons. The teacher will have met many other foreigners, have local connections and speak some English. In other words he or she is the natural starting point in your job hunt. If you make clear that you can only continue paying for your lessons if you earn money too, you've found a highly motivated ally in your search for work.

SURPRISINGLY, IT ISN'T ALWAYS AN ADVANTAGE TO KNOW THE LANGUAGE AS JAMIE MASTERS DISCOVERED IN CRETE:
About speaking Greek. Well, no one told me. I assumed that they'd be quite pleased to have a Greek-speaking English teacher, best of both worlds. It's useful for discipline; the kids can't talk about you behind your back; you can tell when they're cheating on their vocab tests; and, I stupidly thought, you can explain things more clearly, really get them to understand. Well, I was wrong, and was laboriously reprimanded for it when they finally worked out what I was doing. But by that time it was too late: the kids knew I could understand Greek, and so they knew they didn't have to make the effort to speak to me in English. No amount of my playing dumb worked.

WHAT TO TAKE

The research you do on your destination will no doubt include its climate, which will help you choose an appropriate range of clothing to take. But there is probably no need to equip yourself for every eventuality. EFL teachers usually earn enough to afford to buy a warm coat or boots if required. Be sure to pack enough smart clothes to see you through the academic year; blue jeans are rarely acceptable in the classroom.

Even though you are expecting to earn a decent salary, you should not arrive short of money. It is usual to be paid only at the end of the first month. Plus you may need sizeable sums for rent deposits and other setting-up expenses.

A generous supply of passport photos and copies of your vital documents (birth certificate, education certificates, references) should be considered essential. Recreational reading in English will be limited, so you should take a good supply of novels, etc. It could take time to establish a busy social life, leaving more time for reading than usual. In such circumstances, having access to the World Service can be a godsend. You will need a good short-wave radio with several bands powerful enough to pick up the BBC. 'Dedicated' short-wave receivers which are about the size of a paperback start at £65. If you are travelling via the Middle East or Hong Kong, think about buying one duty-free.

A further advantage of having access to the BBC is that you can tape programmes for use in the classroom. Up-to-date details of BBC World Service frequencies are available at www.bbc.co.uk/worldservice/schedules/frequencies/ or similarly, Voice of America's webpage (www.voa.gov) has the latest listings of its broadcasting frequencies.

The other possibility, if possible, is to secure a fast and reliable internet connection and listen online. Radio programmes as podcasts are available outside the UK at www.bbc.co.uk/radio/podcasts/directory/. News programmes are available outside the UK at http://news.bbc.co.uk/2/hi/video_and_audio/default.stm and BBC sport highlights are available at http://news.bbc.co.uk/sport. The fantastic BBC iPlayer sadly isn't available when you're abroad at the moment, but BBC worldwide is working on it so watch this space.

Find out from returned travellers what items are in short supply or very expensive (eg deodorant in Greece, cigarette papers in Scandinavia). Some items which recur on teachers' lists are vitamin tablets, a deck of cards, ear plugs and thermal underwear.

TEACHING MATERIALS

Try to find out which course your school follows and then become familiar with it. Depending on the circumstances, there may be a shortage of materials, so again enquire in advance about the facilities. (For example, English texts being used in a few places in Cambodia dated from 1938 and contained such useful sentences as, 'I got this suit in Savile Row'.) If you are going to have to be self-reliant, you may want to write to the major EFL publishers, primarily Oxford University Press, Cambridge University Press, Longman, Heinemann, Penguin and Phoenix to request details of their course books with a sample lesson if possible, and the address of their stockist in your destination country.

Before leaving home, you should visit a specialist ELT bookshop or the EFL department of a bookshop and obtain a detailed catalogue of ELT materials. KELTIC (Kensington English Language Teaching Information Centre) is a major specialist ELT international mail order service offering an extensive range of materials, information and a free catalogue to teachers and schools worldwide. The former Keltic London shop is now managed by St Giles College at 154 Southampton Row, London WC1B 5AX (nearest tube Russell Square). The opening hours for the shop are Monday to Friday 1pm–5pm (0207 833 2773). KELTIC International Mail Order Department is now part of the YBP UK operation in Bicester, Oxford. You can use their user-friendly website (www.keltic.co.uk) anywhere in the world to get information and advice or to order materials including the *Keltic Guide*. You can contact Keltic by telephone (01869 363589), fax (01869 363590) or email (keltic@ybp.com).

Another major stockist is BEBC the Bournemouth English Book Centre (Albion Close, Parkstone, Poole, Dorset BH12 3LL; ✆ 01202 712934; fax 01202 712913; elt@bebc.co.uk; www.bebc.co.uk). The company supplies books, tapes, videos and ELT software by mail order to teachers worldwide. All popular ELT titles are available on BEBC's Online Bookshop (www.bebc.co.uk). For a list of recommended titles, see the following section.

Waterstones (82 Gower Street, London WC1E 6EQ; ✆ 020 7636 1577; arts@gowerst.waterstones.co.uk) has a large ELT department including courses for adults and children, examinations, grammars, specialist areas and teaching skills. There is also a worldwide mail order service.

In North America those looking for TEFL titles can resort to purchasing online from Barnes and Noble (www.barnesandnoble.com) or www.amazon.com. There are also a few specialist online bookstores including Alta Book Center (14 Adrian Court, Burlingame, CA 94010; 800 ALTA-ESL or fax 800 ALTA-FAX; info@altaesl.com; www.altaesl.com) and Delta Systems Co (1400 Miller Parkway,

McHenry, IL 60050 7030; © 800 323 8270; fax 800 909 9901; www.delta-systems.com). Both Alta and Delta also do orthodox mail order.

Here is a list of items to consider packing which most often crop up in the recommendations of teachers of conversation classes in which the main target is to get the students talking. Teachers expecting to teach at an under-resourced school might think about taking some of the following:

- Good dual language dictionary and picture dictionary
- Cassettes/CDs (including pop music with clear lyrics such as Pink Floyd, Beatles, Simon & Garfunkel, Tracy Chapman, early Billy Bragg)
- Blank tapes/CDs (and a cassette recorder/CD player/iPlayer if necessary with spare batteries)
- Games and activities book
- Illustrated magazines such as *National Geographic* or unusual publications like old comic books, teen mags or the *Big Issue* (interesting to many language learners in former communist countries)
- Maps (for example of London)
- Tourist guides to your home country, travel brochures, blank application forms
- Flash cards (which are expensive if bought commercially; home-made ones work just as well)
- Grammar exercise book
- Old Cambridge exam papers (if you are going to be teaching First Certificate or Proficiency classes).

Postcards, balloons, stick-on stars and photos of yourself as an infant have all been used to good effect. If you know that there will be a shortage of materials, it might even be worth taking general stationery such as notebooks, carbon paper, Blu Tack, plastic files, large pieces of paper, coloured markers, etc. Most employers would be willing to pay the postage costs if you don't want to carry it all in your luggage. (If you are entering a country without a pre-arranged work visa, bear in mind that teaching aids in your luggage will alert customs officers that you intend to work.)

Koober Grob spent an enjoyable time in Russia trying to hone the conversation skills of her highly motivated students. Her main regret was that she hadn't brought with her a 10-page list of possible discussion topics to help them practise their colloquial English because she found that she was sometimes at a loss for topics (which may account for the conversation one day turning to chocolate-covered ants in Africa).

Richard McBrien, who taught English in China, recommends taking a collection of photos of anything in your home environment. A few rolls shot of local petrol stations, supermarkets, houses, parks, etc. can be of great interest to pupils in far-off lands. It may of course be difficult to anticipate what will excite your students' curiosity.

THE ANTHROPOLOGIST NIGEL BARLEY, WHO WRITES AMUSING BOOKS ON HIS FIELD-WORK, DESCRIBES BEING ENLISTED TO ATTEND AN IMPROMPTU ENGLISH CONVER-SATION CLUB IN A REMOTE CORNER OF INDONESIA IN HIS BOOK NOT A HAZARDOUS SPORT:
I answered questions about the royal family, traffic lights and the etiquette of eating asparagus, and gave a quick analysis of the shipbuilding industry. At the end of the evening, I fled back to the hotel.

EFL teachers cannot escape so easily, so you should be prepared to be treated like a guru of contemporary British or American culture.

The range of materials available for teaching English has increased at an amazing pace over recent years. Not only are there more course books and supplementary books available than ever before, but the expansion of the internet has led to an ever-growing choice of online materials. Faced with this bewildering selection, how can you find the resources you need quickly and easily, which you can match exactly to your teaching objective and, most of all, whose quality and reliability is assured? A useful place to start is www.onestopenglish.com.

Onestopenglish is a resource site for teachers run by Macmillan Publishers which claim that more than 420,000 English language teachers use it worldwide. It offers access to a database of free resources including vocabulary worksheets, speaking practice activities, news and culture lessons, lesson plans, methodology articles, professional support and an interactive forum for airing views and sharing ideas. It also has a job vacancy section. Onestopenglish's premium content area for subscribers is called the Staff Room. Staff Room members (£30 per year) are able to access a far greater collection of teaching resources, including a fully-searchable database of worksheets and weekly news lessons published in conjunction with the *Guardian Weekly*.

RECOMMENDED RESOURCES AND REFERENCE BOOKS

There is such a plethora of books and materials that the choice can be daunting to the uninitiated. Every teacher should have a basic manual of grammar handy, such as:

Advanced Grammar in Use by Martin Hewings (Cambridge University Press, 1999; £12.25 with answers).

English Grammar (Collins, Gem, 2004; £4.99). Genuinely pocket-sized. (Dubbed by at least one novice, 'the Teacher's Friend'.)

English Grammar In Use by Raymond Murphy (Cambridge University Press, 2004 edition; £12.50 with answers; £11.50 without answers). Plus Supplementary Exercises with answers £6.95.

The Good Grammar Book by Michael Swan and Catherine Walter (Oxford University Press, 2001; £14.50; ISBN 978 019 431519 7). Elementary to lower intermediate. Explains the rules of grammar, shows how language works and gives plenty of practice.

Grammar for English Language Teachers by Martin Parrott (Cambridge University Press 2000; £15.15).

Practical English Usage, Third Edition by Michael Swan (Oxford University Press; £22.00; ISBN 978 019 442098 3). Intermediate to advanced. Explanations, sample sentences and lots of practice material.

A Practical English Grammar by AJ Thomson and AV Martinet (Oxford University Press, 1990; £14.50; ISBN 978 019 431342 1). Exercises 1 & 2: £11.00 each (ISBN 978 019 431343 8 and 978 019 431344 5). Intermediate: explanations, sample sentences and lots of practice material.

Understanding and Using English Grammar by B Schrampfer Azar (Pearson Education, 2001; £20.90).

Here is a selected list of recommended books and teaching aids which you could consider:

Advanced Learners English Dictionary (Collins, 2004; £16.99). Collins publishes a range of dictionaries for the language learner.

Cambridge Advanced Learners Dictionary (Cambridge University Press, 2003; Hardback £25; Paperback £23). Also available as a CD ROM (£16).

Children Learning English (Macmillan, 2000; £15). Introduces the theory behind good classroom practice with examples from around the world.

ESL Teachers' Activities Kit by Elizabeth Claire (Prentice Hall Direct; £16.06). Aimed at ESL teaching to children.

Freestanding by Maurice Jamall (Delta Systems; £11.95). Elementary to Upper Intermediate. Teachers' resource book suitable for children and young adults.

Grammar Games & Activities by Peter Watcyn-Jones (Longman; £25.95). Other titles by the same author include *Instant Lessons, Vocabulary Games* and *Fun and Games*.

The Grammar Lab by K Bourke (Oxford University Press ; Book 1: £10.00; ISBN 978 019 433015 2; Book 2: £11.00; 978 019 433016 9; Book 3: £12.00; 978 019 433017 6). Beginner to intermediate grammar practice for children aged 9–12.

Grammar Practice Activities by Penny Ur (Cambridge University Press, 1988; Paperback only £16.20). For all levels and ages. Includes photocopiable texts and visuals (£13.50).

How English Works by Michael Swan and Catherine Walter (Oxford University Press ; £16.00; ISBN 978 019 431456 5). Intermediate to lower-advanced. Specially suitable for self-study.

Learning Teaching (Scrivener; £15.00). Useful for teachers in training and as a quick resource of lively lesson ideas.

Lessons from Nothing by Bruce Marsland (Cambridge University Press, 1998; £12.95). From the Cambridge Handbooks for Language Teachers series.

More Grammar Games by M Rinvolucri and P Davis (Cambridge University Press, 1995; £16.80). Includes activities for all levels.

Oxford Advanced Learner's Dictionary, 7th edition (Oxford University Press[LS4] ; £24.00; ISBN 978 019 400116 8). The world's best selling advanced learner's dictionary. Available with COMPASS CD-ROM and Vocabulary Trainer.

Oxford Learner's Thesaurus (Oxford University Press; £22.00; ISBN 978 019 475200 8). Upper-intermediate to advanced. Groups and defines similar words and explains the differences between them, helping the learner choose exactly the right word for the context. Available with CD-ROM.

Oxford Practice Grammar (Oxford University Press; Basic: £17.00; ISBN 978 019 457978 0; Intermediate: £17.50; ISBN 978 019 457980 3; Advanced: £18.00; ISBN 978 019 457982 7). Basic, Intermediate and Advanced. A grammar practice series that offers the right balance of explanation, practice and testing at every level. Available with Practice-Boost CD-ROMs.

The Practice of English Language Teaching, 3rd edition, by Jeremy Harmer (Longman; £18.95). A well-known core reference work for teachers. From the same author *How to Teach English*, straightforward introduction to TEFL for new teachers.

Source Book for Teaching English as a Foreign Language by Michael Lewis and Jimmie Hill (Macmillan, 1993; £15.00). Practical guide for those with little formal training.

The Standby Book Lindstromberg (Cambridge University Press, 1997; £16.20). Teacher's resource book of 110 language learning activities for all types of teaching situation.

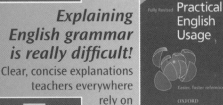

Word For Word by Stewart Clark and Graham Pointon (Oxford University Press, 2003; £13.50; ISBN 978 019 432755 8). Intermediate to advanced. Compares and defines about 3,000 of the most commonly confused words in English.

Anyone who is likely to be teaching young children might like to request the catalogue of Ladybird's Books for English Learning, since the well-known children's publisher has an inexpensive series Key Words Scheme for children. Customers should order through Customer Services (Penguin Group Distribution Ltd, Bath Road, Harmondsworth, Middlesex UB7 0DA; ✆ 020 8757 4000).

If your place of work has an internet connection, you can download teaching materials from the web. Try for example the *Guardian*'s www.educationunlimited.co.uk/tefl which provides lesson ideas based on current events. Oxford University Press's website (www.oup.com/elt) has good quality worksheets mostly tied in with its own books. Lesson plans can also be printed off from http://esl.about.com/library/lessons.

PROBLEMS

Potential problems fall into two broad categories: personal and professional. You may quickly feel settled and find your new setting fascinating but may discover that the job itself is beset with difficulties. On the other hand the teaching might suit but otherwise you feel alienated and lonely. Those who choose to uproot themselves suddenly should be fairly confident that they have enough resources to rely on themselves, and must expect some adjustment problems. Only you can assess your chances of enjoying the whole experience and of not feeling traumatised. Women may encounter special problems in countries where women have little status. An informative site is www.journeywoman.com among many others.

PROBLEMS AT WORK

Anyone who has done some language teaching will be familiar with at least some of the problems EFL teachers face. Problems encountered in a classroom of Turkish or Peruvian adolescents will be quite different from the ones experienced teaching French or Japanese business people. The country chapters attempt to identify some of the specific problems which groups of language learners present.

Although you are unlikely to be expected to entertain 200 people for four hours with a plastic bowl there may be a fairly complete lack of facilities and resources. The teacher who has packed some of the teaching materials listed above will feel particularly grateful for his or her foresight in such circumstances. Some schools, especially at the cowboy end of the spectrum go to the other extreme of providing very rigid lesson plans from which you are not allowed to deviate and which are likely to be uncongenial and uninspiring. Even when reasonable course texts are provided, supplementary materials for role play and games can considerably liven up classes (and teachers). You can obtain extra teaching aids after arrival from the nearest English language bookshop or make them yourself, for example tape a dialogue between yourself and an English speaking friend or cut up magazines or use postcards to make flashcards. If the missing facilities are more basic (eg tables, chairs, heating, paper, pens) you will have to improvise as best you can and (if appropriate) press the administration for some equipment.

PROBLEMS WITH PUPILS

A very common problem is to find yourself in front of a class of mixed ability and incompatible aims. How do you plan a lesson that will satisfy a sophisticated business executive whose English is fairly advanced, a delinquent teenager and a housewife crippled by lack of confidence? A good school of course will stream its clients and make life easier for its teachers. But this may be left to you, in which case a set of commercially produced tests to assess level of language acquisition could come in very handy. Alternatively you can devise a simple questionnaire for the students to describe their hobbies, studies, family or whatever. This will not only display their use of English but also give you some clues about their various backgrounds. One way of coping with gross discrepancies is to divide the class into compatible groups or pairs and give tasks which work at different levels. Subdividing a class is in fact generally a good idea especially in classes which are too large.

IN SOME PLACES YOU MAY EVEN HAVE TO CONTEND WITH RACIAL OR CULTURAL FRICTION AMONG PUPILS, AS BRYN THOMAS ENCOUNTERED IN EGYPT:
One of the problems I found in the class was the often quite shocking displays of racism by the Egyptians towards their dark-skinned neighbours from Somalia. Vast amounts of tact and diplomacy were required to ensure that enough attention was given to the Somalis (who tend to be shy, quiet and highly intelligent) without upsetting the sometimes rowdy and over-enthusiastic Egyptians.

Your expectations of what teaching is supposed to achieve may be quite different from the expectations of your students. Foreign educational systems are often far more formal than their British or American counterparts and students may seem distressingly content to memorise and regurgitate, often with the sole motivation of passing an exam. But this doesn't always operate. Many teachers have had to face pupils who don't seem to care at all about learning any English and merely want to be entertained.

In many countries free discussion is quite alien, whether because of repressive governments or cultural taboos. It is essential to be sensitive to these cultural differences and not to expect too much of your pupils straightaway. The only way of overcoming this reluctance to express an opinion or indeed express anything at all is to involve them patiently and tactfully, again by splitting them into smaller units and asking them to come up with a joint reply.

Discipline is seldom a serious problem outside Europe; in fact liberal teachers are often taken aback by what they perceive as an excess of docility, an over-willingness to believe that 'teacher is always right'. In some cases, classes of bored and rebellious European teenagers might cause problems (especially on Fridays), or children who are being sent to English lessons after school simply as an alternative to babysitting for working mothers. Unfortunately, a couple of troublemakers can poison a class.

You may even have to contend with one or two downright uncontrollable students as **Jamie Masters** did in Crete:

> *At least two of my pupils were very malevolent. There was one, Makis, who used to bring a 'prop' to every lesson, some new way of disrupting the class – an air pistol, a piece of string with a banknote tied to it, a whistle, white paint. He used to slap my cheeks, hug me and lift me off the floor, was quite open about not wanting to work ... and then claimed I was picking on him when I retaliated. Well, call me ... humourless, unfeeling, but ...*

One teacher in Turkey found the majority of his students 'bouncy, bright, enthusiastic and sharp' but with one class he was always amazed that they walked upright when they got out of their chairs. It often turns out that each class develops a certain character.

Some months after Jamie Masters returned home to London, he confessed:

> *Even now you only have to say the words 'D class Mastamba' to strike terror into my heart. But the A class in the same school was a joy to teach: rowdy, yes, but I had a lot of time for them. Within a class there are different personalities of course but they tend to get subsumed into the personality of the group. So I had good classes and bad classes in all the places I taught. When I left, some classes cheered; others wept and drew hearts all over their vocab tests. The main line of demarcation may in fact be age rather than income: the younger students more or less accept that they have to work; the older ones are beginning to rebel.*

Marta Eleniak, who taught in Spain, recommends taking a hard line:

Be very stern at the start. The kids can be very wicked and take advantage of any good nature shown. Squash anyone who is late, shouts, gossips, etc. the first time or it'll never stop. The good classes make you love teaching. The bad make you feel as if you want to go back to filing.

Each level and age group brings its own difficulties. Anyone who has no experience of dealing with young children may find it impossible to grab and hold their attention, let alone teach them any English. A lack of inhibition is very useful for teaching young children who will enjoy sing-songs, nursery rhymes, simple puzzles and games, etc. A firm hand may also be necessary if **Aine Fligg**'s experience in Hong Kong is anything to go by. She was bitten on the ankle by one of her less receptive students. When the headmaster came in and remonstrated (with Aine!) the child bit him on the nose. The brat was then incarcerated in a cupboard, and emerged somewhat subdued.

ONLY 18 HIMSELF, SAM JAMES HAD TO TEACH A VARIETY OF AGE GROUPS IN BARCE-LONA DURING HIS GAP YEAR AND DESPITE THE PROBLEMS, ENDED UP ENJOYING IT:
The children I taught were fairly unruly and noisy. The teenagers were, as ever, pretty uninterested in learning, though if one struck on something they enjoyed they would work much better. Activities based on the lyrics of songs seemed to be good. They had a tendency to select answers at random in multiple choice exercises. On the other hand they were only ever loud rather than very rude or disobedient. The young children (8–12) were harder work. They tended to understand selectively, acting confused if they didn't like an instruction. Part of the problem was that the class was far too long (three hours) for children of that age and their concentration and behaviour tended to tail off as the time passed.

Beginners of all ages progress much more rapidly than intermediate learners. Many teachers find adolescent intermediate learners the most difficult to teach. The original fun and novelty are past and they now face a long slog of consolidating vocabulary and structures. (The 'intermediate plateau' is a well-known phenomenon in language acquisition.) Adolescents may resent 'grammar games' (which are a standard part of EFL) thinking that games are suitable only for children.

The worst problem of all is to be confronted with a bored and unresponsive class. This may happen in a class of beginners who can't understand what is going on, especially a problem if you don't speak a word of their language. It can be extremely frustrating for all concerned when trying to teach some concept or new vocabulary without being able to provide the simple equivalent. If this is the case, you'll have to rely heavily on visual aids. Whole books have been written to show EFL teachers how to draw, for example *1000+ Pictures for Teachers to Copy* by Andrew Wright (£29.99). For a very low-level class, you may need to resort to your bilingual dictionary for lesson plans. On the other hand some teachers enjoy the challenge: 18-year-old **Hannah Bullock** found teaching her class of Czech beginners good fun '*because each lesson was like an invigorating game of charades*'. Many new teachers make the mistake of doing all the talking. During his year of teaching in Slovenia, **Adam Cook**, like many others before him, came to the conclusion that silence is one of the teacher's most effective tools.

The best way to inject a little life into a lethargic class is to get them moving around, for example get them to do a relaxation exercise or have them carry out a little survey of their neighbours and then report their findings back to the class. A reluctance to participate may be because the pupils do not see the point of it. In many countries foreign teachers come to feel like a dancing bear or performing monkey, someone who is expected to be a cultural token and an entertainer. If the students are expecting someone to dance a jig or swing from the chandelier (so to speak) they will be understandably disappointed to be presented with someone asking them to form sentences using the present perfect. At the other extreme, it is similarly disconcerting to be treated just as a model of pronunciation, and you may begin to wonder whether your employer might be better off employing a tape recorder.

PROBLEMS WITH YOURSELF

Of course lessons which fizzle or never get off the ground are not always the fault of the students. One of the most common traps into which inexperienced teachers fall is to dominate the class too much. Conversational English can only be acquired by endless practice and so you must allow your pupils to do most of the talking. Even if there are long pauses between your questions and their attempts to answer, the temptation to fill the silences should be avoided. Pauses have a positive role to play, allowing pupils a chance to dwell on and absorb the point you have just been illustrating. Avoid asking 'Do you understand?' since the answer is meaningless; it is much more useful to test their comprehension indirectly.

A native speaker's function is seldom to teach grammar, though he or she should feel comfortable naming grammatical constructions. You are not there to help the students to analyse the language but to use it and communicate with it. It has been said that grammar is the highway code, the catalogue of rules and traffic signs, quite useless in isolation from driving, which gets you where you want to go. Grammar is only the cookery book while talking is cooking for other people to understand/eat. Persuading some students, whose language education has been founded on grammar rather than communication, that this is the priority may be difficult, but try not to be drawn into detailed explanations of grammatical structures.

This is probably not a very great temptation for many teachers who can barely distinguish prepositions from pronouns. Being utterly ignorant of grammar often results in embarrassing situations. You can only get away with bluffing for so long ('Stefan, I don't think it matters here whether or not it's a subjunctive') and irate pupils have been known to report to school directors that their teachers are grammar-illiterate. One useful trick suggested by **Roberta Wedge** is to reply, 'Very good question – we're going to deal with that in the next class.' Usually it will suffice to have studied a general grammar handbook such as *Practical English Grammar* or *Practical English Usage* (see Resources above). If you contradict yourself between one lesson and the next, and an eager student notices it, take Richard Osborne's advice and say 'Ah yes, I'm sorry about that. You see, that's the way we do it at home. Bizness is always spelled with a z in Canada.'

The worst fate which can befall a teacher is to run dry, to run out of ideas and steam completely before the appointed hour has arrived. This usually happens when you fail to arrive with a structured lesson plan. It is usually a recipe for disaster to announce at the beginning of the lesson 'Tonight let's talk about our travels/hobbies/animals' or whatever. Any course book will help you to avoid grinding to a halt. Supplementary materials such as songs and games can be lifesavers in (and out) of a crisis. If you are absolutely stuck for what to talk about next, try writing the lyrics of a popular song on the board and asking the class to analyse it or even act it out (avoiding titles such as 'I Want Your Body'). Apparently songs which have worked well for many teachers include George Michael's 'Careless Whispers', the Beatles' 'Here Comes the Sun' and 'When I'm 64' and 'Perfect Day' by Lou Reed. Another way of stepping outside the predictability of a course book might be to teach a short poem which you like, or even a short story (eg by Saki) if the class is sufficiently advanced.

A very popular way to structure a lesson is in 'notions'; you take a general situation such as 'praising' or 'complaining', teach some relevant vocabulary and structures and then have the class put them into practice in role-play situations. Unfortunately repetition is the key to language learning, although you have to avoid boring drills that will kill any interest in the language.

Culture shock is experienced by most people who live in a foreign country in whatever circumstances (see below), but can be especially problematic for teachers. Unthinkingly you might choose a topic which seems neutral to you but is controversial to them. A little feature on the English pub for example would not be enjoyed in Saudi Arabia. A discussion about whaling might make a class of Norwegians uncomfortable. Asking questions about foreign travels would be tactless in many places where few will be able to afford international travel.

ONE OF THE MORE SUBTLE PROBLEMS IS KNOWING HOW TO APPROACH TEACHING AS JW ARBLE DISCOVERED:

I was caught up with trying to work out how to present myself to my students: whether to assume the role of friend, exotic or mentor: whether to be 'charismatic' or reserved, enthusiastic or dry, serious-minded or idiot savant. Given the limited time, I persuaded myself the aim was to make the subject interestingly different; with the hope a few might be triggered into curiosity. Less worthily, I just wanted to be liked.

One of the hardest problems to contend with is teacher burn-out. If you invariably arrive just as the class is scheduled to begin, show no enthusiasm, and glance at the clock every 90 seconds, you will not be a popular teacher. Getting hold of some new authentic materials might shore up your flagging enthusiasm for the enterprise. If not, perhaps it is time to consider going home (bearing in mind your contractual commitments).

PROBLEMS WITH EMPLOYERS

All sorts of schools break their promises about pay, perks and availability of resources. The worst disappointment of all, however, is to turn up and find that you don't have a job at all. Because schools which hire their teachers sight unseen often find themselves let down at the last moment, they may over-hire, just in the way that airlines overbook their flights in the expectation of a certain level of cancellation. Even more probable is that the school has not been able to predict the number of pupils who will enrol and decides to hire enough teachers to cover the projected maximum. Whatever the reason, it can be devastating to have the job carpet whipped from under your feet. Having a signed contract helps. It may also be a good idea to maintain contact with the school between being hired and your first day of work. If the worst does happen, you could try losing your temper, threatening to tarnish their good name, and demand a month's pay and your return airfare. Or you could try playing on the guilt of the director and ask him or her to help you get a last-minute job in another school.

Just because a school does not belong to the EFL establishment does not mean that teachers will be treated badly (and vice versa). However the back street fly-by-night school may well cause its foreign teachers anxiety. The most common complaints revolve around wages – not enough or not often enough or both. Either you will have signed a contract (possibly in ignorance of the prevailing conditions and pay levels) or you have nothing in writing and find that your pay packet does not correspond with what you were originally promised. It is probably not advisable to take up a confrontational stance straightaway since this may be the beginning of a year of hostility and misery. Polite but persistent negotiations might prove successful. Find out if there is a relevant teachers union, join it and ask them for advice (though EFL is notorious for being non-unionised). As the year wears on, your bargaining clout increases, especially if you are a half-decent teacher, since you will be more difficult to replace mid-term.

One recourse is to bring your employer's shortcomings to the attention of the British Council or in extreme cases of exploitation, your Embassy/Consulate. If you are being genuinely maltreated and you are prepared to leave the job, delivering an ultimatum and threatening to leave might work. Remember that if there are cowboy schools, there are also cowboy teachers. Many honest and responsible employers have fallen victim to unreliable and undisciplined individuals who break their promises, show up late and abuse the accommodation they are given. Try not to let your employer down unless the provocation is serious.

Language schools must function as businesses as well as educational establishments and in some case the profit motive overtakes everything else. In those cases, teachers soon realise that they matter less to the people in charge than the number and satisfaction of students. You may be asked to conduct a conversation class in a room not much smaller than the Albert Hall. Some employers leave you entirely to your own devices and even look to you for teaching ideas. Others interfere to an annoying degree; we've heard of one school director in Spain who bugged the classrooms to make sure the staff were following his idiosyncratic home-produced course outlines.

JAYNE NASH WORKED FOR A CHAIN OF SCHOOLS IN FRANCE WHICH USE THEIR OWN METHOD; CLIENTS LEARNED BASIC PHRASES AND WORDS FOR EVERYDAY SITUATIONS IN PARROT FASHION:
The courses were aimed at local business people, therefore students learned mostly spoken English to introduce themselves, their company or product, language for meetings, telephone conversations, etc. The method seemed very effective, but can prove extremely tedious for the teacher. After you have repeated a word 10–20 times with 10 students, 4 times a day, 5 days a week.

One of the most commonly heard complaints from teachers concerns their schedule. Eager only to satisfy clients, employers tend to mess around with teachers' timetables, offering awkward combinations of hours or changing the schedule at the last moment, which is extremely stressful. A certain amount of evening work is almost inevitable in private language schools where pupils (whether of school or working age) must study English out-of-hours. Having to work early in the morning and then again through the evening can become exhausting after a while. It can also be annoying to have several long gruelling days a week and other days with scarcely any teaching at all (but still not days off).

One trick to beware of is to find that the 24 hours a week you were told you would be working actually means 32, 45-minute lessons (which is much harder work than teaching 24 one-hour lessons). Even if the number of hours has not been exaggerated, you may have been deluded into thinking that a 24-hour week is quite cushy. But preparation time can easily add half as many hours again, plus if you are teaching in different locations, travel time (often unpaid) has to be taken into consideration.

In some situations teachers may be expected to participate in extra-curricular activities such as dreary drinks parties for pupils or asked to make a public speech. Make an effort to accept such invitations (especially near the beginning of your contract) or, if you must decline, do so as graciously as possible. There might also be extra duties, translating letters and documents, updating teaching materials, etc. for which you are unlikely to be paid extra.

PROBLEMS OUTSIDE WORK

Your main initial worry outside your place of employment will probably be accommodation. Once this is sorted out, either with the help of your school or on your own, and you have mastered the essentials of getting around and shopping for food, there is nothing to do but enjoy yourself, exploring your new surroundings and making friends.

CULTURE SHOCK

Enjoying yourself won't be at all easy if you are suffering from culture shock. Shock implies something which happens suddenly, but cultural disorientation more often creeps up on you. Adrenaline usually sees you through the first few weeks as you find the novelty exhilarating and challenging. You will be amazed and charmed by the odd gestures the people use or the antiquated way that things work. As time goes on, practical irritations intrude and the constant misunderstanding caused by those charming gestures – such as a nod in Greece meaning 'no' or in Japan meaning 'yes, I understand, but don't agree' – and the inconvenience of those antiquated phone boxes and buses will begin to get on your nerves. Unless you can find someone to listen sympathetically to your complaints, you may begin to think you have made a mistake in coming in the first place.

Experts say that most people who have moved abroad hit the trough after three or four months, probably just before Christmas in the case of teachers who started work in September. A holiday over Christmas may serve to calm you down or, if you go home for Christmas, may make you feel terminally homesick and not want to go back. Teachers who survive this, often find that things improve in the second term as they cease to perceive many aspects of life as 'foreign'.

The best way to avoid disappointment is to be well briefed beforehand, as emphasised in the chapter Preparation. Gathering general information about the country and specific information about the school before arrival will obviate many of the negative feelings some EFL teachers feel. If you are the type to build up high hopes and expectations of new situations, it is wise to try to dismantle these before leaving home. English teaching is seldom glamorous.

Even if you are feeling depressed and disappointed, do not broadcast your feelings randomly. Feeling contempt and hostility towards your host country is actually part of the process of adjusting to being abroad. But not everyone seems to appreciate that it has more to do with their own feelings than with the inadequacies (real or imagined) of the country they are in. So if you feel you have to let off steam about the local bureaucracy or the dishonesty of taxi-drivers or the way one simply cannot walk ten yards down the pavement without people crossing the street for the express purpose of bumping into you, at least have the common courtesy to do it in private, in letters or when there are no local people around.

This is especially important if you have colleagues who are natives of the country. They may find some of the idiosyncracies of their culture irritating too but, unlike you, they have to live with them forever. Some native-speaker teachers have found an unpleasant rift between local and foreign staff, which in some cases can be accounted for by the simple fact that you are being paid a lot more than they are. Sometimes new foreign teachers find their local colleagues cliquey and uncommunicative.

No doubt they have seen a lot of foreigners come, and make a lot of noise, and go, and there is no particular reason why they should find the consignment you're in wildly exciting and worth getting to know.

LONELINESS

Creating a social life from scratch is difficult enough at any time, but becomes even more difficult in an alien tongue and culture. You will probably find that many of your fellow teachers are lots of fun and able to offer practical help in your first few weeks (especially any who are bilingual). If you find yourself in a one-foreigner village, surely there's another lonely teacher across the mountaintop. You could meet for a drink at the weekend to commiserate and to draw up a charter and call yourselves 'The Wonga Plateau EFL Teachers' Association' (and remember to put yourself down as founder the next time you are revising your CV).

You may want to take some positive steps to meet people and participate in activities outside the world of English language instruction. This may require uncharacteristically extrovert behaviour, but overcoming initial inhibitions almost always pays worthwhile dividends.

If you are tired of conversations about students' dullness or your director of studies' evident lunacy, you might want to try to meet other expatriates who are not EFL teachers. The local English language bookshop might prove a useful source of information about forthcoming events for English-speakers, as will be any newspapers or magazines published in English such as the *Bulletin* in Belgium or the *Athens News* in Greece. Seek out the overseas student club if there is a university nearby (though when they discover what line of work you are in they may well have designs on you). Even the least devout teachers have found English-speaking churches to be useful for arranging social functions and offering practical advice. If there is a bar in town which models itself on a British pub or American bar, you will no doubt find a few die-hards drinking Guinness or Budweiser, who might be more than willing to befriend you.

The most obvious way to meet other foreigners is to enrol in a language course or perhaps classes in art and civilisation. Even if you are not particularly serious about pursuing language studies, language classes are the ideal place to form vital social contacts. You can also join other clubs or classes aimed at residents abroad, for example some German cities have English amateur dramatics groups.

Making friends with locals may prove more difficult, though circumstances vary enormously according to whether you live in a small town or a big city, with some gregarious colleagues or by yourself, etc. The obvious source of social contact is your students and their friends and families (bearing in mind that in certain cultures, a teacher who goes out to a bar or disco with students risks losing their respect). As long as you don't spend all your free time moping at home, you are bound to strike up conversations with the locals, whether in cafés, on buses or in shops. Admittedly these seldom go past a superficial acquaintance, but they still serve the purpose of making you feel a little more integrated in the community. Local university students will probably be more socially flexible than others and it is worth investigating the bars and cafés frequented by students. If you have a particular hobby, sport or interest, find out if there is a local club where you will meet like-minded people; join local ramblers, jazz buffs, etc. – the more obscure the more welcome you are likely to be. You only have to become friendly with one other person to open up new social horizons if you are invited to meet their friends and family.

Make an effort to organise some breaks from work. Even a couple of days by the seaside or visiting a tourist attraction in the region can revitalise your interest in being abroad and provide a refreshing break from the tyranny of the teacher's routine.

COMING HOME

For some, teaching abroad can be addictive. The prospect of returning home to scour the local job advertisements becomes distinctly unappealing as they drink Retsina, eat sushi or spend the weekend at a Brazilian beach. Once you have completed one teaching contract, it will be very much easier to land the next one, and it can be exhilarating to think that you can choose to work in almost any corner of the globe.

By the same token, many people who go abroad to teach English get burned out after a year or two. The majority of English teachers do not think of TEFL as a long-term proposition. They talk about their colleagues who move on to other things as getting a 'proper job', ie one that does not require an early start followed by a long idle morning, where shabby treatment by bosses is not the norm and where you do not have to correct anyone's phrasal verbs.

Homesickness catches up with most EFL teachers and they begin to pine for a pub or bar where repartee is quick and natural and for all the other accoutrements of the culture of their birth. The bad news is that there are few jobs in EFL in Britain except at summer schools. Even professional English language teachers can find it difficult to land a reasonable job in the UK. American teachers will probably fare better due to the growth industry of ESL in the USA, though the majority of openings are part-time with few fringe benefits and opportunities for career development. The good news is that a stint of teaching English abroad is an asset on anyone's CV/résumé. Employers of all kinds look favourably on people who have had the get-up-and-go to work at a respectable job in a foreign land. On returning home from teaching in Chile, **Heidi Resetarits** began looking for jobs and found that having international work experience on her résumé was invaluable. Potential employers were intrigued by the fact that she'd lived in Chile. Such experience can always be presented as valuable for increasing self-assurance, maturity, a knowledge of the world, communication skills and any other positive feature which comes to mind. Very few teachers have regretted their decision to travel the world, even if the specific job they did was not without its drawbacks and difficulties.

PART 2
COUNTRY BY
COUNTRY GUIDE

WESTERN EUROPE
CENTRAL AND EASTERN EUROPE
MIDDLE EAST
AFRICA
ASIA
LATIN AMERICA
CENTRAL AMERICA AND THE CARIBBEAN
NORTH AMERICA
AUSTRALASIA

NB: Most wages and prices are given in local currencies. For conversion to sterling and US dollars, see Appendix 1 on page 525.

Embassies and Consulates will usually provide information on working visas to supplement the information provided in this book. A selective list of diplomatic representatives in London and Washington can be found in Appendix 2 on page 527.

British Council offices abroad are frequently referred to in these chapters. A list of the relevant addresses is provided in Appendix 3 on page 531.

AUSTRIA

The attraction to English in Austria is proved by the number of English bookshops with names such as Shakespeare & Co. and the popularity of English language newspapers such as *Austria Today* and the online www.austrianews.com. The market for ELT in Austria is largely dominated by English for the business community so teachers with any kind of experience of the business world, even if just temping in an office, have a sharp advantage over those with experience only of teaching general English.

As in Germany and Switzerland, most private language institutes depend on freelance part-time teachers drawn from the sizeable resident international community. An estimated 90% of EFL teachers in Austria are freelancers which means that they do not have a contract with just one school and must pay tax as self-employed workers.

FINDING A JOB

The British Council in Vienna has a list of 19 English language institutes in Vienna. This list is annotated so that the kind of English tuition in which the company specialises is given, eg executive training and conversation classes etc. It can be consulted online (www.britishcouncil.org/austria-english-courses-in-austria.htm).

Teachers with a professional profile might find it worthwhile contacting the Austrian Cultural Forum in London (28 Rutland Gate, SW7 1PQ; ✆ 020 7584 8653; fax 020 7225 0470; culture@austria.org.uk; www.austria.org.uk). They can provide general information on possible teaching jobs in Austria. Qualified teacher status would be essential for teaching jobs in state sector schools. Further sources of information are www.bmukk.gv.at and www.magwien.gv.at/ssr.

The online *Yellow Pages* for Austria are very straightforward to use (www.gelbeseiten.at). They are fully usable in English and links to potential employers can be found under the heading 'Language Schools and Language Instruction'. Professional teachers may wish to contact and join the organisation Teachers of English in Austria (www.tea4teachers.org). Annual membership costs €33 or €22 for students and there are currently about 600 members.

Most Volkshochschulen (adult education centres) offer English courses in their programmes. The coordinating office for the provinces in Austria is situated in Vienna. Browse www.vhs.or.at/volkshochschulen for more information (there is an English summary) and www.adulteducation.at (English). The umbrella organisation is Verband Osterreichischer Volkshochschulen (Weintraubengasse 13, 1020 Vienna; ✆ 1 216 4226; fax 1 214 3891). See the 'List of Employers' for details about salary/working conditions for Vienna's Adult Education centres.

More than 200 English Language Teaching Assistants from the UK and USA are placed in Austrian secondary schools from 1 October to 31 May by the British Council and the Fulbright Commission (Schmidgasse 14, 1080 Vienna; ✆ 1 31339; fax 1 408 7765). The British Council is looking for about 120 assistants with a decent level of German to work 15 hours a week for €1010 net per month (www.britishcouncil.org/languageassistants-austria.htm). The Fulbright Commission is responsible for recruiting American graduates with a working knowledge of German and interest in teaching for the same scheme. The net monthly salary paid to assistants is $1,330 for 13 hours work per week. Detailed information and an application form can be downloaded from their website (www.fulbright.at).

New arrivals in Austria should visit a number of institutes and try to piece together a timetable. After working for three or four schools, it is better to cultivate just one or two since it is unrealistic to try to work for any more than this on a longer-term basis. A smart appearance and confident manner are always assets when looking for work teaching within the business community. Most Austrians will have an intermediate or higher level of English. Berlitz is well represented with four separate premises in Vienna alone, including the main ones at Graben 13, 1010 Vienna (01 512 82 86) and Mariahilferstrasse 27, 1060 Vienna (01 586 56 93; www.berlitz.at). All centres look for people with British, Irish, American or Australian nationality who are at least 23 years of age (business and university background advantageous). European Union (EU) working permission is required; applications can be emailed to wien02@berlitz.at.

To give an idea of qualifications needed, MHC Business Language Training in Vienna asks for teachers who have some business background, ideally in a specialised area such as marketing, finance or law; it does not insist on a degree but welcomes a teaching certificate such as the CELTA. By contrast English Connection in Salzburg requires a TEFL qualification plus at least three years' teaching experience, whereas experience and/or knowledge of business, law, medicine, tourism, etc. are seen as useful bonuses.

The rate at reputable institutes starts at €17 per lesson (usually 45 minutes) and more for 60-minute lessons (€20–€30). This is none-too-generous when the high cost of living in Vienna is taken into account, although taking seminars can pay fairly well (between €300 and €400 per seven-hour day). Life in the provinces is less expensive of course. At the interview stage, always find out whether quoted rates are gross or net, if travelling time is covered and when you will be paid. Some schools pay after the course has finished which will leave you a pauper for an extended period.

SUMMER CAMPS

The demand for teachers of children and young people is very strong in Austria as elsewhere in Europe. Summer camps provide scope for EFL teachers, as indicated in the entries for English Language Day Camps and English For Kids. The summer camp organisation Young Austria runs specialist English language camps near Salzburg attended by children aged from 10 years. Monitors organise the outdoor programme and help the teachers with the social programme as well as with the lessons.

SOME FOREIGN YOUNG PEOPLE WHO WORK AS AU PAIRS IN AUSTRIA FIND THAT THEIR PRIMARY TASK IS TO HELP TEENAGE CHILDREN WITH THEIR ENGLISH, WHICH MAREE LAKEY FROM AUSTRALIA FOUND MORE TAXING THAN SHE EXPECTED:

I am basically here to help the four children (aged between 11 and 17) with their English learning, although this is not always easy. On the whole, they have little desire to learn and see their lessons with me as more of a chore than anything else, but I guess that is not so unusual. I've found out how hard it is to try to speak correct English with them and to explain grammar rules which I have forgotten. It's also a bit difficult sometimes, as my Australian English is different from what the children have to learn. The children are of course not sympathetic to my difficulties, insisting that I should be infallable [sic] being a native speaker.

REGULATIONS

British and Irish teachers are preferred because of their membership in the EU. Most schools are not prepared to embark on the difficult procedures for hiring native-speaking English teachers from outside Europe, unless their working papers are already in order. Some, however, may make the investment if the candidate is deemed good enough after a trial period (for example see entries for MHC Business Language Training and Delphin Sprachservice).

One complication is the reciprocal social security arrangements within the EU. Contributions into a health and pension scheme are reciprocal with the UK. Because schools have to register their staff for a social security card and also pay part of the contributions on their behalf, they are generally not willing to hire someone who is ineligible. Fifteen per cent of earnings will be deducted at source (or should be) of any teacher who earns more than €550 per month. The only people entitled not to have these deductions made are licensed translators (certified in Austria) who are permitted to take care of their contributions independently.

Austria (again like Germany) has many bureaucratic layers. New arrivals need to register with the police, organise a bank account (into which their wages will be paid directly) and get a tax number from the local tax office.

LIST OF EMPLOYERS

BFI/BERUFSFOERDERUNGSINSTITUT WIEN
Alfred-Dallinger-Platz 1, U3 Schlachthausgasse, 1034 Vienna
- 1 811 78 10150; fax 1 811 78 10118
- anmeldung.bat@bfi-wien.or.at
- www.bfi-wien.at

NUMBER OF TEACHERS: approximately 40.
PREFERENCE OF NATIONALITY: English native speakers.
QUALIFICATIONS: CELTA preferred.
CONDITIONS OF EMPLOYMENT: freelance basis.
SALARY: approx. €19–€24 per 45 minute unit.
FACILITIES/SUPPORT: no assistance with finding accommodation.
RECRUITMENT: local interviews essential.

BUSINESS LANGUAGE CENTER
Charles La Fond & Co. KEG, Trattnerhof 2, 1010 Vienna
- 1 533 70 010; fax 1 532 85 21
- blcoffice@blc.co.at
- www.blc.co.at

NUMBER OF TEACHERS: 15.
PREFERENCE OF NATIONALITY: none, but must be native speaker of English.
QUALIFICATIONS: university degree, CELTA or equivalent, experience preferred, an interest in the business world.

CONDITIONS OF EMPLOYMENT: minimum stay 12 months. Teachers work on freelance basis and must sort out their own visa and tax requirements. No guarantee of fixed number of hours.
SALARY: starting fee of €19.80 per 40 minute lesson, net of VAT (not including 30% approx. deduction at source for social security contributions).
FACILITIES/SUPPORT: monthly training, continuous pedagogical support but also chance to work independently. Possibility of LCCI/ARELS Certificate for Teaching English for Business course being offered in the future. No assistance with accommodation.
RECRUITMENT: personal interview necessary.
CONTACT: Tony Hayes, Pedagogical Manager.

DELPHIN SPRACHSERVICE
Getreidemarkt 17, 1060 Vienna
- 1 5855347; fax 1 5855347 11
- ils@dolphin.at
- www.dolphin.at

NUMBER OF TEACHERS: 17.
PREFERENCE OF NATIONALITY: GB, Ireland, USA.
QUALIFICATIONS: charisma and competence, experience and appearance, resourcefulness and reliability, diligence and dynamics.
CONDITIONS OF EMPLOYMENT: stage 1, freelance contracts from 1 to 6 months, starting at 1 hour/week; stage 2,

fixed contract (including health care and pension), open end, starting at 10 hours/week.

SALARY: stage 1, €15–€35 per unit of 55 minutes. Stage 2: €10–€25 per hour.

FACILITIES/SUPPORT: centres provide preliminary accommodation for the first weeks and help teachers find a place on their own. Assistance with work permit only after a trial period.

RECRUITMENT: interview essential. Face-to-face, over the phone, review of references.

CONTACT: Mag. Elke Enzlmüller, Recruitment Officer.

DIE WIENER VOLKSHOCHSCHULEN
Hollergasse 22, A – 1150 Vienna
1 89 174; fax 1 89 174 991
info@vhs.at www.vhs.at

18 Vienna Adult Education Centres (Life long learning). English courses according to CEFR levels, European language portfolio for adults (Verband Österreichischer Volkshochschulen), Cambridge Exams in collaboration with British Council Vienna, TELC Certificate English.

NUMBER OF TEACHERS: varies according to demand. All teachers are freelance.

PREFERENCE OF NATIONALITY: none.

QUALIFICATIONS: EUROLTA (ICC- The European Language Network, Die Wiener Volkshochschulen), EUROLTA-EUROVOLT Diploma (ICC- The European Language Network, Die Wiener Volkshochschulen), CELTA, RSA Dip. TEFLA and/or university training, OR varied extensive experience of language teaching in upper secondary/adult/university education (at least 2 years of work experience).

CONDITIONS OF EMPLOYMENT: self-employed freelancers. Minimum commitment 15 weeks (one term). Teaching hours Monday to Saturday between 6am and 9pm.

SALARY: €16.90 per 50-minute lesson. Maximum: €537.78 per month.

FACILITIES/SUPPORT: workshops and other training available. Library and media facilities available.

RECRUITMENT: courses planned 6 months in advance. European CV, letter of intent, and local interview essential.

ENGLISH CONNECTION
Am Rainberg 7, 5020 Salzburg; tel 662 876210
office@english-connection.at
www.english-connection.at

NUMBER OF TEACHERS: 4–6 teachers of business English.

PREFERENCE OF NATIONALITY: British, preferably resident in Austria and plan to remain medium-term.

QUALIFICATIONS: TEFL qualification required plus 3+ years teaching experience. Experience and/or knowledge of business, the law, medicine, tourism, etc. very useful. Technical, chemical or engineering experience also advantageous.

CONDITIONS OF EMPLOYMENT: freelance contract. Variable hours: 20–30 per week. Longer term fixed contract possible.

RECRUITMENT: face-to-face interview preferred; sometimes possible in UK.

CONTACT: Jim Thomson, Course and Company Director.

ENGLISH FOR CHILDREN (EFC)/ENGLISH LANGUAGE DAY CAMP (ELDC)
Weichselweg 4, 1220 Vienna, Austria
1 958 1972 ext. 0; fax Ext. 14
scott.matthews@englishforchildren.com
www.englishforchildren.com

NUMBER OF TEACHERS: EFC – varies according to need. ELDC – on average about 25.

PREFERENCE OF NATIONALITY: none, but must be an English native speaker.

QUALIFICATIONS: minimum age 20. Experience of working with children is preferred.

CONDITIONS OF EMPLOYMENT: EFC – freelance 10-month contract (September to June). ELDC summer camp runs during month of July for 4 weeks.

FACILITIES/SUPPORT: for the EFC programme teachers need to be living in Austria. Full training given, free of charge, before and during contract. All course materials provided. Housing not provided. ELDC – 4-week summer camp programme, lunch provided during camp days, 5 days a week, housing not provided, however relevant contacts to student housing, hostels etc. available.

RECRUITMENT: direct applications, local advertising and interviews.

CONTACT: Director, Scott Matthews.

ENGLISH FOR KIDS
Postgasse 11/19, 1010 Vienna
1 667 45 79; fax 1 667 45 79–400
magik@e4kids.co.at
www.e4kids.co.at

NUMBER OF TEACHERS AND CAMP COUNSELLORS: 6–8 for residential summer camp in Lachstatt near Linz in Upper Austria; 8–12 for day camps in Vienna.

PREFERENCE OF NATIONALITY: EU or others with work permit for Austria.

QUALIFICATIONS: CELTA or Trinity Certificate (minimum grade B) and some formal teaching preferred/required. Camp counsellors require no formal training/experience but must be outgoing, enjoy working with children and should like outdoor activities and sports.

CONDITIONS OF EMPLOYMENT: duration – mid-July to the end of August. 4 weeks in Vienna and 3 weeks in Upper Austria. Pupils aged from kindergarten to age 10 and 10–15. Full-immersion courses with in-house methods following carefully planned syllabus and teachers' manual, supplemented with CD-ROMs etc.

SALARY: varies depending on qualifications. From €1,188 per month gross, plus full board and accommodation.

FACILITIES/SUPPORT: good standard of accommodation and full board provided for teachers. Computer room, internet and video room available.

RECRUITMENT: personal interviews essential.

CONTACT: Irena Köstenbauer, Principal.

ENGLISH IS FUN CAMP

Döblinger Hauptstr. 38/3, 1190 Vienna

1 369 68 33; fax 1 369 68 77

claudia.millwisch@ins.at or claudia
_millwisch@chello.at

www.englishisfun.at

PREFERENCE OF NATIONALITY: English native speakers (also Spanish, Italian and French native speakers). Must have EU nationality.

QUALIFICATIONS: experience of working with children needed.

CONDITIONS OF EMPLOYMENT: hours according to demand. Freelance basis.

RECRUITMENT: personal interviews held.

CONTACT: Claudia Millwisch, Director.

ESDC

Paul Schmückplatz 18, A-7100 Neusiedl am See

2 167 3371

v.burg@esdc.net or virg.burg@gmail.com

www.esdc.net

NUMBER OF TEACHERS: 50 during the summer months, 8 during the school year.

PREFERENCE OF NATIONALITY: EU.

QUALIFICATIONS: TESOL experience abroad required.

CONDITIONS OF EMPLOYMENT: 6–12 week summer contracts and 10-month term time contracts available. To work Monday to Friday 9am–5pm plus preparation.

SALARY: €180 per week plus B&B.

FACILITIES/SUPPORT: bed and breakfast accommodation provided free of charge. Help with work permits also provided.

RECRUITMENT: online.

CONTACT: Virginia Burg, Owner.

MHC BUSINESS LANGUAGE TRAINING

Wiedner Hauptstrasse 54/13A, 1040 Vienna

650 74 85 160; fax 1 603 05 63

office@mhc-training.com

www.mhc-training.com

NUMBER OF TEACHERS: 15.

PREFERENCE OF NATIONALITY: none.

QUALIFICATIONS: people who have some business background, ideally in a specialised area such as marketing, finance or law. A degree is not necessary, although a teaching certificate such as CELTA would be welcomed.

CONDITIONS OF EMPLOYMENT: freelance, teaching 20–30 hours per week.

SALARY: €20–30/hour, depending on experience and course feedback. Seminars €300–400/day (7 hours). Trainers are responsible for paying their own taxes (about 21%) and social security (variable).

FACILITIES/SUPPORT: willing to assist trainers with their accommodation using school's private network to locate vacant apartments around the city. Later, trainers are helped to find a more long-term residence. Trainers from non-EU countries require working papers and assistance is given if candidate is the right person. In some circumstances, a position is guaranteed once the necessary permits/visas have been obtained in order to speed up the process.

RECRUITMENT: online adverts. Interviews are essential and normally take place at premises. Possibility of telephone interviews if the applicant is based abroad.

CONTACT: Mark Heather, Managing Director.

MIND&MORE, MANAGEMENT AND EDUCATION SERVICES GmbH

Fischerstiege 10/16, 1010 Vienna

1 535 9695; fax 1 533 3073

office@mindandmore.at

www.mindandmore.at

Management and Education Services is the Representative Office of the British Open University and OU Business School in Austria, South Germany, Slovenia and Hungary.

NUMBER OF TEACHERS: approx. 70 language trainers in Vienna and more in many locations around the country and across the borders, plus Management Skills Faculty trainers.

PREFERENCE OF NATIONALITY: none.

QUALIFICATIONS: minimum university degree plus CELTA and teaching experience; preferably also business experience.

CONDITIONS OF EMPLOYMENT: freelance contracts. Hours vary.

SALARY: minimum rate is €22 per unit for 45-minute units/€28 for 60-minute units; more for specialised training and seminars.

FACILITIES/SUPPORT: support given.

RECRUITMENT: via internet, partner institutions including British Council, Bfi and related institutions. Interviews essential.

CONTACT: Sylvia Sage, Deputy Director (s.sage@mindand-more.at) and/or Stephen Hardaker, Director of Studies for ELT (s.hardaker@mindandmore.at).

PRO ACTIVE ENGLISH

Don Bosco-Gasse 39a, A-1230 Vienna

✆ 1 6650989; fax 1 66509898

🖰 office@pae.co.at

🖳 www.pae.co.at

NUMBER OF TEACHERS: about 12.

PREFERENCE OF NATIONALITY: none. Teachers must be from English-speaking countries, or have been to school/university in an English-speaking country, or grown up in a non-English speaking country with English speaking parents (mother tongue).

QUALIFICATIONS: CELTA or equivalent, experience is less important.

CONDITIONS OF EMPLOYMENT: one single block of lessons is usually 15 weeks, but these overlap and teachers work for as long as they do a good job. Usual hours are weekdays 8am–6/7pm.

SALARY: €24 per hour, teachers must register and pay all deductions themselves.

FACILITIES/SUPPORT: none.

RECRUITMENT: through word of mouth, British Council website, etc. Local interview essential.

CONTACT: Francis Montocchio, Director.

SPIDI SPRACHENINSTITUT

Franz-Josefs-Kai 27/10, 1010 Vienna

✆ +43 1 236 17 17 0; fax +43 1 236 17 17 9

🖰 office@spidi.at

🖳 www.spidi.at

NUMBER OF TEACHERS: about 20 English teachers.

PREFERENCE OF NATIONALITY: EU citizens.

QUALIFICATIONS: minimum CELTA or equivalent. Business English and ESP teaching experience preferred.

CONDITIONS OF EMPLOYMENT: freelance. Flexible hours.

SALARY: €25–€28 per hour, depending on qualifications and experience.

FACILITIES/SUPPORT: no assistance with accommodation. Library with PCs for trainers. Monthly teacher development sessions.

RECRUITMENT: local interview essential.

CONTACT: Kitty Loewenstein.

BENELUX

Belgium

The list of language schools in the Brussels *Yellow Pages* runs to four pages, under the heading Langues (Ecoles de)/Talensholen. Prospects for business-oriented language teachers are very good in Belgium. Several language teaching organisations are represented in more than one Belgian city, especially Berlitz which employs about 150 freelance teachers in 10 branches. Linguarama Belgium also recruits freelance native speaker teachers with a TEFL teaching qualification and at least two years' experience of teaching non-native adults. CVs and letters of application can be emailed to brussels@linguarama.com. CLL (Centre de Langues) based in Louvain-la-Neuve employs about 100 teachers to work on a freelance basis.

As one of the capitals of the European Union, there is a huge demand for all the principal European languages in Brussels. Yet, despite the enormous amount of language teaching in Belgium, there are also a large number of well-qualified expatriate spouses who take up teaching. This may meet some demand, but not all, as Karin Derochette, Head of English at Thema Language School is quick to point out. She hopes that her school's entry in the 'list of organisations' will result in more British and North American teachers getting in touch because the school is always recruiting for the English section.

FINDING A JOB

To find contact details for language schools in Belgium, the online *Yellow Pages* are a useful tool. A search for 'Language Schools' in the Brussels Region on www.yellowpages.be will turn up more than 90 institutes. If possible, get hold of the special 'Schools Guide' edition published in April by the weekly English language magazine *The Bulletin* (1038 Chaussée de Waterloo, 1180 Brussels; ✆ 02 373 9909; www.thebulletin.be, www.ackroyd.be). *Newcomer* is a bi-annual publication from the publishers of *The Bulletin* which contains information and contact addresses of interest to the newly arrived teacher including a listing of major language schools, the *Expat Directory* is an annual catalogue of useful addresses and phone numbers. Occasionally the classified ads include some requests for live-in helpers willing to teach English, or you can of course advertise yourself, though there will be plenty of competition from highly qualified teachers. Two other sources of language school addresses are the websites www.living-in-belgium.com and (to a lesser extent) www.xpats.com.

The casual teacher will probably steer clear of the schools which undertake to teach senior EU bureaucrats, but there are plenty of other schools. Telephone teaching has caught on in Belgium, especially among French learners of English; see entry for Phone Languages.

As throughout continental Europe, children attend summer camps which focus on language learning. Companies such as Kiddy and Junior Classes and Ski Ten International organise holiday English courses. Pro Linguis is another company which arranges week long residential language courses in Thiaumont, a remote southern corner of Belgium near Luxembourg (✆ +32 63 22 03 62; www.prolinguis.be) for which it is known to employ some native speaker teachers. Courses are put on for all ages including children, so teachers may also be given pastoral duties patrolling dorms, etc.

FREELANCE TEACHING

The British Council has two teaching centres in Brussels, although to stand a chance of securing a freelance job you will need a degree, CELTA/DELTA and three years' full-time teaching experience.

If your CV falls short of these, it is quite feasible to put up notices in one of the large university towns (Brussels, Antwerp, Gent, Leuven, Liège, etc.) offering conversation practice.

Almost all foreign teachers who begin to work for an institute do so on a freelance basis and will have to deal with their own tax and social security. Officially they should declare themselves *indépendants* (self-employed persons) and pay contributions which amount to up to one-third of their salary. In fact many English teachers take their gross salary without declaring it, and don't work long enough to risk being caught. Once a teacher has worked black (*en noir/in het zwart*) it is difficult to regularise his or her status, since they then have to declare all previous earnings. Therefore anyone who plans to spend more than a few months teaching in Belgium should consider this question.

LIST OF EMPLOYERS

BERLITZ LANGUAGE CENTERS
Avenue de Tervueren 265, 1150 Brussels
2 763 08 30; fax 2 771 01 70
joke.vandaele@berlitz.be

NUMBER OF TEACHERS: about 150 (for Brussels, Waterloo, Namur, Charleroi, Liège, Antwerp, Bruges, Mouscron-Tournai, Courtrai, Nivelles).

PREFERENCE OF NATIONALITY: British or Irish.

QUALIFICATIONS: university degree.

CONDITIONS OF EMPLOYMENT: employee contract. Trial period of 3 months. Flexible hours (mornings, evenings plus Saturday morning).

SALARY: €9.89 per 40-minute teaching unit for employees and €15 per 40-minute unit for freelancers.

FACILITIES/SUPPORT: no assistance with accommodation. In-house training lasts 8 days.

RECRUITMENT: via adverts and direct applications.

CONTACT: Joke Van Daele, Area/Country Manager of Instruction.

CALL INTERNATIONAL
25 rue des Drapiers 25, 1050 Brussels
2 644 95 95; fax 2 644 9495
brussels@callinter.com
www.callinter.com

Centres for Accelerated Language Learning in Brussels, Waterloo, Tournai and Lille.

NUMBER OF TEACHERS: 150.

PREFERENCE OF NATIONALITY: none.

QUALIFICATIONS: degree necessary. Experience an advantage. Good communication skills needed.

CONDITIONS OF EMPLOYMENT: freelance. Flexible hours.

FACILITIES/SUPPORT: no assistance with accommodation.

RECRUITMENT: all year through.

CONTACT: Sylvie Laurent.

CERAN LINGUA INTERNATIONAL S.A.
Avenue des Petits Sapins, 27, 4900 Spa, Belgium
87 791 122/791 514; fax 87 791 188
www.ceran.com/en/about/jobs.php

NUMBER OF TEACHERS: 15

PREFERENCE OF NATIONALITY: must have work permit or EU nationality and be native English speaker (or perfectly bilingual).

QUALIFICATIONS: university degree or relevant work experience and some teaching experience. TEFL background not essential.

CONDITIONS OF EMPLOYMENT: open-ended after 6-month trial. 9am–5.30pm and occasional evenings and weekends. (Residential course commences on Sunday evening.)

FACILITIES/SUPPORT: accommodation provided for first 6 months. In-house training provided.

RECRUITMENT: newspaper and magazine adverts, website (www.jobs-career.be) and word of mouth.

CLL CENTRE DE LANGUES
Place de l'Université 25, 1348 Louvain-la-Neuve
010/47 06 28; 010/47 06 29
jobs@cll.ucl.ac.be
www.cll.be

NUMBER OF TEACHERS: 100.

PREFERENCE OF NATIONALITY: from English speaking countries.

QUALIFICATIONS: experience in teaching English as a foreign language and, if possible, with a degree in languages.

CONDITIONS OF EMPLOYMENT: freelance, variable hours (daytime, evenings, Saturdays etc.)

SALARY: between €22.10 and €27.50 per hour according to experience.

FACILITIES/SUPPORT: none.

RECRUITMENT: interviews in Belgium essential, followed by an integration session.

CONTACT: Sabine Thirion, Recruiting Officer.

INLINGUA SCHOOL OF LANGUAGES
Maaltecenter 165 Blok E, Derbystraat 165, B-9051
Gent – SDW
℡ 9 232 50 50; fax 9 232 50 54
✉ info@inlingua-gent.com
🖥 www.inlingua-gent.com

NUMBER OF TEACHERS: variable.

PREFERENCE OF NATIONALITY: British.

CONTACT: Philippe Smetryns, General Manager.

LANGUAGE STUDIES INTERNATIONAL SPRL
Kiddy and Junior Classes ASBL
Rue du Taciturne 50, 1000 Brussels
℡ 2 217 23 73/2 218 39 20; fax 2 217 64 51
✉ info@kiddyclasses.net/info@lsi-be.net
🖥 www.kiddyclasses.net/www.lsi-be.net

NUMBER OF TEACHERS: 30–60.

PREFERENCE OF NATIONALITY: no.

QUALIFICATIONS: for the adult school, qualified university level teachers with TEFL experience. For the children's school, qualified teachers or would-be teachers with experience in children's entertainment.

CONDITIONS OF EMPLOYMENT: freelance, although 1–2-month contracts during the summer. Adult school hours: 9am–8pm. Children's school: 9am–5pm.

SALARY: varies.

FACILITIES/SUPPORT: none, although for the 2-month summer contract assistance is given finding accommodation.

RECRUITMENT: via internet, newspaper, universities, company brochure. Interviews essential unless excellent references received. Interviews are carried out in Brussels.

CONTACT: Sylvaine Drablier, Director.

LC LANGUAGE CENTRE
Avenue de Broqueville, 113, 1200 Brussels
℡ 2 771 71 31; fax 2 770 90 09
✉ language.centre@skynet.be
🖥 www.lclanguagecentre.com

NUMBER OF TEACHERS: 20.

PREFERENCE OF NATIONALITY: UK and USA.

QUALIFICATIONS: TEFL or TESL and experience.

CONDITIONS OF EMPLOYMENT: Flexible contracts and work hours.

SALARY: Flexible.

FACILITIES/SUPPORT: none.

RECRUITMENT: direct application. Interview essential.

CONTACT: Annick Lombard, General Manager.

MAY INTERNATIONAL TRAINING CONSULTANTS
55 rue de Bordeaux, 1060 Brussels
℡ 2 536 06 70; fax 2 536 06 80
✉ info@mayintl.com
🖥 www.mayintl.com

NUMBER OF TEACHERS: approximately 30.

PREFERENCE OF NATIONALITY: EU.

QUALIFICATIONS: TEFL qualification, minimum 1 year's teaching experience with adults.

CONDITIONS OF EMPLOYMENT: self-employed, no contracts, but minimum commitment of 1 year. Day-time work, although evening work is available. Pupils are all adults, and mostly in business/professions. ISO 9001 Quality System in operation.

SALARY: minimum €10 per hour. Higher rates depending on experience/performance.

FACILITIES/SUPPORT: informal training/assistance given.

RECRUITMENT: internet and local newspaper adverts. Interviews essential.

CONTACT: Valerie McConaghy, Director.

PHONE LANGUAGES
Rue des Echevins 48, 1050 Brussels
℡ 2 647 40 20; fax 2 647 40 55
✉ info@phonelanguages.com
🖥 www.phonelanguages.com

NUMBER OF TEACHERS: 65 throughout Belgium and France (including 20 English teachers).

PREFERENCE OF NATIONALITY: all nationalities, especially English and American.

QUALIFICATIONS: BA preferably with TEFL diploma. Must be online at home.

CONDITIONS OF EMPLOYMENT: all teachers are freelance and teach in cycles of 10, 30, 50 or 100 half-hour lessons over the phone. Flexible hours of work between 8am and 10pm; the favourite times are 8am–10am, lunchtime and 5pm–8pm. Pupils are all adults (usually business people).

Teachers work from their own homes over the telephone and no longer need to be in Belgium to work. All teachers must have a telephone plus email and internet access at home.

SALARY: €10 per hour.

FACILITIES/SUPPORT: no assistance with accommodation. Free training given for 4–6 half-hours. Course books supplied free of charge.

RECRUITMENT: send CV and accompanying letter to info@phonelanguages.com.

SKI TEN INTERNATIONAL
Chateau d'Emines, 45, 5080 Emines la Bruyere (Namur)
℡ 81 21 30 51
martine@ski-ten.be
www.ski-ten.be

NUMBER OF TEACHERS: 1 for English (plus 1 for tennis).
PREFERENCE OF NATIONALITY: none.
QUALIFICATIONS: experience with children. Some knowledge of French useful.
CONDITIONS OF EMPLOYMENT: student contract for July or August. 6 hours of work per day including teaching and 'animation', ie supervising camp activities.
SALARY: €1,000 per month.
FACILITIES/SUPPORT: board and lodging provided at camp.
RECRUITMENT: university exchanges, word of mouth.
CONTACT: Martine Goffinet, Directrice.

THEMA LANGUAGE SCHOOL
Rue du Tabellion, 64–B 1050 Ixelles
℡ 2 640 59 82; fax 2 640 59 87
info@themalingua.be
www.themalingua.be

NUMBER OF TEACHERS: 10–12.
PREFERENCE OF NATIONALITY: none.
QUALIFICATIONS: a minimum teaching experience *or* open and interesting personality, energy, culture.
CONDITIONS OF EMPLOYMENT: Freelance, although good relations can lead to a contract. Hours: daytime from 9am, evening, to 9.15pm at the latest and/or Saturday mornings 10am–1pm for courses at Thema. In-company from 8am to 7pm, most of the time daytime or lunchtime.
SALARY: Freelance starts at €25 per hour plus travel expenses if teaching outside the school. Contract salary depends on number of hours. Freelancers should save between 20% and 40% of gross income for social security and taxes and may deduct travel expenses or any other expenses related to work.
FACILITIES/SUPPORT: does not assist teachers with work permits, but works with a non-profit making society called SMART asbl, which usually takes care of artists etc. and can do all the paperwork and calculations related to taxes and social security, enabling teachers to get paid their net salary.
RECRUITMENT: internet or Belgian publications. Interviews essential.
CONTACT: Karin Derochette (k.derochette@themalingua.be) Head of English.

Luxembourg

With only a handful of private language schools in the country, Luxembourg does not offer much scope for ELT teachers. Phone Languages in Belgium has a network of telephone teachers in Luxembourg, but runs the operation from the Brussels office.

The national employment service (l'Administration de l'Emploi) at 10 rue Bender, L-1229 (2 478 53 00; info@adem.public.lu; www.etat.lu/ADEM) has a EURES adviser who may have information about language teaching openings. Informal live-in tutoring jobs are possible. Luxembourg Accueil Information (10 Bisserwee, L-1238 Luxembourg-Grund; ℡ 241717; www.luxembourgaccueil.com) is a centre for new arrivals and temporary residents. They provide a range of services on their premises from October to May, including workshops and language courses, and might be able to advise on teaching and tutoring possibilities. The British-Luxembourg Society promotes British culture and the English language in Luxembourg, and it also might be a source of information.

If you want to check newspaper adverts which will mainly be for professionals, buy the *Luxemburger Wort*, especially on Saturdays (www.wort.lu).

PRO LINGUIS

Place de l'Eglise, 6717 Thiaumont, Belgium

63 22 04 62; fax 63 22 06 88

secretariat@prolinguis.be

www.prolinguis.be

NUMBER OF TEACHERS: 14 (freelancers) to work near Arlon (Luxembourg).

PREFERENCE OF NATIONALITY: British.

QUALIFICATIONS: EFL training, BA (Hons) in English or business.

CONDITIONS OF EMPLOYMENT: minimum 1-year contracts or 2-month contracts in summer. 7 hours a day, 4–5 days per week.

SALARY: €40–€50 per day plus full board and lodging on campus.

RECRUITMENT: personal contacts. Phone interviews.

The Netherlands

Dutch people have a very high degree of competence in English after they finish their schooling. Educated Dutch people are so fluent in English that the Minister of Education once suggested that English might become the main language used in Dutch universities, a suggestion which caused an understandable outcry. However, the schooling system has become increasingly international and university staff are being challenged to lecture and publish in English and to advance their English language skills.

FINDING A JOB

Yvonne Dalhuijsen, Project Manager at UvA Talen (see list of employers), sees an increasing need for advanced levels of English within both companies and universities. She is always on the lookout for teachers who are native speakers of English.

Most private language schools tend to provide specific training in, eg business English, and are looking for language trainers with extensive commercial or government experience as well as a teaching qualification and – particularly outside the capital – some fluency in Dutch. Business English, legal English and academic English (writing papers, abstracts, etc.) are in high demand. So many native English speaking citizens have settled in the Netherlands, attracted by its liberal institutions, that most companies depend on long-term freelancers.

It might also be possible to fix up some freelance lessons with university students from non-Dutch backgrounds, including Spanish, whose level of English is less advanced than their local counterparts.

The *Yellow Pages* are easy to search online (www.goudengids.nl). An even better way to access a list of language training companies is to contact VTN, the Dutch Association of Language Institutes (Postbus 1592, 3800 BN Amersfoort; VTN-Taleninstituten@pep.nl; www.vtn-online.nl, in Dutch). The British Council in Amsterdam maintains a list of language institutes throughout the country which prepare candidates for the Cambridge exams. Highly qualified teachers or those with expertise in tutoring in an executive context should contact these language institutes.

The British Language Training Centre in Amsterdam offers the CELTA course (see Training chapter) and may be able to give advice to qualified job-seekers and recommend other institutes to try for work. CPLS Corporate Communication Services (Eeneind 2, 5674 VP Nuenen; 40 292 81 63; fax 40 223 81 98; office@cplsnet.com; www.cplsnet.com/jobs_fr.htm) is a typical training company employing project-based trainers to deliver business-to-business programmes all over the Netherlands. Applicants should be well qualified (MA TEFL/Applied Linguistics or similar plus a PGCE or RSA Dip) and with a good track record of training business clients. Similarly Linguarama Nederland has a sizeable operation in the business training field with centres in Amsterdam, the Hague and Soesterberg; enquiries may be sent to personnel@nl.linguarama.com. Only applicants with a full TEFL/TESOL or CELTA qualification will receive a response (www.linguarama.nl).

Outside the mainstream language institutes, it might be possible to arrange some telephone teaching. Phone Languages has an office in the Netherlands at Van de Spiegelstraat 33, 2518 ES Den Haag (℃ 70 365 43 43; netherlands@phonelanguages.com).

Another possibility for those not interested in a corporate atmosphere is the network of Volksuniversiteit, adult education centres. Branches can be found in Amersfoort, Amsterdam, Delft, Groningen, Haarlem, Hertogenbosch, Hilversum, Leiden, Rotterdam, Utrecht and many others, all listed at www.volksuniversiteit.nl.

LIST OF EMPLOYERS

BERLITZ LANGUAGE CENTRES
Rokin 87–89, 1012 KL Amsterdam
℃ 20 622 13 75; fax 20 620 39 59
info@berlitz.nl
www.berlitz.com

NUMBER OF TEACHERS: 10.
PREFERENCE OF NATIONALITY: none.
QUALIFICATIONS: minimum first degree.
CONDITIONS OF EMPLOYMENT: 1-year contract. Working hours are between 7.30am and 9.45pm.
SALARY: from €1,000–€2,500 per month depending on qualifications and hours worked.
RECRUITMENT: via the website or on the spot. Interviews essential.
CONTACT: Eric Werbrouck, Manager.

BOGAERS TALENINSTITUUT B.V.
Groenstraat 139 155, 5021 LL Tilburg
℃ 13 536 21 01; fax 13 535 81 99
info@bogaerstalen.nl
www.bogaerstalen.nl

NUMBER OF TEACHERS: 5 foreign out of total of 50.
PREFERENCE OF NATIONALITY: British.
QUALIFICATIONS: degree and TEFL Cert. Experience in teaching conversational and business English preferred.
CONDITIONS OF EMPLOYMENT: from 1 week to 9 months. Lessons last from 1 hour.
SALARY: €18.50 per hour.

FACILITIES/SUPPORT: will help with accommodation if needed.
RECRUITMENT: speculative CVs and applications.

EBC TALENINSTITUUT
Keldermanslaan 3, 4611 AL Bergen op Zoom
℃ 164 265679; fax 164 266576
lvkerkhof@ebc.nl
www.ebc.nl

NUMBER OF TEACHERS: 8.
PREFERENCE OF NATIONALITY: no preference but native speaker of English.
QUALIFICATIONS: experience in teaching EFL and ESP to adult learners.
CONDITIONS OF EMPLOYMENT: open contracts with flexible hours.
CONTACT: Elizabeth van Kerkhof, Managing Director.

FEEDBACK TALEN
Achillesstraat 79, 1076 PX Amsterdam
℃ 20 671 67 09; fax 20 662 05 51
miranda@feedbacktalen.nl
www.feedbacktalen.nl
Also at Rotterdam, Amersfoort and the Hague.

NUMBER OF TEACHERS: 25.
PREFERENCE OF NATIONALITY: none but must be native speakers.
QUALIFICATIONS: TEFL Cert. Business or technical experience highly valued.

CONDITIONS OF EMPLOYMENT: contract from September to June. 15–25 hours of classes per week. Lessons last 1–2 hours.

SALARY: €19–€23 per hour.

FACILITIES/SUPPORT: 60 hours compulsory in-house training. No accommodation so applicants must live in or near Rotterdam or Amsterdam.

RECRUITMENT: personal interview essential.

CONTACT: Miranda Bensing.

FRANGLAIS LANGUAGE SERVICES
Molenstraat 15, 2513 BH, The Hague

✆ 70 361 17 03; fax 70 361 17 34

✉ jobs@franglais.nl

🖥 www.franglais.nl

NUMBER OF TEACHERS: 25.

PREFERENCE OF NATIONALITY: none.

QUALIFICATIONS: teaching degree required, preferably with a business background. Native English speakers only.

CONDITIONS OF EMPLOYMENT: 3 months or 6 months renewable. From 3 hours a week up to a maximum of 25 per week. Opportunities also available to edit texts by non-native speakers; pay is 5 eurocents per word.

FACILITIES/SUPPORT: no assistance with accommodation. Applicants should already be in the Netherlands.

RECRUITMENT: advertisements in newspapers and on-the-spot interviews.

CONTACT: Maaike van Eijk/Hayley Doidge

PCI – PIMENTEL COMMUNICATIONS INTERNATIONAL
Bachlaan 43, 1817 GH Alkmaar

✆ 72 512 11 90/515 65 18; fax 72 511 64 09

✉ info@pcitalen.nl/info@pcilanguages.com

🖥 www.pcitalen.nl/www.pcilanguages.com

NUMBER OF TEACHERS: 50+.

PREFERENCE OF NATIONALITY: mostly British, Irish or North American. Australians, New Zealanders and South Africans also welcome.

QUALIFICATIONS: experience in business and technical English. Cross-cultural communication skills and familiarity with modern teaching methods needed.

CONDITIONS OF EMPLOYMENT: freelancers working mostly in-company nationwide.

SALARY: starts at €27 per hour.

FACILITIES/SUPPORT: most teachers are already living in the Netherlands.

RECRUITMENT: advertisements, word-of-mouth and recommendations.

CONTACT: Ms. Iona de Pimentel.

SUITCASE TALEN
De Paal 104 -106, 13 51 JJ Almere

✆ 36 536 74 82

✉ info@suitcase.nl

🖥 www.suitcase.nl

NUMBER OF TEACHERS: 15 freelancers.

PREFERENCE OF NATIONALITY: none.

QUALIFICATIONS: native speakers. Pedagogical background and experience in the world of business is an advantage.

CONDITIONS OF EMPLOYMENT: freelance. Standard length of contract normally 20 hours per month, daytime or evening.

SALARY: €27.50–€32.50 per hour, depending on experience.

FACILITIES/SUPPORT: no assistance with accommodation or work permits.

RECRUITMENT: open applications. Interviews essential.

CONTACT: Mrs. M. E. A. Kwakernaak, Director.

THE LANGUAGE ACADEMY (UvA Talen)
Roetersstraat 27, NL-1018 WB Amsterdam

✆ 20 525 46 37

✉ jobs@thelanguageacademy.nl

🖥 www.thelanguageacademy.nl

NUMBER OF TEACHERS: about 30 per year.

PREFERENCE OF NATIONALITY: none, provided native speaker (with widely understood dialect).

QUALIFICATIONS: experience in teaching adults. Working knowledge of Dutch and/or European Framework Reference (A-B-C) is sometimes required, though not always.

CONDITIONS OF EMPLOYMENT: freelance assignments or on a temporary contract for the duration of a course, from 2–20 weeks. Extensions possible.

SALARY: from €25 per hour, plus compensation for preparation work or corrections.

FACILITIES/SUPPORT: no assistance with accommodation or work permits. Project Manager monitors contents of the courses and is happy to advise teachers on content and materials.

RECRUITMENT: teachers submit CVs and cover letter; face-to-face interviews required on arrival.

CONTACT: Yvonne Dalhuijsen, Project Manager at UvA Talen (an independent language institute which is associated with the 'Universiteit van Amsterdam' and consists of a translation agency and a training centre).

FRANCE

The French used to rival the English for their reluctance to learn other languages. A Frenchman abroad spoke French as stubbornly as Britons spoke English. But things have changed, especially in the business and technical community. French telephone directories contain pages of language training organisations and the law continues to put pressure on companies to provide on-going training for staff. The Droit de Formation Continue stipulates that companies have to devote a minimum of 1.5% of their payroll to employee training. English and computing are the most popular objects of investment, and therefore many private language institutes cater purely to the business market. In fact a quick browse through the entries in the List of Employers at the end of this chapter will lead you to the conclusion that all adult language training in France is business oriented, with most of it taking place on-site and the rest taking place in business and vocational schools. In this setting the term *formateurs* or 'trainers' is often used instead of English teachers. Private training companies involved with formation often produce very glossy brochures which look more like the annual report of a multinational corporation than an invitation to take an evening course. Most offer one-to-one tuition.

A considerable number of town councils (*mairies*) and Chambres de Commerce et d'Industrie (CCI) have their own Centres d'Etude des Langues. Pariglotte is the CCI Centre d'Etude de Langues in Paris (6 Av de la Porte de Champerret, 75838 Paris Cedex 17; ✆ +01 44 09 33 10/11; pariglotte@ccip.fr; www.pariglotte.com/template.asp), but there are many centres all over France (www.reseau-cel.cci.fr).

Teaching young children is left mostly to French teachers of English, although foreign language assistants are typically placed in schools (see later). Native teachers might be able to find a freelance opening. Some municipalities have introduced projects to teach English to 4-year-olds. The most popular times are Wednesdays (when state schools are closed) and Saturdays. The fashion for telephone teaching, a concept invented by a Parisian yuppie (or so it is said), continues and can be lucrative for teachers who are online at home and have their own telephones.

PROSPECTS FOR TEACHERS

Advanced ELT qualifications seem to be less in demand in France than solid teaching experience, particularly in a business context. But an increasing number of schools require a relevant educational background, eg BEd, PGCE, CELTA or DELTA. Few schools accept candidates on the basis of being a native speaker and candidates may be asked to provide an *attestation de durée d'études* to show the educational level they have reached. However, anyone who has a university degree in any subject and who can look at home in a business situation (and possesses a suit/smart clothes) has a chance of finding teaching work, particularly if they have a working knowledge of French. Having your own transport is a huge advantage as **Helen Welch** reported. She arrived in the Toulouse area (from Thailand) in August, was offered two jobs almost straightaway and immediately got a car which she claims is 'absolutely necessary for teaching here' since so much is done on different businesses' premises.

In some circles it is fashionable to learn American English which means that, despite the visa difficulties for non-EU nationals, it is possible for Americans to find work as well. Many institutes claim to have no preference as to the country of origin of their native-speaker teachers though most expect to hire foreigners already resident in France with appropriate working papers. France is such a popular and obvious destination for British and Irish people and also for North Americans that a speculative job hunt from abroad can be disappointing. Major language teaching organisations receive speculative CVs every day and can't promise anything until they meet the applicant.

FINDING A JOB

IN ADVANCE

A comprehensive list of English language institutes in France is hard to come by. One source of reputable language schools is the French Training Federation (Fédération de la Formation Professionnelle – FFP) which is based in the centre of Paris (6, rue Galilée, 75016; ✆ +01 44 30 49 49; fax 01 44 30 49 18; ffp@ffp.org; www.ffp.org). The *Pages Jaunes* (*Yellow Pages*; www.pages-jaunes.fr) is another possibility, if you search under the headings Enseignement: Cours de Langues or Ecoles de Langues. The *Dicoguide de la Formation* published by Génération Formation (27 rue du Chemin Vert, 75543 Paris; ✆ +01 48 07 41 41; www.generation-formation.fr) is a directory of training organisations in France, but because it retails for €389 it is best to consult it in a library. The Centre Regional Information pour Jeunesse also lists English language schools (www.crij.org), as does the Paris Anglophone website (www.paris-anglo.com), minus email addresses.

The British Council in Paris (9 rue de Constantine, 75340 Paris; ✆ +1 49 55 73 00; fax 1 49 55 73 02; www.britishcouncil.fr) teaches English to adults, and to children and teenagers during the school holidays and may have vacancies for well-qualified teachers. They also have a useful online teaching resource centre (www.britishcouncil.org/fr/france-english-teaching-english-teaching-resources.htm) which offers a weekly collection of links to free materials from British Council websites.

The Centre International d'Etudes Pédagogiques (CIEP) in France offers about 1,500 assistantships in France for students from many different countries (✆ 1 45 07 60 00; www.ciep.fr). Undergraduates and graduates under the age of 30 (35 in some countries) can spend an academic year working as English language assistants in secondary and (increasingly) primary schools throughout France. In return for giving conversation classes 12 hours a week, providing classroom support and teaching pupils about their country, assistants receive a gross allowance of approximately €940 a month for between six and nine months, beginning 1 October. Similar posts are also available in other francophone countries such as Belgium, Canada (Québec) and Switzerland.

Assistants must have a working knowledge of French so modern languages students are encouraged to apply. Applications are encouraged from students who have at least AS level, higher grade or equivalent in French. Some posts in primary schools require degree-level French because any help offered by colleagues and all discussion of pupil progress, curriculum, lesson planning etc. is likely to be in French. English and Welsh applicants should contact the Language Assistants Team at Contracts and Projects, British Council (10 Spring Gardens, London SW1A 2BN; ✆ 020 7389 4596; assistants@britishcouncil.org; www.britishcouncil.org/languageassistant). Scottish and Northern Irish students can contact the British Council Language Assistants teams in Edinburgh/Belfast (www.britishcouncil.org/languageassistants-contact-us.htm). American students can participate in the scheme by applying through the French Embassy (Assistantship Program French Embassy, 4101 Reservoir Road N.W. Washington DC 20007; for further information contact Marjorie Nelson at: assistant.washington-amba@diplomatie.gouv.fr or browse www.ciep.fr/en/assistantetr/index.php).

EMILY SLOANE FROM AMERICA WAS POSTED AS AN ASSISTANT TO A SMALL TOWN IN LORRAINE (WHERE THE QUICHE COMES FROM), UNKNOWN TO ANY ENGLISH-LANGUAGE GUIDEBOOK THAT SHE COULD FIND:

I taught English to about 170 students in three different primary schools, two 45-minute sessions per class per week, for a total of 12 hours of work each week. In general, the teaching and lesson planning were thoroughly enjoyable, although I wasn't given much guidance and received no feedback throughout the year, so I'm sure the fact that I was already comfortable and experienced with teaching and working with children made a big difference in my enjoyment. The kids, although adoring and very enthusiastic, were a lot rowdier than I had expected, and I was obliged to spend a lot more time on behavior management than I'd anticipated. The kids were never mean, just excitable and chatty, especially so because my class offered a break from their usual blackboard-and-worksheet style routine. The fact that I was the only assistant in my town meant that my French improved noticeably, especially my slang and listening comprehension, although it made for some lonely weekends, because I was forced to get by in French all the time.

The Alliance Française has centres throughout the world, with about a dozen teaching centres in the UK (www.alliancefrancaise.org.uk) and many more in the USA and worldwide. Anyone who can converse in French might find it useful to make contact before leaving home. Most centres have a notice board where requests for tutors, au pairs, etc. are occasionally posted. In London, the Alliance Française of Grande Bretagne is located at 1 Dorset Square, London NW1 6PU (℗ 020 7723 6439; info@alliancefrancaise.org.uk) and in New York at 22 E. 60th St, New York, NY 10022 (℗ 212 355 6100; languagecenter@fiaf.org; www.fiaf.org).

THERE IS ALSO DEMAND FOR EXPERIENCED ENGLISH TEACHERS FROM FRENCH UNIVERSITIES, ALTHOUGH YOU REALLY NEED TO BE LIVING IN FRANCE TO STAND A CHANCE OF SECURING A JOB (AS IS OFTEN THE CASE). MICHAEL BUXTON, WHO HAS BEEN A NATIVE ENGLISH TEACHER FOR 15 YEARS, TAUGHT AT THE UNIVERSITY OF LYON:

Today, students are much keener to communicate and the university gives them exams based around student life and the four elements speaking/listening/reading/writing. Students are also able to make use of the extremely up-to-date facilities.

The university has several systems of employment. Lyon 2 employs about 45 native English teachers by a system called 'vacataire', which means you need to have a principal employer. There is also another system called '*travailleurs indépendants*' where the teachers can work at two/three/four universities, but are classed as self-employed and have to pay their own social security. The disadvantage of working at the university is that although they pay relatively well with good conditions of employment, they often pay late; you could be waiting for up to six months.

It remains to be seen what impact president Nicolas Sarkozy's public sector reforms will have on the universities and their recruitment patterns.

Advertisements for teaching jobs in France seldom appear in the UK press and virtually never in American journals. French newspapers carry few teaching advertisements though very occasionally one may be seen in *Le Figaro* especially on Mondays and Tuesdays and in the Paris edition of the *International Herald Tribune*.

WHEN APPLYING TO A TRAINING ORGANISATION, TRY TO DEMONSTRATE YOUR COMMERCIAL FLAIR WITH A POLISHED PRESENTATION INCLUDING A BUSINESS-LIKE CV (OMITTING YOUR HOBBIES) PREFERABLY ACCOMPANIED BY A HAND-WRITTEN LETTER IN IMPECCABLE FRENCH. ANDREW SYKES FELT THAT HE OWED THE SUCCESS OF HIS JOB-HUNT TO HIS MISGUIDED AND UNSUCCESSFUL ACCOUNTANCY TRAINING RATHER THAN TO HIS TEFL CERTIFICATE:

I wrote to more or less all the schools from your book in France and elsewhere that didn't stipulate 'experience required' and was fairly disheartened by the few, none-too-encouraging replies along the lines of 'if you're in town, give us a call.' Sitting in a very cheap hotel bedroom halfway down Italy in early November feeling sorry for myself and knowing that I was getting closer and closer to my overdraft limit and an office job back in the UK, I rang the schools that had replied and so picked up the phone and rang through to BEST in Tours. 'Drop in,' the voice said, 'and we will give you an interview'. So I jumped on the next train, met the director on Monday and was offered a job on the Tuesday morning, initially on an hour-by-hour basis and then in December on a contract of 15 hours which was later increased to 20 hours a week.

OK, I was very lucky. I have since learned that the school receives several phone calls and letters per week; it's an employer's market. What got me the job was not my TEFL certificate nor my very good French. It was the fact that I was an ex-accountant. I had been one of the thousands enticed by the financial benefits of joining an accountancy firm after graduation. But I hated the job and failed my first professional exams. Ironically the experience gained during those two and a half years of hell was invaluable. Whereas in Italy they want teaching experience, in France they want business experience.

You will in the end be teaching people not objects, and any experience you can bring to the job (and especially the job interview) will help. However ashamed you may be of telling everyone in the pub back home that you were once a rat catcher, it may be invaluable if the school's main client is 'Rent-o-kil'.

The technique of making a personal approach to schools in the months preceding the one in which you would like to teach is often successful. On the strength of her Cambridge Certificate from International House, **Fiona Paton** had been hoping to find teaching work in the south of France in the summer but quickly discovered that there are very few opportunities outside the academic year. On her way back to England, she disembarked from the train in the picturesque town of Vichy in the Auvergne just long enough to distribute a few self-promotional leaflets to three language schools. She was very surprised to receive a favourable reply from one of them once she was home, and so returned a few weeks later for a happy year of teaching.

Teaching English in exchange for room and board is very widespread and is normally arranged on the spot, but can also be set up in advance. While looking for something to do in her gap year, **Hannah Start** was put in touch with a French bank executive who had done an English language course in Hannah's home town and who wanted to keep up her English at home in Paris by having someone to provide live-in conversation lessons. So, in exchange for three hours of speaking English in the evening (usually over an excellent dinner), Hannah was given free accommodation in the 17th *arrondissement*.

ON THE SPOT

The British Institute in Paris has a notice board advertising very occasional teaching vacancies as well as live-in tutoring and au pair jobs. Among the services cut back by the Paris British Council is its notice board.

Prospective teachers should not automatically head for Paris but bear in mind that provincial cities have many language schools too. Not only is it hard to find work in Paris, but of course rents are very high in the capital. If you do decide to give it a go in Paris, watch for advertisements in the métro for English language courses, since these are usually the biggest schools and therefore have the greatest number of vacancies for teachers. Certain streets in the 8th *arrondissement* around the Gare St. Lazare abound in language schools.

Non-EU nationals are bound to encounter problems (see section on Regulations below) as **Beth Mayer** from New York found:

I've tried to get a job at a school teaching, but they asked for working papers which I don't have. I checked with several schools who told me that working papers and a university degree were more important than TEFL qualifications.

It is also worth visiting your local ANPE (agence national pour l'emploi), which may direct you to the 'right place' if it can't help you directly (www.anpe.fr).

FREELANCE TEACHING

As is increasingly common in many countries, schools are often reluctant to take on contract teachers for whom they would be obliged to make expensive contributions for social security (19%–22% of gross pay). So there is a bustling market in freelance teachers. Self-employed workers (*travailleurs indépendants*), however little they earn, are obliged to register at the social security office (www.urssaf.fr/general/les_urssaf/votre_urssaf/fiche.phtml). The hourly fees (*honoraires*) paid to freelance teachers should be significantly higher than to contract workers (*salariés*) since they are free of deductions. It is very difficult to earn a professional living as a freelancer in the big cities, especially in Paris, since competition is ferocious, the market saturated, and taxes and social charges very high. **Michael Buxton** tried his hand at freelancing in Lyon and found it '*a difficult way to earn a living.*'

However at a more casual level, language exchanges for room and board are commonplace in Paris; these are usually arranged through advertisements or word-of-mouth. You can also offer English lessons privately in people's homes, which should pay at least €18 a session. In addition to the British Institute notice board mentioned above, there are many other *panneaux* which might prove useful to someone looking for private tutoring. This is especially appealing to Americans who do this without worrying too much about visas.

AS PART OF A WELL-ORGANISED TEACHING JOB HUNT IN MARSEILLE, AMERICAN BRADWELL JACKSON TRIED TO ARRANGE TO TEACH SOME PRIVATE LESSONS:

Besides searching for jobs in schools, I also tried my hand at the tutoring market. I put up petites annonces in the local boulangeries and bars, and I also put an ad in a free local paper called 13 (treize), also called Top Annonces (www.topannonces.fr). The cost of placing the ad was not free, but it wasn't expensive (maybe €10). This did turn out to be fruitful, as I did get responses. My big disadvantage was that I didn't have a cell phone, and I was told that the French are not inclined to respond to someone only by email. I decided to counteract this by putting in a very low asking price, only €10 per hour. With that price, I got several responses, even with only an email address advertised. The problem was that there was a time lag of two weeks between my placing the order and its appearance, by which time I had booked a plane ticket back to Mexico. I also advertised on a free website service called Kelprof (www.kelprof.com). It was indeed free, but to contact referrals you have to use a password and 08 numbers which, I learned the hard way, are very expensive.

There are expatriate grapevines all over Paris, very helpful for finding teaching work and accommodation. The notice board in the foyer of the Centre d'Information et de Documentation Jeunesse (CIDJ) at 101 Quai Branly; ✆ 1 44 49 12 00; www.cidj.com (métro Bir-Hakeim) is good for occasional student-type jobs, but sometimes there are advertisements for a *soutien scolaire en Anglais* (English tutor). It is worth arriving early to check for new notices (the hours are Monday, Tuesday and Friday 10am–6pm, Thursday 1pm–6pm and Saturday 9.30am–1pm).

The other mecca for job and flat-hunters is the American Church at 65 Quai d'Orsay (Métro Invalides) which has very active notice boards upstairs, downstairs and outside. There is a charge for posting a notice (eg for au pair jobs and accommodation) and they are kept up to date. In the basement, the free corkboard is much more chaotic; it can take about half an hour to rummage through all the notices.

The American Cathedral in Paris (23 Avenue George V; www.americancathedral.org) near the métro stations Alma Marceau and George V, also has a notice board featuring employment opportunities and housing listings. The two British churches may be of assistance: St Georges at 7 rue Auguste Vacquerie in the 16th *arrondissement* and St Michael's (www.saintmichaelsparis.com) at 5 rue d'Aguesseau in the 8th (métro Madeleine). The notice board of St Michael's carries notices of accommodation both wanted and available, as well as very occasional advertisements for conversation exchanges (eg English for French). The church administrator says she often gets asked if she can help with finding jobs, but really is unable to offer any assistance. She adds that people are welcome to come and look at the noticeboard, but that it is entirely separate from the church's activities. The church is open Monday, Tuesday, Thursday, Friday and Sunday between 10am and 5.30pm.

Although the notice board at the Alliance Française (101 Boulevard Raspail; métro Notre Dame des Champs) is for the use of registered students of French, you may be able to persuade a student to look at the advertisements for you, some of which involve free lodging in return for babysitting and/or teaching. The notice board is in the annexe around the corner at 34 rue de Fleurus (near the métro Notre Dame des Champs). The Alliance Français can be contacted on 1 42 84 90 00; www.alliancefr.org.

Most of the above expat meeting places distribute the free bilingual newsletter *France-USA Contacts* or *FUSAC* (www.fusac.org) which comes out every other Wednesday. It can also be picked up at English language bookshops such as WH Smith at 248 rue de Rivoli near Place de la Concorde, Attica, the largest language learning bookseller in Paris (www.attica.fr) or at the eccentric Shakespeare & Company bookshop, 37 rue de la Bǔcherie (opposite Notre-Dame). *FUSAC* comprises mainly classified advertisements including some for English teachers which are best followed up on the day the paper appears. An advertisement in *FUSAC* costs from €24 for 20 words, and can be ordered online.

DURING BETH MAYER'S FIRST YEAR IN PARIS SHE FOUND THAT ADVERTISING IN FUSAC WAS VERY EFFECTIVE:

I placed an advertisement to teach English and offer editing services (I was an editor in New York City before moving here) and received many responses. I charged the equivalent of $12 per hour but found that after I had spent time going and coming, I cleared only half that. So perhaps it would be better to have the lessons at your apartment (if centrally located). I not only 'teach' English but offer English conversation to French people who don't need a teacher but more a companion with whom to practise. I've met a lot of nice people this way and earned money to boot.

It may be worth including a reminder here that anyone who advertises their services should exercise a degree of caution when arranging to meet prospective clients.

OUTSIDE THE BIGGER CITIES, YOUR CHANCE OF PICKING UP FREELANCE WORK IS GREATLY IMPROVED. WORKING AS A LANGUAGE ASSISTANT IN A SMALL TOWN IN LORRAINE, EMILY SLOANE HAD NO PROBLEM FINDING FREELANCE WORK:

Through word-of-mouth and no active self-promotion, numerous townspeople contacted me about private English tutoring. By the middle of the school year I had 5 private students, whom I taught once a week each for €10, with sometimes a meal on top of that. It was nice to be able to work through more complicated material with older students and really nice to have an inside look into various French households. Plus, the tutoring sessions kept me busy. I also earned some extra cash by doing freelance writing work for the mother of one of my students, which helped to supplement my fairly meagre salary and allowed me to take long and stress-free vacations during the numerous school breaks.

REGULATIONS

EU NATIONALS

Since 2003, EU citizens have been free of the obligation to obtain residence permits to live and work in other EU countries so the *carte de séjour* is now obsolete for most. Long-stayers may choose to apply for one since it can be a useful piece of identification, but they will have to be prepared to provide a battery of translated documents.

Once you take up paid employment in France, your employer must complete all the necessary formalities for registering you with social security (*sécu*) and you will be issued with a registration card and then pay a percentage of your wages as contributions. After working a summer season at Disneyland Paris **Keith Leishman** offers what he considers a crucial piece of advice, which is to take a certified copy of your birth certificate translated into French. It must include your father's full name and your mother's maiden name. Keith arrived without this abstruse document and as a result had trouble registering for social security and furthermore in getting paid.

As mentioned, self-employed workers (*travailleurs indépendants*) are obliged to register at the social security office (URSSAF). Some employers may claim that they cannot hire you without a *sécu*, and employment agencies may not be willing to register you without one, however, you should insist on your rights.

Legal employers will deduct as much as 20% for social security payments, even before you have a number. These can be counted towards National Insurance in Britain, if you subsequently need to claim benefit. You may also lose a further 5% in tax. It is worth pointing out that legal residents of France may be able to reduce their rent bill significantly, provided their earnings two years prior to applying were low. The benefit is administered by the Caisse d'Allocations Familiales (CAF) to whom you must furnish a signed/stamped declaration from your landlord, a declaration of income for the calendar year preceding the year of benefit, a Fiche Individual d'Etat Civile and various other bits and pieces.

NON-EU NATIONALS

In France, it is difficult for Americans, Canadians, Australians and all other non-EU nationalities to get a work permit. Even with a job offer, applicants are not automatically granted work permits unless they are married to a French national. Americans should check www.ambafrance-us.org/spip.php?article360. Non-EU nationals must obtain work documents before they leave their home country, either a *carte de séjour temporaire salarié* (valid for one year and specifying where and in what sector they may work) or a *carte de résident* (valid for 10 years and for any activity anywhere in continental France). The only way to get either visa is to have a signed contract in hand and to obtain authorisation from the French Department of Employment. A handful of employers are willing to tackle the bureaucracy which involves applying to the Direction Départementale du Travail, de l'Emploi et de la Formation Professionelle for permission to hire a foreigner. American participants in the Assistants scheme mentioned earlier will be guided through the process.

Note that the TEFL training organisation WICE (20 Boulevard du Montparnasse, 75015 Paris; ℰ 1 45 66 75 50; www.wice-paris.org), which is affiliated to Rutgers University in the USA, is familiar with the necessary steps but cannot assist in the application process. In its standard letter E7, the CIDJ writes in no uncertain terms about the difficulty of obtaining working papers. It might also be worth obtaining fiche 5.570: Séjour et travail des étrangers en France.

A FIRST-HAND ACCOUNT OF THE DIFFICULTIES AMERICANS FACE WAS KINDLY SUPPLIED BY BRADWELL JACKSON BASED ON HIS RECENT EXPERIENCES IN MARSEILLE. AFTER A NEAR EFFORTLESS JOB-HUNT IN MEXICO, BRADWELL DECIDED THAT HE WANTED TO TEACH IN A FRENCH-SPEAKING COUNTRY, AND SO HE TRAVELLED TO FRANCE. THE DESCRIPTION OF HIS JOB-HUNT MAKES DEPRESSING READING, SINCE AT EVERY TURN HE FOUND HIS LACK OF A WORK PERMIT AN OBSTACLE:

The first school I went to enquire at was Berlitz. They were somewhat encouraging the first day, but the next day, they said they needed the work visa first and also said that Berlitz does not help with the process of getting one. The second company I went to was the American Center. The woman there said that they needed teachers with more experience than I have, meaning teachers with a specific degree in English or a comparable amount of experience. I was very encouraged at first by my visit to the Wall Street Institute. I happened to arrive at the right time when they very much needed a teacher. The coordinator asked me into her office and requested that I tell her about myself and my experience. After about a minute of explanation, she was showing me the schedule of where she wanted me to work. It seemed that I was in and that the old magic from Mexico had returned. When she said that I needed a car, and I had to tell her that I didn't have one, things cooled down a bit, but it still looked promising since she liked me.

The next day, I met the big boss, and he seemed to like me too. He asked if I had a work visa, and we did the same 'visa dance' where I maintained that I needed a job offer first. Things still looked good, as he indicated that he might sponsor me with the process. I returned the next day, only to be told that the boss had checked out the situation and decided, firmly, that he would not go through the hassle of sponsoring someone through such a labyrinthine process. The coordinator was kind enough to refer me to other places where she had contacts and also told me of a free internet site for registering my name as a tutor.

> *Next I went to the World Language Center, an upscale place for businessmen, where the boss told me of how essential the work visas were. My credentials, which are limited to four months teaching in Mexico, some tutoring of ESOL students in Tampa, and no teaching degree (my degree is in psychology) also seemed to be substandard. He was not keen on the idea of helping me get a work visa, but he was very kind in giving me advice which was useful. The fifth place just wanted to take my CV for future reference and at the next (Master Institute) I wasn't able to wangle my way in to see an upper level staff, as is my style, so I settled for simply handing in my CV to a secretary.*

In fact thousands of Americans (and other nationalities) are teaching English in France on a part-time basis. All foreign students, including those arriving for the first time or enrolled in their first year of study, have the right to work during their studies provided that they are enrolled in an education institution that entitles them to student coverage under the French national health insurance system (Sécurité Sociale) (and that they have a residence permit if they are non-EU nationals). French legislation authorises foreign students to work a maximum of 964 hours per year. The guaranteed minimum salary in France, the SMIC, is €8.44 gross per hour (before the average 20% deduction for social security contributions). Students are no longer required to obtain a temporary work permit (*autorisation provisoire de travail* (APT)) in order to work part-time during their studies. Once a student has obtained a degree equivalent to a Master's or higher degree, they may request a temporary residence permit (*autorisation provisoire de séjour*) after expiration of the 'student' residence permit. The temporary residence permit is valid for six months and is non-renewable. This permit authorises an ex-student to work in any kind of salaried job up to a limit of 60% of the legally permitted number of working hours. If an employment contract is signed in a field related to their studies and whose remuneration is at least equal to one and a half times the SMIC, an ex-student will then be able to work full-time and request a change in status (from student to employee) from the Préfecture administrative offices. Further information is available in a digestible form at www.campusfrance.org/en.

One possibility open to some Americans with Irish or Greek ancestry is to obtain an EU passport. An easier route is to teach on a voluntary basis; or you can always work on the 'black market', which is not really easy or advisable, but is something that the French, as well as foreigners, continue to do all the same.

CONDITIONS OF WORK

Teaching 'beezneezmen' is not everyone's cup of tea, but it can be less strenuous than other kinds of teaching. Provided you do not feel intimidated by your pupils' polished manners and impeccable dress, and can keep them entertained, you will probably be a success. As mentioned above, one-to-one teaching is not uncommon, for which ELT training (including the CELTA or Trinity Certificate) does not prepare you. However, if you develop a rapport with your client, this can be the most enjoyable teaching of all. As mentioned earlier, language schools which offer this facility to clients may well expect you to drive, perhaps even own, a car so that you can give lessons in offices and private homes. Most schools pay between €18 and €25 (gross) per lesson.

Salaried teachers should be covered by a nationally agreed and widely enforced Convention Collective which makes stable contracts, sick pay, holiday pay, etc. compulsory as well as guaranteeing a monthly salary. The Convention Collective also obliges language schools to contribute to a mutual fund (*une prévoyance*) which provides employees and their families with financial protection in the case of accident or handicap. Many language schools feign to ignore this so you should ascertain whether your prospective future employer respects this obligation.

The annual holiday allowance for full-time teachers is five weeks plus an extra five days.

Telephone and internet teaching are popular for their convenience and anonymity. For many people, making mistakes over the phone is less embarrassing than face-to-face. Apparently this method of teaching is great fun for teachers since the anonymity prompts people to spill out all their secrets. Many have been surprised by the good results. It is not necessary to be able to speak French and possibly even an advantage to be monolingual, so you won't be tempted to break into French in frustration. The standard rate of pay for telephone teaching is about €10 for half an hour plus telephone expenses.

An unusual feature in France is that some schools calculate the salary according to a certain number of teaching hours per 9 or 12 months, and will pay overtime for hours worked in excess of this. Obviously the total can't be calculated until the end of the contract, which is a drawback for anyone considering leaving early.

Partly because of France's proximity to a seemingly inexhaustible supply of willing English teachers, working conditions in France are seldom brilliant. Although **Andrew Boyle** enjoyed his year teaching English in Lyon and the chance to become integrated into an otherwise impenetrable community, he concluded that even respectable schools treated teachers as their most expendable commodity. By contrast, **Fiona Paton** was well looked after and had no trouble finding a comfortable and affordable flat in Vichy (which is often easy in popular holiday resorts outside the summer season). Her impression was that flat-sharing is not as commonplace in France as in other countries.

THE FRENCH DO NOT OFTEN COME ACROSS AS THE MOST APPROACHABLE OF PEOPLE, HAVING A FIRMER COMMITMENT TO PRIVACY THAN IS COMMON IN SOME COUNTRIES (THEY REMAINED DISTINCTLY UNIMPRESSED WHEN SARKOZY BEGAN TO FLAUNT HIS LOVE LIFE IN THE MEDIA), BUT THEY CAN BE GREAT COMPANY, AS EMILY SLOANE DISCOVERED:

I joined the French Alpine Club, which had a thriving and spirited branch in my village. In addition to weekly indoor rock climbing sessions, I accompanied club members on various weekend hikes and climbing trips in the Jura and Vosges Mountains in France and Switzerland and even attended a 10-day climbing clinic in northern Provence. Learning French climbing vocabulary while suspended 100 feet above the ground, when misunderstandings could have pretty serious consequences, was an experience I won't soon forget. The club members were fantastic people who generously shared the tight space of their homemade 'camping cars' and handcrafted liqueurs. I even convinced them to dress as Americans and speak English one night at the climbing wall. In return for their effort, I provided American snacks and music and a cheat sheet of useful American slang and insults that they enthusiastically tried out on each other. Through the club I even found my very own French lover, which proved to be the most efficient way to improve my language skills.

LIST OF EMPLOYERS

ANGLESEY LANGUAGE SERVICES (ALS)

1 bis, 3 Avenue du Maréchal Foch, 78400 Chatou

1 34 80 65 15; fax 1 34 80 69 91

als@alschatou.com

NUMBER OF TEACHERS: 40.

PREFERENCE OF NATIONALITY: native speakers.

QUALIFICATIONS: CELTA plus 2 years of experience preferred but possibilities for trainees.

CONDITIONS OF EMPLOYMENT: 1-year open contract. 15–25 hours per week. Pupils are adults and many are taught in their workplaces. Recent expansion, so group lessons at all levels offered in evenings and during the day. Some Saturday work available.

SALARY: €21.50 per hour plus 12% on top for holiday pay.

FACILITIES/SUPPORT: some help with accommodation possible. No initial training provided but on-going professional development provided for teachers.

RECRUITMENT: initial contact by email, then one-to-one interviews held in the school.

CONTACT: Mike Webster.

APPLILANGUE

3 rue du 6 Juillet, 21000 Dijon

3 80 52 98 98; fax 3 80 58 80 66

applilang@wanadoo.fr

www. appli-langue.com

NUMBER OF TEACHERS: 12+.

PREFERENCE OF NATIONALITY: none.

QUALIFICATIONS: TEFL diploma and/or business experience.

CONDITIONS OF EMPLOYMENT: open-ended contracts. Hours of teaching between 8.30am and 7.30pm.

SALARY: €1,449 per month starting, less about 20% for contributions.

FACILITIES/SUPPORT: school has contact who rents rooms while teachers are looking for an apartment. Help given with work permit applications including recommending a registered translator.

RECRUITMENT: spontaneous CVs, word of mouth from former teachers.

CONTACT: Karen Bonvalot-Noirot.

BTL

82 Boulevard Haussmann, 75008 Paris

1 42 93 45 45; fax 1 42 93 99 19

swragg@btl.fr

www.btl.fr

NUMBER OF TEACHERS: 50.

PREFERENCE OF NATIONALITY: mother tongue English.

QUALIFICATIONS: TEFL qualification required. University degree and experience teaching professionals preferred. Will take other work experience into account.

CONDITIONS OF EMPLOYMENT: Open-ended contracts. Flexible hours according to the teacher's preferences. 25 hours per week is considered full-time.

SALARY: variable depending on experience and assignments.

FACILITIES/SUPPORT: when required, help is given with accommodation and work permits.

RECRUITMENT: via *FUSAC* magazine, word of mouth and speculative applications. Interviews are essential and can be done in the UK.

CONTACT: Stephen Wragg.

CITYLANGUES

Le Triangle de l'Arche–Bât. C 11, cours du Triangle, La Défense 12, 92937 Paris la Défense Cedex

1 55 91 96 70; fax 1 55 91 96 76

8 rue Louis Blériot, 92500 Rueil Malmaison

1 47 49 79 46

sw@citylangues.com

www.citylangues.com

NUMBER OF TEACHERS: 25.

PREFERENCE OF NATIONALITY: none, but employ only teachers resident in Paris.

QUALIFICATIONS: degree and TEFL certificate.

CONDITIONS OF EMPLOYMENT: teaching represents 70% of total paid hours as per mandatory French law.

SALARY: according to profile, graded accorded to experience.

FACILITIES/SUPPORT: no assistance with accommodation. Training available in how the French system works, emphasis on team work in school.

RECRUITMENT: local interviews essential.

CONTACT: Stephan Wheton, elected president of the French Training Federation.

ENGLISH POINT

14E rue Pierre de Coubertin, Parc de Mirande,
Dijon, 21000

- 0380631953; fax 0380711623
- contact@englishpoint.fr
- www.englishpoint.fr

NUMBER OF TEACHERS: 3 (founded 2007), in the process of recruiting more.

PREFERENCE OF NATIONALITY: None. UK, NZ, US, Canada.

QUALIFICATIONS: preferably a CELTA or equivalent and/or significant teaching experience and business work experience. The majority of courses are business based so knowledge of how a business works is essential.

CONDITIONS OF EMPLOYMENT: contracts are from 3 months – permanent. School open 8am–9pm, Monday to Friday (possible Saturday mornings).

SALARY: €17–€24 per hour depending on age/experience/ flexibility etc.

FACILITIES/SUPPORT: school can help find accommodation for teachers, from organising viewings to full accommodation management.

RECRUITMENT: through websites, training schools, word of mouth, etc. Telephone interviews essential followed by face-to-face meeting.

CONTACT: Tony Holland, Director.

EXECUTIVE LANGUAGE SERVICES

20 rue Sainte Croix de la Bretonnerie, 75004 Paris
(ELS Hotel de Ville in centre of Paris next to La
Défense, the main commercial district)

- 1 44 54 58 88; fax 1 48 04 55 53
- info@els-france.com
- www.els-france.com

NUMBER OF TEACHERS: 30 English teachers, 20 of other languages.

PREFERENCE OF NATIONALITY: none, but must be a native speaker.

QUALIFICATIONS: TEFL grade B; minimum qualifications include at least a year's experience, and an ability to teach groups and Business English.

CONDITIONS OF EMPLOYMENT: 1 year minimum. Full-time and part-time positions available. Team teaching in school and on-site in company premises.

SALARY: 25% deductions for tax and social security.

FACILITIES/SUPPORT: 2 fully equipped resource centres for staff. No help with accommodation. Work permits are

possible for highly qualified American and Canadian teachers with 2–3 months processing time needed; these are the responsibility of the applicant.

RECRUITMENT: interview after CV and handwritten letter (can be interviewed by telephone). Observation of a class and demo lesson for the same class the following day.

FONTAINEBLEAU LANGUES & COMMUNICATION

47 Boulevard Marechal Foche, 77300 Fontainebleau

- 1 64 22 48 96; fax 1 64 22 51 94
- contact@flc-int.com or dianne_riboh@ calv.flc.com
- www.flc-int.com

NUMBER OF TEACHERS: 15 English teachers, 35 in total.

PREFERENCE OF NATIONALITY: British/Irish. Australians, Canadians and Americans or other native English speakers with EU nationality or French working papers.

QUALIFICATIONS: TEFL training (eg CELTA). Must be dynamic, creative, versatile and able to work in a team.

CONDITIONS OF EMPLOYMENT: 1 year minimum. Majority of teaching takes place in company premises so a car is necessary (transport costs are reimbursed at a rate of €0.45 approx. per kilometre depending on the horsepower of the car). Variety of teaching situations including groups, one-to-one lessons and business English. Hours are grouped as much as possible between 9am and 7pm Monday to Friday.

SALARY: starting at €17.92 per hour which includes 12% holiday pay. Social security deductions are about 22%.

FACILITIES/SUPPORT: Training workshops held regularly. Large teachers' library.

RECRUITMENT: interview essential – usually by phone.

CONTACT: DiAnne Riboh, Director of Human Resources.

ILC FRANCE – IH PARIS (INTERNATIONAL LANGUAGE CENTRE)

13 Passage Dauphine, 75006 Paris

- 1 44 41 80 20; fax 1 44 41 80 21
- info@ilcfrance.com
- www.ilcfrance.com

NUMBER OF TEACHERS: 34.

QUALIFICATIONS: CELTA or approved equivalent. Experience of business world essential.

CONDITIONS OF EMPLOYMENT: teaching hours between 8.30am and 7pm. Contracts according to French labour laws. 80% of teaching is in-company.

SALARY: variable according to contract.

FACILITIES/SUPPORT: assistance with finding accommodation, teacher development and training. ILC offers the CELTA course (see Training chapter).

ECRUITMENT: spontaneous CVs and local advertisements, although priority given to IH network. Interviews in Paris essential.

CONTACT: Marlene Regaya, Director.

INLINGUA PARIS

109 rue de l'Université, 75007 Paris

C 1 45 51 46 60; fax 1 47 05 66 05

invalides@inlingua-paris.com

www.inlingua-paris.com/versionAnglaise/emploisUk.php

NUMBER OF TEACHERS: many teachers required for eight branches in Paris (others at Bastille, La Défense, Levallois Peret, Roissy, Versailles, etc.).

PREFERENCE OF NATIONALITY: none.

QUALIFICATIONS: TEFL plus 2 years' experience preferably with adult professionals. Preferred minimum age 25.

CONDITIONS OF EMPLOYMENT: minimum 12 months; open-ended contracts. Flexible hours, with guaranteed minimum, mostly 20–30 hours per week.

SALARY: approx. €15.85–€30.49 per hour.

FACILITIES/SUPPORT: assistance with accommodation, work permits and training.

RECRUITMENT: interviews essential in UK or France.

INSTITUT FRANCAIS RIERA

15, Boulevard d'Alsace, 06400 Cannes

C +4 92 99 26 63; 4 92 99 26 37

sec@ifr.fr

www.ifr.fr

NUMBER OF TEACHERS: 14.

PREFERENCE OF NATIONALITY: mother tongue.

QUALIFICATIONS: teaching experience of adults needed.

CONDITIONS OF EMPLOYMENT: permanent contract, usual hours from 8am to 9pm.

SALARY: about €16 per hour.

FACILITIES/SUPPORT: none.

RECRUITMENT: through advertising on English local radio, newspapers, employment agencies. Interviews essential in France.

CONTACT: Paskiewiez Nives, Administration Manager.

INSTITUTE OF APPLIED LANGUAGES

8 rue de la Michodière, Paris 75002

C +1 42 68 79 90; fax 1 42 68 05 65

ial@wanadoo.fr

www.ial.fr

NUMBER OF TEACHERS: 50.

PREFERENCE OF NATIONALITY: none.

QUALIFICATIONS: CELTA or TESOL or other TEFL diploma.

CONDITIONS OF EMPLOYMENT: indefinite. Between 10 and 30 hours per week.

SALARY: €19 per hour, less 23% deductions.

RECRUITMENT: spontaneous CV.

CONTACT: Elisabeth Pichon, Director of Studies.

LE COMPTOIR DES LANGUES

12 Rue de Madrid, 75008 Paris

C +1 45 61 53 53/56; fax 1 45 61 53 30

support@langues.fr

www.comptoirdeslangues.fr

NUMBER OF TEACHERS: 70.

PREFERENCE OF NATIONALITY: British, plus American, Canadian and Australian if they have valid working papers.

QUALIFICATIONS: university degree and at least 2 years of teaching experience in a school.

CONDITIONS OF EMPLOYMENT: 1 year contracts, 4–6 hours work per day between 8am and 9pm within Paris, between 9am and 8pm in the suburbs. All clients are business executives.

FACILITIES/SUPPORT: no assistance with accommodation. Training provided.

RECRUITMENT: local interviews essential.

LINGUARAMA

Tour Eve, 7e étage, La Défense 9, 92806 Puteaux Cedex

C +1 47 73 00 95; fax 1 47 73 86 04

paris@linguarama.com

www.linguarama.com

NUMBER OF TEACHERS: 30.

PREFERENCE OF NATIONALITY: none.

QUALIFICATIONS: 4-week certificate course plus 1 year's teaching experience. Driving licence useful.

CONDITIONS OF EMPLOYMENT: full-time teachers work 25 hours per week September to June. Part-time teachers work flexible hours. Teaching is business English, taught in-company and at school.

SALARY: approx. €1,400 per month.

FACILITIES/SUPPORT: advice on finding accommodation. Regular training available.

RECRUITMENT: via Linguarama in England and also locally.

METROPOLITAN LANGUAGES
151 rue de Billancourt, 92100 Boulogne Billancourt
+1 46 04 57 32; fax 1 46 04 57 12
cmarthe@metropolitan.fr
www.metropolitan.fr

NUMBER OF TEACHERS: 20.

PREFERENCE OF NATIONALITY: British, American, Australian, Irish.

QUALIFICATIONS: university and/or TEFL. Experience not essential.

CONDITIONS OF EMPLOYMENT: 1 year. Hours between 9am and 6pm.

SALARY: approx. €1,300 per month less 15% deductions.

FACILITIES/SUPPORT: no help with accommodation or work permits.

RECRUITMENT: newspapers, TEFL journals, word of mouth and email applications.

SYNDICAT MIXTE MONTAIGU-ROCHESERVIERE
35 Avenue Villebois, Mareuil, 85607 Montaigu
+2 51 46 45 45; fax 2 51 46 45 40
smmr.anglais@cc-montaigu.fr
www.explorer.com/english

NUMBER OF TEACHERS: 4.

PREFERENCE OF NATIONALITY: British.

QUALIFICATIONS: experience of and interest in teaching and a love of France.

CONDITIONS OF EMPLOYMENT: standard contract length 9 months. To teach 20 hours per week.

SALARY: allowance of €177 per month.

FACILITIES/SUPPORT: accommodation provided with local host families/resident project coordinator.

RECRUITMENT: UK interview essential.

CONTACT: Julie Legrée, Project Co-ordinator.

TEFL JOBS IN FRANCE
147 Rue Etienne Pédron, 10000 Troyes
contact@tefljobsinfrance.com
www.tefljobsinfrance.com.

PREFERENCE OF NATIONALITY: none, but applicants must hold a European passport.

QUALIFICATIONS: minimum experience of 1 year.

CONDITIONS OF EMPLOYMENT: minimum contract 1 year. To work 25 hours per week, with some evening work.

SALARY: varies according to qualifications and experience. Starting salary is approx. €1,400 per month gross.

RECRUITMENT: interview required, can be done by phone.

CONTACT: Roy Sprenger, Director.

TELAB LANGUAGE COURSES BY TELEPHONE
Head Office, En Verdan, 71520 Saint Point
+3 85 50 58 58; fax 3 85 50 56 05
s.evans@telab.com
www.telab.com

NUMBER OF TEACHERS: 80.

PREFERENCE OF NATIONALITY: None but must be native speaker, resident in France and with necessary working papers.

QUALIFICATIONS: language teaching qualifications (TOEFL, TEFL or equivalent), at least 2 years' experience in teaching languages to company employees, work experience in or knowledge of a specific field (eg marketing, finance, medical, technical, etc.), excellent communication abilities, independent, organised and rigorous at work. Must have a computer and know how to use the internet.

CONDITIONS OF EMPLOYMENT: teachers work from home, flexible hours between 7am and 9pm.

FACILITIES/SUPPORT: assistance given with social security registration (about 20% of gross salary is taken at source as contributions). No help with work permits or accommodation.

RECRUITMENT: referrals, internet, press.

CONTACT: Stephanie Evans, Manager.

TRANSFER
4 schools: 15 rue de Berri, 75008 Paris
+1 56 69 22 30; fax 1 56 69 22 35
info@transfer.fr
www.transfer.fr
Also: 20 rue Godot de Mauroy, 75009 Paris; 303 Square des Champs Elysees, Evry; 39 Bd Vauban, 78280 Guyancourt

NUMBER OF TEACHERS: 80.

PREFERENCE OF NATIONALITY: none.

QUALIFICATIONS: either professional or technical experience (law, finance, etc.) or solid teaching experience,

Cambridge CELTA or similar qualification and degree.

CONDITIONS OF EMPLOYMENT: short-term, long-term or permanent. Teaching takes place generally from 9am to 6pm and some evenings.

SALARY: on application. About 20% is deducted for tax and social security.

FACILITIES/SUPPORT: Americans must have their own work papers as no assistance is given with arranging these.

RECRUITMENT: direct application and CV. Interview.

WALL STREET INSTITUTE

www.wallstreetinstitute.fr/Cours-Anglais-Recrutement

NUMBER OF TEACHERS: fluctuating number needed for about 50 franchised branches.

PREFERENCE OF NATIONALITY: none.

QUALIFICATIONS: CELTA or equivalent TEFL qualifications.

CONDITIONS OF EMPLOYMENT: Permanent contracts offered. To work part-time hours or more if necessary.

SALARY: from €15 per hour.

RECRUITMENT: via local advertising and the internet.

GERMANY

The excellent state education system in western Germany ensures that a majority of Germans have a good grounding in English, so very little teaching is done at the beginner level, although there are still quite a lot of lower-level learners in the eastern part of Germany. If German students want exposure to a native speaker they are far more likely to enrol in a language summer course in Britain than sign up for extra tuition at a local institute. Furthermore, many secondary schools in Germany (including the former East) employ native speakers of English to assist in classrooms (programme details below). English is also offered at Volkshochschulen or adult education centres where various subsidised courses are run.

Cities in the former East Germany such as Leipzig, Dresden and Erfurt are less popular destinations for job-seeking teachers than Munich and Freiburg, and may therefore afford more opportunities, especially since provision of English in the schools lags behind that of western Germany.

The greatest demand for English in Germany continues to come from the business and professional community. Despite some economic strains, some German companies are still expanding their EFL training programmes. This means that there are many highly paid in-company positions for EFL and ESP teachers, and the agencies and consultancies which supply teachers to business clients have increased the number of native speaker teachers they recruit. Demand is greatest outside cities such as Munich, where teachers complain about a lack of work.

PROSPECTS FOR TEACHERS

Many of the companies that market in-company English courses are desperate for good teachers and trainers, though there is no shortage of inexperienced teachers looking for teaching opportunities. Any graduate with a background in economics or business who can speak German has a very good chance of finding work in a German city. A TEFL Certificate and a university degree have less clout than relevant experience, as **Kevin Boyd** found when he arrived with his brand new Cambridge Certificate in September:

> *I was persuaded by a teaching friend to go to Munich with him to try to get highly paid jobs together. As he spoke some German and had about a year's teaching experience, he got a job straightaway. Every school I went to in Munich just didn't want to know as I couldn't speak German and only had four weeks' teaching experience. After two days of this I decided to try my luck in Italy.*

Experience in business is often a more desirable qualification than an ELT qualification. The question is not so much whether you know what a past participle is but whether you know what an 'irrevocable letter of credit' or a 'bank giro' is. Many schools offer *Oberstufe*, advanced or specialist courses in, for example, Banking English, Business English, or for bilingual secretaries, etc. Full-time vocationally-oriented courses in languages for business and commerce are called *Berufsfachschule* and this is by far the most buoyant part of the market. For none of these is a Cambridge or Trinity Certificate or even a Diploma the most appropriate training. However, for language schools at the better end of the market, a TEFL qualification is regarded very favourably. There is a move among more serious schools and the regional English Language Teachers' Associations (ELTAs) to professionalise the industry and to offer and require more training in ELT skills. Qualifications such as a degree in physics may also impress and lead to scientific translation work, according to Penny, a teacher in Berlin. Very few schools are willing to consider candidates who can't speak any German. Although the 'direct method' is in use everywhere (ie total immersion in English), the pupils may expect you to be able to explain things in German. Penny was not put off so easily:

> *At the beginning they all expected me to talk to them in German. True to my CELTA training I insisted on English except in emergencies and they got used to it!*

If the school prepares its students for the London Chamber of Commerce exams (LCCI), the teacher will be expected not only to understand the syllabus but to interpret and teach it with confidence. Some schools employ the now unfashionable 'contrastive' method, again making a knowledge of conversational German essential. There is still a preference for British English, but the increasing number of course participants working for global or American companies prefer Canadian/American English.

Fees charged to companies by the most established and specialist teachers and trainers can be very high, which means few openings occur in this sought-after sector. These teachers also have high overheads and a staggeringly large percentage of their incomes will disappear in compulsory contributions (described below) and expenses. One further requirement of many employers is a driving licence, so that teachers can travel easily from one off-site assignment to another.

FINDING A JOB

Posts as English language classroom assistants are available at secondary schools throughout Germany. Applications are encouraged from students who have at least AS level, higher grade or equivalent in German. UK applicants should contact the Language Assistants Team at the British Council (10 Spring Gardens, London SW1A 2BN; ✆ 020 7389 4596; assistants@britishcouncil.org, www.britishcouncil.org/languageassistants). Language Assistants such as **Sarah Davies** (who was sent to a small town in the east) advises against agreeing to teach in a small village where conditions may be basic and the sense of isolation strong.

American students and graduates can apply to work as assistants through the Fulbright Program (administered by the Institute of International Education, 809 UN Plaza, New York, NY 10017 3580). Candidates planning to go on to become teachers of German are strongly preferred for this programme, which pays a reasonable monthly stipend in addition to free flights and insurance.

University students and graduates can often find out about possible employers from their university careers office or local English schools, as happened to **Catherine Rogers**. She wrote on spec to a number of local language schools to get some experience before working abroad and ended up being interviewed by two British contacts of a government scheme for teaching English to unemployed engineers and secretaries operating in the Dresden area of the former East Germany.

Like so many embassies, the German Embassy in London is not noted for its helpful attitude to aspiring teachers or other job-seekers. Apart from directing students to enquire about the exchange programme run by the British Council and providing addresses of the state Ministries of Education, it recommends applying to the Zentralstelle für Arbeitsvermittlung. ZAV (Villemombler Strasse 76, 53123 Bonn; ✆ +228 713 1330; fax 228 713 1035), which is the Central Placement Office of the Federal Department of Employment. Although ZAV primarily deals with German teachers who want to go abroad, they also help foreign applicants, who would need to speak a decent level of German to be able to manage filling out all the forms. Try calling 0228 713 1313 (correct department) or browse www.ba-auslandsvermittlung.de (only in German). A letter addressed to one of the 184 Arbeitsämter (job centres) around the country will be forwarded to the Zentralstelle for processing. A personal visit to an Arbeitsamt is more likely to produce results, though you are likely to be told that there are far more qualified teachers and translators than there are vacancies.

As usual, it is much more difficult to arrange a job by sending written applications and CVs from the UK than by presenting yourself in person to language school directors and training companies, CV in hand. Determination, qualifications, experience and being on the spot are often deciding factors when an employer has to choose between large numbers of similarly qualified applicants.

The best source of language school addresses is once again the *Yellow Pages* (*Gelbe Seiten*) which can be consulted online (www.gelbeseiten.de). Another way of accessing potential employers is via the local English Language Teachers Association, a branch of which can be found in most major cities. The Munich Association (MELTA) is especially vigorous and devotes one page of its website to potential employers (www.melta.de/employer.htm). There is also a forum for English teachers in Germany, which can be found at http://elt.yuku.com. Look for English-language magazines aimed at expats and you should come across some relevant advertisements. For example the English-language magazine *Munich Found* (www.munichfound.de) carries occasional TEFL vacancies.

All the major language school chains have a significant presence in Germany including Berlitz, Language Link, Inlingua (with 70 training centres), Linguarama, which specialises in language training for business in eight cities, and Wall Street Institute, which is opening about six or seven new centres a year. Rates of pay vary, however, some employers pay inexperienced teachers in the range of €13–€16 for a 45-minute lesson.

Throughout Germany, more than 2,000 adult education centres or Volkshochschulen teach the English language (among many other courses) to adults. Native speakers with teaching experience might find a role within the Deutscher Volkshochschul-Verband e.V (Obere Wilhelmstrasse 32, 53225 Bonn; ✆ /fax 228 975 69 20; www.vhs.de).

The European Language Network, formerly the International Certificate Conference (ICC), is based in Germany (Berner Heerweg 183, D-22159 Hamburg; ✆ 40 428 853 233; www.icc-europe.com)

and acts as an umbrella organisation for adult education associations such as VHS, working on teaching foreign languages in Europe, but it cannot send a list of addresses.

INTERVIEWS

Most schools and institutes in Germany cannot under normal operating circumstances hire someone unseen merely on the basis of his/her CV and photo. Applicants should arrange for a face-to-face interview and make themselves available at a moment's notice. Professional presentation is even more important for securing work in the German business world than elsewhere. Vacancies occur throughout the year since businessmen and women are just as likely to start a course in April as in September. Germans tend to be formal, so dress appropriately and be aware of your manners at an interview. Also good references (*Zeugnisse*) are essential.

A good starting place is Frankfurt am Main, known to locals as 'Bankfurt' or 'Mainhattan'. Frankfurt has the highest concentration of major banks and financial institutions in the country (nearly 400) and a correspondingly high number of private language schools. It is helpful, though not essential, to have some basic knowledge of German and business experience. In a job interview with a language school director, demonstrating a detailed knowledge of a handful of commonly used textbooks may be more important than business experience. A former teacher who spent two years teaching in dozens of banks and multinational companies recommends *Build Your Business Vocabulary* by J Flower and *New International Business English* by L Jones and R Alexander.

You can also impress a potential employer by showing some familiarity with current major German business news (bank mergers etc.). This can easily be done by scanning the English language press or listening to the BBC's *World Business Report*. Language schools are looking for teachers who can pose intelligent questions to business students about their jobs. There is a considerable demand from the business community for guidance on conducting 'small talk' in English, which is crucial in building rapport with clients and colleagues.

If asked about permits, visas, etc. (especially in the case of non-EU nationals), reassure the interviewer that you are waiting for your paperwork to be finalised.

FREELANCE TEACHING

The majority of native speakers teaching for commercial institutes are not on contracts, but are employed on a freelance contract basis (Honorarvertrag) to work for between two and 20 hours per week. Schools employing freelance teachers are not in a position to make deductions, because they cannot know a teacher's full expenses. Teachers may also work for several different schools. Freelance teachers are responsible for paying their tax, pension, insurance contributions and health insurance (a must).

ON SUCCESSFUL COMPLETION OF A TRINITY TESOL CERTIFICATE COURSE IN ENGLAND, ANN BARKETT FROM ATLANTA WENT TO MUNICH TO LOOK FOR FREELANCE WORK, BUT FOUND IT TOUGH GOING:
During the period December to March, I was putting up flyers for private and group lessons but received no response. I finally answered an advert for a private student whom I taught for a few weeks, but there just wasn't enough work or money coming in and I was tired of trying at that point.

MANY FREELANCE TEACHERS FIND THEMSELVES FOR THE FIRST TIME REQUIRED TO DESIGN AN ESP COURSE (ENGLISH FOR SPECIFIC PURPOSES), INDIVIDUALLY TAILORED TO THE NEEDS OF THEIR BUSINESSMEN AND WOMEN STUDENTS. NATHAN EDWARDS FOUND THAT HE GOT BETTER AT THIS:

Experience has shown me that such a syllabus must be flexible, open to change and short-term adjustment so as to accommodate the complex and evolving needs of students who are also full-time working professionals. Students and their employers must be given the assurance of a clearly structured course outline, but this must be partly generated by an ongoing negotiated process with all the participants. Finally don't forget that the students themselves can be a valuable source of ESP course material such as authentic English fax or email messages, business letters and company brochures from their offices.

REGULATIONS

EU nationals are free to travel to Germany to look for work, but are still subject to the labyrinthine German bureaucracy. If your German is poor or non-existent you may have to impose on the good offices of a German-speaking friend or colleague to help you since not all German civil servants speak English. Very useful guidance is available on the internet, for example on the website of the Munich English Language Teachers Association (MELTA; http://elt.yuku.com) where detailed information about the procedures has been provided by **John Sydes**, the MELTA committee member who contributed most of the information in this section. Also try www.expatica.com/de/main.html which covers topics such as taxation, pensions and insurance.

The first step is to register your address with the local authority of the district you are living in (*Einwohnermeldeamt*) or at your local registry office (*Meldestelle*), as German citizens must also do. For this you will need proof that you are living locally, eg a copy of your contract with your landlord. You should do this within 14 days of arriving in Germany.

Only after doing this is it possible to apply for a residence permit (*Niederlassungserlaubnis*) from the residence office (*Landeseinwohneramt*) or from the aliens' authority (*Ausländerbehörde*) probably located in the *Rathaus* (town hall) or the *Kreisverwaltungsreferat* (local authority's offices). You have to go to your local authority in person with a completed residence permit application form, a valid passport and a recent passport photograph.

NON-EU NATIONALS

As a non-EU citizen, you need to find a job and to obtain a work permit before you can apply for a residence permit. Once you have found a job, you can apply for a work permit. You will need a letter from your employer stating that they will employ you through the German Employment Office (*Arbeitsamt*). The form your employer has to fill out can be downloaded from most local authorities' websites.

To apply for a work permit you need a valid passport, a letter from your employer stating what the position you have been offered is and how much your salary will be and the completed application form for a work permit.

Once you have the work permit you can then apply for a residence permit. You will need:

- The completed application form
- Valid official identification or passport

- An up-to-date passport photograph
- Accommodation: proof of sufficient room for all members of the family and statement of rental costs (including heating, water and electricity) and mortgage (where applicable)
- Work permit
- Employees: proof of employment (written statement by employer or a contract)
- Self-employed applicants: statement of registration of business
- Proof of sufficient means to support yourself
- Detailed statement and proof of regular income (wages for the past three months, wages of spouse and children, if they have an income)
- Proof of health insurance in Germany
- Students: statement of matriculation and proof of sufficient means to support yourself (a written statement from your parents stating they will support you is sufficient).

According to a new law (*AufenthG*) that governs residence permits for non-EU citizens, applicants must prove that they have a secure and regular income which is next to impossible for freelance teachers. The only exceptions are if you can show that you can invest at least a million euros and/or create at least 10 new jobs and/or prove that the business will benefit the region economically.

Most of the sections of the new German immigration laws require discretionary decisions from the individual authorities, so prospects for non-EU freelancers will differ from region to region. Only a work permit which has been issued by the district/city you live in is valid.

Americans who find an employer while still in the USA might seek advice on documentation from the Carl Duisberg Society (CDS International, 871 United Nations Plaza, 15th Floor, New York, NY 10017 1814; ✆ 212 497 3500; info@cdsintl.org; www.cdsintl.org) which specialises in arranging six-month business internships.

As soon as a teacher from outside the EU obtains a promise of salaried employment, he or she should take steps to get the necessary permits. The teacher must first register his or her name and address (as for EU nationals) and then report to the Ausländersamt (foreigners' office). There they must present a contract or letter from a school claiming that they are the best candidate for the job (difficult). Further requirements may include a certificate of good conduct (notarised by the US embassy for a fee), proof of address and health insurance and also a health certificate from a German doctor. If approved, a one-year residence permit will be affixed to the passport, with a hand-written explanation that the bearer is allowed to work as an English teacher in private language schools only.

Unfortunately, Canadians, Australians, New Zealanders and other nationalities experience more difficulties since they require a residence visa which has been applied for in their country of origin. If within the three months of their tourist stay they manage to obtain a formal written offer of employment, they must return to their home country in order to apply for a working visa at the German Consulate. The application process takes up to one month and there is always a risk that the application will be refused. Successful applicants are issued with a one-year renewable work visa. Not all employers are willing to wait one month for a new teacher to begin working and may prefer to hire British or Irish teachers in the meantime.

TAX, HEALTH INSURANCE AND SOCIAL SECURITY CONTRIBUTIONS

About 95% of all the EFL teaching work in language schools and companies in Germany is offered on a freelance or self-employed basis.

The hourly rates you are offered might sound good, but freelancers and self-employed teachers have to pay 19.5% (2008) of their income after expenses and before tax into the German pension scheme. This is a compulsory contribution for all freelance teachers regardless of whether they already have a private pension scheme. Compulsory pension contributions and health insurance payments (also a must to obtain a work and residence permit) can easily make up 30–35% of a freelance or self-employed teacher's 'expenses', and then there is still income tax to think about. John Sydes mentioned above says that these 'expenses' plus rent to be paid, means that most hard-working teachers are left with very little disposable income.

Sylvia Weismiller, Director of Euro-Lingua, based in Freiburg, writes:

> *Yes, it's very complicated, and lots of grey areas, unenforced requirements, etc. One of my American teachers is having problems getting his permits renewed. They said if he paid his pension contributions, they would renew it. What those two have to do with each other is a mystery! However, I don't know any foreigners who pay it, even though it is an official policy.*

Sylvia also mentions solidarity tax (about 1%) and church tax (about 1%), which you can avoid by registering as an atheist. However, medical insurance can be painful, particularly if you're a woman:

> *Official health insurance depends on age, sex, etc. Also complicated. As a 40 year old female (women pay about double) I was paying €400 per month. It doesn't depend on your income. If you are a registered student however, you can get a much lower rate, I think €80 per month. As a student you can only work a limited number of hours, but as there aren't any tuition fees it's not a bad idea. There are also ex-pat programmes which charge, I believe, €90 per month. They are limited to 5 years. You have to have health insurance to get your residence permit extended.*

If you are a non-EU citizen you can ask the Deutsche Rentenversicherung (German pension authority) to repay the contributions you have made if you have paid into the state scheme for less than five years, ie have paid less than 60 pension contributions.

Foreigners working in Germany should obtain a *Lohnsteuerkarte* (tax card) if they are employees, or a *Steuernummer* (tax number) if they are self-employed or freelance from their local *Finanzamt* (tax office).

CONDITIONS OF WORK

You can almost guarantee that you will be teaching adults (since school children receive such a high standard of English tuition at school), and usually before or after office hours. Contracts for full-time work are usually at least a year long, often with a three-month probation period. But it is rare to be *Angestellt*, ie fully employed by a school with guaranteed minimum hours, sick pay, holiday pay, etc.

Hourly rates can be high: typically €17–€22 per lesson and double that and more for established teachers of business English. Off-site teaching hours often incur a premium of €2–€5 to compensate for travel time, or sometimes employers pay 'three hours for two'. Freelancers who earn high incomes have usually been in Germany a long time, speak excellent German and have invested in acquiring relevant specialisations, resources, materials, etc. They have built up their clientele and reputation over years and defend their patch with understandable vigour. However, rates do vary. Even established employers such as the Goethe Institute may offer only around €15 per hour for examining work.

The majority of newcomers gain their initial experience at smaller or chain language schools where the pay is much lower, sometimes on a par with cleaners, and where poor working conditions and no job security prevail. A 30-hour working week could consist of 40 45-minute lessons, which would be a very heavy workload. However, after walking into a tiny English school on her street in Berlin and asking the owner if she needed any help, **Penny**, a British widow in her 50s, has built up an enviable client base. She describes her experiences in Berlin in 2008.

> *I do two classes a week, one in the morning and one in the evenings. The morning class is made up of retired ladies who come for fun and I have difficulty keeping them speaking English. I keep reminding them that I am being paid to teach them English and not to learn German from them. We have a good relationship and go out to the cinema occasionally. The members of the evening class are slightly more serious about learning English. Some of them sometimes join in the cinema outings.*
>
> *The classroom has a table with eight chairs, which limits the size of the class. There is a black board – I would dearly love a white board – and a CD/tape player. Most of my work, however, is one-to-one teaching, which I originally obtained through the school. I charge €14 and pupils come to me. Now, many pupils are recommended by a former or current pupil, so I have several German-Russians and several art historians together with some business ladies – there is a big demand for business English.*

Penny doesn't depend on her teaching, because otherwise her standard of living would be much lower than it is. If you are depending solely on one employer for your income try to find an institute which guarantees a monthly minimum number of hours. Monthly salaries for full-time Angestellter (employees) can be from €1,200 to €2,000 gross, with the possibility of paid overtime. Considering that a one-bedroom flat in one of the big cities can easily cost €400–€600 per month, excluding bills, salaries need to be high. Quite a few schools assist with accommodation. Teachers often turn to agencies though their fees can be very steep, as much as two or three months rent plus VAT. Try answering advertisements in the local paper, or look up *Wohnung* (apartments/flats) in the phone book or try the local *Mitwohnzentralen* which charges a more reasonable fee (usually one month's rent) for finding flats, though they may charge less if you end up renting a room or flat from owners who are temporarily absent. It is customary to pay your rent directly out of a bank account, so open a basic current account (Girokonto) as early as you can. By law, the deposit you pay (usually three months rent) is put in a bank account, which should be a joint savings account in the tenant's and landlord's name, so that neither can withdraw money without the approval of the other.

LIST OF EMPLOYERS

ACADEMY OF BUSINESS COMMUNICATION (ABC)
ABC Franchise GmbH, Asperger Weg 14, 71732 Tamm
📞 7154 797 5044; fax 7154 279 8331
📧 info@abc-stuttgart.de

PREFERENCE OF NATIONALITY: none.
QUALIFICATIONS: teaching experience or business background plus university degree in any subject.
CONDITIONS OF EMPLOYMENT: freelance only.

RECRUITMENT: Interviews preferred and are occasionally available in UK.
CONTACT: Mr. Kurt Zeller, Director (kurt.zeller@abc-stuttgart.de).

ACADEMY OF EUROPEAN LANGUAGES
Prinz-Albert-Str. 73, 53113 Bonn
📞 228 24 25 840; fax 228 24 25 842
📧 info@sprachakademie-bonn.de
🖥 www.sprachakademie-bonn.de

NUMBER OF TEACHERS: 370.

PREFERENCE OF NATIONALITY: none.

QUALIFICATIONS: advanced qualifications needed and much experience.

CONDITIONS OF EMPLOYMENT: negotiable hours; open freelance contracts.

SALARY: €18 for a 45-minute lesson.

FACILITIES/SUPPORT: help can be given with accommodation and work permits if necessary.

RECRUITMENT: personal recommendations.

CONTACT: Tony Westwood, Director.

ANGLO ENGLISH SCHOOL
Dammtorstrasse 21a, 20354 Hamburg
- 40 350 9090; fax 40 350 90 950
- liz.bodemer@anglo.de
- www.anglo.de

NUMBER OF TEACHERS: 40 freelance trainers and 1 contract trainer.

PREFERENCE OF NATIONALITY: none but must be native speaker.

QUALIFICATIONS: TEFL, CELTA, DELTA, TESOL.

CONDITIONS OF EMPLOYMENT: open-ended contracts. Normal load is 10–20 90-minute classes per week, mainly mornings and evenings.

SALARY: negotiable.

FACILITIES/SUPPORT: assistance given with accommodation and to non-EU teachers in obtaining work and residence permits.

RECRUITMENT: word of mouth and indirectly through advertisements for courses.

CONTACT: Liz Bodemer, Director of Studies.

BERLIN SCHOOL OF ENGLISH
Dorotheenstrasse 90, 10117 Berlin
- 30 229 04 55; fax 30 229 04 71
- info@berlin.school-of-english.de
- www.berlin.school-of-english.de

NUMBER OF TEACHERS: 30–40.

PREFERENCE OF NATIONALITY: none (native speakers only).

QUALIFICATIONS: university degree plus TEFL/CELTA Certificate and minimum one year's experience.

CONDITIONS OF EMPLOYMENT: minimum 1 year on freelance basis. Between 16 and 30 hours per week. Focus on business English and ESP in a diverse range of professions and industries.

SALARY: Details given at interview stage.

FACILITIES/SUPPORT: in-house training provided: accredited Cambridge CELTA Centre, regular teaching workshops and seminars, internet access for teachers, school library.

CONTACT: John Wills, School Manager.

BERLITZ DEUTSCHLAND GmbH
- http://careers.berlitz.com

Job vacancies and information about working conditions are posted on the Careers Services website. Hiring is done locally by one of the 61 schools in Germany. All contact information is provided on the above website or on www.berlitz.de. At the time of writing, more than 20 Berlitz schools had vacancies but most were open to people already residing in the vicinity or having the required documents to work in Germany (visa and work permit).

NUMBER OF TEACHERS: varies depending on the size of the language centre. Over 1,000 instructors employed in Germany.

PREFERENCE OF NATIONALITY: English native speakers preferred.

QUALIFICATIONS: Teaching abilities, a professional attitude, good communication skills, willing to work a flexible schedule, and preferably have a business background.

CONDITIONS OF EMPLOYMENT: open-ended, freelance contracts. Flexible hours between 8am and 9.30pm.

FACILITIES/SUPPORT: training in the Berlitz Method given before start. Assistance with accommodation and work permits occasionally given.

RECRUITMENT: advertisements and personal referral.

CAMBRIDGE INSTITUT
Hildegardstr. 8, 80539 Munich
- 89 22 11 15; fax 89 290 47 38
- info@cambridgeinstitut.de
- www.cambridgeinstitut.de

NUMBER OF TEACHERS: approximately 15.

PREFERENCE OF NATIONALITY: British.

QUALIFICATIONS: PGCE (preferably in modern languages) or CELTA certificate.

CONDITIONS OF EMPLOYMENT: 11-month contracts, renewable for a further 11 months. 29 hours per week. Lessons 9am–11.40am and 5.30pm–9.15pm.

SALARY: €2,046 per month less social security payment.

FACILITIES/SUPPORT: assistance with accommodation. Induction course and ongoing workshops.

RECRUITMENT: interview in UK or Munich essential.

CONTACT: Philip Moore, Principal.

CONTEXT SPRACHEN – UND MEDIENDIENSTE GmbH

Elisenstr. 4–10, 50667 Cologne

221 925 456 12; fax 221 925 456 16

teaching@contextinc.com

www.contextinc.com

NUMBER OF TEACHERS: 15–20.

PREFERENCE OF NATIONALITY: none.

QUALIFICATIONS: must be native speakers with academic education and experience.

CONDITIONS OF EMPLOYMENT: freelance basis. Hours vary between 8am and 8pm, Monday to Friday.

SALARY: varies according to qualifications/experience and degree of difficulty of class taught.

FACILITIES/SUPPORT: accommodation and visas are responsibility of teachers. Some training given.

RECRUITMENT: newspaper advertisements, followed by local interviews.

CONTACT: Patrick O'Sullivan, Project Manager.

DESK

Blumenstr. 1, 80331 Munich

89 26 33 34; fax 89 260 56 00

info@desk.sprachkurse.de

www.desk-sprachkurse.de

NUMBER OF TEACHERS: 30 (70 teachers in total).

PREFERENCE OF NATIONALITY: none.

QUALIFICATIONS: degree. Experience teaching English as a foreign language to adults.

CONDITIONS OF EMPLOYMENT: duration of contract to suit. One of the few schools in Munich offering a full contract, rather than freelance conditions. Teaching hours mainly early mornings and evenings.

SALARY: €22 per 45-minute lesson.

FACILITIES/SUPPORT: no help with accommodation.

RECRUITMENT: CV and interview.

CONTACT: Erwin Schmidt-Achert, Owner.

DIE NEUE SCHULE

Gieselerstrasse 30a, D-10713 Berlin

30 873 03 73; fax 30 873 86 13

info@neueschule.de

www.neueschule.de

NUMBER OF TEACHERS: 80–110.

PREFERENCE OF NATIONALITY: British, American, Irish, Canadian.

QUALIFICATIONS: Cambridge or TEFL Certificate and teaching experience needed. Mostly adults (ages 25–40) in small groups of no more than 8.

CONDITIONS OF EMPLOYMENT: open-ended freelance contracts and some employed teachers. Variable hours in the daytime (9am–3pm) and evenings (6pm–9.15pm).

SALARY: approx. €19 per hour.

FACILITIES/SUPPORT: help with accommodation.

RECRUITMENT: personal interview necessary, application link on website.

ENGLISH STUDIO

Killanstrasse 121, D-90425 Nürnberg. Also branches in Regensburg and Munich.

911 599073; fax 911 592872

jobs@englishstudio.de

www.englishstudio.de

NUMBER OF TEACHERS: 15–20.

PREFERENCE OF NATIONALITY: native speakers.

QUALIFICATIONS: minimum teaching/training qualification eg PGCE, CELTA/Trinity, Tefl/TESOL Certificate. Relevant business experience and commercial/industrial training experience will also be considered.

CONDITIONS OF EMPLOYMENT: open-ended contract for freelancers; contract teachers receive a 2-year contract after a 3- or 6-month trial. 24 contact hours per week at any time between 7.30am and 8pm.

SALARY: Minimum starting salary €1,500 gross per month. Salaries can be much higher for teachers with relevant qualifications and experience.

FACILITIES/SUPPORT: confirmation of employment can be provided for non-EU staff. May be able to advise on accommodation.

RECRUITMENT: word of mouth. Interviews essential.

CONTACT: Thomas Hintze (thintze@englishstudio.de).

EURO FREMDSPRACHENSCHULE

Esplanade 36, 85049 Ingolstadt

841 17001; fax 841 17193

sw@euro-ingolstadt.de

State-recognised vocational language college.

NUMBER OF TEACHERS: 25.

PREFERENCE OF NATIONALITY: British, American, Canadian.

QUALIFICATIONS: at least a BA (including German studies). PGCE preferred. At least 3 years' experience.

CONDITIONS OF EMPLOYMENT: permanent contracts. Part-time work possible. 30 hours per week.

SALARY: based on German state salary scale.

FACILITIES/SUPPORT: assistance given with accommodation and work permits.

RECRUITMENT: interview in Ingolstadt necessary.

CONTACT: Stuart Wheeler.

EURO-LINGUA

Ricarda-Huch-Str. 10, 79114 Freiburg

📞 179 693 1898

📧 info@euro-lingua.de

🖥 www.euro-lingua.de

NUMBER OF TEACHERS: 13.

PREFERENCE OF NATIONALITY: none, but natives speakers preferred.

QUALIFICATIONS: university degree, teaching experience, foreign language ability, preferably TOEFL or teacher training.

CONDITIONS OF EMPLOYMENT: freelance.

SALARY: €15 per 45-minute lesson.

FACILITIES/SUPPORT: advice given on local accommodation agencies. Non-EU teachers applying for a work permit outside Germany can be supplied with statement of projected income etc. Support available as needed for lesson planning, books and other materials.

RECRUITMENT: word of mouth, local advertisements, contact with schools abroad.

CONTACT: Sylvia Weismiller, Director.

GERMAN AMERICAN INSTITUTE TUEBINGEN

Karlstrasse 3, 72072 Tübingen

📞 07071 795 260; fax 07071 7952626

📧 mail@dai-tuebingen.de

🖥 www.dai-tuebingen.de

NUMBER OF TEACHERS: 15.

PREFERENCE OF NATIONALITY: American.

QUALIFICATIONS: BA or MA minimum.

CONDITIONS OF EMPLOYMENT: freelance positions only. To work 3–9 hours per week, mostly teaching adult students.

SALARY: hourly wage.

RECRUITMENT: local interview required.

CONTACT: Melinda Markus-Leal, Language Program

Co-ordinator (07071 795 2614; Melinda.markus@dai-tuebingen.de).

HAMBURG SCHOOL OF ENGLISH

Main Office: Eppend. Landstr. 93, 20249 Hamburg

📞 40 480 21 19; fax 40 460 69 076

📧 info@hamburg.school-of-english.de

🖥 www.hamburg-school-of-english.de

Teacher Training Centre: Isekai 19, 20249 Hamburg

📞 +40 480 21 19; fax 40 432 61687

📧 celta@hamburg.school-of-english.de

🖥 www.hamburg-school-of-english.de

NUMBER OF TEACHERS: 60–70.

PREFERENCE OF NATIONALITY: British.

QUALIFICATIONS: university degree plus TEFL Certificate. Preferably minimum 1 year's experience.

CONDITIONS OF EMPLOYMENT: minimum 1 year on freelance basis. Between 16 and 30 hours per week. 2-year full-time contracts also available.

SALARY: approx. €26–€41 for 90-minute teaching session.

FACILITIES/SUPPORT: assistance given with finding accommodation and obtaining work permits. CELTA courses (Certificate in Teaching Business English) and teacher development workshops offered on-site.

RECRUITMENT: via local or telephone interviews.

HARDIE INTERNATIONAL LANGUAGE TRAINING & COACHING

Quer Str. 4, 44139 Dortmund

📞 +231 779300; fax 231 797 9307

📧 info@hardie-iltc.com

🖥 www.hardie-iltc.com

NUMBER OF TEACHERS: 15.

PREFERENCE OF NATIONALITY: none.

QUALIFICATIONS: highest possible. Usually branch specialists are retrained as coaches, consultants or trainers.

CONDITIONS OF EMPLOYMENT: open freelance contracts. Lessons take place 7 days a week between 7am and 10pm.

SALARY: above average (depending on qualifications and experience).

FACILITIES/SUPPORT: accommodation can be provided or at least advice given.

RECRUITMENT: through partner organisations. Interviews compulsory and sometimes carried out in UK or by telephone.

CONTACT: James Hardie, Owner.

ICC SPRACHINSTITUT

Am Nordplatz 9, 04105 Leipzig

📞 +341 550 36 73; fax 341 550 36 74

✉ info@icc-sprachinstitut.de

🖥 www.icc-sprachinstitut.de

Also premises in Chemnitz: An der Markthalle 3, 09111 Chemnitz (📞 371 520 21 92)

NUMBER OF TEACHERS: 35.

PREFERENCE OF NATIONALITY: none.

QUALIFICATIONS: university degree, CELTA and/or 6 months TEFL experience.

CONDITIONS OF EMPLOYMENT: fixed term or freelance. Teaching in-company business courses, intensive and evening courses.

SALARY: €13–€16 per 45-minute lesson.

FACILITIES/SUPPORT: assistance with accommodation and work permits (if necessary). Induction and regular training including TEB. Good career prospects throughout the ASSET group.

RECRUITMENT: walk-ins mainly though email applications welcome. Local interview essential.

CONTACT: James Parsons, Director.

INLINGUA SPRACHSCHULE HANNOVER

Andreaestrasse 3, Ecke Schillerstrasse, D-30159 Hannover

📞 +511 324580; fax 511 363 2931

✉ info@inlingua-hannover.de

🖥 www.inlingua-Hannover.de

NUMBER OF TEACHERS: 15.

PREFERENCE OF NATIONALITY: English, American, Canadian native speakers.

QUALIFICATIONS: minimum 1 year TEFL experience.

CONDITIONS OF EMPLOYMENT: 12 months minimum. Average at least 25 school lessons (45 minutes each) per week.

SALARY: approx. €15 per lesson.

FACILITIES/SUPPORT: assistance finding accommodation.

RECRUITMENT: newspaper advertisements and internet.

INTERACT!

Die Sprachexperten, Rissener Strasse 58, 22880 Wedel/Hamburg

📞 +4103 702468; fax 4103 702469

also Achter de Weiden 10, 22869 Hamburg-Schenefeld

📞 +40 8309 9009

✉ info@interact-experts.com

NUMBER OF TEACHERS: 42.

PREFERENCE OF NATIONALITY: none.

QUALIFICATIONS: TEFL plus experience, business background.

CONDITIONS OF EMPLOYMENT: minimum 1-year contracts. Various hours Monday to Friday mornings and evenings.

SALARY: approx. €15–€18 per hour.

FACILITIES/SUPPORT: assistance given with accommodation. Training. Access to internet/ materials.

RECRUITMENT: via advertisements, agencies, internet and word of mouth.

LINGUA FRANCA

Mauer Strasse 77, 10117 Berlin

📞 +30 8639 8080; fax 30 8639 8082

✉ info@lingua-franca.de

🖥 www.lingua-franca.de

NUMBER OF TEACHERS: 50.

PREFERENCE OF NATIONALITY: none.

QUALIFICATIONS: university degree plus TEFL experience and/or certificate. Experience in ESP preferred.

CONDITIONS OF EMPLOYMENT: freelance only. Can generally give good teachers as many lesson hours as they want.

FACILITIES/SUPPORT: no help with accommodation. Will write the necessary letter to the employment office to support work permit application. In-house training available.

RECRUITMENT: local interviews.

CONTACT: Charles Arrigo, Director.

LINGUARAMA SPRACHENINSTITUT DEUTSCHLAND

Sendlinger-Tor-Platz 7, 80336 Munich

📞 +89 200 009 3 0; fax 89 200 009 333

✉ munich@linguarama.com

🖥 www.linguarama.com

NUMBER OF TEACHERS: from 25 in the smaller Linguarama schools to 70 in the larger ones; Linguarama schools located in Berlin, Cologne, Düsseldorf, Frankfurt, Hamburg, Leipzig, Munich and Stuttgart with significant in-company work also in Bonn.

PREFERENCE OF NATIONALITY: native speakers only who must have valid working papers for the EU.

QUALIFICATIONS: minimum university degree or equivalent and a basic TEFL qualification (eg CELTA). Experience of teaching business English is preferred but at least teachers should have a keen interest in business.

CONDITIONS OF EMPLOYMENT: mixture of contract and freelance teachers. Freelance teachers work variable hours, usually early mornings and evenings. Contract teachers usually contracted for 1 year, extendable to 2 years, but occasionally shorter contracts available. 23 days paid holiday per 12-month contract.

SALARY: depends on experience.

FACILITIES/SUPPORT: contract teachers are given an initial 2-week accommodation entitlement and assistance with finding permanent accommodation. Travel expenses to the city are paid from the UK if recruitment is through head office. Help is given with obtaining a residence permit, etc. All teachers are given an induction course and paid training is held monthly.

RECRUITMENT: usually local interviews for freelance teachers. Contract staff are sometimes recruited locally or via Linguarama Group Personnel Department, 1 Elm Court, Arden Street, Stratford-upon-Avon CV37 6PA (see introductory chapter Finding a Job).

CONTACT: Danny Coughlan, Personnel Manager, Linguarama; Jason White, Centre Manager, Linguarama Munich.

PROFESSIONAL ENGLISH TRAINING (PET–Sprachen)
Wittelsbacherstr 13, 80469 Munich
+89 202 386 55; fax 89 202 386 54
info@pet-sprachen.de
www.pet-sprachen.de

NUMBER OF TEACHERS: 50 freelancers.

PREFERENCE OF NATIONALITY: none.

QUALIFICATIONS: TEFL qualification and/or degree preferable, as are business experience and friendly, outgoing disposition.

CONDITIONS OF EMPLOYMENT: travelling to companies to hold in-company courses on a freelance basis.

SALARY: €21 per teaching unit (45 minutes) plus travel.

FACILITIES/SUPPORT: no assistance with accommodation. Materials support given. Teachers' workshops held.

RECRUITMENT: direct applications. Local interviews necessary.

CONTACT: paul.bacon@pet-sprachen.de

SPRACHZENTRUM SUD
Marktplatz 20, 83607 Holzkirchen
+8024 1733; fax 8024 91782
info@sprachzentrum-sued.de
www.sprachzentrum-sued.de

NUMBER OF TEACHERS: 15.

PREFERENCE OF NATIONALITY: British, American, Australian.

QUALIFICATIONS: Teaching certificate (eg CELTA, DELTA) or university degree. Teaching experience needed especially in Business English.

CONDITIONS OF EMPLOYMENT: freelance, employment possible after 1 year successful freelance.

SALARY: between €15 and €25 per hour, depending on the qualification and contract.

RECRUITMENT: telephone interviews possible. Candidates in Europe will be invited to interview and to teach practice lesson with volunteer students.

CONTACT: Dr. Karin Wiebalck-Zahn, Managing Director.

STEVENS ENGLISH TRAINING
Rüttenscheiderstr. 68, 45130 Essen
+201 8770770; fax 201 793783
office@stevens-english.de
Also Kaiser-Wilhelm-Ring 14 16, 50672 Cologne; Westenhellweg 112, 44137 Dortmund; Am Wehrhahn 67, 40211 Dusseldorf; Petersilienstrasse 1–3, 38100 Braunschweig, Olferstrasse 6, 48153 Münster.

NUMBER OF TEACHERS: approx 80 full and part-time.

PREFERENCE OF NATIONALITY: native speakers of English.

QUALIFICATIONS: TEFL Certificate or business experience.

CONDITIONS OF EMPLOYMENT: 2-year contracts. Hours between 7.30am and 8.45pm Monday to Friday. 80% of teaching is in-company with high element of ESP.

SALARY: paid on points system per 45-minute session.

FACILITIES/SUPPORT: furnished flats available near the school for trainers recruited from the UK. Extensive workshop training programme for trainers. Opportunity to take the LCCI exam 'Further Certificate in Teaching Business English' (FTBE). Extensive library of teaching materials.

RECRUITMENT: interviews essential and regularly held in Essen. Candidates receive €100 towards travel expenses and one night accommodation provided.

CONTACTS: Sigrid and Michael Stevens, Managing Directors.

VINCE NET ENGLISH
Ledererstrasse 9, 84428 Buchbach
+8086 1645; fax 8086 1581
John@VinceNetEnglish.de
www.VinceNetEnglish.de

NUMBER OF TEACHERS: 17 freelancers.

PREFERENCE OF NATIONALITY: none, but must be English native speaker.

QUALIFICATIONS: prefer teaching certificate and degree. Experience of teaching EFL and of business English essential. Candidate must have taught and/or worked in a business environment.

CONDITIONS OF EMPLOYMENT: teachers contracted to teach between 26 and 30 90-minute lessons per school year.

SALARY: €52–€62 per 90-minute lesson plus travel.

RECRUITMENT: direct application, personal recommendation or via adult education centres. Interviews essential.

CONTACT: John Vince, Commercial Director.

WALL STREET INSTITUTE (WSI)
ZHd. Matthew Duffy, Rosental 5, 80331 Munich
℮ +89 552 989 0; fax 89 552 989 10
teach@wallstreetinstitute.de
www.wallstreetinstitute.de

NUMBER OF TEACHERS: approximately 100, at 24 locations.

PREFERENCE OF NATIONALITY: none, but it is easier to employ EU nationals or those who have citizenship due to visa restrictions.

QUALIFICATIONS: teachers must be native speakers with CELTA or equivalent TEFL qualification, experience in teaching English as a second language, ability to work within an existing, structured teaching method, excellent organisational and interpersonal skills, and be motivated, energetic and dedicated.

CONDITIONS OF EMPLOYMENT: contracts of at least 1 year, usually unlimited. Between 10 hours per week and 25 hours per week, plus paid overtime (occasionally 30 hour contracts are offered).

SALARY: depends on the city. There is also the opportunity to earn bonuses and be paid commission.

FACILITIES/SUPPORT: can help teachers find accommodation through informing them about various, reputable websites and organisations when they arrive in the city of employment. Also, if the applicant does not speak German, WSI may accompany them to the Immigration office and help them register as a citizen and obtain their work permit. WSI gives a letter of intent to the employment authorities. Once the employment authorities have given their permission, the applicant receives a contract.

CONTACT: Carolyn Hutchison.

GREECE

The ELT industry in Greece is huge. Thousands of private language schools (frontisteria) continue to supplement the language education of most children aged 6–16. A few years ago the state school system lowered the age when students began to learn English so parents want very young children to 'get ahead of the game' and have a good grounding in English before they start their state school lessons. An increasing number of older students are also enrolling, because many jobs require proof of advanced attainment in English, not just the basic secondary school level.

Greek language schools are often run by local entrepreneurs without much more than basic English themselves and can be housed in buildings which were not purpose-built as schools. Secondary school pupils in Greece are obliged to study 15 subjects, all of which they must pass before being allowed to proceed to the next year. In most areas the teaching of English in state schools is considered inadequate so that the vast majority of pupils also attend frontisteria, and it is not uncommon for a 15-year-old to have two or three hours of lessons a day (in other subjects as well as English) in one or more private establishments to supplement the state schooling. Not surprisingly, the students are not always brimming over with enthusiasm; in fact, quite often they are not even awake.

English language teaching in Greece has been described as an exam industry, and there is fierce competition among the international exam bodies. At one time Cambridge First Certificate and Cambridge Proficiency examinations ruled the roost, only to be replaced a few years ago by University of Michigan exams. Recently, there has been intense competition between the London Tests of English and the University of Central Lancashire exams, eating into Michigan's share of the market. These are administered by two rival associations of language schools, PALSO and EUROPALSO. A newcomer has just arrived on the scene in Greece, the City and Guilds, which is marketing its exams very aggressively. The terminology for exam levels can be confusing. Some teachers and students still refer to the exams by exam board names such as First Certificate and Proficiency (Cambridge), Michigan and Michigan Proficiency, Edexcel, etc. A new structure for language learning and assessment has been laid down by the EU and is gradually gaining acceptance. B2 denotes someone who can function in English as an 'Independent User' and C2 denotes the highest level 'Mastery' of English.

PROSPECTS FOR TEACHERS

The employment situation for teachers is still booming with a number of agencies busily recruiting EFL teachers throughout the summer for the following academic year. Prospects for EU nationals with a university degree are good, particularly outside Athens. A fairly recent development is that ESP classes are also booming in Greece and institutions organising company classes are always on the lookout for professional, highly trained teachers.

Be aware that an increasing number of *frontisteria* are looking for teaching qualifications such as a Cambridge or Trinity Certificate, although few school employers insist on experience. The government stipulates that in order to obtain a teacher's licence, English teachers must have at least a BA in English language and literature or education, so that all but the most dodgy schools will expect to see a university certificate. Having a TEFL qualification, as always, will make the job hunt easier. Given the size of the ELT market in Greece, it is surprising that so few training centres offer the CELTA or the Trinity TESOL Certificate in Greece. The main teacher training organisations in Greece tend to concentrate on training Greek speakers to become English teachers.

Anglo-Hellenic: PO Box 263, 201 00 Corinth (✆ +27410 53511; fax 27410 85579; train@ anglo-hellenic.com; www. anglo-hellenic.com). Via Lingua TEFL Certificate course (www .teflcorinth.com) held monthly (see Directory of Training Courses).

CELT: 77 Akademias St, 10678 Athens (✆ +210 330 2406/201 330 1455; fax 210 330 1202; info@celt.edu.gr; www.celt.edu.gr). Website has limited Teacher Recruitment information.

Linguistic Lab: PO Box 12, 20400 Xylokastro, Corinth (✆ +/fax 27430 22135; info@linguis- ticlab.com; www.linguisticlab.com/tesol-certification-course.html). Courses run by Global TESOL (www.globaltesol.com) offered monthly.

Study Space: 86 Tsimiski St, 54622 Thessaloniki (fax 2310 269697; studyspa@otenet.gr; www.studyspace.gr). Specialises in CELTYL because the local market mainly comprises 7–16-year-olds but also offers CELTA package which includes a promise to graduates of employment in their network of 200 schools.

Americans and other non-EU nationals will find it difficult to find a school willing to hire them, purely because of immigration difficulties. The government can impose stiff penalties on employers who break the rules, and few, at least in the major cities, will risk it, as **Tim Leffel** found out:

> *We had planned on teaching in Greece, but as Americans, we were not exactly welcomed with open arms in Athens; they told us to try the countryside.*

Tim moved on to Turkey instead. Another complicating factor is the high number of Greek emigrés to North America and Australia who have returned (or whose children have returned) to Greece. In many cases, they are virtually native speakers of English but are favoured because of their ancestry. Of course there will always be schools prepared to hire Americans and others if well qualified, such as the Hellenic American Union which has one of the largest programmes in adult EFL in Athens.

One reason why EU nationals with basic qualifications can expect to land a job in Greece is that wages are not high enough to attract a great many highly qualified EFL teachers. Greece tends to be a country where people get their first English teaching job for the experience and then move to more lucrative countries. Also, few schools place any emphasis on staff development or provide in-house training, so serious teachers tend to move on quickly. The majority of advertised jobs are in towns and cities in mainland Greece. Athens has such a large expatriate community that most of the large central schools at the elite end of the market are able to hire well qualified staff locally. But the competition will not be so keen in Edessa, Larissa, Preveza or any of numerous towns of which the tourist to Greece is unlikely to have heard.

FINDING A JOB

IN ADVANCE

Unless you elect to register with one of the recruitment agencies (that deal primarily with Certificate-qualified teachers), it may not be worthwhile trying to fix up a job in advance, since so much in Greece is accomplished by word of mouth. Getting a list of language schools from outside Greece is not easy. A considerable proportion of *frontisteria* belong to the Pan-Hellenic Federation of Language School Owners (PALSO Headquarters, 2 Lykavitou St & Akademias St, 106 71 Kolonaki, Athens; ✆ +210 364 0792). There are local branches of PALSO all over Greece though they are unlikely to offer much help to job-seeking teachers until they are on-the-spot. Note that the Athens association of language school owners has recently split from PALSO and now calls itself EUROPALSO (Akademias 98–100, Athens 10677; ✆ 210 3830 752; www.europalso.gr). EUROPALSO consists of more than 2,500 schools in the Athens area and they keep a file of applications submitted by teachers who visit in person and school owners often look for teaching staff there. PALSO-Chania has a separate web presence at www.palso-chania.gr (Partheniou Kelaidi 72, Chania 73100; ✆ 2810 92622) while the Heraklion branch is at www.palsoher.gr and only in Greek (✆ 2810 322002).

An alternative association of language schools is QLS (Quality in Language Services) which aspires to be a Panhellenic Association of Accredited Language Schools. Overseeing its 17 member schools, the main office is in Volos (Aristotelous 53, Volos 38333; ✆ /fax 24210 37171; qls@vol .forthnet.gr; www.qls.gr) with secondary offices in Athens (Evrinomis 73, Zografou, Athens 15771) and Thessaloniki (Tsimiski 104, Thessaloniki 54622). The prestigious European language school association EAQUALS has nine accredited member schools in Greece (see www.eaquals.org/schools/ members_printable.asp).

The internet is not as widely used in Greece as in some other countries but increasingly Greek vacancies are being advertised on the main ELT websites. Some of the main Greek internet service providers maintain lists of language schools; try http://dir.forthnet.gr/1651–0-en.html and the Hellenic search engine www.robby.gr for language schools and Foreign Language education listings in English. If you can transliterate from the Greek alphabet, have a look at www.schools.gr.

Most schools do their hiring for the following academic year between March and June. Obviously the major chains of schools offer the most opportunities, and it is worth sending your CV in the spring to organisations like the Stratigakis Group with about a hundred schools in northern Greece (✆ 2310 264263; www.stratigakis.gr). Another major group is The Scholars Group (www.the-scholars.gr).

Fortunately there are several active recruitment agencies which specialise in Greece with offices in Greece and/or Britain. These recruitment agencies are looking for people with at least a BA and normally a TEFL qualification and/or experience (depending on the client school's requirements). All client employers provide accommodation. The following undertake to match teachers (with EU nationality) with frontisteria and do not charge teachers a fee: Anglo-Hellenic Teacher Recruitment, Cambridge Teachers Recruitment and Hyphen (see list of organisations for more information). When discussing your future post with an agency, don't be lulled into a false sense of security. It is wise to check contractual details for yourself and verify verbal promises. Check to see whether you are entitled to any compensation if the employer breaks the contract and similarly whether you will have to compensate the school if you leave early. Find out if there will be any other native speaker teachers in the area, and ask about the possibility of contacting your predecessor in the job.

ON THE SPOT

So many *frontisteria* rely on agents to find teachers for them, that it can be difficult to walk into a job. After gaining a lot of on-the-ground experience of Greece, **Jane McNally** from County Derry in Ireland concluded that knocking on school doors can be discouraging, a view corroborated by **Jain Cook**:

> *There do not seem to be as many vacancies for teachers as there used to be in the Peloponnese. I have interviewed about 15 British teachers in the past few weeks, all of whom have stressed the difficulty of finding work in this area. They were all personable, smartly dressed, well qualified and experienced, but as yet have received no definite job offers.*

The majority of schools have filled all their vacancies by June, so September is usually too late for prospective teachers to be looking for work. One of the best times to look is January. Greece is far less attractive in mid-winter than in summer, and many foreign teachers do not return to their posts after Christmas. Finding work in the summer is virtually impossible; most English language summer courses in resorts or on the islands are staffed by people who have taught for an academic year. Marisa Constantinides of CELT Athens suggests trying the islands of Naxos and Syros, or any of the larger islands for on-the-spot summer vacancies.

Will Brady is one of the co-founders of Atlantis Books on the island of Santorini (www.atlantis-books.org). He picked up a teaching job on the island:

> *It was just an opportunistic thing. I knew that I needed to earn some money so having recently got a TEFL qualification I thought I'd try my hand at a bit of TEFL teaching. I wondered around Fira and asked if there were any language schools, discovered that I was facing one, and walked in. I met a very strange man, who was the manager (the owner didn't speak English). This guy had studied psychology in England. I think he took a liking to me because I was English. I asked if I could do some work for them and he more or less told me straight away that I could, but kept things on very vague terms. Whilst I was back in England to arrange a few things, I negotiated with him over the phone. Then when I got back to the island I just went in and started. There was no interview whatsoever.*

Although Will had enquired about working legally, he concluded that advice from the Greek Embassy in London, 'seemed to lead to no certain conclusions about what was the correct protocol.' He ended up working under the table, an arrangement that suited both himself and the school owner, and was paid a wage equivalent to the British minimum. Work was part-time, teaching (or assisting in the classroom) about two to three hours a day, three to four times a week. The language school had never hired a native speaker before and all the Greek teachers would defer to Will on grammatical points, something he found 'quite strange,' because he was considerably younger.

Cassandra Filio worked in Ioannina, in the north western part of Greece, where the school and officials were not very concerned with her (non-legal) work status: 'Had I tried to get a work permit there would have been quite a lot of wait, paperwork and headaches.' However, despite not having a contract that was legally binding (a risk), Cassandra did have an agreement that she would teach for a year and re-evaluate the situation towards the end of the year. Her employer found and paid for her apartment, a block away from the school in a nice part of town, and the wages were enough to live on, but did not stretch to foreign travel.

Although **Jamie Masters** knew that October was not prime time for job-hunting, that is when he arrived in Heraklion to look for work:

> *I advertised (in Greek) in the Cretan newspapers, no joy. I lowered my sights and started knocking on doors of frontisteria. I was put onto some guy who ran an English-language bookshop and went to see him. Turned out he was a lynch-pin in the frontisterion business and in fact I got my first job through him. Simultaneously I went to the PALSO office and was given a list of schools which were looking for people. The list, it turned out, was pretty much out of date. But I had insisted on leaving my name with them (they certainly didn't offer) and that's how I found my second job.*

Once you arrange an interview, be sure to dress well and to amass as many educational diplomas as you can. This will create the right aura of respectability in which to impress the potential employer with your conscientiousness and amiability.

When you elicit interest from a language school owner or a family, take your time over agreeing terms. Greece is not a country in which it pays to rush, and negotiations can be carried out in a leisurely and civilised fashion. On the other hand, do not come to an agreement with an employer without clarifying wages and schedules precisely. Make sure you read your contract very carefully so that you are familiar with what you should be entitled to.

FREELANCE TEACHING

Private lessons are not as easy to find as they were even two or three years ago. Established EFL teachers might now have three or four private pupils when before they had as many as 15. This is partly because of the falling birth rate in Greece but also because the middle classes have less disposable income and prefer to send their children to frontisteria. If you are lucky enough to arrange to tutor privately, the going rate is about €25 per hour for B2 and €30 per hour for C2, probably more in Athens.

Private tutoring jobs seem to materialise either from the language schools (whose directors seldom seem to mind their teachers earning on the side) or from conversations in a *kafeneion* (café). Trading English lessons for board and lodging is a common form of freelance teaching in Athens and elsewhere. Sometimes contracted teachers are offered free accommodation in exchange for tutoring children. In Athens, the rich suburbs of Kifissia and Politia are full of families who can afford to provide private English lessons for their offspring. The suburbs of Pangrati and Filothei are also well-heeled as is the more central suburb of Kolonaki. It is also possible to start up private classes for children, provided you have decent accommodation in a prosperous residential area, though this will normally be too expensive if your only source of income is private teaching. **Leah White** solved her accommodation problem in Athens by approaching managers of blocks of flats to see whether they could arrange for her to have a rent-free flat in exchange for teaching their children.

REGULATIONS

English teachers must first obtain a teacher's licence and then a residence permit (which is also a work permit) and the bureaucratic procedures involved can be stressful, even with a supportive employer. The two documents needed for a teacher's licence used to be a health certificate and a degree certificate. The Ministry of Education considers a BA or higher degree in English literature or a degree in Education a sufficient qualification, though a TEFL Certificate strengthens your application of course. You must have your degree certificate officially translated and notarised, either before you leave home (which is usually cheaper) or in Greece (ask the British Council for advice). The health certificate can be obtained only in Greece, and involves a chest X-ray and in some cases a blood or stool test.

However, it's soon to become law that native speakers of English will have to take a Greek proficiency exam to prove they are fluent in Greek and know something of Greek history and culture. The Catch 22 to this is that teachers have to take the exam before they get a job and cannot apply for a Teacher's Licence until they prove they have the Proficiency Certificate. If teachers work illegally, they will not be paying IKA (national health insurance) so will not be eligible for unemployment benefits, bonuses, pension, etc. There is a movement afoot to try to scupper the whole idea, although the Greek Embassy in London stipulates on their website that to acquire a permit to teach you need a validated university degree and a certificate of proficiency in Greek. Teachers are advised to contact the Hellenic Ministry of Education/Department of Private Education which issues the permit (Mitropoleos 15, Athens 101 85; © 210 3231656; www.ypepth.gr). London Embassy staff are underinformed about this change in requirements. Harry J Nikolaides, School Director of Lord Byron School, says that in practice, a teacher with a degree can enrol in a Greek language course and ask for a certificate, whereupon he/she can be declared an assistant or trainee teacher.

ENGLISH SPEAKERS OF GREEK ANCESTRY FIND IT MUCH EASIER TO OBTAIN A TEACHER'S LICENCE IN GREECE AND HAVE GENERALLY MORE ATTRACTIVE PROSPECTS, AS EXPLAINED BY JAIN COOK:

Australian, Canadian, South African and American Greeks are classed as native speakers because English is their first language, but most have a Greek passport which makes it all much simpler for them. As Director of Studies at the Koutsantonis School, I have interviewed dozens of such teachers. Although many have no teaching experience or qualifications, they have already obtained a teacher's licence and therefore school owners are more than willing to consider them.

The paperwork is supposed to be getting simpler, but I haven't seen any signs of it myself. I've been here 11 years now, and have only recently been given a five-year residence permit. Until now I have been doing all the running around for the paperwork every year.

When the teacher's licence arrives from Athens, the teacher must take it along with his or her pass-port, photos and a lot of patience to the police station to apply for a residence permit, which should come through in about a month. The health certificate and residence permit must be renewed an-nually, though if you protest loudly enough you can usually get away with just having a chest X-ray. You will however have to take your IKA book (see below) to renew your residence permit and a form from your employer which shows the length of your term of employment. The first residence permit is normally valid for just six months, subsequent ones for one to three years. Keep photocopies of all forms.

Frontisteria usually tend to leave all the bureaucratic legwork to the teachers. Employers will take on the necessary transactions only if they are convinced that a candidate will be an asset to their school. Non-EU teachers often find that the Ministry of Education delays and even turns down their applications for a teacher's licence. Officially they must obtain a letter of hire from a language school which must be sent to an address outside Greece. The teacher takes the letter to the nearest Greek consulate and applies for a work permit; the procedures take at least two months.

It is mandatory for Greek employers to register employees with the Greek national health insur-ance scheme (IKA) and pay employer contributions which amount to 27.97% of the salary; the employee's contribution is 16% and should be deducted from the salary at source. Be sure to find out ahead of time whether the salary quoted is before or after the IKA deduction. You should go with your employer to the local IKA office in order to apply for an IKA book 60 days after starting to pay contributions; thereafter you are entitled to free medical treatment and reduced cost prescriptions on production of the book. Most IKA payments are now done online and further information regarding the Greek Social Insurance scheme can be found at www.ika.gr. Once you have paid IKA and tax for two consecutive years, you are entitled to unemployment benefit; some teachers have been known to claim over the summer when they are out of the country, though the authorities may clamp down on this. Very few teachers declare their private earnings for tax purposes. Income tax is paid annually and it is up to the teacher to register with the tax officer.

Detailed information for US citizens is available from the US Consular Services in Athens (http://athens.usembassy.gov). Information and permits are available from the Police Aliens Bureau; the suburban Athens one is located at Petrou Ralli 24, Tavros (℃ 210 340 5829), and the central Ath-ens one is at Mezonos 45 near the Metaxourgio metro station (℃ 210 523 4466); both are open 8am–2pm.

CONDITIONS OF WORK

Standards vary enormously among *frontisteria*. Although there is specific legislation which is meant to regulate the operation of language schools, this is seldom enforced. The way to recognise a good *frontisterion* is by its exam results and by its ability to retain staff.

In general the large chains are better, probably for no other reason than that they have a longer history of employing native English speakers. You also have some back-up if you have been hired through a mediating agency. Some of the small one-man or one-woman schools are cowboy outfits run by barely qualified entrepreneurs who have had little contact with the English language; their teaching techniques involve shouting (usually in Greek) at their students and getting them to recite English irregular verbs parrot fashion. In fact this kind of school is on the decline, helped by the fact that foreigners are now allowed to run language schools in Greece, which has had the effect of raising standards.

The minimum hourly rate of pay for 2007–2008 is €8.81 gross, minus 15.89% national insurance contribution, leaving a net balance of €7.41, though this increases if the teacher is married, has children, a master's degree, and for each year of experience teaching. It can be a combination of all or some of these, putting the minimum hourly rate up to €12 per hour. No teacher should accept less than the legal rate and annual increases are decided by the government, not by school owners. Usually these are announced in March and backdated to September or October. In 2008 there was a 3.5% increase. Although the hourly rates are very low compared to those paid in other European countries, jobs bring a range of statutory benefits, eg holiday pay and bonuses as described below. Teachers should be paid an extra hour's wage for marking for every 10 hours of teaching, though some employers try to evade this.

Always keep a copy of your contract safe in case difficulties arise, as they did in the case of **Belinda Michaels** while working at a *frontisterion* in Patras:

> *In November, the school owner told me that the students wanted me back after Christmas. On January 29th the following year, she dismissed me with no notice and no holiday pay. Her excuse was that there was low student attendance during the university exam period. The next day the landlady was very rude to me saying that I had left the school. I had to pay a large sum for my January electricity bill which I never saw. She also asked for money to cover the water bill and a month's rent in advance. I immediately left the accommodation. When I went into the school to ask for one month's severance pay to which I was legally entitled, the owner started attacking me verbally and ordered me out of the school. She refused to give me a copy of my contract, nor had the UK agent given me a copy.*

The basic salary should be augmented by compulsory bonuses at Christmas, Easter and summer. Teaching unions have negotiated some reasonable conditions, though not all schools offer them. Bonuses, holiday pay and health insurance should all be stipulated. Contracts may be dissolved by either party giving a month's notice.

The teaching year has been shrinking, so that an increasing number of schools now start their courses at the beginning of October and finish at the end of May. So some schools offer eight month contracts rather than the nine months that used to be standard. Teachers should always check beforehand the date up to which they will be paid. Native speakers are often employed to teach exam classes that actually finish earlier than the end of May. For example, classes for Michigan exams in 2008 finished on 9 May, just before the ECCE and the ECPE exams. Teachers should check that they will be paid until the end of the month if they are not going to continue at least a few hours a week doing oral work with their students. Schools have been known to break the contract by paying off teachers as soon as their classes have taken the exams.

The majority of employers allow two paid fortnight holidays at Christmas and Easter (remember that the Greek Easter is usually later than elsewhere). Bonuses are calculated according to the number of days worked. For every nine days you have worked before Christmas you get one day's pay (ie five hours). For every 13 days worked between 1 January and 30 April you get two days' pay. This usually approximates to an extra month's pay at Christmas and half a month's pay at Easter. If you have queries about the collective labour agreement, contact the Greek Labour Office (OEAD) at Ethnikis Antistasis 8 str, 16610 Ano Glyfada.

You also get a lump sum at the end of your contract which is not in fact a bonus. It is two weeks' holiday pay and two weeks' severance pay (both tax-free). Beware of employers who pay for your accommodation out of your gross salary and then try to calculate your bonuses as a percentage of your net salary. This is illegal. Employers who have suffered from staff desertions in the past may hold back some of your monthly pay as a bond (*kratisi*) against an early departure. The number of hours of teaching available from an average *frontisterion* is also decreasing, which of course means lower earnings. According to **Jain Cook**, the average working week is now 18 hours and it is unusual for new teachers to get more than that. Some schools offer as few as 10 hours which means that teachers are forced either to work at more than one school (which school owners are not keen on) or to take on private students. Teachers working fewer than 18 hours are not eligible for full national insurance contributions. Split shifts are now very uncommon except in technical colleges or universities. Almost all teaching at *frontisteria* takes place between 5pm and 10pm.

It is not unusual to be expected to teach in two or more 'satellite' sites of the main school in villages up to 10 miles away. Local bus services are generally good and cheap but you could find yourself spending an inordinate amount of (unpaid) time in transit and standing around at bus stops.

All areas have a local Workers' Office where you can go if you are in dispute with your employer or fear that you are being ripped off. These have improved enormously and are very willing to help teachers.

PUPILS

Most native English speakers are employed to teach advanced classes, usually the two years leading to pre-university exams. Because of the Greek style of education, pupils won't show much initiative and will expect to be tested frequently on what they have been taught. **Andrew Boyle** found the prevailing methodology of 'sit 'em down, shut 'em up and give 'em lots of homework' was moderately successful.

There is a great deal of pressure to assign pass marks just to retain the students' custom. Some school owners are so profit-motivated, they have euros for eyeballs. Students expect to be told the answers and teachers are expected to be lenient with the marking so that the students all pass and parents will re-enrol them.

Will Brady, teaching on the island of Santorini, found the pupils quite challenging, particularly the girls:

> *The job was littered with problems because the kids, for a start, were pretty uninterested They were the offspring of hotel owners on the island, for the most part, whose only reason for having their kids learn English was so that they could be of use in the family business when the tourists came in summer. They had a level of MTV English but that was about it. They weren't motivated to learn and it was quite difficult to get them interested in the subject. I had a particular problem with a class of 15–16-year-old girls who were quite difficult to discipline. For some lessons I was alone and they took advantage of the fact that I didn't speak Greek. They were not even bothering to whisper, but talking openly to each other, and playing footsie with me under the table, and it was very difficult to know how to handle that. The manager took me aside and told me in no uncertain terms that I should not respond to any of the advances. Thankfully, I hadn't entertained the idea.*

The link 'Teaching in Greece' on the website of TESOL Greece (www.tesolgreece.com/teaching_in_greece.htm) describes the approach to teaching under such headings as 'Teachers do not take risks in class' and 'Students do not see the value of any learning unless it is tested'.

ACCOMMODATION

Since most schools provide a flat or at least help in finding a flat, teachers are often not too concerned about their living arrangements. Placements arranged by the recruitment agencies offer free accommodation in addition to the full salary. It is definitely worth checking in advance about furnishings. Flats are sometimes quite spartan but some of the better ones are comfortably furnished and may have a washing machine and television in addition to the essentials. However some flats, especially in Athens, are unfurnished which is a serious nuisance for someone on an eight-month contract.

Utility bills come every two months, and winters in Greece can be surprisingly cold. Even in a small flat, the electricity bill will run to hundreds of euros. Water bills are very cheap however. Before taking over accommodation, try to find out if the bills have been paid. Changing the name is such a major hassle (involving tax returns, etc.) and unfortunately it is not uncommon for tenants to move on without paying their bills and the new tenant becomes liable. Non-payment of electricity and phone bills (but not water bills) will result in disconnection, and no final reminders are sent out.

LEISURE

Teachers in Athens should have no trouble constructing a social life. The monthly paper *The Athenian* available from kiosks in Omonia Square among other places contains details of clubs and events of interest to expats. Outside Athens, the social order is still fairly conservative. A further problem is the enormous language barrier in a country where it will take some time to learn how to read the alphabet. Watching Greek television is a good way to learn the language plus Greek lessons are run free of charge in many locations. Cassandra, based in the north of Greece, found that '*teaching was a bit more difficult and isolating than I expected, but once I was used to the lifestyle I enjoyed it . . . with hindsight I would have enrolled in Greek lessons sooner and tried to get out and meet more people.*'

Most teachers find the vast majority of Greek people to be honest, friendly and helpful and are seldom disappointed with the hospitality they receive.

As anyone who has visited Greece knows, the country has countless other attractions, not least the very convivial and affordable tavernas. Eating out, wine and cigarettes are more or less the only things that have not become expensive. *Kafeneions* are a largely male institution in which women teachers may not feel comfortable. Travel, particularly ferry travel, is relatively cheap and a pure delight out of season.

The cost of living is higher than it used to be. All imported goods are expensive, for example cosmetics, deodorant, shampoo, cleaning products, shoes, etc. Don't expect to have much left out of your net weekly take-home pay for saving or splurging. Despite all the hassles, most people enjoy a year in Greece.

LIST OF EMPLOYERS

ANGLO-HELLENIC TEACHER RECRUITMENT
PO Box 263, 201 00 Corinth
/fax 27410 53511
jobs@anglo-hellenic.com
www.anglo-hellenic.com

NUMBER OF TEACHERS: about 80 vacancies every year in a wide choice of locations.
PREFERENCE OF NATIONALITY: UK.
QUALIFICATIONS: university graduates with a TEFL Certificate.
CONDITIONS OF EMPLOYMENT: most vacancies are in September, several in January and a few come up throughout the year.
SALARY: 9-month contracts pay the going rate of about €900 per month plus bonuses and 4 weeks' paid holiday.
FACILITIES/SUPPORT: accommodation in a furnished flat. A 4-page contract will be provided by agency (specimen copy available beforehand). Anglo-Hellenic also take care of the bureaucratic essentials, and encourage meetings and exchange visits of their teachers and provide interactive web-based facilities for information, opinion and social chat. TEFL certificate courses (120 hours) are run every month, with shorter professional development courses also being offered throughout the year.
RECRUITMENT: interviews are conducted in London, Athens or Corinth throughout the summer.

BETSIS LANGUAGE SCHOOLS
Thivon 109, 18542 Piraeus
210 492 0871; fax 210 493 3661
abetsis@hol.gr

NUMBER OF TEACHERS: 15–20.
PREFERENCE OF NATIONALITY: British.
QUALIFICATIONS: BA and Cambridge exams.
CONDITIONS OF EMPLOYMENT: 8-month contracts. 18–24 hours per week. Also opportunities for teachers to work at the publishing company, Andrew Betsis ELT, specialising in ELT exam books. Positions are available in the editorial and marketing departments.
SALARY: €8,000–€9,000 per year.
FACILITIES/SUPPORT: school helps teachers find rental accommodation and with the bureaucracy involved in applying for a work permit.
CONTACT: Lawrence Mamas, Director of Studies.

CAMBRIDGE TEACHERS RECRUITMENT
17 Metron St, 143 42 Athens
/fax 210 258 5155
macleod_smith_andrew@hotmail.com

NUMBER OF TEACHERS: about 50–60 per year in vetted schools.
PREFERENCE OF NATIONALITY: British.
QUALIFICATIONS: degree and TEFL certificate, a friendly personality and conscientious attitude.
CONDITIONS OF EMPLOYMENT: contracts usually between September and May, although some summer work. Usual hours are Monday and Friday afternoons, 4pm–10pm.
FACILITIES/SUPPORT: applicants can expect to receive a wealth of information about working in Greece.
RECRUITMENT: comprehensive interviews are conducted between mid-June and the end of August. Interviews are held in hotels in central London.
UK CONTACT ADDRESS OF MAIN INTERVIEWER DURING THE SUMMER: Andrew MacLeod-Smith, 53 Green Acres, Parkhill, Croydon CRO 5UX; fax 020 8686 3733.

HYPHEN
Vas. Olgas 24b (4th floor), 54641 Thessaloniki
2310 888125; fax 2310 887208
hr@hyphen.gr
www. hyphen.gr (go to career opportunities/ careers in ELT)

NUMBER OF TEACHERS: Hyphen is approached by approximately 1000 foreign language centres regarding vacancies each year and receives over 2000 CVs from potential teachers from throughout the world.

KOUTSANTONIS SCHOOL OF LANGUAGES
35 Gounari Ave, 26221 Patras
2610 273925; fax 2610 623 340
kapaflc@otenet.gr

NUMBER OF TEACHERS: out of staff of 35, only about 2 are British.
PREFERENCE OF NATIONALITY: native speakers with Greek ancestry.
QUALIFICATIONS: university degree. Preferably a teaching qualification and some experience.

CONDITIONS OF EMPLOYMENT: 8-month contracts. 12–18 teaching hours per week, evenings only Monday to Friday.
SALARY: from legal minimum of €9 gross according to qualifications and experience.
FACILITIES/SUPPORT: school owner will help with search for an apartment and might be able to lend furniture.
RECRUITMENT: generally teachers leave their CVs in person and are called back for interview when a vacancy occurs. Very occasional interviews held in UK.
CONTACT: Jain Cook, Director of Studies.

LAMBRAKI FOREIGN LANGUAGES CENTRES
El. Venizelou 194, Gazi, Heraklion, Crete
2810 822 292; fax 2810 2111 65
info@lambraki.gr
www.lambraki.gr

NUMBER OF TEACHERS: 10.
PREFERENCE OF NATIONALITY: Britain.
QUALIFICATIONS: university degree and TEFL qualification.
CONDITIONS OF EMPLOYMENT: most teachers stay 2–3 years. 18–25 hours per week
SALARY: €700–€1000 per month, less 16% deductions.
FACILITIES/SUPPORT: assistance given in finding accommodation. School assists with residence permit after teacher provides a verified copy of his/her degree; official translation can be done in Heraklion.
RECRUITMENT: via newspaper advertisements, personal contact and PALSO Association. Telephone interviews.
CONTACT: Irene Lambraki, School Director.

LORD BYRON SCHOOL
104,Tsimiski St, Diagonios, 54622 Thessaloniki
2310 278804; fax 2310 268639
school@lordbyron.gr
www.lordbyron.gr

NUMBER OF TEACHERS: 3–5 native English speakers.
PREFERENCE OF NATIONALITY: EU nationals.
QUALIFICATIONS: university degree, TEFLA or CELTYL or CELTA and EFL teaching experience.
CONDITIONS OF EMPLOYMENT: Standard contract 8 months. 24–26 hours per week.
SALARY: €800 to €1,000 according to qualifications. 17% deductions for tax and social security.
FACILITIES/SUPPORT: assistance finding accommodation and obtaining a legal status/teaching permit.

RECRUITMENT: via detailed CV, interview, model lesson (with lesson plan). Interviews are carried out in Thessaloniki every May and June.
CONTACT: Harry J. Nikolaides, School Director.

MICHALOPOULOS ENGLISH SCHOOLS
30 E. Anistasis, 59300 Alexandria
+233 302 2890

NUMBER OF TEACHERS: 2.
PREFERENCE OF NATIONALITY: British, Canadian, American.
QUALIFICATIONS: BA.
CONDITIONS OF EMPLOYMENT: Standard contract 1 year. 25 teaching hours per week.
SALARY: Above average. Depends on qualifications and experience.
FACILITIES/SUPPORT: Free accommodation provided near to the school.
RECRUITMENT: Personal interview not necessary.
CONTACT: Kostas Michalopoulos, Director.

PAPAELIOU SCHOOLS OF FOREIGN LANGUAGES
111 Karaiskou Str, 18532 Piraeus-Athens
+210 417 3892; fax 210 412 1520
papaili@ath.forthnet.gr
www. papaeliou.edu.gr
Branch in Nikea at 124 laodikias 18451.
+210 491 6800

NUMBER OF TEACHERS: 45.
PREFERENCE OF NATIONALITY: British. Majority are Greek-Americans or Greek.
QUALIFICATIONS: BA or MA and teacher training.
CONDITIONS OF EMPLOYMENT: 2–3 year contracts teaching 4–18 hours per week (or less).
SALARY: approx. €850 net; €382 deductions.
FACILITIES/SUPPORT: no help with accommodation.
RECRUITMENT: interviewees teach a demo lesson.
CONTACT: Diana Papaeliou, General Director.

STRATEGAKIS ISON LANGUAGE CENTRES
Central Branch, 24 Proxenou Koromila St, 546 22 Thessaloniki
+2310 264276; fax 2310 228848
centralschool@strategakis.gr
Member of the EG Strategakis SA Group

NUMBER OF FOREIGN TEACHERS: 25 in 100 foreign language centres with 2,000 students all over Northern Greece.

PREFERENCE OF NATIONALITY: British, Irish only.

QUALIFICATIONS: BA/MA, PGCE (or equivalent). TEFL qualifications welcomed but not required.

CONDITIONS OF EMPLOYMENT: 1 academic year renewable contracts. 28 hours per week Pupils mainly aged 9–17 although there are also some adult groups.

SALARY: €760–€800 per month.

FACILITIES/SUPPORT: accommodation arranged; teacher pays rent. Pre-contract training provided.

RECRUITMENT: through advertising and UK universities and colleges. Interviews essential and are often held in UK, usually in May. Note that the Strategakis School in Athens (6 George St, Canningos Square, 106 77 Athens; & +210 38 11 496) is a separate operation.

CONTACT: Konstantinos Nikolaides, Director of Studies.

THE LINGUISTIC LAB

PO Box 12, Xylokastro, Corinthia 204 00

  +27430 41280/31999/22135; fax 27430 22135

  filisbob@hotmail.com or info@ linguisticlab.com

  www.linguisticlab.com or www.linguisticlab.gr

NUMBER OF TEACHERS: variable.

PREFERENCE OF NATIONALITY: must hold a European EU passport.

QUALIFICATIONS: minimum BA plus TESOL certificate and experience. TESOL courses offered at Linguistic Lab.

CONDITIONS OF EMPLOYMENT: minimum contract period 2 years. To work 18–25 hours per week. Classes begin early September and finish either in May or June. Summer classes run in June and July.

SALARY: Depends on qualifications and experience. Salary takes into account home preparation and marking. Also includes 21 days paid holiday and public insurance.

FACILITIES/SUPPORT: free accommodation is provided in new fully furnished 2 bedroom apartments, to be shared between 2 teachers. Option to have a private apartment, with a lower salary.

RECRUITMENT: to apply send a CV, copies of diplomas and passport, reference letters and a recent photo to the above address.

CONTACT: Bob Filis, Director.

ITALY

English language schools are thriving in Italy and opportunities for qualified native speaker teachers are very good, especially in towns and cities which cannot boast leaning towers, gondolas or coliseums. Small towns in Sicily and Sardinia, in the Dolomites and along the Adriatic have more than their fair share of private language schools and institutes, all catering for Italians who have failed to learn English in the state system. (English teaching in Italian schools is generally acknowledged to be inadequate.)

PROSPECTS FOR TEACHERS

A complete range of language schools can be found in Italy, as the *Yellow Pages* will confirm. At the elite end of the market, there are the 44 schools which belong to AISLI, the Associazione Italiana Scuole di Lingue, (www.aisli.com). Prospective teachers should apply directly to the schools and not to AISLI.

Strict regulations mean that only ultra-respectable schools can become AISLI members so there are thousands of good schools outside the association. AISLI schools usually expect their teachers to have advanced qualifications and in return offer attractive remuneration packages and conditions of employment.

At the other end of the spectrum, there is a host of schools which some might describe as cowboy operations, though these are decreasing in number. The CELTA is very widely recognised and respected in Italy (unlike in France, for instance). US qualifications are much less well known for the simple reason that work permits are virtually impossible for non-EU citizens to obtain.

A healthy number of schools wanted their job vacancies to be registered in this book and can be seen advertising on the main ELT websites and relevant journals.

Strict employment regulations and red tape in Italy make small companies reluctant to offer full-time contracts. Some schools offer a British contract (ie one that is not subject to Italian legislation) in which the wages are much lower than on an Italian contract but the benefits much better (see entry for Caledonian Communications for an explanation). Compulsory contributions for social security and expensive perks (such as the compulsory severance pay of one month's pay) make hiring a permanent member of staff very costly so most of the jobs available are eight or nine month contracts. The majority of English teachers in Italy work on a freelance basis with no long-term job security, which is acceptable for those who only want to spend one or two years in the country.

FINDING A JOB

IN ADVANCE

There is no single compendium of the hundreds of language school addresses in Italy. The relevant *Yellow Pages* (Pagine Gialle) are user friendly; go to www.paginegialle.it and choose the handy English version of the site. Typing in 'language school' produced 585 entries in 2008.

International language school groups such as Benedict Schools, Linguarama, Berlitz and inlingua are major providers of English language teaching in Italy. International House has 13 affiliated schools throughout the country. Wall Street Institutes now has about 50 centres in Italy and actively recruit native speakers; one of the centres is in Udine at Via Maniago 2; ✆ 0432 481464; www.wsi.it.

Several Italian-based chains of language schools account for a large number of teaching jobs. But because many of them operate as independent franchises, it is difficult to get a master list of addresses. Chains include the British Schools Group (www.britishschool.com) with more than 60 member schools who carry out a lot of their recruitment through Saxoncourt. Another major chain is British Institutes (www.britishinstitutes.it) with 50+. If you are in Italy, go into a branch of the student tourist bureau CTS, for example at Via Genova 16, 00184 Rome, and ask for the leaflet listing all the British Institutes in Italy. (Most language schools in Italy seem to incorporate the word British, English, Oxford or Cambridge randomly combined with Centre, School or Institute, which can result in confusion.)

American citizens have a lot of difficulty finding work in Italy, largely because it is so difficult to obtain a work permit. However, a solution suggested by **Carla Valentine**, an English teacher in Venice, is to try working for one of the Department of Defence US army schools on the military bases in Italy. Under these circumstances, work permits are processed in the USA.

Peter Murrell, a recruiter based in Genoa, claims to have client schools in Italy and might be worth contacting if you are a mother tongue speaker of English with EU nationality and a Cambridge or Trinity certificate (www.genovaweb.net/tii). The English Conversation Club in Genoa was advertising for summer staff in 2008 – contact smurrell@thetrainingcompany.org (✆ 010 540964).

ON THE SPOT

THE *YELLOW PAGES* IS PROBABLY STILL THE BEST SOURCE OF POSSIBLE EMPLOYERS, WHETHER YOU BROWSE ONLINE IN A CAFÉ OR LOCATE A PRINT COPY IN A TELEPHONE OFFICE. WHEN BRUCE NAIRNE AND SUE RATCLIFFE WENT JOB-HUNTING IN ITALY A FEW YEARS AGO, THEY RELIED ON THE *YELLOW PAGES* AS A SOURCE OF POTENTIAL EMPLOYERS:

Rather unimaginatively we packed our bags and made for Italy in the middle of the summer holidays when there was no teaching work at all. Nevertheless we utilised the Yellow Pages in the SIP telephone office in Syracuse and proceeded to make 30 speculative applications, specifying our status as graduates who had completed a short course in TEFL. By the end of September we had received four job offers without so much as an interview.

Unfortunately, the jobs in Bari which Bruce and Sue chose to accept never materialised and so they once again resorted to the Yellow Pages, this time in Milan railway station, where they managed to secure the interest of three or four establishments for part-time work.

Often a few hours teaching can gradually be built up into a full-time job by those willing to say 'Yes'. If you're there when they need you, you can usually get something. Most find that the longer they stay, the more hours they get, though there is still no job security working this way.

Although it is difficult to get work without TEFL training it is not impossible. **Laurence Koe** visited all the language schools in Como and Lecco, some of them on several occasions, and was told that he needed a qualification or that he was there at the wrong time (October). After three weeks of making the rounds he was asked to stand in for an absent teacher on one occasion, and this was enough to secure him further part-time work. After a few more weeks he found work teaching an evening class of adults. He began to attend the weekly English Club and was offered a small fee to answer questions on the plot after the showing of a James Bond film. Most towns have an English Club (Associazione Italo-Britannico) which may offer conversation classes and employ native speakers on a casual basis.

Scouring advertisements in English language newspapers has worked for some. Try the fortnightly publications *Rome Metropolitan* and *Wanted in Rome*, and also the Italian-language classified advertisements paper *Porta Portese*. (If you happen to see a request for 'mothers only', this means that they are looking for someone whose mother tongue is English, not a female with small children.)

FREELANCE TEACHING

Another possibility is to set up as a freelance tutor, though a knowledge of Italian is even more of an asset here than it is for jobs in schools. You can post notices in supermarkets, tobacconists, primary and secondary schools, etc. In Rome, the notice board at International House's training centre (Accademia Britannica, Viale Manzoni 22, 00185 Rome) displays requests for teachers. Also in Rome, check out the notice boards at English language bookshops such as the Lion Bookshop on Via Babuina and the Economy Bookshop on Via Torino, or frequent the right pubs such as Ned Kelly's near Palazzo Valdassini and Miscellania near the Pantheon. University students looking for private tuition might consult the notice boards at the Citta Universitaria.

Porta Portese is also a good forum in which to advertise your availability to offer English lessons in Rome; advertisements placed by women should not betray their gender and meetings with prospective clients should not take place in private homes. It cost **Dustie Hickey** about £15 to advertise in four editions of the free paper in Rimini. As long as you have access to some premises, you can try to arrange both individual and group lessons, though competition is so cut-throat in some places that hourly fees are less than they once were.

Whatever way you decide to look for work, remember that life grinds to a halt in August, just as in France. Competition is keenest in Rome, Florence and Venice, so new arrivals should head elsewhere. **Peter Penn** recommends Trieste where he was offered two jobs with no experience.

Freelance teaching can be very lucrative and you can expect to make around €20 an hour, which is still undercutting most of the language schools (who charge around €26 per hour and take over half themselves).

Universities throughout Italy employ foreigners as *lettori* (readers/lecturers) who teach English as well as other subjects such as business and science in English. There are probably around 1,000 *lettori* on yearly contracts (maximum three years) earning about the same as EFL teachers in private institutes. Although personal recommendation often plays a part in getting this work, it may be worth contacting various faculties directly and asking for work, preferably in September/October. After flouting EU legislation for many years, Italian universities have come into line and are starting to accord the same status and benefits to foreign teachers as to Italian ones.

SUMMER WORK

Young English teachers are in great demand to work at summer language camps; see for example the entries for ACLE and International House Campobasso. The cheerfully named organisation Smile (V. Vigmolese 454, 41100 Modena; ✆ /fax 059 363868) employs summer tutors to supervise games as well as teach English. The North American agency Scotia Personnel runs an organised scheme whereby young North Americans are recruited to work on language and sports camps in Italy in exchange for pocket money; details from Scotia Personnel, 6045 Cherry St, Halifax, Nova Scotia B3H 2K4, Canada (✆ 902 422 1455; scotiap@ns.sympatico.ca; www.scotia-personnel-ltd.com).

REGULATIONS

The bureaucratic procedures for EU nationals are fairly straightforward and teachers don't need a work permit or a residence permit, although the latter can be helpful for long-stayers. To obtain one teachers must take their passport and other papers (including a declaration of residence/consular declaration from your country's consulate in Italy) to the local *Questura* (police department) to obtain a *permesso di soggiorno* (residence permit). As mentioned above, non-EU citizens have very little chance of getting their papers in order unless they are dual nationals or receive a firm offer of a job while they are still in their home country. According to the Italian Embassy in Washington, language teachers from the US need a visa for *lavoro subordinato*. To qualify they must first obtain from their employer in Italy an authorisation to work issued by the Ministry of Labour or a Provincial Office of Labour (Servizio politiche del lavoro) plus an authorisation from the local *Questura*. The originals of these plus a passport and one photo must be sent to the applicant's nearest embassy or consulate. These procedures can take up to a year to complete and as **Carla Valentine**, an English teacher in Venice points out; '*no school director in his right mind is going to bother going through that proc-*

ess when there are plenty of British teachers here who can work without visa red tape'. It is for this reason that so many Americans and other non-EU citizens work in Italy without work visas. However, there are two legal alternatives for US citizens. The first is to go to Italy as a student, which allows you to work for up to 20 hours a week (enough to live on). This is the route that Carla took:

> *Getting a student visa is very easy. I paid $500 to enrol for a year at Instituto Venizia to learn Italian. With a letter of enrolment from the school I was able to get a student visa from the Italian Consulate in Boston for one year (whether or not I attend class is irrelevant, although obviously I do).*

The second option is to become an independent contractor. This involves registering for the equivalent of VAT (*Partita IVA*) from the local town government. To get this number, you simply need a codice fiscale (tax ID number), which is available from the local town hall upon presentation of a passport. With this number it is possible to obtain the Partita IVA from the municipal authorities. With these numbers it seems that you can find work and get paid, even though technically without a permesso di soggiorno you are still an illegal immigrant. Australians and New Zealanders can take advantage of working holiday schemes, which allow a 12-month stay, although holders are not meant to work for more than three months.

Tax is a further headache for long-stay teachers. As soon as you sort out the work documents, you should obtain a tax number (codice fiscale). The rate of income tax (ritenuta d'acconto) is usually about 20% in addition to social security deductions of up to 10%.

CONDITIONS OF WORK

A good salary for a full-time timetable would be about €1,000 net per month though many novice teachers earn less. Staff on a *contratto di collaborazione* are paid by the hour, usually ranging from €12–€18 net. Always find out if pay scales are quoted net or gross, since the two figures are so different. Take-home pay is not as high as might have been expected because of the high cost of compulsory national insurance, social security and pension contributions. Salaries tend to be substantially higher in northern Italy than in the south to compensate for the much higher cost of living. Business English, as always, can be very lucrative. Intensive Business English, based in Milan (see list of employers) offers a gross salary of between €1,700 and €3,250. However, some teachers in Rome, Milan, Bologna, etc. have had to reconcile themselves to spending up to half their salaries on rent.

Only professional teachers will benefit from the Contratto Collettivo Nazionale del Lavoro (CCLN) which sets a high salary for a regulation 100-hour working month. Because of the high costs of legal employment, there is a lot of dubious practice in Italy and prospective teachers should try to talk to an ex-teacher before committing themselves, especially if offered a job before arrival. **Rhys Sage** was disappointed at the discrepancy between what he had been promised by a language institute in Chivasso near Torino and what he found when he arrived:

> *They had given a glowing description of the locality and of the cost of living, of the flat they were offering and of the high wages. Upon arrival, it transpired that the wages were minimal, the prices quite high and the flat shoddy. The toilet didn't work and neither did the heating. The school also wanted a sizeable deposit in advance for the first month and would then deduct from my salary for the rent. When I discovered the extent to which I'd been told a tissue of lies, I regretted going to Chivasso and left. In the end my Italian trip turned into a holiday.*

Few teachers complain about their students. Even when pupils attend English classes for social reasons (as many do in small towns with little nightlife) or are generally unmotivated, they are usually good-natured, hospitable and talkative in class. In contrast to Greece, many language school directors are British rather than local.

LEISURE

Italian culture and lifestyle do not need to have their praises sung here. A large number of teachers who have gone out on short-term contracts never come back – probably a higher proportion than in any other country. While rents are high, eating out is fairly cheap and public transport is quite affordable. Women teachers should be prepared to cope with some Mediterranean machismo, particularly in the south.

Compared with many languages, Italian is easy to learn, though courses are expensive. It may be possible to swap English lessons for Italian ones, which might lead to further freelance teaching.

LIST OF EMPLOYERS

A.C.L.E. – SUMMER & CITY CAMPS
Via Roma 54, San Remo, 18038
+0184 506070; fax 0184 509996
info@acle.org
www.acle.org

NUMBER OF TEACHERS: 400+ for both day camps and residential camps.

PREFERENCE OF NATIONALITY: all native English speakers between 20 and 30 years of age.

QUALIFICATIONS: minimum age 18. Must have experience working with children and the ability to teach English through the use of theatre and outdoor activities. A fun-loving personality and genuine interest in children, high moral standards and a flexible attitude to work required, preferably with some experience of living and travelling abroad.

CONDITIONS OF EMPLOYMENT: Camps start in June and run until September. Minimum of 3 weeks commitment required. The average tutor works for 4 weeks or more.

SALARY: €220–€260 per week (City Camp, Summer Camp respectively) plus full board and accommodation. Transport between camps provided + bonus.

FACILITIES/SUPPORT: intensive 4/5-day introductory TEFL (Teaching English to Foreign Learners through Theatre and Play) course provided for fee of €150 usually deducted from wages.

RECRUITMENT: Application online at www.acle.org.

ANDERSON HOUSE (QFG)
Via Bergamo 25, 24035 Curno (Bergamo)
+035 46 30 74; fax 035 437 5698
info@andersonhouse.it
www.andersonhouse.it

One of the founder members of QFG (Quality First Group, www.qfg.it) a circuit of schools specialised in corporate language training. AH is a centre for language testing and certifications (Cambridge, BULATS, TOEIC and TOEFL) and a translation company. This year AH will be offering summer Italian courses with the brand ITALIAN IN BERGAMO.

NUMBER OF TEACHERS: 1 Director of Studies, 10 full-time, 5 part-time for English. 10 part-time for other languages.

PREFERENCE OF NATIONALITY: British and Irish. European passport essential.

QUALIFICATIONS: degree plus CELTA (min. grade B) or DELTA and min. 2 years' experience. Min. age 25. Couples with car a bonus.

CONDITIONS OF EMPLOYMENT: Contracts from October to June (8/9 months) or from January for 5 months. All contracts renewable. To work 25 hours per week, 8am–10pm (one period of the day free). Some Saturday morning work; some summer work (June, July, September).

SALARY: €1,200 net for qualified teachers with 2 years' experience. Salary negotiable for those with more experience.

FACILITIES/SUPPORT: Italian lessons at cost. Seminars and workshops with the Director of Studies and 2 Assistant DOSes and experts during the year. 90% is company work (general and business) both on and off-site. School has 2 small company cars, and helps teachers with accommodation. Excellent facilities, staff resource centre, free internet access, video club.
RECRUITMENT: via www.tefl.com and direct application.
CONTACT: Peter Anderson, Director and Owner.

ANGLO-AMERICAN CENTRE
Via Mameli 46, 09125, Cagliari, Sardinia
☎ +070 654 955; fax 070 670 605
✉ aacentre@tiscali.it
🖥 www.angloamericancentre.it

NUMBER OF TEACHERS: 20.
PREFERENCE OF NATIONALITY: native English speaker teachers only.
QUALIFICATIONS: university degree, CELTA / Trinity Cert, 2 years' experience, valid driving licence, basic Italian.
CONDITIONS OF EMPLOYMENT: standard 11-month contract. 25 contact hours a week.
SALARY: €1050–€1300 a month net. All INPS and INAIL contributions are paid.
FACILITIES/SUPPORT: centre assists teachers in dealing with landlords, visiting apartments, providing financial loans etc.
RECRUITMENT: through internet, local newspaper and employment agencies. Interview usually carried out in Italy or UK.
CONTACT: Guido Diana, General Director.

BENEDICT SCHOOL
C. so Alberto Pio 68, 41012 Carpi (MO)
☎ +059 695921; fax 059 622 1007
✉ info@benedict-carpi.it
🖥 www.benedict-carpi.it/job.asp

NUMBER OF TEACHERS: 10.
PREFERENCE OF NATIONALITY: British or American.
QUALIFICATIONS: minimum TEFL (CELTA or equivalent certification).
CONDITIONS OF EMPLOYMENT: mid-September until mid-July. Minimum 90 hours per month guaranteed (average 120 hours). 80% of work is with companies; 20% with private students.

SALARY: to be discussed at interview.
FACILITIES/SUPPORT: accommodation provided by school. Assist non-EU and EU teachers with permits.
RECRUITMENT: internet and recruitment agency.

BENEDICT SCHOOL
Via Crispi 32, 1 80122 Naples
☎ +081 662 672
✉ info@benedictschool.it
🖥 www.benedictschool.it

NUMBER OF TEACHERS: 6 for 4 branches in the Campania region.
PREFERENCE OF NATIONALITY: British and Irish nationals.
QUALIFICATIONS: Minimum CELTA plus degree and 1 year of teaching experience.
CONDITIONS OF EMPLOYMENT: 8–9-month contracts (November to June) and 2 year contracts available. To work 25 hours per week, teaching children and adults.
SALARY: €8 per hour net plus free accommodation.
FACILITIES/SUPPORT: furnished flat provided for teachers in Naples. Opportunities to qualify for a Trinity CertTESOL.

BRITISH INSTITUTE
Viale Duca D'Aosta 19, 21052 Busto Arsizio (VA)
☎ +0331 627479; fax 0331 634280
✉ britba@tin.it

NUMBER OF TEACHERS: 8.
PREFERENCE OF NATIONALITY: EU citizens.
QUALIFICATIONS: TEFL, TESOL or CELTA certificate plus 1 year's experience and valid driving licence.
CONDITIONS OF EMPLOYMENT: October to June. 25 hours of teaching per week.
SALARY: €820 per month net, plus €640 bonus for completing the 8-month contract.
FACILITIES/SUPPORT: free accommodation supplied close to the school.
RECRUITMENT: internet.
CONTACT: Pasquale Tallarida.

BRITISH LANGUAGE SERVICES
Division of Linguaviva, Via C. De Cristoforis 15, 20124 Milan
☎ +02 659 6401; fax 02 2900 2395
✉ job@linguaviva.net
🖥 www.linguaviva.net/job.htm

NUMBER OF TEACHERS: 20–25.

PREFERENCE OF NATIONALITY: British and Irish (EU only).

QUALIFICATIONS: minimum CELTA or equivalent, degree plus some experience, must be dynamic.

CONDITIONS OF EMPLOYMENT: September to June/July. 28 hours per week.

SALARY: guaranteed monthly salary plus benefits.

FACILITIES/SUPPORT: teachers can stay in a residence sharing with another teacher for the first month or the whole contract period.

RECRUITMENT: advertisements followed by personal interviews in London or Milan. Send full CV with photo and email addresses of 2 referees.

BRITISH SCHOOL BARI

Via C. Rosalba 47/o, 70124 Bari

+0 80 5615275; fax 0 80 5617105

bari2@britishschool.com

www. britishbari.com

NUMBER OF TEACHERS: 18.

PREFERENCE OF NATIONALITY: from Great Britain and Ireland.

QUALIFICATIONS: minimum CELTA and 1 year's experience.

CONDITIONS OF EMPLOYMENT: standard 8-month contract, 25 hours a week.

SALARY: €950 net.

FACILITIES/SUPPORT: assistance finding furnished accommodation.

RECRUITMENT: through an agency, interviews sometimes carried out in the UK.

CONTACT: Richard Udall, Director.

BRITISH SCHOOL VICENZA

Viale Roma, 8, 36100 Vicenza

+0444 542190; fax 0444 323444

info@britishschoolvicenza.net

NUMBER OF TEACHERS: 8.

PREFERENCE OF NATIONALITY: must have EU passport.

QUALIFICATIONS: degree, Cert TEFL and 1–2 years' experience plus some Italian.

CONDITIONS OF EMPLOYMENT: mid-September to mid-June. 26 hours per week Mainly evening work.

SALARY: guaranteed €1,114 (net) per month plus end of contract bonus.

RECRUITMENT: direct applications from June to September.

CONTACT: Mrs Marianne Clement, Director.

BRITISH s.r.l.

Via XX Settembre 12, 16121 Genoa

+010 593591; fax 010 562621

britishsrl@libero.it or britishgenova@libero.it

www.britishgenova.it

NUMBER OF TEACHERS: 12.

PREFERENCE OF NATIONALITY: EU only.

QUALIFICATIONS: BA plus CELTA and minimum experience. Italian useful.

CONDITIONS OF EMPLOYMENT: 25+ hours per week between mid-September and mid-June. Most pupils aged 16–40.

SALARY: variable according to hours worked.

FACILITIES/SUPPORT: assistance given with accommodation, teaching materials and course programming.

RECRUITMENT: interviews not essential, but usually take place in Italy.

BYRON LANGUAGE DEVELOPMENT

Via Sicilia 125, 00187 Rome

+06 4201 4436; fax 06 482 8556

info@byronschool.it

www.byronschool.it

NUMBER OF TEACHERS: 18.

PREFERENCE OF NATIONALITY: none.

QUALIFICATIONS: TEFL qualification, degree and minimum 3 years' teaching experience. Smart professional attitude and appearance needed.

CONDITIONS OF EMPLOYMENT: freelance contracts of flexible length. To work either morning and afternoon or afternoon and evening.

SALARY: €14–€15 per hour (net).

FACILITIES/SUPPORT: assistance given with obtaining a tax number.

RECRUITMENT: local advertising. Interview required.

CONTACT: Bob Ratto, Principal (bobratto@byronschool.it).

CALEDONIAN COMMUNICATIONS

Viale Vigliani 55, 20148 Milan

+02 4802 0486/1086; fax 02 4819 4706/02 4819 4706

info@caledonian.it

www.caledonian.it

NUMBER OF TEACHERS: 15–35, depending on time of year.

PREFERENCE OF NATIONALITY: EU citizens or others with permits already. British nationals can be hired on UK contract and given help to find accommodation. First two weeks are provided free and in some cases up to one month.

QUALIFICATIONS: degree (preferably in a business subject) followed by TEFL qualification.

CONDITIONS OF EMPLOYMENT: 4–12 months, renewable. 40 hours per week, split up into max 30 contact hours and the rest didactic and travelling to clients.

SALARY: choice of UK (if you are British) or Italian contract. UK contract pays between £725 and £1,100 monthly depending on age and experience, plus benefits including tax-free daily living allowance of £10, two return flights to UK per year, 2 days paid leave for every month worked plus Italian public holidays and statutory sick pay. To qualify you must have a UK bank account. Italian contract starts at €1,800 per month with no benefits or accommodation. Deductions on UK contract vary according to amount earned, can be tax-free initially. Deductions on Italian contract, 24%–39%.

RECRUITMENT: word of mouth, newspapers, magazines, internet and CVs sent on spec.

CONTACT: Maria McCarthy (Managing Director), maria@caledonian.it; or Carlos Galvez (Didactic Assistant), carlos@caledonian.it.

CAMBRIDGE INSTITUTE
Viale Cappuccini 45, 66034 Lanciano (CH)
- +0872 710291 or 727175; fax 0872 724390
- info@cambridgeinstitute.it
- www.cambridgeinstitute.it

NUMBER OF TEACHERS: 4–7.

QUALIFICATIONS: TOEFL/TEFL qualification.

CONDITIONS OF EMPLOYMENT: one year contracts. 15–30 hours per week. Institute also a Liceo Linguistico or high school, and teaches English to children.

FACILITIES/SUPPORT: assistance with accommodation and work permits. Training available.

RECRUITMENT: Interviews can sometimes be arranged in UK, and are not always essential.

CENTRO LINGUISTICO BRITISH INSTITUTES
Corso Umberto I, 17–62012 Civitanova Marche (MC)
- /fax 0733 816197
- info@centrolinguistico.it
- www.centrolinguistico.it

NUMBER OF TEACHERS: 10.

PREFERENCE OF NATIONALITY: British.

QUALIFICATIONS: BA essential (MA preferred) and TEFL

Certificate or Diploma. One year's experience abroad. A little spoken Italian preferred.

CONDITIONS OF EMPLOYMENT: 8-month contracts from October. 25 hours per week minimum.

SALARY: approx. €1,000 per month.

FACILITIES/SUPPORT: training, free Italian lessons, assistance finding accommodation.

RECRUITMENT: phone interviews are possible.

CONTACT: Loretta Muzi.

CLM-BELL
Via Pozzo 30, 38100 Trento
- 0461 981733; fax 0461 981687
- clm-bell@clm-bell.eu
- www.clm-bell.it

NUMBER OF TEACHERS: 25.

PREFERENCE OF NATIONALITY: UK.

QUALIFICATIONS: minimum 2 years' experience with CELTA/DELTA qualification.

CONDITIONS OF EMPLOYMENT: 9-month contracts. To work 22 hours per week can be extended.

SALARY: from £900 to £1,100 per month.

FACILITIES/SUPPORT: Shared or single subsidised accommodation. Help provided with work permits.

RECRUITMENT: Via TEFL.com or direct applications. Interview required.

CONTACT: Eugen Joa, Managing Director.

DARBY SCHOOL OF LANGUAGES
Via Mosca 51, Villino 14, 00142 Rome
- +06 51962205; fax 06 51965012
- darby@darbyschool.it
- www.darbyschool.it

NUMBER OF TEACHERS: 30–40.

PREFERENCE OF NATIONALITY: none, but must be native English speaker.

QUALIFICATIONS: TEFL Cert. CELTA.

CONDITIONS OF EMPLOYMENT: freelance. Teachers can choose their hours which usually are an average of 20–25 hours per week. More hours available if wanted.

SALARY: the average salary of about €1,400 is sufficient and more to live on in Italy.

FACILITIES/SUPPORT: new teachers are helped to find accommodation.

RECRUITMENT: relevant CVs and interviews.

CONTACT: Gilda Darby.

ENGLISH ACADEMY SNC

Via Carlo Zucchi 64, 41100 Modena

℡ /fax 059 33 4737

✎ callan@englishacademy.it

💻 www.englishacademy.it/insegnanti.php

QUALIFICATIONS: no special teaching certification necessary because teachers are trained in the Callan Method.
CONDITIONS OF EMPLOYMENT: no lesson preparation necessary, no homework to be set or corrected, all lessons last 50 minutes; small groups of mainly adults (max. 6 per group).
FACILITIES/SUPPORT: training given. Assistance given with finding accommodation. Airfares (via no-frills flights from Stansted to Bologna) are reimbursed.
CONTACT: Mr. MT Di Salvo, Director of Studies.

IIK ANCONA SCUOLA DI LINGUE

Scalo Vittorio Emanuele II, 1, 60121 Ancona

℡ +071 206610; fax 071 207 0169

✎ info@iik.it

💻 www.iik.it

NUMBER OF TEACHERS: 5–6.
PREFERENCE OF NATIONALITY: British preferred; EU nationals.
QUALIFICATIONS: minimum 3 years' teaching experience and TEFL/TESOL Certificate. (Taster weekend courses and distance learning courses without observed and assessed teaching practice will not be considered.)
CONDITIONS OF EMPLOYMENT: generally from September until end of June. Guaranteed minimum 25 hours per week. Teaching takes place between 8.45am and 9pm.
SALARY: €10 net per hour.
FACILITIES/SUPPORT: assistance given with finding accommodation but teacher responsible for paying rent. School advises EU teachers on getting residence permit, fiscal code and enrolling in health services.
RECRUITMENT: direct contact and www.tefl.com.
CONTACT: Maria Margherita Gargiulo, Director of Studies.

INTENSIVE BUSINESS ENGLISH

Via Colautti, 1 20125 Milano

℡ +0269002017; fax 0269002064

✎ info@ibeschool.com

💻 www.ibeschool.com

NUMBER OF TEACHERS: 40.
PREFERENCE OF NATIONALITY: UK, Ireland, Australia and New Zealand.

QUALIFICATIONS: minimum 3 years experience and relevant certificate/qualification.
CONDITIONS OF EMPLOYMENT: 12-month contract. Usual hours are 9am to 7pm, Monday to Friday.
SALARY: from €1700 to €3250 gross depending on type of contract and experience. Between 20–30% deductions for taxes.
FACILITIES/SUPPORT: accommodation in flats owned by the school at very low rates.
RECRUITMENT: by the internet, advertising in local magazines and through the teacher network in Milan. Interviews essential.
CONTACT: Gordon Doyle, Director of Studies.

INTERLINGUE – LANGUAGE SYSTEM and ROME – TEFL INTERNATIONAL

Via Ennio Quirino Visconti 20, 00193 Rome

℡ +06 321 5740/321 0317; fax 06 323 5709

✎ info@interlingue-it.com

💻 www.interlingue-it.com

Accredited Centre: Trinity College, City and Guilds–TOESL Exam and ACE, London Chamber of Commerce. Recognised as efficient by the Italian Department of Education (DPR 389 – 18/04/1994 and DM 5 – 13/01/09).
NUMBER OF TEACHERS: approx. 20.
PREFERENCE OF NATIONALITY: none.
QUALIFICATIONS: minimum TEFL certificate, university degree, some teaching experience.
CONDITIONS OF EMPLOYMENT: 9-month contracts, working between 20 and 30 hours per week.
SALARY: between €12.50 and €19 per hour, depending on the type of contract.
FACILITIES/SUPPORT: students receive support in their search for accommodation.
RECRUITMENT: via students on their TEFL course and other methods. Interviews required, must be carried out in Rome.
CONTACT: Angela Giordano, General School Manager.

INTERNATIONAL CLUB

P.le A. Moro, 6, 20034 Giussano (MI)

℡ +0362 354057; 0362 352333

✎ info@internationalclub.it

💻 www.internationalclub.it

NUMBER OF TEACHERS: 10.
PREFERENCE OF NATIONALITY: UK, Ireland.

QUALIFICATIONS: for adult classes, CELTA/TESOL or any other TEFL qualification. At least 1 year's experience with teaching groups at all levels. For children's classes, any qualification for teaching children (not necessarily as an EFL teacher) and experience with teaching children.

CONDITIONS OF EMPLOYMENT: standard contract is 9 months or longer. Permanent teachers welcome. Sometimes teachers are employed shorter term and summer contracts from June to July are also offered. Teachers work an average of 25 hours per week.

SALARY: €12 net per hour /€1,200 net per month.

FACILITIES/SUPPORT: accommodation in flats owned by the school at very low rates.

RECRUITMENT: by direct contact or recruitment agencies. Interviews can be carried out on the phone or by internet. Sometimes, interviews are arranged in the UK or USA during the summer.

CONTACT: Mary Sposari, Director of Studies.

INTERNATIONAL HOUSE (CAMPOBASSO)
Via Zurlo 5, 86100 Campobasso
+0874 481321; fax 0874 63240
mary@ihcampobasso.it

NUMBER OF TEACHERS: 20 for summer camp in Italy.

PREFERENCE OF NATIONALITY: British/American.

QUALIFICATIONS: CELTA qualification and experience teaching children and teenagers essential.

CONDITIONS OF EMPLOYMENT: contract 2/4 or 6 weeks from end of June to August. 6 hours teaching per day. Pupils aged 8–16.

SALARY: approximately €650 per shift.

FACILITIES/SUPPORT: accommodation and all meals provided.

RECRUITMENT: direct application.

CONTACT: Mary Ricciardi.

INTERNATIONAL HOUSE (PALERMO)
Via Quintino Sella 70, 90139 Palermo
+091 584954; fax 091 323965
ihpa1@ihpalermo.it
www. ihpalermo.it
Mailing address: Via Q Sella 70, 90139 Palermo

NUMBER OF TEACHERS: 8 plus 1 Director of Studies and 1 Children Coordinator.

PREFERENCE OF NATIONALITY: British; others considered (only European passport).

QUALIFICATIONS: degree and CELTA (minimum grade 'B'). School interested in career teachers only.

CONDITIONS OF EMPLOYMENT: 8-month contracts. 25 hours per week Normally 1pm–9.30pm.

SALARY: from €1,200 plus increments.

FACILITIES/SUPPORT: assistance with finding accommodation (rent €350–€400 per month). Weekly seminars and workshops. School will subsidise in-service Diploma course by distance learning for suitable candidates. Italian survival lessons. CELTA courses offered in June every year.

RECRUITMENT: via IH London or directly. Interviews essential.

INTFLEX S.R.L.
Via F.lli Cairoli 9 (Isolago), 23900 Lecco
+0341 369383; fax 0341 366138
info@intflex.com
www.intflex.com

NUMBER OF TEACHERS: 12.

PREFERENCE OF NATIONALITY: European.

QUALIFICATIONS: TEFL or TESOL diploma.

CONDITIONS OF EMPLOYMENT: October to May. 25 hours per week.

SALARY: varies with experience.

FACILITIES/SUPPORT: flats available for teachers' use.

RECRUITMENT: via internet (www.tefl.com, etc.).

KEEP TALKING
Via Roma 60, 33100 Udine
+0432 5015256; fax 0432 228216
info@keeptalking.it
www.keeptalking.it

NUMBER OF TEACHERS: 10.

PREFERENCE OF NATIONALITY: none but must be native speakers.

QUALIFICATIONS: university degree and CELTA or equivalent required plus minimum 1 year of experience.

CONDITIONS OF EMPLOYMENT: 9-month contracts (contratto a progetto). Min. 700–800 hours per year. 25 hours per week. Lessons mostly at lunchtimes and evenings until 9.30pm and Saturday mornings.

SALARY: starting hourly wage of €14.40–€16 (net); monthly €1,200–€1,330 depending on qualifications and experience.

FACILITIES/SUPPORT: training seminars once a month. Excellent facilities. Income tax, pension, medical/accident insurance paid by employer. Accommodation provided.

RECRUITMENT: advertisements via internet
(www.tefl.com).

NUMBER OF TEACHERS: 3.
PREFERENCE OF NATIONALITY: UK, North America,
Australia and New Zealand. Candidates must have an EU
passport and be native English speakers.
QUALIFICATIONS: minimum TEFL certificate and at least 1
year's experience.
CONDITIONS OF EMPLOYMENT: average contract is
9 months. Teachers need to be flexible and can be asked to
work at any point from 8am until 10pm, Monday to Friday,
and 8am–3pm Saturday. On average, teachers work
approximately 20–30 hours a week.
SALARY: on average, approximately €1,000 net a month.
FACILITIES/SUPPORT: none.
RECRUITMENT: through tefl.com. Interviews are essential.
Telephone interviews might be offered to candidates outside
of Italy, who meets the school's requirements and mandate.
CONTACT: Jennifer Ginevra, Director of Studies/Owner.

NUMBER OF TEACHERS: 8.
PREFERENCE OF NATIONALITY: mother tongue speakers
of English.
QUALIFICATIONS: TEFL, CELTA.
CONDITIONS OF EMPLOYMENT: 9-month renewable
contracts. British contract. Teaching hours from 3pm to 9pm
Monday to Friday.
SALARY: approx. €826 (net) per month for an inexperienced
teacher.
FACILITIES/SUPPORT: help given with accommodation.
RECRUITMENT: via advertisements. Interviews sometimes
carried out in UK.

NUMBER OF TEACHERS: 6.
PREFERENCE OF NATIONALITY: UK, Ireland.
QUALIFICATIONS: two-years' exposure to YL after the CELTA.
CONDITIONS OF EMPLOYMENT: 8/9-month contracts.
Usual hours are 8am–1pm or 3pm–9pm.
SALARY: gross approx €1,220, net approx €950.
FACILITIES/SUPPORT: school usually provides temporary
accommodation. Some help with bureaucracy.
RECRUITMENT: through interviews and reference checking.
Interviews essential; usually carried out over the phone.
CONTACT: Susanne Fuchsberger, Director of Studies.

One of the largest independent language schools in Italy,
with more than 35 years' experience. Authorised by Italian
Ministry of Education and member of EAQUALS (European
Association for Quality Language Services).
NUMBER OF TEACHERS: 30 full-time, 20 part-time.
PREFERENCE OF NATIONALITY: British nationals. Canadian, American and Australian applicants can be considered
only if they have dual European citizenship.
QUALIFICATIONS: degree, TEFL qualification, at least 1
year's teaching experience and knowledge of a foreign
language.
CONDITIONS OF EMPLOYMENT: 8/9-month contracts
October to the end of May or 5-month contracts from January,
renewable. National insurance and pension coverage. 27
hours per week including paid training and development
hours. Students of all ages and levels but mainly young adults.
SALARY: starting from about €900 net per month. Paid
orientation week. 5 weeks' paid holiday.
FACILITIES/SUPPORT: free in-house DELTA course for
teachers with minimum 1,200 hours teaching experience.
Large self-access centre with videoclub, cinema, large TEFL
resource centre and library and staff internet access. Free
Italian course. Assistance finding accommodation and accommodation allowance given for first week.

RECRUITMENT: email or postal applications with full CV, recent photograph, the names and email addresses of two teaching-related references, copies of degree, TEFL qualification and passport. Interviews and hiring mainly in June/July for October start and in December for January.

CONTACT: John Credico, Director of Studies.

MAC LANGUAGE SCHOOL
Via Rasella 152, 00187 Rome
+0697747699; fax 0642823927
hr@maclanguage.biz
www.maclanguage.biz

NUMBER OF TEACHERS: 57.

PREFERENCE OF NATIONALITY: none, if mother tongue.

QUALIFICATIONS: 3 years' experience or certified teachers.

CONDITIONS OF EMPLOYMENT: 4–8 hours per day.

FACILITIES/SUPPORT: none.

RECRUITMENT: internet, newspapers, other. Interviews essential. Sometimes, phone interviews can be arranged.

CONTACT: Ms Carmen Lora, Director of Studies.

MADRELINGUA SCHOOL OF ENGLISH
Via San Giorgio, 640121 Bologna
+051 267 822; fax 051 267 822
info@madrelinguabologna.com
www.madrelinguabologna.com

NUMBER OF TEACHERS: around 10.

PREFERENCE OF NATIONALITY: no, but must be eligible to work legally in Italy.

QUALIFICATIONS: degree plus certificate or PGCE diploma preferred.

CONDITIONS OF EMPLOYMENT: academic year is October to June. Teachers work evenings and Saturday mornings.

SALARY: depending on experience but above average for the local market. Minimum €20 an hour gross. Taxes are around 20%.

FACILITIES/SUPPORT: school can arrange a 'homestay' on a temporary basis.

RECRUITMENT: receives lots of CVs.

CONTACT: Daniel Stephens, Director.

NEW SCHOOL
Via de Ambrosis 21, 15067 Novi Ligure (AL)
+0143 2987; fax 0143 767678
new.school@libarnanet.it
www.newschool.it

NUMBER OF TEACHERS: 8.

PREFERENCE OF NATIONALITY: British, Irish.

QUALIFICATIONS: TEFL Diploma/degree plus 1 year's experience.

CONDITIONS OF EMPLOYMENT: 9 months, renewable. Average of 25 hours per week.

SALARY: €10 per hour net.

RECRUITMENT: via www.tefl.com.

CONTACT: Daniela Oddone, Director.

OXFORD INSTITUTE
10/12 Via Adriatica 10/12, 73100 Lecce
fax 0832 390312
info@oxfordiamo.com
www.oxfordiamo.com

NUMBER OF TEACHERS: 15 (another branch in Maglie).

PREFERENCE OF NATIONALITY: none.

QUALIFICATIONS: CELTA plus 2 years' experience.

CONDITIONS OF EMPLOYMENT: 9-month contracts October to June. 30 hours per week

SALARY: approx. €650–€700 (net).

FACILITIES/SUPPORT: free accommodation provided. Help given with obtaining all necessary documents. Training available.

RECRUITMENT: interviews in London.

OXFORD SCHOOL OF ENGLISH s.r.l.
Administrative Office, Via S. Pertini 14, 30035 Mirano, Venice
041 570 23 55; fax 041 570 2390
oxforditalia@tin.it
www.oxforditalia.it

NUMBER OF TEACHERS: 20–30 for 13 schools in northeast Italy of which most are independent franchises (60–70 teachers employed altogether).

PREFERENCE OF NATIONALITY: British.

QUALIFICATIONS: degree, TEFL and knowledge of Italian needed.

CONDITIONS OF EMPLOYMENT: 9-month contracts or longer. 22 hours per week

SALARY: varies according to hours and length of contract. Tax deductions of about 23% give minimum health and welfare cover.

FACILITIES/SUPPORT: accommodation at teacher's own expense, but school will help to find it.

RECRUITMENT: interviews in London from mid-May or Italy.

QUAGI LANGUAGE CENTRE

Via Manzoni, C Santa, 91100 Trapani, Sicily

fax 0923 557748

quagi@quagi.com or quagi@quagi.org

www.quagi.org

NUMBER OF TEACHERS: 7.

PREFERENCE OF NATIONALITY: native English speakers with an EU passport.

QUALIFICATIONS: preferably 2 years' experience but not essential. However, a degree and CELTA or TESOL are required.

CONDITIONS OF EMPLOYMENT: usually 8 months October to the end of May. 4-month contracts also offered (January to May).

SALARY: €1,500 per month, guaranteed base salary.

FACILITIES/SUPPORT: modern, up-to-date school which offers training to become an official Cambridge Esol oral examiner, internet, a large range of resources and a return flight to the UK at the end of the contract term and holidays are fully paid. The school will also help teachers find fully furnished accommodation, arrange tax file numbers and medical visits.

RECRUITMENT: direct. Telephone interviews possible.

CONTACT: Teresa Matteucci, quagi@quagi.org.

REGENCY SCHOOL

Via Arcivescovado 7, 10121 Torino

+011 562 7456; fax 011 541845

regency@tin.it or regency.international@regency.it

www.regency.it

NUMBER OF TEACHERS: 35.

PREFERENCE OF NATIONALITY: European nationals or applicants from other countries who also have an EU passport.

QUALIFICATIONS: university degree essential plus CELTA or equivalent or DELTA or equivalent.

CONDITIONS OF EMPLOYMENT: full-time and part-time contracts. Maximum 7 hours per day in 2 of possible 3 blocks. Pupils are mainly adult professionals.

SALARY: negotiable (according to experience and qualifications).

FACILITIES/SUPPORT: regular seminars and workshops for teachers.

RECRUITMENT: through network of contacts or internet (eg www.tefl.com). Interviews essential in Italy.

SUMMER CAMPS

Via Roma 54, San Remo, 18038

/fax 0184 506070

See entry for ACLE above

THE CAMBRIDGE SCHOOL

Via Rosmini 6, 37123 Verona

+045 800 3154; fax 045 801 4900

info@cambridgeschool.it

www.cambridgeschool.it

NUMBER OF TEACHERS: 12–15.

PREFERENCE OF NATIONALITY: none, but should be native English speaker.

QUALIFICATIONS: CELTA (or similar), degree and preferably 2 years' experience.

CONDITIONS OF EMPLOYMENT: 9 months for 10/15 or 20 hours per week. Hours are mainly evenings (5pm–10pm).

SALARY: depends on hours, qualifications and experience.

FACILITIES/SUPPORT: the school has one apartment which can be shared by two teachers; otherwise assistance given with finding accommodation. School runs CELTA courses (see Training). On-going assistance and training.

RECRUITMENT: on presentation at the school.

THE ENGLISH CENTRE

Via P. Paoli 34, 07100 Sassari, Italy

+079 232154; fax 079 232180

theenglishcentre@tin.it

www.theenglishcentreonline.com

NUMBER OF TEACHERS: 4.

PREFERENCE OF NATIONALITY: none.

QUALIFICATIONS: CELTA (or equivalent) and 2 years' experience.

CONDITIONS OF EMPLOYMENT: 9-month contracts, working between 2pm and 9.20pm.

SALARY: €1100–€1500 per month, net.

FACILITIES/SUPPORT: assistance with finding accommodation.

RECRUITMENT: dedicated website, recruitment agency. Interviews essential, these are sometimes carried out in the UK.

CONTACT: Dr Paul Rogerson, Director.

UNITED COLLEGE
Ronco a Via Von Platen 16/18, 96100 Siracusa

📞 fax 0931 22000

📧 info@unitedcollege.it or carolyn.davies@
unitedcollege.it

NUMBER OF TEACHERS: 10.

PREFERENCE OF NATIONALITY: British (work contracts for non-Europeans much more difficult to arrange).

QUALIFICATIONS: degree plus Certificate (Trinity or Cambridge) plus 1 year's experience. Basic knowledge of Italian preferable.

CONDITIONS OF EMPLOYMENT: mid-September to mid-June. Hours between 3pm and 9pm.

SALARY: approximately £800 per month (depending on experience).

FACILITIES/SUPPORT: accommodation arranged and school car available.

RECRUITMENT: through www.tefl.com.

CONTACT: Carolyn Davies, Director of Studies.

WALL STREET INSTITUTE

📧 staff@wallstreet.it

💻 www.wallstreetinstitute.it/lavoro-
scuola-inglese.asp

Branch vacancies given on website.

WALL STREET INSTITUTE (FERRARA)
Via Zandonai 4, 44100 Ferrara

📞 +0532 977703; fax 0532 907446

📧 reception@wallstreetferrara.it

💻 www.wallstreetferrara.it

NUMBER OF TEACHERS: 6–7.

QUALIFICATIONS: CELTA or other TEFL qualification; teaching experience (minimum 1 year) needed. Driving licence may be needed.

CONDITIONS OF EMPLOYMENT: 10-month contracts (September to June). 25 hours per week. Mostly adults.

SALARY: approx. €1,200 per month.

FACILITIES/SUPPORT: assistance with finding accommodation and obtaining working papers. Training in Wall Street method.

RECRUITMENT: direct application and recruiting agencies.

CONTACT: Service Manager.

WINDSOR SCHOOL OF ENGLISH
Via Molino delle Lime 4/F, 10064 Pinerolo (TO)

📞 349 1229255; fax 0121 795555

📧 info@windsorpinerolo.com

💻 www.windsorpinerolo.com

NUMBER OF TEACHERS: 15–20.

PREFERENCE OF NATIONALITY: British or EU applicants only.

QUALIFICATIONS: minimum CTEFL.

CONDITIONS OF EMPLOYMENT: 9–10 months.

SALARY: from €600–€1,300 net per month.

FACILITIES/SUPPORT: flat provided.

RECRUITMENT: advertisements, contacts in the UK. Interviews can be carried out in UK.

CONTACT: Sandro Vazon Colla, Director

PORTUGAL

Relations between Portugal and Britain have always been warm and the demand for English tuition remains strong, even if the lacklustre state of the Portuguese economy has put a damper on the market. There are some excellent native Portuguese English teachers, but students tend to prefer a native English speaker, so schools will continue to employ foreigners. Most schools cater for anyone over the age of seven, so you should be prepared to teach children. The Portuguese government has been pushing for English to start at 1st grade and as a result parents are eager to start their children very young in private English classes. The enrolment for children's courses has really gone up. The Centro Anglo-Americano (see list of employers) is fairly typical: 90% of its student body is under 17. They find it hard to recruit teachers who have experience of teaching children and a basic knowledge of Portuguese, which is useful when teaching young children.

In fact, some schools organise courses in nursery/primary schools for children from the age of three, sometimes as part of the Ministry of Education's 'Teaching and Understanding of the first level of basic English' programme. The language school, Self Escola de Linguas, based in Madeira, teaches very young children through this programme, as well as older students and businessmen and women.

The vast majority of British tourists flock to the Algarve along the southern coast of Portugal, which means that many Portuguese in the south who aspire to work in the tourist industry want to learn English. Schools such as the Wall Street Institutes in Portimao and Faro, and the Centro de Linguas in Lagos cater for just that market. But the demand for English teachers is greatest in the north and central Portugal. Jobs crop up in historic centres such as Coimbra, Braga and Viseu and in small seaside towns like Aveiro and Póvoa do Varzim. These can be a very welcome destination for teachers burned out from teaching in big cities, first-time teachers who want to avoid the rat-race, or teachers who simply want to secure a good wage and accommodation. The British Council (www.britishcouncil.org/portugal) has English language centres in Coimbra, Greater Lisbon and Porto and recruits teachers with a degree, TEFL certificate and two years' post-TEFL qualification EFL teaching experience.

FINDING A JOB

Most teachers in Portugal have either answered advertisements or are working for one of the large chains. International House (IH) has 12 affiliated schools in Portugal. Wall Street Institute is well represented with 34 centres.

About three-quarters of all IH students in Portugal are children, so expertise with young learners is a definite asset. IH and the British Council, among others, also offer 'courses to help professionals,' so expertise in law/finance and business should also prove helpful when trying to secure a job.

Outside the cities where there have traditionally been large expatriate communities, schools cannot depend on English speakers just showing up and so must recruit well in advance of the academic year (late September to the end of June).

The Bristol Schools Group offers the only possibility of which we have heard for working in the Azores, so if you want to work in the most isolated islands in the Atlantic Ocean – more than 1,000 km west of Portugal – this is your chance. Small groups of schools, say six schools in a single region, is the norm in Portugal. A number of the schools listed in the directory at the end of this chapter belong to such mini-chains. One of the most well-established is the Cambridge Schools group which every year imports up to 100 teachers.

Many schools are small family-run establishments with fewer than 10 teachers, so sending off a lot of speculative applications is unlikely to succeed. Some recruit through sites such as www.tefl.com, whilst others place advertisements in the local press.

As is true anywhere, you might be lucky and fix up something on the spot. The Cambridge CELTA is widely requested by schools and can be obtained at IH in Lisbon.

REGULATIONS

The red tape for EU nationals working in Portugal is refreshingly painless. All that is required (as throughout the EU) is to obtain a residence permit (*Autorizacao de Residencia*) after an initial six-month stay by taking documents to show proof of accommodation, health insurance and means of support. If you are employed, you must show that you have been registered in the social security system and are not being paid less than the Portuguese minimum wage. These must be presented to the local authorities, ie any office of the Serviço de Estrangeiros e Fronteiras (SEF) or Aliens Office. The headquarters are at Rua Conselheiro José Silvestre Ribeiro 4, 1649 007 Lisbon (✆ +21 711 5000; www.sef.pt).

NON-EU RESIDENTS TEND TO HAVE A MUCH MORE DIFFICULT TIME TRYING TO WORK IN PORTUGAL THAN EU RESIDENTS, AS RACHEL BEEBE, AN AMERICAN, DISCOVERED IN 2008:

I was not able to obtain a work visa of any kind: I found that this is very difficult for Americans living and working in Portugal. I had to work using recibos verdes ('green receipts'), which are intended for use by temporary workers in the country. This situation prevented me from securing a contract with my school; a contract would have allowed me a more permanent position as well as vacation time and other benefits. To get a work visa, you need a work contract in hand. While my school offered me a letter of their intent to employ me, you are required to have a legal contract when applying for the visa, which can then take upwards of a year (or more) to process. In the meantime, you are only allowed to stay in the country on a 'temporary stay visa,' which will allow you to stay up to nine months from the time of your arrival in Portugal. Needless to say, this period of time will expire before you are able to obtain a work visa. After the nine months, you would be expected to leave the Schengen area (which includes most western European countries, with the notable exception of the UK) for an equal period of time. Ostensibly, this would prevent most would-be American teachers from being able to teach long-term in Portugal. You could always try to secure a contract 12 months in advance of your planned arrival date, but I have never heard of a school hiring more than five or six months before the start date. In my case, I managed to get my hands on a book of green receipts and taught for a few months using those. However, many government offices will give you conflicting information, and I was only able to get the receipts with the help and direction of a friend who was able to tell me exactly where to go and what to say to whom.

The other alternative is to seek employment with schools that seem likely to prefer American speakers: any school with 'American' in the title is probably a good bet. Try the American School of Languages (Av. Duque de Loule, 22–1, 1050 090, Lisbon; ✆ 21 314 6000; www.americanschooloflanguages.com) or the Centro Anglo-Americano (see entry). The Centro Anglo-Americano is a family-run school that prefers to hire EU citizens because they are cheaper, although they'd make an exception for qualified candidates (who rarely apply).

Since most teachers working for nine months are working on a freelance basis, they are responsible for paying their own taxes and contributions. There are seven income tax brackets ranging from 10.5% to 42% and an array of tax deductions, credits and special benefits. Tax laws and regulations are frequently subject to change, so it is best to check with the relevant authorities (Direcção-Geral dos Impostos, dsdsitarp@dgci.min-financas.pt).

CONDITIONS OF WORK

The consensus seems to be that wages are low, but the cost of living, at least outside the major cities, is reasonable. Imported consumer goods are taxed and expensive and the cost of domestic fuel and tolls on roads and bridges are high, but local produce such as olive oil, fruit, vegetables and wine are still relatively inexpensive. Public transport is quite cheap, as well as eating out. Working conditions are generally relaxed and students are generally helpful, as **Rachel Beebe** discovered: '*Most students had a good attitude and tried very hard to speak the language. I spoke virtually no Portuguese in encounters or classes, and the students made every effort to use what they were learning to communicate with me.*'

The normal salary range is €700–€1,000 net per month. Full-time contract workers are entitled to an extra month's pay after 12 months, which is partly why most teachers are employed on 9/10-month contracts. Some schools pay lower rates but subsidise or pay for flights and accommodation. Several provide free Portuguese lessons. Teachers being paid on an hourly basis should expect to earn €10–€17, but they will of course not be eligible for the 13th month bonus or paid holidays. Rates per hour can sink as low as €6.50, which isn't enough to live on unless you can also secure free accommodation. If you are living in an urban centre, then you'll also need to factor in any unpaid travel time to find out how much you are 'really' getting paid.

LIST OF EMPLOYERS

BRISTOL SCHOOLS GROUP

Bristol School – Instituto de Línguas da Maia, Trav. Dr. Carlos Pires Felgueiras, 12–3°, 4470 158 Maia

📞 22 948 8803; fax 22 948 6460

🖱 bsmaia@bristolschool.pt

💻 www.bristolschool.pt

Comprises a group of 9 small schools: 4 in Oporto area, 2 in the Azores and 3 inland (Castelo Branco and Fundão and Colvilha). Addresses on website.

NUMBER OF TEACHERS: 25.

PREFERENCE OF NATIONALITY: British only (couples preferred).

QUALIFICATIONS: BA and TEFL qualification. 1 year's experience essential.

CONDITIONS OF EMPLOYMENT: minimum period of work 15 September to 30 June, 25 hours per week Pupils aged from 8 to Proficiency level.

SALARY: basic salary plus Christmas bonus and end-of-contract bonuses plus tax rebate. Legal contract of work.

FACILITIES/SUPPORT: assistance with accommodation given. No training.

RECRUITMENT: direct application preferred.

CAMBRIDGE SCHOOL S.A.

Avenida da Liberdade 173, 1250 141 Lisbon

📞 21 312 4600; fax 21 312 4694

🖱 info@cambridge.pt

💻 www.cambridge.pt

Portugal's largest private language school with 8 centres in Lisbon and other major cities

NUMBER OF TEACHERS: 90-110.

PREFERENCE OF NATIONALITY: Native speakers of English, EU citizens or in possession of a Portuguese residence permit.

QUALIFICATIONS: BA plus CELTA, Trinity TESOL or an equivalent EFL qualification. Non-mainstream qualifications must be accompanied by an official course programme.

CONDITIONS OF EMPLOYMENT: All contracts are for full-time positions (22 hrs/week).

COMPENSATION: At the moment, in a typical month, most starting teachers (2008-2009) will average between €1200 and €1300 after deductions and extras. Two bonus salaries paid per year (Christmas and summer). One month's paid summer holiday. All staff currently receive a monthly meal subsidy of €132.00. In addition to joining the Portuguese National Health scheme, the school employs its own medical officers. Salaries are adjusted at the beginning of October.

FACILITIES/SUPPORT: All schools have 2 or 3 senior staff.

RECRUITMENT: adverts on tefl.com. Applicants should send CV, recent photograph, contact telephone number and copies of degree and EFL Certificate. Interviews are usually held in London in May and possibly mid-summer depending on requirements. Visitors to Portugal can be interviewed in Lisbon by prior arrangement.

CONTACT: Jeffrey Kapke (Pedagogical Director) or Richard Nicholas (General Director of Studies).

CENTRO ANGLO-AMERICANO
Travessa da Viscondessa, Ed. D. João, loja 5,
R/C 5400 567, Chaves; Rua Miguel Torga 18 R/C
5000 524, Vila Real
1 276 333 469 and 1 259 321 471
caaenglish@caaenglish.com
www.caaenglish.com

NUMBER OF TEACHERS: 7.
PREFERENCE OF NATIONALITY: no.
QUALIFICATIONS: teaching degree, CELTA, or equivalent. Experience with children/young learners is essential.
CONDITIONS OF EMPLOYMENT: 9-month contracts. 20–28 hours a week.
SALARY: from €600 to €1000 depending on qualifications and experience.
FACILITIES/SUPPORT: school accountant is able to assist teachers with work permit.
RECRUITMENT: via walk-in, personal recommendation, face-to-face interview essential.
CONTACT: Tulia Pilomia Vogensen, Director of Studies.

CENTRO DE INGLES DE FAMALICAO
Edificio dos Correios, n° 116–4° Dto, Rua S. Joao de Deus, 4760 V.N. de Famalicao
/fax 252 374233
cif@esoterica.pt

NUMBER OF TEACHERS: 4.
PREFERENCE OF NATIONALITY: EU preferred.
QUALIFICATIONS: degree and CELTA or equivalent essential; experience an advantage but not essential.
CONDITIONS OF EMPLOYMENT: 9-month renewable contracts. 24 contact hours p.w.
SALARY: at least €935 per month (net).
FACILITIES/SUPPORT: fully furnished flat near school provided rent-free. Help given with work permit procedures. Lessons are regularly observed and feedback given.
RECRUITMENT: via advertisements in the *Guardian*. Interviews essential, usually held in London.
CONTACT: David Mills, Director of Studies.

CIAL – CENTRO DE LINGUAS

Avenida Republica 14–2, 1050 191 Lisbon

☎ 213 533 733; mobile 918 500 300;
   fax 213 523 096

✉ linguas.estrangeiras@cial.pt

🖥 www.cial.pt

NUMBER OF TEACHERS: 15–17.

PREFERENCE OF NATIONALITY: EU.

QUALIFICATIONS: university degree, CELTA, EFL teaching experience (to adults; minimum 2 years); business English teaching experience.

CONDITIONS OF EMPLOYMENT: contracts October to June. Early morning, lunch-time and evening teaching hours.

SALARY: depends on work agreement. Possibility of full-time, part-time or hourly basis. Monthly performance evaluation bonus paid as well as free Portuguese lessons and free health insurance as fringe benefits.

FACILITIES/SUPPORT: family accommodation can be arranged for first 4 weeks if requested.

RECRUITMENT: pre-selection through detailed CV; personal interviews compulsory.

CONTACT: Isabel Coimbra, Director (isabelcoimbra@cial.pt).

ENCOUNTER ENGLISH

Av. Fernão Magalhães 604, 4350 150 Oporto

☎ 225 367916; fax 225 366 339

Also at Rua da Estação Velha, 2628, 4460
306 Senhora da Hora

☎ 229 542 675

✉ info@encounterenglish.com

🖥 www.encounterenglish.com

NUMBER OF TEACHERS: 14.

PREFERENCE OF NATIONALITY: British.

QUALIFICATIONS: recognised 1-month intensive TEFL course plus 2 years' solid teaching experience.

CONDITIONS OF EMPLOYMENT: contracts last from 15 September to 30 June. Up to 24 lessons per week lasting 50 minutes. Mostly evenings and Saturday mornings. Extended holidays at Christmas, Easter and Carnival.

SALARY: €1,000–€1,200 gross plus 2 bonuses per academic year depending on qualifications and experience.

FACILITIES/SUPPORT: assistance given with finding accommodation. Training available. Senior staff available to support less experienced teachers.

RECRUITMENT: interviews held locally or in England.

CONTACT: Stephen Cassidy.

ENGLISH LANGUAGE CENTRE

Rua da Palmeira 5, 1A/B, Cascais

☎ 214830716

✉ caroline.darling@elc-cascais.com

🖥 www.elc-cascais.com

NUMBER OF TEACHERS: 5.

PREFERENCE OF NATIONALITY: UK.

QUALIFICATIONS: CELTA and 1 year experience.

CONDITIONS OF EMPLOYMENT: 10-month renewable contract. 15–18 hours per week.

SALARY: 15 hours €850.

FACILITIES/SUPPORT: teachers introduced to local estate agents. No other help.

RECRUITMENT: through tefl.com/local advertisements. Face-to-face interviews essential.

CONTACT: Caroline Darling, Director.

ENGLISH SCHOOL ÉVORA

Praça da Muralha, 12–1º esq. 7005 248
Évora

☎ 266743231/938512574; fax 266743231

✉ englishschoolevora@gmail.com

🖥 www.englishschoolevora.com

NUMBER OF TEACHERS: 3.

PREFERENCE OF NATIONALITY: EU national, native English speaker so Ireland or UK.

QUALIFICATIONS: degree, TEFL qualification, minimum 2 years' experience.

CONDITIONS OF EMPLOYMENT: 9-month renewable contract, 23 hours plus possible overtime.

FACILITIES/SUPPORT: some assistance with finding accommodation.

RECRUITMENT: through the internet. Interviews are often by phone.

CONTACT: Michael W Lewis, Director.

INSTITUTO BRITANICO DE BRAGA

Rua Conselheiro Januario 119 123, Apartado 2682,
4701 908 Braga

☎ 253 263298; fax 253 619 355

✉ efl.ibb@alb-minho.pt

🖥 www.alb-minho.pt

NUMBER OF TEACHERS: 16.

PREFERENCE OF NATIONALITY: English native English speaker.

QUALIFICATIONS: degree plus TEFL Cert, CELTA etc. and experience of teaching.

CONDITIONS OF EMPLOYMENT: one school year. 22 contact hours per week.

SALARY: €1,120 per month (approx).

FACILITIES/SUPPORT: no assistance with accommodation.

RECRUITMENT: direct application – with CV. Interview at the school essential.

CONTACT: Dr. Vergilio Rodrigues (v.rodrigues@alb-minho.pt).

INSTITUTO DE LINGUAS DE S. JOAO DA MADEIRA
Largo Durbalino Laranjeira S/N, 3700 S. João da Madeira
- 256 833906; fax 256 835887
- institutodelinguas@hotmail.com or instituto .de.linguas@netvisao.pt

PREFERENCE OF NATIONALITY: British.

QUALIFICATIONS: DELTA/COTE plus 2 years' experience.

CONDITIONS OF EMPLOYMENT: 9-month contracts from October.

SALARY: dependent on qualifications.

FACILITIES/SUPPORT: no help given with accommodation, work permits or training.

RECRUITMENT: interview essential.

CONTACT: Dr. Helena Borges, Director.

INTERLINGUA INSTITUTO DE LINGUAS
Lg. 1° de Dezembro 28, 8500 538 Portimao
- 282 427690; fax 282 416030
- interlingua@mail.telepac.pt or interlingua@ netcabo.pt

NUMBER OF TEACHERS: 4.

PREFERENCE OF NATIONALITY: British.

QUALIFICATIONS: TEFL Cert. able to teach children (6–10 years) as well as adults.

CONDITIONS OF EMPLOYMENT: 9 months to a year.

SALARY: €14 per hour.

FACILITIES/SUPPORT: assistance with finding accommodation.

RECRUITMENT: letters of application. Interviews in Portugal not essential but preferred.

CONTACT: Zita Segall Neto, Director.

INTERNATIONAL HOUSE (LISBON)
Rua Marquês Sá da Bandeira 16,
1050 148 Lisbon
- 21 315 1493/4/6; fax 21 353 0081
- info@ihlisbon.com
- www. ihlisbon.com

NUMBER OF TEACHERS: 18.

PREFERENCE OF NATIONALITY: native English speakers.

QUALIFICATIONS: CELTA minimum.

CONDITIONS OF EMPLOYMENT: standard length of stay 9 months. Flexible working hours to include evening and Saturday work. Pupils range in age from 8 to 80.

SALARY: €1,440 per month for first year teachers.

FACILITIES/SUPPORT: assistance with finding accommodation. CELTA and IHCYL courses offered regularly (see Training chapter).

RECRUITMENT: through local advertisements and by IH, London.

CONTACT: Colin McMillan, Director.

INTERNATIONAL HOUSE (PORTO)
Rua Marechal Saldanha 145–1°, 4150 655 Porto
- 22 617 7641
- info@ihporto.org
- www.ihporto.org
Also Leça da Palmeira, Rua Oliveira
Lessa 350, 4450 Matosinhos
- 22 995 9087
- business@ihporto.org

NUMBER OF TEACHERS: 10.

PREFERENCE OF NATIONALITY: British, Canadian, Australian, New Zealander and American.

QUALIFICATIONS: CELTA/Trinity.

CONDITIONS OF EMPLOYMENT: 1-year contracts. 22 hours per week. Pupils aged from 7.

SALARY: depending on qualifications and experience.

FACILITIES/SUPPORT: assistance with accommodation. Portuguese lessons available. Training provided.

RECRUITMENT: direct application.

CONTACT: Phil Rich, Business Services Manager.

LANCASTER COLLEGE
Praceta 25 de Abril 35–1, 4430 Vila Nova de Gaia
- 22 377 2030; fax 22377 2039
- info@lancastercollege.pt
- www.lancastercollege.pt

Also at Covilhã, Espinho, Estarrega, Santa Maria da Feira, Fafe, Arcozelo, Vizela, Porto, Viana do Castelo, Bragança, Lisboa, Amarante, Seixal, Póvoa do Varzim, Braga, Felgueiras, Paredes, Paços de Ferreira, and Estoril (phone, fax and email details on website). Also in Spain (Madrid).

NUMBER OF TEACHERS: up to 150 for all schools.

PREFERENCE OF NATIONALITY: EU (British and Irish preferred but also will consider Australian, New Zealanders, Canadian, American, English-speaking Africans).

QUALIFICATIONS: CELTA, Trinity Cert or equivalent (minimum).

CONDITIONS OF EMPLOYMENT: 9-month contracts. 16–20 contact hours per week; 25 hour working week.

RECRUITMENT: via internet and EFL press.

CONTACT: Personnel Manager.

MANITOBA INSTITUTO DE LINGUAS
Apartado 184, 4491 909 Póvoa de Varzim
(C) /fax 252 683014
🖳 www.manitoba.com.pt

NUMBER OF TEACHERS: 10–12 in 2 schools (other one is in Vila do Conde).

PREFERENCE OF NATIONALITY: American, Canadian, British, Australian, etc.

QUALIFICATIONS: B.Ed./MA plus TEFL qualifications and experience.

CONDITIONS OF EMPLOYMENT: 1–2 year contracts. 25 hours per week. Pupils aged 7–60. Also run children's summer schools.

SALARY: above average for Portugal.

FACILITIES/SUPPORT: assistance with finding accommodation. Training provided.

RECRUITMENT: applicants should send proof of degrees and other certificates, at least two references and a recent photograph. Interviews not always necessary.

CONTACT: Isabel Boucanova, Pedagogic Director.

OXFORD SCHOOL
Lisbon: Rua D. Estefania, 165–1°, 1000 154 Lisbon
(C) 21 354 6586; fax 21 314 1152
Also: Av. Marques Tomar 104–4°dto,
1050 157 Lisbon
(C) 21 796 6660; fax 21 795 1293
🖰 oxford-school@mail.telepac.pt
Cacém: Av. Bons Amigos, 37–1° Dto, 2735 077
Cacém
(C) 21 914 6343
🖳 www.oxford-school.pt

Member of AEPLE and ELITE (Excellent Language Institutions Teaching in Europe)

NUMBER OF TEACHERS: about 40 for two branches in Lisbon and one in Cacém.

PREFERENCE OF NATIONALITY: British.

QUALIFICATIONS: minimum TEFL course and some experience.

CONDITIONS OF EMPLOYMENT: October to June. Evening hours mainly.

SALARY: minimum €17 per 1 teaching hour.

RECRUITMENT: direct application.

CONTACT: – Zilda Amaro.

POMBALINGUA ESCOLA DE INGLES
Rua de Ansiao 29, 3100 474 Pombal
(C) 236 214 319; fax 236 211 064
🖳 www.pombalingua.com

NUMBER OF TEACHERS: 9.

PREFERENCE OF NATIONALITY: British.

QUALIFICATIONS: EFL certificate; experience preferred but not essential.

CONDITIONS OF EMPLOYMENT: 9-month renewable contracts available, usually contracted on a freelance basis. To work 18 hours per week.

SALARY: €11 per hour.

CONTACT: Paul A. Araújo, Headmaster/Director.

ROYAL SCHOOL OF LANGUAGES – ESCOLAS DE LINGUAS, LDA
Headquarters: Rua José Rabumba 2, 3810 125 Aveiro
(C) 234 429 156 or 234 425 104; fax 234 382 870
🖰 rsl@royalschooloflanguages.pt
🖳 www.royalschooloflanguages.pt

Schools also in Porto, Agueda, Guarda, Ovar, Viseu, Mirandela, Macedo de Cavaleiros, Iihavo and Albergaria-a-Velha. Languages taught: English, French, German, Italian, Spanish and Portuguese

NUMBER OF TEACHERS: 28–33 in group of 10 schools.

PREFERENCE OF NATIONALITY: British, Australian, Canadians and Americans.

QUALIFICATIONS: university degree plus TEFL Certificate (Trinity, Cambridge or equivalent).

CONDITIONS OF EMPLOYMENT: 9-month contracts. 25–27 teaching hours per week.

FACILITIES/SUPPORT: assistance with accommodation and working papers.

RECRUITMENT: via CVs or interviews, which sometimes take place in UK.

SELF ESCOLA DE LÌNGUAS
Rua Bela São Tiago No 16, Funchal,
Madeira, 9060 400
- 291 234 225/ 291 224 017/962192323;
  fax 291225 429
- info@e-self.net
- www.e-self.net

NUMBER OF TEACHERS: 5
PREFERENCE OF NATIONALITY: none.
QUALIFICATIONS: a degree or teaching experience preferred. A TEFL certificate and proven social skills are also useful.
CONDITIONS OF EMPLOYMENT: 6-month, 9-month or 1-year contracts, or part-time. To work 4–25 hours per week, depending on type of contract.
FACILITIES/SUPPORT: advice given on finding accommodation. Sometimes the company assists with additional costs.
RECRUITMENT: school usually puts an advertisement in the paper, sends out emails to embassies etc. Then the applicants send their CV. Interviews are face-to-face or by phone.
CONTACT: Rebecca Jardim, Director of Studies.

SINTRALINGUAS CENTRO DE LINGUAS
Avenida Movimento das Forças, Armada
14–3D, 2710 431 Sintra
- /fax 21 923 4941
- sintralingua@mail.telepac.pt
- www.sintralinguas.com

NUMBER OF TEACHERS: 15.
PREFERENCE OF NATIONALITY: British; must be native English speaker.
QUALIFICATIONS: minimum BA and 2 years' experience.
CONDITIONS OF EMPLOYMENT: 1-year contracts. Part-time hourly work also available. Lots of evening teaching (5.30pm–9.30pm) but other times possible.
SALARY: full-time teachers €850 per month (14 months paid per year), part-time teachers €16 per hour. Petrol allowance for travelling to give language training in companies €9 per trip.
FACILITIES/SUPPORT: assistance given with finding accommodation. Observation and feedback programme.

RECRUITMENT: online or mail applications; interviews in UK or locally.
CONTACT: James Scott MA, Director.

SPEAKWELL ESCOLA DE LINGUAS
Head office: Praça Mário Azevedo Gomes,
N 421, 2775 240 Parede
- 21 456 1771; fax 21 456 1775
- speakwell@speakwell.pt
- www.speakwell.pt

NUMBER OF TEACHERS: 10 full-time and 20 part-time.
PREFERENCE OF NATIONALITY: none, but must be native English speakers.
QUALIFICATIONS: TEFL certificate, preferably plus some business experience, or experience teaching children.
CONDITIONS OF EMPLOYMENT: can guarantee full-time hours October to June. School opening times are weekdays and Saturday mornings. Business trainers and qualified school teachers also required.
SALARY: above the average hourly rate for Portugal.
FACILITIES/SUPPORT: nothing formally, but will help people to find accommodation through contacts, etc.
RECRUITMENT: internet, local advertising, word-of-mouth.
CONTACT: Director of Studies.

THE NEW INSTITUTE OF LANGUAGES
Rua Cordeiro Ferreira, 19C 1°Dto, 1750 071 Lisbon
- /fax 21 759 0770 or 21 943 5238
- nilportugal@gmail.com
- www.nil.edu.pt

NUMBER OF TEACHERS: 11/12 English teachers for four schools in and around Lisbon.
PREFERENCE OF NATIONALITY: British preferred.
QUALIFICATIONS: experienced and inexperienced graduates who have successfully completed a TEFL course.
CONDITIONS OF EMPLOYMENT: 9/10 months, renewable at the end. 20–25 contact hours per week.
SALARY: depends on experience.
FACILITIES/SUPPORT: secretarial and administrative help in finding and renting accommodation. The school acts as guarantor for rentals. 3-month teaching course on a once a week basis to aid teachers in the classroom.
RECRUITMENT: website advertising followed by possibility of London interviews in June/July and September.
CONTACT: Nicholas Rudall, Director of Studies.

SCANDINAVIA

Certain similarities exist in ELT throughout Scandinavia. The standard of English teaching in state schools is uniformly high, as anyone who has met a Dane or a Swede travelling abroad (and mistaken them for a Brit) will know. Yet many ordinary Scandinavians aspire to fluency so keep up their English by attending evening classes, if only for social reasons. Sweden, Denmark and Norway have excellent facilities for such people, which are variations on the theme of 'folk university', a state-subsidised system of adult education. Classes at such institutions are the ideal setting for enthusiastic amateur teachers.

But as elsewhere in Europe the greatest demand for the English language comes from the business community, particularly in Finland. Enthusiastic amateurs tend to be less in demand in this setting than mature professionals. Yet Scandinavia is not a very popular destination for such teachers, despite its unspoilt countryside, efficient public transport and liberal society So there is scope for most kinds of teacher to work in Scandinavia, particularly in Finland, whose language schools sometimes advertise in the British press.

Since Finland and Sweden are EU members, red tape is straightforward for EU teachers. But even in Norway, whose people voted by a referendum not to join, the formalities are straightforward for EU nationals and language institutes employ foreign teachers. Billington Recruitment Consultants (1 Mariners Close, St James Court, Victoria Dock, Kingston Upon Hull, East Yorkshire, HU9 1QE; ✆ 1482 611008; www.billingtonuk.com) provides a recruitment consultancy to employers in Scandinavia, especially those looking to hire teachers of business English with some professional work experience.

Denmark

There is little recruitment of English teachers outside Denmark, apart from the Cambridge Institute Foundation which is Denmark's largest EFL institution with 38 branches and which specialises in English for business. The Danish government has tightened up the immigration laws in Denmark making it virtually impossible for non-Europeans to get working permits. However, it decided on a slight change of tack after the Minister for Employment launched 'a 13-point plan for providing assistance to Danish companies in connection with the recruitment of foreign labour', and 30% more residence permits were issued (mainly to European IT experts, nurses, etc., but not exclusively).

Many schools expect their teachers to speak Danish, and there seem to be almost enough fully bilingual candidates resident in Denmark to satisfy this requirement. It is worthwhile for any native English speaker with an appropriate background who is staying in Denmark to enquire about part-time openings.

Like Scandinavians generally, Danes are enthusiastic self-improvers which means that evening classes in English (and hundreds of other things) are very popular. These are purely recreational and are meant to be fun and informal (*hygge* in Danish). Folkehøjskoler (folk high schools) offer residential courses of varying lengths where working conditions are generally so favourable that there is very little turnover of teaching staff. The tradition of voluntary organisations including trade unions running courses is still strong in Denmark. It might be worth tracking down one of the voluntary organisations which run evening classes countrywide:

- Arbejdernes Oplysnings Forbund (AOF), Teglvaerksgade 27, 2100 Copenhagen Ø; ✆ 3929 6066; www.aof.dk. AOF means Workers' Education.
- Netop, Gammel Kangevej 39G, 1, 1610 Copenhagen K; ✆ 3393 0096; info@netoplysning.dk; www.netoplysning.dk.

Addresses of the Danish Folkeuniversitet can be found on its website at www.folkeuniversitetet.dk.

Wages in Denmark are set by law and teaching English is no exception. The minimum is about DKK50, and that is what most new arrivals earn. However once you're established you can expect to earn £25 an hour teaching in the state sector (which is much better funded and resourced than its UK counterpart). Denmark has among the highest taxes in the world, ie 45%.

Finland

Although Finland's second language is Swedish, English runs a close second. Finns are admirably energetic and industrious in learning foreign languages, possibly because their own language is so impenetrable (belonging to the Finno-Ugric group of languages along with Hungarian and Estonian). English is taught in every kind of educational institution from trade and technology colleges to universities, in commercial colleges (*Kauppaloulu*) and in Civic and Workers' Institutes. Private language schools flourish too and traditionally have not been too fussy about the paper qualifications of their native English speaker teachers. They seldom teach straight English courses but tailor courses to clients, eg 'English for presentation skills', so they are not looking for young first-timers to teach their wealthy corporate clients. Still, some private schools (such as Berlitz) may take on native English speakers without a teaching qualification.

Children start their primary education at age 7, and many children between the ages of 3 and 7 are sent to private kindergartens, many of which are English (as well as German, American, etc). These sometimes welcome a native English speaker with experience of teaching children. (The only skill which concerned one of these nurseries-cum-kindergartens looking to hire a young British graduate was singing.) Local teachers all have an MA degree since this is the minimum requirement. Provision of English is so good in state schools that there is little scope for picking up slack from disgruntled school leavers who feel they can't speak enough English. Neither is there a demand from an immigrant population since there are few foreigners or refugees in Finland.

FINDING A JOB

One or two members of the Federation of Finnish-British Societies in Finland (Fredrikinkatu 20 A 9, 00120 Helsinki; ✆ 9 687 70 20; 9 687 70 210; finnbritt@finnbrit.fi) take on a few mostly experienced teachers for their teaching centres, notably Helsinki and Jakobstad/Pietarsaari (Ostermalmsgatan 29B, 68600 Jakobstad). The other societies have given up on teaching in the face of stiff competition from commercial institutes and because of lack of staff and time for teaching, which was largely done on a voluntary basis in the past. Any teacher who is hired at an English Club usually finds that it is considered compulsory to participate in regular social evenings, for example giving a talk about British life, or accompanying classes on excursions and ski trips.

Another big player in the provision of English language teaching is Richard Lewis Communications (RLC) with offices throughout Finland and Sweden as well as England (see entry). RLC draws most of its students from senior management in both the public and private sector, and also provides cross-cultural training in Finland.

Of course not all the teaching takes place in the capital. There is a significant demand for freelance teachers for business in Turku, Oulu and other cities.

Teachers without European nationality will still encounter serious problems. American university students and recent graduates (within two years) over 21 can apply to the American-Scandinavian Foundation (58 Park Avenue, New York, NY 10016; ✆ 212 879 9779; trainscan@amscan.org; www.amscan.org/tefl.html) which can arrange English teaching placements in Finland in companies and in schools from kindergarten to colleges. Placements coincide with the terms of the Finnish academic year from the end of August until the end of May. Monthly salaries vary from US$500 to US$1,000 (paid in euros) with monthly rent bills falling between US$250 and US$310 for accommodation arranged by the employer. Flights, insurance and internal travel are also at the teacher's expense. There is no strict application deadline but placements are made between April and June.

CONDITIONS OF WORK

Freelance arrangements have largely replaced contracts which means that fewer institutes pay travel expenses and arrange accommodation for their teachers. A teaching unit of 45 minutes is the norm, with less evening work than elsewhere. Wages are high, but so is the cost of living. Some schools compress the teaching into four days a week, leaving plenty of time for weekend exploration of the country.

Taxes are high and are usually the responsibility of the teacher, whereas contributions should be paid by the employer; social security and unemployment insurance deductions will amount to at least 6% of the salary. Note that there is virtually no possibility of accepting payment 'under the table'. The system is highly controlled and everybody pays his or her taxes.

The Finnish Embassy in London's website (www.finemb.org.uk) has information about living and working in Finland, which points out that as their baby-boomers retire, vacancies will open up.

Helsinki has about 35 museums and art galleries plus a high density of sports facilities, ice rinks, etc. The long dark winters are relieved by a wide choice of cheerful restaurants, cafés, bars and clubs in the cities, and saunas almost everywhere.

Norway

The trend in Norwegian EFL is similar to that in Denmark, and most schools rely on a pool of native English speakers already resident in Norway. The instructional Supervisor for Berlitz Norway says that he finds it next to impossible to recruit teachers from abroad because, '*they don't have a place to stay, a bank account, a work permit, can't attend interviews or training "next week". On top of this I have so many applicants who have all of these things in place and are in the Oslo area.*' Most jobs are for part-time work and of course do not offer accommodation. At least things are easier from an immigration point of view than they used to be. Although Norway is not a member of the EU, it does allow the free reciprocity of labour so that EU nationals are allowed to work in Norway without a work permit. Immigration restrictions on non-EU teachers remain stringent.

The *Yellow Pages* for Norway are online at www.gulesider.no, though typing in Sprakinstitut produced only one result: Norsk Språkinstitutt AS (Kongens, g9 0153 Oslo; ✆ 23 10 01 10).

As throughout Scandinavia, the Folkuniversity of Norway plays an important role in language tuition and hires many native English speakers, mostly on an occasional basis; the main office is at Christian Krohgsgate 34, 0186 Oslo (✆ 22 98 88 00; info@fu.no; www.fu.no). There are branches in 300 Norwegian municipalities with fairly major teaching operations in Stavanger, Skien, Kristiansand and Hamar. Berlitz hires native English speakers with no TEFL background including students and trains them in their method.

The basic hourly wage is about NKK140, though this can double for high-level business teaching. Expect to lose about a third in deductions.

CASUAL OPPORTUNITIES MAY CROP UP IN UNPREDICTABLE PLACES IN NORWAY. DAVID MOOR WAS SIMPLY INTENDING TO SPEND A MONTH ON HOLIDAY SKIING WHEN HE SAW AN ADVERTISEMENT IN A LOCAL SUPERMARKET FOR A NATIVE ENGLISH SPEAKING TEACHER AND JUMPED AT THE CHANCE:

A teacher put me up and fed me. I'd intended to stay in the hostel or a cheap hotel, but was finding Norway expensive. I was just working for keep, teaching three days a week, so I had lots of spare time. I had a fantastic time, much better than a normal holiday.

Sweden

For many years the EFL market has been in a slow but inexorable decline, as standards of English among school leavers have improved. The Folkuniversity of Sweden has a long-established scheme (since 1955) by which British and other native English speakers may be placed for nine months (one academic year) at a time in a network of adult education centres throughout the country, but they no longer have a policy of actively recruiting applicants from abroad. They take on new staff who are already resident in Sweden and even then, the work is part-time, at least initially (Box 2116, S-22002 Lund; ✆ 46 19 77 00; fax 46 19 77 80; peter.baston@folkuniversitetet.se; www. folkuniversitetet.se).

Originally the teaching at the Folkuniversity consisted of evening classes called a 'Study Circle', an informal conversation session. Circumstances have changed, however, and the range of pupils can be very varied from unemployed people to business executives, as well as people who want to prepare for Cambridge examinations or IELTS. People who need English at work are in the majority these days.

FINDING A JOB

Advertisements seldom appear in the educational press. Teachers with a solid ELT background might try the main state universities who put on English courses or the language schools listed in the *Yellow Pages* of Stockholm, Malmö, Gothenburg, Orebro and Uppsala.

Charlotte Rosen decided to do a TEFL course in London before going to Sweden to be with her Swedish fiancé:

> *I had visited Sweden several times before going to Gothenburg to work. After I'd been in Sweden for about six weeks, I looked through the* **Yellow Pages** *for language schools and sent off my CV in English which wasn't a problem because everyone speaks English really well. I was offered several interviews, including by the British Institute. Many of them said they were interested but the terms only start in September and January so you have to time your applications quite carefully.*
>
> *Another possibility is to try some of the private schools in Sweden (not fee paying, as in Britain), particularly if you are interested in staying in Sweden longer term. The Swedish school system has changed dramatically over the last years and private schools (friskolor – free schools) are now plentiful. There are a few English schools within the state system but most of them are independent. Internationella Engelska Skolan (www.engelska.se) is one of Sweden's leading independent schools, founded by an American, and branches are opening all over the country. The schools follow the Swedish curriculum, are authorised by* **Skolverket** *and are free for the students.*

Cathryn Lock, who has a Swedish fiancé, started working at one of the secondary schools in 2007. She found the job through the employment service Arbetsförmedlingen (www.ams.se), sent in a letter of application and was interviewed by the headmaster. She had a degree from an English university. Cathryn has since gone on to pass a teacher exam in Sweden and she believes that it is pretty easy to get a job if you come from the UK.

Although a business background will stand you in good stead, some of the private language schools accept certification, or even just a degree. The British Institute was interested in hiring CELTA/ TEFL qualified teachers in 2008 (see listing), whilst English i2i Language Consultancy (see listing) are also recruiting native English teachers, with a BA and 'great' personality.

Making a breakthrough as a freelancer is difficult without a knowledge of the Swedish labour market and a functioning network of contacts. Note that FU teachers are officially forbidden to take on private pupils.

CONDITIONS OF WORK

Teachers must pay tax in Sweden on a scale, which varies according to the municipality. Swedish income tax is notoriously high, and the FU estimates that teachers lose about 30% in deductions. However, the upside of paying lots of tax is that Sweden is famous for the quality of its public services, its generous child-care and sick day policies, and its efficient and moderately priced public transport system. Although Swedes groan about tax, they do not often express frustration that their money is 'wasted', as often seems to be the case when British citizens talk about the beleaguered National Health Service (NHS), rail network etc.

> **CONSTRUCTING A LIVELY SOCIAL LIFE IN SWEDEN CAN BE A CHALLENGE. ANN HUNTER POINTS OUT THAT IT CAN BE DIFFICULT TO MAKE SWEDISH FRIENDS:**
> *The only Swedes you meet regularly are your pupils and the professional relationship can make it awkward to socialise, though after your first term you can get to know ex-pupils quite well. Learning Swedish, if it is possible, is a good way to meet people, though your fellow students are foreigners of course.*

Andrew Boyle had mixed feelings about Sweden and Swedish people.

> *Sweden is a pleasant place to live, if a little dull at times. It is a generally liberal place, although the increasingly multicultural nature of society is causing Swedes to have to face up to their own prejudices. The students are generally of a high level and although initially quiet not unfriendly and even chatty after they know you a little better.*

Still, once you meet one outgoing Swede you'll find yourself quickly drawn into a group, which manages to avoid the horrific cost of dining out/drinks by meals and parties in people's homes, trips to free galleries and museums and various meetings of social clubs/interest groups. There are also of course cheaper places to eat out, which you'll discover once you're able to find you way around. Stockholm has a great vibe, although the stylishness of its inhabitants can sometimes be intimidating. Gothenburg has a younger feel, and is the city of choice for hip young Scandinavians (and other nationalities since the Swedish government is remarkably supportive of promising artists).

Outside the major cities, especially further north, you have to be independent and comfortable with your own company for long periods to enjoy Sweden. During the seven months of the winter the locals either hibernate or devote all their leisure to skiing. Anyone who enjoys outdoor activities will probably enjoy a stint in Sweden, especially ramblers and hill-walkers, who take advantage of the Allemannsrätt, the law which guarantees free access to the countryside for everyone. Island hopping around the (car free) Stockholm archipelago with a tent is an excellent and cheap way to enjoy nature, eat far too many cinnamon buns and lie around in the sun. Summers are usually very warm, certainly more so than in Britain, which is why so many Swedes have an enviable golden tan.

LIST OF EMPLOYERS

DENMARK

CAMBRIDGE INSTITUTE FOUNDATION
Vimmelskaftet 48, 1161 Copenhagen K
- 3313 3302; fax 3313 3323
- info@cambridgeinstitute.dk
- www.cambridgeinstitute.dk

NUMBER OF TEACHERS: 39 in various schools in the Greater Copenhagen area.

PREFERENCE OF NATIONALITY: British, Irish.

QUALIFICATIONS: BA, TEFL qualification and at least 1 year's TEFL experience abroad.

CONDITIONS OF EMPLOYMENT: 7-month renewable contracts (October to May). Minimum 20 hours per week Students aged 18–70.

SALARY: approximately £20 per teaching hour.

FACILITIES/SUPPORT: assistance with accommodation. Training given.

RECRUITMENT: through advertisements in UK newspapers.

SANWES SPROGINSTITUT APS
Kokholm 1, 6000 Kolding
- 7551 7410; fax 7551 7490
- sanwes@sanwes.dk
- www.sanwes.dk

Also branches at Horsensvej 39C, 7100 Vejle
- 7572 4610 and Fredericia Uddannelsescenter, Mosegardsvej, 7000 Fredericia
- 7594 1411

NUMBER OF TEACHERS: 20–22.

PREFERENCE OF NATIONALITY: British, American, Australian.

QUALIFICATIONS: should have some business background, be open-minded, cheerful and have lots of initiative.

CONDITIONS OF EMPLOYMENT: freelance; preferred minimum period 6 months. Daytime hours; total number depends on clients.

SALARY: approximately DKK172 per hour.

FACILITIES/SUPPORT: no assistance with accommodation. Pre-service training from other teacher. Help given with work permits.

RECRUITMENT: local interviews.

FINLAND

AAC GLOBAL
Tammasaarenkatu 5, 00180 Helsinki;
- 9 4766 7800; fax 9 4766 7810
- info@aacglobal.com
- www.aacglobal.com

NUMBER OF TEACHERS: With growing operations in Sweden and Russia, the company has over 300 trainers (80 native English speakers) and a total of eight offices in Finland, including Helsinki, Tampere, Turku, Jyväskylä, Kouvola, Kuopio, Vaasa and Oulu.

PREFERENCE OF NATIONALITY: British, American, Canadian.

QUALIFICATIONS: University degree plus CELTA/TEFL or equivalent or degree plus business background; teaching experience preferred. Driving licence is an asset.

CONDITIONS OF EMPLOYMENT: AAC Global is the market leader in Finland and it is expanding its operations in Sweden. It trains over 20,000 professionals yearly. ACC's clients are dynamic international companies, and the company offers them an interesting range of challenging language courses.

FACILITIES/SUPPORT: Possibility of one-way airfare being paid. Induction training provided and a system of Head Trainers to support the trainers in each language.

RECRUITMENT: Direct application (see AAC home page/jobs), newspaper advertisements, recruitment websites.

CONTACT: recruitment@aacglobal.com

RICHARD LEWIS COMMUNICATIONS
Länsituulentie 10, 02100 Espoo (Helsinki)
- 9 4157 4700; fax 9 466 592
- info.finland@rlcglobal.com
- www.crossculture.com

Offices also in Turku, Tampere, Oulu, Jyväskylä and Kuopio (addresses on website); and in the UK: Riversdown House, Warnford, Southampton, Hampshire SO32 3LH;
- 01962 771111

RLC has a network of offices worldwide, especially Scandinavia, specialising in cross-cultural and communication skills training and language teaching.

PREFERENCE OF NATIONALITY: British or American.

QUALIFICATIONS: university degree and TEFL preferred.

CONDITIONS OF EMPLOYMENT: full-time contracts, 9-month contracts (September until the third week in June) and freelance work.

FACILITIES/SUPPORT: assistance with finding accommodation. New teachers are given thorough training in RLC's methods and cross-cultural tools/courses.

RECRUITMENT: apply online.

NORWAY

BERLITZ A/S
Akersgate 16, 0158 Oslo
22 33 10 30; fax 22 33 10 03
info@berlitz.no
www.berlitz.no

NUMBER OF TEACHERS: varies.

PREFERENCE OF NATIONALITY: none.

QUALIFICATIONS: Minimum bachelor's degree and/or business-related work experience. Must be energetic, outgoing and creative. Non-EU citizens must hold a valid residency and work permit.

CONDITIONS OF EMPLOYMENT: freelance basis. Instructors choose their hours of availability between 8am and 9pm. Trainee teachers receive an initial qualification programme and learn to teach using the Berlitz Method.

SALARY: to be negotiated.

FACILITIES/SUPPORT: no assistance with accommodation given.

CONTACT: Marc Stevens, Instructional Supervisor; marc.stevens@berlitz.no.

FOLKEUNIVERSITETET/FRIUNDERVISNINGEN OSLO
Torggata 7 (P.B. 496 Sentrum), 0105 Oslo
22 47 60 00; fax 22 47 60 01
info@fuoslo.no
www.fuoslo.no

NUMBER OF TEACHERS: 2 full-time, 8–12 part-time.

PREFERENCE OF NATIONALITY: none, but must be native English speaker.

QUALIFICATIONS: TEFL experience and/or qualification(s) (min. CELTA or equivalent).

CONDITIONS OF EMPLOYMENT: no contracts. Non EEA residents will need a work permit. Students aged 18–65.

SALARY: varies according to course (NKK250–285 per 45-minute lesson).

FACILITIES/SUPPORT: no assistance with accommodation. Monthly teacher development workshops. Possibility of working at other centres around Norway.

RECRUITMENT: local interviews only.

CONTACT: Marcus Borley.

INTERNATIONAL LANGUAGE SCHOOL
Fredensborgveien 24D, 0177 Oslo
22 35 10 70/22 35 40 05
anne.tufte@ils.as
www.ils.as

NUMBER OF TEACHERS: 15.

PREFERENCE OF NATIONALITY: none but must be native English speakers.

QUALIFICATIONS: pedagogical or English language degree or TEFL/TESOL certificate and teaching experience.

CONDITIONS OF EMPLOYMENT: freelance basis. School hours are from 8am to 4pm.

SALARY: varies.

FACILITIES/SUPPORT: no assistance with finding accommodation. School only hires those already in possession of a valid work visa.

RECRUITMENT: advertisements in local paper and the university career centre. CV and interview essential for on spec applications (CVs and covering letters welcome). All teachers are interviewed and observed in a practice lesson before they are offered work.

CONTACT: Anne Tufte or Elisabeth D Aehlie.

NORSK SPRAKINSTITUTT
Kongens Gate 9, N-0153 Oslo
23 10 01 10; fax 23 10 01 27
post@nsionline.no
www.nsionline.no

NUMBER OF TEACHERS: 7 (but varies).

PREFERENCE OF NATIONALITY: British or American without marked accent.

QUALIFICATIONS: TEFL, etc. and teaching experience. Work experience in other fields such as business is a valuable asset. Must be resident in Oslo.

CONDITIONS OF EMPLOYMENT: freelance only. Hours vary according to course requirements.

SALARY: hourly rate. Holiday pay based on previous year's earnings.

RECRUITMENT: direct contact.

NUMBER OF TEACHERS: 12.

QUALIFICATIONS: native English speakers with education in business, pedagogy or psychology and teaching experience.

CONDITIONS OF EMPLOYMENT: standard contract is 2 years.

SALARY: 210 kroner per hour.

CONTACT: Richard Stephenson.

SWEDEN

NUMBER OF TEACHERS: 10, set to increase.

PREFERENCE OF NATIONALITY: native English speakers.

QUALIFICATIONS: BA hons degree or higher. Good communication skills, great personality (charming, funny, boisterous and intelligent), with range of professional experience, passion for teaching, talent for improvising with materials and some knowledge of grammar.

CONDITIONS OF EMPLOYMENT: freelance. Long-stay teachers preferred. Teaching hours of up to 20 per week. Teachers are offered more hours the longer they work at the school.

SALARY: minimum SEK440 per teaching session (90 minutes).

FACILITIES/SUPPORT: Teachers must find their own accommodation.

RECRUITMENT: initial email enquiries with CV (not phone or fax). Phone interviews and face-to-face interviews in the UK sometimes possible.

CONTACT: Richard Whale, Manager.

NUMBER OF TEACHERS: 40.

PREFERENCE OF NATIONALITY: must be native English speakers.

QUALIFICATIONS: an EFL qualification, teaching experience in Business English and some personal business experience would be an advantage.

CONDITIONS OF EMPLOYMENT: various locations in Europe, mainly UK, Finland, Sweden and Germany. Full-time and freelance positions available.

SALARY: depends on location and experience.

FACILITIES/SUPPORT: varies depending on location.

RECRUITMENT: send CV to info@crossculture.com, with a covering letter.

CONTACT: David Lewis.

NUMBER OF TEACHERS: 12 for centres in Stockholm.

PREFERENCE OF NATIONALITY: British.

QUALIFICATIONS: CELTA or DELTA.

CONDITIONS OF EMPLOYMENT: short-term or permanent contracts. 1,760 hours per year.

SALARY: permanent staff get paid an annual salary; temporary staff earn less. Deductions of 30%–35% for tax and contributions.

FACILITIES/SUPPORT: no assistance with accommodation. Training provided.

RECRUITMENT: local interview essential.

CONTACT: Principal.

SPAIN

Despite an economic slowdown, Spain continues to offer plenty of opportunities for native English teachers. Major companies in every sector from transport to fashion employ English teachers to improve their staff's English skills; language schools continue to attend to the massive demand from students and young adults just out of university keen to improve their CVs, and from parents who continue to send their young children and teenagers to English classes, so they can pass school exams and eventually cope with a job market that often demands fluency in English.

There is a national push to introduce English early; it is compulsory in state schools from the age of 8, and in some regions they are trying to start even earlier (each *Comunidad Autonoma* is responsible for taking decisions about education). In conjunction with the Spanish Ministry of Education and Science, the British Council has been recruiting experienced EFL teachers to work in primary schools (www.britishcouncil.org/spain-education-bilingual-project.htm). This trend has filtered through to private language providers, some of whom organise summer language camps for children and teenagers (see Baker Street and TECS in the list of employers).

There are thousands of foreigners teaching English in language schools (*academias*) from the Basque north (where there is a surprisingly strong concentration) to the Balearic and Canary Islands, as well as Madrid and Barcelona. The entries for language schools occupy about 18 pages of the Madrid *Yellow Pages* and 512 listings in the online *Yellow Pages*. Almost every back street in every Spanish town has an Academia de Ingles. *Academias* are privately run and unregulated by the Ministerio de Educación.

Spain has always been a popular destination for EFL teachers. Who can fail to be attracted to the climate, scenery, history and culture? And yet, many new arrivals in Spain soon realise that Spain and the Spanish people of their imagination bear little resemblance to what they find, at least in the major cities. Economic expansion and increased prosperity has brought about a dynamic, fast-paced society, while traditional stereotypes of flamenco and toros are completely out of context in the centre and north, where Basques and Catalans have their own culture and language.

In some places, the ELT business has become cut-throat with academy owners doing their best to squeeze out every last euro of profit, which can lead to poor working conditions. High inflation and rising costs mean that a teacher's salary does not go all that far, although it is still possible to have a three course meal with wine for €8, and even cheaper outside the big cities: if you ask for a caña (small glass of beer) or a glass of tinto in Granada you're given decent portions of several tapas for free. A travel pass for 10 journeys in Madrid's metro and bus system costs €6.70. Teaching wages rarely allow more than a tolerably comfortable lifestyle, and certainly do not allow you to save. These are points to bear in mind when visions of paella and beaches dance before your eyes.

PROSPECTS FOR TEACHERS

The days are gone when any native English speaker of English without a TEFL background could reasonably expect to be hired by a language academy. Almost all self-respecting schools these days require a solid TEFL certificate and shorter or distance learning courses are frowned upon. Many schools in some major cities echo the discouraging comments made by the director of a well-established school in Barcelona who said that he has found that there is a large supply of well-qualified native English speakers on hand so that his school cannot possibly reply to all the CVs from abroad that they receive as well. However, despite this trend, schools report that the number of applications from candidates with a recognised TEFL certificate has increased simply because so many more centres in the UK and worldwide are churning them out. At least one director is not terribly impressed by the standard of applicants and wonders why certificate courses continue to concentrate on teaching adults when increasingly it is children and adolescents who are the main market. In the case of his school the number of adults has remained static in recent years whereas the number of young learners has doubled. Another problem he has encountered more than once is being let down by selected candidates late in the day so that he has to do rushed telephone interviews to fill the posts.

Opportunities for untrained graduates have all but disappeared in what can be loosely described as 'respectable' schools, though there are still more opportunistic language academy directors who might be prepared to hire someone without qualifications, particularly part-time. A number of schools fall into this category. To take a random example, the expatriate director of a well-established school in Alicante estimated that of the 20 or so schools in town, only four operate within the law (ie keep their books in order, pay social security contributions for their staff, etc).

Many Britons and Irish people with or without TEFL qualifications set off for Spain to look for work on spec, preferably in early September, visiting, calling in and faxing across their CVs once they get there. Many employers do much of their recruitment locally, and at the last minute, which is one Spanish habit that hasn't changed. A very high percentage of schools depend on word-of-mouth and local walkins for their staff requirements, or advertise heavily in the local press. Anyone with some experience and/or a qualification should find it fairly easy to land a job this way. With a knowledge of Spanish, you can also fill one of the many vacancies for teachers of children, or low-level adult classes, but speaking Spanish is not a must for most jobs. The usual process is to put together a timetable from various sources and be reconciled to the fact that some or all of your employers in your first year will exploit you to some degree. Those who stay on for a second or further years can become more choosy.

The situation for Americans has become almost impossible if they want to work legally (see section on Regulations below).

Companies such as ModLang in Zaragoza cunningly interweave sport and language learning by running intensive English and sports summer courses for children aged 5–18. For these, native English speakers are recruited in large numbers to teach the language and coach sports and/or supervise swimming.

FINDING A JOB

Because schools run the whole gamut from prestigious to cowboy, every method of job-hunting works at some level. Many independent language schools are run by expatriate Britons, and a few of these will actually offer some guidance and support for newer teachers and as well as opportunities for further professional development.

IN ADVANCE

Candidates who know that they want to teach in Spain should consider doing their TEFL training with an organisation with strong Spanish links such as Oxford TEFL in London with schools in Barcelona and Cadiz (see Training: Trinity College TESOL Courses and the List of Employers below). Better still, do your training in Spain, which will allow you to get to know the country, and the specific needs of the students, to take advantage of the job guidance of trainers that know the local job market well, as well as being on the spot for job vacancies. This option is often even cheaper than staying in the UK, given the lower cost of living and the fact that many centres offer a package that includes low-priced accommodation. International House has centres in Barcelona and Madrid, while CLIC offers courses in Seville. Astex (see below) runs an intensive teacher training programme that begins in early September. The cost at the time of writing was €1,200 (£950), accommodation not included. This amount may be waived if candidates graduate from the course and accept a full-time contract with Astex. Interested candidates should send an updated CV, and a letter explaining why they want to pursue a career in teaching to dwarner@astex.es or call 91 590 3474.

For a listing of English language schools in Spain, the best source is the *Yellow Pages* which can be accessed on the internet (www.paginas-amarillas.es) – you need to type in 'Academias de Idiomas' and the city or town of interest. You may be able to access the list of 350 members of FECEI, the national federation of English language schools (Federación Española de Centros de Enseñanza de Idiomas). FECEI is concerned with maintaining high standards, so its members are committed to providing a high quality of teaching and fair working conditions for teachers. In order to become a member, a school has to undergo a thorough inspection; therefore FECEI schools represent the elite end of the market and are usually looking for well-qualified teachers. However they list only a fraction of the thousands of language schools that exist, and there are many quality language institutions that are not members of FECEI.

Successful candidates from Teacher Training Madrid (see entry in Part 1, section on Training Courses Abroad) are guaranteed an interview with Training Express, one of the largest teaching agencies in Madrid (jobs@trainingexpress.es; www.trainingexpress.es) which also offers teaching by telephone.

British or Irish nationals with a TEFL qualification or PGCE might want to make use of a recruitment agency, whether a general one or one which specialises in Spain such as English Educational Services (Alcalá 20–2°, 28014 Madrid; ✆ 91 532 9734/531 4783; fax 91 531 5298). The owner Richard Harrison has been interviewing, assessing and recommending teachers to client schools since 1986 and charges no fee to teachers and can advise and help with both short-term and long-term accommodation in Madrid. He suggests that candidates with just a degree and TEFL qualification come to Spain in early September and contact his agency on arrival since he is at his busiest through September and well into October trying to satisfy requests for teachers from client schools all over Spain. However, schools continue to request teachers throughout the academic year and for summer intensive and residential courses and applications are welcome at any time. Richard Harrison also runs a small English-speaking theatre company based in Madrid called Moving Parts (richardinmadrid@gmail.com) which tours Spain throughout the academic year and offers paid work to young teachers with performance ability, especially those applying in pairs. Speculative applications are welcome at any time.

Link to Teach is the only agency specialising in the recruitment of English language teachers for English language schools within Andalucía (✆ 677 263 610 or in the UK +44 777 5755966; applications@linktoteach.com; www.linktoteach.com). They are based in Seville and will consider candidates with a passion for teaching plus a Cambridge CELTA or Trinity TESOL.

ON THE SPOT

Most teaching jobs in Spain are found on the spot. Interlang Business Language Centre in Madrid (address below) is hardly unusual in stipulating that they meet all candidates in person before hiring so do all their interviewing in Madrid only. With increasing competition from candidates with solid TEFL qualifications it is more and more difficult for the under-qualified to succeed. The best time to look is between the end of the summer holidays and the start of term which falls in the first two weeks of October, although you can find jobs in late October too. Since a considerable number of teachers do not return to their jobs after the Christmas break and schools are often left in the lurch, early January may also be possible. Try outlying towns and suburbs if work is scarce in the city centres. In Madrid there are usually at least part-time jobs going most months of the academic year, though after Easter demand dies down. Many schools shut over the summer, but there is some work to be had in those that remain open, since most of their teachers disappear over the summer too, as well as teaching kids in a number of English summer camps dotted around the country, and advertised in the local press.

Once in Spain, the local press is very useful: the twice-weekly *Cambalache* in Seville, the *Vanguardia* newspaper on Sunday and the daily *Segundamano*. In *El Pais*, look in the classified section of the salmon-coloured supplement *Negocios*, under *Idiomas*, and in *Segundamano* under *Ofertas de Empleo – Profesores*. The classified advertisements papers *Cambalache* and *Segundamano* are also good for flat hunting, as is the website www.loquo.com for Barcelona.

In Madrid (www.in-madrid.com) and *Madrid Insider* (www.madridinsider.com) are good for just about anything. *In Madrid* also allows you to post free 'job wanted' advertisements online and in the print edition.

The website www.madridteacher.com is a comprehensive source of information about teaching opportunities in Madrid (specifically), and also in the rest of Spain. It is run by a group of freelance bilingual English, German and French teachers who teach in small and mid-sized companies, academies, schools and with private students in Madrid. The Expatriate Café website (www.expatriatecafe .com/index.php?option=weblinks&Itemid=4&topid=7) contains useful information about language schools, as well as TEFL training, certification and ESL.

You can visit the regional British Council offices which maintain lists of language schools in their region (which partially duplicates FECEI lists) apart from Madrid, which does not keep a register of schools. Some British Council centres disappointingly seem to see other language schools as competition to their own courses rather than helping to actually promote the activities of other schools and the practice of English language teaching in general, and will provide very little help in this field.

Local magazines may advertise the possibility of *intercambio* which means an exchange of English for Spanish or Catalan conversation practice – a great way to meet locals. The Irish pubs not only offer the opportunity to meet other expats but often organise weekly *intercambio* nights, which will be listed in the English-speaking press. English language bookshops sometimes have a notice board with relevant notices, as do the EOIs (Escuelas Oficial de Idiomas) in major cities (these are enormous state-sponsored official language schools with up to 10,000 students).

After finishing A levels, **Sam James** and **Sophie Ellison** decided to spend their gap year in Barcelona if possible. After acquiring their Trinity certificates in their destination city, they did the rounds of the language schools. Sam says:

> *Though tedious, this did work and we doubt we would have found work any other way. Job availability didn't seem that high in Barcelona when we were looking in October and we both accepted our only job offers. (Our age may have put off some employers.) Most schools seem to have recruited in September, so October was a bit of a lean month. I got my job by covering a class at two hours notice for a teacher who had called in sick. When this teacher decided to leave Barcelona, I was interviewed and offered her classes on a permanent basis. I got the job permanently about a fortnight after handing out CVs. Sophie was asked to her first interview after about three weeks of job-hunting. She was selected but then had to wait for several more weeks while her contract was finalised.*

The conventional wisdom says that the beginning of summer is the worst time to travel out to Spain to look for work since schools will be closed and their owners unobtainable. However, Sam James handed round his CV again in May (when his hours were cut) and was given some encouragement. He thinks that because so few teachers look for work just six weeks before the end of the academic year, employers are sometimes in need of replacements and this might well be a way for teachers to get ahead of the queue for September jobs. With so many no-frills cheap flights on the market, it might be worth a gamble.

When knocking on doors, bear in mind that most language academies will be closed between 2pm and 4pm when directors are invariably away from their desks. Try to leave a CV with a contact telephone number (most pensions won't mind). It is a good idea to buy a mobile or at least an inexpensive local SIM card with a local number if you already have a phone. A serious director will probe into any claims of experience and will soon weed out any bogus stories. Other directors are just checking to see that you are reasonably competent.

A more probable scenario for the untrained is that they will elicit some mild interest from one or two schools and will be told that they may be contacted right at the beginning of term and offered a few hours of teaching. Spanish students sign up for English classes during September and into early October. Consequently the academies do not know how many classes they will offer and how many teachers they will need until quite late. It can become a war of nerves; anyone who is willing and can afford to stay on has an increasingly good chance of becoming established.

The great cities of Madrid and Barcelona act as magnets to thousands of hopeful teachers. **Sam James** blamed his lack of job security and bitty hours on Barcelona's popularity, '*the result of the great supply of willing teachers here keeping working conditions down and making it hard to exert any leverage on an employer when one is so easily replaced.*' For this reason other towns may answer your requirements better. There are language academies all along the north coast and a door-to-door job hunt in September might pay off. This is the time when tourists are departing so accommodation may be available at a reasonable rent on a nine-month lease.

LIVE-IN POSITIONS

If you want a base from which to look for work and some contact with Spaniards who are eager to learn English, you might like to consider a live-in position with a family who wants an English tutor for their children or a voluntary position as an English assistant on summer language/sports camps. Further details may be sought from Relaciones Culturales, the youth exchange organisation at Calle Ferraz 82, 28008 Madrid (✆ 91 541 71 03; fax 559 1181; spain@clubrci.es; www.clubrci.es), which also places native English speakers with Spanish families who want to practise their English in exchange for providing room and board. One other agency that makes live-in placements is GIC, Centro Comercial Arenal, Avda del Pla 126, 2.22 03730 Alicante (✆ 96 646 0410; fax 96 646 2015; gic-spain@telefonica.net; www.gic-spain.com).

The American organisation InterExchange (161 Sixth Avenue, New York, NY 10013; ✆ 212 924 0446 ext. 109; fax 212 924 0575; info@interexchange.org; www.interexchange.org) places mainly women (aged 18–35) with Spanish families for one to three months as language tutors (fee US$695).

MICHELLE MANION FROM AUSTRALIA ENJOYED TAKING PART IN AN EXCHANGE PROGRAMME:
I would recommend live-in tutoring to anyone in my situation, ie anyone who wants to live in Spain but not as an au pair and is not entitled to a work permit. I was placed with a family with two boys aged 11 and 14. In the morning I went off for my Spanish lesson and then gave a lesson to the boys in turn. Spanish boys are notorious for being spoilt and impossible to control, but also for possessing wonderful personalities and great senses of humour. Carlos and César were typically Spanish and always managed to be both delightful and infuriating. Anyone interested in undertaking this venture should try to ascertain the children's level of English before arriving in Spain and to bring textbooks, magazines and children's books to work with, since English books are difficult to find in Spain. Also, when you arrive in Spain try to make as many friends and take up every opportunity you're given as this is the best way to learn Spanish.

FREELANCE TEACHING

As usual, private tutoring can pay better than contract teaching because there is no middle man. **Stuart Britton** easily found private pupils to supplement his school income in a small town in the untouristy north of Las Palmas de Gran Canaria. However when his employer found out, he was told to drop them or risk being sacked, even over the summer when the school was closed and Stuart had no other source of income. He resented this so much that he advises not bothering with small schools, and simply concentrating on obtaining private students.

As always, it is difficult to start up without contacts and a good knowledge of the language; and when you do get started it is difficult to earn a stable income due to the frequency with which pupils cancel. The problem is particularly acute in May when undergraduates and school pupils concentrate on preparing for exams and other activities fall by the wayside. Spaniards are fond of taking off the days between a mid-week fiesta and the weekend known as *puente*, meaning bridge.

Getting private lessons is a marketing exercise and you will have to explore all the avenues which seem appropriate to your circumstances. Obviously you can advertise on notice boards at universities, EOIs, community centres (*centros cívicos*), public libraries, corner shops and wherever you think there is a market. Major stores are a good bet, for example Jumbo and Al Campo in Madrid. A neat notice in Spanish along the lines of '*Profesora Nativa da clases particulares a domicilió*' might elicit a favourable response. Send notices to local state schools asking them to pin it up broadcasting your willingness to ensure the children's linguistic future. Compile a list of addresses of professionals (eg lawyers, architects, etc.) as they may need English for their work and have the wherewithal to pay for it. Try export businesses, distribution companies, perhaps even travel agencies. Make the acquaintance of language teachers who will know of openings.

Because private classes can be so much better paid than institute teaching, they are much in demand, including by contract teachers, most of whom are engaged in some private tutoring. The ideal is to arrange a school contract with no more than 15–20 hours and supplement this with private classes which are lucrative although unstable.

REGULATIONS

All EU citizens planning to live in Spain for more than three months are obliged to register in person at the Foreigners' Office (Oficina de Extranjeros) in the province of residence or at a designated police station. You will be issued with a Residence Certificate stating your name, address, nationality, identity number and date of registration. The number on your resident card is your NIE (*Número de Identidad/Identificación de Extranjero*), an identification number necessary for filing taxes, establishing a business, opening a bank account (not necessary for foreign accounts), and for almost any other form. Once you start work, your employer should apply for a social security number on your behalf; if you are self-employed, this is your responsibility.

Many long-stay foreigners engage a specialist lawyer called a *gestoria* to assist negotiating the bureaucracy, especially if they are buying property. Further details are contained in the Notes Settling in Spain available from the British Embassy, Madrid or from the website Spain Expat (www.spainexpat .com), which is full of useful information about living and working in Spain.

The immigration situation for people from outside Europe is very difficult indeed. Most of the schools that once hired North Americans now refuse to tackle the lengthy procedures involved in obtaining work permits. Berlitz cautions, '*unfortunately, the European Union (EU), of which Spain is* a part, seldom issues work permits to non-EU citizens unless they are married to an EU national.' Americans with Irish or Italian ancestry often prefer to chase the papers which will get them an EU passport.

This pessimistic view of the chances for Americans and Canadians was voiced by so many schools that it seems almost superfluous to describe the procedures. Briefly, you need to submit a slightly dizzying array of documents to the Subdelegación del Gobierno in the city you are trying to move to and work in, including, but not restricted to, an official job offer form, original official company fiscal identity document, and official certification that the job on offer has already been advertised in the official Provincial Unemployment Office and that no suitable European candidate has applied. Then you need to make an appointment with the Spanish Consulate serving your official home address (in country of origin) in order to process all the documentation which they require for a work visa, including, among others, a formal job offer from an employer in Spain, a recent medical certificate, *antecedents penales* (police certificate of good character), notarised degree certificate and seven passport photographs. Once your home country's Spanish Consulate has processed your work visa, you have to fetch it in person. It cannot be handed to anyone other than you. Then you can return to Spain and finalise applications for a work/residence permit. According to Institut Nord-America (IEN) in Barcelona (listed below), who have a vested interest in employing people with a North American accent, visa processing takes 12–16 months. They go on to stipulate that they prefer 'applicants with Spanish/European work permit/citizenship' for obvious reasons.

None of this means that there aren't any Americans or other nationalities teaching in Spain without permits. According to **Jon Loop**, many post-Hemingway Americans go to Spain for a year to learn Spanish and '*find themselves man*' (or maybe even find themselves a man). The teacher training schools in major cities are full of American as well as British trainees, and Americans, Australians and New Zealanders also find work, not just teaching private classes but through numerous intrepid academies who hire them off-contract and send them off to teach in companies rather than on school premises. Anyone who works on a tourist visa will have to renew it every three months by leaving the country. Weekend trips to France or Portugal can be organised for this purpose.

Social security (*seguridad social*) contributions are between 4% and 7% of earnings, typically 6.4%. Tax residents will need to pay income taxes in Spain and are generally defined as those who live in Spain for more than 183 days in each calendar year. However, www.spainexpat.com suggests that in many cases you only need to file a tax return in Spain when you make more than €22,000 per year; unlikely if you are a language teacher. Spain and Britain have a double taxation treaty: for more information visit www.hmrc.gov.uk/cnr/dtdigest.pdf (although it's heavy going).

Under EU legislation, language schools must give contracts and make contributions for all staff, whether full-time or part-time. In practice, this does not always happen. After a few months of teaching for one academy, Jon Loop asked for a contract and was given a special 11-hour contract (though at the time he was teaching 20 hours a week). Contracts for less than 12 hours a week do not require more than minimal social security contributions. **Joanna Mudie** from the Midlands describes the situation which results from this:

> There's a great deal of uncertainty and insecurity about all aspects of work: hours, days, rates of pay, insurance, etc. Contracts (if you're lucky enough to get one) are a load of rubbish because employers put down far fewer hours on paper to avoid paying so much insurance, and also to protect themselves if business dwindles. My advice is, forget your English sense of honesty and obeying the law. 'When in Rome . . .' Relax and simply don't worry about the legalities. It usually seems to work out okay, and if not, well, it's a nice life in the sun.

Schools that sidestep the regulations to maximise profits and who do not pay contributions to cover their employees' social security might well be the ones willing to employ non-Europeans and pay cash-in-hand.

CONDITIONS OF WORK

Salaries are not high in Spain and have not increased significantly over the past decade. A further problem for teachers in Madrid and Barcelona is that there is not much difference between salaries in the big cities where the cost of living has escalated enormously and salaries in the small towns. The minimum net salary is about €850 per month, though most schools offer €900–€1050 after deductions for 25 hours of teaching a week. A standard hourly wage would be €12, although some pay their starter teachers more; for example Hot English Language Services in Madrid (Calle Fernandez de los Rios 98, 2a, 28015 Madrid; ✆ 91 455 0273; classes@hotenglishmagazine.com) pays its 50–75 teachers between €12 and €25 an hour. The highest hourly wages are paid by centres specialising in sending teachers out to firms or those teaching short courses which are funded by the EU.

Spanish TEFL is no different from TEFL in other countries in that there are lots of employers offering low pay, long hours and exploitative conditions. For example, teachers have discovered that pay has been deducted when they have been unavoidably absent or that their bonuses have been withheld with no explanation. **Sam James** was taken aback when his hours were drastically cut by his employer in Barcelona with no notice. The simple explanation was that Sam was working without a contract that would have guaranteed a certain number of hours. He advises getting a contract if at all possible, even on a lower rate of pay, since contracts bring security, a reliable income and holiday pay (which he knows because his girlfriend Sophie had one).

Barry O'Leary taught in Seville for three years. In his first year he worked for a slightly disorganised and crafty academy where there was no mention of a contract, classes started at 8am and staggered throughout the day until 10pm and it was difficult to predict how much you would earn from month to month because of all the unpaid festivals in Spain. Luckily in his second year, after mingling with the other ex-pat teachers, he was able to land himself a job with a more professional establishment. He now works fixed hours from 4pm until 10pm, Monday to Thursday leaving the mornings free, and there are excellent on-going training sessions on Friday mornings. The language school is one of the most successful in Seville with 12 academies scattered throughout the city and it takes care of its teachers, offering fixed contracts for long-term prospects:

> *The students, who are often passionate and keen to learn English, range in age from 6 to 60 so there is never a dull moment. Classes have a maximum of 12, all material is provided and there is scope to move away from the syllabus now and then. A lot of extra work is necessary in February and June when the exams take place but it's worth the agony.*
>
> *Life in Seville is fun and varied, with an abundance of festivals including the religious Semana Santa and the livelier Feria. The city is a great place to live and a base for exploring Andalucía. Evenings can be spent in the many bars enjoying tapas, watching flamenco or Sevillanas (a local dance) or just mingling with the locals. Seville is generally safe and with the year-round blue skies it's a great place to brush up on your Spanish and experience a different way of life.*

Sophia Brown worked in a school in Barcelona and objected to the terrible timetable (always late evenings), the lack of organisation and the low pay of €10 an hour. She also didn't really like the city, although her American friend, Dylan, is still working at the school and at last report was hoping to be trained as a tester, which is much more lucrative.

The Madrid school director rang me to inform me that I had got the job and I was to start nine days later. When, as instructed, I rang to confirm the arrival time of my plane, I was told that there was no job for me after all since the school had gone bankrupt. I think what really made me angry was that I had rung him rather than the other way round. He did not even say sorry or sound in the least remorseful. It is just possible that the bankruptcy was just an excuse in the face of insufficient pupils.

Some schools tend to work their teachers very hard, expecting them to teach around 30 hours. Considering that preparation and travelling is extra, this can result in a gruelling schedule. The ideal full-time timetable is 25 teaching hours a week. Dennis Bricault refers to the notoriously uncongenial timetable of most EFL teachers (and not just in Spain) as a 'bookend schedule', whereby you might have to teach between 8am and 10am, then again through the evening. Most teachers put up with the late finishing time without too many murmurs because they are not deprived of Spanish nightlife even if they have to work until 10pm.

According to Spanish law, workers are not entitled to paid holiday until they have been working for 12 months, hence the near-universality of nine-month contracts. Most teachers find it impossible to save enough in nine months to fund themselves abroad for the rest of the year. Most pay agreements also already include the bonuses (*pagas extraordinarias*) which have already been pro-rated, of which there are two or three a year. Legal schools will pay *finiquito* (holiday pay) at the end of a contract which should work out to be about two and a half days of every month worked, based on your base (not full) salary.

If the terms of a contract are being breached and the employer does not respond to the teacher's reminders, recourse can be taken by means of a *denuncia*, which involves informing the authorities (either in person or via a union, such as the Commissiones Obreros) that your school is not complying with tax and social security rules or fire regulations or whatever. The *denuncia* can effectively close a school if it is taken seriously and if the school does not have the proverbial friends in high places. In fact the procedure is complicated and time-consuming but the mere mention of it might improve your working conditions.

The children learned English for three hours in the morning with one half hour break (but not for the teacher on morning snack duty trying to fight off the hordes from ripping apart the bocadillos). Then we had another three or four hours of duties ranging from sports and/or arts to shop/bank duty. For many of us, inexperienced with dealing with groups of kids, there were a few problems of discipline. It was the kids' holiday and they quickly cottoned on that we English teachers in general were a bunch of hippies.

PUPILS

SPANIARDS HAVE THE REPUTATION FOR BEING SOMEWHAT CHALLENGED AT LEARN-ING LANGUAGES. THIS IS MORE TOLERABLE IN MOTIVATED ADULTS BUT OFTEN HARD-GOING WITH CHILDREN. THIS WAS ONE OF DAVID BOURNE'S BIGGEST PROBLEMS AND ONE WHICH HE THINKS IS UNDERESTIMATED, ESPECIALLY AS A HIGH PROPORTION OF ENGLISH TEACHING IN SOME ACADEMIES IS OF CHILDREN AND TEENAGERS:

I have found that a lot of the younger students only come here because their parents have sent them in or-der to improve their exam results. The children themselves would much rather be outside playing football. There are days when you spend most of the lesson trying (unsuccessfully in my case) to keep them quiet. This is especially true on Fridays. I have found it very hard work trying to inject life into a class of bored 10-year-olds, particularly when the course books provided are equally uninspiring.

In such cases it might be a good idea to change your aim, from teaching them English to entertain-ing them (and paying your rent). If students don't want to learn, you will only break your heart trying to achieve the impossible. Adults are usually an easier proposition, willing to listen and think and with a good sense of humour.

In general the Spanish will welcome opportunities to speak animatedly in class and express their opin-ions, though **Sophie Ellison** found some to be lacking in enthusiasm and imagination; for example when she asked her class to discuss what might constitute an ideal justice system in Spain, some stu-dents' reply was a disappointing 'I don't know' which made it hard to work on the students' fluency.

A GOOD KNOWLEDGE OF SPANISH IS HELPFUL IF NOT ESSENTIAL WHEN TEACHING JUNIOR CLASSES AS PETER SALIBA, DIRECTOR OF THE CROSS SCHOOL IN MALAGA, EXPLAINS:

We need teachers with a fluent command of Spanish, not the typical grasp of elementary phrases which may get them by in a social context. On a limited two or three hour per week teaching timetable, there simply is not time for cumbersome English explanations of English grammar and vocabulary. It is worse still with young learners and teens, who will 'run riot' or at the very least run circles round non-Castilian speaking teachers.

Classes differ enormously as **Jon Loop** found during his year of teaching at an academy in Madrid:

A lot of my groups were civil servants. They were excruciating because they didn't want to be there. The government has to spend its language training budget and picks people at random. I taught other classes of university students who were very enthusiastic and were great to work with. I taught a group of technicians at the meteorological office who were keen because it was directly linked to their work. Then I taught groups from companies who were not very keen to start with, but by the end of the year we were having a great time. It's classes like this that make teaching worthwhile.

Jon recommends making good use of your students, since so many Spaniards are friendly and eager to help. If you are having trouble with a recalcitrant landlord, perhaps a letter from a trainee lawyer you happen to be teaching might solve the problem. Students may lend you an unoccupied holiday house or put you in touch with friends looking for private English lessons. In Jon's case, a student arranged for him to spend the harvest at a family vineyard and another helped him to fix up work editing technical papers.

Needless to say, Spaniards are a nation of talkers. If things seem to be going awry in your classes, for example students turning up late or being inattentive, don't pussyfoot around. Make your feelings known, just as Spaniards do.

ACCOMMODATION

Rents usually swallow up at least a quarter of a teacher's income, more in the big cities and much more if you don't share. In small towns, it is not uncommon for schools to arrange accommodation for their teachers at least for an initial period. Many Spanish students want to live with English students so check language school, Escuela de Idiomas, and university notice boards for flat shares, especially in the Facultad de Filologia which includes the Department of English. Some teachers even arrange to share a flat rent-free in exchange for English lessons.

If you are renting a flat expect to pay a month's rent in advance, plus one or two months' rent as deposit. Since your first pay cheque may not arrive until November, you should arrive with up to £1,000 to tide you over. Try to avoid using an *inmobiliaria* (property agency) which will charge a further month's rent (at least). Be aware of the agencies or associations with seedy premises that charge you a fee before showing you anything. You will quickly distinguish their advertisements from private ones in the classifieds. In Madrid and Barcelona many people use the free advertisements paper *Segundamano;* if you do decide to compete for a flat listed in this paper, get up early since most flats are gone by 8am. **Barry O'Leary** advertised in Spanish for a two-bedroomed apartment in central Seville and indicated a maximum rent of €550 between two. His chosen forum was the university notice board website (http://sevilla.campusanuncios.com). It is easier flat hunting in July and August, than in September/October or February.

LEISURE

Once you acquire some Spanish, it is very easy to meet people, since Spaniards are so friendly, relaxed and willing to invite newcomers out with them. Of course there is also a strong fraternity of EFL teachers almost everywhere. With luck you will end up socialising with both groups in bars, at parties, *romerías* (pilgrimages), fiestas, etc.

Eating, drinking, smoking, entertainment and transport (including taxis) are all still fairly cheap, though this advantage is cancelled out for some by the high cost of other things such as clothes, cars and electrical items, not to mention contraceptives, standard chemists' products and dental care. As anywhere, the cost of living gets lower the longer you stay and discover where the locals get their bargains.

If you're looking for traditional Spanish culture, don't go to Madrid, and certainly don't look for it in Barcelona which is not Spanish at all but Catalan. Seville, Granada and Valencia are lovely Spanish cities. While teaching in Andalucia, **Joanna Mudie** appreciated the chance to learn about the traditional but still very much alive dances of Spain, eg Sevillanas, Malagueras and Pasadoble.

Some Spanish customs are less well known. Galicia is the province on the undiscovered Atlantic Coast of Spain, brilliant for long beaches, seafood and also for bagpipes, intriguingly enough. Its climate has also something in common with its northern cousin, but you can't have everything.

Glen Williams describes his spare time activities in Madrid, a city with an enormous variety of nightlife where he was clearly enjoying himself to the full:

> *Madrid is a crazy place. We usually stay out all night at the weekend drinking and boogying. During the gaps in my timetable (10–2 and 4–7) I pretend to study Spanish (I'm no natural) and just wander the back streets. I suppose I should try to be more cultural and learn to play an instrument, write poetry or look at paintings, but I never get myself in gear. I think most people teach English in Spain as a means to live in Spain and learn the Spanish language and culture. But there is a real problem that you end up living in an English enclave, teaching English all day and socialising with English teachers. You have to make a big effort to get out of this rut. I am lucky to live with Spanish people (who do not want to practise their English!).*

A few schools offer free or subsidised Spanish lessons as a perk to teachers. Otherwise investigate the government-run Escuela Oficial de Idiomas.

So many kinds of people find themselves teaching English in different situations that there is no average profile. **Jon Shurlock** worked alongside both reformed alcoholics whose lives had fallen apart and the usual middle class 'jolly nice' people taking a year or two out. While one teacher finds the locals cold and hostile and money-grabbing, another finds them warm and supportive. If the idea of teaching in Spain appeals at all, it is almost always a rewarding and memorable way for people with limited work experience to finance themselves as they travel and live abroad for a spell.

LIST OF EMPLOYERS

All schools prefer to hire teachers who are EU nationals – most will not consider non-EU applicants – and have a university degree, some knowledge of Spanish and a quality TEFL qualification. Although some may be prepared to consider less, especially from candidates with some business experience or experience teaching children, the ever-increasing number of qualified applicants means that the occasions when schools need to do so are diminishing.

The standard negotiated contract is about €1,100 per month gross for a 25-hour-a-week full-time teacher, though gross salaries tend to fluctuate between €1,000 and €1,200 depending on number of hours worked. The average range for an hourly wage is €12–€24 gross with rates in Madrid and Barcelona at the upper end.

The best plan is to pick out the schools in the city or province which appeals to you, and email or write for details enclosing a CV and photograph. Most schools carry out their selection procedure of new teachers locally between April and July (some schools hold interviews for more experienced teachers in the UK throughout the summer), though if you arrive in person to look for a job in September at one of the listed schools, your chances of success are reasonable.

Because of the shift from a teachers' to an employers' market over the past 10 years in many parts of Spain, quite a few schools are reluctant to publicise expected job vacancies for fear of being inundated with applications. Madrid at one end of the spectrum still has Directors of Studies searching for teachers to cover their last remaining vacancies in October; **Fran McAleer** a recent graduate from Liverpool did his TEFL at the Advanced Institute in Madrid and found himself in the right place at the right time: '*It helped me find work straightaway*'. Barcelona on the other hand is a mecca for tourism, and subsequently for more teachers competing for the same jobs. Bear in mind that a personal visit is always more likely to lead to success than an unsolicited CV by email, fax or post.

Instead of including full entries for the schools, we have provided a skeletal list of names and addresses of schools willing to consider applications, followed by the number of native English speaker teachers which they expect to employ each year and in some cases some brief annotations and a contact name. Many schools make reference to the CELTA qualification as a minimum requirement as that has been around the longest, but in Spain that should be taken to mean any quality TEFL qualification. Note that the international prefix for Spanish telephone numbers is 34.

ACADEMIA BRITÁNICA INTERNATIONAL HOUSE, CORDOBA: C/ Rodríguez Sánchez, 15,14003 Córdoba; ✆ +957 470350; fax 957 470627; info-cordoba@acabri.com; www.acabri.com. 19 teachers; EU passport holders who can get residence permits easily. A or B in CELTA plus minimum 1 year's experience, especially in teaching younger learners. 9-month contracts, October to June. Teachers work 22–25 per week. Salary is on average €1,400 gross (2007/8). Average 12% tax; 6.5 % social security deductions. Assistance with finding accommodation. Residence Permits are applied for by the school and the teacher is accompanied to the permits office soon after arrival. Recruitment through IH Recruitment system, or locally via IH Seville. Interviews in the UK if teacher recruited through IH World.

ACADEMIA CATS: C/ Poeta Andres Bolarin 1, 30011 Murcia; ✆ +968 346733; academia-cats@yahoo.com; www.academiacats.com. Must be native English speakers, must be EU or have work permit for Spain; prefer CELTA or Trinity. To teach equal numbers of children, teenagers and adults. Offer free training for teaching children and direct method. See website for full recruitment details, ambience, salaries, etc. Contact: Marc Turner, Director.

ACADEMIA DE IDIOMAS BIG BEN: Ronda Eloy Sanz Villa, no. 8, local 11 12003 Soria; ✆ +975 230 217; fax 975 230217; bigben.3017@cajarural.com. 2 teachers required with TEFL qualifications and experience. 9-month part-time (25 hours per week) and full-time (15 hours per week) contracts available. Full-time salary €800 net per month. Part-time salary €500 net per month. Telephone and 'netmeeting' interviews required. Contact: Béthy Rodriguez, Headmistress.

ACADEMIA YES: Avda. Lopez Laguna 9, bajos, 50009 Zaragoza; ✆ +976 350505; yess@arrakis.es or info@academiayes.com; www.academiayes.com. 3 teachers with experience teaching children. Summer work available. €1,000 per month. Can arrange shared accommodation with other teacher.

ADVANCED INSTITUTE: Travessera de Gracia, 15, 5°, 3a, 08021 Barcelona; ✆ +934 143 125; fax 934 141 103; tefljobs@terra.es. 10 (preferably British) teachers with at least a TEFL certificate and 1–2 years' experience of teaching. Part time and full-time positions available for 8-month contracts. Accommodation available in school flats. Contact: the Centre Manager at the above address.

ADVANCED INSTITUTE: Fernandez de los Rios, 75, 28015 Madrid; ✆ +915 431 992; fax 915 431 992; tefljobs@terra.es. 20 (preferably British) teachers required with at least a TEFL certificate or a diploma and 2 years' experience. To teach 25 hours per week on an 8-month contract. Gross salary approx. €1,100 per month. Interview necessary, periodically held in London. Contact: the Director of Studies at the above address.

ALGINET ENGLISH CENTRE: Avenida Reyes Católicos, 52, 2°, Pto. 4, 46230 Alginet, Valencia; ✆ +961 752 747. 2 (preferably British) teachers required from September to June, to work 30 hours per week. Applicants must hold a TEFL certificate and have at least one year of experience. Gross salary €1,000 per month. Help finding accommodation provided. Interview essential. Contact: Carol Luscombe, Director.

AMERICAN LANGUAGE ACADEMY: Calle Rodríguez San Pedro 2, 28015 Madrid; ✆ +91 445 5511; fax 91 445 5800; efl@americanlanguage.es or ala@americanlanguage.es;

www.americanlanguage.es. 25+ North American, British, Irish and Australian teachers with a degree, TEFL training and experience. 3 Directors of Studies. Teachers are provided with free Spanish classes, a Teacher Development Programme and a computer room with internet connection and word processing and printing facilities. Candidates will be invited to do the interview process, including a demonstration class. 9–12-month contracts to successful candidates who must be interviewed in Madrid and offered a position by June (in order to allow time for visa processing by early October). Salary is highly competitive and all teachers work on contract.

ASTEX SERVICIOS LINGUISTICOS: C/ Hermanos Bécquer 7–6°, 28006 Madrid; ✆ +91 590 3474; fax 91 563 8466; selem@astex.es/dwarner@astex.es; www.astex.es. Require CELTA or equivalent and minimum 2 years EFL teaching experience. ASTEX employs around 300 ESL teachers at any one time, and usually hires 30 new teachers each September/October, with vacancies needing to be filled throughout the year. Most classes are in companies, but there is a possibility of working with young learners as well, or in the case of more experienced teachers taking part in immersion programmes. ASTEX recruits teachers mostly in Madrid, but also Barcelona, Valencia and other cities.

BAKER STREET INTERNATIONAL: Calle Sangre, 7–13, 46002, Valencia; ✆ +963 516 312; valencia@bkstreet.com; www.bkstreet.com. Runs 1-month summer camps. 25–35 teachers from UK/Ireland with a university degree, TEFL certificate and experience with kids. Net salary approximately €1,200 per month, accommodation included. Teachers work all day. Contact: Joshua C Goldblatt, Director.

BETA GROUP: Paseo de Los Parques, El Encinar, La Moraleja, 28109 Madrid; ✆ +91 650 72 32; fax 91 650 76 12; thebetagroup@tsai.es; www.betagroup.com. 30 teachers with degree plus TEFL experience to teach Business English only. Require minimum 3 years' experience and European passport.

BRIAN SCHOOL: Magdalena 19, 33009 Oviedo; ✆ +98 522 04 08; brianschool@fade.es; www.brianschool.com. 5+ native English speakers with EFL qualifications. Sometimes teachers without experience are accepted if they are really keen and talented. American teachers require a vast amount of Spanish bureaucracy so they have got to be outstanding to make it worthwhile. School now has ISO Certificate from Lloyds E201000. Also recognised as an official training centre by the Spanish Ministry of Work – state-funded courses include business English, commercial English and client attention.

BRITISH INSTITUTE OF SEVILLE: Federico Rubio 14, 41004 Seville; ✆ +95 422 0240; fax 95 450 1081; abenvenuty@ibsevilla.es. 20 full-time qualified teachers (CELTA/DELTA, university degree and 2 years' valid experience). Contracts of 9 and 11 months. Salary according to qualifications and experience €1,275–€1,450 (gross) per month. Full and founder member of EAQUALS and affiliated to Bell Schools (www.bell-centres.com/contactus/employment/spain.html). Contact: Alexia Benvenuty.

BRITISH LANGUAGE CENTRE: Calle Murillo 377–2°, 28020 Madrid; ✆ +91 733 07 39; fax 91 314 50 09; ted@british-blc.com; www.british-blc.com. 40 or more teachers with CELTA minimum. Also offers CELTA/CELTYL/DELTA courses. Teacher interviews in Spain essential. Contact: Director of Studies.

BRITISH SCHOOL: Plaza Ponent, 5–2nd floor, 43001 Tarragona; ✆ +/fax (+34) 977 211 605; british@bstarragona.com; www.bstarragona.com. Established in Tarragona since 1973. 5 teachers with degree, CELTA or Trinity teaching qualification and minimum 1 year's experience teaching English abroad. Gross salary €1,037 per month for 21 class hours a week; new-year bonus €240 and end-of-contract holiday pay €528 and travel expenses €211. Contact: Bernard Tingle, Director.

BVRNS ACADEMY: Artekale 3–1°, Durango, 48200 Vizcaya; ✆ +946 203 668; bvrnsacademy@euskalnet.net. English teacher with a TEFL qualification and experience required. Standard contract 9 months, working 25 hours a week. Salary €1000 per month. Telephone interview required. Contact: Ana Lopez, Director.

CALEDONIA SCHOOL OF ENGLISH: Avenida Del Quinto Centenario, Edificio Mirasol 3, local 2, 11540 Sanlúcar de Barrameda (Cádiz); ✆ +956 380097; fax 956 368125; caledon@arrakis.es; www.caledoniaschool.es. 5 teachers. Native of UK or Ireland. University graduate, preferably in Spanish or Modern Languages. Need recognised TEFL qualification or PGCE, 1–2 years' experience in TEFL or minimum 150-hour TEFL course for newly-qualified graduates. Interview, held at school, essential. Contracts 9 months or indefinite. 21–24 teaching hours a week. Salary highly competitive. Help with finding accommodation. Contact: Iain Cunningham.

CAMBRIDGE ENGLISH STUDIES: Avenida de Arteijo 8–1°, 15004 La Coruña; ✆ +981 160 216; fax 981 145 694; camcor@arrakis.es. Staff of 16 teachers. 10 in La Coruña and 6 in Ferrol. Teachers must be EU nationals and hold a CELTA or TESOL certificate or equivalent. Courses run from September to June, teaching 25 hours per week. Basic salary is €900 per month plus increments for experience and qualifications. Taxes and social security paid by the school. Interviews required, but telephone interview is acceptable. Contact: Nick Shaw, Director.

CAMBRIDGE HOUSE: C/ Lopez de Hoyos, 95 1°A, 28002 Madrid; ✆ +91 519 4603/64 795 0087; teachers@cambridge-house.com; www.cambridge-house.com. 25 British or Irish teachers with degree, EFL Certificate and some teaching experience. Full-time block timetables in the afternoon/evening teaching all age ranges. Contact: Penny Rollinson, Director of Studies.

CAMBRIDGE SCHOOL: Placa Manel Montanya 4, 08400 Granollers, Barcelona; ✆ +93 870 2001; fax 93 879 5111; admin@cambridgeschool.com; www.cambridgeschool.com. 65 teachers with at least CELTA or equivalent to teach in one of four schools (the others are in Caldes de Montbui and Cardedeu, La Garriga). Average salary is €1,260 a month for 20 contact hours per week Contact: Sarah Edge, Director.

CANADIAN LANGUAGE INSTITUTE: Avenida de Europa No. 28, Edificio Paraiso 1, Montequinto, Seville 41089; ✆ +95 412 9016; fax 95 412 9016; forymed@auna.es; www.canadian languageinstitute.com. 5 Canadian or American teachers (in addition to British staff). Minimum 2 years' teaching experience, TESOL/CELTA and dynamic. €11 an hour. Contact: Victoria Mantecon, Director EFL Department.

CENTRAL PARK IDIOMAS: C/ Ronda del Ferrocarril, 37 bis, 09200 Miranda de Ebro, Burgos; ✆ fax 94 733 2547. Warm, friendly and professional working atmosphere. Students aged 4 to adults, all levels, classes at school and off-site (transport provided, displacement time considered). Small groups, emphasis on Communicative Methodology. Preparation for Trinity exams. Working from Monday to Thursday (some Fridays only for teaching meetings). Help with finding accommodation. Qualifications required: native English speaker of English, BA (MA, BSc), TEFL (CELTA; Trinity, etc.) certificate, EU citizenship. Basic knowledge of Spanish and some relevant previous experience is desirable. EU passport only. Salary: from €1,000–€1,050 minimum after taxes for a full-time contract, 22 contact teaching hours. Extra hours are available. Contract from the end of September to mid June. The school usually contracts 6–7 native English speaking teachers, others are Spanish. Contact: Ismael Perez centerpark@terra.es or centralparkidiomas@hotmail.com or centralparkidiomas@gmail.com.

CENTRO DE IDIOMAS SANTA ANA: Calle Pasión 10, 1°b, 47001 Valladolid; ✆ fax 983 358242; beatriz@idiomassantaana.es; www.idiomassantaana.es. Small, friendly, reputable language school in the centre of Valladolid est. 1982. 3 full-time teachers with degree plus TEFL Cert. 20 hours per week guaranteed with contract, social security paid. Interview in Spain essential. Contact: Beatriz Martinez.

CENTRO EDIMBURGO IDIOMAS: Edificio Edimburgo, Plaza Niña, 21003 Huelva; ✆ +959 263821/263865; fax 959 280778. Also: Alfonso XII (esquina Padre Andivia, 21003 Huelva; ✆ +959 250168; info@centroedimburgo.com; www.centroedimburgo.com. 20 teachers with degree, CELTA plus 1 year's experience. Must speak conversational Spanish. Interviews in London end of June. The school helps find flats.

CENTRO FRANCES: C/ Isilla 3, 09400 Aranda de Duero (Burgos); ✆ +947 505117; fax 947 510551; info@escuelacf.com; www.escuelacf.com. 2 teachers with BA and TEFL Cert. Phone interviews essential. Contracts from 9 months to one year; 25 or 28 hours a week. Salary €1,100 a month with 2% tax and 6% social security deductions. Help to find accommodation. Contact: Mercedes Calvo.

CENTRO INGLÉS SEGOVIA SL: Avda Fernández Ladreda 22, Segovia 40002; ✆ +921 461820; fax 921 466016; centroinglessegovia@yahoo.com or cening@terra.es. Typically, 4 native ESL teachers. Salary: €900 per month. Contact: Jose Emigdio Bernardos Sanz.

CHELSEA ENGLISH STUDIES: Paseo Pamplona 17, 1° dcha, Zaragoza 50004; ✆ +976 219868; fax 976 229016; zaragoza@chelseaenglishstudies.com; www.chelseaenglishstudies.com. 5 teachers preferably British and preferably long term, although take on short-term teachers during the summer months.

CHESTER SCHOOL OF ENGLISH: Jorge Juan 125, 28009 Madrid; ✆ +91 402 58 79/431 28 39; fax 91 431 50 54; tefl@chester.es or info@chester.es; www.chester.es. 24 teachers with degree, Cert. TEFL and basic Spanish. €1,040 per month; supplement of €360 for higher qualifications and experience. Help with finding accommodation. 1-week induction training course at the end of September. Contact: Sandra Bradwell, Director.

CIC: Via Augusta 205, 08021 Barcelona; ✆ +93 200 1133; fax 93 200 7680; idiomes@iccic.edu; www.iccic.edu. 20 teachers with Cambridge Certificate and 1 year's experience.

CLIC INTERNATIONAL HOUSE: Albareda 19, 41001 Seville; ✆ +95 450 21 31; fax 95 456 16 96; dos@clic.es; www.clic.es. Approx 30 teachers. Must have TEFL Certification (recognised versions, such as CELTA or TESOL), experience desirable. Personal interviews preferable. Recruitment normally takes place from June/July onwards.

COVENT GARDEN ENGLISH SCHOOL: Calle Sofia nº 48, 28022 Madrid; 91 306 27 34; info@coventgarden.e.telefonica.net. 5 teachers with TEFL training; experience is a plus. Interviews in Madrid. Contact: Elena Medina, Director.

CROSS SCHOOL OF LANGUAGES: C/ Esperanto 19, 29007 Malaga; ✆ +95 228 01 48; fax 95 228 01 48; crossidiomas@spansurf.com or crossidiomas@hotmail.com. 1 part-time experienced teacher directly employed from unsolicited applications, according to school's needs. Modern languages degree, appropriate TEFL Cert. and fluent Spanish essential. Contact: Peter Saliba, MA

EIDE SCHOOL OF ENGLISH: Genaro Oraa 6, Santurce 48980; ✆ +94 493 7005; fax 94- 461 5723; eide@eide.es; www.eide.es. 2 teachers with BA degree and some teaching experience. Interview essential. 9-month contract; 15 hours per week in the evenings. €12 per hour plus bonus for holidays at the end of contract; 8% tax and social security deduction. Help finding accommodation. Contact: Marisol Largo, Director.

EL CENTRO DE INGLES: C/ Calderos 7, 23740 Andújar (Jaén);✆ +/fax 953 506821; elcentro-deingles@infoandujar.com. 2–3 new teachers required every year for September start. To work until June of the following year. Teachers work 21 contact hours per week (34 hours with preparation, meetings and teacher training). Usually there are no morning classes. CELTA/Trinity and 2 years' experience, especially valued if with children. Emphasis on teacher development. Contact: Julie Hetherington, Owner.

ENGLISH 1: Marqués del Nervión 116, 41005 Seville; ✆ +95 464 20 98; info@english1sevilla .com; www.english1sevilla.com. 7 teachers with degree and TEFL Cert (or Diploma) and some experience with young learners. 23 contact hours per week Monday to Thursday only. Starting salary €980 gross plus extra payments for Cambridge exam preparation classes. In-house training and great support in a friendly and harmonious working atmosphere. Assistance with finding accommodation given. Contact: Jennifer Fricker.

ENGLISH CENTRE: Carrer Odena 26, 08700 Igualada (Barcelona); ✆ +93 804 45 54; fax 93 805 58 42; info@centreangles.com; www.centreangles.com. The centre teaches adults, companies and children. 6 teachers with degree, recognised TEFL Certificate and 1 year's experience. All teachers must be EU nationals. Salary €1,200 per month. School can assist with finding accommodation. Contact: Rowland Norris, Principal.

ENGLISH CENTRE: Calle Nuñez de Balboa 17, Bajo Derecha, 28001 Madrid; ✆ +91 577 91 22; fax 91 577 97 43; empresas@theenglishcentre.org or info@theenglishcentre.org. Well established school since 1967. Approx. 60 teachers. CELTA qualification or equivalent and preferably at least 1 year's experience. Part-time and full-time contracts offered from September/October to June. Paid holidays during contract. Classes mainly in companies in central Madrid and own school. Contact: Julia Hoare.

ENGLISH COLLEGE: Carrer Empedrat 4, 03203 Elche, Alicante; ✆ +965 458401; fax 965 452 302; englishcoll@teleline.es. 3–5 teachers with degree, TEFL qualification and 1–2 years' experience of similar kind of teaching. Some knowledge of Spanish desirable but not essential. 9-month contract. 29 hours per week. €1,030 per month (gross). School will assist in finding accommodation. Contact: Mark Harper, Director.

ENGLISH GROUP: Calle General Aranaz, 49 Local 2, 28027, Madrid; ✆ +915101030; fax 914135256; info@english-group.com; www.english-group.com. Employs 'lots' of English teachers, British/Irish or American, with TEFL/CELTA of value and/or experience, also of value. Standard 1-year contract, hours are variable, although the best teachers are given up to 28/30 hours a week. Company assists teachers in any way possible. Interviews essential, always carried out in Madrid, never over the phone or in the UK. Contact: Marianna Chidley, Head of Studies.

ENGLISH HOUSE: Avda. De Alemania, 22, 41012 Seville;✆ +/fax 95 461 06 36. 6 teachers required to teach a maximum of 24 hours per week, mainly from 4pm–10pm Monday to Friday, on a 9-month contract. Teachers must hold CELTA or equivalent qualification and have a minimum of 1 year's experience. Net salary of approx. €995. Assistance with accommodation and work permits offered. Candidates must be available in Seville for interview. Contact: Jennifer Gaudette, Director.

ENGLISH LANGUAGE INSTITUTE: C/ Eduardo Dato 36, 41005 Seville; ✆ +95 464 00 26; fax 95 464 95 03; eli@eli.es; www.eli.es. 10 centres, with headquarters in Seville. 30 teachers with TEFL qualification and experience of teaching children and adolescents. Interviews essential (in Seville and occasionally UK). Help given with finding accommodation.

ESIC IDIOMAS: Sancho el Fuerte 38, Bajo, 31011 Pamplona;✆ +/fax 948 173011; idiomas. pam@esic.es; www.esicidiomas.com. 28 teachers (some part-time), sometimes interviewed by phone. Recognised TEFL qualification and relevant experience. €1,094–€1,128 depending on experience. Contact: Michael John Kerr, Co-ordinator (michael.kerr@esic.es).

EUROLOG IDIOMAS: C/ Valencia, 289 1° 3a 08009 Barcelona; ✆ +93 415 99 44; fax 93 415 33 42; eurolog@eurolog.es; www.eurolog.es. 40 teachers (full and part-time) with CELTA or equivalent and minimum 1 year's teaching experience. Contact: Jon Green, Director of Studies.

EUROPEAN LANGUAGE SCHOOLS: Plaza de la Independencia, Regueiro 2, 36211 Vigo; ✆ +986 291748; euroschools@moriartys.com. 15 EU teachers with good degree preferably in English, Spanish or modern languages, TEFL qualification, some experience preferred. Candidates need references, knowledge of Spanish, outgoing, friendly personality. Contact: John Moriarty.

IDIOMASTER LANGUAGE CENTRES: C/ Juan Rico 8, Apartado de Correos 591, 14900 Lucena (Cordoba); ✆ +957 591678; fax 957 511857; idiomaster@terra.es; www.idiomaster.net. 8 EU teachers with degree, CELTA and at least 1 year's experience preferably with children. Minimum monthly net salary €1,000 plus end of contract bonus of 2.5 days salary per month worked. Full social security and national health insurance cover. Ongoing internal teacher training and support plus external teaching conferences and courses. Help with finding accommodation. Preparation centre for the Cambridge suite of exams. A registered Trinity College, London examination centre and member of ACEIA and FECEI. Contact: Alan McDyre, Director.

INLINGUA LAS PALMAS: C/ Francisco Gourie 67–3°, 35002 Las Palmas de Gran Canaria; ✆ +928 765237; fax 928 372586; inlingua@idecnet.com. 8–10 teachers with TEFL Cert + 2 years' experience.

INLINGUA SANTANDER: Avenida de Pontejos 5, 39005 Santander; ✆ +942 278465; fax 942 274402; inlingua.santander@inlingua.com; www.inlinguasantander.com. 9 qualified teachers. Minimum €970/992. Contact: Ms Ingrid Antons, Director.

INSTITUT NORD-AMERICA (IEN)/INSTITUTE OF NORTH AMERICAN STUDIES: Via Augusta 123, 08006 Barcelona; ✆ +93 240 2847; fax 93 202 0690. 70 Americans (and Canadians). BA plus EFL Certificate (eg Cambridge or Trinity) or MA in Applied Linguistics/EFL/ESL. Minimum 2 years' experience teaching both adults and children (aged 8–17). Work permit processing takes 12–16 months, therefore prefer applicants with Spanish/European work permit/citizenship. Contact: Silvia Cardus, Academic Director.

INSTITUTE OF MODERN LANGUAGES: Puerta Real 1, 18009 Granada; ✆ +958 225536; fax 958 221455; director@imlgranada.com. 12 teachers with degree and TEFL qualification and relevant experience. Member of FECEI (Association of Recognised Language Schools in Spain). Examination Centre for University of Cambridge ESOL examinations. Contact: Jonathan Baum.

INTER-COM ENGLISH: Paseo del General Martinez Campos 28, 28010 Madrid; ✆ +91 308 28 22; fax 91 308 47 75; info@inter-com.com; www.inter-com.com. 65 teachers to teach children and adults. Must have degree, TEFL cert and preferably a year's experience. Contracts of a minimum of 18 hours a week. Gross salary €1,160 per month. School pays social security and income tax. All teaching materials supplied. Workshops and teaching support given. Contact: Alan Crisp.

INTERLANG: C/ Velázquez, 117, 1ª, Madrid; ✆ +91 5158422; fax 91 5642443; formacion@interlang.es; www.interlang.es. Employs 50 native English teachers, no preference of nationality (but must have permission to work in EU if non-EU citizen). Required qualifications are a CTEFLA plus 2 years TEFL experience and some business experience. Standard

9-month contract, working 8.30am to 11am/1pm to 6pm, €18hr gross on contract, €23hr gross for registered freelancers. Tax deductions vary, but for freelancers there is a 7% deduction for the first two years and then 15%. Recruitment via the internet: the school has a permanent page on www.madridteacher.com. A face-to-face interview in Madrid is essential. Contact: Sean O' Malley, Director of Studies.

INTERNATIONAL HOUSE: Calle Trafalgar 14, 08010 Barcelona; ✆ +93 268 4511; fax 93 268 0239; ihbarcelona@bcn.ihes.com; www.ihes.com/bcn. IH Barcelona is a large school with about 40 classrooms, 1,500 students and a busy teacher training department which runs CELTA courses throughout the year. IH Barcelona also hires teachers who have passed the CELTA for both part-time and full-time contracts to teach a mixture of kids, teenagers and adults. There are currently 15–20 teachers, typically working for 20 hours per week €1,221 per month (gross). Teachers who work at IH Barcelona are encouraged to develop professionally and there are substantial subsidies available for training courses within IH Barcelona.

INTERNATIONAL HOUSE MADRID: Calle Fernando el Santo 24 28010 Madrid; ✆ +34 91 3197224; fax +34 91 7027932; rrhh@ihmadrid.com; www.ihmadrid.com. Employs approximately 170 teachers in 5 centres in Madrid, all native English speakers with legal permission to work in Spain. RSA CELTA/Trinity TESOL or RELSA/IH Certificate required. Teachers should ideally have two years' of experience and some knowledge of Spanish. 10-month contract if starting in October. The usual hours are between 18 and 25 a week. Full-time salary packages start from €1,372 plus supplement based on experience and qualifications. Depending on individual circumstances, between 12% and 20% deductions are made for tax and social security. An accommodation officer is able to provide teachers with contact addresses, but will not be able to accompany them to visit flats. Due to the size of the school, recruitment is constant. IH Madrid advertises on various websites, but all candidates are interviewed face-to-face and must be prepared to come to Madrid. In exceptional cases only, candidates are interviewed in London. Contact: Kate Baade, Human Resources Manager.

INTERNATIONAL HOUSE MATARÓ: Jaume Balmes 29, 08301 Mataró, Barcelona; ✆ +93 796 01 25; fax 93 755 1158; ihmataro@mat.ihes.com; www.ihes.com/mat/. Employs 7–10 English teachers from the UK (for legal reasons), and any English teacher from the States etc. has to have an EU passport. Minimum CELTA. DELTA is good and PGCE interesting. 9 or 10-month contracts, but options for longer. Starting contract hours are 18 a week. Salary from €900 net a month. Assistance with deposits as long as there are guarantees of recoupment. Recruitment through IHWO and website. Interviews are preferred and can be done in London, but often on-site.

KINGSBROOK LANGUAGES and SERVICES: Travesera de Gracia, 60, 08006 Barcelona; ✆ +932 093 763; fax 932 021 598; info@kingsbrookbcn.com; www.kingsbrookbcn.com. Approx. 20–30 teachers required annually to work either 3, 6 or 9-month contracts. Personal interview in Barcelona required. Contact: Carmen, Assistant Director of Studies.

LA ACADEMIA DE INGLES: Avda. De Moratalaz, 139 (Lonja), 28030 Madrid; ✆ +914 305 545; fax 914 379 259; www.lacadeintop.com. 25 teachers required. Must be university graduates with at least intermediate level Spanish. 9-month contracts working from 3 hours per week to 27 hours per week. Gross salary approx. €840 per month, with approx. 5% deducted for taxes and social security. Personal interviews essential. Contact: Ana Aparicio, Director at the above address.

LANGUAGE CENTRE IDIOMAS E INFORMATICA: C/ Convento, 5 bajo, 46970 Alaquas (Valencia); fax 96 150 67 60; info@languagecentre.es; www.languagecentre.es. 5 teachers per year with some knowledge of Spanish, degree and TEFL, or 1 year's experience. Approximately €792 a month based on 18 hours per week. Contract according to Spanish Law. Contact: Carmen Ros, Director.

LINGUACENTER BUSINESS LANGUAGE SCHOOL: Calle Juan de Austria 30, 28010 Madrid; ✆ +91 447 03 00; fax 91 447 07 81; joelle@linguacenter.es or info@linguacenter.es; www.linguacenter.es. General and business English teachers mainly for company classes in the Madrid area. Educated to degree level, plus CELTA (or equivalent) and relevant experience. Contact: Joëlle Brossier.

LINGUARAMA IBERICA: Orense 34, 28020 Madrid; ✆ +91 555 04 85; fax 91 555 09 59; madrid@linguarama.com; www.linguarama.com. 80 native English speaker teachers in Spain alltogether (Barcelona address given below). University degree required, TEFL certificate required.

LINGUARAMA IBERICA: Edificios Trade, Torre Norte, Gran Via de Carlos III 98–2°, 08028 Barcelona;93 330 1687; fax 93 330 8013; barcelona@linguarama.com or personnel@linguarama.com; www.linguarama.com. University degree required, TEFL certificate preferred. Package includes flights, initial accommodation and on-going training.

MAUCAL SL: Pol. Argualas Nave 35, 50012 Zaragoza; ✆ +976 350 205; fax 976 350 205; maucal@maucal.com; www.maucal.com. Approx. 4 teachers a year, depending on work demand. Application via www.tefl.com or CV. Interview essential. EFL qualification and BA (Hons) preferable. Contracts of 9–10 months; from 12 to 34 hours a week. Salary depends on hours a week. Contact: Natalia Alastuey.

MERIT SCHOOL: Campo Florido 54–56, 2a, 08027 Barcelona; ✆ +93 243 15 24; fax 93 408 24 53; dos@meritschool.com or www.meritschool.com. 30–40 teachers with at least a TEFL Certificate and 2 years' experience. Business English useful. Hourly rate is €12–€15. Contact: Sam Whiteley, Director of Studies.

MOD LANG: C/ Residencial Paraíso, 2 local 56, 50008 Zaragoza; ✆ +976 33 33 33; modlang@modlang.es; www.modlang.es. Native English teachers for children's summer camps. Candidates need degree-level education plus qualifications and/or experience in teaching EFL or sports/swimming.

NUMBER NINE – THE ENGLISH LANGUAGE CENTRE: C/ Sant Onofre 1, Ciutadella de Menorca, Menorca, Balearic Islands; ✆ +971 384058; fax 971 484001/384058; number9@supersonik.com. 3 native and 2 non-native English speakers with degree, preferably in modern languages and min Cert. TEFL (prefer Dip.). Starting salary €1021. Contact: James R Easton.

OXFORD TEFL: Girona 83, 08009, Barcelona; ✆ +93 4580111; fax 93 458 66 38; tesol@oxfordtefl.com; www.oxfordtefl.com; 40 teachers. No preference regarding nationality. Trinity TESOL certified. Standard 9-month contract to be renewed. 25 hours per week. €1,200 per month gross. 10% deductions for tax and social security.

PRO-LENGUA: C/ Músico Martín Soler, 7–8 46022 Valencia; ✆ +96 5045 28 14; info@prolengua.org; www.prolengua.org. 10 or more teachers required. Must be native English speakers and have a minimum of 2 years' experience. Courses run from September/October to June/July, teaching both company classes and private classes. Salary €12–€15 per hour. Interview essential. Contact: Eugene Bolger, Director.

SAM'S ACADEMY: Dtres. Castroviejo, N° 29, 1° Izda-Logroño, La Rioja; ✆ +941 259 125. 2 teachers required to work afternoons and evenings for one full school term. Applicants must hold a TEFL certificate. Gross salary €1,000 per month. Personal interview at the school essential. Contact: Amparo Busto, Director of Studies.

SECOND LANGUAGE: Autonomia, 26–6°A, 48010 Bilbao; ✆ +94 444 80 62/66; fax 94 444 8066; info@secondlanguage.net; www.secondlanguage.net. 15 teachers with in-company training and Cambridge Certificate.

SPEAK ENGLISH SCHOOL: Cimadevilla 17 Ent F, 33003 Oviedo, Asturias; ✆fax +98 522 61 36; speakschool@hotmail.com; www.speakschool.com. 2 (preferably British) teachers required with a TEFL certificate and a minimum of 2 years' experience. 9–10-month contracts, to work 24–25 hours per week. Net salary of €1,045 per month. The school can help with finding accommodation. Interviews essential, but can be carried out in the UK. Telephone interviews may be possible. Contact: Mick Gordon, Director.

STANTON SCHOOL: Antonio de Trueba, 23, 3, Izq, 03001, Alicante; ✆ +965 20 75 81; fax 965 20 75 81; stanton.school@telefonica.net. About ten teachers, native English speakers of the EU, with a degree plus CELTA or Trinity College teaching certificates. Standard contracts are usually 8–9 months, some summer work, working early morning, mid-afternoon and evening. About 20 hours a week. €12 per hour minimum (net). A teacher helps new recruits to find accommodation. Recruitment through advertisements on the internet and by recommendation. Interviews are essential and usually carried out in Spain. Contact: Mark Smith, Director.

TECHNICAL COLLEGE: C/ Maria Costal, 22, Zaragoza; ✆ +976 227 909; fax 976 233 676; info@academiatechnical.com; www.academiatechnical.com.5 teachers required to work 20–25 hours per week. Must be native English speakers with a degree in languages. Gross salary €800–€1,000 per month. Interview may be required. Contact: Felicidad Segura, Manager.

TECS: Apdo. Correos 85, 11500 El Puerto de Santa María, Cadiz; ✆ +902 350 356; fax 956 860 553; tecscamp@tecs.es; www.tecs.es (commercial) and www.tecs.es/employment (employment site with online application). 15–20 teachers required throughout the year. More than 130 staff employed in summer (40–50 teachers, 50–60 monitors and 20–30 management and support staff) at two residential camps in southern Spain, close to Cadiz in Andalucia. For right applicants there is opportunity for employment all year round. Employees must be team players who are young at heart and full of energy, with a mature and responsible personality. A 'camp' personality (energy, enthusiasm and positivity) is essential for summer work. Apply online.

TENIDIOMAS: C/ Caracuel 15, 11403 Jerez de la Frontera (Cadiz); ✆ fax +956 324707; info@ tenidiomas.com. Contact: Gerry Rylance, Director.

THE LANGUAGE CLUB: C/ Rosalia de Castro 63, 08025 Barcelona; ✆/fax +93 450 33 70; gillian@thelanguageclub.org; www.thelanguageclub.org. Groups of children, adolescents and adults as well as one-to-one and in-company classes.

VAUGHAN SYSTEMS SL: Edificio Master 1, Avenida General Perón, Nº 38–2ª, Planta, 28020 Madrid; ✆ +91 748 59 50; fax 91 556 42 21; recruitment@vausys.com; www.vaughanteacher.com. 315 teachers with EU nationality to commit for at least a year. Interviews held in Madrid and London. Starting salary of €19.30 per hour gross; teachers on contract earn €144 gross per day.

VAUGHANTOWN or PUEBLO INGLES: Eduardo Dato 3, 1a planta, 28010 Madrid; ✆ 91 591 48 30; fax 91 445 87 82; anglos@vaughantown.com; www.vaughantown.com. Cultural exchange project. Native English speakers exchange conversation in return for room and board in a high-standard hotel in rural villages (one in Avila, another in Caceres) where speaking Spanish is not allowed. The programme lasts 7 days and takes place almost every week of the year. Volunteers are required to speak English to Spanish business executives via a schedule of well-orchestrated and fun-packed activities.

YOUR HOUSE IDIOMAS: C. Sant Antoni 4, 08500 Vic and Pl. Nova 15, 08570 Torelló, Barcelona; ✆ 609 11 2475; yhouse@yourhouse.es; www.yourhouse.es. 5–6 teachers; TEFL qualification not essential. Furnished flat provided. Contact: Ferran Pérez.

SWITZERLAND

The status of English is steadily rising. Partly in response to parental pressure, some cantons (including Zurich) decided in 2001 to teach English rather than French as the first-choice second language, to the consternation of many Swiss. According to the Superintendent of Education in Zurich, the decision was taken because children and young people are far more motivated to learn English than any other language and he believes that this should be the starting point for success in teaching. English will become compulsory throughout the curriculum in all Swiss schools by 2010 which will involve massive retraining of Swiss teachers and possibly more demand for foreign teachers of English.

Yet prospects are gloomy for people who fancy the idea of teaching the gnomes of Zürich or their counterparts in other parts of Switzerland, unless they are ultra-qualified. Although immigration regulations are not as restrictive as they once were (see next section), Switzerland will not suddenly be welcoming an army of foreign language teachers. Teachers may also like to consider whether they wish to face the barrage of regulations that are part and parcel of living in Switzerland, from attempting to open a bank account without possessing a small fortune, to falling foul of strict rubbish disposal regulations.

The Swiss economy remains solid, but is not as invincible as it was once considered to be, as the director of a Sprachschule in Basel explained:

> *As a small language school in a country and region which has been experiencing severe withdrawal symptoms (from full employment, job and financial security), it is unlikely that we will be recruiting staff from outside Switzerland, especially as there is a large reservoir of potential candidates here in the Basel region and work permits for staff from outside Switzerland are now a rarity.*

Very few native English speakers are recruited abroad except at a very advanced level. Those schools that do not insist on very advanced qualifications, for example the network of adult education Ecoles Club Migros, generally hire only teachers who already reside legally in Switzerland. Bell Switzerland, based in Geneva, is located close to the United Nations and to the head offices of many global companies. The school specialises in providing English and a range of other languages for professional people working in a multinational or international context, and celebrated 25 years in 2008. Bell Switzerland also offers English language courses for children aged 4½ to 17 and a range of English, French, Spanish, German, Russian, Portuguese, Arabic, Chinese, Italian and Japanese courses for adults. The One World Nursery School introduces children aged 2½ to 5 to English through activities, stories and songs. For further information on teaching opportunities with Bell visit www.bell-worldwide.com/jobs or email recruitment@bell-centres.com.

There are eight Wall Street Institute centres and nine Bénédict schools in Switzerland; a list of addresses and email contact numbers is available at www.wallstreetenglish.ch and www.benedict-international.com. One of the biggest is the one in Lausanne at Rue du Simplon 34, 1006 Lausanne (✆ 21 614 66 14; wsi.lausanne@wallst.ch). If you are hired by a Swiss language school, wages are high, ranging from CHF30 to CHF60 for a 50-minute lesson.

PRIVATE TUTORING IS A POSSIBILITY FOR THOSE WHO LACK A PERMIT, AS THE AMERICAN WORLD TRAVELLER AND FREE SPIRIT DANNY JACOBSON DISCOVERED WHEN HE WAS LIVING WITH HIS SWISS GIRLFRIEND IN BERN:

A Swiss friend advised me to apply at one of the English schools but I didn't think it would work without a permit. So I just made my own flyer and put it up around town and the next thing I knew I had a bunch of people calling me up to help with proofreading seminar papers/assignments and to give private lessons. I figured I'd go for quantity and low-ball the market, charging only CHF20 per hour. But I found a few advertisements for people looking for teachers and with those, I went with their offered price which was much more.

A qualified teacher can charge about CHF80 an hour in the cities, so even CHF40 might be considered a bargain.

Potentially useful websites are ETAS (English Teaching Association in Switzerland; www.e-tas.ch/other/index.asp), which has a blog where teachers share information, and the newsgroup http://groups.yahoo.com/group/swissenglish, which is aimed at EFL teachers already in Switzerland.

REGULATIONS

Switzerland is not a member of the EU. However a bilateral agreement with the EU has been concluded and the main obstacles to free movement of persons were removed in 2004. This means that the Swiss have had to undergo a huge shift in their attitudes to immigration and employment. Not everyone welcomed the change, but the Swiss electorate recently rejected a people's initiative that would have tightened the requirements for acquiring Swiss citizenship. Now the immigration system is more in line with the rest of Europe so that EU job-seekers can enter Switzerland for up to three months (extendable) to look for work. If they succeed they must show a contract of employment to the authorities and are then eligible for a short-term residence permit (valid for up to one year and renewable) or a long-term permit (up to five years) depending on the contract.

VACATION WORK

More possibilities for teaching English exist at summer camps than in city language institutes, as can be seen from the programmes listed in the directory below. There are a number of international schools in Switzerland, some of which run English language and sports summer schools. The Swiss Federation of Private Schools produces a list of summer schools in Switzerland held at its member private schools indicating which ones teach English. This is available at www.swiss-schools.ch.

Watch for occasional advertisements or, if you are in Switzerland, make local enquiries. **Susanna Macmillan** hitch-hiked from Italy to Crans-Montana in the Swiss Alps in the autumn and within three days had arranged a job as a monitrice at the International School there. The job, which was to teach English and sport, came with room and board and paid an additional SFr850 per month. (Perhaps one reason the job was so easy to get was because of the 60-hour weeks and compulsory overtime with no compensation.)

In addition to the organisations with entries below, the following organisations offer summer language courses between June and September and may need teachers or monitors (or some combination of the two):

Aiglon Summer School: 1885 Chesières – Villars; ✆ 24 495 2348; www.aiglon.ch/new/ welcome.shtm.

Beau Soleil Holiday Language Camp: EPTA Organisation, CH-1884 Villars-sur-Ollon.

Institut Le Rosey: Camp d'Eté, Route des Quatre Communes, CH-1180 Rolle. Winter address January-March: CH-3780 Gstaad;30 435 15; www.rosey.ch. Qualified or experienced EFL teachers for coeducational summer camps with sports coaching on Lake Geneva. Teachers must be capable of carrying out boarding school duties.

Institut le Vieux Chalet: CH-1837 Chateau d'Oex.

Institut Monte Rosa: 57 Avenue de Chillon, CH-1820 Montreux; ✆ 21 965 4545; info@ monterosa.ch; www.monterosa.ch.

Leysin American School in Switzerland: CH-1854 Leysin; ✆ 24 493 37 7; fax 24 494 15 85; www.las.ch.

St George's School in Switzerland: 1815 Clarens/Montreux; www.st-georges.ch.

Surval Mont-Fleuri: Route de Glion 56, CH-1820 Montreux 1; www.surval.ch.

TASIS (The American School in Switzerland): Summer Language Programs, Via Collina d'Oro, 6926 Montagnola-Lugano; ✆ 91 960 5151; fax 91 994 2364; administration@tasis.ch; www.tasis.com/switzerland/. Employ Americans in Lugano.

LIST OF EMPLOYERS

BERLITZ
Steinentorstr. 45, 4051 Basel
✆ 61 226 90 40; fax 61 226 9041/281 6206

NUMBER OF TEACHERS: 15.
PREFERENCE OF NATIONALITY: must have work permit.
QUALIFICATIONS: BA or professional experience, eg business, banking.
CONDITIONS OF EMPLOYMENT: no limit on contract length. Flexible hours of work. Pupils are adults whose average age is between 30 and 40.
SALARY: SFr22.50 per 40-minute lesson plus 10–20% supplements for some programmes.

FACILITIES/SUPPORT: no assistance with accommodation. Training provided.
RECRUITMENT: through advertisements. Local interviews essential.

HAUT-LAC INTERNATIONAL CENTRE
1669 Les Sciernes
✆ 26 928 42 00; fax 26 298 42 01
info@haut-lac.com or jobs@haut-lac.com
www.myswisscamp.com

NUMBER OF TEACHERS: teacher/monitors needed for summer, spring, autumn and winter language camps for adolescents.

PREFERENCE OF NATIONALITY: language teachers must be mother-tongue.

QUALIFICATIONS: TEFL CELTA or equivalent plus it is useful to have experience in sports, drama, art or games organisation.

CONDITIONS OF EMPLOYMENT: summer camp (mid-June to end of August); winter ski camp (end of December to early April); spring camp (early April to early May) and autumn camp (late September to mid-October).

FACILITIES/SUPPORT: full board and lodging provided in single, twin or three-bedded rooms. Help given with travel expenses. Free laundry facilities and use of sports equipment.

RECRUITMENT: send for an application form to jobs@ haut-lac.com.

CONTACT: Steve McShane (stephen.mcshane@ haut-lac.com).

VILLAGE CAMPS
Personnel Office, Department 342, Rue de la
Morache 14, 1260 Nyon
☎ +41 22 990 9405; fax +41 22 990 9494
✍ personnel@villagecamps.ch
🖥 www.villagecamps.com/personnel

Language summer camp at Leysin near Lake Geneva in French-speaking Switzerland (also in Hurstpierpoint, Sussex, England).

PREFERENCE OF NATIONALITY: European, North American, Australian, New Zealand passport holders may apply.

QUALIFICATIONS: Applicants must be at least 21 years of age, possess a recognised qualification in language teaching (minimum 4 weeks) and be a native English speaker of the language of instruction. A second language is desirable and experience in sports, creative and/or outdoor activities is essential. A valid first aid and cardio-pulmonary resuscitation (CPR) certificate is required while at camp.

PERIOD OF EMPLOYMENT: Periods vary from 3 to 8 weeks between June and August.

ALLOWANCE: room and board, accident and liability insurance and a weekly allowance provided.

RECRUITMENT: starts in December. There is no deadline to submit applications, but positions are limited. Interviews are by telephone. Please specify department 342 on application. For information on dates, locations, positions available and to download an application form, visit www. villagecamps.com.

THE REST OF EUROPE

Outside the mainstream European nations, demand for native speaking teachers of English obviously exists though immigration problems often occur. This chapter contains a miscellany of European opportunities in some quite obscure corners of the continent.

Albania

Information about teaching in this European country wedged between Greece, Macedonia, Serbia and Montenegro has not always been easy to find, but Albania is now fairly stable and offers some opportunities for teachers keen to escape the traditional EFL circuit.

The number of paid teaching jobs is still limited by the country's poverty, but in June 2006 Albania signed a Stabilisation and Association agreement with the EU, so there is perhaps hope that demand might increase if the country's economy slowly continues to grow.

English is certainly the favoured foreign language and is compulsory from the fifth grade through to university. Language schools have begun to open and most at least aspire to employ a native-speaking English teacher, although few can currently afford it.

FINDING A JOB

The Language Schools in Albania Foundation (LSIA) is the largest non-profit private language tuition provider in Albania, founded in April 1994 by a group of Albanian university teachers and students. It currently enrols around 3,500 students in 14 locations across Albania and Macedonia, with plans to expand into Kosovo and Montenegro. Out of 120 English teachers a handful are native English speakers. The salary is €300 per four weeks (no taxes and social security paid). Accommodation is free and the association organises the work permit.

Albania might be a good bet for newly qualified teachers, as the LSIA website explains (www.lsiaal .com/teachforus.php): '*There are relatively few native-speaker teachers in Albania, and we offer rapid career development not normally available to new or recently qualified teachers.*'

Other institutions that may be worth contacting include the Memorial International School of Tirana (Ish Shkolla Partise Rr. Dumes, Tirana; ℂ 4 237379; info@mistedu.net; www.mistedu.com) that currently employs one American, one Briton, and three Canadians. The school's minimum requirement is that teachers have some years of experience in their own fields, although the majority have completed university courses with components in education. The Abraham Lincoln Professional Studies Center in Tirana offers English language courses for all levels and special English programmes for several professional institutions in Albania. It employs a few American teachers with English degrees at their two branches in Tirana: Rruga Qemal Stafa, Nr. 184, and Rruga Ismail Qemali, Nr. 31 (ℂ 4 230880; info@lincoln.org.al; www.lincolnalbania.org).

Blerina Gjonaj, Head of the Overseas Department at LSIA, suggests that volunteering might lead to a paid job:

> *The demand for native English speakers is increasing every day, and the same can be said for paid employment, although that is not yet at the level that everybody wants. It is still easier to find a teaching job if you are a volunteer (maybe at the beginning), and then you can get involved as a paid employee. Albanian people are very interested in learning English. Language schools in Albania enrol children, mature students, adults and even parents of the students.*

REGULATIONS

Visa guidelines can be checked at the Embassy of the Republic of Albania in the UK or USA, although the LSIA site (www.lsiaal.com/download/expat-orientation.doc) says the following about visas: '*Most western nationalities don't need to apply for a Visa in advance, but do check to make sure. Visitors will be required to pay $10 upon entering Albania and if the stay extends 20 days, you may need to start the process of a residence visa. Airport fees can be waived by presenting your Residence Permit (entry) or a letter stating that you work for a foundation (exit).*'

Living costs are reasonable by US and UK standards, and Albania has plenty of scenic attractions, including rugged mountains and a marvellous stretch of Adriatic coastline, blissfully free of package holiday tourists.

LANGUAGE SCHOOLS IN ALBANIA (LSIA), FOUNDATION 'PRAKTIKIMI I GJUHES'

P.O.Box 1400, RR. Bardhyl NR.76/1, Tirana, Albania

42 361 498; 42 376 740

lsiaheadquarter@abcom-al.com

www. lsiaal.com

NUMBER OF TEACHERS: 6.

PREFERENCE OF NATIONALITY: no, but have to be native English teachers.

QUALIFICATIONS: University, master's degree in any specialisation, job experience.

CONDITIONS OF EMPLOYMENT: 1-year contract (possibility of renewal). Usual hours are 6 weekly.

SALARY: €300 per 4 weeks. No taxes and social security paid.

FACILITIES/SUPPORT: school provides accommodation and assists with work permit.

RECRUITMENT: interviews are very important and are carried out In the UK or USA, depending on the occasion. If the teacher is in Albania, then a face-to-face interview will be possible.

CONTACT: Blerina Gjonaj, Head of Overseas Department.

Andorra

Andorra lies in the heart of the Pyrenees between Spain and France, and can be seen as an extension of both countries, though it has its own elected government. It is too small to have many language schools, but the one listed here is a possibility (and you would be there over the skiing season).

CENTRE ANDORRA DE LLENGUES (CALL)

15 Carrer del Fener, Andorra-la-Vella, Andorra

80 40 30; fax 82 24 72

centrandorra.lang@andorra.ad

www.call.ad

NUMBER OF TEACHERS: 2.

PREFERENCE OF NATIONALITY: British and North Americans.

QUALIFICATIONS: BA in English or foreign language plus TEFL qualification and 2–3 years' experience abroad most welcome. A good knowledge of Spanish and/or French can help. Non-smokers preferred.

CONDITIONS OF EMPLOYMENT: 9–10-month renewable contract which runs from October to June. 27 hours per week 5 days a week. Teaching hours spread throughout the day. Teaching very young learners (6–7 years) and all other ages including professionals.

SALARY: €1,800 per month (plus overtime if any available).

FACILITIES/SUPPORT: board and lodging available within walking distance from €500 per month. Work permit arranged and paid for by the School.

RECRUITMENT: direct application with CV and photo by email.

CONTACT: Claude Benet.

Bosnia-Herzegovina

There are still not many private language schools in Bosnia. You could try Studio Byblos (Kralja Petra I, Karadordevica 119, 78000 Banjaluka, BIH; +751215612; info@studio-byblos.com; www.studio-byblos.com), Globe Language Centre (Kralja Petra I Karađorđevićća 103 Banja Luka; 𝒞 065 028 018; info@globecentre.rs.ba; www.globecentre.rs.ba) or Seal (Vase Todorovića 2 Bijeljina i Dvorovi; 𝒞 55 222 772/222 777; seal_bn@yahoo.co.uk; www.seal-rs.com).

SOROS FOREIGN LANGUAGE SCHOOL

Safvet-bega Bašagića 6, 71000 Sarajevo

𝒞 ++387 33 533077

✏ school@soros-school.com

🖳 www.soros-school.com

NUMBER OF TEACHERS: 2–6 full-time and a number of part-time.

PREFERENCE OF NATIONALITY: none.

QUALIFICATIONS: minimum CELTA or equivalent.

Experience preferred.

CONDITIONS OF EMPLOYMENT: 10 months, 96 hours per 4 weeks max.

SALARY: about €500 per month (net) in local currency.

FACILITIES/SUPPORT: school provides free accommodation in a shared flat, plus utilities (apart from telephone bill).

RECRUITMENT: advertisements. Short-listed applicants are interviewed by phone.

Croatia

Building on its strong indigenous English teaching infrastructure, Croatia's private language schools flourish in Zagreb, Varazdin and Karlovac, as well as in other towns. For many schools, the idea of employing a native English speaker teacher is very attractive, particularly given Croatia's popularity as a British tourist destination, accessible by cheap flights. However, until fairly recently, there was little tradition of employing native English speakers and teachers who go to work in Croatia are likely to find themselves being made welcome and treated well, certainly outside the usual tourist hot spots. Salaries are likely to be quoted in euros.

The market for private teaching is strong, although increasingly native English speakers are penetrating the market, because the country is so geographically accessible – and beautiful. As a result, and perhaps because of the high standards demanded by pupils of teachers and of themselves, native English teachers need to be well qualified to secure a job. The Foreign Language School, Ziger, is fairly modest in size, with only 1 or 2 native teachers, but they still ask for a degree, at least 1 year's experience, and a TEFL/CELTA/DELTA certificate.

Anyone wishing to work in Croatia must apply to the Embassy of the Republic of Croatia for a visa. An application form must be completed by your employer and returned together with a passport, two photographs and details of the job (eg a copy of your contract, length of employment, type of work, location and full address of employer).

The British Council in Zagreb can offer informal assistance to prospective teachers and should be able to put you in touch with the Association of Croatian Teachers of English (HUPE) which organises teacher development activities but can't help foreign teachers to find jobs. The voluntary placement organisation Services for Open Learning (see Eastern Europe chapter: Finding a Job) sends teachers to Croatia but posts are dependent on an unpredictable Ministry.

FOREIGN LANGUAGE SCHOOL – ZIGER
S. Vraza 37, 42000 Varazdin
+42 330 385; fax 42 330 385
irena.ziger@vz.htnet.hr
www.skola-ziger.hr

NUMBER OF TEACHERS: 1–2.
PREFERENCE OF NATIONALITY: UK, USA, Canada.
QUALIFICATIONS: at least 1 year's experience, TEFL/
CELTA/ DELTA, university degree.
CONDITIONS OF EMPLOYMENT: minimum 1-year contract,
teaching hours are usually late afternoon and evenings.
FACILITIES/SUPPORT: assistance with finding accom-
modation and work permit (school applies and translates
necessary documents).
RECRUITMENT: via email contact. Interviews by phone.
CONTACT: Irena Ziger, Principal.

LANCON ENGLISH LANGUAGE CONSULTANCY
Kumiciceva 10, 10 000 Zagreb
+1 485 4985; fax 1 485 4984
lmo@lancon.hr
www.lancon.hr

NUMBER OF TEACHERS: 10.
PREFERENCE OF NATIONALITY: must be native speaker
of English.
QUALIFICATIONS: university degree, a TEFL qualification and
2 years' experience. Knowledge of Business English useful.
CONDITIONS OF EMPLOYMENT: 1 academic year contracts, renewable. Salary paid monthly over 12 months. 750
teaching hours (45 minutes) per year, averaging 24 per week
during term time.
FACILITIES/SUPPORT: teachers need to enter the country
with a work permit stamped in their passports at a Croatian
embassy/consulate in their country of residence. The issue of
the work visa requires a letter from Lancon offering employment and also depends on the official quota on foreign
employees. Assistance with finding accommodation.
RECRUITMENT: via the internet and direct application.
Interviews in Zagreb or by telephone.
CONTACT: Martin Doolan.

Cyprus

A visitor to the Republic of Cyprus will be struck by the similarities with Greece – cuisine, architecture, landscapes and culture – but then surprised at the relative prominence of English. Signs
are printed in both Greek and English, many (if not most) local people even outside the cities speak
some English, and the British influence can be noticed everywhere. Because of the longstanding
relationship between Cyprus and Britain, the English language is given much prominence in the state
educational system. As a result the density of *frontisteria* is not as high as it is in Greece, though there
are still a fair number of private institutes preparing children for external examinations.

Cyprus has a small population of not much more than one million people and therefore opportunities are not extensive. Also a large number of Cypriot students leave the island each year to study in the
UK and USA, although there are still a number of afternoon language schools in the cities and towns.

PROSPECTS FOR TEACHERS

To find an ELT job in Cyprus before you arrive is extremely difficult because very few of the ELT
schools actually advertise on the internet and there is a sizeable expat community, from which native
teachers can be drawn. Some expats will also informally help Cyprian friends with their English over
a glass of beer.

Sending speculative CVs is unlikely to succeed. It is more fruitful to visit schools in person and
hand in your CV. Furthermore, state school jobs are extremely hard to come by for foreigners as you
need at least a three-year degree in the relevant subject (eg English literature for teaching English)

as well as a good knowledge of Greek. Therefore, most foreign teachers aim to find a job in a language school in the private sector, which will probably mean working in the afternoons or evenings, although some schools also have morning classes. Summer posts are very rare, with few schools offering summer courses.

One freelance opportunity might be to approach businessmen and women in the booming property sector, who have (or would like to have) English and American clients. You'd need a solid business background to succeed, and would be required to provide specialist vocabulary ('grouting', anyone?).

Since Cyprus has joined the European Union, visas are no longer a major hurdle. The country has also adopted the euro. If you wish to advertise your services as a tutor in the English language press of Greek Cyprus, contact the *Cyprus Mail* which has an online edition (www.cyprus-mail.com) or the *Cyprus Weekly* published on Fridays by Cyweekly (PO Box 24977, 1306 Nicosia; ✆ +22 666047; www.cyprusweekly.com.cy).

Major English institutes include the Papantoniou Institute founded in 1999 (see entry) which offers English at all levels. Most schools offer a contract of 20–25 working hours a week for the academic year September to May/June. The hourly pay is above average for southern Europe, starting at about €12 per hour. As in Greece, there are usually two paid holidays during the academic year: two weeks over Christmas and two weeks for the Greek Orthodox Easter.

Most Cypriot schools have very good facilities, although they may be lagging behind somewhat in technology. Teacher support is readily available with regular free seminars organised by various publishers. In language classrooms, there is a wide range of levels for all ages. The majority of children enrol at language schools when they are about eight and finish around the age of 16, attending lessons twice a week. However, there is a growing demand for children as young as 4 to start learning English as a foreign language, so schools are introducing classes for younger children. A lesson can last from one to two hours for higher levels. Young students and adults are usually motivated and love interactive teaching. However, those teaching teenagers will need to be firm and to make lessons particularly interesting.

People move to Cyprus nowadays more for the lifestyle than for cheap living. The downside is that eating out, etc. is not cheap; however the improved infrastructure (like the very good motorways) makes life easier. Over the next few years many marinas and golf courses are due to be built indicating that the island is going up-market as the government intends. If reunification with the Turkish north takes place on the island (a long way off but positive talks have started) then the country could really flourish. A decent studio apartment can be rented for about €350 euros per month. Eating out is not too ruinous at €17 per person. Public transport, on the other hand, is sparse. There are no trains, although the motorways have been much improved if you have a car. Look at the English newspapers to find out what's on and where to meet new friends. If you want to find out more about life in Cyprus for ex-pats, visit www.cyprusliving.org and www.easterncyprus.com.

PAPANTONIOU INSTITUTE
30a Ippocratous, 2122 Nicosia
✆ +22455724; fax 99821634
✉ papantoniouinstitute@yahoo.co.uk
🖥 www.papantoniou-institute.com

NUMBER OF TEACHERS: 6.
PREFERENCE OF NATIONALITY: none.
QUALIFICATIONS: degree normally required but TEFL certificate also valued. Teaching ability is the most important factor.

CONDITIONS OF EMPLOYMENT: 9-month contracts.
SALARY: from €12 per hour.
FACILITIES/SUPPORT: training courses offered onsite, LTTC and LCCI full range of courses lasting 6 to 8 weeks.
RECRUITMENT: from onsite TEFL course (see Directory of Training Courses). Local interviews essential.
CONTACT: Tina Papantoniou, Director.

Turkish Cyprus

There are six private universities, four private schools and at least two language schools in the Turkish Republic of Northern Cyprus (TRNC). The main industry in Northern Cyprus is tourism, largely catering for an English-speaking clientele, so there is strong local demand to master the languages for employment purposes. However, it should be pointed out that the expatriate community numbers more than 4,000 so there is already a substantial pool of native English speakers on hand to fill any teacher vacancies that occur.

Malta

Although somewhat off the beaten track and although English is the first language of the tiny island, EFL is booming in Malta. A number of private language schools cater to groups coming from other Mediterranean countries on short courses in the spring, summer and at other times. Even the National Tourist Office of Malta distributes a leaflet 'Learning English in the Sun' or check the list on www.visitmalta.com (which devotes a whole section to 'language learning'). Their interests are represented by FELTOM, the Federation of English Language Teaching Organisations Malta (c/o Victoria Hotel, Triq Paul Borg Olivers, Sliena SLM 1807; ✆ 2744 5422); the website has good links to all the member schools and information about the courses they offer (but nothing about teaching jobs).

Bell Malta, Malta is a major centre for English language training as English is an official language and spoken everywhere on the island. For further information on teaching opportunities visit www.bell-worldwide.com/jobs or email recruitment@bell-centres.com.

The following 16 schools are members of FELTOM (contact details given below) though there are others on this island nation: inlingua, Geos, am Language Studio, English Language Academy, English Communication School, Institute of English Language Studies, International English Language Centre and Linguatime all in Sliema; elsewhere: Sprachcaffe Languages Plus (St Andrew's), Academy Master and European Centre of English (St Julian's), NSTS English Language Institute (Valletta and Sliema), Lasalle Institute (Floriana, Valletta), Global Village (St Paul's Bay) and BELS (Gozo) and the Voice School of English.

REGULATIONS

All EU nationals have the right to live and work in Malta, although it is necessary to obtain an employment licence before you start teaching. These are granted on application and can be obtained from the Department of Citizenship and Expatriates Affairs (3 Castille Place, Valletta CMR 02; ✆ 2 50868; fax 2 237513; www.mjha.gov.mt). Applications are screened by the work permit office, the training and employment corporation, the labour office and finally the immigration authorities. Employment licences are usually valid for one year in the first instance. Further details may be requested from the Malta High Commission in London (Malta House, 36–38 Piccadilly, London W1J 0DP; ✆ 020 7292 4800; fax 020 7734 1832) or direct from the Department for Citizenship and Expatriate Affairs in Malta. The rate of tax is progressive starting at 15% and rising to 25%–35% for high earners. There is a €8,150 tax free allowance (Malta adopted the euro on 1 January 2008).

The NSTS English Language Institute (220 St Paul St, Valletta VLT07; ✆ 2558 8000; fax 2558 8200; nsts@nsts.org; www.nsts.org) markets its English courses in conjunction with sports holidays for young tourists to Malta. NSTS run weekly vacation courses from June to August, and it might be worth approaching them for a job, particularly if you are a water sports enthusiast. NSTS was keen to hire **Robert Mizzi** from Canada once it learned that he was half-Maltese:

I was offered a job quite casually when NSTS found out I was volunteering conversational English in the main youth hostel in Valletta. Perhaps one reason they wanted to hire me was they knew the visa would not be a problem. However I was surprised by how relaxed the offer was. It was just mentioned in passing rather than at an actual interview. I guess it is the Maltese way: once you are one of them, then everything is gravy.

GLOBAL VILLAGE ENGLISH CENTRE

St George's Street, St. Paul's Bay SPB 02

📞 21 573417; fax 21 578280

✉ dos@gvmalta.com

🖥 www.gvmalta.com

NUMBER OF TEACHERS: all staff are native English speakers.

PREFERENCE OF NATIONALITY: none.

QUALIFICATIONS: experience and TEFL qualification needed plus minimum 1-year experience.

CONDITIONS OF EMPLOYMENT: open-ended contracts. 15–20 hours per week in low season, 20+ hours per week in peak season.

SALARY: varies according to experience and qualifications.

FACILITIES/SUPPORT: advice given on rental accommodation in area.

RECRUITMENT: mainly via teacher training courses run on-site. Interviews are essential and are usually carried out face-to-face with the Director of Studies and include analysis of lesson planning.

CONTACT: Rebecca Portelli, Director of Studies.

INLINGUA SCHOOL OF LANGUAGES

9 Triq Guzi Fava, Off Bisazza St, Sliema SLM 15

📞 +2133 6384/2131 3158;

　 fax 2133 6419/2131 8903

✉ info@inlinguamalta.com

🖥 www.inlinguamalta.com

Member of FELTOM

NUMBER OF TEACHERS: 30–100+ depending on time of year.

PREFERENCE OF NATIONALITY: Maltese and native English speakers if they are able to work in Malta. (inlingua does not apply for work permits.)

QUALIFICATIONS: matriculation standard of education, 'A' level English and TEFL qualification minimum.

CONDITIONS OF EMPLOYMENT: casual and freelance employment only.

SALARY: depends on qualifications.

RECRUITMENT: local interviews essential.

CONTACT: Ms Kathleen von Schloss Cremona, Managing Director.

Slovenia

As in Croatia, there are a good many private schools and many opportunities can be created by energetic native English speakers both as freelance teachers for institutes or as private tutors. Slovenia is a sophisticated little country with high standards of education and many well-qualified native teachers of English.

The English Studies Resource Centre at the British Council in Ljubljana (www.britishcouncil.org/slovenia) has a list of private language schools throughout the country (see www.britishcouncil.org/jp/slovenia-exams-cambridge-how-to-prepare-language-schools.htm). The council remains closely in touch with language schools and will refer qualified candidates to possible employers. There is also a British Council resource centre in Maribor, located in the university library. The average hourly wage starts at about €8.

As one of the countries that joined the EU in May 2004, Slovenia now has fairly straightforward regulations for EU members. The euro has replaced the Slovenian tolar. All EU nationals are able to work in Slovenia under the same conditions as Slovene citizens in their countries. However, teachers should obtain a temporary residence permit within three months of entering the country, and will need a valid passport whose expiry date exceeds by at least three months the intended period of stay, health insurance, sufficient means of subsistence and a legitimate purpose for their residence (like a job). The Embassy in London (10 Little College Street, London SW1P 3SH; ✆ 020 7222 5700; www.slovenia.embassyhomepage.com) handles external applications for both British and Irish nationals; the average processing time is one month. Slovenia joined the Schengen agreement in 2007/2008.

Your school should report that you are working for them to the Employment Service of Slovenia, Zavod za zaposlovanje (Rono dolino Cesta IX/6, 1000 Ljubljana; ✆ 1 4790 0900; www.ess.gov.si) within eight days of starting the job.

LIST OF EMPLOYERS

BERLITZ LANGUAGE CENTER

Gosposvetska 2, 1000 Ljubljana;

✆ +386 1 433 13 25; fax +386 1 433 20 42

Svetozarevska 6, 2000 Maribor

✉ berlitz.ljubljana@berlitz.si

🖥 www.berlitz.si

NUMBER OF TEACHERS: 40.

PREFERENCE OF NATIONALITY: none.

QUALIFICATIONS: sound educational background, good communication skills, professional attitude and appearance.

CONDITIONS OF EMPLOYMENT: minimum 1 year. 4–8 teaching hours per day.

SALARY: €10+ per unit (40 minutes).

FACILITIES/SUPPORT: try to assist teachers with accommodation. Compulsory training in Berlitz method. Regular support through observations and workshops.

RECRUITMENT: advertisements and personal recommendation. Interviews necessary in most cases, occasionally held abroad.

CONTACT: Beatrice Slamberger, Director of Berlitz Ljubljana; Ian Jan, Director of Berlitz, Maribor.

EVROPA BLED d.o.o.

Finzgarjeva 15, 4260 Bled

✆ 4 57 41 563/64 49 88; fax 4 57 68 850

✉ evropabl@s5.net

NUMBER OF TEACHERS: 1–2.

PREFERENCE OF NATIONALITY: none.

QUALIFICATIONS: experience essential. Teacher training course for TEFL required.

CONDITIONS OF EMPLOYMENT: school year from October to May. Minimum 30–40 lessons a month.

SALARY: starting salary about €6.50 net per 45-minute lesson.

FACILITIES/SUPPORT: help is given with finding accommodation but the rental charge is borne by the teacher.

RECRUITMENT: contacts through the British Council.

CONTACT: Cilka Demsar, Manager.

GLOTTA NOVA

Poljanska cesta 95, SI-1000 Ljubljana

✆ 0 1520 0670; fax 0 1520 0676

✉ info@glottanova.si

🖥 www.glottanova.com

QUALIFICATIONS: teaching experience, good language knowledge, willingness to learn and use Global Method Learning.

CONDITIONS OF EMPLOYMENT: 1-year contract. To work Thursdays to Sundays.

SALARY: €10 per hour.

RECRUITMENT: Interviews essential but can be carried out in the UK if necessary. Successful applicants will then be trained in Global Method Learning.

CONTACT: Marusa Jovanovic.

NISTA LANGUAGE CENTER

6 Smarska C.5D, 6000 Koper

✆ 0 5625 0400; fax 0 5625 0404

✉ nista@siol.net

🖥 www.nista.si

Located on the Adriatic not far from Trieste, Italy.

NUMBER OF TEACHERS: 15.

PREFERENCE OF NATIONALITY: England, Scotland, New Zealand, Australia.

QUALIFICATIONS: BA (hons) and TEFL Certificate plus a year's teaching experience. Business background useful.

CONDITIONS OF EMPLOYMENT: minimum 10 months' September to June (preferably longer). Usual 24–26 hours contact time per week.

SALARY: about €10 per lesson. No tax or social security deductions.

FACILITIES/SUPPORT: the school finds accommodation for teachers and provides necessary documents for obtaining a temporary visa which the teacher has to obtain. Visa fees reimbursed.

RECRUITMENT: email, internet.

PANTEON COLLEGE

Vojkova 1, 1000 Ljubljana

(C) 1 280 3220/280 3225; fax 1 280 3230

info@panteon.si

www.panteon.si

NUMBER OF TEACHERS: 5.

PREFERENCE OF NATIONALITY: British/American.

QUALIFICATIONS: English teacher with a variety of TEFL experience.

CONDITIONS OF EMPLOYMENT: standard length of contract 1 year. 20 hours per week including morning, afternoon and evening lessons.

SALARY: €10 per hour (45 minutes of teaching).

FACILITIES/SUPPORT: help is given with finding accommodation and acquiring the necessary permits.

RECRUITMENT: CV must be submitted. Successful applicants will be invited to attend an interview.

YURENA

Glavni Trg 11, 8000 Novo Mesto

(C) 7 337 2100; fax 7 337 7210

yurena@siol.net

www.yurena.si

NUMBER OF TEACHERS: 2–3.

PREFERENCE OF NATIONALITY: English.

QUALIFICATIONS: TEFL qualification.

CONDITIONS OF EMPLOYMENT: 1-year contracts. 25–30 hours per week.

SALARY: approx. €1,000 per month.

FACILITIES/SUPPORT: accommodation and help with work permits provided.

RECRUITMENT: Interviews essential.

CONTACT: Kati Golobic, Director.

Serbia and Montenegro

With the short-lived union of Serbia and Montenegro breaking down in 2006, followed by Kosovo's declaration of independence from Serbia in 2008, the dissolution of the former Yugoslavia seems finally complete, even if underlying tension remains.

The nascent ELT industry looks set to develop, perhaps rapidly, if the region remains stable. Possible leads include the Bejza Education centre (Ul. Vuka Karadžića br.7 11000, Belgrade; *(C)* 11/328 14 49; info@bejza.edu.rs; www.bejza.edu.rs), ELS Language School (Beogradska 70/I; *(C)* 11 30 868 18; office@els.co.yu; www.els.co.yu) the Oxford Centar (081/234 425; oxford-centar@cg.yu; www.oxfordcentar.com) and Speak Up English Language School, (ul. Visnjiceva 31, 34000 Kragujevac; *(C)* 34 67472; speakup@ptt.yu).

In order to get a residence/work permit for Serbia and Montenegro, you must submit a contract of employment and a translated copy of your diploma. Further information on the regulations for entering and working in Serbia can be found at www.serbianembassy.org.uk.

NEW VISIONS SCHOOL

Narodnog fronta 75, Novi Sad

✆ 21 466 343; fax 21 368 766

office@newvisions.co.yu

www. newvisions.co.yu

NUMBER OF TEACHERS: 3 (1 full-time, 2 part-time).

PREFERENCE OF NATIONALITY: none.

QUALIFICATIONS: EFL experience.

CONDITIONS OF EMPLOYMENT: standard contract

1 school year, made up of 2 semesters: September to December, January to June. Hours flexible from 15 to 40 hours per week.

SALARY: agreed personally.

FACILITIES/SUPPORT: help offered with finding the right accommodation and with registering for a work permit.

RECRUITMENT: via website, British Council or on the spot applications.

CONTACT: Dragana Djurkovic-Tasic, Principal.

Macedonia

The Strategakis Organisation (see Greece chapter) has 15 schools in Macedonia and Albania, administered under the umbrella of Pharos Schools from Sofia (Bulgaria). Qualified EL teachers might try IH Skopje (Nikola Parapunov b.b., Skopje 91000; ✆ 91 364 625) or St George's School (Partizanski odredi 3–315, 1000 Skopje; 91 212 916).

CENTRAL AND EASTERN EUROPE

The transition to a market economy throughout the vast area of eastern and central Europe has resulted in a huge demand for professional assistance at all levels, especially when it comes to improving the skills of communication. The dramatic changes which have taken place in the former Communist Bloc since 1989 mean that in every hotel lobby, office boardroom and government ministry from Silesia to Siberia, deals are being struck, export partnerships forged and academic alliances developed between East and West. The east Europeans benefitting from this new commerce tend to be the ones who have acquired the English language.

While Russia and many of its former satellites have continued to wrestle with their political and economic demons, the more stable central European states of Hungary, Poland, the Czech Republic, Slovakia, the Baltic States and most recently, Bulgaria and Romania, have been welcomed into the European fold by acceding to the European Union (EU).

In some quarters of central Europe there has been a noticeable backlash against what has been seen as a selling out to the West, especially in the major capitals which are now swarming with foreigners. School directors are now perfectly aware of the English-speaking foreigner who masquerades as a teacher but really intends to indulge in cheap beer and all-night discos. They are suspicious of anyone projecting this hidden agenda, disliking the fact that so many foreigners used the region as an extended party venue early on.

In the years just after the revolution, teachers up and down the countries of eastern Europe chucked their ancient textbooks and joyfully embraced the new communicative methodologies. Everybody craved English lessons, assuming that to learn was to earn, parents as well as children and teenagers. Many foreigners, some representing religions such as the Mormons and Bahai, arrived and set up schools. The people thought that knowing English would make them happy and rich. It didn't. Furthermore, they learned that learning a language is very difficult, and much of that initial enthusiasm has subsided.

Yet despite having moved past making 'Western' synonymous with 'desirable', they are still remarkably welcoming to British and American ELT teachers. On most street corners, private language schools employ native English speaker teachers. Working in central and eastern Europe may not seem as attractive as it did just after the 'revolution', but thousands of Britons and Americans continue to fall under the spell of famous destinations such as Prague, Budapest, Krakow, as well as beautiful towns in Slovakia and Bulgaria. Even those who find themselves in the less prepossessing industrial cities normally come away beguiled by central European charm.

Even if ordinary people no longer see English as an automatic passport to higher wages and a better life, they have not stopped wanting to learn it. The English language teaching industry in those countries has grown up, and is now much more likely to hire teachers with proven experience or an appropriate qualification. Massive amounts of money have been invested in Poland, Hungary and the former Czechoslovakia in retraining local teachers for the teaching of English in state schools and these programmes have been largely successful. Thousands of young people from central Europe move to English-speaking countries to earn some money and improve their English. Yet, demand continues for native speakers in state schools, private language schools and universities, often for native English speakers with a sophisticated understanding of linguistic methodology.

Yet outside the major centres, the need remains substantial. While the wealthy elite can afford to pay for extra tuition in English (and other subjects), most citizens must endure fairly small education budgets in their local schools, particularly in countries such as the Slovak Republic where local teachers hardly earn enough to live on. It is worth bearing these issues in mind when considering where to head to teach EFL, as emphasised by **Steve Anderson** from Minneapolis who spent two years teaching in Hungary, the first in a well resourced urban school, the second in an impoverished rural one which he found much more fulfilling.

The explosion in the number of training centres for TEFL/TESL teachers in all English-speaking countries means that the pool of certified available teachers is fairly large. Teachers who can claim to specialise either in teaching young learners or in teaching Business English are especially attractive since both these areas of ELT are buoyant. Tourism training colleges in Hungary, the Czech and Slovak republics and the Baltics are especially keen on encouraging conversational English, while some schools in Poland are offering practical conversation classes which teach pupils to fill in English forms and rent a flat. Failing that, the easiest way to become more employable is to acquire a TEFL qualification which could prove especially useful (and incidentally cheaper) if obtained in eastern Europe. For example International House in Prague, Budapest, Krakow and Wroclaw all offer the CELTA course while ITC Prague offers a TESOL certificate (see the training directory).

North Americans may find that the accession of some of the former Eastern bloc countries to the EU has resulted in immigration regulations favouring English teachers from Britain and Ireland. Note that former Yugoslav republics (i.e. Slovenia, Croatia and Macedonia) are included in the previous chapter 'The Rest of Europe', though some placement organisations mentioned here include them as part of central and eastern Europe.

One of the first language teaching organisations, International House, to break into eastern Europe has continued to be one of the most active and energetic in the region. In the past few years a number of International House affiliated schools have opened in Belarus, Macedonia, Lithuania, Ukraine, Poland, Romania and the Republic of Slovakia. The affiliation agreement with all International House schools states that the schools can employ only teachers who have passed the CELTA course. Similarly the British Council is often in need of suitable candidates to fill vacancies in its teaching centres in Bulgaria, Romania and Ukraine, among others worldwide.

Local salaries can seem absurdly low when translated into a hard currency. Some schools pay what is usually a generous salary by local standards but which can leave little after paying for food and accommodation. It is difficult to generalise but a typical package would include a monthly net salary of £400–£600 in addition to free accommodation and possibly some other perks such as a travel stipend. The best paid jobs are for firms which teach in-company courses, especially in Poland, though they are unlikely to offer accommodation.

A host of private language schools which are either independent or part of larger language teaching organisations are represented in eastern and central Europe. Most of the central European schools listed in the directory are well established and offer above average working conditions. Some mainstream schools in the stable democracies have delegated to specialist recruiters the task of finding teachers. But in the more volatile climate of Russia and former Soviet republics (which are several years behind the Central European nations), locally managed schools come and go, and tend to choose their teachers from the pool of native English speakers on the spot, who also come and go. Intrepid travellers visiting the Central Asian Republics with no intention to work are still often invited to stay a while and do some English teaching, as was happening in off-the-beaten-track towns in Poland and Czechoslovakia 15 years ago.

One interesting option for those who do not wish to commit themselves for a full academic year is to work at one of the many language summer camps which are offered to young people, usually in scenic locations from Lake Balaton in Hungary to Lake Baikal in Siberia.

CONDITIONS OF WORK

The financial rewards of working in the old Russian Empire are usually so negligible that trained/ experienced teachers cannot be enticed to teach there unless they have an independent interest in living in that part of the world or are supported by a voluntary organisation such as the Soros Foundation. Even the large language chains which offer reasonable working conditions (e.g. flat provided, plenty of support) do not pay high enough wages to allow ordinary EL teachers to save any money.

Russia itself can offer reasonable wages, particularly now that the economy is performing well, but the cost of living can be very high in Moscow and St Petersburg and inflation continues to be a problem.

Volunteering programmes arrange for eager but unqualified volunteers in search of a cultural experience to spend time in this part of the world, provided they don't mind being out-of-pocket at the end of a short stint of teaching in the Ukraine etc. The role of native speaking volunteers is to conduct practical English classes (i.e. conversation classes) to supplement grammar taught by local school staff.

The scarcity of accommodation in the major cities of Eastern Europe is less acute than it was but it is still difficult to find something affordable and comfortable. Fortunately, many employers of native speaker teachers supply accommodation. Unfortunately, the flats they provide can be less than luxurious, although some builders have become very imaginative about transforming concrete blocks into modern living spaces with designer interiors.

Most of the central European cities and larger towns have sprouted Western-style supermarkets and other consumerist outlets, often to the disgruntlement of the older generations who have a fondness for their local shops. Living in these cities begins to feel not so very different from living in France or Italy, particularly with the influx of international companies. Smaller towns and rural areas can still be a very different proposition (until you come across expats who have bought property on the cheap in Bulgaria etc).

However, the entry of these countries into Europe, with its capitalist ideals, has been attended by problems and pitfalls such as an absence of coordinated educational policies (or political infighting on the topic) and the possibility of shoddy or exploitative working conditions for teachers, not to mention price rises, unemployment and an increase in crime. Similarly, locals worry about the 'Westernisation' of their countries, the unfortunate influx of English-speaking tourists determined to get very drunk or buy up prime local property, and the exodus of their own young people to wealthier countries.

The bubble of opportunism about EU integration has probably burst for just about all concerned; although the up side of this for qualified native English teachers is that the market is more stable, realistic and developed.

FINDING A JOB

A range of vacancies in central and eastern Europe, particularly in Poland, continues to be advertised in the educational press or on the internet, which is fast usurping the role of recruitment agencies.

Many British and American programmes that were set up in the wake of the 1989 revolution have now been cancelled, a loss to the state schools in much of eastern Europe, and also to the many young Britons and Americans who would still be willing to spend a year earning very little. The need for native speakers in state schools hasn't disappeared, but the number of mediating agencies has certainly diminished.

As has been stressed elsewhere, the possibility of creating your own job in this region is still strong. Much of what takes place happens by chance, and protocol is often given a back seat to friendly encounters. Obtaining work often comes down to the right (or wrong) hairstyle or whether you've got any Polish/Lithuanian/Slovak/Azerbaijani ancestry. Looking professional, being persistent and asking as many questions as you answer, rather than sitting back on your heels, usually pays off.

EU teachers will have an advantage in securing 'on the spot' jobs in private language schools, although public school jobs may involve more red tape, particularly in the case of Hungary.

If you want to arrange a position through a mediating organisation, here are the main ones in the UK which continue to recruit teachers for· more than one country in the region. (Organisations that deal only with one country are included in the relevant chapter.) Note that a number of general ELT recruitment agencies included in the introductory chapter Finding a Job have vacancies in eastern Europe. In addition to International House, the major chains have franchise schools in the region, chief among them EF English First which sends teachers to Lithuania, Poland and Russia, and Language Link with affiliated schools in Russia, the Czech Republic, Poland and Central Asia.

International TEFL Certificate: Kaprova 12, 110 00 Prague 1; ✆ +2 481 4791; fax 2 2481 7530; info@itc-training.com. For those wishing to teach English abroad certification is often required. ITC offers the internationally recognised TEFL certificate with a guarantee of immediate employment in Eastern Europe. Lifetime worldwide job guidance included (see Training).

Language Link: 21 Harrington Road, London SW7 3EU; ✆ 020 7225 1065; fax 020 7584 3518; recruitment@languagelink.co.uk; www.languagelink.co.uk. Mainly active in Russia and Central Asia (see entries). Contracts for new teachers pay US$800–$1200 per month.

Projects Abroad: Aldsworth Parade, Goring, Sussex BN12 4TX; ✆ 01903 708300; fax 01903 501026; info@projects-abroad.co.uk; www.projects-abroad.co.uk. Recruits volunteers to work as ELT assistants for the summer or during the academic year in Moldova and Romania, as well as many countries worldwide. No TEFL background required. Packages cost from £995 for one month's teaching in Moldova (excluding airfares), £1,795 for three months. Prices include placement, food and accommodation and back-up.

Sharing One Language (SOL): 2 Bridge Chambers, The Strand, Barnstaple, Devon EX31 1HB; ✆ 01271 327319; fax 01271 376650; info@sol.org.uk/sol@sol.org.uk; www.sol.org.uk. Non-profit-making organisation which annually recruits teachers with a degree (ideally in Education or Languages) plus at least an introductory TEFL/TESOL certificate to teach in schools in the state sector in some Eastern and Central European countries, especially Hungary, Slovakia and Romania. All posts include local salary and free independent housing thus giving enough to live reasonably on. The teacher's only expense is the cost of getting there and back.

FOR NORTH AMERICANS

Several US organisations are actively involved in teacher recruitment for the region:

Bridges for Education: 167 E. Main Street, Springville, NY; ✆ 14141 1205/fax 716 592 4090; www.bridges4edu.org. Recruits American volunteer English teachers for peace camps organised with the Ministries of Education and UNESCO. Camps are held for 3 weeks in July followed by 1 week of travel. Participants pay their own airfare plus an administration fee (about US$1,000).

Central European Teaching Program (CETP): 3800 NE, 72nd Avenue, Portland, OR; ✆ 97213; 503 287 4977; mary@cetp.info or hajni@cetp.info; www.cetp.info. CETP places approximately 60 native speakers of English in Hungary, and is currently looking into expanding into an additional central European country or two. The placement fee in 2008/9 is US$2,500 which helps to pay for the many programme costs which include a full-time Hungarian coordinator plus a week-long orientation in Budapest. A furnished apartment with utilities is provided free and monthly standard teacher's salary the equivalent of about US$550–US$600 is paid in local currency.

Peace Corps: 1111 20th St NW, Washington DC 20526; (toll-free) ✆ 1 800 424 8580; www .peacecorps.gov. Provides volunteer teachers on 27-month contracts to many countries in Eastern Europe, with the largest numbers in Ukraine, Bulgaria, Kyrgyz Republic and Romania. Must be US citizen, over 18 and in good health. All expenses, including airfare and health insurance, are covered. They recruit people to teach at both secondary and university level and to become involved with teacher training and curriculum development.

The rest of this chapter is organised by country. Bulgaria, Czech Republic, Hungary, Poland and Romania are followed by Russia and its former satellite states (Baltics, Ukraine and Central Asian Republics) and finally by Slovakia.

BULGARIA

Since Bulgaria joined the EU in 2007 it has attracted EU tourists in large numbers, while property speculators and foreign business have not been far behind. There is a substantial demand for English teachers, although the market has moved on from the excitable years following the 1989 transition to a market economy. Those without a degree or teaching qualifications are much less likely to secure a position than they once were. The schools listed at the end of this section all ask for at least a degree and teaching certificate; two also require experience.

FINDING A JOB

The Sofia-based organisation Teachers for Central and Eastern Europe (21 V 5 Rakovski Boulevard, Dimitrovgrad 6400; www.tfcee.8m.com) is active in Bulgaria. Since 1993 TFCEE has been recruiting native speaker teachers for English medium secondary schools, schools of natural sciences or universities in cities of over 50,000 for an academic year. A TEFL certificate is not required, but teaching experience is an advantage.

The weekly teaching load is 19 40-minute classes per four-day week. The salary in Bulgarian leva is equivalent to £100 (which is 20% higher than that of a Bulgarian teacher). Benefits include free furnished accommodation, 60 days of paid holiday, paid sick leave, free Bulgarian language instruction, internet, free healthcare and free multiple-entry visa and work permit.

The British Council in Sofia has a thriving English centre, which offers courses for young learners, adults and businessmen and women, although they reported no teaching vacancies at the time of writing. Young learners can also attend three-week BC summer schools, which may present opportunities for well qualified candidates with experience of teaching young learners. Language camps are popular in Bulgaria and are a good way for teachers to enjoy the country without committing themselves for a year. Bell Bulgaria is situated in central Sofia, the capital of Bulgaria. The school offers a wide range of courses for adults and young learners: General English at all levels from beginner to advanced, Cambridge Exams preparation (FCE, CAE, CPE), English for Communication, Business English, including in-company tailor made modules. In most cases native speakers work in tandem with Bulgarian teachers, sharing the lessons equally. For further information on teaching opportunities visit www.bell-worldwide.com/jobs or email recruitment@bell-centres.com.

American teachers could try the AUBG, a private American-style liberal arts university located in Blagoevgrad (www.aubg.bg). All classes are in English and the university's English Language Institute prepares future AUBG applicants for the TOEFL and SAT exams, as well as teaching courses every semester to absolute beginners and intermediate students. Unfortunately they have discontinued their English language camps. Outside of the official education system there are a reasonable number of language institutes and educational establishments and these tend to be on the look out for well-presented, confident candidates. A chain of private schools under the auspices of the Greek company Strategakis (see Greece chapter) has penetrated the market as the first and biggest network of schools for foreign languages and computing. There are 30 Pharos schools whose contact details are given on www.pharos.bg, though none replied to an invitation to include their details in this book.

One of the first private schools to be established after the revolution of 1990 was the AVO-3 School of English (2a Krakra St, Sofia 1504; ℂ +2 944 3032; fax 2 943 3943; infoavo@avo-3.com; www.avo-3.com) now affiliated to Bell Worldwide. It runs CELTA courses (see entry in training directory) and employs highly qualified staff.

The English Academy has two centres in Plovdiv and Varna (www.englishacademybg.com), while the Real English School (www.realenglishschool.eu), run by Vicky and Collin Williams, is based in the beautiful old town of Veliko Turnovo (see entries below). The Real English School sends teachers to work at the local private high school, which also employs a few native teachers of their own.

Many companies run in-house English language training, and jobs with them tend to be well paid and stable.

REGULATIONS

Bulgaria's recent accession into the EU has now made it easier for teachers in terms of red tape. EU nationals only need a letter from their employer in order to get permission to stay for one year. It's a little time consuming, but basically unproblematic, and is done at the local police station. US citizens, on the other hand, need a visa obtained from the Bulgarian Embassy. For this reason the Real English School only employ EU citizens or non-EU citizens who have a right to stay for some other reason (e.g. marriage to a Bulgarian).

The English Academy, however, will consider employing US citizens who are responsible for their own visas, although some assistance is given with paperwork.

LEISURE TIME

VICKY WILLIAMS, CO-DIRECTOR OF THE REAL ENGLISH SCHOOL BASED IN VELIKO TURNOVO, FINDS THAT LIVING IN BULGARIA IS NEVER DULL:
As for living and working in BG, it is a country which is changing rapidly. There are still plenty of vestiges of communism around in terms of architecture, cars, bureaucracy and lack of choice in shops etc, but on the other hand there is a huge amount of building going on and many people now do have a lot of money. It's a fascinating place to live in at the moment – it is a country of contrasts. There are American style malls springing up everywhere full of designer clothes shops that are frequented by people who drive 25-year-old Ladas. In the countryside you will see peasants with donkeys and carts and stooped old ladies lugging branches of trees home to burn for firewood. Go into town and the place is packed with bars, nightclubs, casinos, Ray-Banned teenagers and flashy 4 x 4s parked all over the crumbling pavements.

LIST OF EMPLOYERS

ENGLISH ACADEMY PLOVDIV

38 Gladstone Street, Plovdiv 4000

- +0 32 623 457
- plovdiv@englishacademybg.com
- www.englishacademybg.com

NUMBER OF TEACHERS: 4.

PREFERENCE OF NATIONALITY: only native speakers.

QUALIFICATIONS: first degree and recognised teaching certificate such as the Cambridge CELTA.

CONDITIONS OF EMPLOYMENT: 3, 6 and 12 month contracts. Full-time: Tuesday to Friday, 5.40pm–9.40pm and Sat 9am–1pm and 2pm–6pm. Part-time: less than 24 hours per week within the same time frame.

SALARY: 15 Bulgarian Leva per hour, 10% flat rate tax.

FACILITIES/SUPPORT: Facilities/support: arranges with local agents for accommodation viewings and assists with translation. Non-EU citizens are responsible for their own visas although assistance is given by the school.

RECRUITMENT: telephone and/or in person interviews.

CONTACT: Mark A Faulkner, Director of Studies.

ENGLISH ACADEMY VARNA

23 Bratya Skorpil, Varna, 9000

- +52622351
- varna@englishacademybg.com
- www.englishacademybg.com or www.varnaschool.com

NUMBER OF TEACHERS: 10.

PREFERENCE OF NATIONALITY: only native speakers. Non-EU citizens are responsible for their own visas, but assistance given with the relevant paperwork.

QUALIFICATIONS: degree, TEFL and 2 years experience.

CONDITIONS OF EMPLOYMENT: 10-month or 1-year contracts, 24 teaching hours a week, 5 days a week (Monday to Friday or Tuesday to Saturday).

SALARY: 19 leva per hour (approx. €10), 25 leva for technical/non-standard teaching. 10% flat rate tax.

FACILITIES/SUPPORT: arranges a selection of properties for the teacher to view in the first week depending on requirements, but teachers pay rent.

RECRUITMENT: through the internet (www.tefl.com, school website, local advertising). Interviews essential, either by telephone or face-to-face.

CONTACT: Mark Mctaggart, Director of Studies.

THE REAL ENGLISH SCHOOL

21 Hadji Dimitar Street, Veliko Turnovo, 5000

- +062 605 749/0886 171753
- information@realenglishschool.eu
- www.realenglishschool.eu

NUMBER OF TEACHERS: 6.

PREFERENCE OF NATIONALITY: must have EU passport, native speakers only.

QUALIFICATIONS: CELTA or equivalent, prefer minimum 1 year's experience. Without CELTA, must have BA/MA English or PGCE plus 2 years' TEFL experience. Experience teaching any exam courses (FCE, CAE, CPE, TOEFL, SAT, IELTS, ILEC) will be an advantage. The school teaches general and business English (students are aged from 8 to adult) and supplies teachers to a local high school.

CONDITIONS OF EMPLOYMENT: 1-year standard contract. 24 contact hours a week.

SALARY: 700–900 Bulgarian levas per month (net).

FACILITIES/SUPPORT: Free Bulgarian lessons. Assistance with locating accommodation and registering with the police, etc.

RECRUITMENT: through www.tefl.com, www.eslbase.com, and local hire. Interviews are essential, and can be by phone. Very occasionally interviews are carried out in the UK.

CONTACT: Vicky and Collin Williams, Directors.

CZECH REPUBLIC

Because of the worldwide increase in the number of trained EFL teachers as well as the popularity of Prague and the Czech Republic, the standard of native speaker teacher has improved. In Prague, the glut of well-qualified teachers is so bad that salaries are actually lower than in smaller cities like Brno, even though the cost of living is higher.

There is still some scope for novices outside Prague, but in general the proliferation of TEFL-qualified teachers has allowed language schools to become far more discerning. They generally do not accept online TEFL certificates, and adhere to the international standard of at least 106 class hours in a four-week minimum on-site programme, with at least six hours of observed teaching practice. Some of the smaller Czech towns including some rather uninspiring places in the steel-producing heart of the country and the Moravian capital Brno offer interested teachers much more scope for employment than the tourist-clogged capital.

> **KATIE BOLAND OF THE BOLAND SCHOOL (SEE ENTRIES IN TRAINING CHAPTER) HIGH-LIGHTS THE PROBLEMS OF WORKING IN THE CZECH REPUBLIC'S STUNNING CAPITAL:**
> *Living and working conditions change dramatically as soon as you leave the capital, especially in terms of the TEFL market. Prague offers low pay, dreadful hours, split shifts and cutthroat competition between language schools that leads to a lot of job insecurity for teachers. However, the rest of the country is a delight, offering the opportunity to earn some decent money and enjoy a wonderful teaching experience. I would advise people to look around a bit before jumping into a position.*
>
> *Teaching private lessons is the most lucrative but the most difficult to fix up for new arrivals. Private lessons now go as high as 300 crowns an hour for businesses, but most earn the teacher about 200 crowns. A good way to attract pupils initially is to charge at the lower end of the scale but to teach in groups of three or four.*

FINDING A JOB

Most schools express no preference for nationality, and prefer a mixture of accents. Americans are still in the ascendancy (it has been estimated that there are between 20,000 and 30,000 in Prague alone), but Canadians, Britons, etc. are all welcome. Australians are generally well received partly because of the large number of Czechs (about 20,000) who emigrated to Australia, though they will encounter more visa difficulties than teachers from Britain, Ireland or the USA. The Czech Republic's entry into the EU also gives Britons a red-tape advantage. At least one school in the list below (St James, which employs 125 teachers) stipulates that they prefer EU nationals.

STATE SCHOOLS

Qualified teachers are recruited to teach in Czech primary and secondary schools, usually on a one-year contract with low-cost or free accommodation and a salary of 11,000–20,000 Czech crowns net per month. The centralised contact is the Academic Information Agency (AIA) in Prague (see entry). AIA is part of the Ministry of Education, and distributes its literature through Czech Embassies abroad. In the UK write to the Cultural Section, Czech Embassy, 26 Kensington Palace Gardens, London W8 4QY (© 020 7243 1115; fax 020 7727 9654; london@embassy.mzv.cz).

The AIA assists people interested in teaching English at primary and secondary state schools. Most of the teaching positions are at schools in smaller towns. The school year runs for 10 months from 1 September to 30 June 30, though some vacancies occur in January between semesters. Although the minimum requirement is a BA/MA in English/Applied Linguistics, additional teaching qualifications (TEFL or PGCE) and experience give an applicant priority. Applications should be submitted before the end of April. The AIA simply acts as a go-between, circulating CVs and applications to state schools that have requested a teacher. Schools then contact applicants directly to discuss contractual details.

Kathy Panton is just one of the AIA's satisfied customers: '*I really recommend the AIA; they helped me out of a bad hole when I moved from Liberec to Prague and tried harder than I had any right to expect to get me out of another one, when I was assigned flea-ridden and expensive accommodation.*'

Another important Czech organisation for TEFLers is the Akademie JA Komenského, which actively recruits native speakers to participate in the Czech adult education programme. As mentioned in the introduction to this chapter, the organisation based in Bulgaria, Teachers for Central & Eastern Europe, cooperates with the ministries of education of the countries in which it is active (including the Czech Republic) in order to place native speakers for an academic year in state schools.

THE GROWTH OF A FREE MARKET ECONOMY MEANS THAT THE ROLE OF VOLUNTARY ORGANISATIONS HAS DIMINISHED. ALTHOUGH SOL (SEE INTRODUCTION TO EASTERN EUROPE) IS MORE ACTIVE IN ROMANIA AND HUNGARY, IT IS ABLE TO PLACE EFL TEACHERS IN CZECH STATE SCHOOLS FOR AN ACADEMIC YEAR, AS IT DID FOR BRIAN FARRELLY:

I taught in two state schools in the Czech Republic and had a really great time in both. I felt really privileged to teach the students there. My first job in a 'gymnasium' secondary school in a small town called Sedlcany south of Prague was arranged by SOL. The staff and students made me tremendously welcome. I also greatly enjoyed the freedom to teach as I saw fit, although I felt initially very daunted by the lack of guidance regarding what I should be doing with the students. My next job was found by the AIA in Prague. After visiting, I was offered a number of schools and I chose another gymnazium [secondary school] in another small town called Jevicko, north of Brno.

PRIVATE SCHOOLS

There is now a wide range of well-established schools offering high standards of instruction. The main international chains of language schools like Berlitz have large established operations in the country. Most teachers are recruited locally, often through their TEFL training centre (such as TEFL Worldwide) or via notice boards for example at the British Council and the Globe English language bookshop. Others recommended by the *Prague Post* (see below) are the notice boards at Radost FX, Laundry Kings and the Meduza Café. The site www.jobs.cz is aimed primarily at Czech job-seekers and, although there is a section in English, it contains only occasional teaching vacancies.

Most schools in Prague can count on receiving plenty of CVs on spec from which to fill any vacancies that arise. Anyone who is well qualified or experienced should have few difficulties in finding a job on the spot, particularly if they are lucky with their timing. The *Yellow Pages* (Zlaté Stránky) is an excellent source of addresses under the heading Jazykove skoly. The market in Brno is booming, with more than 80 language schools listed as operating in the country's second largest city (many will be one person outfits), catering to a population of just 380,000. However, only four schools are members of the Association of Language Schools and are therefore externally vetted and their quality standards monitored (see Brno English Language Centre in the List of Employers). Bell Prague is committed to providing high quality language training for students and to providing teachers with the conditions where they can perform to their potential and develop professionally. They pride themselves in offering strong teacher support both on an academic and administrative level. For teachers newer to the profession they offer a lot of one-to-one support. For further information on teaching opportunities visit www.bell-worldwide.com/jobs or email recruitment@bell-centres.com.

MOST PEOPLE WAIT UNTIL THEY ARRIVE IN PRAGUE BEFORE TRYING TO FIND TEACHING WORK, WHICH IS WHAT LINDA HARRISON DID:

The best time to apply is before June. I arrived in September which was too late, but if you persevere there are jobs around. A lot of teaching work here seems to be in companies. Schools employ you to go into offices, etc. to teach English (though not usually business English). After a short job hunt, I was hired by a company called Languages at Work which paid well and provided food and travel vouchers as well as helping with accommodation.

Languages at Work has recently been taken over by the St James Language Centre (see entry). People end up teaching in Prague via the most circuitous routes as **Anne Morris** from the USA describes:

Although I'm near retirement age, I'm still a free spirit and am living in Prague now more or less by chance. I ran into an American couple at a jam-packed event in Old Town Square on a visit to Prague two years ago who said they were teaching English here. I've always loved this city so I asked how one would get a job like that and they scratched out a website on the back of an envelope (TEFL Worldwide). I lost them in the crowd but on return to the US came across the envelope in a coat pocket and decided to check it out – and now here I am teaching English. Just wish I'd made this discovery much earlier in my life!

Outside of Prague, it is fairly easy to find jobs in the private sector all year round, with the greatest selection available in late August through to November and in January/February.

Those without qualifications or experience will find it very difficult. Even with a year and a half of teaching experience in a Czech town, **Kathy Panton** got turned down in Prague because she didn't have a TEFL Certificate. She warns that you can't count on picking up work for at least a month, though living expenses shouldn't be too crippling during that time. Unlike state schools, private schools in Prague do not necessarily offer accommodation, and will give preference when hiring to anyone who already has accommodation fixed up.

If you are stuck for a job during the summer months, then a good option is to work in a summer camp until the school year starts. There are a number of good summer camp options, particularly teaching children, as well as intensive one-week courses for adults at holiday resorts. Children's camps do not generally pay very well, but food and accommodation are included, and many teachers use the camps as an opportunity to get to know a bit more of the country before going back to their city jobs in September.

There are a few advertisements for teaching jobs in the local English press, primarily the *Prague Post* (Stepanska 20, 110 00 Prague 1; © +2 9633 4400; www.praguepost.com). The classifieds can be read online at www.praguepost.com/classifieds.html. At the time of writing a couple of language schools were advertising, as were native English teachers offering private lessons. It is very cheap to place your own advertisement of 25 words or less by contacting classifieds@praguepost .cz. It may be worth advertising your speciality as an English tutor (e.g. marketing, law, etc.) ahead of time. **Kathy Panton** suggests enlisting the help of a Czech friend:

> *A better way to find work is to get someone (the Czech embassy will probably do it if you catch them on a slow day) to translate 'Native speaker will tutor English to intermediate or advanced students' and send it to a newspaper like* **Mláda Fronta Dnes** *or* **Annoncé.**

REGULATIONS

EU nationals do not require a visa or work permit. However, those who stay for more than 30 days are required to register with the Alien and Border police by filling in an application form and presenting a copy of their contract. They should then be given a long-term stay card, which is valid for five years. It is possible, although not obligatory to apply for a temporary or permanent residence permit.

For non-EU nationals the situation is slightly more complex. It is necessary to apply for a long-stay Czech visa before arrival in the country. Anyone who intends to work or for any other reason stay in the Czech Republic for longer than 90 days must obtain the visa in advance. This requires gathering a raft of documents including a birth certificate and proof of no criminal record with certified translations, proof of accommodation with a document from a Czech landlord proving ownership of the property, and so on, all presented in the original or a notarised copy. Many non-EU teachers enter the Czech Republic as tourists (valid for three months) then cross a border to renew their tourist status or ask their employer to sort out the paperwork and then apply for the visa at the Czech embassy in Vienna or other neighbouring capitals.

Those who hail from outside the EU must also ensure that their employer obtains a work permit from the local employment office (*Urad práce*). They will need a signed form from you plus a photocopy of your passport (valid for at least three months longer than the intended stay) and the originals or notarised copies of your education certificates.

All of this is quite a palaver and (realistically) takes at least three months. The necessity of conforming with these procedures puts some candidates off. In Prague many schools simply hire teachers without worrying about the legal issues – a luxury they can afford due to the over-supply of teachers in the city. Outside the capital however, schools are much more cooperative. Indeed several schools in Brno will actually take their teachers to the embassy to submit the paperwork and then take them again the following month to pick up the visa.

The Czech Republic has a working holiday agreement with New Zealand, which allows New Zealanders aged 18–30 who meet the acceptance criteria, to reside in the Czech Republic for up to 12 months (www.mzv.cz/wwwo/default.asp?id=53835&ido=15718&idj=2&amb=153).

CONDITIONS OF WORK

Most English teachers agree that working conditions in state schools are generally better than in private schools. People teaching at private institutes in Prague where there is a definite glut of foreign teachers, attracted by the cultural chic of the city, have been called the 'sweat shop labourers' of the TEFL world because of the low wages employers can get away with paying. The guaranteed salary at state schools, even if you're sick or there is a holiday, is a definite advantage. If you are lucky enough to be teaching mostly final year students, your working hours in the exam month of June will be minimal. Even though the teaching day at a state school might start at 8am. This counts as a lie-in compared to teaching in private companies which is often underway by 7am or 7.30am. And of course in state schools there is no evening or weekend work.

Compared with the monthly wage in state schools of 14,000–22,000 crowns gross, private sector wages are higher, e.g. 15,000–30,000 crowns gross. But this does not usually include accommodation which will account for between a quarter and third of a teaching salary. Hourly fees start at 180 crowns net, though a more usual wage is 200–250 crowns less 25%–30% for tax and deductions. A full-time salary should be adequate to live on by local standards but will not allow you to save anything, unless you take on lots of private tutoring.

In Brno, 15,000–20,000 crowns net is a reasonable wage, but you should expect a few thousand less in smaller cities such as Olomouc, Xlin, Hradec Kralove, etc. However, outside the Czech Republic's major cities the cost of living drops dramatically and many teachers in smaller cities and towns find that they are able to save much more despite actually earning a lower monthly salary.

The majority of private language school clients are adults who are available for lessons after work, so most teaching takes place between 4pm and 8pm Monday to Thursday. (Some schools do specialise in teaching children, for which a basic knowledge of the Czech language, or a TEFL qualification which includes some training in teaching children is essential.)

Anne Morris warns that it will take time to find your financial feet:

> *Do not plan on living on your income for several months at least. Schools usually only give you a few classes to start out. Also you are not paid when classes are cancelled for one reason or another or school is on vacation (I found this out the hard way in February when classes stopped during winter break) and there are a lot of initial expenses involved in housing, agency fees, health insurance, phone, internet, etc. etc. so best to have a bit of a stash to fall back on.*
>
> *One reward has been the opportunity to, if not totally assimilate, be a part of the native culture to some extent. An example was last night when I attended my high school's prom or 'ball' as they call it. Such fun to compare this universal ritual to a US prom! For starters, it was held in a palatial hall by any standards – not a crepe paper decorated basketball court as I remember high school dances and, heaven forbid, alcohol was served! A definite no-no in the US. And of course the kids outdid themselves with originality of style and sophistication. Really fun to be an onlooker.*

Accommodation in Prague is more plentiful than it used to be. If you have a friend to translate for you, you can try the accommodation listings in *Annoncé*, the Prague free advertisement paper. Most employers are prepared to help newcomers to find accommodation, usually a room in a small shared flat or university hostel. In the rest of the country there is less competition for affordable accommodation. However, those moving to Brno or Zlin will find that the real estate agents have taken over the market, so those without local support will find themselves having to pay one month's rent to the agent as a finder's fee. On the other hand, agents do offer the advantage of providing a wide selection of furnished flats covering a range of budgets and in a variety of neighbourhoods. Many people place an advertisement in the local *Inzert Expres* or other classifieds magazine, looking for accommodation. Many Czech students welcome the opportunity to share a flat with a native English speaker in order to practise their English for free.

Students are reported to be '*a delight to teach, alert, intelligent, fun-loving, keen and interested*'. Many English teachers avail themselves of the excellent resource centres run by the British Council in most of the Czech Republic's major cities, although these are gradually being phased out as the British Council attempts to move everything online (www.teachingenglish.org.uk). The British Council also occasionally has openings for teachers who are TEFL certified with two years' relevant experience. They were recently advertising for part-time positions.

One of the strongest motivations among secondary school (*gymnazium*) students to learn English is the prospect of the 'Maturity' (school-leaver's) exam. At the beginning of the year they are given 25 topics (e.g. the British Royal Family, the influence of the media) and at the end of the year they must talk in English about one topic (chosen at random) for 15 minutes. This is a very good incentive for class participation.

LEISURE

The cost of living in Prague continues to creep up, though most things are still affordable in other towns. For example a decent midday meal at a Brno restaurant (soup, main course and beer) will cost 80–90 crowns, while Brno rents are around 6000 crowns minimum a month. Due to the fact that the Czech crown has appreciated rapidly against the dollar/pound/Euro, everything has become a lot more expensive when recalculated to other currencies.

Prague has a vibrant nightlife with clubs and cafés, cinema, opera, poetry and dance. There is so much expat culture, that a new arrival serious about getting into Czech culture will encounter difficulty. There is also something of a backlash among Czechs against Western 'good-for-nothings' who spend Czech currency as if it were Monopoly money. In Prague theft is a serious problem, though walking the streets is still safe.

IN SMALL TOWNS, ENGLISH TEACHERS ARE STILL LIKELY TO BE TREATED AS HONOURED GUESTS WITH MANY OFFERS OF HOSPITALITY AND INVITATIONS, FOR EXAMPLE TO JOIN SKIING TRIPS (WHICH ARE VERY CHEAP), AS HANNAH BULLOCK FROM OXFORD DISCOVERED IN HER YEAR OUT BETWEEN SCHOOL AND UNIVERSITY IN THE TOWN OF STRAKONICE:

I've got some great Czech friends here. A colleague of mine has been very kind (as I've found most Czechs are) and has been a mentor-cum-grandpa to me, taking me to visit castles, nearby towns, beautiful little villages and to walk in the mountains which border Germany. Most of this would have been very difficult without a car (the trains go very infrequently and at unsociable hours). I've spent many weekends in Prague since it's only one and a half hours by bus. I had to do double takes on hearing English spoken and seeing the Guardian being passed round the bars. Now instead of seeing Prague as the opening to Central Europe with its old-fashioned trams and cobbled streets as I did when I first arrived in September, I now think of it as the door back to Westernisation.

One final tip: if you play a musical instrument, take it with you since it's a great way to make local friends.

LIST OF EMPLOYERS

ACADEMIC INFORMATION AGENCY (AIA)
Dum zahranicních sluzeb MSMT,
Senovázné nám. 26, P.O Box 8, 110–06 Prague 1
- +2 2422 9698; fax 2 2422 9697
- aia@dzs.cz
- www.dzs.cz/scripts/detail.asp?id=599

NUMBER OF TEACHERS: teachers needed for state primary and secondary schools throughout the Czech Republic (very few in Prague).

PREFERENCE OF NATIONALITY: native speakers from UK, Canada, USA, Australia.

QUALIFICATIONS: college or university degree in relevant subject required (e.g. English or Linguistics) or MA/BA in other subject plus TEFL/TESL qualification. Previous experience in TEFL highly valued.

CONDITIONS OF EMPLOYMENT: 10-month contracts September to June. 24 hours per week.

SALARY: 11,000–20,000 Czech crowns per month.

FACILITIES/SUPPORT: accommodation provided by schools (free or subsidised). Non EU citizens – work and residence permits organised before arrival.

RECRUITMENT: interested applicants register their availability with AIA who circulate details to schools looking for a teacher. Actual vacancies with contact details are posted at www.dzs.cz/scripts/detail.asp?id=612.

CONTACT: Karla Benesová.

ACADEMY OF PRAGUE SCHOOLS TEFL
Evropska 35, Prague 6, 160–00
- +2 3332 2742; fax 2 3332 3779
- info@tefl.cz
- www.tefl.cz

NUMBER OF TEACHERS: 20.

PREFERENCE OF NATIONALITY: none.

QUALIFICATIONS: MA TEFL, MA TESOL, Dip. TESOL, Dip. TEFL.

CONDITIONS OF EMPLOYMENT: 1 year contracts. 100+ hours per month.

SALARY: 30,000 crowns (gross) per month.

FACILITIES/SUPPORT: teachers are provided with school flats. Help provided with work permits.

RECRUITMENT: Submitted CVs. Interview required.

CONTACT: Martin Müller, Director.

AKCENT INTERNATIONAL HOUSE PRAGUE
Bitovská 3, 140–00 Prague 4
- +2 6126 16 38/6126 16 75; fax 2 6126 18 80
- info@akcent.cz
- www.akcent.cz

NUMBER OF TEACHERS: 120+ for third largest language school in the country.

PREFERENCE OF NATIONALITY: none (need to comply with Czech immigration laws).

QUALIFICATIONS: degree + CELTA or equivalent (minimum).

CONDITIONS OF EMPLOYMENT: 10 or 12 months from September/October. Approximately 21 contact hours per week. Mostly teaching general English to adults, though some YL teaching. Teaching both on site and in company.

SALARY: 10,000–19,000 crowns (before tax) per month plus accommodation and other benefits.

FACILITIES/SUPPORT: health insurance covered and 25 days paid holidays per calendar year. Contribution made to cost of travelling to Prague. Offers CELTA/ICELT/DELTA courses plus courses in teaching young learners and business English.

RECRUITMENT: e-mail helena.linkova@accent.cz.

BELL SCHOOL
Nedvezská 29, 100–00 Prague 10
- +2 7481 5342; fax 2 7482 2961
- info@bellschool.cz
- www.bellschool.cz

NUMBER OF TEACHERS: 100 (full-time and part-time).

PREFERENCE OF NATIONALITY: British, American.

QUALIFICATIONS: DELTA or CELTA or equivalent, plus minimum 1 year of teaching experience.

CONDITIONS OF EMPLOYMENT: contracts start in September.

FACILITIES/SUPPORT: emphasis on teacher development. Czech lessons, assistance with work visa process. Attractive salary.

RECRUITMENT: local interviews essential.

NUMBER OF TEACHERS: 15–20.

PREFERENCE OF NATIONALITY: English-speaking country including Commonwealth countries.

QUALIFICATIONS: Certificate TEFLA (Trinity or Cambridge) and degree. Some experience teaching teenagers or adults.

CONDITIONS OF EMPLOYMENT: Teaching adults September/October to June. Max 20 hours per week in Prague or Pilsen. Part-time work also available.

SALARY: 16,333 crowns per month (fixed salary). Compulsory deductions of 3,000 crowns.

FACILITIES/SUPPORT: can guarantee furnished flat accommodation to be shared with another teacher. Assistance with work permit application provided after arrival; teacher should bring a TEFL certificate, birth certificate, photos, copy of passport and declaration of no criminal convictions. Australians and Canadians advised of special procedures in information pack sent by school.

RECRUITMENT: adverts in TES and Guardian. Send a CV with dates and a detailed covering letter to the above addres – followed by interview in UK or Prague or (rarely) by telephone.

CONTACT: David Camidge, Principal.

NUMBER OF TEACHERS: 14

PREFERENCE OF NATIONALITY: none.

QUALIFICATIONS: a university degree plus an internationally-recognised TEFL/TESOL qualification (not online), together with a minimum of 1 year teaching with a similar institution.

CONDITIONS OF EMPLOYMENT: standard contract is from September to May (i.e. nine months). 18–20 hours of teaching per week, plus preparation, training and meetings.

SALARY: around 24 000 CZK per month. The average teacher would take home about 18,000–19,000 CZK.

FACILITIES/SUPPORT: centre finds affordable accommodation, pays the fees associated with this and advances the

first month's rent. Work permits are generally not a major problem. It is more problematic gaining the residence permit needed for non-EU citizens, although the centre provides assistance.

RECRUITMENT: normally by direct application. The centre does not go through agencies or intermediaries. Interviews are essential and can, in theory, be carried out in the UK or else by phone.

CONTACT: Simon Hooper, Director.

NUMBER OF TEACHERS: 300+ in locations in Prague and in schools around the Czech Republic (also in Slovakia).

PREFERENCE OF NATIONALITY: none.

QUALIFICATIONS: BA plus Trinity CertTESOL or CELTA or equivalent.

CONDITIONS OF EMPLOYMENT: 10-month contracts from mid-September to end of June plus possible summer teaching. 20–26 45-minute lessons. School teaches adults and young adults, in-school and in-company.

SALARY: approx. 20,000 crowns per month for qualified teachers. Free local transport pass. Free healthcare plan. Free Czech lessons. Spanish, German, Italian and French with 50% discount.

FACILITIES/SUPPORT: school arranges and pays for flats for teachers who teach in the out-of-Prague sites. Regular teacher development workshops held, usually twice a month. Library has over 3,000 EFL titles, photocopiers and internet access for teachers. Social events at the Caledonian café for staff.

RECRUITMENT: Steven Koehler, jobs@caledonianschool.com. School hires year round.

CONTACT: Steven Koehler, Personnel and Placement Coordinator.

NUMBER OF TEACHERS: 25 full-time native English speakers, 5 part-time native English speakers. 20 full-time Czech teachers of English and other languages, over 60 part-time Czech teachers.

PREFERENCE OF NATIONALITY: anywhere English is the first language (UK, USA, Australia, New Zealand, Ireland, Canada, South Africa). Applicants also accepted from countries where English has equal status or is the second language, but these teachers may not qualify for a work visa.

QUALIFICATIONS: university degree preferred plus CELTA (or equivalent) and at least 6 months' full-time TEFL teaching experience.

CONDITIONS OF EMPLOYMENT: 10-month contract throughout teaching year from September to June. 24 contact teaching hours per week (45-minute lessons).

SALARY: hourly teaching according to experience, qualifications and length of service. Legal deductions of 28%–30% at source (income tax, health insurance and social security). End of contract bonuses, public transport travel passes reimbursement, visa costs, training attendance bonus.

FACILITIES/SUPPORT: limited school-owned accommodation; otherwise flat-finder service (free to full-time teachers). Assistance given with work permits prior to arrival; processing takes up to 4 months. Monthly teacher development training sessions; mini-group teacher training; observed lessons with feedback; large resource library and computer/internet facilities.

RECRUITMENT: applicants abroad should submit CV and cover letter, submit a lesson plan (on requested subject), have telephone interview and provide two referees who will be contacted directly. Applicants already in Prague must teach demonstration lesson.

THE CITY OF PRAGUE LANGUAGE SCHOOL
Skolska 15, 116–72 Prague 1
+2 2223 2237; fax 2 2223 2236
sekretariat@sjs.cz
www.sjs.cz

NUMBER OF TEACHERS: approx. 10 (approx. 95 teachers of 25 languages).

PREFERENCE OF NATIONALITY: none.

QUALIFICATIONS: university degree preferably in languages or humanities with teaching qualification (CELTA, DELTA, TEFL, TEFLA, TESOL, TOEFL) and/or experience.

CONDITIONS OF EMPLOYMENT: 10-month contracts, covering the school year from September to June. To teach 21 lessons (45 minutes) per week between the hours of 8am and 8pm, either at the school (in the centre of Prague) or on the premises of various firms and institutions in Prague. Extra

work available helping with placement tests or state exams. Also possible to work part-time as a substitute teacher.

SALARY: starting salary of 17,900 crowns per month (gross). Includes 18 days paid holiday during the school year, plus 33 days paid holiday during the summer if the contract is renewed. Extra part-time teaching paid at 250 crowns per lesson.

FACILITIES/SUPPORT: teachers can attend 6 lessons a week, free of charge, in one of the 25 languages taught at the school (including Czech for foreigners). Help with documents provided.

RECRUITMENT: Speculative applications and recommendations. Teachers in Prague are always invited for interview. A telephone interview may be sufficient.

CONTACT: Eva Zahradnickova, Head of the English Department.

DAVID'S AGENCY
Dr. Veseleho 1042, 763–26 Luhacovice
420 603 346 618
davidsagency@hotmail.com

NUMBER OF TEACHERS: 2 in Zlin and Luhacovice spa town.

PREFERENCE OF NATIONALITY: British or other native speakers.

QUALIFICATIONS: university degree and TEFL.

CONDITIONS OF EMPLOYMENT: 10-month contracts. Hours are 8am–noon and 1pm–4.30pm.

SALARY: 18,000 crowns (gross) less about 25% for tax, health insurance and social benefits.

FACILITIES/SUPPORT: accommodation arranged for 4,000 crowns per month. Assistance with work visa process. Training given in Czech language and culture.

RECRUITMENT: via e-mail. Early application encouraged to allow visa processing time. Interviews are held in Britain in the summer.

CONTACT: David Catto, Director (davidsagency@hotmail.com).

HAMPSON CS LTD.
Vaclava Klementa 601, 293–01 Mlada Boleslav
+326 732732; fax 326 320807
hampson@hampson.cz
www.hampson.cz

NUMBER OF TEACHERS: 4.

QUALIFICATIONS: native English speakers.

CONDITIONS OF EMPLOYMENT: contracts last for 1 school year. To work 20–27 hours per week.

SALARY: on application.

FACILITIES/SUPPORT: teachers provided with apartment and help given with accommodation.

RECRUITMENT: apply to the above address.

LONDON SCHOOL OF MODERN LANGUAGES
Podolská 54, Prague 4, 14700
℡ +2 226 096 140/2
🖱 office@londonschool.cz

NUMBER OF TEACHERS: 10.

PREFERENCE OF NATIONALITY: none.

QUALIFICATIONS: CELTA or TEFL required.

CONDITIONS OF EMPLOYMENT: 1-year contract. Teaching approx. 25 lessons per week.

SALARY: approx. 15,000 crowns net per month.

FACILITIES/SUPPORT: permits arranged by school. Free internet. Free Czech lessons.

CONTACT: Eva Straková, Director.

PHILADELPHIA ACADEMY
T.G.M. 916/111, 293–01 Mlada Boleslav
℡ fax +326 733 386
🖱 philadelphia@dragon.cz
🖥 www.philadel.com

NUMBER OF TEACHERS: approx. 40 in total (around 5 native teachers).

PREFERENCE OF NATIONALITY: none (though visas for Canadian and Australian citizens are problematic).

QUALIFICATIONS: BA/MA English plus TEFL/TESOL/CELTA.

CONDITIONS OF EMPLOYMENT: 1 school year at least. About 25 hours per week (20 guaranteed – more is possible).

SALARY: 200 crowns per hour. Deductions depend on agreement.

FACILITIES/SUPPORT: fully furnished flat with satellite dish, DVD player etc. in 15 minutes walking distance from the school building – paid for by school, except for utilities.

RECRUITMENT: internet advertising. Interviews essential.

CONTACT: Dana Zbiralova, Owner.

ST JAMES EDUCATION CENTRE
Namesti Miru 15, 120–00 Prague 2
℡ +222 517 869; fax. 222 517 870
🖱 info@stjames.cz
🖥 www.stjames.cz
Member of Czech Association of Language Schools (www.ajscr.cz)

NUMBER OF TEACHERS: 125

PREFERENCE OF NATIONALITY: must be a native English speaker, EU nationals preferred

QUALIFICATIONS: minimum requirements are university degree and a recognised TEFL certificate. Formal EFL teaching experience is valued and rewarded. Professionalism, reliability, enthusiasm and smart appearance expected.

CONDITIONS OF EMPLOYMENT: 10-month renewable contracts. 80 teaching units per month (more if requested). Teaching adults only, mainly in-company General and Business English, small groups and individuals.

SALARY: approx. 22,000 crowns (gross) per month plus performance bonus and contract completion bonus.

FACILITIES/SUPPORT: accommodation assistance (optional company furnished housing within easy reach of city centre by public transport), full assistance with visas, free internet access, well-stocked library. Full academic support. Rich social life.

RECRUITMENT: school recruits year-round but main recruiting month is September. Resumés/CVs and cover letter welcomed by e-mail with 'Recruitment' in subject line. Interviews conducted in Prague or via Skype/telephone.

CONTACT: Petra Schneidrova, ADOS (schneidrova@stjames.cz)

STATE LANGUAGE SCHOOL BRNO
Statni Jazykova Skola Brno,
Kotlárská 9, 611–49 Brno
℡ +5 4124 8999; fax 5 4124 9001
🖱 pilarova@sjs-brno.cz
🖥 www.sjs-brno.cz/old/jo.htm

NUMBER OF TEACHERS: 5–7.

PREFERENCE OF NATIONALITY: British.

QUALIFICATIONS: must have TEFL qualification.

CONDITIONS OF EMPLOYMENT: 1 academic year (September to June). Approximately 20 hours per week.

SALARY: about 14,500 Czech crowns per month.

FACILITIES/SUPPORT: assistance with finding accommodation, full help with work permits and training available at staff meetings.

RECRUITMENT: liaise with other schools.

CONTACT: Marie Pilarová, Deputy Head.

VISTA WELCOME
Konevova 210, 130–00 Prague
℡ fax +2 8486 2345
🖱 vista@iol.cz
🖥 www.vista-welcome.cz

NUMBER OF TEACHERS: 11 native speakers. 42 Czech teachers.

PREFERENCE OF NATIONALITY: British, Canadian, American.

QUALIFICATIONS: TEFL Certificate and/or proven ESL teaching experience. Mature teachers preferred, though enthusiasm important. School does not want to hire people who are just looking for a way to see the world. Experience in teaching Business English a plus.

CONDITIONS OF EMPLOYMENT: 1-year contract minimum. Teaching hours vary. Full-time teachers guaranteed at least 20 lessons (45 minutes each) per week. Courses aimed at firms and organisations looking for in-house courses. Teachers often work for more than one school to get enough teaching hours.

SALARY: 220 crowns per hour if the school pays medical and social insurance; 300 crowns without insurance.

FACILITIES/SUPPORT: no accommodation provided though advice may be given to new arrivals.

RECRUITMENT: adverts in the local English-language newspaper for expats (Prague Post), the internet and via other schools in Prague.

CONTACT: Ela Struzkova, Principal.

HUNGARY

English is compulsory for all Hungarian students who wish to apply for college or university entrance, and university students in both the Arts and Sciences must take courses in English. Apart from the much-hated Russian, the second language of Hungary was traditionally German, a legacy of the old Austro-Hungarian Empire. But in most contexts German has been overtaken by English.

The Hungarian education system has much to be proud of, not least the efficacy with which it retrained its Russian teachers as English teachers after the return to democracy in 1989. The network of bilingual secondary schools (*gimnazia*) has produced a large number of graduates with a sophisticated knowledge of English. In cities and even some small towns, bilingual schools now operate at the elementary level as well. From first grade onwards, students study basic subjects in English and Hungarian. The vast majority of private language schools are owned and run by Hungarians rather than expats. Even though the calibre of Hungarian teachers is very high, schools still seem keen to employ native English teachers.

The invasion of foreigners in Budapest was never as overwhelming as it was (and is) in Prague, but still Budapest has a glut of teachers, among them some who have fled over-crowded Prague. The opportunities that do exist now are mostly in the provinces. Even in the more remote parts of the country, formal academic qualifications are important. It is a legal requirement that the bilingual schools employ a native speaker as lector. Most *gimnazia* liaise with the Fulbright Commission or the Central European Teaching Program and take on Americans, though Britons are also eligible.

Teachers are poorly paid in Hungary, aside from in the top-notch private schools. Rents in Budapest are high and take a major proportion of a teacher's salary; some schools help by subsidising accommodation, or it may be possible to arrange accommodation in return for English lessons. Teachers through the Central European Teaching Program (see entry) have housing and utilities provided. Low as the salaries may seem, native speakers can console themselves with the thought that they are usually better paid than Hungarian university lecturers.

FINDING A JOB

Very few jobs in Hungary are advertised in the UK and only one or two UK sending organisations (notably Sharing One Language; www.sol.org.uk) include Hungary in their list of destinations. Only a scattering of language schools replied to an invitation to be included in this book.

In the USA, recruitment of teaching assistants takes place via the Central European Teaching Program (CETP). The programme offers 'cultural immersion through teaching' and is open to anyone with a university degree, and preferably some experience of TEFL and overseas teaching/study experience. CETP liaises with the relevant government department in Hungary to place teachers in state schools as well as in some parochial schools throughout the country.

AFTER ARRIVAL

The British Council in Budapest (www.britishcouncil.org/hungary.htm) closed its teaching operations in 2007 and now works with partner libraries known as Gateway UK networks. These provide UK 'information services,' including an extensive English language teaching collection that members can borrow and host teacher training and events for those interested in British culture and learning English. Partner libraries are located in Budapest, Bekescsaba, Debrecen, Eger, Gyor, Kecskemet, Szeged, Szekszard, Szolnok, Tatabanya and Veszprem. Although these networks and access points are mainly aimed at Hungarians, they might be good places for picking up contacts. The British Council employs well-qualified native English teachers to supervise exams (and mock exams).

A useful resource for native English teachers is the 'Book of Lists' from the *Budapest Business Journal* which contains about 40 addresses of private language institutes.

Of interest to Americans is the Regional English Language Office located in the Public Diplomacy section of the US Embassy (Szabadság tér 12, 1054 Budapest; ✆ +1 475 4400). The Regional office does not run its own English teaching programme but provides some assistance to Hungarian teacher training programmes by providing access to English language materials. A small lending/resource collection of professional ELT materials is available to professionals in the field in the Information Resource Center in the Embassy's Public Affairs section.

PRIVATE SCHOOLS

While it has become increasingly difficult for foreigners to find teaching jobs in Hungarian state schools, private institutes have mushroomed, primarily to meet the needs of the business community and also for children whose parents are keen for them to supplement the English teaching at state schools. It is estimated that there are over 100 private language schools in Budapest alone and 300 around the country, both very fluid numbers since schools open and close so quickly. Many private schools use native speakers as live commercials for the schools, though nowadays they want to advertise the qualifications of their teachers too.

Anyone with a recognised TEFL Certificate and experience of the business world has a good chance of finding at least some hourly teaching after arrival in Budapest or elsewhere. British and American accents are both in demand. International House offers one-year contracts for qualified teachers of both adults and children and (according to **Dennis Bricault**) '*a wonderful social and professional atmosphere*'.

To find the less well-established schools on the spot, keep your eyes open for the flyers posted in the main shopping streets or check out the English language weeklies. To find out what new institutes have opened or expanded, look at Hungarian papers such as *Magyar Nemzet* or the free advertisement paper *Hirdetes* to see if any courses in Angol are being advertised at *Nyelviskola* (language schools).

Private tutoring provides one way of supplementing a meagre salary. Freelance teachers may find a developing market for their linguistic expertise in companies. Many executives need English for business as Hungary seeks to integrate with the economies of the West and attract foreign investors. The Department of Commerce, for example, employs teachers to train bankers, traders and top electrical engineers. Many professionals now need English as part of their work and are both able and prepared to pay for it.

Another option is the Teach Abroad agency SELTI (Sheppard English Language Teacher Institute) in Budapest. This company (info@selti-hungary.com; www.selti-hungary.com) recruits native speakers with a qualification and some higher education to teach English for a variety of language schools throughout Budapest. Candidates must acquire some TEFL training, for example the i-to-i online TEFL course; the fee (currently US$199) is reimbursed after the first month of teaching. The package provides accommodation, meals, group activities and a stipend in exchange for 20 contact hours per week for 6–12 months.

REGULATIONS

Hungary joined the EU in 2004 but until the reciprocal transitional controls expire, employing schools must obtain a labour permit for their foreign teachers from the appropriate Hungarian labour office (Munkaügyi Központ) stating that no Hungarian national is available to do the job. The application for a labour permit must include originals (notarised copies will not suffice) of your university diploma, TEFL certificate (if applicable) and recent medical report stating that you have no communicable diseases (including HIV). The costs involved in having all these tests done in Hungary is at least US$200. All documents must be officially translated into Hungarian, which is more cheaply carried out by the Central Translation Office in Budapest (about US$100) than by Hungarian embassies abroad.

British nationals who have found a Hungarian employer willing to go through all this and obtain a work permit do not need to apply to the Embassy for a work visa. Instead they must report to the Hungarian police within 15 days of arrival and obtain a residence permit for the period covered by the work permit. General information for Britons is available from the Embassy of Hungary at www.huemblon.org.uk.

Americans, Australians and Canadians have to apply for their residence permit at the Hungarian Embassy or Consulate in their country. Applicants need to present their contract of employment, their work permit, and insurance to cover the duration of their intended stay in Hungary. They also have to prove that they can pay for their own housing. Some organisations such as CETP take care of the paperwork and pay the permit cost of US$120.

There are now legal consequences if somebody stays in Hungary for more than 90 days without a residence permit.

CONDITIONS OF WORK

Salaries vary, but currently teachers in the state sector can expect about 100,000 forints (net) a month for teaching full-time. The hourly rate at commercial centres is normally in the range 1,200–

1,800 forints. Freelance teachers can ask for about 1,700 forints per lesson. It is essential to find out whether pay is net or gross since Hungarians lose more than a quarter of their already meagre wages on tax and contributions. It is also important to check whether your employer is taking out insurance on your behalf: an insurance mix-up turned Ellen Parham's 'satisfactory' high-school salary into something worse than meagre.

RECENT AMERICAN GRADUATE AND CETP PARTICIPANT GENEVIEVE PIERCE, FINDS THAT TEACHING TEENAGERS IN A STATE SCHOOL CAN BE CHALLENGING:
They are totally uninterested in learning, don't complete their homework, and lack any opinion or viewpoint. This is a result of the political situation in Hungary and the low salaries. I am sure my students overhear their parents complain about money and politics constantly which has to drain the students' hope for a future. I think they feel trapped in Hungary. One student even said, 'Why should I do my homework when I'm going to live in Hungary and be a shop clerk like my mother?.'

On a more positive note, Genevieve found that going to class with a topic that everyone could talk about and allowing lessons to evolve was a more successful teaching strategy than following a strict lesson plan. In general students in the rural areas of eastern Hungary are better behaved than their counterparts in Budapest, though their level of English will be lower.

LEISURE TIME

The Opera House in Budapest is one of the most beautiful in the world, the Széchenyi thermal baths are the perfect place to unwind graciously and the coffee houses are ideal for watching the world go by. It is easy to make a strong argument for living in Budapest, but there are downsides, as long-stay American teacher **Ellen Parham** explains, '*Everything is convenient for me here in Budapest, but some of the others in the CETP programme who are teaching in smaller towns are treated like celebrities and everyone knows them. Living in a big city is hindering my ability to speak Hungarian, too. Everyone speaks English and I am never forced to speak Hungarian.*'

Being made to speak this notoriously difficult language, however, can be a mixed blessing, as **Genevieve Pierce** discovered while living in a quaint city on the Romanian border:

Teaching in a place where you don't speak the language is difficult because you feel like a child. I seriously need a babysitter if I'm going to do anything of grave importance (i.e. visit the doctor, purchase a bicycle, arrange a postage delivery). Though, with all that said, teaching abroad has been the best experience of my life. I love to see a student's face when they finally realise what I'm talking about. I have enjoyed all the school functions such as dances, initiation ceremonies, and graduation. The best part has been learning about another culture, understanding their way of life. It's like nothing I could learn from a book.

LIST OF EMPLOYERS

CENTRAL EUROPEAN TEACHING PROGRAM
3800 NE, 72nd Avenue, Portland, OR 97213

503 287 4977

mary@cetp.info or hajni@cetp.info

www.cetp.info

NUMBER OF TEACHERS: 50+.

PREFERENCE OF NATIONALITY: USA, Canada, Australia, New Zealand, and European.

QUALIFICATIONS: must be native English speaker, hold a BA or BSc. Those with no teaching certificate must be willing to undertake an online TEFL certificate. Retired people welcome.

CONDITIONS OF EMPLOYMENT: standard contract 1 school year, although teachers can be placed for 1 semester. To teach 20–22 hours per week.

SALARY: US$500–$550 per month after taxes.

FACILITIES/SUPPORT: All teachers receive a furnished apartment with utilities paid. Apartments range from a small studio to a spacious 1 or 2 bedroom flat. All are equipped with TV and washing machine, among other amenities. CETP provides teachers with all necessary documents for residence visas.

RECRUITMENT: via word of mouth, the internet and university placement offices.

CONTACT: Mary Rose, Director.

INTER-EX CENTRE
4/a Budaörsi Str. 1118 Budapest

+1 361 0248; fax 1 209 6229

interex@hu.inter.net

www.interexcentrum.hu

NUMBER OF TEACHERS: 1–2.

PREFERENCE OF NATIONALITY: none.

QUALIFICATIONS: any TEFL qualification and Cambridge CELS language exams.

CONDITIONS OF EMPLOYMENT: 20 hours per week. Open-ended contract.

SALARY: 200,000–300,000 forints per month.

FACILITIES/SUPPORT: possibility of some assistance with accommodation.

RECRUITMENT: candidates must be interviewed in Hungary or occasionally UK.

CONTACT: George Gallo, Director.

INTERNATIONAL FURTHER STUDIES INSTITUTE – IFSI
2 Petofi S. u., 6000, Kecskemet

fax +76–418 560

info.desk@ifsi.hu

www.ifsi.hu

NUMBER OF TEACHERS: 3–5.

PREFERENCE OF NATIONALITY: British and Irish preferred as there is no need for a work permit, but it is possible to obtain work permits for other nationalities.

QUALIFICATIONS: minimum BA degree, TEFL certificate and 2 years experience.

CONDITIONS OF EMPLOYMENT: Renewable 1-year contracts. Usual working hours are early mornings and late afternoons. Number of lessons varies from 24–30 sessions (45 minutes) per week.

SALARY: 1200 forints per lesson. The school pays all taxes, social security and insurance.

FACILITIES/SUPPORT: Free accommodation provided: fully-equipped flats with private bedrooms, close to the school. If necessary the school helps teachers to obtain a work permit.

RECRUITMENT: usually via the internet. Telephone interview required.

CONTACT: Marjan Abdi, Principal.

INTERNATIONAL HOUSE
Language School & Teacher Training Institute, Vermezo Ut 4, 1012 Budapest

+1 212 4010, ext 20; fax 1 316 2491

dos@ih.hu

www.ih.hu

NUMBER OF TEACHERS: 40.

QUALIFICATIONS: minimum Cambridge CELTA.

CONDITIONS OF EMPLOYMENT: contracts are for 25 contact hours per week including in-company teaching, groups, one-to-one and special projects.

SALARY: 180, 000 forints per month (net).

FACILITIES/SUPPORT: assistance given with finding accommodation. In-service teacher development.

RECRUITMENT: through direct application. Interviews essential, conducted if necessary by telephone or Skype.

CONTACT: Steve Oakes.

KARINTHY FRIGYES GIMNAZIUM

Thököly ucta 7, Pestlorinc, 1183 Budapest

+1 291 2072; fax 1 291 2367

ba@karinthy.hu

www.karinthy.hu

NUMBER OF TEACHERS: approx. 100.

PREFERENCE OF NATIONALITY: native speakers of English.

QUALIFICATIONS: MA preferred in English or teaching English. BA in English or teaching English, or in any subject plus teaching certificate for English as a foreign language.

CONDITIONS OF EMPLOYMENT: 1–2 year contracts; 22 lessons a week.

SALARY: National salary plus all costs of accommodation in a pleasant, fully furnished and equipped flat near the school. 10% taxes and social security deduction.

FACILITIES/SUPPORT: Assistance with work permits; authorised copies of degrees and/or certificates are needed by the end of June.

RECRUITMENT: Application directly through agencies and foundations. Interviews preferred and conducted via Skype, web cam or telephone.

CONTACT: Dr Anikó Bognár, Deputy Head.

LIVING LANGUAGE SEMINAR

Elő Nyelvek Szemináriuma,

Fejér György u. 8–10, 1053 Budapest

+1 317 9644; fax 1 317 9655

elonyelv@t-online.hu

www.elonyelvek.hu

NUMBER OF TEACHERS: 3–5 (natives).

PREFERENCE OF NATIONALITY: British, American, Canadian.

QUALIFICATIONS: a great deal of ESL teaching experience, registered City and Guilds, Local State Examinations centre. Preparation for City and Guilds, Cambridge and local ITK-Origó exams, TOEFL, Business English.

CONDITIONS OF EMPLOYMENT: contracts from 3 months. Negotiable hours. Mainly teaching adults (aged 16–40).

SALARY: high by local standards.

FACILITIES/SUPPORT: no assistance with accommodation at present.

RECRUITMENT: through adverts. Interviews required.

CONTACT: Paul Biró.

SELTI HUNGARY

Garay utca 37, Budapest 1076

+17857743

info@selti-hungary.com

www.selti-hungary.com

NUMBER OF TEACHERS: 20.

PREFERENCE OF NATIONALITY: native English speaking countries.

QUALIFICATIONS: some background in tertiary/higher education

CONDITIONS OF EMPLOYMENT: 6–12 month contracts. 20 contact hours per week plus preparation and travel time.

SALARY: complete package is 120,000 forints per month after tax.

FACILITIES/SUPPORT: accommodation is provided in the package. Also, assistance with work permits.

RECRUITMENT: online advertising agencies, Interview are essential and carried out by telephone.

CONTACT: Ryan Sheppard, Managing Director.

TUDOMANY NYELVISKOLA

Tavasz u.3, 1033 Budapest;

+/fax 1 368 1156

info@tudomanynyelviskola.hu

www.tudomanynyelviskola.hu

NUMBER OF TEACHERS: 10–15.

PREFERENCE OF NATIONALITY: British and American.

QUALIFICATIONS: TEFL/TESL preferred.

CONDITIONS OF EMPLOYMENT: 10-month contracts. Hours vary.

FACILITIES/SUPPORT: assistance with accommodation not normally given. Training sometimes available. Affiliated with ELT training centre Via Lingua Budapest (see training listings).

RECRUITMENT: local interviews essential.

CONTACT: Zsuzsanna Tölgyesi, Director of Studies (zsuzsa@tudomanynyelviskola.hu or dos@tudomanynyelviskola.hu).

VOCATIONAL ACADEMY

Teleki u 18, 9022 Györ

+96 512010; fax 96 315665

nagyotto@vocational.hu

www.vocational.hu

NUMBER OF TEACHERS: 34.

PREFERENCE OF NATIONALITY: Britain, USA, Canada.

QUALIFICATIONS: TEFL and/or MA. University degree needed, preferably in economics.

CONDITIONS OF EMPLOYMENT: minimum 1 year. Hours of teaching 7.30am–4.30pm.

SALARY: €580 per month + 5 weeks' paid holiday per year and extra benefits (e.g. flat, cheap meals, etc.). Deductions amount to about €65.

FACILITIES/SUPPORT: student residence or block of flats owned by school, or employer helps teacher find other rental accommodation. School provides work and residence permit provided teacher passes medical test and has relevant documents and certificates to hand.

RECRUITMENT: advertising. Face-to-face interview not essential.

CONTACT: Paul Rogerson, Principal (paul.rogerson@ihh.hu).

POLAND

Prospects for English teachers in Poland, western Poland in particular, remain reasonable, even if the seemingly insatiable demand for English teachers that has characterised the past 15 years is now a thing of the past. Poles are still incredibly keen to learn English, but with the explosion of cheap flights to and from Poland and the opening of borders, millions of Poles simply get on a plane and come to Britain, mainly to work but sometimes to sign up for English language courses.

This is bound to have a knock-on effect in terms of the quality of Polish English teachers working in their home country, although the reverence for 'native speakerhood' still runs very high. A famous Polish poet recently described (in perfect English) how his teenage daughter and her friends largely communicate in English, or at least a form of English picked up from TV shows and pop songs, and that some of the older generation are worried that Poland is becoming swamped by the English language and Western culture.

For now, certain types of English classes, largely taught by native English speakers are increasingly popular; according to one director of studies: 'realistic' conversation classes teach Poles how to rent a flat or order a drink, while others teach students how to fill in forms (good luck to them).

Major cities such as Warsaw, Wroclaw, Krakow, Poznan and Gdansk are possible destinations, especially for people with experience of preparing for Cambridge exams or those looking for in-company work. The smaller towns for example in Silesia in southern Poland are more promising destinations, where the competition for jobs will be less intense and you may still receive preferential 'foreigner' treatment if you gain a dependable reputation as a teacher. Foreign teachers normally find their students friendly, open and keen to learn more about the world. Discussion classes are likely to be informed and lively, with students well up to date on developments and very well motivated to practise their English. In some companies, promotion depends on the level of English achieved, which spurs students from the business world to be especially committed. On the other hand, if the company is paying for an employee's lessons, there may be little incentive to attend regularly or with enthusiasm.

FINDING A JOB

Interested teachers should not expect to be snapped up unless they have at least a TEFL certificate and some sort of teaching experience.

International House has a big presence in Poland with schools in Bielsko-Biala, Bydgoszcz, Katowice, Kielce, Koszalin, Krakow, Opole, Torun and Wroclaw, some of which are listed in the directory. Bell has three partners in Poland: ELS-Bell located in Gdansk, Gdynia, Sopot Szczecin, Bydgoszcz, Warsaw, Bell Kraków and PROGRAM-Bell in Poznan and Konin. ELS-Bell provides tuition to over 4,500 students on general English and exam courses as well as in-company courses in both general and Business English, and summer camps for young learners and teenagers. Bell Kraków operates a language school and also a teacher training college. PROGRAM-Bell is a private language school teaching on or off site. For further information on teaching opportunities visit www.bell-worldwide. com/jobs or email recruitment@bell-centres.com. These high profile ELT organisations are founding members of PASE, the Polish Association for Standards in English which promotes ethical practices in the private sector. PASE has 33 member schools which are linked from www.pase.pl (PASE Sekretariat, ul. Sedziowska 5, 02–081 Warsaw; ✆ +22 825 5512).

The TEFL pages of the *Guardian* and the main ELT job search websites continue to carry advertisements for schools in Poland but far fewer than in the 1990s.

ON THE SPOT

Semesters begin on 1 October and 15 February, and the best time to arrive is a month beforehand. After arrival, try to establish some contacts, possibly by visiting the English department at the university. Although some school directors state a preference for British or American accents, many are neutral provided you are a native speaker.

Private language schools catering for all kinds of English teaching sprang up everywhere as soon as private enterprise was legally possible. The Warsaw *Yellow Pages* carry several pages under the heading *Jezykowe Kursy*, *Szkolenia*. The very busy British Council in Warsaw (near Central station) and the smaller British Council offices and libraries in other cities may be able to assist personal callers. The Gdansk office has a list of the dozen biggest private language schools.

If you base yourself in Warsaw and wish to advertise your availability for private English tuition, try placing a notice just to the right of the main gate of Warsaw University or in one of the main dailies, *Gazeta Wyborcza* or *Zycie Warszawy*. A further idea is to visit the Irish pub on ul. Miodowa near the castle which many English speakers use as their watering-hole.

Most Polish teachers of English work 'on the side' and it may be possible to work in partnership with one of them as a teaching aide, earning a reasonable wage for speaking as instructed (and incidentally picking up some teaching ideas for future use). Freelancing is very popular, and there has been a huge increase in demand for tailor-made one-to-one courses. **Kathy Cooper**, based in the small town of Raciborz in Silesia, has worked for three language schools over the past seven years and has also freelanced on the side: '*currently I have no time for private students, however, in the past, I had a waiting list. Once you are established your name gets around town, if you are dependable.*' Banks are likely clients and often pay very well by Polish standards. Kathy has also taught large corporate clients (signed through the school), including '*food/chocolate, cement, power plants, furniture, steel, industrial cleaning and sanitation, automotive, banking, industrial equipment, manufacturing, legal profession, doctors, and hotel industry. Yes, I am in Poland, land of opportunity for teachers.*'

For this work, teachers should have enough ELT awareness to be able to devise their own syllabus. They will also have to put up with early or late hours (8am/9pm) and the inevitable cancelled lessons as business execs reschedule due to important meetings. Kathy Cooper gets around this problem simply by calling another business client who wants to make up lost hours.

ACADEMIC INSTITUTES

NKJOs are teacher training colleges which specialise in training teachers of foreign languages. Some of the 60 or so NKJOs are eager to hire qualified, experienced teachers. University Centres for English Teaching (known as UCETs) were originally set up by the British Council and eight leading Polish universities (Warsaw, Wroclaw, Gdansk, Poznan, Lodz, Katowice, Gliwice and Szeczecin). They now comprise the only group of schools in Poland entitled to use the marque 'In Association with the British Council'. Their requirements differ slightly according to parent university but basically they offer plum jobs normally taken up by people with a higher degree (see entries for several UCET ELCs in the directory).

Virtually every institute of higher education (universities, medical academies, technical universities, economics academies, art schools, etc.) has a Studium Jazykow Obcych (Foreign Language Department) which is where the students who aren't language majors fulfil their foreign language requirements. The learners are less advanced and possibly less motivated in English than at the NKJOs, and they may be prepared to accept less well qualified native speaker assistants while offering the attractions of an academic setting.

Jobs attached to universities usually offer stability and a light workload, say 12–15 classroom hours a week during the two 15-week semesters. The salary is paid over 12 months and includes full health insurance, housing perks and discounts on train travel. Bear in mind that if you are tutoring some of them privately, this income will vanish over the summer vacation.

HOLIDAY LANGUAGE CAMPS

Private language teaching organisations run short-term holiday courses in summer and sometimes winter, which require native speakers. The English School of Communication Skills whose Personnel Department is located in the charmless city of Tarnów (℡ fax +14 690 87 49; personnel@escs.pl; www.escs.pl), hires 100 EFL teachers for five language schools in southern Poland and summer language camps at the Polish seaside. Pay is 25–30 zloties an hour, 2,200 zloties a month. ESCS offers its own three-week TEFL training course in August at a cost of US$400. American **Alicia Wszelaki** was full of praise for ESCS after spending a year immersing herself in Polish culture in the southern town of Myslenice. Similarly, **Will Gardner** greatly enjoyed his summer job with ESCS which he had fixed up from England in the spring:

> I spent one month working for ESCS at their summer camp on Poland's Baltic Coast. The camps were well organised and great fun. As an experienced teacher who has worked in several different countries for a range of schools, I would just like to say what a pleasure it was to work with such a well organised group of people and for a school that completely lived up to its promises. The school supplied a wide range of resources to assist teachers, although a lot of emphasis was placed on originality. The focus was always on communication and fun. The camp facilities were perfect for the situation. Food and accommodation were supplied and the weather was beautiful. Although the students were attending lessons daily, a holiday atmosphere prevailed over all activities.

The Anglo-Polish Universities Association (APASS) based in Leeds used to run two summer schemes, but since the organiser died recently these are not operating at the time of going to press.

REGULATIONS

Poland's requirements for EU teachers are broadly in line with the rest of Europe. They no longer need to apply for a work permit, however, teachers wishing to stay for more than three months must obtain a residence card from the regional governor of their chosen city/town. Applicants will need to justify their stay in Poland and confirm that they have sources of income (e.g. a statement from a bank account). Employers should assist with the documentation and the necessary translation of official documents into Polish.

Non-EU nationalities will have to jump through the usual hoops prior to departure from their home country. The required documents must be presented in person to a Polish Consulate: a promissory work permit from your Polish employer, your passport, two photos, a completed application form and the current fee for a work visa. In order for your employer to obtain permission to employ a foreign teacher, he or she will have to submit originals or notarised copies of your degree diploma and TEFL Certificate (if applicable) with official translations. After arrival with the visa, you will need to obtain a work permit. Most schools will assist with the documentation but may not bear the financial cost. When the initial visa expires (after three months), it is possible to apply for a residency card from inside Poland which will be valid for two years. Most employers who take on foreign teachers are well aware of the procedures which, according to one, could fill a book on their own.

The information portal of the Ministry of Foreign Affairs of the Republic of Poland (www.poland.gov.pl) contains information about work permits etc. as does the embassy website (www.polandembassy.org).

CONDITIONS OF WORK

Generally speaking, private language schools in Poland offer reasonable working conditions. Instead of hearing complaints from teachers of employers, it tends to be more often the other way round, as the Director of Studies of a private language school makes clear:

My boss, who has been employing British native speakers for seven years and who has proved to be a very patient person, could provide you with some hair-raising stories of teachers signing their contracts and withdrawing at the very last minute (having probably found a more lucrative job in Japan), teachers returning a couple of days late after the Christmas break without presenting any adequate excuse (or not returning at all), not to mention the state of flats and equipment which, after being used for nine months, is often left in a wrecked condition.

Wages are much higher than they used to be, but the cost of living has crept up too. Wages that look low on paper may come with free accommodation. Accommodation does not present as major a problem as it did in the early days because most employers either offer staff accommodation or will assist in a flat hunt. The terms of service are seldom exploitative. It is not uncommon for overtime to be paid to teachers for hours worked in excess of the contracted number (typically 24) and for transport perks to be offered.

ERICA JOLLY AND PAUL ROBINSON DESCRIBE THE SITUATION IN GDANSK:
The big schools in and around Gdansk all seem similar. They are well equipped but don't pay that well. Class sizes are around 12–15 students and hours are usually a minimum of 18 teaching hours per week. The director in charge of teaching is an experienced EFL teacher and teacher-trainer herself, and is always available to help and advise. My only criticism is the propensity towards paperwork: each teacher is obliged to complete forms after each lesson giving details of everything covered, comments, etc.

The current average net salary in the private sector starts at about 2,000 zloties (£450) per month. Foreigners do not have to pay income tax for the first two years of residence, though a deduction will be made for social security.

HEIDI ROTHWELL-WALKER ENJOYED COMPANY TEACHING, WHICH WAS A CONTRAST WITH THE BASIC ADULT EDUCATION SHE HAD BEEN DOING IN BRITAIN:

I was expected to work any time from 7am to 6pm. Sometimes the early hours (especially in the long winter) can get you down, but you will be rewarded financially for starting at 7am. There was a lot of travelling and waiting at bus stops, but working conditions in the companies were excellent. Not every company gave you access to a white board, overhead projector or cassette player but they could be made available upon request.

Once you are working either in the public or private sector, you may be approached with various proposals, from 'verifying' English translations of scientific research papers or restaurant menus, to coaching actors and singers preparing for English performances and doing dubbing or voice-overs for films and TV.

KATHY COOPER IS AN AMERICAN GRANDMOTHER WHO SUDDENLY DECIDED TO LIVE IN EUROPE. IMMEDIATELY AFTER OBTAINING A TRINITY CERTIFICATE IN TESOL IN THE UK, SHE WAS OFFERED A JOB IN SOUTHERN POLAND AND HAS FALLEN IN LOVE WITH HER LIFE THERE, THE CHEMICAL-FREE FOODS, THE TEACHING AND THE CULTURE. SHE BEGAN HER POLISH TEACHING CAREER IN THE TOWN OF OPOLE, WHERE SHE WAS THROWN IN AT THE DEEP END. WITH TIME, SHE HAS REFINED HER TEACHING SCHEDULE:

Teaching varies from school to school, and from classroom to classroom. Starting out, I was thrown immediately into a range of beginning children to executive business and British Council exam classes. It was either to be my death or destiny. I now specialise in only executive business and exam classes. Periodically I embark on a student who wants to attend either high school or university in America whence I teach TOEFL exams for both. SLEP testing is the new format for high school entrance in America, it is part of the TOEFL system. I can proudly relate that my last student attending a foremost university in the States has just been asked to return, and on scholarship, to obtain her MA in graphic design. She was their first Pole of several thousand foreign students. Teachers are a mix of English speaking nationalities; I have worked with all, including other Americans. It is most common to tandem teach with Polish teachers. In my case, I have some executives and advanced students that require only native speakers because of their language level. Facilities vary, and I have been lucky enough to have had beautifully renovated and comfortable buildings and classrooms. It's not always the norm. Conditions depend on the age of the company, and the size of the resource library. I am with a young school now, and we are stocking year by year.

DESPITE A CONSIDERABLE AMOUNT OF DISORGANISATION AT MANY SCHOOLS, NO ONE COMPLAINS OF A LACK OF HOSPITALITY FROM THE POLES. ONCE THEY GET TO KNOW THE TEACHER, STUDENTS WILL OFFER WHATEVER SERVICES THEY CAN FROM MENDING SHOES TO GIVING LARGE QUANTITIES OF HOME-PRESERVED FRUIT OR SPLENDIDLY ARRANGED FLORAL DISPLAYS. MARTA ELENIAK ESPECIALLY ENJOYED HER EXPERIENCE TEACHING CHILDREN:

Teaching in the primary school was really enjoyable as the little kids make you feel so appreciated by giving you flowers, drawing pictures for you and performing songs, poems or dances for you. They always wanted to continue after the bell had gone. One class was so keen that they invited themselves for a lesson even though it was my break.

All of this makes a refreshing contrast with the lot of the EFL teacher in many other parts of the world. Poles even seem to have the ability to crack jokes in English when their English is very elementary, so lessons are not usually dull. On the whole they are also very well-motivated and hard-working, including adolescents.

LEISURE

Poland offers no shortage of sights to see, pubs to visit, museums, theatres and parks to enjoy. Films are usually in English with Polish subtitles. Travelling is fairly cheap and easy. The transport system in Warsaw and some other cities looks complicated at first glance but is in fact straightforward. People in shops and so on can seem rude and abrupt, though this should not be taken personally.

The language is difficult, comprising such wonderful names as, 'Sczcyrk,' a tiny ski village, but it can make for a good atmosphere in the classroom as you struggle with Polish pronunciation while your students try to get their tongues round English words.

Kathy Cooper has fallen for the food, '*Poland yields the most amazing hams, kielbasas and bacon that have ever melted in my mouth. Add the dense and daily purchased homemade breads that taste like my grandmother's, the variety of local and international cheeses, harvests of the freshest chemical free fruits and vegetables that can be found – finalising – ice creams, baked goods, and phenomenal yogurts abound. Need I say more?*' Although she does go on to say that the Western plague of hypermarkets is starting to lead to the closure of traditional small shops.

Heidi Rothwell-Walker is convinced that she made the right decision when she chose to work for a school in Poland rather than at one of the other schools around the world that offered her a job:

> *Poland can seem a bit of a backwater, but it's a tremendous experience. It'll change your thinking completely and you'll either love it (like 98% of people) or hate it, but you must try it. I have just renewed my contract for another year because I have been very impressed by them and am very happy here.*

LIST OF EMPLOYERS

ABILITY ES LTD.

ul. Jerozolimskie 49 IIp, 00–697 Warsaw

+22 622 61 39

biuro@ability.com.pl

www.ability.com.pl

NUMBER OF TEACHERS: 12.

PREFERENCE OF NATIONALITY: none.

QUALIFICATIONS: TEFL Cert. or equivalent. Experience preferred but not essential.

CONDITIONS OF EMPLOYMENT: from October to June. 20–25 45-minute lessons a week.

SALARY: depends on experience. Newly qualified teachers are paid about £110; those with 1 year experience about £120 (net) per week.

FACILITIES/SUPPORT: the school will assist in obtaining appropriate housing and assist with bills and any problems. As much assistance as possible is given with work permits when required. Teacher training and observation.

RECRUITMENT: by interview (in person if possible). Some-

times teachers are required to give a demonstration lesson and are offered a job on the basis of this.

CONTACT: Eric Rohe, Director of Studies.

ADAM MICKIEWICZ UNIVERSITY ENGLISH LANGUAGE CENTRE

Studium Jezyka Angielskiego,

ul Slowackiego 20, 60–823 Poznan

fax +61 829 2825

sjauam@main.amu.edu.pl

NUMBER OF TEACHERS: 12.

PREFERENCE OF NATIONALITY: none.

QUALIFICATIONS: BA/MA in Humanities; CELTA/TEFLA plus experience a major advantage.

CONDITIONS OF EMPLOYMENT: 1-year renewable contracts, September to end of June. Annual workload 520 hours. Morning, afternoon or evening work. Students from age 16.

SALARY: 1,600 zloties per month (tax free for first two years) plus overtime.

FACILITIES/SUPPORT: free accommodation in teachers' hostel. Work permit arranged (cost of permit reimbursed by Studium). Teacher development programmes. Mentoring system for new teachers. Insurance provided.

RECRUITMENT: detailed CV and references sufficient. Interviews not essential, could be by phone. Applications welcome by e-mail or post.

CONTACT: Krystyna Mikulska MA, Director of Studies.

ANGLOSCHOOL
ul. Ks. J. Popieluszki 7, 01786 Warsaw
+/fax 22 663 8833
popieluszki@angloschool.com.pl
www.angloschool.com.pl

NUMBER OF TEACHERS: 12 native speakers in 7 centres in Warsaw.

QUALIFICATIONS: CELTA or equivalent and a university degree. Teaching experience preferred.

CONDITIONS OF EMPLOYMENT: 9-month contract from mid-September. Up to 28 hours per week. teaching 3pm–8.30pm Monday to Friday. Some morning classes 8.30am–10am and in-company classes.

SALARY: competitive. School pays taxes and social security (45%).

FACILITIES/SUPPORT: accommodation is provided by the school in the form of two or three roomed shared flats or single rooms in a house. Accommodation includes all necessary facilities, ie furniture, a phone, cable TV, a washing machine, kitchen with necessary equipment. Initial training course and ongoing workshops.

RECRUITMENT: cooperates with schools running CELTA, TEFL courses which provide a job placement service. Advertising in newspapers, internet (www.tefl.com) and recruitment agencies. Direct application with CV welcomed.

BELL – see ELS-Bell, Gama-Bell and Program Bell.

BRYTANIA SCHOOL OF ENGLISH
Ul. Ogrodowa 12, 39–200 Debica
fax +14 670 3811
brytania@pro.onet.pl
www.brytania.com.pl. Also: Ul. Powroznicza 5, 33–100 Tarnow (14 628 68 00).

NUMBER OF TEACHERS: 5–7.
PREFERENCE OF NATIONALITY: British, Irish, Canadian, American.

QUALIFICATIONS: BA or MA degree in humanities plus recognised TEFL Certificate. At least 1 year of teaching experience.

CONDITIONS OF EMPLOYMENT: academic year. 20–24 hours per week, mainly in the afternoons.

SALARY: about £5 per hour. Bonus based on performance.

FACILITIES/SUPPORT: accommodation provided and help given with visas and work permits. In-house teacher training and teaching resources available. Recognised by PASE, the Polish Association of Standards for English (www.pase.pl). Authorised Centre for London Tests of English (www.pearsonlanguageassessments.com).

RECRUITMENT: advertises in Dave's Café, EL Gazette and Polish newspapers.

CONTACT: Bozena Kula.

CAMBRIDGE SCHOOL OF ENGLISH
Ul. Konwiktorska 7, 00–216, Warsaw
+22 622 30 19; fax 22 635 66 14
cambridge@cambridge.com.pl
www.cambridge.com.pl

NUMBER OF TEACHERS: 20 for 1,000 students, all levels and ages.

PREFERENCE OF NATIONALITY: EU native speakers.

QUALIFICATIONS: CELTA or TESOL and university degree.

CONDITIONS OF EMPLOYMENT: 9 month contracts (September to June). Working hours are Monday to Thursday, and either Friday or Saturday. Up to 22 hours contact time per week. Teachers should be prepvared to teach children (aged 6 and upwards) and adolescents, carry out exam preparation courses (FCE, CAE, CPE) and give lessons to individuals and companies.

FACILITIES/SUPPORT: professional development seminars, one senior staff member per four teachers for advice and help. Established course syllabus used.

RECRUITMENT: directly through the school, adverts in established newspapers, TEFL.com or via agency.

COSMOPOLITAN PRIVATE LANGUAGE SCHOOL
Grunwaldzka 42, 45054 Opole
+77 453 0818; fax 77 454 8773
info@cosmopolitan.com.pl
www.cosmopolitan.com.pl

NUMBER OF TEACHERS: 6.
PREFERENCE OF NATIONALITY: EU teachers.
QUALIFICATIONS: applicants must be native English

speakers with a university degree plus TEFL/TESOL or similar certification and at least 1 year's experience.

CONDITIONS OF EMPLOYMENT: 10-month contract from end of September to the end of June. 24 teaching hours per week, 3.30pm–5pm, 5.10pm–6.40pm, 6.50pm–8.20pm Monday to Friday.

SALARY: very competitive, bonus upon renewal of contract for the following year.

FACILITIES/SUPPORT: computer/internet lab, EFL library, DVD equipment, induction for new teachers, regular observations and workshops, professional teacher development programme, accommodation arranged by and paid for by the school.

RECRUITMENT: info@cosmopolitan.com.pl, email applications followed by telephone interviews required.

EF ENGLISH FIRST
ul. Petczyńskiego 30, 01–471 Warsaw
+48 22 666 00 55/ 666 05 67
tomasz.urban@ef.com
www.englishfirst.pl

There are currently 15 EF schools in Poland: 4 in Warsaw and the rest in Lodz, Katowice, Radom, Poznan, Myszkow, Wloclawek, Bielsko Biala, Kielce, Wroclaw, Tychy.

NUMBER OF TEACHERS: 20 teachers for Poland.

PREFERENCE OF NATIONALITY: none but must be native speaker.

QUALIFICATIONS: minimum CELTA/TESOL Certificate or equivalent.

CONDITIONS OF EMPLOYMENT: 9 month renewable contract with possible part-time work in the summer.

SALARY: 3,850–4,750 zloties (net) per month.

FACILITIES/SUPPORT: visa arranged. Help with accommodation: temporary accommodation provided in a hotel on arrival then agent to assist with flat finding.

RECRUITMENT: directly through Warsaw school or through EF offices worldwide including North America, UK or Australia.

CONTACT: Tomasz Urban.

ELS-BELL SCHOOL OF ENGLISH
Al. Niepodleglosci 792/2, 81–805 Sopot
recruitment@elsbell.com
In association with Bell Educational
Trust of Cambridge.

NUMBER OF TEACHERS: 90 for centres in Gdansk, Gdynia, Bydgoszcz, Sopot, Szczecin and Warsaw. Other Bell affiliates are Program Bell in Poznan, and Gama Bell in Krakow.

PREFERENCE OF NATIONALITY: British and Irish. Non-EU considered with relevant experience.

QUALIFICATIONS: CELTA or Trinity TESOL plus university degree. Experience preferred.

CONDITIONS OF EMPLOYMENT: September to June. Up to 24 lessons a week (45 minutes each). Annual workload is 680 hours. Also run summer camps for young learners (aged 9–17).

SALARY: 2,400–2,800 Zloties net, plus end-of-contract bonus of 1,000 Zloties. Warsaw wages are higher: 3,000–3,600 Zloties.

FACILITIES/SUPPORT: accommodation found. Cost of obtaining work permits is reimbursed by school. Health insurance taken out. In-house teacher development programme. Warsaw centre also runs CELTA and DELTA courses.

RECRUITMENT: advertisement on internet. Interviews necessary, usually by phone.

CONTACT: Chris Bogner.

ENGLISH LANGUAGE CENTRE 'RIGHT NOW'
Pszczynska 17, 44–240 Zory, Silesia
+48 32 434 2929 fax 48 32 434 7201
info@rightnow.com.pl
www.rightnow.pl

NUMBER OF TEACHERS: 2–3.

PREFERENCE OF NATIONALITY: EU passport holder.

QUALIFICATIONS: TESOL certificate or equivalent, and at least a year's teaching experience to speakers of other languages.

CONDITIONS OF EMPLOYMENT: 9–10 months September to mid-June. 12 90-minute lessons per week.

SALARY: about 2,000 zloty per month after deductions and taxes.

FACILITIES/SUPPORT: free accommodation in a two-person flat within walking distance of the school.

RECRUITMENT: internet advertisement followed by interviews in person or by telephone.

CONTACT: Rafal Zurkowski, Owner/Manager.

ENGLISH SCHOOL OF COMMUNICATION SKILLS (ESCS)
Ul. Walowa 2, 33–100 Tarnow
fax +14 690 87 49
personnel@escs.pl
www.escs.pl

NUMBER OF TEACHERS: 100 for 5 schools in southern Poland (Tarnow, Bochnia, Krakow, Nowy Targ, and Katowice). Also hold summer courses/camps at Polish seaside.

PREFERENCE OF NATIONALITY: English as mother tongue.

QUALIFICATIONS: degree level of education plus TEFL methodology certificate or ESCS's own training course offered in August.

CONDITIONS OF EMPLOYMENT: 1-year contracts. 20 hours per week. 600 teaching hours per school year (October to June) plus 36 project hours. Teaching all ages (6–60). Pre-selected course books, standardised texts and many extracurricular activities for students (baseball, drama club, video club, etc.)

SALARY: hourly rate; base salary 2,200 zloties per month; varies according to experience and qualifications.

FACILITIES/SUPPORT: seminars and workshops held. Teacher resource centre includes videos, cassettes and supplementary material. Photocopying and computers on-site.

RECRUITMENT: via universities. Interviews held whenever possible. Applications should be sent to the Personnel Department.

CONTACT: Renata Bogucka-Wisniewska, ESCS Personnel Dept.

ENGLISH UNLIMITED
ul. Podmlynska 10, 80–855 Gdansk
+/fax 58 301 3373
k.anflink@eu.com.pl
www.eu.com.pl

NUMBER OF TEACHERS: 8–12 for 11 centres around the Tri-City (Gdansk, Gdynia and Sopot) and in Poznan, Bydgoszcz, Szczecin, Chojnice and Starogard Gdanski. Also possibility of teaching at the Teacher Training College in Gdansk.

PREFERENCE OF NATIONALITY: none; must be native speakers (EU citizens preferred).

QUALIFICATIONS: BA/MA and Cambridge Cert. or Dip. plus experience of overseas teaching.

CONDITIONS OF EMPLOYMENT: 9-month contracts from September. Varied hours of teaching. Courses offered in ESP (e.g. business English).

SALARY: ca. £350 per month (net).

FACILITIES/SUPPORT: accommodation arranged. Training provided.

RECRUITMENT: adverts in the *Guardian*. Interviews essential.

CONTACT: Kamila Anflink, Director of Studies.

EUROPA 2000
Szkoła Jezykow Obcych,
ul. Dabrowskiego 24, 40–032 Katowice
+32 255 10 53 SJO
ul de Gaulle'a 8, 43–100 Tychy
+32 327 34 83
e2000c@europa2000.edu.pl
www.europa2000.edu.pl

NUMBER OF TEACHERS: 6–10.

PREFERENCE OF NATIONALITY: British, American, Canadian.

QUALIFICATIONS: MA, BA, experience in English teaching and leading courses.

CONDITIONS OF EMPLOYMENT: 1–3 years. Usual hours 3pm–8pm.

SALARY: £7–£10 per hour less 21% income tax.

FACILITIES/SUPPORT: assistance with finding accommodation and obtaining permits. Health insurance provided.

RECRUITMENT: References essential. Minimum telephone interviews.

CONTACT: Edyta Stasiak-Ulfik, Language Centre Manager.

GAMA-BELL KRAKOW
ul. Michalowskiego 4, 31–126 Krakow
+12 634 12 49; fax 12 634 12 79
bell@bell.pl
www.gamabell.pl

NUMBER OF TEACHERS: 10.

PREFERENCE OF NATIONALITY: British.

QUALIFICATIONS: BA plus CELTA or equivalent plus at least 1 year's experience.

CONDITIONS OF EMPLOYMENT: 9–12 month renewable full-time contracts. 20–26 lessons per week. Part-time contracts also available and subject to negotiations. Students from age 10.

SALARY: Monthly salary calculated on the basis of agreed total amount of hours per year.

FACILITIES/SUPPORT: 7 days free accommodation on arrival and assistance given with finding accommodation. Monthly teacher development seminars and workshops. Work permit and visa costs covered. Health insurance allowance. Free 'survival Polish' lessons.

GLOBAL VILLAGE

Al. Legionów 42, 25–035 Kielce

fax +41 362 1393

office@gv.edu.pl

www.gv.edu.pl

NUMBER OF TEACHERS: 7.
PREFERENCE OF NATIONALITY: EU nationals preferred.
QUALIFICATIONS: BA or MA in any subject plus a CELTA, DELTA or TEFL certificate.
CONDITIONS OF EMPLOYMENT: standard contract length 1 academic year. To work 3pm–8pm Monday to Friday.
SALARY: competitive.
FACILITIES/SUPPORT: The school organises accommodation.
CONTACT: Urszula Szczepanczyk, Director.

GREENWICH SCHOOL OF ENGLISH

ul. Gdanska 2, 01 633 Warsaw

+22 833 24 31; fax 22 833 36 02

school@greenwich.edu.pl

www.greenwich.edu.pl

NUMBER OF TEACHERS: 20 full-time, 10 part-time for 4 branches in Warsaw and 1 in Gdansk.
PREFERENCE OF NATIONALITY: British or any native English speaker.
QUALIFICATIONS: accredited EFL teaching certificate and degree (BA/BSc).
CONDITIONS OF EMPLOYMENT: 1 school year contract, end September to end June. Guaranteed minimum 80 hours per month plus up to 15 hours overtime. Full sick and holiday pay.
SALARY: approx. £470–£600 basic per month (net guaranteed) depending on experience, qualifications and ability. Plus end of contract bonus.
FACILITIES/SUPPORT: accommodation found by school, usually in shared flats. Rent is approximately £160 per calendar month. Fully paid work visa. Regular programme of seminars.
RECRUITMENT: adverts in the Guardian or on the internet. Interviews essential and held in various locations in the UK in July or by phone where necessary.

INTERNATIONAL HOUSE – BYDGOSZCZ

ul Piotrowskiego 6, Bydgoszcz, 85–098

fax +52 322 3515

bydgoszcz@inthouse.pl

www.inthouse.pl/index.php

NUMBER OF TEACHERS: approximately 12, but up to 25.
PREFERENCE OF NATIONALITY: none.
QUALIFICATIONS: a CELTA, Trinity or IHC good pass or better.
CONDITIONS OF EMPLOYMENT: 9-month standard contract, 25 teaching hours per week (each teaching hour is 50 minutes), either Monday-Friday or Tuesday to Saturday. Some morning work, but the bulk is between 3pm and 9pm.
SALARY: dependent on experience and qualifications, between 1,600 Zloties and 1,900 Zloties.
FACILITIES/SUPPORT: arranges and pays for flats (including bills), flights (to and from London) and healthcare.
RECRUITMENT: either through IHWO Recruitment Services or directly, usually through adverts on websites such as TEFL.com
CONTACT: Grzegorz Chruszcz, School Director.

INTERNATIONAL HOUSE – INTEGRA BIELSKO

ul. Zielona 32, 43–300 Bielsko Biala

+33 822 33 52; fax 33 822 33 51

recruitment.bielsko@ih.com.pl

www.ih.com.pl/bielsko

NUMBER OF TEACHERS: 12–14.
PREFERENCE OF NATIONALITY: EU nationals preferred, other nationalities are acceptable if they apply before the end of June to allow for visa applications.
QUALIFICATIONS: minimum degree and CELTA or equivalent, with one year's experience.
CONDITIONS OF EMPLOYMENT: 9-month contracts, October to June. 21 contact hours.
SALARY: from 2,200–3,050 Zloties per month with paid holidays.
FACILITIES/SUPPORT: the school arranges either shared or single accommodation. After acceptance of the position an offer of work is produced and sent to the teacher who then applies for a work visa from the Polish Consulate. All costs are reimbursed on arrival in Poland.
RECRUITMENT: through IH World and www.tefl.com. Interviews essential, usually carried out by telephone.
CONTACT: David Massey, Director of Studies.

INTERNATIONAL HOUSE – KATOWICE

ul. Sokolska 78/80, 40–128 Katowice

/fax 32 259 99 97

katowice.dos@ih.com.pl

www.ih.com.pl

NUMBER OF TEACHERS: approx. 30.

PREFERENCE OF NATIONALITY: EU citizens preferred.

QUALIFICATIONS: minimum CELTA or equivalent.

CONDITIONS OF EMPLOYMENT: 9-month contracts. 20 contact hours per week, plus 90 minutes standby and 90 minutes training seminar and administration meeting. Students are all ages and there are several in-company contracts.

FACILITIES/SUPPORT: free Polish lessons. Extensive in-service support and development. Subsidised DELTA, Teaching Younger Learners and Business English Certificate courses available.

RECRUITMENT: via IH Central Department (London) or direct to the school.

CONTACT: Bronwen Allen, Director of Studies.

INTERNATIONAL HOUSE – KRAKOW
ul. Pilsudskiego 6, 31–109 Krakow
- 48 12 421 94 40; fax 48 12 422 64 82
- admin@ih.pl
- www.ih.pl

NUMBER OF TEACHERS: 20.

PREFERENCE OF NATIONALITY: none.

CONDITIONS OF EMPLOYMENT: 1-year contracts. 24 contact hours per week. Students from 9 years up. Classes may include in-company Business English for suitably qualified/experienced teachers.

SALARY: basic 2,500 zloties per month.

FACILITIES/SUPPORT: assistance given with accommodation. Fortnightly training workshops plus regular developmental observations. In-house intensive courses for teaching young learners and Business English.

CONTACT: Director of Studies.

INTERNATIONAL HOUSE – OPOLE
ul. Reymonta 30, 45–072 Opole
- +77 454 66 55; fax 77 454 63 09
- opole@ih.com.pl
- www.ih.com.pl

NUMBER OF TEACHERS: 14.

PREFERENCE OF NATIONALITY: EU native speakers preferred. US/Australian/South African with high level of experience.

QUALIFICATIONS: B pass CELTA preferred. Strong C pass CELTA with good report possible.

CONDITIONS OF EMPLOYMENT: approx. 6 weeks holiday and bank holidays per year (3 days per month worked).

20 hour teaching timetable per week plus stand-by duties, input and admin meeting.

SALARY: on a sliding scale dependent on qualifications and experience. B pass/C pass plus one year's experience, 1,640 zloties per month plus shared flat and travel allowance of £30 for every month worked.

FACILITIES/SUPPORT: shared accommodation.

CONTACT: Rod Fricker, Director of Studies.

INTERNATIONAL HOUSE (IH) – WROCLAW
Ul. Leszczynskiego 3, 50–078 Wroclaw
- +/fax 71 372 3698 or 71 78 17 290
- ttcentre@ih.com.pl
- www.ih.com.pl

NUMBER OF TEACHERS: 12.

PREFERENCE OF NATIONALITY: EU passport holders, but non-EU passport holders may also be considered.

QUALIFICATIONS: minimum CELTA or Trinity Certificate. 1 year's experience or CELTA Pass 'A' or 'B' preferred.

CONDITIONS OF EMPLOYMENT: 9 month standard contract. 21 contact hours per week.

SALARY: 2,400–3,200 zloties per month net (in first year) depending on qualifications and experience.

FACILITIES/SUPPORT: The school helps new teachers find suitable accommodation on arrival.

RECRUITMENT: via IH Human Resources in London or direct at wrocdos@ih.com.pl. Interviews are carried out by IH Human Resources in London or else directly in Wroclaw in person or by phone.

CONTACT: John Fowler, Director of Studies.

INTERNATIONAL LANGUAGE CENTERS (ILC)
ul. Karmelicka 10/7, 31–128 Krakow
- +48 12 429 67 88; fax 48 12 429 67 88
- info@ibes.pl or info@learnpolish.net
- www.ibes.pl, www.learnpolish.net

NUMBER OF TEACHERS: variable, according to need.

PREFERENCE OF NATIONALITY: none as long as native speaker.

QUALIFICATIONS: No qualifications/experience necessary, although teaching experience with the Callan Method is useful, as is other teaching experience. Other useful skills include an ability to multi-task, clear projecting voice, and an ability to remain active and engaging throughout the lesson.

CONDITIONS OF EMPLOYMENT: full-time load is 25 hours per week, with a possibility of working up to 30 depending on school needs. Part-time work available.

SALARY: commensurate with experience and qualifications.

FACILITIES/SUPPORT: accommodation listings supplied and assistance with translation. In-house training required upon arrival, free for teachers. Training courses conducted for those who wish to obtain Callan certification for use elsewhere, although these courses are paid for by recipient. Teachers are supplied with necessary documents and translations to obtain residency, usually after 3 months.

CONTACT: Roza Urban, Assistant Director of Studies.

LANG LTC

Sedziowska 5, 02–081 Warsaw

+/fax 22 825 1648

lang@lang.com.pl

www.lang.com.pl

NUMBER OF TEACHERS: approx. 25–30.

PREFERENCE OF NATIONALITY: British.

QUALIFICATIONS: Minimum first degree plus TEFL, CELTA or TESOL.

CONDITIONS OF EMPLOYMENT: Standard length of contract 1 year. 16 hours per week including mornings and afternoons.

SALARY: 50 zloties per 45-minute teaching session.

FACILITIES/SUPPORT: Help with work permits and resident cards provided for non-EU citizens.

RECRUITMENT: local newspapers, internet. Interviews are essential and must be carried out in person or over the phone. During interviews candidates must describe a lesson plan and discuss their teaching experiences.

CONTACT: Klara Malowiecka.

LEKTOR SZKOLA JEZYKOW OBCYCH

ul. Olawska 25, 50–123 Wroclaw

+71 343 2599; fax 372 5292

rmyszkowski@lektor.com.pl or metodyk@lektor.com.pl

NUMBER OF TEACHERS: 50.

PREFERENCE OF NATIONALITY: British, Irish, American, Canadian, Australian.

QUALIFICATIONS: Certificate in TEFL required (CELTA, DELTA or equivalent).

CONDITIONS OF EMPLOYMENT: contracts for one or more years. 20–25 lessons per week. Students are young adults.

SALARY: from 55 zloties per hour.

FACILITIES/SUPPORT: assistance with finding accommodation and obtaining work permit.

RECRUITMENT: personal interviews essential.

CONTACT: Roman Myszkowski or Anna Lukiewicz-Kawalek.

MULTISCHOOL SZKOLA JEZYKOW OBCYCH

Ul. Olawska 5, 01 494 Warsaw

+22 638 23 39; mobile 604 97 33 49; fax 22 638 23 40

biuro@multischool.pl

www.atut.edu.pl

NUMBER OF TEACHERS: 20–25 in 5 branches in Warsaw.

QUALIFICATIONS: TEFL course, higher education. Experience not necessary.

CONDITIONS OF EMPLOYMENT: 6–12 months. Teaching hours 8am–11am and 3pm–8pm.

SALARY: US$1,000 a month average, varies according to timetable. Less 10% for deductions.

FACILITIES/SUPPORT: help given in finding a flat to rent and in obtaining a work permit.

RECRUITMENT: prefer to interview candidates but can rely on CVs, letters of motivation and telephone conversations.

NKJO (TEACHER TRAINING COLLEGE OF FOREIGN LANGUAGES) – LESZNO

pl. Kosciuski 5, 64–100 Leszno

+65 529 9426; fax 65 529 5798

koleszno@kolegium.pl

www.kolegium.com

NUMBER OF TEACHERS: 2.

PREFERENCE OF NATIONALITY: British, American.

QUALIFICATIONS: MA or BA, TEFL.

CONDITIONS OF EMPLOYMENT: minimum stay one year. 15–24 hours per week.

SALARY: 2,000–3,000 zloties per month.

FACILITIES/SUPPORT: free accommodation in a flat with all facilities. Some training through the University of Poznan to which this NKJO is affiliated or assistance from the college.

RECRUITMENT: direct application. Interviews not essential.

CONTACT: Anna Geremek, Director.

OXFORD LEARNING CENTER, PROFESSIONAL SCHOOL OF ENGLISH

ul. 25 Czerwca 60, 26–600 Radom

+/fax 48 360 2166/1416

recruitment@ats.radom.pl

www.oxford.radom.pl

NUMBER OF TEACHERS: 12.

PREFERENCE OF NATIONALITY: native speakers.

QUALIFICATIONS: minimum degree plus Cambridge/Trinity Certificate or equivalent.

CONDITIONS OF EMPLOYMENT: contract from September to June; 24 lessons per week. General English, Business English, Cambridge exam classes, conversational classes for adults based on practical exercises such as ordering a drink in a bar or filling out a form in English. All age groups.

SALARY: from 2,432 zloties per month. Performance-related bonus at the end of each semester. Lessons over and above 24 hours are paid on overtime basis.

FACILITIES/SUPPORT: teachers are provided with help and support with lesson planning and everyday queries and problems. School has excellent teaching resources, ie a library with over 2,500 books for teachers. Teacher development programme, eg school pays for course leading to DELTA for teachers who commit to stay on. School provides free of charge a single, furnished studio flat within walking distance of school, travel allowance, 4 weeks paid holiday if contracted for more than 1 year, to be taken between September and June. School provides and pays for the visa, work permit, residence card and private medical insurance (visas and residence card relevant for non-EU only). New staff met at airport upon arrival.

RECRUITMENT: via e-mail to Recruitment Coordinator, from February until the end of June.

CONTACT: Inga Gorzkowska, Recruitment Coordinator.

POLANGLO
02–508 Warsaw
+22 848 89 39; fax 22 848 89 85
szkola@polanglo.pl
www.polanglo.edu.pl

NUMBER OF TEACHERS: 5.

PREFERENCE OF NATIONALITY: British.

QUALIFICATIONS: BA plus CELTA, DELTA or equivalent.

CONDITIONS OF EMPLOYMENT: minimum 8–12 hours per week for one semester. General and business English for adults.

SALARY: 45–55 zloties per 45-minute lesson.

FACILITIES/SUPPORT: candidates must apply in advance if assistance with work permits is needed. No help with accommodation.

RECRUITMENT: local adverts. Local interviews essential.

CONTACT: Jolanta Dobrowolska, Director, Justyna Martin, Director of Studies.

PROGRAM–BELL
ul. Fredry 1, 61 701 Poznan
+61 8519 250; fax 61 855 18 06
office@program–bell.edu.pl
www.program–bell.edu.pl/english/work
_for_us.htm

NUMBER OF TEACHERS: 4–5.

PREFERENCE OF NATIONALITY: Irish, British.

QUALIFICATIONS: Cambridge Certificate or Diploma with experience of teaching young children.

CONDITIONS OF EMPLOYMENT: 9-month contracts. 16 hours per week. Pupils of all ages including classes for 7–10 year olds. Summer language camps also organised where teachers/sports monitors are needed for 6 weeks from the end of June. Winter possibilities too.

SALARY: 1,900 zloties net.

FACILITIES/SUPPORT: 1-room furnished flat provided. Extensive choice of teaching materials.

RECRUITMENT: website advertisements. E-mail and telephone interviews.

SPEAK UP ENGLISH
Al. Solidarnosci 117, 00–140 Warsaw
+22 652 58 70
praca@lsp.edu.pl
www.speak-up.pl

NUMBER OF TEACHERS: native speaker teachers needed for schools in Warsaw, Lodz, Sosnowiec, Katowice and Gliwice.

PREFERENCE OF NATIONALITY: Great Britain, USA, Canada, South Africa and Australia.

QUALIFICATIONS: university degree, teaching experience; any certificates more than welcome. Enthusiasm also important.

CONDITIONS OF EMPLOYMENT: teachers employed on job contracts – so they are insured and entitled to paid holidays, dependent on visa. Looking for teachers who can explain structures of language and English grammar.

SALARY: competitive with incentive bonus scheme.

FACILITIES/SUPPORT: school can help teacher find an apartment close to the school

RECRUITMENT: direct approach and internet advertisements. Interviews essential but no telephone interviews.

UCET ELC – SILESIAN UNIVERSITY OF TECHNOLOGY

English Language Centre, ul. Akademicka 2A,
44–100 Gliwice
+/fax 32 237 1838
gliwice@ucet.pl
www.ucet.pl/gliwice

NUMBER OF TEACHERS: about 2.
PREFERENCE OF NATIONALITY: British or other native speakers.
QUALIFICATIONS: MA/BA plus a certified teaching qualification if MA/BA is not in teaching/English/pedagogy. No preferences as far as experience is concerned.
CONDITIONS OF EMPLOYMENT: 1–2 years. 540 teaching hours per academic year, ie 18 hours per week. 2 semesters of 15 weeks.
SALARY: standard university salary with paid holidays and bank holidays, less legal deductions for ZUS (social security, medical insurance, pension scheme and tax deduction) or mandatory agreements at hourly rates.
FACILITIES/SUPPORT: university accommodation, school contributes towards 50% of accommodation costs.
RECRUITMENT: internet, personal contacts, teacher training colleges. Telephone interviews suffice.
CONTACT: Mrs. Katarzyna Buch-Gasz, Director of Studies (Katarzyna.Buch-Gasz@polsl.pl or gliwice@ucet.pl).

UNIVERSITY OF LODZ

English Language Centre, Lindleya 8, 91–131 Lodz:
+42 66 55 755/42 66 55 760
magda.matz@elc.pl
www.elc.pl

NUMBER OF TEACHERS: 3.
PREFERENCE OF NATIONALITY: British preferred.
QUALIFICATIONS: CELTA, DELTA or equivalent teaching qualification. Candidates with higher education preferred.
CONDITIONS OF EMPLOYMENT: October to mid-June. Lessons take place 3pm–8.30pm and Saturday mornings 10am–1pm.
SALARY: approximately €13 per hour before tax. Minimal deductions for social security.
FACILITIES/SUPPORT: help to arrange accommodation and hope in the future to offer accommodation.
RECRUITMENT: after initial contact, applicants are sent questionnaire with some methodological questions, referees are contacted and then a phone interview.
CONTACT: Magdalena Matz, Director of Studies.

WORD SCHOOL OF FOREIGN LANGUAGES

ul. Wyszynskiego 1, 39–400 Tarnobrzeg
+15–823 83 33; /fax 15–823 79 63.
Also: Al. Jaba Pawla II 2 G, 39–450 Stalowa Wola
+15 844 5566
word@word.edu.pl
www.word.edu.pl

NUMBER OF TEACHERS: 10.
QUALIFICATIONS: minimum BA in a language/arts related subject. CELTA/Trinity/TESOL. Teaching experience preferred.
CONDITIONS OF EMPLOYMENT: contract from October to June. 26 teaching hours (45 minutes) a week plus 2 hours a week of social programmes, tutoring etc. School hours between 3.30pm and 8.30pm.
SALARY: US$750 a month plus US$400 travel stipend paid at end of contract.
FACILITIES/SUPPORT: apartments provided with basic furnishings, within walking distance of the school (single or shared).
RECRUITMENT: via internet. Interviews by telephone.
CONTACT: Artur Roman, Director.

WORLDWIDE SCHOOL

Popieluszki 21 paw 21, 01–591 Warsaw
+/fax 22–833 91 12
praca@worldwideschool.pl
www.worldwideschool.pl

NUMBER OF TEACHERS: 16 for business clients.
QUALIFICATIONS: native speakers with a university degree and EFL qualification, preferably with a general awareness of the corporate environment. Computer literacy is essential. Must have a strong personality and drive.
CONDITIONS OF EMPLOYMENT: 9–10 month contracts. Early mornings and late afternoons with lots of travel around Warsaw.
FACILITIES/SUPPORT: assistance with paperwork may be given to North American teachers.
RECRUITMENT: local research, screening submitted CVs. Interviews done locally.

YORK SCHOOL OF ENGLISH

ul. Mackiewicza 12, 31–213 Krakow
+12 415 1818/415 1444
info@york.edu.pl
www.york.edu.pl
PASE (www.pase.pl) and Quality English (www.quality-english.com) recognised school, City and Guilds and LCCI-approved examination centre.

NUMBER OF TEACHERS: 40, including approximately 15 native speakers.

PREFERENCE OF NATIONALITY: British and Irish, also American, Canadian or Australian (EU visa holders).

QUALIFICATIONS: BA/MA (preferably in English or Linguistics). TEFL certificate (CELTA/Trinity or equivalents). Teaching experience, references.

CONDITIONS OF EMPLOYMENT: one year contract (September to June). 28 hours per week. Excellent working conditions.

SALARY: monthly average salary €1000 gross depending on qualifications and experiences.

FACILITIES/SUPPORT: help given with accommodation. Bonuses. Professional development, regular workshops and conferences.

RECRUITMENT: www.tefl.com and Google.

CONTACT: Ewa Krupska MA, Director of Studies (e.krupska@york.edu.pl).

ROMANIA

English was barely taught before the downfall of Ceaucescu in 1989 and the collapse of communism and there are few private language schools in Romania at present, though with Romania's admission to the EU in January 2007 and increased investment from Brussels, this is changing. Romania's economy has been slow to develop, but strong consumption and investment expansion will result in real gross domestic product (GDP) growth of 6.6% in 2008.

Anyone seriously intent on teaching in Romania regardless of remuneration should be able to find an opening.

The Ministry of Education (Strada Gen Berthelot 28–30, 010174 Bucharest; ✆ +21 405 6200; www.edu.ro) does not recruit EFL teachers directly, though it cooperates with the British Council to improve standards of local teachers and place volunteers. The British Council has been very active in promoting English in Romania at all levels and in 2000 opened its own Teaching Centre in Bucharest at Calea Dorobantilor 14 (✆ +21 307 9600; fax 21 307 9601). The British Council Romania webpage (www.britishcouncil.ro) has relevant information. In the last few years the government has made a foreign language exam compulsory for graduating from school and university.

Bell Bucharest have developed Corporate Language Programmes and a dynamic and interactive package, ideal for learners who wish to develop their managerial and linguistic communicational abilities. The centre caters for over 1300 students from more than 30 companies. For a list of current vacancies visit http://www.bell-worldwide.com/jobs/list.asp or email recruitment@bell-centres.com.

Despite the demand for native English speakers, however, the government doesn't always make it easy for foreign teachers to work in Romania. The American organisation CETP used to supply teachers to schools, particularly in the Hungarian-speaking areas of Transylvania, but decided to pull out last year. They found that the government would reassign their teachers to locations such as Bucharest, regardless of promises made by CETP. Also, 2007 saw the government in a state of disarray, with teachers on strike, native English speakers receiving no pay and the education minister resigned.

The vast majority of English teaching is carried out by Romanian teachers who seem to do a splendid job judging from the extremely high pass rate their pupils achieve in the Cambridge exams. Teenagers are also motivated to learn English, at least according to one young person, because they aspire to live and work abroad.

The Cultural Counsellor at the Romanian Embassy in London (Arundel House, 4 Palace Green, London W8 4QD; ✆ 020 7937 9666) deals with education and can advise on contacting the Ministry of Education or regional education departments which process all teaching jobs in state schools. There is no point contacting individual schools because recruitment is centralised.

QUEST Romania (www.quest.ro), the Romanian Association for Quality Language Services, operates as a quality control system on the basis of an inspection scheme. The Language Centre members of QUEST employ well-qualified teachers (most of them Romanian) and operate as private language schools registered as NGOs and recognised by the Ministry of Education. The addresses of its founder, full and observer members and one other are available from QUEST's website (which may not be completely up to date) or from its office at the Prosper-ASE Language Centre (Calea Grintei 2–2A, 2nd Floor, Suite 4211, 010731 Bucharest 1; ✆ +21 211 7800; prosper1@prosper. ro; www.prosper.ro). Under the heading Limbi Straine – Cursuri in the *Yellow Pages* there are about 24 addresses though these are unlikely to employ a native speaker.

The arrival of Western investment and companies such as McDonald's and Hilton Hotels is creating more demand for commercial English though not necessarily the prosperity to pay for it.

ROMANIAN LANGUAGE SCHOOLS FIND IT NEXT-TO-IMPOSSIBLE TO ATTRACT NATIVE SPEAKER TEACHERS BECAUSE THEY SIMPLY CAN'T AFFORD TO PAY THEM. AS THE DIRECTOR OF ONE QUEST MEMBER SCHOOL WROTE:

While we would welcome having native English teachers on our staff (we do occasionally receive enquiries from interested people), it is true that given how small our school is (approximately 400 students a year altogether) we cannot afford spending too much on employing them. For the moment, we only employ highly qualified local teachers on part-time contracts. I do not want to mislead people before we reach a more secure position and financial situation, in a very unstable country, economically speaking.

Wages will be equivalent to those earned by Romanian teachers, from US$250 a month. Accommodation is normally provided; if it isn't, it takes a good part of a teacher's salary. Rent for a one-bedroom flat in a provincial city can even take all of a local salary, though teachers may receive an extra allowance to help cover this. Plumbing, heating and standards of construction do not match those of Western European countries. Resident foreign teachers are eligible to obtain an AVIZ card, which in theory entitles them to pay the Romanian rate for hotels, etc. (a quarter of the tourist rate) though many hoteliers insist on charging the higher rate. Obviously it is possible to live on the salary earned but not if a teacher indulges in Western luxuries in high-price supermarkets catering to privileged Romanians.

Pupils are lively and curious about life in the West, and children are often up-to-date with the latest Western fashions and music from MTV. Teachers would be advised to take as many teaching materials as possible, eg magazine articles, postcards, language games, photos, and pictures. Information about the teacher's hometown always goes down well.

Wages on a volunteer placement scheme will be equivalent to those earned by Romanian teachers. **Sean Roberts** participated on a scheme called SCROLL (Scottish Romanian Language Link; scroll.edinburgh@gmail.com) on which Scottish university students enjoy a cultural exchange by teaching English at Romanian summer camps. Although the group the year before had been attached to an orphanage and others had been placed in the middle of nowhere, Sean's placement was very comfortable:

The Echo Language School in Baia Mare was in charge of running the primary camp for 7–10 year olds and the 2-week secondary school camp. We had access to teaching materials such as puzzle books, drawing books and craft materials. Photocopies could be requested a day in advance. The schools also had sports equipment. The family I stayed with struck a wonderful balance between introducing me to their country and leaving me to discover it for myself. They took me on day trips on two weekends and I was introduced to the town centre and their friends. At the same time, they didn't mind me com-

ing home late after being out with the other SCROLLies. They have an enormous heated swimming pool, jacuzzi, sauna, cable TV, Broadband Internet (which they let me use at my leisure, along with the phone) and table-tennis table. In their large garden they grow fruit, vegetables and berries which I got to sample at almost every meal. They also keep bees and have fresh honey every day. I was thrilled to have such a luxurious base for my stay.

British-Romanian Connections is an organisation that has been set up primarily to run an English club in Piatra-Neamt. New graduates (and others) can obtain details from PO Box 86, Birkenhead, Merseyside L41 8FU (℃ /fax 0151 512 3355). The voluntary organisation Youth Action for Peace Romania (Str. Emile Zola nr. 2 ap. 7, 400112 Cluj-Napoca; ℃ +0264 590717; office@yap.ro; www .yap.ro) arranges for a few foreign volunteers to teach English to village children in the mediaeval town of Sighisoara; enquiries should be made to partner organisations, eg YAP UK (www.yap-uk.org).

After the 2007 accession of Romania to the EU, red tape, at least for Europeans, should become simpler. Any teacher wishing to stay for longer than 120 days should apply for a temporary resident permit, preferably in their home country: work visas can be obtained from the Ministry of Labour and Social Protection, after you provide proof of employment by a Romanian employer. It is recommended that you begin proceedings about five weeks in advance of your arrival. Since laws and rules change often, contact the Ministry of Labour and Social Protection to get a current list of required documents. As usual, the process for non EU teachers requires effort from both employer and teacher. Contact the Romanian Embassy in Washington for more information on specific requirements at 1607–23rd St. NW, Washington, D.C. 20008, ℃ 202 232 4747, or at one of the Romanian consulates in Los Angeles, Chicago, or New York City. The Romanian Embassy maintains a web site at www.roembus .org. American citizens are not required to obtain Romanian visas for stays up to 90 days within 6 months. Upon arrival in Romania, foreigners who plan to stay more than 10 days must register their presence with the nearest Police Precinct.

LIST OF EMPLOYERS

ACCESS LANGUAGE CENTRE
Str. Tebei No. 21, 3400 Cluj-Napoca
℃ +/fax 264 420476
✍ office@access.ro
🖥 www.access.ro

PREFERENCE OF NATIONALITY: British, or from Commonwealth countries and the USA.
QUALIFICATIONS: CELTA/DELTA or equivalent.
CONDITIONS OF EMPLOYMENT: classes are mainly from 2pm, 4pm or 6pm. Local teachers tend to work part-time, eg 32–48 teaching hours per month.
SALARY: approximately US$6 an hour for local, part-time teachers. Deductions for tax and contributions are more than a third.
FACILITIES/SUPPORT: help could be given to find affordable accommodation.

RECRUITMENT: personal recommendation, CV, demonstration class.
CONTACT: Ovidiu Ursa (Mr) director.

ENGLISH FOR ALL
str. Horea, nr.2, Targu-Mures, Mures 540050
℃ +265 225355
✍ romania@wegoglobal.com
🖥 www.weteachenglish.go.ro

NUMBER OF TEACHERS: 10–15.
PREFERENCE OF NATIONALITY: any native speaker.
QUALIFICATIONS: prefer TESOL or equivalent, or working towards certificate in first term of teaching. Committed Christian interested in outreach opportunities.
CONDITIONS OF EMPLOYMENT: 1 term/1 year/2 years.
SALARY: volunteer. Flat rent and utilities paid.

FACILITIES/SUPPORT: assists teacher with residence permit.

RECRUITMENT: via internet, magazine adverts, mailings, churches. Interview on Skype/Yahoo by internet or telephone.

CONTACT: Kevin Sissons, Director/Head Teacher.

PROFESSIONAL LANGUAGE CENTRE
197 1 Decembrie 1918, St. Targu-Mures 4300
 +265 256 041
 acotoara@rdslink.ro
 www.professionalcentre.ro

NUMBER OF TEACHERS: 1.

QUALIFICATIONS: BA or equivalent.

CONDITIONS OF EMPLOYMENT: 1-year contracts. To work 4pm–8pm, 5 days a week.

SALARY: US$5 per hour. Taxes and social security paid by the school.

FACILITIES/SUPPORT: assistance with finding accommodation and acquiring work permits.

RECRUITMENT: interview required.

CONTACT: Angela Cotoara, Director.

RUSSIA

It seems that you can't pick up a paper these days without reading one alarming headline or another: '*Former Russian security chief dies of suspicious causes*' '*Russian bomber enters British airspace*' or '*British Council ordered to close its doors in Russia*'. But this is hardly the full story and there are still plenty of opportunities for native English teachers who wish to experience this vast and diverse country safely.

Russia is no longer an emerging market; it has fully emerged and Russians are taking full advantage of their new found capital to pay for homes and cars, travel and tourism and, of no less importance, to pay for English lessons. Russians are still basically conservative and concerned by the need for good education, but there is a constant shortage of Russian English teachers in state schools so private language schools continue to be popular. The large chains such as Language Link, BKC-International House and EF are constantly recruiting teachers for their schools. The number of applications remains steady, although as Robert Jensky, Director of Language Link Russia points out, the numbers of qualified and/or fully experienced teachers are down. Rather than employ an under-qualified native English teacher, most language schools would rather turn to home-grown English teachers for whom teaching English is a profession and not simply a one to two year past-time. Russian English teachers are also far cheaper and do not require visa support and other costly add-on benefits such as accommodation, healthcare and travel allowances.

Native English teachers with a CELTA or Trinity College London TESOL Certificate are likely to impress. Most schools will also accept applicants who hold TEFL certificates obtained on courses which roughly approximate either of those certificate courses, ie are 100–120 hours long with six to eight hours of observed teaching practice. If you do not hold a certificate but have gained valuable experience teaching general English, business English and/or international examination courses (IELTS, FCE, CAE, etc) and you have taught both adults and children, you should have little difficulty finding a job teaching English in Russia.

ROBERT JENSKY, WHO KINDLY PROVIDED MOST OF THE INFORMATION FOR THIS CHAPTER, IS CONVINCED THAT HIGH STANDARDS ARE ESSENTIAL:
I have personally seen many unqualified teachers fail because they did not fully realise the difference between speaking English and teaching English. Although Russians can vary in temperament and personality, they share a respect for education. Russians who under communism did not have to pay for education have come to accept the fact that it is now necessary to do so. There is little debate among Russians as to

the significance of the English language both domestically and globally. Their only concern is that they get their full money's worth from each and every lesson. Russian students are demanding and place high expectations on their teachers, and so do the companies which employ them (including those that hire EFL teachers illegally). Given these circumstances, it is strongly recommended that any teacher coming to Russia has with him or her a good grammar book, a dictionary and a concise guide to TEFL methodology.

Many young Russians are already fairly competent in the language and want to become more conversant with Western culture, not just for its own sake but to enhance their career prospects. Jobs in international firms are often advertised only in English. Russians young and not-so-young who want to work in advertising, banking, computing and so on need to speak English and therefore are drawn to the intensive English courses advertised all over the Moscow metro and on lampposts.

There are also plenty of jobs tutoring and looking after young children, as affluent parents hope to give their children a head start. This sector seems to be expanding, with several companies and individuals posting adverts in newspapers/websites such as www.expat.ru. One advertisement posted in 2008 was for a 22–40-year-old native speaking woman to engage in 'dialogues, conversation, play activities and developmental games' with a 9-month old baby. Kindergartens and specialist companies that offer tutors, nannies and governesses for children have also realised that native English speakers 'create a good image for your company,' according to Sveta Kotwani, Director of Little Angels Kindergarten in Moscow (see list of employers). Kid's Estate in Moscow (✆ +985 7631942; julia-zeligman@yandex.ru; www.kid-estate.ru) looks for native speakers to work with children aged 3–7, full-time or part-time. Bonne International with offices in London and Moscow (✆ 495 933 2893; info@bonne.ru; www.bonne-int.com) has recently started taking on native English speakers and have posted a number of vacancies, mainly in and around Moscow, for ESL-qualified native English speakers to tutor children aged 4–10. MsPoppins (✆ 744 0651; www.mspoppins.com) also advertises for native English tutors for children aged from 4 to 12.

FINDING A JOB

Finding a school vacancy in Russia shouldn't be too difficult. Russia is, after all, the largest country on earth spanning 11 time zones. You only need to decide where in Russia you'd like to settle down to teaching English. As a rule, salaries can drop the further you go from Moscow. A lower salary however is usually more than made up for by the lower costs of living found in many of the big away-from-Moscow cities of Russia; and a lower cost of living usually means a higher standard of living. Likewise, you're more likely to experience real Russia and real Russians.

ROB JENSKY CAUTIONS AGAINST FOCUSING YOUR JOB HUNT ENTIRELY AROUND SALARY AND PERKS:
For newly qualified teachers, academic support can mean the difference between success and failure as a teacher. And speaking of success as a teacher, having tons of personality is imperative. Students want to like their teachers and the way to gain their affection is by truly liking them back. Teachers who like their students will spend the time needed to prepare for their lessons adequately and this is where the value of proper academic support cannot be underestimated. The availability of a good director of studies and other experienced teaching staff who can help you with lesson preparation is a benefit that cannot be counted in terms of dollars and cents or pounds and pence.

Teachers who are capable of performing in a variety of EFL classroom settings (young learners, adults, general, business English, examination preparation) are in the greatest demand. Likewise, teachers who are prepared to be flexible with regard to teaching schedules will find a far greater number of employment opportunities. This is especially true in the great metropolitan areas where the number of both business and one-to-one clients is on the rise, many of whom want to be taught before or after the working day.

The three most popular websites used by Russian employers looking to hire English teachers are: www.TEFL.com, www.ESLcafe.com and www.goabroad.com. When writing to potential employers in Russia make sure that the company has the right to invite and employ teachers in Russia (see visa section for details), check whether the salary is net or gross and ask if accommodation is free/included.

Some companies such as the Samantha School of English in Moscow (see list of employers) have a UK recruiter who can interview prospective candidates in the UK.

An estimated 900 tertiary institutes offer English courses, and many employ one or two highly educated native speakers to assist. One is St Petersburg University of Humanities and Social Sciences whose Department of Foreign Languages (15 Fuchika St, 192238 St Petersburg; ✆ +812 269 6707; www.uhss.spb.ru) employs a couple of Britons to assist in the English Language Department. Most universities and polytechnics offer free or subsidised accommodation and a civilised timetable but usually can't pay more than a couple of dollars an hour.

Some of the main language chains recruit abroad, including Language Link and EF English First. EF recruits for Russia on reasonable terms with return flight, medical insurance and visa costs included. Saxoncourt fills vacancies in Siberia on behalf of IH-affiliated schools, among others. Many foreign teachers prefer the security of working for a Western-owned company. Even if the wages are not brilliant, the support and fringe benefits usually make up for it.

BARRY ROBINSON SPENT A NUMBER OF YEARS IN MOSCOW WORKING THE EFL CIRCUIT AND HAS PROVIDED A SNAPSHOT OF THE MAIN EMPLOYERS. HE ADMITS THAT HIS OPINIONS ARE TOTALLY SUBJECTIVE AND ARE MEANT PURELY AS A GUIDE:

EFL in Moscow can often be more rewarding financially on a freelance basis, but for those who prefer to tie in with an all-inclusive contract, here is some info on what's on offer. BKC have an excellent reputation for teacher development and you get loads of professional support. They always pay on time and for work finished, and they are a decent company who will always look good on your CV. The same applies to Language Link who are friendly, fair, very supportive and will find you a flat. EF English First probably offer the best contract. They allow teachers to find their own flat (and pay for temporary accommodation during house-hunting) and their schools are always well-equipped. They insist that you stick to the EF book so there isn't much room for teacher development.

A thriving English language press has established itself in Moscow and St Petersburg. Check advertisements in the *Moscow Times* and the *St Petersburg Times*. Look out also for the free advertisement paper *Iz Ruk v Ruki* in about 15 towns in Russia and check the online message-boards community for English speakers living in Moscow on www.expat.ru.

Since 1982 the Serendipity Russian-English Program has been sending Americans to work at the American Home in Vladimir Russia, a city 200km east of Moscow. Not only do they teach English but also deliver lectures on American culture. Contracts last eight to nine months (renewable) starting in mid-August. The annual deadline for applications is 15 March. The project is located at the American Home (Ulitsa Letneperevozinskaya 3, 600000 Vladimir; ✆ +7 4922 323687; ah@amhome.elcom

.ru) though the programme is administered from Illinois (Dr. Ron Pope, President, 1403 Kingsridge Drive, Normal, IL 61761 2860; ✆ 309 454 2364; fax 309 452 6332; ronpope42@cs.com; www .serendipity-russia.com/engculture.htm#teaching%20opportunity).

> **JIM CLOST FROM CANADA DOES NOT HAVE A TEFL CERTIFICATE BUT HE HAD STUDIED RUSSIAN AT UNIVERSITY AND JOINED A VOLUNTARY TEACHING SCHEME ORGANISED BY A LOCAL TRAVEL AGENCY:**
>
> *I was required to work between four and six hours a day, only conversation and listening. Accommodation and meals were provided with a local family (normally one of the students) however no wages were paid as the position was voluntary. I met wonderful students, kids and adults and made friends that I go back to see regularly. The pupils were in general quite shy but some were ready to speak up and chat with me right away. Once we got to know one another conversation flowed more freely. Many of my students were quite eager to have me in their home for dinner. This is normal in Russian society where meeting with foreigners on a personal basis is a rarity. In my free time, I skated, swam, visited friends for tea and dinner, walked and talked.*

Further information about this scheme in Izhevsk (for which the application fee is less than US$150) can be obtained from SV, Izhevsk Karla Marxa 288a, 426008 Izhevsk (or PO Box 2040, 426000 Izhevsk); tel/fax 3412 450037; svezhyveter@gmail.com; www.sv-agency.udm.ru.

Koober Grob from Chicago was also impressed with the SV arrangement and found lots of scope for initiative:

> *I corresponded with the teacher I would eventually work with for seven months before I went to Izhevsk. The students and I would discuss various topics such as domestic violence, cooking, nature, war or even manure and chocolate-covered ants. There was never any pretence in any of the classes. Eventually I started a theatre club for teenagers at school no. 27 and then accompanied a 6-week school trip around Siberia helping students individually with their English. The students were all so motivated, respectful and friendly. I only spent US$600 for the three-month period that I was in Russia since Russia is very inexpensive and my students and friends paid for most of my expenses.*

Students of Russian should investigate the programme run by the Pro-Ba Centre in St Petersburg where four or eight weeks of intensive study of Russian is followed by a period of work in schools, kindergartens or summer camps (www.studyrussian.spb.ru). Fees are from €2,250 for two months to €3,250 for four months.

UK ORGANISATIONS

The Language Assistants Team, Education & Training Group, British Council: 10 Spring Gardens, London SW1A 2BN; ✆ 020 7389 4596; assistants@britishcouncil.org; Places English language assistants in universities in Russia. This programme is open to applicants with graduate-level Russian or equivalent who have already spent a period of work or study in Russia. The monthly allowance is minimum 5,000 roubles plus a £175 supplement from the British Council and accommodation is provided free of charge. The deadline for applications is the end of February.

CHRIS JONES HAD A WONDERFUL YEAR AS A TEACHING ASSISTANT IN NIZHNY NOVGOROD (SEVEN HOURS FROM MOSCOW) AND HIS EXPERIENCES ARE REPRE-SENTATIVE OF OTHERS' WHO HAVE GONE THROUGH A MEDIATING ORGANISATION TO TEACH IN THE RUSSIAN STATE SYSTEM:

I had no relevant teaching experience, but the fact that I had been to Russia several times before seemed to be a big selling factor; I obviously knew what I was in for. During the interview, discussion concentrated on how you thought you would cope with living in Russia for nine months.

My institution was very conscious of not over-burdening me with work and I regularly had to press for more hours. I was expected to concentrate on phonetic and conversational practice but was allowed almost to do my own thing once they realised that I was competent. I used articles from newspapers and magazines for listening and reading comprehensions and made extensive use of popular songs.

There were problems with resources. There were only two video recorders in my university and these had to be booked well in advance. Hand-outs are virtually unheard of in university teaching in Russia and getting photocopying done for lessons was very difficult. Certainly all copies had to be handed back in at the end of each lesson and saved for other groups to use. Sometimes I paid for photocopies myself, as the official channel for using the photocopier (there was only one) involved much wearisome justification to those in authority.

Language Link offers an array of different employment opportunities designed to fit the needs of most EFL applicants. In addition to jobs for qualified EFL teachers, Language Link also recruits for its Teacher Internship, Work-Study and Volunteer programmes. For details visit www.language link.ru.

With Travellers (7 Mulberry Close, Ferring, West Sussex BN12 5HY; ✆ 01903 502595; www .travellersworldwide.com) paying volunteers teach conversational English in Russia. Prices start at £2,145 for three months teaching in St Petersburg, excluding international travel.

The youth exchange company CCUSA runs a Summer Camp Russia Programme whereby teacher/counsellors are placed on youth camps in Russia lasting four or eight weeks between mid-June and mid-August. Camps are widely scattered from Lake Baikal in Siberia to the shores of the Black Sea. The programme fee, from £800, includes round-trip travel from London to Moscow, visa, travel insurance, orientations on arrival and room and board. In the UK, contact CCUSA at 2 Brunswick Road, Pudsey, Leeds LS28 7NA; ✆ 0113 257 4308; caityw@ccusa.com; www.ccusa.com.

WORKING AND LIVING CONDITIONS

The unregulated housing market makes it difficult for foreign teachers to find independent accommodation. Furthermore rents in Moscow and St Petersburg are staggering relative to the quality on offer. Company-provided accommodation is easily a US$600–$900 add-on benefit. Of course, as you leave the bright lights of Moscow and St Petersburg, rental costs come down. Employers normally arrange accommodation for their teachers in small shared flats. As single flats are much more expensive, your employer is unlikely to cover the extra cost of providing you with this luxury. Teachers might also lodge with landladies, of whom there is no shortage considering how many widows there are trying to make ends meet on vanishingly small pensions.

Russians generally take a far more laid back attitude to work than their counterparts in Western society. This sometimes results in standards of efficiency and service that are somewhat lower than people generally expect in the UK or the USA. As Robert Jensky puts it: '*Whereas in America every-thing should be done ten minutes ago and in the UK it should be done right now, in Russia it probably won't get done until the end of the working day (or week)*'. This is particularly true of those working in administrative and official capacities who are often slow, unhelpful and inconsistent, but is less so in some of the larger chains of language schools where a high level of professionalism prevails. Teachers need to be flexible in their approach to the working world in Russia and be prepared to compromise and adapt to an unfamiliar working environment.

A CULTURAL DIFFERENCE WHICH MANY NEWCOMERS FIND DIFFICULT TO ACCEPT IS THE APPARENT UNFRIENDLINESS OF THE RUSSIAN PEOPLE. HOWEVER THE COLD FACE OF RUSSIAN OFFICIALDOM COULD NOT BE IN STARKER CONTRAST TO THE WARMTH THAT WILL GREET YOU WHEN YOU GET TO KNOW RUSSIANS BETTER. ELIZABETH BEARMAN, A TEACHER IN MOSCOW GOES SOME WAY TO UNRAVELLING THE MYSTERY OF THE COLD RUSSIAN EXTERIOR:

The Russian man in the street does not smile unless he is happy, he does not engage complete strangers in meaningless conversation and he does not suffer fools gladly. There is a Russian proverb that perhaps sums it up: 'Only a fool smiles all the time'. However, while Russians can appear rude and unfriendly, when you get to know them they are considerate, helpful, generous and friendly. The Russian concept of friendship is much deeper and less superficial than elsewhere.

With a serious shortage of teaching aids in many places, resourcefulness will be necessary. Not surprisingly, the younger generation seems more willing to embrace new communicative teaching methods than the older one, according to the director of the Sunny Plus English School in Moscow (© +495 727 1431; www.sunnyplus.ru/job):

'Adults cause headaches. They get upset with grammar. Many of them can't easily accept modern methods of teaching. The progress is very slow. For many weeks they can't understand a teacher. They demand changing him. Their pronunciation is terrible, but during classes they keep silent'.

However, **Joanna Graham**, a teacher trainer at BKC Moscow (affiliated to International House), has had quite a different experience of teaching adults in Russia:

The students here are great, and one of the main reasons I have stayed at this school for so long. English lessons are not cheap (about a quarter of most people's monthly wage) and because more companies require it to communicate with overseas clients etc. adult students tend to be very motivated. They want to learn and, for most of the classes I have taught, the more homework I give them the better (I've actually been told off by students for not giving them enough!).

Don't be fooled into believing that just because you choose to work for a chain school, you are go-ing to be working in either a large school or one staffed by native English-speaking teachers. Many major chains operate small teaching operations in far-flung locations. Proximity to good healthcare cannot be taken for granted, and could be an issue for people with medical conditions. If proximity to cultural and recreational outlets such as theatres, cinemas, museums, parks, circuses and other tourist attractions is important to you psychologically, then be sure to investigate locations prior to accepting a job.

REGULATIONS

There's an old saying that goes, 'The more things change, the more they remain the same'. In that spirit, the essentials of working in Russia have not changed. It is not difficult to obtain a working visa. The difficulty lies in finding an organisation which is registered with the authorities and has permission to invite foreigners to Russia for the express purpose of working for them. Many language schools would prefer to avoid this route as it necessitates their having to pay both income and social welfare taxes on their foreign employees. Companies employing English teachers legally must pay 30% income tax on the teachers' salaries during their first 183 days on Russian soil, and thereafter 13%. Social welfare tax is another 26.5%.

Obviously, the easiest way for language schools to avoid these costly taxes is not to employ teachers legally. In the past, this was done by employing English teachers who had arrived in Russia on 12-month multiple entry business visas. Certain underhanded employers even went so far as to tell their newly hired teachers that possessing a business visa allowed them to work legally in Russia. This is not true. Business visas allow foreigners wishing to do business in Russia the right to enter the country for the purpose of doing their business. Multiple entry business visas are issued to foreigners with the understanding that they will be paid (and taxed) for their work back home and that they will leave the country once they have concluded their business.

The number of companies willing to employ foreigners illegally and the number of foreigners including teachers willing to work illegally was so large that the authorities started to crack down. The first crackdown came a few years ago. At that time, foreigners who entered Russia on one-year multiple entry business visas could only have their visas registered for six months before they were required to leave Russia for at least one day. Most foreigners simply crossed the nearest border and then immediately returned. When this 'inconvenience' didn't solve the problem of illegal employment, the authorities passed Government Decree 635 in October 2007. Now, foreigners entering the country on one-year multiple entry business visas may only remain on Russian soil for a maximum of three months before having to leave Russian territory for at least three months, in other words they may remain in Russia for only three months during any six-month period.

To obtain a work visa, you need a visa sponsor. If you have accepted a teaching job with an organisation which has the right to invite and employ foreign teachers, then your employer will become your visa sponsor and their name will appear on your visa. If the name is anything other than the company which is offering you employment, then it is advisable to ask why this is so. Once you have been accepted for employment, you will need to send your visa sponsor a scanned copy of your passport details. These along with the necessary documentation will then be used to procure a letter of invitation for you from UFMS (Federal Migration Service Organisation). Obtaining a letter of invitation (LOI) can take up to a month. As these letters are obtained at the local level, they can be prepared for your visa sponsor in as little as three days (as in the case of Samara), two weeks (in Moscow) or a month (in St Petersburg). Once obtained, your visa sponsor will post your LOI to you along with a letter of support and, if necessary, proof of health insurance, which you then submit to the local Russian consulate. Application forms are available online.

The three-month single or double entry business visa that you will be granted in the first instance can be extended to one year by your employer. Processing normally takes between two days and two weeks. Although most Russian consulate websites state that a human immunodeficiency virus (HIV) test is not required for issuance of a three-month visa, you will undoubtedly be required to submit proof of being HIV-negative.

A new law imposes a mandatory two-week wait before getting your visa if you are applying for a visa in a country in which you do not hold residency.

Teachers travelling to Russia will be required to fill in and submit a migration card along with their passport and visa when arriving at passport control. The migration card is paper and is easily completed as it only asks for basic passport and visa information. The migration card has two identical sides, one which is retained by the border guard and the other which is returned to you with a stamp on it. Be sure that you get back your half and that it is stamped. The migration card is necessary to your proper registration in Russia.

Once you have entered Russia, your visa sponsor has 72 hours to register you with the authorities. It is imperative that you turn over your passport, visa (usually already in your passport) and migration card to your visa sponsor for registration with the authorities. Failure to register visas on time can incur a fine which you will be responsible for paying.

Once registered, your documents should be returned to you. If, while in the employ of your visa sponsor, you desire to travel to another city for more than three working days, you should notify your visa sponsor so that they can inform the authorities. Failure to do so can again result in fines.

Work visas are tied to the named employer. If you wish to change employers, you must also change your visa sponsor. This will involve the process previously explained and necessitate your leaving Russian territory within 72 hours of stopping your employment.

FOREIGNERS DO WORK IN RUSSIA WITHOUT PROPER AUTHORISATION, BUT RUN THE RISK OF BEING FINED OR EVEN DEPORTED. RHYS SAGE BECAME SUSPICIOUS OF A LANGUAGE SCHOOL WHICH SENT HIM THE WRONG VISA:

After a fiasco in Latvia, it has become apparent to me that if a company is not willing to obtain the proper visa then they must be up to something dodgy. When I negotiated my contract with a school in Novosibirsk, they accepted some pretty excessive demands on my part which made me suspicious that the contract was worthless. This, combined with the fact that they sent me a visa form for a transit visa claiming it was a work visa, resulted in my complete loss of interest in them. A transit visa means nothing. It just means that you have permission to cross Russia, and therefore you have no redress if the employer decides to withhold your wages.

WHATEVER YOU ATTEMPT TO ACCOMPLISH IN RUSSIA YOU WILL NEED PATIENCE, A QUALITY THAT JIM CLOST THINKS IS ALMOST UNKNOWN IN 21ST-CENTURY NORTH AMERICA:

If you're from the West you have to understand some things about Russian people and bureaucracy. At first glance it may seem that they don't function at all. But this is a deceiving picture. Don't expect anything to happen instantly. If you are trying to register a visa or book a plane ticket, don't hound the government desk-slave or tour operator to the ends of the earth looking for answers. They'll get done what you've asked and in good order – eventually.

My final point is this: 99% of the Westerners who visit Russia never set foot outside the Moscow–Golden Ring–St Petersburg circuit. If you think this is a discovery of Russian culture, then you might as well be off to Disneyland Paris to learn about French culture. To get a true feeling for Russia and her people, visit the regions to the east and the south. This is the real Russia, away from the throngs of foreign tourists, the Pizza Huts and the English language newspapers.

LIST OF EMPLOYERS

BENEDICT SCHOOL

4 Admiraltejskaya Nabereznaya,
St Petersburg 190000

✆ +812 315 3596; fax 812 325 7573

✁ benedict@peterlink.ru

The biggest English language school in
St Petersburg and north-west Russia.

NUMBER OF TEACHERS: 18–20 for St Petersburg and
the surrounding cities.

PREFERENCE OF NATIONALITY: British, American,
Canadian, Australian.

QUALIFICATIONS: TEFL qualification preferred. Benedict
school offers intensive 4-week TEFL course in
cooperation with the Via Lingua. www.vialingua.org/
tefl-petersburg.asp).

CONDITIONS OF EMPLOYMENT: 3–12 months.
15–25 hours per week.

SALARY: US$800–$1,500 per month.

FACILITIES/SUPPORT: visa support and help with accommodation given. Library and resource centre.

CONTACT: Natalya Rostovtseva, Director.

BKC – INTERNATIONAL HOUSE

Starovagankovsky Peruelok 15, office 1,
121019 Moscow

✆ +495 737 5225; fax 495 737 6579

✁ recruit@bkc.ru or recr@bkc-ih.com

🖥 www.bkcih-moscow.com

NUMBER OF TEACHERS: around 200 contract and hourly
paid teachers in Moscow, 50 teachers in the Moscow region.

PREFERENCE OF NATIONALITY: none.

CONDITIONS OF EMPLOYMENT: 9 or 6-month contracts;
paid holidays; 30, 27or 24 teaching hours per week. Typical
timetable includes some teenager or children as well as
adults' classes; general English, conversational, exam and
business English classes.

SALARY: US$905–$1310 net depending on qualifications
and experience, plus accumulating bonus paid on completion
of contract.

FACILITIES/SUPPORT: visa support, shared accommodation
(rent and all utilities except long-distance phone calls paid
by BKC), airfare allowance and healthcare provided. Monthly
seminars and regular observations. Discounts are offered to
teachers who want to learn Russian.

RECRUITMENT: contact the Recruitment Department,
BKC-IH Moscow.

CONTACT: Nadya Maximova or Tanya Chibireva, Recruitment
Managers.

BRITISH-AMERICAN LANGUAGE CENTRE

Novo-Sadovaya 106–526, 443068 Samara

✆ +/fax 846 2703700/2703573

✁ volgacentre@mail.ru

🖥 www.the_world.ru

Otherwise known as the Volga Centre for Education
& Information.

NUMBER OF TEACHERS: 50 for centres in Samara and
Togliatti.

PREFERENCE OF NATIONALITY: British, American,
Canadian, Australian, New Zealand.

QUALIFICATIONS: BA/BEd, TEFL Cert, experience.

CONDITIONS OF EMPLOYMENT: 12-month renewable
contract for 100–135 hours per month September to May,
65 hours per month. July-August.

SALARY: US$600 per month September to May, US$390
per month July-August.

FACILITIES/SUPPORT: visa invitation sent to relevant
Russian Embassy. Free single flat provided.

RECRUITMENT: via internet. Face-to-face interviews not
necessary.

CONTACT: Vadim Kamaev, Director; Olga Makarova,
Personnel Manager.

EF ENGLISH FIRST

5th Floor, Building No. 15, 1st Brestskaya Street,
125047 Moscow

✆ +495 937 3887; fax 495 937 3889

✁ Svetlana.shulzhik@ef.com

🖥 www.englishfirst.com

NUMBER OF TEACHERS: about 40 for 30 schools
(19 including one business school in Moscow, 2 in Vladivos-
tok, 3 in St Petersburg, 1 in Stavropol, Rostov, Tyumen,
2 Nizhny Novgorod, Novosibirsk, Almatievsk, Yuzhno Sakha-
linsk and Tver).

PREFERENCE OF NATIONALITY: British, North American,
Australian, New Zealand, South African, Irish.

QUALIFICATIONS: CELTA/TESOL/EF TEFL Certificate plus a
university degree.

CONDITIONS OF EMPLOYMENT: 9-month or 12-month renewable contracts. Schools open from 9am to 9pm Monday to Friday, 9am–6pm Saturday. 24 contact hours per week. Modern classrooms all fitted with computers and LCD screens with on-line supplementary materials, support with finding accommodation. Visas arranged. Paid holidays. Flights paid. Orientation on arrival and ongoing training. Medical insurance provided.

CONTACT: Stewart MacPherson (stewart.macpherson @ef.com) or Alexander Titov (alexander.titov@ef.com).

GLOBUS INTERNATIONAL
Myasnitskaya 40/16 office 415, Moscow 101000
✆ +495 6213112
✉ crichtonb@globus-int.ru
🖥 www.globus-int.ru

NUMBER OF TEACHERS: 26.

PREFERENCE OF NATIONALITY: UK, Ireland, Australia, New Zealand, Canada, USA.

QUALIFICATIONS: minimum CELTA or equivalent, plus ideally 2 years' experience.

CONDITIONS OF EMPLOYMENT: 12-month standard contract, 26 academic hours per week.

SALARY: from £950 net per month.

FACILITIES/SUPPORT: a housing manager helps to accommodate all teachers based on what they would like. Centre organises a work visa invitation, then when the teacher is in Russia, organises all the necessary documents to make sure the teacher is fully registered and has all correct documentation.

RECRUITMENT: through TEFL websites. Telephone interviews are essential. If possible the school tries to set up face-to-face interviews in London.

CONTACT: Crichton Brauer, Managing Director.

LANGUAGE LINK RUSSIA
Novoslobodskaya ul. 5, bld. 2, 127055 Moscow
✆ +495 250 6900; fax 495 250 6360
✉ jobs@languagelink.ru
🖥 www.jobs.languagelink.ru

NUMBER OF TEACHERS: 200 throughout Russia (Moscow, Moscow Region, St Petersburg, St Petersburg Region, Obninsk, Volgograd, Samara, Ekaterinburg, Ufa, Krasnoyarsk, Irkutsk, Rostov na Donu, Zelenograd).

PREFERENCE OF NATIONALITY: British, American, Canadian, Australian, New Zealand and South African.

QUALIFICATIONS: CELTA or Trinity Certificate/Diploma (or equivalents) required. Candidates without a recognised qualification may enter Language Link's Teacher Internship Training Programme.

CONDITIONS OF EMPLOYMENT: 6, 9 or 12 month contracts. 25 teaching hours per week, usually 4 hours a day, 5 days a week. Adult classes, children's classes and in-company. Also runs a number of English language summer camps near major cities (camps@languagelink.ru) starting the beginning of June.

SALARY: US$800–$1200 (net) depending on location and experience. Return airfare (maximum US$800 to America, or £300 to the UK). 4 weeks of paid holiday and health cover (for teachers on 9-month contracts).

FACILITIES/SUPPORT: all teachers provided with free accommodation in 2-room flat (for 2 teachers). Paid medical services and full visa/work permission support. Academic support via on-site director of studies, inset training, seminars and presentations. Teachers at summer camps receive US$400–$500 per month in addition to room and board.

RECRUITMENT: Application is online. Minimum 2 professional references. Telephone interviews are compulsory unless carried out by Language Link in London (21 Harrington Road, London SW7 3EU; ✆ 020 7225 1065; fax 020 7584 3518; recruitment@languagelink.co.uk; www.languagelink.co.uk).

CONTACT: Robert Jensky, Director.

LITTLE ANGELS KINDERGARTEN
St. Novocheremushkinskaya 11/2,
Metro Akademicheskaya, Moscow
✆ +495 7797640; fax 495 7797640
✉ litang@mail.ru
🖥 www.littleangels.ru

NUMBER OF TEACHERS: 3 or 4.

PREFERENCE OF NATIONALITY: preferably from England, Canada or Australia.

QUALIFICATIONS: a strong background in early childhood education and a TEFL qualification. Also he/she should have experience of teaching.

CONDITIONS OF EMPLOYMENT: standard 1 year contract, usual hours are 9am–5pm.

SALARY: depends on qualification and experience but at least US$1,500. If the employee has a work permit from Little Angels they pay 13% of the tax from their salary.

FACILITIES/SUPPORT: no help with accommodation or work permit at the moment. Usually, teachers already have a work permit from a company or agency.

RECRUITMENT: by interview, filling in a questionnaire and taking a class. Interviews are essential.

CONTACT: Mrs. Sveta Kotwani, Director.

SAMANTHA SCHOOL OF ENGLISH

Garibaldi Street 28, building 3,117393 Moscow

☏ +499 794 4384; fax 495 422 0881

🖱 samanthaschool@comail.ru

💻 www.samantha.ru

NUMBER OF TEACHERS: 15 full-time, 10 part-time English teachers.

PREFERENCE OF NATIONALITY: UK, USA, Australia.

QUALIFICATIONS: teaching experience and proof that candidates enjoy teaching children and teenagers. The school does not require TEFL qualifications per se, but when teachers have teaching qualifications, it is an added benefit. Some knowledge of Russian and interest in Russia are also an advantage.

CONDITIONS OF EMPLOYMENT: standard academic year contract, usual hours are Mondays, Tuesdays, Thursdays and Fridays from 2pm until 7.30pm.

SALARY: depends on experience.

FACILITIES/SUPPORT: school tries to help teachers find appropriate accommodation and pays US$100 towards the cost of accommodation. Teachers are assisted with work permits once the school has made the decision to offer a Contract of Employment. Teachers provide passport information, on the basis of which the school issues an invitation to work for the school. This process of issuing the invitation takes 21 days. After 21 days teachers are sent a reference number for their invitation and a copy of the invitation to be taken to the local Russian consulate. Usually the visa is issued within 1 working day.

RECRUITMENT: the school usually recruits teachers by reviewing their CVs, academic background and work experience, as well as having a personal (either phone or in person) interview. Interviews are essential and when possible, they are carried out in the UK because the school has a UK representative. Interviews in the USA always take place by phone. Sometimes existing teachers recommend their friends or ex-colleagues, but the school always reviews applications carefully, paying attention to cover letters to find out what motivates prospective teachers to approach the school and what makes them interested in teaching Russian students.

CONTACT: Marianna Nezhivaya, Recruitment Coordinator.

SUNHILL SCHOOL

Krasnaya Street, 124, 141–500 Moscow Region

☏ +7962 9737271; fax 7495 9941153 (request)

🖱 teachers@sunhillschool.ru;
sunhillschool@gmail.com
or kruglova@sunhillschool.ru

💻 www.sunhillschool.ru/en

NUMBER OF TEACHERS: 4.

PREFERENCE OF NATIONALITY: none.

QUALIFICATIONS: minimum 1 year's experience as a full-time EFL teacher abroad.

CONDITIONS OF EMPLOYMENT: 10-month or 6-month contracts. 24 teaching hours per week plus 2 hours on standby.

SALARY: from US$1,200. 25 days paid holiday per year.

FACILITIES/SUPPORT: accommodation provided by school, close to work.

RECRUITMENT: telephone interview.

CONTACT: Ms Natalia Kruglova, Director.

WINDSOR

Office 7004, 16–1 Olympiysky prospect
129090 Moscow

☏ +495 225 35 07; 495 937 78 48

🖱 job@windsor.ru

💻 www.windsor.ru/eng

NUMBER OF TEACHERS: vacancies almost all year round.

PREFERENCE OF NATIONALITY: Great Britain, Canada, Ireland, USA, Australia, New Zealand.

QUALIFICATIONS: candidates must hold a bachelor's degree or higher and also a certificate in TEFL (Cambridge CELTA, Trinity College London TESOL etc).

CONDITIONS OF EMPLOYMENT: 9 or 12 month contracts.

SALARY: starting salary is US$1250, no deductions.

FACILITIES/SUPPORT: the school provides good quality accommodation and fully assists teachers with obtaining work visas.

RECRUITMENT: Interviews are absolutely essential, usually done by telephone.

CONTACT: Milla Kalinina, Recruitment Manager.

THE BALTICS

Arguably the most Westernised part of the old Russian Empire, the Baltic countries of Lithuania, Latvia and Estonia all became fully-fledged members of the EU on 1 May 2004. This has significantly eased the bureaucracy for EU passport holders, while other citizens will need to apply for a work permit which can take six months. For this reason and due to extra costs, most schools strongly prefer to employ EU citizens. A number of budget airlines as well as national carriers operate to the region (e.g. Ryanair to Kaunas and Riga) and ticket prices can be remarkably low.

Latvia

Of the three Baltic states, Latvia has been slowest to embrace change, although its beautiful capital, Riga, has become a mecca for a certain type of British tourist (at the lager lout end of the spectrum). English is increasingly necessary for anyone working in the hospitality sector, although there are still relatively few commercial language schools and these vary widely in quality. Perhaps because of this shortage, it is quite easy for teachers to pick up private students. There are few TEFL possibilities with state organisations. Qualified ELT teachers should make contact with the Latvian Association of Teachers of English (LATE) in Riga (a/k 1020, Riga LV-1050, Latvia; ✆ fax +371 782 1073; late@acad.latnet.lv; www .late.lv).

Even voluntary opportunities are few and far between. One of the few volunteer and gap year agencies that deals with Latvia is Changing Worlds. **Karen Rich** decided in her 30s to get some TEFL training and do something completely different from her career as airline cabin crew. The country that took her fancy was Latvia, so she made contact with Changing Worlds (www.changingworlds.co.uk), paid the programme fee (currently £2,345 for three months) and ended up enjoying herself enough to extend her three-month stay to a full year, ending in June 2008:

> It's truly been a life-changing year for me. I changed careers, I moved to the small town of Tukums where I'm the only English person and I've travelled to many new and exciting countries including Russia, Lithuania and Estonia. I hadn't expected to have so many students and classes. I had to call a halt at around 50 students and working weeks of 40 hours. I felt so proud that students who had been shy and reserved at the beginning of the year were relaxed and able to chat to me quite openly at the end. However loneliness was a problem. All my colleagues in the school were Latvian and had their own families, so it was difficult to mix with the local people as the culture was different and it's not acceptable for a single woman to sit in a café and drink coffee. I noticed that the people didn't laugh much.

A language school which may be able to offer decent facilities is the Language Centre International House Riga-Satva (A. Kalnina iela 1a-1, LV 1050 Riga; ✆ +371 722 6641; bruce@ihriga.lv; www .ihriga.lv) which can help with visas, flat-finding and teaching support. Occasionally, there are advertisements for TEFL vacancies in Latvia on the internet, usually on TEFL.com or www.ihworld.com.

INTERNATIONAL LANGUAGE SERVICES
Brivibas iela 40–2, Riga LV-1050
✆ +7 240557; fax 7 240560
🖐 info@ilsriga.lv
🖥 www.ilsriga.lv

NUMBER OF TEACHERS: 11.
PREFERENCE OF NATIONALITY: native speaker.
QUALIFICATIONS: minimum CELTA or Trinity Cert.
Experience preferred.

CONDITIONS OF EMPLOYMENT: 10-month or 22-month contracts. 96–120 45-minute lessons per month.
SALARY: approx. US$550–$650 per month after deductions.
FACILITIES/SUPPORT: free flat provided. Travel allowance. All procedures for work permits handled by school.

Regular seminars and teacher development programme leading to LCCIEB Further Certificate in teaching Business English.
RECRUITMENT: internet and TEFL/TESOL press. Telephone interviews.
CONTACT: David Line, Director (david@ilsriga.lv).

Lithuania

There is more scope for teachers in Lithuanian schools, although the three commercial schools listed below all ask for a teaching certificate. The Lithuanian Embassy in Washington distributes a list of programmes including teaching programmes. One of the key organisations is the American Professional Partnership for Lithuanian Education (APPLE), 1114 Golfside Drive, Winter Park, FL 32792 (© 407 671 0189; www.applequest.org). English teachers from the USA are placed in the state system at secondary or tertiary level for an academic year.

Alan Reekie is a Briton who has taught in Lithuania through the Ministry of Education:

Successful applicants receive free accommodation either with a family or in a flat, a Lithuanian teacher's salary and a week's course of lectures on teaching in Vilnius. I am teaching 14–18-year-olds who are fairly eager to learn, though because they only have an examination when they leave at 18, it can be harder to motivate the lower forms. Everyone is friendly which seems to be the case in most of eastern Europe. I would say that the possibility of getting work is very good. An American I have met here found work within a few weeks of arriving here on spec (however he claims to be telepathic so this may have helped).

The teaching hasn't been too hard so far, as the schools accept enthusiasm instead of skill. It also helps when your lessons are only 15 minutes long due to a heating failure. This is quite a good programme for people with no experience of teaching or travelling abroad, as you don't have to worry overly about the logistics, at the same time gaining some experience of dealing with the inevitable problems – like my landlady.

LIST OF EMPLOYERS

AMERICAN ENGLISH SCHOOL
Naugarduko 4, 01141 Vilnius
© +5 279 1011; fax 5 269 1301
egle@ames.lt or vilnius@ames.lt
www.ames.lt

NUMBER OF TEACHERS: 40.
PREFERENCE OF NATIONALITY: none.
QUALIFICATIONS: TEFL Certificate required.
CONDITIONS OF EMPLOYMENT: 5 days per week (mornings and afternoons). Other conditions negotiable. Students are teenagers, adults and corporate clients. private and

public sector.
SALARY: US$9–$12 per contact hour.
FACILITIES/SUPPORT: initial in-house training provided; continuous in-house training and teacher support provided.
RECRUITMENT: demo class to be taught after the interview.
CONTACT: Egle Kesyliene, Director.

EF ENGLISH FIRST
Kosciuskos g.11, 01100 Vilnius
© +5 279 1616/205 1227
vilnius@ef.lt
www.ef.lt

NUMBER OF TEACHERS: approx. 15 (5 native speakers) for several branches.

PREFERENCE OF NATIONALITY: British, Australian, New Zealand or North American.

QUALIFICATIONS: minimum university degree and certificate in TEFL/TESL and preferred teaching experience of 1 year.

CONDITIONS OF EMPLOYMENT: 9–12 month contract (renewable) teaching between 7am and 9pm weekdays. 24 contact hours per week.

SALARY: local equivalent of US$500 a month, plus generous bonuses and annual review.

FACILITIES/SUPPORT: modern facilities, teacher library, computer lab, guidance of an academic counsellor, opportunities for promotion and transfer to other countries. Return flight from London paid. Assistance with finding accommodation. Visas arranged. Paid holidays. Orientation on arrival, ongoing training, local medical insurance and variety of resources provided.

RECRUITMENT: directly to the Director of Studies or via EF English First's Online Recruitment Centre which can be accessed via www.englishfirst.com.

INTERNATIONAL LANGUAGE SERVICES
Lukiskiu g. 5–115, Vilnius 01108
℗ +5 262 5406; fax 5 262 5419
recruitment@ilsvilnius.lt
www.ilsvilnius.lt

NUMBER OF TEACHERS: 10 full-time native speakers plus part-timers in Vilnius, as well as smaller cities such as Kaunas and Klaipeda.

PREFERENCE OF NATIONALITY: native or near-native speakers wanted for full-time positions teaching older teens, adults in school and in companies. EU citizens preferred but the school can assist with work permits for non EU citizens IF candidates have CELTA or Trinity TESOL + 3 years' post certificate experience.

QUALIFICATIONS: minimum CELTA or Trinity Cert. Experience preferred but newly qualified teachers with relevant background experience will find a supportive environment. Other qualifications with practical teaching components will also be considered.

CONDITIONS OF EMPLOYMENT: 9/10-month contracts with paid holidays (or longer/shorter according to demand). Maximum 112 lessons (45 minutes) per month.

SALARY: approx. US$775–840 per month net for full-time teachers depending on experience and responsibilities. Senior salaries according to experience/position.

FACILITIES/SUPPORT: free single flat provided. 23 calendar days paid holiday (per 10 month contract) at Christmas and Easter. Local medical insurance. Flight allowance. Free local travel card. Regular seminars and teacher development programme. Free week-long intensive course leading to the LCCIEB Further Certificate in Teaching Business English. Pan Baltic seminars with sister schools in Riga and Tallinn. Air conditioned premises in the city centre with free wireless internet for teachers.

RECRUITMENT: internet and TEFL/TESOL press. Telephone interviews or face to face in Vilnius. Comprehensive 'Teaching Handbook' available on request. Contacts of previous teachers available on request.

CONTACT: Hannah Shipman, Director.

Estonia

Estonia is arguably the most progressive of the three Baltic countries, and the British Council in Tallinn can send a list headed 'Major Language Schools in Estonia' with about 30 addresses of universities and private language schools. The demand for native speaker teachers is not very high as illustrated by the language institute in Tallinn that communicated in 2008 that they already have plenty of native speaking English teachers in their database with few vacancies.

Some Estonian contacts to try:

Concordia International University: Kaluri Tee 3 & 5, Haabneeme, 74001 Harjumaa; ℗ +60 90077; fax 60 90216; university@university.e).

International House: Pikk 69, 10133 Tallinn; ℗ +64 10 607/64 11 407; ihte@online.ee; www.ihtallinn.ee

Parnu Language School: Malmä 19, Pärnu 80010; 44 31310; fax 44 44002
Vista Education: Linda 4, Narva (3569410)

After her sister had worked in Estonia with a Christian organisation, **Sarah Wadsworth** applied to four schools in Estonia and was offered jobs in three of them. She chose to teach at a specialist music school in the country town of Rapla. She recommends looking in *Opetaja Lent,* the teachers' newsletter, for employment leads in state schools. International House in Tallinn employs about eight ELT instructors.

In order to obtain the right of temporary residence an EU citizen must contact the local government authority nearest to their place of residence within three months from the date of entering Estonia. The right of temporary residence is granted for a period of five years. Within a month, an EU citizen should contact in person a customer service centre of the Citizenship and Migration Board (CMB) to apply for an identity card which certifies their right of temporary residence. European Union citizens do not have to register their short-term employment in Estonia, although they do need to apply for a work permit (which costs about EEK750) if they are staying longer term. Or a residence permit for employment grants an alien the right to stay in Estonia for the purpose of employment. EU teachers can apply in their home country or in Estonia and will need a letter of intent from their employer, ratified by the Labour Market Board. For more information, including a list of state processing fees, browse: www.mig.ee/index.php/mg/eng/.

International Language Services states that non-EU teachers are welcome to apply and that all procedures for work permits are handled by the school.

INTERNATIONAL LANGUAGE SERVICES
Roosikrantsi 8B, 10119 Tallinn
+627 7171; fax 646 4258
info@ils.ee
www.ils.ee

NUMBER OF TEACHERS: 15.
PREFERENCE OF NATIONALITY: native speaker. Non-EU teachers (native speakers) are welcome to apply.
QUALIFICATIONS: minimum CELTA or Trinity Certificate; experience preferred.
CONDITIONS OF EMPLOYMENT: 10-month or 22-month contracts. 96–120 45-minute lessons per month.

SALARY: about €500–€600 per month after deductions, depending on experience and qualifications
FACILITIES/SUPPORT: free flat provided, travel allowance, all procedures for work permits handled by school. Regular seminars and teacher development programme leading to LCCI Further Certificate in Teaching Business English. Sponsorship for the Trinity Dip TESOL by distance for teachers on longer contracts.
RECRUITMENT: internet and TEFL/TESOL press. Phone interviews.
CONTACT: Phil Marsdale, Director (phil@ils.ee).

UKRAINE

The vast republic of the Ukraine's EFL market is still in its infancy, although demand is increasing as citizens realise that they may be able to double their earning power by learning English and open up opportunities for their children by sending them to private tutors. This increase in demand has not been met by an influx of native English teachers, partly because the government appears to have no centralised recruitment policy for foreign teachers and partly because wages can be very low and conditions primitive. Computers and televisions may be in short supply outside the major cities, while books can be out of date and old-school. Students are trying to make the transition from Soviet-style language learning techniques to the more fluid, communicative methods favoured today.

> **TEACHING IN THE UKRAINE CAN BE A VERY REWARDING EXPERIENCE, ESPECIALLY AS ONE OF THE BIGGEST PROBLEMS ENCOUNTERED BY UKRAINIANS STUDYING ENGLISH IS THE LACK OF CONTACT WITH NATIVE SPEAKERS AS SARA COLEMAN DISCOVERED WHEN SHE WENT WITH PROJECTS ABROAD TO TEACH IN THE COUNTRY'S CAPITAL, KIEV:**
>
> *The main concern of Ukrainian English teachers and pupils alike was pronunciation. There are very few exchange programmes for students or teachers and it is almost impossible to receive a visa to visit England even if they could afford it. As I was one of the few English people to have visited the school I was in great demand. I never took over one class for a long time, as they wanted me to go around as many classes as possible, to give everybody the chance to hear a real native speaker!*

Many native teachers in the Ukraine remark upon the enthusiastic reception that they receive from pupils. Many of the younger pupils express an adoration for native teachers which can at first be quite overwhelming and prospective teachers should be prepared for an abundance of invitations to students' homes in order to meet their families. Although this can initially be a little unnerving, most teachers find that the generous hospitality of people so poor is one of the things that makes teaching in the Ukraine such a worthwhile experience. Bell's first partnership with a school in the Ukraine began in 2006 with Chkalovskiye-Bell (Bell Odessa), located in central Odessa. There are 5 more branches in the city and 3 outside Odessa. The centres offer spacious, bright, welcoming premises that are considered to be the best in Odessa. For a list of current vacancies visit http://www.bell-worldwide.com/jobs/list.asp or email recruitment@bell-centres.com.

In addition to the British organisations mentioned at the beginning of this chapter which send volunteers to Ukraine, several emigré organisations in the USA recruit volunteers, warning that teachers must be prepared to accept a modest standard of living. According to **Sara Coleman**, this is no exaggeration:

> *I was fairly shocked by the country's poverty and I had to endure difficult living conditions. I was staying in a small apartment in a tower block in Kiev's suburbs. While my host family were very hospitable and tried to make me as comfortable as possible, the flat would regularly run out of water and conditions were very cramped. The lift regularly broke down and the fact that most of the lights on the stairwell were broken made the long climb to the eighth floor fairly daunting.*

For professional rather than volunteer opportunities, well-qualified candidates can try the British Council in Kiev (4/12 Hryhoriya Skovorody, Kiev 04070; © +44 490 5600; www.britishcouncil.org/ukraine), which has a Teaching Centre and can also supply a list of English language institutes that provide exam preparation (www.britishcouncil.org/ukraine-exams-schools-list.pdf). International House has a strong presence in the country and some of its centres are listed below. Pay is between US$600 and US$800 net, plus a partial accommodation allowance. Most private language institutes will pay in the region of US$10–$15 an hour in Kiev, although specialist or established teachers will earn considerably more.

LIST OF EMPLOYERS

INTERNATIONAL HOUSE – KHARKIV
7 Marshala Bazhanova St. Kharkiv 61002
© +57 760 1060; fax 57 714 1109
ih@ih.kharkiv.com
www.ih.kharkiv.com

NUMBER OF TEACHERS: 5–7.
PREFERENCE OF NATIONALITY: no.
QUALIFICATIONS: CELTA, IH Certificate, Trinity TESOL or SIT TESOL plus 1 year post-certificate experience.

CONDITIONS OF EMPLOYMENT: at least one academic year, 24 hours per week.

SALARY: US$600–800 after deductions.

FACILITIES/SUPPORT: the school helps find accommodation and pays an allowance to cover 70–100% depending on the accommodation standard and obtains a work permit before the arrival of a candidate, who is then to present it to the Ukrainian Consulate to be issued an employment visa.

RECRUITMENT: International House recruitment service. Interviews can be conducted by International House World Organization in London; sometimes the school interviews candidates on the phone.

CONTACT: Igor Manko, Director.

INTERNATIONAL HOUSE (IH) – KYIV

7 Vandy Vasilevskoy str, 03055 Kyiv

+44 238 98 70; fax 44 236 22 64

dos@ih.kiev.ua or info@ih.kiev.ua

www.ih.kiev.ua/en/vacancies.htm

NUMBER OF TEACHERS: 27–30.

PREFERENCE OF NATIONALITY: native speaker.

QUALIFICATIONS: minimum TEFL/CELTA Cert.

CONDITIONS OF EMPLOYMENT: one year contracts. Teach up to 25 hours per week.

SALARY: US$800–$1,000 depending on experience.

FACILITIES/SUPPORT: the school provides the teacher with a single room or shared apartment.

RECRUITMENT: through IH London or locally.

CONTACT: Tetyana Tereshchenko, Director of Studies.

INTERNATIONAL HOUSE – LVIV

109 Zelena Street, 79035 Lviv

+/Fax 32 260 12 68

ihlviv@g-mail.com

NUMBER OF TEACHERS: up to 16.

PREFERENCE OF NATIONALITY: none, but should be native speakers of English.

QUALIFICATIONS: CELTA/TESOL/Trinity certificate.

CONDITIONS OF EMPLOYMENT: 10 months plus 3 weeks paid holidays. 24 teaching hours per week plus one meeting/seminar.

SALARY: from 4,900 hryvnias depending on experience.

FACILITIES/SUPPORT: US$400 of return ticket covered by the school. Furnished accommodation is provided for up to US$200.

RECRUITMENT: locally, via the internet and through IHWO recruitment services.

CONTACT: Marianna Ilyina, Director.

INTERNATIONAL HOUSE – ODESSA

15 Govorova Street, 65063 Odessa

fax +482 429702

tasinip@yahoo.com

NUMBER OF TEACHERS: 11 (mixture of native speaker and local).

PREFERENCE OF NATIONALITY: none, but should be native speaker.

QUALIFICATIONS: CELTA or Trinity Cert.

CONDITIONS OF EMPLOYMENT: 12 months including 4 weeks holiday.

SALARY: US$400 approx.

FACILITIES/SUPPORT: return flight London–Odessa–London provided. Accommodation in flats provided.

RECRUITMENT: through Human Resources at IH London/via the internet.

CONTACT: Tatyana Sinipolskaya, Director.

MONARCH INTERNATIONAL LANGUAGE ACADEMY (ILA)

45 Tolbukhina Str, 03190 Kyiv

+44 451 7839; fax 44 443 3932

monarch@i.kiev.ua

www.monarchila.kiev.ua

NUMBER OF TEACHERS: 4–8.

PREFERENCE OF NATIONALITY: British/American.

QUALIFICATIONS: bachelor's or master's degree in Humanities and valid TEFL qualification. Minimum 2 years' experience teaching English. Business English would be a plus.

CONDITIONS OF EMPLOYMENT: 10 months September to June with 3-week break from Christmas day. 28–40 academic hours per week.

SALARY: approx. US$900–$1,200 per month after tax.

FACILITIES/SUPPORT: help given with finding suitable flat. Help given with visa and school arranges work permit documents.

RECRUITMENT: internet, newspaper advertisements, word of mouth, through other ILA schools worldwide. Internet and telephone interviews possible.

CONTACT: Oksana Yurynts, Managing Director (mila_md @i.kiev.ua).

CENTRAL ASIA

With ever increasing frequency, the former Soviet republics are taking on their own national and regional identities due to geographic, cultural and economic factors. The number of treaty organisations that have emerged since the 'civilised divorce' of the former Soviet Union took place in 1991 is near mind boggling. Whereas the Baltic States (Estonia, Lithuania and Latvia) desire few if any ties with Russia, other former Soviet Republics especially those in North Central Asia (Kazakhstan, Kyrgyzstan, Tajikistan, Turkmenistan and Uzbekistan) have joined with Russia (and China) to form a number of economic and security-related treaty organisations. In between these two extremes are the eastern European states (Belarus, Moldova and the Ukraine) and Caucasian states (Armenia, Azerbaijan and Georgia) which drift from one side to the other depending upon the nature of the area of cooperation. Prospective EFL teachers seeking to find employment in any of these countries or areas (exception being the Baltic states) would do well to investigate the prevailing influences affecting the particular country(ies) or area(s) in which they are interested at the time of their job search.

Though a decision concerning where to look for work will most likely depend on a number of variables, prospective EFL teachers looking for teaching jobs in the former Soviet republics should give some thought as to whether they will be able to tolerate different attitudes to human rights, religious freedoms, etc. On the question of the religious flavour, not to say fervour, of the republic in question, as a general rule, the former Western republics are mostly Eastern Orthodox Christian and the southern Central Asian republics are Sunni Islamic, so there are noticeable differences between levels of tolerance in matters of sexual freedom, alcohol, dietary habits and even smoking.

Once an informed decision has been made to look for work in a former Soviet republic, the most obvious question is where to start. A search on the internet will yield few results. Though most TEFL job sites include these countries in their indexes, teachers will be disappointed to find few if any entries for many of the countries designated as former Soviet republics. Using search engines to turn up prospective TEFL work will likewise be disappointing. Compounding these difficulties is the fact that many established schools operating in the various countries of the former Soviet republics either don't have websites or are simply not found in search engines. That said, a number of universities will be listed who do employ at various times native English speaking teachers. Given the university nature of these jobs, they will no doubt be in either high demand or have teacher requirements above those held by the usual TEFL teacher. Unfortunately as attested to by internet experience, English teaching is still delivered by the state; for example the list of English language institutions sent by the British Council in the Uzbek capital Tashkent comprises only state universities and pedagogical institutes (ie teacher training colleges). For those interested in pursuing such employment, the British Council in Kazakhstan can send a long list of institutes which are likely to offer English language courses and therefore might be interested in employing part-time or full-time teachers of English. Most are state-owned but there are a growing number of private ones. University faculties often have their own international relations office which may have up to three vacancies for highly educated language assistants; try for example Pavlodar University (Gorky Str. 102/4, 637003 Pavlodar; ✆ +3182 454311; fax 3182 326797).

Another source of TEFL employment can be the non-governmental organisations (NGOs) operating in a number of former Soviet republic countries. In response to the increase in demand for English, the Peace Corps has sent a substantial number of volunteer English teachers to Kazakhstan in recent years. Much of this demand has been spurred by the influx of businesses connected with the Caspian oil industry, which has particularly affected Kazakhstan, Uzbekistan, Turkmenistan and Azerbaijan. Opportunities with international companies exist for professional ELT teachers where the salaries are on a par with those of the oil-rich states of the Middle East. The London-based recruitment company Education and Training International (www.educatrain.ge) advertises for staff to join teams in Georgia and Azerbaijan to teach oil company employees, NGO staff and others. Contact Education & Training International which has teaching centres throughout the region (123 Bond St, London W1 or 10 J. Nikoladze St, 100900 Tbilisi, Georgia; ✆ +32 250945; fax 32 291735).

A Georgian language school that hosts intensive English summer courses for which it recruits native speaking teachers is the Caucasus Academic Centre (16 A. Kazbegi Ave, 0160 Tbilisi, Georgia; ✆ +995 32 25 17 30, 38 76 76; www.cac.edu.ge/eng). Teachers are also recruited by IH in Georgia (2 26th May Square, 380015 Tbilisi; ✆ +/fax 32 940515; director@ihtbilisi.ge).

For further possible vacancies, check out www.educatrain.ge/jobs.php where ETI often need teachers for their operations in Baku and Tbilisi, both affiliated to ETI London and catering to both the public and corporate sectors. ETI Tbilisi employs over 20 teachers both Georgian and expatriate, plus support staff, with teaching vacancies for part-time native English speakers among others (applications to Lika Sadunashvili, eti_sales@caucasus.net). In Baku the contact is Nigar Namazova at manager@eti.in-baku.com.

Richard McGeough, a 28 year old teacher from Britain, describes his stint working in the capital of Azerbaijan:

> *My primary motivation for coming to Baku was the salary my post offered, which was £15,000 a year. The students are highly motivated, well-educated and almost embarrassingly hospitable and generous. I'm working in newly modernised premises now, but until recently we had to contend with alternately unheated and unventilated classrooms and regular power cuts in winter. Baku can be too quiet sometimes, although an acquaintance of mine who lived in Ashkhabad, Turkmenistan for two years says that Baku is like Paris compared to there. What Baku lacks in beauty it makes up for in interest. The centre of Baku – the Oil Town and the Old Town – is rustic and charming, and not at all what I'd expected of the old USSR. Having lived in Istanbul before, historical Baku was like a return to the 1950s before ugly modern apartment buildings were put up.*

Chain schools such as Language Link and International House can also provide sources of TEFL employment. In recent months, Language Link has opened teaching centres in Astana, Kazakhstan and Tashkent, Uzbekistan and looks to continue opening centres as long as the petro dollars continue to flow. In Astana, Language Link trades under the name Incom Lingva and is located at Sary Arka Street 6 (✆ +7 7172 99 11 11; jobs@languagelink.ru). In Tashkent, Language Link can be contacted at Language Link, Room 303, Markaziy Hotel, 15 Amir Temur, Tashkent 100000, Uzbekistan (✆ +998 71 138 30 05; jobs@languagelink.ru).

Both International House and the Soros Foundation have also been active in opening up the region to English language learners. The beguilingly named Soft & Safe Co Ltd in Armenia (41 Abovyan St, Yerevan 0009; ✆ +10 2-526364; www.spyur.am/softsafe.htm) might have occasional vacancies.

Belarus is another republic with various language teaching opportunities for example at International House Minsk (Room 306, Gykalo 9, 220071 Minsk; ✆ +172 32 47 12) and SOL Minsk school affiliated to the reputable voluntary organisation SOL described at the beginning of this chapter. Two Soros institutes which might have openings for people with an MA in TESOL are the English Language School, 120 Kievskaya St, 72001 Bishkek, Kyrgyz Republic (℗ +312 212946) and the International Language Training Center, 13 Amreasca St, Chisinau 2012, Moldova (2–541994; vgalii@cepd.soros.md). Another US-oriented school in Chisinau is the American Language Center, 37B Tricolorului St, Chisinau 2012 (℗ +22 225860; fax 22–211253; alc@americancouncils.md) though they tend to hire only local staff. Few foreigners would be able to survive on the monthly stipend is of US$175.

IF SALARY IS NOT A MOTIVATING FACTOR IN YOUR SEARCH FOR TEFL EMPLOYMENT IN A FORMER SOVIET REPUBLIC, THEN JOE SCARANGELLA, EMPLOYED BY THE LONDON SCHOOL IN THE KYRGYZ REPUBLIC, POINTS OUT THAT THERE ARE OTHER BENEFITS TO BE HAD:

For those interested in teaching in Kyrgyzstan, money will certainly NOT be a motivation. The vast majority, dare I say all of the work is located in the capital, Bishkek. With prices equivalent to those in Eastern Europe, it's difficult to save anything on a salary of US$500. But who cares?! With a landscape similar to Switzerland and a genuine hospitality extended by nearly everyone you meet, there is much more here than just money. Trips to the mountains are always breathtaking. And Bishkek has a unique multicultural population making people watching a national sport. Bishkek does wear the scars of its communist era. The architecture is drab and gray. The standard of living is lower than that of some of the other 'Stans'. Power cuts are frequent and hot water is unreliable. But things are on the rise. An increasing number of people have disposable income. This means that shopping, clubbing and general merriment are not just pipe dreams any more. People can now afford English lessons. All students (even the young ones) are highly motivated and remarkably knowledgeable about the world and current events. This makes things like in-class activities and conversation clubs almost a pleasurable experience.

In searching for a job, perhaps the best advice might be to limit your search to a couple of countries and thereafter do your research. A thorough understanding of the country, its culture and its regard for foreigners is absolutely essential. And be sure to check out the legality of any employment that you are thinking to engage in. As William Kinsey found out while working in Almaty, things are not always what they seem. '*Our school was raided by the police who demanded our visas and claimed 'incorrect' registration. Our boss/owner was useless and two of my fellow teachers were brought to the police station and had their apartment raided. Further the boss asked us to lie on his behalf and say that we are not paid rather we are only English consultants not accepting salary. I can only speculate but I surmise it creates a tax escape for him.*' Given this, teachers are well advised to check with consulates rather than potential employers as to how legal working status is obtained. As laws change often, employers may not be lying to potential teachers, they may simply be out-of-date in their current thinking.

LIST OF EMPLOYERS

EF ENGLISH FIRST

82 Sh. Mehdiyev Street, Baku 370141, Azerbaijan

info.baku@englishfirst.com

www.englishfirst.az/baku/index.htm

NUMBER OF TEACHERS: 2.

PREFERENCE OF NATIONALITY: UK, North America, Australia, New Zealand.

QUALIFICATIONS: EFL/ESL Cert.

CONDITIONS OF EMPLOYMENT: 11 month contracts from September. Schools open from 9am–9pm Monday to Saturday. 24 contact hours per week. Mainly adults students.

SALARY: US$900 per month.

FACILITIES/SUPPORT: modern facilities, teacher library, computer laboratory, guidance and support of academic coordinator, flights paid on completion of contract, paid holiday, orientation and ongoing seminars and development. Assistance given with finding flat (not shared). Medical insurance and visa provided.

RECRUITMENT: applications through English First (EF) teacher recruitment in offices worldwide.

INTERNATIONAL HOUSE – ALMATY

InterPress, International House, 46 Mynbayev str, Almaty 050057, Kazakhstan

+727 258 25 11/ 727 258 48 41;
fax 727 258 24 81

recruitment@ih-almaty.com

www.ih-almaty.com

www.ih.kz.

NUMBER OF TEACHERS: about 25.

PREFERENCE OF NATIONALITY: UK, the USA, Ireland, Canada, Australia.

QUALIFICATIONS: Cambridge CELTA, IHC, Trinity TESOL, MA in TESOL and at least 1 year of teaching experience. YL qualification and experience in teaching exam preparation will be an advantage.

CONDITIONS OF EMPLOYMENT: 9 or 12 month contract. 1 contract type: 1080 academic hours of teaching per 9-month contract (about 120 ac.hours or 100 real hours monthly) 2 contract type: 1296 academic hours of teaching per 9-month contract (about 144 ac.hours or 108 real hours monthly).

SALARY: US$ 700–$1200 net, depending on qualifications, experience and contract type. Bonus paid on completion of contract. Paid holidays.

FACILITIES/SUPPORT: free shared accommodation, all bills paid by the school (excluding long distance telephone calls, cable TV and internet) or accommodation reimbursement. Airfare allowance. The school assists and covers the costs of a work permit. For this a degree in humanities is needed (a notarised copy) and a letter from a former employer confirming at least 1 year of teaching experience (original on headed paper).

RECRUITMENT: through IHWO (www.ihworld.com) and recruitment services, www.tefl.com. Phone interviews essential.

CONTACT: Elena Vodolagina, Recruitment Manager.

LANGUAGE LINK KAZAKHSTAN

Sary Arka Street 6, Arman Business centre, 010000 Astana, the Republic of Kazakhstan

+7172 99 11 11; fax: 7172 99 00 99

jobs@languagelink.ru

www.jobs.languagelink.ru

NUMBER OF TEACHERS: 8.

PREFERENCE OF NATIONALITY: British, American, Canadian, Australian, New Zealander and South African.

QUALIFICATIONS: CELTA or Trinity Certificate/Diploma (or equivalents) required. Candidates without a recognised qualification may enter Language Link's Teacher Internship Training Programme.

CONDITIONS OF EMPLOYMENT: 6 and 9 month contracts. 25 teaching hours per week, normally 4 hours a day, 5 days a week. Adult classes, children's classes and in-company.

SALARY: US$800–$1,000 (net) depending on location and experience. Return airfare (maximum US$800 to America, or £300 to the UK). 4 weeks of paid holiday and health cover (for teachers on 9-month contracts).

FACILITIES/SUPPORT: all teachers provided with free accommodation in 2-room flat (for 2 teachers). Paid medical services and full visa/work permission support. Academic support via on-site Director of Studies, inset training, seminars and presentations.

RECRUITMENT: Application is online. Minimum 2 professional references. Telephone interviews are compulsory.

CONTACT: Robert Jensky, Director.

LANGUAGE LINK UZBEKISTAN

Language Link, Room 303, Markaziy Hotel,
15 Amir Temur, Tashkent 100000, Uzbekistan
+/fax: 998 71 138 30 05
info@languagelink.uz
www.languagelink.uz

NUMBER OF TEACHERS: 4

PREFERENCE OF NATIONALITY: British, American, Canadian, Australian, New Zealander and South African.

QUALIFICATIONS: CELTA or Trinity Certificate/Diploma (or equivalents) required. Candidates without a recognised qualification may enter Language Link's Teacher Internship Training Programme.

CONDITIONS OF EMPLOYMENT: 9 or 12 month contracts. 25 teaching hours per week, usually 4 hours a day, 5 days a week. Adult classes, children's classes and in-company.

SALARY: US$800–$1,000 (net) depending on experience. Return airfare (maximum US$1,000). 4 weeks of paid holiday and health cover (for teachers on 9-month contracts).

FACILITIES/SUPPORT: all teachers provided with assistance to find suitable accommodation; full visa/work permission support, paid medical services. Academic support via on-site director of studies, inset training, seminars and presentations.

RECRUITMENT: Application is online (www.jobs.languagelink.ru). Minimum 2 professional references. Telephone interviews are compulsory.

CONTACT: Robert Jensky.

LONDON SCHOOL IN BISHKEK

Sovetskaya 39, 720005 Bishkek, Kyrgyz Republic
+312 54 44 74/54 21 92/54 54 30
ls@tlsbi.com or ls@elcat.kg
www.tlsbi.com/Tefl.htm

NUMBER OF TEACHERS: 8.

PREFERENCE OF NATIONALITY: American or British native speakers.

QUALIFICATIONS: CELTA and at least one year's teaching experience.

CONDITIONS OF EMPLOYMENT: minimum 10 months starting all year round. 22 hours per week, 5 hours per day, 4 days a week plus 1-hour interview with new students four times a month.

SALARY: US$400 a month plus extra US$100 a month to reimburse airfare.

FACILITIES/SUPPORT: free one-bedroom flat provided plus all accommodation expenses. Help given with work permits for which teachers must have CELTA certificate and two references from previous teaching jobs.

RECRUITMENT: via www.tefl.com. Teachers hired on basis of CV and references.

CONTACT: Kendje Aitikeeva, Director.

SLOVAK REPUBLIC

The republic of the Slovaks has been somewhat neglected not only by tourists but by teachers as well. As one language school director put it:

> *Many teachers are heading for Prague, which is why Slovakia stands aside of the main flow of the teachers. That's a pity as Prague is crowded with British and Americans while there's a lack of the teachers here in Slovakia.*

Another wrote from a small Slovakian town, '*It would be wonderful if through your book more native speakers come to Slovakia.*' The density of private language schools in the capital Bratislava and in the other main cities like Banska Bystrika makes an on-the-ground job hunt promising.

Language Link (21 Harrington Road, London SW7 3EU; 020 7225 1065; recruitment@languagelink.co.uk) is affiliated with the Akadémia Vzdelávania, the largest semi-private language school in Slovakia (see entry), and actively recruits ELT teachers from the UK. IH Bratislava, formerly a branch of the Caledonian School, Czech Republic, (Námestie SNP 14 811 06 Bratislava; ✆ +2 52 96 26 75; jurbanova@ihbratislava.sk; www.caledonianschool.sk) is one of the largest private language schools in the Slovak Republic with over 60 teachers based in Bratislava and other towns around the Slovak Republic. They are looking for teachers with a TEFL certificate such as CELTA, Trinity cert. TESOL, IHC etc. Teaching experience and business work experience are an advantage, but not essential.

There is a substantial demand for native English teachers, although the wages are fairly low so many teachers tend to take on private students and/or economise. The average monthly salary in Slovakia is about 20,000 koruna, but local teachers only receive 8,000 as a starting salary, rising to perhaps 25,000 when they retire. Native English teachers may command a higher starting wage of 12,000, certainly in the private sector. Otherwise, they will need to head to the poorer regions in the south or east where living costs are significantly lower.

Dana Piffkova, a young Slovak, explains that it is very important to speak English if you want to secure a good job. She works for an international company where all communication and paperwork is in English. She thinks that knowing English is more important now than it was four years ago, and that although Slovaks are taught English twice a week at high school from the first grade onwards, university language courses are 'rare or very short.' Dana took extra tuition from a local English teacher to help her become fluent (although she'll insist that she isn't). In-company training is also in demand, as attested by the success of International House, which caters to the business market.

University students often leave Slovakia to work abroad during the summer (mostly in English speaking countries). Although students can learn English by immersion, many will wish to be reasonably fluent so they can land a decent job in the first place.

It always used to be a level playing field for English-speaking foreigners wanting to teach in Slovakia, but now EU citizens have a clear advantage, needing only to confirm residency for tax purposes. For candidates from outside the EU, the Slovak visa process is expensive and time-consuming. The main costs are getting a criminal record check from the teacher's home country (cost varies) and the fee in Slovakia (about €170).

Documents may need to be officially translated, and the applicant may need to submit a medical certificate, evidence of accommodation and so on. A blood test must be carried out within a couple of weeks of arriving as a pre-requisite for a residence permit. Most employers guide their teachers through the process but not many will cover the cost.

As well as the British Council at Panska 17 in Bratislava, there are two other British Council offices in Banska Bystrica and Kosice. The main English language newspaper is the Slovak Spectator published every other Thursday. Occasionally the classified column carries an advertisement of interest to people looking for teaching work. You might also consider advertising your availability to give private tuition (www.slovakspectator.sk).

Although wages can be low, prices are not high: an average restaurant meal costs 130 koruna (£3.40), and a loaf of bread between 30 koruna and 50 koruna. Accommodation in Bratislava is about 4,000 korunas a month, but if you go east this drops significantly – to 2,000 korunas in central Slovakia.

Budapest, Vienna and Prague are all within easy reach. Slovakia also offers good conditions for mountain walking along thousands of miles of hiking routes (up to an altitude of 2,500m) and for mountain cycling.

STEPHEN MILLS FROM ENGLAND WAS VERY POSITIVE ABOUT HIS TEACHING EXPERIENCES IN SLOVAKIA:

I am currently employed as the native speaker at Ivega Learning Center in Kosice. I was told about the job by a friend who was working here at the time. I have quite a few private pupils and there is never a lack of people wanting to learn English here. As my mornings are free, there is always plenty of time. I charge up to 200 koruna an hour. The school has a friendly atmosphere and I get on really well with the Slovak teachers. The owner has been incredibly helpful and efficient with the various bureaucratic procedures and very supportive when I had medical problems.

LIST OF EMPLOYERS

ACADEMIA ISTROPOLITANA NOVA
Prostredna 47/A, 900–21 Svaty Jur
+2 4497 0449 453; fax 2 4497 0455
erikas@ainova.sk
www.ainova.sk

NUMBER OF TEACHERS: 6.
PREFERENCE OF NATIONALITY: UK citizens.
QUALIFICATIONS: university graduates preferably with pedagogical degree or holders of CELTA, TEFL or other internationally recognised certificate.
CONDITIONS OF EMPLOYMENT: 1-year contract. 80 teaching hours per month.
SALARY: by agreement.
FACILITIES/SUPPORT: assistance given in finding accommodation but teachers pay rent.
RECRUITMENT: personal recommendation and ELT training centres. Phone interviews possible.

AKADEMIA VZDELAVANIA – ACADEMY OF EDUCATION
Gorkého 10, 81517 Bratislava
+/fax 2 544 100 40
sflint@aveducation.sk
www.aveducation.sk

NUMBER OF TEACHERS: approximately 30 posts in branches throughout Slovakia.
PREFERENCE OF NATIONALITY: native speaker holding an EU passport.
QUALIFICATIONS: CELTA or TESOL qualification (or recognised equivalent) and degree. Energy, enthusiasm and an interest in people required.
CONDITIONS OF EMPLOYMENT: 1 academic year. Teachers' contracts are for a maximum of 22.5 contact hours per week.
SALARY: new teacher without experience in Country, 12,000Sk (term1) 13,000Sk (terms 2&3); new teacher without experience in Bratislava, 13,000Sk (term1) 14,000Sk (terms 2&3); new teacher with minimum 1 year experience in country, 13,700Sk (all terms); new teacher with minimum 1 year experience in Bratislava, 14,700Sk (all terms).
FACILITIES/SUPPORT: paid accommodation provided in shared flats. Work and residency permits organised and paid for. Academic and pastoral support, monthly staff development days including seminars and workshops; orientation for new teachers.
RECRUITMENT: via e-mail: sflint@aveducation.sk.
CONTACT: Simon Flint, Assistant Director of Studies.

EUROTREND 21
Namestie slobody 16, 81332 Bratislava
+2 2562 6394/5262 6395/fax 2 5294 4350
info@eurotrend21.sk
www.eurotrend21.sk

NUMBER OF TEACHERS: 4.
PREFERENCE OF NATIONALITY: none.
QUALIFICATIONS: minimum university degree, TEFL certificate and experience.
CONDITIONS OF EMPLOYMENT: minimum contract 6 months. Hours available mornings, afternoons and evenings.
SALARY: dependent on experience. Starts at 250 koruna per 45 minute lesson.

RECRUITMENT: Interviews are essential and are carried out on site.

CONTACT: Magda Nagyova, Director.

IVEGA LEARNING CENTRE
Moldavska 8, 04011 Kosice

📞 +55 642 7864 or mobile: 905 212 417

✉ gtroskoo@orangemail.sk

🖥 www.ivega.sk

NUMBER OF TEACHERS: 2.

PREFERENCE OF NATIONALITY: none.

QUALIFICATIONS: min. TEFL/TESL certificate plus teaching experience.

CONDITIONS OF EMPLOYMENT: 1 academic year. Approx. 20 hours of teaching per week.

SALARY: approx. 20,000 koruna gross salary.

FACILITIES/SUPPORT: the school takes care of all necessary arrangements for residence and work permits and will assist teachers to find accommodation. Work permits not necessary for EU citizens.

RECRUITMENT: applicants should send CVs and letters of reference by mail. Short-listed candidates will be invited to interview, although interviews are not essential.

CONTACT: Gabriela Troskoova, headmaster and owner.

JAZYKOVÁ SKOLA START
Kriva 18, 040–01 Kosice

📞 421 915 846 728

✉ recruitment@jazykova.sk

🖥 www.jazykova.sk/jobs.php

NUMBER OF TEACHERS: 6.

PREFERENCE OF NATIONALITY: Traditional native-speaker countries, such as UK, USA, Australia etc.

QUALIFICATIONS: TEFL or previous experience is an advantage. Apart from being a native speaker, the only condition a candidate absolutely must fulfil is they must have a university degree (in any subject).

CONDITIONS OF EMPLOYMENT: one academic year. Extendable to a permanent contract. Usual hours are 3pm–8pm with some morning lessons.

SALARY: by negotiation. About €800 per month in term time, or €500 per month out of term. Luncheon vouchers provided.

FACILITIES/SUPPORT: school finds accommodation for teachers. School assists logistically but not financially with visas (e.g. €170).

RECRUITMENT: via the internet. Also, a number of teachers come to Slovakia because they are in a relationship with a local and their partners make the initial contact in response to advertising. Interviews are carried out by phone or Skype. In the case of teachers already in Slovakia they are carried out in person.

CONTACT: Richard Swales, Director.

S-CLUB
Vojenska 30, 934–01 Levice

📞 +36 631 3224; fax 36 633 2170

✉ info@sclub.sk

🖥 www.sclub.sk

NUMBER OF TEACHERS: 8 including one native speaker.

PREFERENCE OF NATIONALITY: British, Irish.

QUALIFICATIONS: TEFL/TESOL and some experience.

CONDITIONS OF EMPLOYMENT: academic year (September to the end of June). 25 teaching units of 45 minutes per week in the afternoons.

SALARY: SKK 140 (net) per lesson.

FACILITIES/SUPPORT: a furnished flat is provided free by the school. No special permits needed for EU citizens.

RECRUITMENT: via the internet. First contact by e-mail. Telephone interviews.

MIDDLE EAST

Oil wealth has meant that many of the countries of the Middle East have long been able to afford to attract the best teachers with superior qualifications and extensive experience. Most employers can afford to hire only professionals and there are few opportunities for newcomers to the profession.

The main exception is Turkey where thousands of native English speaker teachers can find work. Despite its adherence to Islam, Turkey does not fit comfortably into a chapter on the Middle East, and despite its aspirations to join the European Union (EU) and its secular government, neither does it fit logically into a section on western Europe. But whatever its geographical classification, Turkey is a very important country for EFL teachers, whatever their background, and so it's covered at length later in this chapter.

On the one hand, the wealthy countries of Saudi Arabia, Bahrain, Oman and the Gulf states generally employ teachers with top qualifications. On the other hand, countries such as Syria and Jordan may have more casual opportunities. Anyone interested in teaching English to the Palestinians scattered throughout the Arab world is likely to be working on a voluntary basis or for accommodation and a local stipend, rather than for expatriate salaries.

Despite the much publicised hostility to the West in the region, the demand for English has certainly not disappeared. In the aftermath of the infamy perpetrated on the USA in September 2001 and with the continuing enmity between Israelis and Palestinians, the taste for travel and employment in the Middle East has been quelled and some prospective teachers, especially from North America, have been put off by a perceived fear for their personal security. But panicky reactions may be out of place. Perhaps English language teachers can play a small part in diminishing the distrust and tension between the two cultures, bringing people together, allowing individuals on both sides to gain some understanding of the complexity of the world's problems.

SOME COUNTRIES ARE STILL OFF-BOUNDS, NAMELY IRAQ, BUT AS JOE HANCOCK FROM NORTH WALES REPORTED FROM THE TOWN OF BOJNURD IN NORTH-EASTERN IRAN, THERE IS AN UNTAPPED DEMAND FOR ENGLISH IN IRAN, WHICH IS FULL OF 'FRIENDLY, HELPFUL AND RESPECTFUL PEOPLE':

I called in at the local English school to ask if I could assist with conversational English and was immediately asked if I could take a 40-hour English course starting tomorrow. After that they wondered if I could go to Tehran to teach, as they require five expat teachers there. Qualifications were mentioned but not dwelt on. I couldn't accept since my work permit is with the petrochemical company I work for. As a courtesy I asked my employer if I could teach in my spare time (four hours a week) but they forbade it saying that once the school advertised that they had an English native teacher, they would have queues around the block.

Teachers who sign contracts in a strict Islamic country should be aware of extreme differences in culture. People usually spend a year or two teaching in Saudi Arabia to make some money, rather than because they enjoy the lifestyle (unless they are students of Arab culture). When the amount of money accumulating back home is the principal or only motivation, morale can degenerate. The situation can be especially discouraging for women.

Yet not everyone is gasping to get home (or even to Bahrain) to freely available alcohol, etc. A high percentage of teachers are recruited locally from a stable expatriate community, although at least one director is getting rather tired of seeing 'the same old faces'. Demand for native English speaking teachers is increasing in Saudi Arabia, mainly due to the opening of new colleges and universities, both in the public and private sector.

Middle Eastern language schools are also more likely to recruit non-native English speakers, specifically well-heeled teachers with pristine qualifications. Ahad Shahbaz. Director of Interlink Language Center, asks: 'if a non-native speaker is highly educated, has earned his credentials from the Harvards of ESL teacher training institutions, and has near-native and at times superior proficiency and eloquence in the language, should we not be hiring him or her?'

FINDING A JOB

Unless you are more or less resident in the Middle East, it is essential in most cases to fix up a job in advance. Casual teaching is not a possibility in most countries for a number of reasons, including the difficulty of getting tourist visas, the prohibitively high cost of staying without working and the whole tradition of hiring teachers. A few countries can be entered on a tourist visa (ie Qatar, Yemen and the United Arab Emirates) if you want to inspect potential employers, but this would be an expensive exercise. Visa difficulties vary from country to country. In Jordan, for example, schools which would like to hire foreign teachers are often put off by the cost of securing a work permit ($500 straight to the government and $150 in lawyers fees). The American ESL Center, based in Jordan, (see list of employers) employs foreigners as native English speakers.

Single women, no matter how highly qualified, are at a serious disadvantage when pursuing high-paying jobs in Saudi Arabia and other strict Islamic countries. The majority of adverts specify 'single status male' or, at best, 'teaching couples'. Another requirement often mentioned in job details which excludes many candidates is experience of the Middle East, in acknowledgment of the culture shock which many foreigners encounter in this region of the world.

Job advertisements regularly appear on websites such as www.tefl.com, in the educational press and in journals such as the *International Employment Gazette*. The largest display advertisements in the British education press are quite often for Middle East vacancies, many placed by recruitment agencies on behalf of high-spending Saudi clients. It is always worth checking regional newspapers as well. For example both the *Gulf News* (www.gulfnews.com/Classifieds) and the *Khaleej Times* (www.khaleejtimes.co.ae) are published online and sometimes include teaching vacancies in the Emirates (for subscribers only).

The British Council has teaching centres in Bahrain (Manama), Lebanon (Beirut), Oman (Muscat), Qatar (Doha), Saudi Arabia (Riyadh, Jeddah and Dammam), Damascus in Syria and the United Arab Emirates (Abu Dhabi and Dubai). ELS Language Centers/Middle East has 12 centres in the region including Hawally (Kuwait), Muscat, Salalah and Sohar (Oman), Jeddah, Riyadh and Dammam (Saudi Arabia), Dubai, Abu Dhabi, Al Ain and Fujairah (UAE) and Doha (Qatar). These centres employ 30 full-time staff plus many part-time (see entry). Possible leads may be available from Amideast, 1730 M St NW, No 1100, Washington, DC 20036 (© 202 776 9600; fax 202 776 7090; inquiries@amide-ast.org; www.amideast.org) which recruits for international schools in the region. Bell Amman is a newly-established language training centre in Jordan opening in January 2009. The Centre is jointly managed by Luminus Group and Bell. The centre is committed to provide academic excellence, and the highest standards of management and staff development. Bell Amman provides quality language programmes in English Language Teaching, Business and Technical English Language Skills for Adults and Young Learners. For further information on teaching opportunities visit www.bell-world-wide.com/jobs or email recruitment@bell-centres.com.

There are also American language centres in Amman, Damascus and Sana'a. International House (www.ihworld.com/directory/schools.asp) has four schools in Saudi Arabia (Dharan, Medina, Al Jouf, Jeddah), one in Dubai, one in Iran, one in Lebanon and one in Oman. It is worth writing to the embassies (particularly of Saudi Arabia and Oman), which occasionally recruit directly on behalf of their ministries of education or defence. The Saudi Embassy in London (30 Charles St, London W1J 5DZ; ✆ 0 20 7917 3000) occasionally advertises for teachers with high academic qualifications, as does the Saudi Arabian Defence Office (22 Holland Park, London W11 3TD).

If trying to fix up employment directly with a company in the Middle East, try to be sure that you have a water-tight contract. Predictably, there is not a great deal of input by the voluntary agencies. However, the Peace Corps sends a number of English teachers to rural secondary and primary schools in Jordan to participate in a team teaching project.

RECRUITMENT AGENCIES

In theory, being hired by an established recruitment agency in your own country should offer some protection against exploitation. However, this is not always the case. A couple of years ago an educational consultancy with an office in Toronto recruited a large number of EFL teachers to work for the United Arab Emirates military. When a dispute arose between client and recruiter, the teachers were the ones to suffer since they weren't paid promised salaries and their contracts were not honoured.

LEISURE TIME

The majority of teachers live in foreigners' compounds provided by their employers. Most of these are well provided with sports facilities such as tennis courts and swimming pools. In some locations, such as Jubail in Saudi Arabia, water sports are a popular diversion. Some have described expat life in the Middle East as a false paradise.

The principal pastimes are barbecues, reading out-of-date copies of the *International Herald Tribune*, playing with computers (which are cheaply available) and complaining about the terrific heat and the lack of alcohol. (Saudi Arabia and Kuwait are completely dry states.) Others of course try to learn some Arabic and make local friends, always observing the local culture. The constraints of living in these countries are well known. For example, in some countries anyone found drinking or smoking in a public place during the month of Ramadan could face a jail sentence, large fine and/or deportation.

BAHRAIN

Bahrain is among the most liberal of the oil states, and one which attracts foreigners, including women because of its tolerance of women in the workplace. The British Council keeps a list of language schools and may be of assistance in referring a TEFL-qualified teacher to private clients, whether companies, individuals or secretarial colleges. Unlike in Saudi Arabia, it is possible to teach mixed classes of men and women.

ISRAEL

Because of the large number of English-speaking Jews who have settled in Israel from the USA, South Africa, etc. many native speakers of English are employed in the state education system and there is little active recruitment of foreign teachers. There are a number of private language schools for example Wall Street Institute has centres in Tel Aviv, Kiryat Bialik, Ra'anona, Petah Tikva, Rehovot,

Beer Sheba and Haifa, which were hiring at the time of writing. The British Council maintains a presence in Israel and has teaching centres in Tel Aviv and Jerusalem, which recruit qualified EFL teachers mainly from the local English-speaking population. However, there are openings as **Tom Balfour** discovered, shortly after reacquainting himself with a girl he knew in Tel Aviv:

> *I sent emails with my CV to various English schools, mostly branches of the two big companies Berlitz and Wall Street Institute, explaining my situation – that I would be leaving Israel in a week to return to England for my summer job, but that I wanted to come back in September and teach English in Tel Aviv. Most of the schools simply sent me a reply saying 'get back to us when you return' but Wall Street Institute Tel Aviv invited me for an interview. In the interview I was asked various questions about teaching, and then the director pretended to be a low level student and asked me to explain various words to her. When she asked me what a model was, I said 'Naomi Campbell, Kate Moss' and then got up and did a pretend cat-walk round the room. Although I'm sure that my qualifications helped, I think that might be what got me the job: knowing how to keep explanations simple, and being prepared to look silly if it helped. She told me that if I came back I would be offered a contract.*
>
> *I had heard (from this book in fact!) that with the high number of native English-speaking immigrants in Israel there wasn't really a market for English teachers. I think, however, that my Trinity qualification and my planned work at the summer school made me stand out from the native candidates, some of whom were hoping for a job simply on the strength of being English speakers.*

One difficulty that native speakers may run into is getting a visa. Even if you are an English speaker and teacher there is no guarantee that you will get one, unless you improve your chances by being in a relationship with an Israeli (or Jewish).

Tom Balfour has no regrets about choosing Israel:

> *Israel is an amazing country and Tel Aviv is a great, cosmopolitan city with a good beach and fantastic nightlife.*

PALESTINIAN TERRITORIES

Education is all but impossible for many Palestinians and the situation is very difficult for teachers. Although the demand is there, the circumstances do not allow the vast majority of Palestinians to achieve their ambition. Like most international organisations, the British Council has withdrawn from the Palestinian Territories and its educational activities in Nablus, Ramallah, Gaza and East Jerusalem have been halted.

The charity UNIPAL (Universities' Trust for Educational Exchange with Palestinians; BCM UNIPAL, London WC1N 3XX; info@unipal.org.uk; www.unipal.org.uk) operates an educational and cultural exchange with Palestinian communities in the West Bank, Gaza and Lebanon. Volunteers teach English to children aged 12–15 in the refugee camps mid-July to mid-August. Volunteers must be native English speakers, based in the UK and at least 20 years old. Previous work with children is essential, and previous teaching experience preferred. TEFL/TESL qualifications are an advantage, but not necessary. The approximate cost of the programme is £500 to cover airfare and insurance.

Palestinian schools struggle on and anyone who supports their cause might be prepared to become a volunteer teacher. At the time of writing the Sheperd School in Beit Sahour (shepherd-schoolesol@yahoo.com) was looking for volunteers to establish a programme of evening classes for residents of the Bethlehem area, in collaboration with the British Council and Cambridge University.

Volunteer teachers would be asked to teach English up to 20 hours a week in exchange for housing near the school and a monthly stipend.

KUWAIT

Although teaching salaries are no longer in the stratosphere in Kuwait, as some were more than a decade ago, many organisations still seek to lure expat teachers with favourable terms. Educational standards are variable, as encountered by **BP Rawlins** in Kuwait:

> *There are simply too many schools in Kuwait acting like pigs at a trough, all of them out there for the money. They dare not criticise any anti-social behaviour by pupils, parents or adult students for fear of losing fees in a competitive market. Professionalism is viewed with hostile suspicion in some quarters.*

This negative view is not subscribed to by all who have spent time in the region. Many agree that English learners in Kuwait, as throughout the Arab world, can be a pleasure to teach because they are so eager to communicate, and so unhesitant to speak English in class.

As well as keeping an up-to-date list of the many international and English medium schools in Kuwait, the British Council (PO Box 345, Safat 13004; ✆ 2 51 5512; fax 252 0069; bc.enquiries@ kw.britishcouncil.org; www.britishcouncil.org/kuwait) employs teachers year round and for July/August summer courses.

LEBANON

Lebanon has traditionally been an important commercial hub for the Middle East, although the major military campaign launched by Israel in 2006, coupled with the fact that Lebanon has been without a president since November 2007, has set back the progress of an otherwise forward-thinking, artistic and entrepreneurial country. There continues to be heavy United Nations (UN) presence in the south and many foreign embassies advise against non-essential travel to the area.

Most teaching jobs in Lebanon are found in Beirut. Locals are generally open-minded and many speak three languages: English, French and Arabic. Male and female teachers will find it relatively easy to adjust (compared with the major culture shock experienced in some other Middle East destinations), although the pace of life is slower and more conservative outside Beirut.

RECRUITMENT

Finding an English teaching job in Lebanon can be difficult as there is a local pool of qualified teachers. A few schools advertise abroad and recruit on teaching websites, but most do not. If you cannot find a posting, search online; find the contact information of any school and then start sending your CV. Most full curriculum schools are English or French, with the other language plus Arabic taught as second languages, although English continues to gain ground over French, to the chagrin of the French. The popularity of English is increasing due to its status as the international language of business and also to a strong tradition of Lebanese emigration to the USA and Australia.

However, even schools who do not use English as the medium of instruction employ English teachers. The website www.schoolnet.edu.lb has links to some private schools around Lebanon; www .lebweb.com is an online directory for everything from banks to schools in Lebanon and the classified section of www.dailystar.com.lb carries occasional teaching vacancies (but check daily). For information about teaching English to adults try the American Lebanese Language Center, International

House Beirut (Sin El Fil, Confidence Center, 7th floor, PO Box: 55463; © +1 500978/1 489166/ 1 485475; info@allcs.edu.lb; www.allcs.edu.lb) or the British Council (www.britishcouncil.org/leba-non). It's perhaps also worth trying the Lebanese American University (PO Box 13–5053, Chouran, Beirut 1102 2801; www.lau.edu.lb), although classes could be cancelled in times of political instabil-ity. Links to other local universities can be found at www.lebdaleel.com, another online directory.

While the demand for teachers exists, the wages can be low unless you are lucky enough to be hired by a large and foreign-operated school or university. The minimum wage is about $300 per month and local teachers earn about $600 per month as a starting salary. Foreign teachers can expect to earn about $800–$1500 a month, depending on credentials, experience and how the contract is negotiated. Contact hours are often high and teachers may be assigned additional tasks. Lebanon has 20 official holidays, often more for various reasons.

A few larger schools offer on-site housing and those who do not will help teachers find decent accommodation. Finding a flat from abroad is difficult, although some English websites and news-papers list private and shared accommodation.

RED TAPE

Schools will manage your work visa, but expect this to take time. Teachers generally arrive at the airport on a tourist visa. After arrival, the school begins processing your work papers, which may take between two weeks and more than two months. Lebanon is a developing country, and paperwork is not always straightforward and government offices are not easy to negotiate (if they ever are). Be patient. Note that teachers from the UK and USA are sometimes preferred simply because their visas are half the price of Canadians and Australians. However Shelley Beyak-Tarabichi, who works for International House in Beirut, provides words of reassurance: '*Canucks and Aussies still get hired!*' Shelley is originally from Canada and has provided most of the information for this chapter.

INCREASINGLY IT WILL BE WORTHWHILE INVESTIGATING POSSIBILITIES IN THIS TINY BUT FASCINATING COUNTRY. WHILE ACCOMPANYING HER HUSBAND ON A SHORT-TERM CONTRACT IN LEBANON, ANNE CLEAVER (AN EARLY-RETIRED TEACHER) EASILY FOUND WORK (ALBEIT VOLUNTARY) AT A NEW SPECIAL NEEDS CENTRE JUST OUTSIDE BEIRUT:
Even during my short period there, I was tentatively offered a full-time post at a neighbouring school and even an opening in Abu Dhabi. There is a real eagerness to learn English in Lebanon. I found Lebanese edu-cationalists, parents and children most welcoming and enthusiastic. Being a British teacher there made me feel more valued, I regret to say, than back in the UK.

Good education is extremely important and costly in Lebanon and families pay large sums to ensure their child attends a distinguished school and also invest in tutoring outside of school. Children are expected to study hard inside and outside of school, as government tests are difficult.

A very different experience would be to teach in the Palestinian refugee camps. The charity UNIPAL (BCM UNIPAL, London WC1N 3XX; info@unipal.org.uk; www.unipal.org.uk) operates an educational and cultural exchange with Palestinian communities in the West Bank, Gaza and Lebanon. Volun-teers teach English to children aged 12–15 in the refugee camps mid-July to mid-August. However, UNIPAL did not operate in the refugee camps in Lebanon for some time in the recent past due to the on-going fighting in Nahr al-Bared camp near Tripoli. Interested candidates should keep an eye on the website. In the past UNIPAL has been looking for native English speakers, based in the UK who are at least 20 years old. Previous work with children is essential, and previous teaching experience preferred. TEFL/TESL qualifications are an advantage, but not necessary. The approximate cost of the programme is £500 to cover airfare and insurance.

LEISURE

Shelley Beyak-Tarabichi has come to appreciate life in Lebanon:

> *Lebanese hospitality is renowned, the food is fantastic (healthy and vegetarian-friendly) and the weather is comfortable. You can swim at a beach resort in the summer, ski in the winter and hike all year round. There are gyms, malls, outdoor groups, concerts, art schools and mountain resorts along with traditional Arabic cafés, monasteries, mosques and historical sites dating back thousands, if not millions, of years. While the political situation in Lebanon is termed unstable, it is not evident on a day-to-day level as one would expect.*

OMAN

Since the 1970s Oman has had to import the majority of its skilled labour including teachers. Teachers of English are employed from Sudan, Sri Lanka, India and North Africa and many of the private language schools are run by Indian ex-pats. Therefore 'native-speaker' teachers from the West have never really had much of a look in. Some positions do become available each year with the British Council in Muscat but the major employers of Western teachers are employed by the Ministry of Higher Education, Sultan Qaboos University and CfBT.

Despite a fast-expanding EFL market, there's no room at all for visiting job-seekers, since a tight hold is kept on tourist visas. It is important these days to have an MA in TESOL or Applied Linguistics (or at least be enrolled in a distance learning ELT master's degree) with at least three years of experience, preferably at university level. IH Muscat (Polyglot Institute) in Oman asks for teachers with a BA (English major), RSA CELTA or Trinity TESOL, plus three to five years' EFL experience. If the first degree is a BSc, the approving body requires five years' experience post CELTA. The main recruiting season begins in March just prior to the Al-Ain TESOL Arabia conference. Exactly why an MA in TESOL should be necessary is not very clear, at least not to **Sandeha Lynch** who provided some of the information in this section. His wry description of students in higher education could apply equally to students throughout the Middle East:

> *Unfortunately there is a widespread idea that experts in linguistics and the like have what it takes to teach English. It can come as a bit of a shock, therefore, for teachers who have studied phonics, syllabus design, methodology and socio-linguistics to discover that they are teaching 'Headway Elementary' units 1 to 5 to groups of up to 40 students per class. Not exactly what the MA prepares you for. It may also be a bit of a shock to discover that with the same qualifications a teacher can usually earn about 20% more in the UAE, have a greater range of colleges and institutes from which to choose, and even have a social life.*

One could say that the school-leavers who come to the colleges and higher institutes are ill-prepared. Certainly the school-leaving grades for English don't seem to reflect the true level of the students. Although things are gradually changing and entry to the colleges is becoming more rigorous, the teacher still has to get around the idea that these students have had English at school three hours a week for nine years (900 hours of English?) and still can't distinguish 'he' from 'you' or 'did' from 'do'. Teachers raised on communicative or task-based teaching methodology tend to have a rough time in their first few months as they adapt to the quasi-Victorian teaching style of talk and chalk that the students demand. Somewhat short on personal initiative and motivation, the students believe that each of them has a personal relationship with the teacher, and that in the classroom they have the right to direct and exclusive contact. This goes some way towards explaining why 40 students can all shout out the same question within a five-minute period and why the teacher is expected to explain the point to each of them one at a time. This lack of team-playing does not extend to exams, however, when innumerable devices and intrigues are developed so that the students can help each other.

This is not life in the fast lane of academic endeavour but something of an academic lay-by. If you choose to work in one of the colleges of higher education, you may find that the concept of rigorous academic standards is imperfectly understood, and therefore rarely applied. This will change in the future but, for the moment, teachers and students can relax at weekends safe in the knowledge that low examination marks can always be raised by the administration.

CfBT Education Services LLC, Oman, supplies expertise in Education and Training for various public and private sector clients including the Ministry of Education, the Ministry of Higher Education and Petroleum Development Oman (PDO). With more than 20 years experience in-country, CfBT LLC maintains a project office in Muscat and has expanded operations to the Gulf Region. Further details are available at www.cfbtoman.com or www.cfbt.com.

Despite Sandeha Lynch's reservations about the job, he clearly enjoyed Oman which he describes as the best place to be in all Arabia, both summer and winter.

Oman is a great place for camping in the desert, picnicking in the mountain valleys or just haring around in a four-wheel drive. The countryside and coasts are stunning and if you can handle the heat and at time the humidity, mountain walking and diving are popular leisure activities. Just try not to get bored with these activities. There are no others, unless you happen to live near Muscat where you can indulge in wandering around glossy shopping malls, watching Hindi movies and eating sushi.

QATAR

The tiny traditional emirate of Qatar is surrounded by Saudi Arabia, Bahrain, the United Arab Emirates and Iran, and is currently experiencing growth in the ELT industry. Sweeping reforms in 2003 by the Emir of the state, Sheikh Hamad bin Khalifa Al-Thani, promoted English over Arabic as the medium of instruction in the state school curriculum, while trying to balance respect for the heritage and conservative nature of Qatar's people.

AS A COUNTRY HIGH IN NATURAL GAS AND OIL RESERVES, QATAR HAS A PER CAPITA INCOME THAT EXCEEDS SOME OF THE LEADING INDUSTRIAL COUNTRIES OF WESTERN EUROPE, AND AS SUCH OFFERS SOME ENTICING EXPATRIATE PACKAGES TO TEACH-ERS. AFTER COMPLETING A MASTER OF EDUCATION IN CANADA, ARSHIYA-NAGEEN AHMED WENT TO QATAR TO TEACH AND TO RESEARCH EDUCATION PRACTICE IN THE MIDDLE EAST:

I have been actively looking for careers related to my field since February 2006 while volunteering to gain additional experience. The following month I received three job offers and had to decide my best option. The interview procedures were long, however I got the job and have been working ever since. Students are hesitant to speak English at times since they do not want to make mistakes. Thus the best way is to build good student-teacher rapport so that the students become comfortable in an English language environ-ment. I was already aware that students would find some difficulty in adjusting to a foreign accent but from their feedback, they seem at ease in understanding a Canadian accent. Furthermore, it is important to encourage students to speak English with their peers so that they stay in practice.

The main teaching opportunities are to be found in the state schools and post-secondary education institutes. There are also opportunities for in-company development of business English for those with the appropriate qualifications. The British Council has an office in Doha (93 Al Sadd Street, PO Box 2992, Doha; ✆ +4426193 4; fax 4423315; general.enquiries@qa.britishcouncil.org), which offers eight-week English courses to adults and children and may be able to offer advice on finding teaching work. It offers the CELTA course twice a year.

There are also possibilities within private language institutes. Recently, Inlingua Qatar was looking to employ native English speakers (ESL qualifications a plus).

SAUDI ARABIA

EFL teachers in the Kingdom of Saudi Arabia no longer earn fabulously high salaries, and rising violence against foreigners has acted as a further disincentive. But expatriate packages are still very attractive, with substantial salaries, free airfares and accommodation plus generous holidays and other perks.

Teaching in a naval academy or petrochemical company while living in a teetotal expatriate ghetto is not many people's idea of fun, especially after a request for an exit visa has been denied. The rare woman who gets a job as a teacher (at a women's college) may live to regret it when she finds that she is prohibited by law from driving a car and must not appear in public without being covered from head to foot. EFL teachers are required for the world's largest ELT project in the world intensive University Foundation Programme at King Saud University, Riyadh. The preparatory year programme delivers English language teaching to 6,500 students, both male and female. For more information visit www.bell-worldwide.com or email recruitment@bell-centres.com

A sprinkling of companies advertise in the educational press, including Arabian Careers (Berkeley Square House, 7th Floor, Berkeley Square, London W1X 5LB; 020 7495 3285; fax 020 7355 2562; www.arabiancareers.com). Arabian Careers specialises in recruiting healthcare professionals for hospitals but occasionally need English teachers. Candidates must usually be single men with PGCE plus TEFL certificate and four years' full-time experience.

> **PROFESSIONAL TEACHERS TEMPTED BY THE MONEY SHOULD BEAR IN MIND THE DRAWBACKS OF LIVING IN SAUDI ARABIA, AS PHILIP DRAY DID:**
> *I decided against Saudi Arabia. The money was most appealing, but I couldn't think myself into a situation where there was no nightlife and limited contact with women. A year may seem short when you say it fast, but you could get very depressed in a situation like that. Money is nearly everything but it can't buy you peace of mind. So I opted for a job at a school for boys in the UAE which, from the description, sounds sociable, inviting and accessible.*

After Philip's arrival at the Oasis Residence in Dubai, he was well pleased with his decision, since living conditions in his luxury apartment complex complete with pool, steam room, squash court and gym, were just as lavish as he would have been given in Saudi. High salaries can also be earned in the United Arab Emirates.

Caution must be exercised when considering job offers from the Kingdom of Saudi Arabia. We have heard from several American teachers who have been badly burned by a Saudi employer. **Arno Kemp**, writing from Riyadh, says he wouldn't advise anyone to work for any language schools or academic except the British Aerospace training academies in Riyadh or Dahran:

> *All the other 'schools' and 'academies' are run mostly by individuals who have no knowledge about teaching or management and teachers end up being miserable with no way out as they are contractu-*

ally bound. Many employers still keep passports in safes and control the comings and goings of teachers. Teachers are often required to work very long hours in order to make it feasible to stay in Saudi, as salaries are not very good at most schools. Also, very few of the privately-owned schools offer proper accommodation and teachers are left to their own devices in a city/culture where people do not speak any English. Single people have immense difficulty in securing accommodation as most apartments, buildings and villas are exclusive to families. Basically, it is a very harsh culture to deal with . . . teachers need as much help and assistance as possible and sadly this is non-existent. Unless it is a major, international (preferably Western) organisation, offering fully-furnished compound accommodation (check details before accepting any offers). The 'let's see how much money we can make out of this' syndrome has hit the Middle East as well. Teachers need to make sure about contractual details as these are often chopped and changed after arrival to suit employers. Saudi law is not very expat-friendly and employers have a huge advantage over employees once they have signed the contract. There are hundreds of stories from teachers who have been shafted in Saudi. Be very careful.

Rachid Taouil recently started working for Wall Street Institute in Saudia Arabia and is pleased with his job and the country, largely because the Institute was very welcoming and helped him with red tape:

Many teachers are like me and are offshore hires. They are professional and very friendly. I had the pleasure of attending some of their classes whilst receiving my induction. They helped me understand the requirements of the students and their needs. The students on the other hand were two types; private students urged by the need to learn English to forward their studies and company students urged by the necessity and the requirements of their job to learn English.

Morris Jensen, working for Elite Training, points to the good things about Saudi Arabia including the hospitality, ease of finding lucrative private work, excellent sports facilities, shopping and accessibility of places of interest in the Middle East. He also acknowledges the problems, such as the religious and cultural clashes which arise in the classroom and the frustrating bureaucracy. Among the documents required for a work permit are a medical certificate notarised by the Foreign and Commonwealth Office in London, an authorisation from the Saudi Ministry of Foreign Affairs, copies of diplomas, a contract of employment and accompanying letter from the sponsoring company. The fee of 50 riyals payable before leaving your home country is only the beginning. Your passport is held by your sponsoring employer while you carry around an official copy as identification, at least until you are issued with an *iqama* (resident visa). Every time you want to leave the country you must request an exit and re-entry visa which is given at the discretion of your employer. Some foreign workers have reported having to pay a very substantial sum for an exit visa.

SYRIA

The opportunities in Syria are expanding and improving. The Education Adviser at the small British Council office in Damascus is willing to advise individual enquirers and has a list of half a dozen ELT institutions in Syria. The British Council cautions that: '*Teachers wishing to teach here should make sure of their positions before arrival. They should obtain sponsorship from the prospective employer for residence purposes and have an agreed written contract.*'

There's an enthusiastic demand for private tuition, though Syria is a poor country and only a small proportion of the population can afford it. The American Language Center in Damascus (see entry) employs about 40 native speakers for a minimum of three months in its programme of American English courses for adults. Anyone with a TEFL background has a good chance of getting some part-time hours. Occasionally they run their own training programme for EFL teachers. They may also know of individuals who want private tutoring in English.

To enter Syria, you should have an entrance visa from the Syrian Embassy in your country, and you must also obtain an exit visa every time you leave. (The journey from Damascus to Beirut takes four hours and costs about $15.) If you do teach for one of the schools, it is usually possible to obtain a resident visa after arrival, which entitles you to stay in hotels at local prices (one quarter of the tourist price in some cases).

YEMEN

Many people consider Yemen to be the most beautiful and interesting of all Middle Eastern states. Several professional schools employ a sizeable number of expat (especially American) teachers, mainly the similarly named YALI (Yemen-American Language Institute) and MALI (Modern American Language Institute). MALI is the largest privately owned and operated ESL institute in Yemen with an average of 500 students per term, expanding to 800 in the summer in Sana'a and Aden.

TEACHING SALARIES AT THE RESPECTABLE INSTITUTES IN YEMEN ALLOW A GOOD LIFE-STYLE SINCE THE COST OF LIVING IS SO LOW. A FEW YEARS AGO, MARY HALL WORKED FOR AN AID AGENCY IN YEMEN AND BECAME FAMILIAR WITH THE TEACHING SCENE:

There are more and more places teaching English here. The main ones recruit mostly qualified teachers from England or the US. Some others hire any old bod who turns up and don't pay very well. I had a lodger who was teaching at one place for a pittance as the boss took money out of her wages to pay for her lodgings, even after she moved in with me. I think she was getting a couple of dollars an hour. This is something you sort of get used to. It can be very cheap living here, with rent about $50 a month or less if you're not fussy.

Although Yemen has attracted a growing number of tourists, rebels trying to force concessions from the authorities have kidnapped foreigners.

Three-month visas can be obtained after submitting to an HIV test and paying a fee.

LIST OF EMPLOYERS

ELS LANGUAGE CENTERS – MIDDLE EAST
PO Box 3079, Abu Dhabi, United Arab Emirates
+2 6426640 1516; fax 2 66426643
jobs@elsmea.com
www.elsmea.com

NUMBER OF TEACHERS: 30 full-time plus many part-time in 12 centres throughout the Middle East including Hawally (Kuwait), Muscat, Salalah and Sohar (Oman), Jeddah, Riyadh and Dammam (Saudi Arabia), Dubai, Abu Dhabi, Al Ain and Fujairah(UAE) and Doha (Qatar).
PREFERENCE OF NATIONALITY: American, Canadian, British, New Zealander, Australian, though other nationalities are sometimes accepted.

QUALIFICATIONS: Preferred MA in TEFL/TESL and 2 years' experience with recognised TEFL Certificate plus 3 years' experience. Minimum BA plus TEFL plus experience.
CONDITIONS OF EMPLOYMENT: 1- or 2-year contracts. 30 contact hours plus 15 administrative hours per week for full-time teachers.
SALARY: varies according to qualifications, experience and location. Some salaries are tax free and come with benefits such as housing, airfares and medical insurance.
FACILITIES/SUPPORT: furnished accommodation provided, though teachers may choose to find their own within their housing allowance. Work and residence permits arranged in all countries, usually involving a medical examination and blood test and a notarised and attested copy of the teacher's

degree and qualifications. Standard orientation for all new teachers and monthly workshops.

RECRUITMENT: through TESOL USA and TESOL Arabia, and also via the internet. Telephone interviews sometimes sufficient. Face-to-face interviews arranged where possible.

BAHRAIN

BRITISH COUNCIL – BAHRAIN
146 Shaikh Salman Highway, PO Box 452,
Manama 356
+261555; fax 258689
www.britishcouncil.org/bahrain

NUMBER OF TEACHERS: 11.
PREFERENCE OF NATIONALITY: British.
QUALIFICATIONS: minimum DELTA or equivalent plus 2 years' overseas EFL experience.
CONDITIONS OF EMPLOYMENT: 2-year contracts. 36 hours per week (24 contact hours). Saturday to Wednesday. Most teaching between 3pm and 9pm.
FACILITIES/SUPPORT: accommodation arranged plus medical insurance.
RECRUITMENT: via British Council Recruitment Unit in London.

CAMBRIDGE INSTITUTE OF BAHRAIN
PO Box 24914, Muharraq
+17 331919; fax 17 331717
Branch in Rafa.

PREFERENCE OF NATIONALITY: none.
QUALIFICATIONS: must be male. BA in English language or humanities plus CELTA or TEFL qualification. 3 years of experience preferred.
CONDITIONS OF EMPLOYMENT: to teach military and civil adults using Headway and Side by Side books. 1- or 2-year contract. Hours 7am–2pm with a chance to work overtime in the afternoons.
SALARY: US$700–US$1,200 per month tax free (increase in second year).
FACILITIES/SUPPORT: free accommodation in shared furnished flat (or housing allowance per month in lieu), travel expenses including ticket flights to Bahrain and return ticket at mid-term, free medical care (excluding dental).
RECRUITMENT: via internet (www.tefl.com).
CONTACT: Mr Abdul Jamsheer.

ISRAEL

TASP
Teach and Study Program, PO Box 2320,
Kadima 60920
+9 899 5644; fax 9 899 5711
zdank@netvision.net.il
www.tasp.org.il

NUMBER OF TEACHERS: 18 annually.
PREFERENCE OF NATIONALITY: none but English as a mother tongue.
QUALIFICATIONS: BA and some meaningful experience (formal or informal) of working with children or young adults.
CONDITIONS OF EMPLOYMENT: 22 months. Internships 15 hours per week, study of Hebrew and study for an MA in Teaching English to Speakers of Other Languages at Tel Aviv University. Interns are placed in schools in Tel Aviv and surrounding area from 1 September teaching English to primary and secondary school children. There are 3 days a week in schools and 2 days a week studying on the campus of Tel Aviv University.
SALARY: approx. US$500 (2,000 shekels) per month. Tuition fee of US$10,500 includes special programme in English at Tel Aviv University in TESOL, supervision and support while working in the public schools, health insurance and Hebrew language classes over the 22-month period.
FACILITIES/SUPPORT: help given finding appropriate accommodation.
RECRUITMENT: via the internet. Full programme information and application online at www.tasp.org.il.
CONTACT: Dr Zvi Dank, Director.

JORDAN

LONDON EDUCATIONAL CENTRE
PO Box 850272, Amman 11185
fax 6 585 4466; fax 6 585 4477
londoncentre@cyberia.jo
www.lec-jordan.com

NUMBER OF TEACHERS: 8 in total.
PREFERENCE OF NATIONALITY: none.
QUALIFICATIONS: TEFL Certificate.
CONDITIONS OF EMPLOYMENT: 1-year renewable contract. 25 contact hours per week plus 5 hours at centre preparing lessons. Specialise in teaching for business.
SALARY: 500 Jordanian dinars (US$700) per month. Additional hours paid at JD7 (US$10) an hour.

FACILITIES/SUPPORT: assistance in locating accommodation; rent will be about JD150. Emergency insurance provided. Paid holidays and 21 days paid vacation.

RECRUITMENT: via internet.

CONTACT: Darwish Najia, Managing Director.

THE AMERICAN ESL CENTER

PO Box 1240, Al Jubeiha, Amman 11941

+6 534 1421; fax 6 534 1376

admin@aeslc.com

www.aeslc.com

NUMBER OF TEACHERS: 10

PREFERENCE OF NATIONALITY: native English speakers.

QUALIFICATIONS: ESL Qualification and ESL Teaching Experience.

CONDITIONS OF EMPLOYMENT: standard 1-year contract, mostly teaching afternoons and evenings (usually 12pm–8:30pm).

SALARY: $700–$1000 per month (average salary in Jordan is $350). No deductions.

FACILITIES/SUPPORT: assistance in locating accommodation near the centre. The company lawyer has offered a very low fee to process work permits for foreign employees. Cost of work permit $500 (paid to government). Cost of lawyer's fees is $150.

RECRUITMENT: through internet/newspaper. 1-minute recording of the applicant's voice to be sent by email to determine language ability and accent.

CONTACT: Kara Murphy, Academic Director.

KUWAIT

AMIDEAST

Block 3, Corner of Fourth St and Yousef Al-Qanaie St, Building 15, Salmiya

+575 0670; fax 575 0671

kuwait@amideast.org

www.amideast.org

NUMBER OF TEACHERS: all part-time.

PREFERENCE OF NATIONALITY: North American. Amideast emphasises American-style English.

QUALIFICATIONS: Bachelor of Arts or Education and MA in TESL is essential. 5 years of teaching experience is required.

CONDITIONS OF EMPLOYMENT: hired as independent contractors. Contracts are usually 6 weeks long and renewable according to demand. Average 1 hour a day, 3 days a week;

generally evenings.

SALARY: depends on qualifications and experience.

RECRUITMENT: newspaper advertisements and referrals.

CONTACT: Maureen Aldakheel, Country Director.

INSTITUTE FOR PRIVATE EDUCATION & TRAINING (IPETQ)

Munther Tower, Near Kuwait TV, Soor Street, Kuwait City

+2 403571/403671/403581; fax +965 2 403362

John@ipetq.com.kw

www.ipetq.com.kw/currentopenings.asp

NUMBER OF TEACHERS: about 90.

PREFERENCE OF NATIONALITY: British, Irish, American, Canadian, Australian.

QUALIFICATIONS: English language instructors ideally need a degree in English or related subject from a recognised university, EFL teaching qualification such as CELTA/ DELTA or TEFL, minimum of 5 years' teaching experience with adult students, experience in teaching ESP and CALL experience.

CONDITIONS OF EMPLOYMENT: 1 year. Hours vary according to project requirements; split shifts are common. 6 weeks paid leave per year plus standard insurance and annual gratuity.

SALARY: approx. £14 000–£18,000 per year.

FACILITIES/SUPPORT: furnished, air-conditioned accommodation and flights provided. Regular schedule of in-service training.

RECRUITMENT: directly to John Forrester, Recruitment Officer, via the internet (eg Dave's ESL Café) or through the Human Resources Department of TQ Education and Training Ltd (Garden Court Pavilions, Lockington Hall, Main Street, Lockington, Derby DE74 2SJ; 0 1509 678442; hr@tq.com). Recruitment booklet available. Staff never hired without interview which is held in UK, Kuwait or Egypt (via the American University in Cairo).

LEBANON

ALLC IH BEIRUT

American Lebanese Language Center – International House Beirut

P.O. Box 55463, Confidence Center, 7th Floor, Sin el Fil, Beirut

1 500978/1 489166, 1 485475; fax 1 510485

info@allcs.edu.lb

www.allcs.edu.lb

NUMBER OF TEACHERS: varies, most locally hired.

PREFERENCE OF NATIONALITY: USA, UK.

QUALIFICATIONS: CELTA certified, 2 plus years experience. Business English experience essential.

CONDITIONS OF EMPLOYMENT: 12 month standard contract. 26 contact hours per week, split shift between 11am and 9:30pm.

SALARY: US$900–1200, depends on experience and qualifications. No deductions.

FACILITIES/SUPPORT: will assist in finding suitable accommodation ready on arrival and at teacher's expense. All work permit paperwork is done by the centre.

RECRUITMENT: normally through IH recruitment page, unsolicited applications and emails. Interviews are essential, usually carried out via telephone.

CONTACT: Elaine Kniveton, Director of Studies.

UNIPAL
BCM UNIPAL, London WC1N 3XX
- info@unipal.org.uk
- www.unipal.org.uk

NUMBER OF TEACHERS: 30.

PREFERENCE OF NATIONALITY: native English speakers.

QUALIFICATIONS: experience with children or teaching. TEFL a bonus.

CONDITIONS OF EMPLOYMENT: 5-week contracts, 5 hours a day.

SALARY: none – volunteers pay £500 for flight, accommodation, food, insurance, etc.

FACILITIES/SUPPORT: accommodation provided.

RECRUITMENT: through application form and interview, which is essential. UK only in March for programme in July/August. Training provided.

CONTACT: Brenda Hayward, Director.

OMAN

CFBT EDUCATION SERVICES
PO Box 2278, PC 112 Sultanate of Oman
- +244 85290; fax 244 85852
- gen@cfbtoman.com

NUMBER OF TEACHERS: 12 approx. in British Training Institute in Muscat. 40 approx. in projects with Ministries of Education and Higher Education.

PREFERENCE OF NATIONALITY: British, North American, Australian, New Zealand.

QUALIFICATIONS: usually DELTA.

CONDITIONS OF EMPLOYMENT: 1-year renewable. Up to 25 teaching hours a week.

SALARY: approximately £16,000 per annum. Tax-free.

FACILITIES/SUPPORT: free accommodation or accommodation allowance; work permit; annual return flight.

RECRUITMENT: usually through advertisements on internet (tefl.com, edufind.com), agents abroad; CfBT database and www.cfbt.com.

CONTACT: Tim Eyres, Country Manager.

IH MUSCAT – POLYGLOT INSTITUTE
PO Box 221, Ruwi, Post Code 112, Sultanate of Oman
- +2483 5777; fax 2483 4602
- polyglot@omantel.net.om
- www.polyglot.org

NUMBER OF TEACHERS: 12.

PREFERENCE OF NATIONALITY: speakers of British English.

QUALIFICATIONS: BA (English major), RSA CELTA or Trinity TESOL, plus 3–5 years EFL experience post CELTA. If the first degree is a BSc, the approving body requires 5 years experience post CELTA.

CONDITIONS OF EMPLOYMENT: 2-year contracts, up to 30 hours per week, but most of the year 20.

SALARY: RO750 ($1935) per month.

FACILITIES/SUPPORT: furnished accommodation or an additional allowance of RO200 ($516) and medical cover, flights, gratuity.

RECRUITMENT: through online/telephone interviews. Interviews are essential, but rarely face to face owing to location.

CONTACT: Karima Scroxton, Director of Language Studies.

SUR UNIVERSITY COLLEGE
PO Box 400, Postal Code 411, Sur
- /fax +968 2554 4210
- job@suc.edu.om
- www.suc.edu.om

NUMBER OF TEACHERS: 30.

PREFERENCE OF NATIONALITY: native English speakers.

QUALIFICATIONS: first degree plus TEFL component.

CONDITIONS OF EMPLOYMENT: 1-year renewable. 25 hours per week. To teach on foundation course for Omani students who want to study business and IT at university.

SALARY: US$2,000–$2,350 (800–900 Omani Rials) per month (tax-free).

FACILITIES/SUPPORT: free furnished accommodation and assistance with work permit. Transport provided plus medical insurance, utilities allowance and bonus.

RECRUITMENT: interviews in UK.

QATAR

QATAR AERONAUTICAL COLLEGE
PO Box 4050, Doha
✍ qataraerocol@qatar.net.qa

NUMBER OF TEACHERS: 20–25.

PREFERENCE OF NATIONALITY: none, but native English speaker-like proficiency required.

QUALIFICATIONS: TEFL certificate, diploma or masters plus minimum 3 years' experience.

CONDITIONS OF EMPLOYMENT: length of contract ranges from 2 months to 1 year. Working hours are 7am–2pm.

SALARY: $3,000–$3,400 per month.

FACILITIES/SUPPORT: furnished accommodation and assistance with work permits provided.

RECRUITMENT: interviews required, usually carried out in the United Arab Emirates or in the UK.

CONTACT: Pamela Ohlenschlager, Head of English Language Teaching.

SAUDI ARABIA

AL-FALAK
P.O. Box 1963, Al-Khobar 31952
☎ +3 8591990 ext. 155; fax 3 8592810
✍ msaeed@alfalak.com or alfalakjobs@gmail.com

Al-Falak is an HR Outsourcing Partner with many universities and colleges in KSA.

NUMBER OF TEACHERS: around 15–20 every academic year, but expecting around 50 new openings.

PREFERENCE OF NATIONALITY: native speakers from the USA, UK, Canada, Australia, New Zealand, South Africa, etc.

QUALIFICATIONS: preferably MA in TESOL/English BA plus TESOL/CELTA/TEFL.

CONDITIONS OF EMPLOYMENT: 1-year renewable contract, 20 contact hours per week.

SALARY: $39K–41K (all inclusive). No deductions.

FACILITIES/SUPPORT: salaries include housing allowance. Company assists in arranging accommodation, either within their own compounds or if employee opts to live elsewhere. Work visa and other formalities all taken care of by the company.

RECRUITMENT: interviews are usually by telephone.

CONTACT: Muhammad Saeed, Recruitment & Manpower Projects Administrator.

AL-RAJHI CO FOR HRD
European Centre for Languages & Training, PO Box 60617, Riyadh 11555
☎ +505 36 31 09; fax 1 479 3328
✍ euro3@al-rajhi4hrd.com or euro@zajil.net
🖥 www.theeuropeancentre.com

NUMBER OF TEACHERS: approx. 40 full-time in Jubail, Riyadh and in other cities.

PREFERENCE OF NATIONALITY: none

QUALIFICATIONS: CELTA/DELTA/Trinity Diploma/BA Hons/MA depending on assignment.

CONDITIONS OF EMPLOYMENT: 12-month contracts. 27 contact hours per week; 40 hours per 5-day week.

SALARY: from £1,400 per month (net) upwards. Increments for qualifications and length of service. Overtime available up to £475/£950 per month (net). Company provides full legal work visas and residence permits with Tawuniya medical cards. (Staff pay £75 approx. only per annum of the medical card cost; company pays the remaining full balance of medical card costs. Medical cards provide medical insurance coverage.)

FACILITIES/SUPPORT: free furnished accommodation plus transport allowance. Flights provided. Annual leave allowance plus annual leave flight ticket. British academic management. All classes comprise adult learners. Centre uses labs, tactile learning and simulator facilities, plus Adobe format materials for projectors and smart boards. On-the-job training provided.

RECRUITMENT: interviews in person or by telephone.

ELITE TRAINING PROGRAMS CENTER
PO Box 11015, Gulf Building, Jubail Industrial City 31961
☎ +3 347 7060/1/3; fax 3 347 7064
✍ training@etpc.com.sa
🖥 www.etpc.com.sa

NUMBER OF TEACHERS: 5 for Jubail and Yanbu City.

PREFERENCE OF NATIONALITY: male UK passport holders only.

QUALIFICATIONS: minimum CELTA or equivalent plus 3–5 years' experience (preferably 1 abroad). Also require 2 technically trained teachers (male only) who also have an EFL background.

CONDITIONS OF EMPLOYMENT: contracts from 6 weeks to 1 year (usually the latter). 25 contact hours per week plus 15 hours admin.

SALARY: $3,000–$3,500 per month plus Western-style accommodation, transport and related expenses.

FACILITIES/SUPPORT: free furnished single accommodation. Work permits obtained. Free medical insurance.

RECRUITMENT: personal recommendation and via the internet (www.eslcafe.com and www.tefl.net).

CONTACT: Ali Mowlana, Consultant (Marketing & Operations).

ENGLISH LANGUAGE CENTER
King Abdulaziz University, PO Box 80200, Jeddah 21589, Saudi Arabia
℡ +2 695 2468; fax 2 695 2471
✉ elc@kau.edu.sa
🖥 www.kau.edu.sa/CENTERS/ELC (with a Jobs icon)

NUMBER OF TEACHERS: 10+.

PREFERENCE OF NATIONALITY: none.

QUALIFICATIONS: Native English speakers preferred. 2 years of teaching experience outside the teacher's country preferred (especially if in the Middle East). Married couples preferred. Prescribed combinations of experience needed: MA in TEFL/TESL/Applied Linguistics/English or BA in English with 3–6 years of ELT experience.

CONDITIONS OF EMPLOYMENT: 1-year contracts. Approximately 18 contact hours per week

SALARY: US$1,765–US$2,465 per month depending on experience.

FACILITIES/SUPPORT: housing allowance given but teachers find their own accommodation. Teachers purchase their work permits (approximately US$135).

RECRUITMENT: CVs considered after January for the following academic year. Interviews essential and sometimes can be carried out abroad.

ENGLISH LANGUAGE CENTER
King Fahd University of Petroleum & Minerals, College of Applied and Supporting Studies, Box 5026, Dhahran 31261, Saudi Arabia
℡ +/fax +966 3 860 2341
✉ recruite@kfupm.edu.sa

NUMBER OF TEACHERS: 70.

PREFERENCE OF NATIONALITY: American, Australian, British, Canadian, Irish, New Zealander.

QUALIFICATIONS: MA or full-time postgraduate diploma in TESOL/Applied Linguistics, or CAMBRIDGE DELTA, plus minimum 2 years' overseas experience. CAMBRIDGE CELTA or equivalent may be acceptable with particularly relevant experience.

CONDITIONS OF EMPLOYMENT: male, native speakers of English. 2-year contracts starting September and February. 40 hour working week Saturday to Wednesday. Pupils aged 18–20.

SALARY: SR111,800–SR157,000 ($30,000-$42,000).

FACILITIES/SUPPORT: married or single status. On-campus furnished accommodation with all services. Annual airfares. Local education. Contract completion bonus.

RECRUITMENT: send cover letter and CV by email to Dean of Educational Services. Personal interviews required and can be held in US, Canada, UK and locally or by video-conferencing.

INTERLINK LANGUAGE CENTER
Al Yamamah College, PO Box 45180, Riyadh 11512, Saudi Arabia
✉ yamamah@mines.edu
🖥 www.eslus.com

NUMBER OF TEACHERS: about 50, 80%–85% of whom are native speakers.

PREFERENCE OF NATIONALITY: selection isn't based on whether teachers are native or non-native, but on their philosophical orientation, linguistic and cross-cultural competence, past experience, and many other attributes determined through 'dialoguing', questionnaires, and final interviews.

QUALIFICATIONS: MA in TESL, at least 2 years of teaching experience, and good cross-cultural background, either working or living in another culture.

CONDITIONS OF EMPLOYMENT: minimum 1-year contract, longer preferred. 20–25 hours per week.

SALARY: $38,000–$43,000, tax-free.

FACILITIES/SUPPORT: free housing, medical insurance and transportation.

RECRUITMENT: resumés collected through multiple websites. Interviews are essential and can be organised by conference call.

CONTACT: Ahad Shahbaz, President.

JUBAIL INDUSTRIAL COLLEGE
PO Box 10099, Jubail Industrial City 31961, Saudi Arabia
℡ +3 340 2071; fax 3 340 2073
✉ elc@jic.edu.sa
🖥 www.jic.edu.sa

NUMBER OF TEACHERS: 50.

PREFERENCE OF NATIONALITY: none, native speakers from all recognised English speaking countries.

QUALIFICATIONS: minimum 1-year full-time postgraduate degree or an MS/MA/MAT in TEFL/TESL or related field. At least 4 years' full-time TEFL experience preferably in the Middle East after BA or 2 years' after MA.

CONDITIONS OF EMPLOYMENT: 2-year contract renewable for a further year. 20 hours per week (lecturers) teaching EAP to 1,500 male students preparing to take courses leading to technical and business diplomas and specialised courses at a higher level.

SALARY: SR8,015–SR12,817 (tax-free) depending on number of years of experience after the BA or MA. Plus allowances for transport (SR600), settling in and relocation gratuities, end-of-service bonus, air tickets and education of dependent children. Teachers are paid according to the Hijri calendar and therefore receive payment for an extra 13 days a year.

FACILITIES/SUPPORT: free accommodation and medical and dental care.

RECRUITMENT: mail, fax or email cover letter and detailed résumé and recent photograph. Interviews essential. College hires throughout the year for semesters starting end of January and August.

CONTACT: Duleim Al-Qahtani.

SDT COMPANY (TOTAL TRAINING SOLUTIONS)
PO Box 67775, Riyadh 11517, Saudi Arabia

+966 1 220 0078; fax +966 1 220 0164

enquiries@sdt.com.sa

www.sdt.com.sa

British-Saudi joint venture with centre in Jeddah as well as Riyadh.

NUMBER OF TEACHERS: 16 (occasional vacancies).

PREFERENCE OF NATIONALITY: must be native speaker; no preference otherwise.

QUALIFICATIONS: minimum CELTA or equivalent and university degree plus 3 years' recent teaching experience.

CONDITIONS OF EMPLOYMENT: 2-year open-ended contract. Up to 30 contact hours per week

SALARY: about SR10,000 per month, tax free.

FACILITIES/SUPPORT: free accommodation provided in Western compounds. Arrangements for work permit coordinated through SDT HR department. Free use of car with fuel allowance. Flights to and from Jeddah at beginning and end of contract. Free life insurance and medical care in Saudi Arabia.

RECRUITMENT: via internet (www.tefl.com) and newspaper advertisements. Apply online or email a CV. Interviews sometimes held in UK or can be conducted by telephone.

THE KNOWLEDGE ACADEMY OF LEARNING
PO Box 63440, Hofuf 31982

+3 5811131; fax 3 5805055

mosharyhol@hotmail.com

NUMBER OF TEACHERS: 10.

PREFERENCE OF NATIONALITY: UK.

QUALIFICATIONS: BA university degree (preferably in English) and a DELTA or CELTA.

CONDITIONS OF EMPLOYMENT: contracts are 2 years, renewable, although the target is long-term employment, 5 years+; 6 hours teaching a day.

SALARY: based on qualification and experience.

FACILITIES/SUPPORT: furnished family housing. Processing of work permit all done by academy.

RECRUITMENT: through contacts. Interviews sometimes take place in the UK or USA.

CONTACT: Moshary AlHolaibi, MD.

YANBU INDUSTRIAL COLLEGE
EFL Center, PO Box 30436, Yanbu Al-Sinaiyah, Saudi Arabia

+4 394 6111; fax 4 392 0213

itmgr@rc-ynb.com

www.yic.edu.sa/job.htm

NUMBER OF TEACHERS: 8.

PREFERENCE OF NATIONALITY: American, Canadian, British, Australian.

QUALIFICATIONS: MA in TEFL/Applied Linguistics preferred; degree in English. EFL teaching and Middle East experience might also be acceptable.

CONDITIONS OF EMPLOYMENT: 2-year contract (renewable).

SALARY: $3,000 per month free of deductions.

FACILITIES/SUPPORT: furnished accommodation provided.

RECRUITMENT: advertisements followed by interviews (in person or by phone).

SYRIA

AMERICAN LANGUAGE CENTER/AMIDEAST
PO Box 29, (Abou Roumaneh, Rawda Circle), Damascus

+11 333 7936 or 332 7236; fax 11 331 9327

syria@amidest.org

www.amideast.org/syria

One of AMIDEAST's largest English language teaching centres in the Arab world

NUMBER OF TEACHERS: 45.

PREFERENCE OF NATIONALITY: none as long as native English speakers.

QUALIFICATIONS: degree and TEFL Certificate.

CONDITIONS OF EMPLOYMENT: 1 year or more contract. Flexible hours. Full range of courses including business English, conversation, TOEFL preparation and drama.

SALARY: $9–$13 per hour.

FACILITIES/SUPPORT: no assistance with accommodation but assistance given with work permit.

RECRUITMENT: locally from candidates already in Damascus.

DAMASCUS LANGUAGE INSTITUTE
PO Box 249, Damascus
+11 444 0575; fax 11 332 4913
nouresham@mail.sy

Affiliated with an English language book distributor in Damascus.

NUMBER OF TEACHERS: 72.

PREFERENCE OF NATIONALITY: Syrians and British.

QUALIFICATIONS: Minimum 5 years' TEFL experience.

CONDITIONS OF EMPLOYMENT: on term basis that lasts for 13 weeks. Working hours are three 75-minute sessions a week.

SALARY: approx. US$7 per session.

FACILITIES/SUPPORT: The school supplies work permits and does its best to find accommodation for staff.

RECRUITMENT: Interviews essential.

CONTACT: Maher Abul-Zahab, Principal.

UNITED ARAB EMIRATES

BERLITZ LANGUAGE CENTER
P. O. Box 41720, Abu Dhabi
+2 6672287; fax 2 6672289
berlitz@emirates.net.ae
www.berlitz.ae

NUMBER OF TEACHERS: around 6 full-time teachers and 20 part-time teachers.

PREFERENCE OF NATIONALITY: none.

QUALIFICATIONS: University graduates with teaching diplomas. CELTA/TEFL. For candidates with non-education or teaching university degrees, a CELTA or TEFL certificate is essential. All instructors need to undergo and successfully complete training in the Berlitz Method of instruction.

CONDITIONS OF EMPLOYMENT: minimum contract is 1 year. Usual hours are Sunday to Thursday, between 7.30am and 9:30pm, Saturdays between 9am and1.30pm. A weekly schedule is provided by the Center Director specifying working days and hours.

FACILITIES/SUPPORT: accommodation is provided in a shared teachers' apartment. A work visa and labour card are issued to new candidates on full time contracts. Original degrees/diplomas and an Experience Letter are necessary, with attestation from the UAE Embassy or Ministry of Foreign Affairs in country of origin.

RECRUITMENT: through email applications, referrals and advertisements in newspapers or on their websites. Interviews are important, for international applicants phone interviews are carried out.

CONTACT: Manal Mahshi, Director.

HIGHER COLLEGES OF TECHNOLOGY (HCT)
PO Box 47025, Abu Dhabi
+2 681 4244; fax 2 681 0933
recruit@hct.ac.ae
http://recruit.hct.ac.ae

NUMBER OF TEACHERS: about 450 English Faculty teachers involved in teaching ESL.

PREFERENCE OF NATIONALITY: none.

QUALIFICATIONS: English Faculty minimum requirements are MA in TEFL (preferred) or BA and TEFL Diploma; 3 years' teaching experience (tertiary preferred); experience in curriculum development and student assessment; knowledge of contemporary teaching practices and computer assisted learning.

CONDITIONS OF EMPLOYMENT: standard contract is 3 years, renewable upon mutual interest. 40 hours a week, usually with a class of 20.

SALARY: Tax-free income. Salary based on experience and education. Annual rises are given upon receiving positive performance evaluations.

FACILITIES/SUPPORT: visa arranged by HCT. Singles and families welcome. Unfurnished accommodation and a furniture allowance, excellent benefit package offered – details provided upon request or to short-listed candidates.

RECRUITMENT: Online HCT application required. Interviews are conducted worldwide in person or video teleconference.

UGRU (UNITED ARAB EMIRATES UNIVERSITY)

PO Box 17172, United Arab Emirates University,
Al Ain, United Arab Emirates

☏ +3 7131 354

✎ HR_dept@uaeu.ac.ae or e-recruitment
@uaeu.ac.ae

🖥 www.uaeujobs.com

NUMBER OF TEACHERS: 200.

PREFERENCE OF NATIONALITY: none.

QUALIFICATIONS: MA or MEd in TESOL. All teachers with an MA must also possess a BA. 3 years of experience also a pre-requisite.

CONDITIONS OF EMPLOYMENT: 3-year contract. 40 hours per week (18 contact hours). Teachers should be on campus for 6-hour shifts at variable times: 8am–2pm, 10am–4pm, 12pm–6pm or 2pm–8pm but will teach 2 classes (consisting of 2 50-minute periods) in that time.

SALARY: 10,000–12,500 dirhams per month.

FACILITIES/SUPPORT: rent-free accommodation provided. Flats are unfurnished but teachers receive furniture allowance. University processes visa paperwork.

RECRUITMENT: job advertisements, interviews in Middle East, US or via video conferencing.

CONTACT: Academic Co-ordinator – English Programme.

ZAYED UNIVERSITY

English Language Center, PO Box 19282, Dubai,

☏ +4 264 8899; fax 4 264 8690

✎ zayed_recruitment@zu.ac.ae

🖥 www.zu.ac.ae

NUMBER OF TEACHERS: 90.

PREFERENCE OF NATIONALITY: none.

QUALIFICATIONS: minimum MA TESOL or applied linguistics from an accredited Western institution plus at least 3 years' experience in a tertiary English programme.

CONDITIONS OF EMPLOYMENT: 3-year contract, starting August or January. Teaching hours are between 8am and 5pm, 5 days per week.

SALARY: 8,500–15,000 dirhams per month (tax-free).

FACILITIES/SUPPORT: free housing, furniture allowance, subsidised healthcare, semester breaks (up to 9 weeks), annual vacation airline tickets for the employee and his/her family members, educational subsidies for children and end of contract gratuity.

RECRUITMENT: via TESOL or websites. Job application should be submitted online (www.zu.ac.ae under 'Employment').

YEMEN

AMIDEAST YEMEN

Box 6009, 162 Miswat Street, Khormaksar,
Aden

☏ /fax 2 232345

✎ aden@amideast.org

Sana'a: Box 15508, Off Algiers St., Sana'a, Yemen

☏ /fax 1 400279/80/81

✎ sanaa@amideast.org

Mukalla: HST Business College, Fuah,
Mukalla, Yemen

☏ /fax 5 371560

✎ mukalla@amideast.org

🖥 www.amideast.org

NUMBER OF TEACHERS: 4–8

PREFERENCE OF NATIONALITY: American.

QUALIFICATIONS: TESOL/CELTA certification and minimal teaching experience.

CONDITIONS OF EMPLOYMENT: 1-year contracts. 4–6 hours per day.

SALARY: US$10–US$14 per instructional hour.

FACILITIES/SUPPORT: furnished housing or monthly housing allowance provided.

RECRUITMENT: internet and word of mouth. Interviews can be by phone/email.

CONTACT: Nafisa Bin Tayeh, Academic Coordinator.

MODERN AMERICAN LANGUAGE INSTITUTE (MALI)

44 Djibouti St, Hadda, PO Box 11727, Sana'a

☏ +1 441036; fax 1 446104

✎ admin@arabicinyemen.com

🖥 www.arabicinyemen.com/employment.htm

NUMBER OF TEACHERS: 38 for centres in Yemen, Sana'a, Aden and Mukalla.

PREFERENCE OF NATIONALITY: British, Canadian, American.

QUALIFICATIONS: minimum college degree and CELTA certificate, although TEFL certified applicants will be considered. Prefer experienced ESL/EFL instructors. Should be enthusiastic, motivated and willing to adapt to a different culture.

CONDITIONS OF EMPLOYMENT: minimum 1 year. 30 hours per week.

SALARY: US$800 a month for teaching 6 hours, 5 days a week. If accommodation is provided, the monthly salary is US$580 and if Arabic lessons are included US$400.

FACILITIES/SUPPORT: single room accommodation provided. There is also an exchange programme of English lessons in return for accommodation and Arabic lessons (2 hours daily). Residence visa provided.

RECRUITMENT: phone interviews sometimes sufficient.

YEMEN-AMERICAN LANGUAGE INSTITUTE (YALI)
PO Box 15766 (located near Baghdad Street), Sana'a
📞 +1 448 039/445 482/3; fax 1 448 037
📧 yali@amideast.org
🖥 www.yali.org.ye

NUMBER OF TEACHERS: teaching staff numbers around 40–45 of which a quarter are native English speakers. Student enrolment varies from 1,200 to 2,000.

PREFERENCE OF NATIONALITY: none, but a knowledge of American culture is helpful.

QUALIFICATIONS: BA degree and CELTA or equivalent, some teaching experience and some experience of living in a developing country, preferably in an Arab context, are desirable.

CONDITIONS OF EMPLOYMENT: term-by-term contracts, with teaching load of 4–6 hours per day, 5 days per week. Terms last 5 weeks with the sixth week off.

SALARIES: hourly rate from US$8 to US$12, depending on experience and qualifications. Salaries are exempt from Yemeni taxes and other deductions. US citizens may be subject to taxes and deductions in the USA.

FACILITIES/SUPPORT: YALI can help find accommodation and temporary housing can be provided until teachers find their own. No travel or housing allowance, but local rents are reasonable. YALI arranges visas and work permits.

TURKEY

The ELT industry in Turkey still absorbs an enormous number of globe-trotting English teachers although schools in Istanbul have been cutting back on pay, free accommodation and holidays, while increasing their teachers' workload. By describing the problems which many have encountered on short teaching contracts in Turkey, it is to be hoped that readers can guard against them. Every single one of the teachers who has complained about employers breaking their promises, run-down accommodation, sexual harassment and so on, has concluded by saying that Turkish people are wonderful and the country fascinating.

PROSPECTS FOR TEACHERS

Turkey's ambition to join the EU, together with a remarkable expansion in tourism during the past two decades of the 20th century, means that Turkey's prosperous classes are more eager than ever to learn English. It also means that they may have the money to pay for it because 'pre-accession assistance' alone was worth €500 million (earmarked by the EU in 2007). The boom in English is not confined to private language schools (*dershane*) which have mushroomed in the three main cities of Istanbul, Ankara and Izmir. In order to prepare students for an English language engineering, commerce, tourism or arts course, many secondary schools hire native English speaking teachers. Hundreds of private secondary schools (*lises*) consider as one of their main priorities the teaching of the English language. Similarly at the tertiary level, some universities, both private and public, use English as the medium of instruction.

Turkey is a good choice of destination for fledgling teachers of any nationality. Not only are there a great many jobs, but a number of schools still offer a package which includes free accommodation and free airfares (London–Istanbul) on completion of a contract. Virtually all of these employers want to see a university degree and a TEFL Certificate of some kind, preferably the Cambridge CELTA or equivalent. Both a degree and a specialist qualification are required by the Turkish Ministry of Education before it will approve a work permit (see Regulations below).

The bias in favour of British English over American is not particularly strong. Many schools claim to have no preference and yet because they advertise in the UK press and are more familiar with British qualifications, there is a preponderance of British teachers. Also, the requirement that work visas should be applied for in the country of origin makes matters more difficult for teachers from the USA, Australia, etc.

A messageboard of interest to prospective teachers is www.teflturkey.net.

FINDING A JOB

IN ADVANCE

The British Council offices in Istanbul, Izmir and Ankara have lists of private language schools, primary schools and high schools and run a wide range of teacher training courses including Drama for English Language Teachers as well as the usual suspects.

There is also a Job File where local institutions advertise for TEFL teachers. For a privately compiled list of schools see www.geocities.com/sandyhoney2/privatelanguageschools.html.

Bilkent University School of English Language (teacher@bilkent.edu.tr; www.bilkent.edu.tr/~busel) in Ankara regularly recruits EFL/EAP instructors through agents or directly. This privately funded English-medium university offers excellent facilities and career opportunities together with campus accommodation, fares, etc. Applicants will need to possess as a minimum an honours degree, CELTA and two years' relevant experience, though often they are looking for staff with doctorates. (Teacher Services department ✆ 312 290 1712/fax 312 266 4320.)

Some of the British recruitment agencies included in the introductory chapter 'Finding a Job' have contacts in Turkey. Among the main language teaching organisations in Turkey are English Fast with several big operations in Istanbul and the Turco-British Association and its American counterpart, the Turkish-American Association. Dilko English, English Time, Interlang and City of London College (www.clc-turkiye.com) are all well established in Istanbul. Most of the language chains have come in for criticism over the years, with words such as 'cowboy', 'unprofessional' and 'untrustworthy' being bandied about by disappointed teachers. Browsing the web will eventually bring you to sites which name and shame schools that sack their teachers to save money, slash wages, fail to honour contracts, withhold certificates to prevent staff from leaving prematurely and so on. But it isn't always easy to establish how current some of this information is.

Quite a few advertisements for Turkish schools appear on the main TEFL job sites and the educational press in the spring and through the summer. If you are considering accepting a job with an advertiser, ask for the name and telephone number of a previous teacher for an informal reference. An even better indication is if they have been able to keep their teachers for two or more years. If the school is reluctant to provide this kind of information, be suspicious. It may also be worth phoning the British Council office in the relevant city, since they keep a file of complaints about language schools.

ON THE SPOT

ALTHOUGH NOT THE CAPITAL, ISTANBUL IS THE COMMERCIAL, FINANCIAL AND CULTURAL CENTRE OF TURKEY, SO THIS IS WHERE MOST OF THE EFL TEACHING GOES ON. ON THE NEGATIVE SIDE, THERE MAY BE MORE COMPETITION FROM OTHER TEACHERS HERE AND ALSO IN IZMIR THAN IN ANKARA OR LESS OBVIOUS CITIES. DANIEL ELDRIDGE FROM SEATTLE SPENT FOUR MONTHS TEACHING IN ISTANBUL:

The English teaching scene in Istanbul is absolutely huge and insane. Without the necessary charisma and connections (and confidence, maybe) I stayed on the bottom rung. I also had no TEFL certification which seemed to be important to some and not to others.

Given the huge demand for native speaker teachers, Turkey is one country where scouting out possibilities on the ground can pay off, rather than signing a contract at a school you have never seen. After **Bruce Lawson** had a terrible experience with a private language teaching organisation in Istanbul ('their contract was a fiction that Tolstoy would have been proud of'), he concluded that he could have earned half as much again if he had been hired by a school which hired its teachers in Turkey.

Tim Leffel and **Donna Marcus** from New Jersey were amazed by the contrast between job-hunting in Greece (where Americans encounter visa problems even when they have a Cambridge Certificate as Tim and Donna had) and Turkey:

There's a huge demand for teachers (any nationality really) in Istanbul. We lined up work on our second day of interviews. We interviewed at three schools and all of them offered us positions. We chose one in Bakirköy because there were two jobs available in the same place and we were allowed to wear anything within reason (no ties, no new clothes to buy). They were satisfied that we could only commit ourselves for four months. We did see a lot of applicants turned away, even when there was a need for new teachers, because they lacked TEFL credentials.

Fewer and fewer schools are willing to employ people with no formal TEFL background.

FREELANCE TEACHING

The standard Ministry of Education contract prohibits private teaching outside the bounds of the signed contract. In fact, unless you are blatantly pinching students from the institution that employs you, most employers turn a blind eye. University English departments might be a place to look for private pupils. The top rate of pay goes up to £20 an hour.

REGULATIONS

It is necessary to apply for a visa before arrival in Turkey as the Vice Consul at the Turkish Consulate General in London clearly explains:

> *Anyone who intends to work in Turkey has to obtain a work visa before departing for Turkey. Otherwise, he/she will not be permitted to take up employment in the country, unless he/she chooses to work illegally. Applications from teachers are usually processed quicker than the other professions. We believe that an application made four weeks before the intended departure would be sufficient. Applications to the Ministry of Education should be done by the prospective employer in Turkey on behalf of the teachers. Written approval of the Undersecretariat for the Treasury also has to be obtained by the Turkish employer.*

Employers may be willing to undertake some of the bureaucratic steps and expense of the visa application but this is not given automatically.

Teachers are required to submit their degree and ELT certificate. These have to be translated into Turkish by an official Turkish translator and then notarised. If the teacher undertakes this step then there is no need to submit the originals to the school. They will of course want to see them, but they do not need to keep a copy. The Turkish employer needs to send permission from the Ministry of Education that he or she is authorised to employ foreign teachers and a document from the Undersecretariat for the Treasury. Once these have arrived, the teacher takes them with the original contract of employment and completed forms in person to the Consulate to apply for a work visa, preferably six weeks before the proposed departure. New regulations do allow you to leave and re-enter the country without having to pay again for a visa, as long as your work and residence permits are still valid. Work permits cost around £75.

If you stay in Turkey longer term (ie longer than the tourist visa) you are meant to obtain a residence visa, which costs about £85.

The complications involved in obtaining a work visa have created a rise in language teachers who are working on just a tourist visa. In fact the majority of transitory language teachers opt for this route and as a result are forced to make a trip to either the border or the immigration office every three months, in order to renew their tourist visa. At the immigration office you will have to show that you have the means to support yourself; for example having a Turkish friend undertake to support you would help. However, it is more common to leave the country and obtain a new tourist visa, which costs £10 in sterling at the point of entry (or US$20 for US citizens). Usually people cross the border to Greece, though a trip to northern Cyprus is more pleasant. If you do this too many times the border officials will become suspicious. If you have overstayed, you become liable for a hefty exit fine of about US$250.

Before agreeing to work on a tourist visa, teachers should negotiate financial help or at least a subsidy for their border run. Schools are often happy to do this as it is still cheaper for them than arranging a work visa.

All salaries in Turkey are quoted net of deductions which amount to about 25% for contributions and tax. If the school makes social security contributions on your behalf, you will have medical cover from your first day of work. The scheme pays all your doctor's bills and 80% of prescriptions. Once again it is prudent to confirm that your employer keeps any promises he makes. More than one teacher has realised at a critical moment that, despite assurances, insurance premiums have not been paid by the school.

A complication for people who intend to teach English in a *lise* or secondary school is that the Ministry of Education insists that teachers of English have a university degree in English, Linguistics or related degree and preferably a PGCE or a BEd with English as a main subject. **Barry Wade**'s degree in philosophy with a minor in English was deemed inadequate to teach English at an Istanbul secondary school, despite what he had been told by an agent in England, and he was fobbed off with having to work for less money at a private language school instead.

CONDITIONS OF WORK

The normal deal is a one-year contract with airfare out and back from London, free or subsidised shared accommodation and a monthly salary in Turkish lire equivalent to about US$1,000 in private language schools, more in primary and secondary schools. Hourly employment used to be fairly unusual in Turkey, but increasingly employers are finding it more profitable to pay by the hour, especially during low seasons when the number of teaching hours decreases dramatically.

> **IT IS A MISTAKE TO EXPECT WESTERN ATTITUDES TOWARDS EMPLOYEES TO PREVAIL. IN TURKEY, THE MANAGER IS THE BOSS AND IN MANY CASES DOES NOT FEEL IT INCUMBENT ON HIM TO WORK EFFICIENTLY OR TO LOOK OUT FOR THE WELFARE OF HIS STAFF. SOME PEOPLE IN THE ELT BUSINESS BELIEVE THAT THE SITUATION IS GRADUALLY IMPROVING, AMONG THEM A DIRECTOR OF STUDIES AT A MAJOR ISTANBUL SCHOOL:**
>
> *I have worked for approximately four years in Turkey, in Istanbul and in a small remote town in the south. Prospective teachers always hear many horror stories about working in Turkey and to an extent they are well founded. In the past, schools and employers openly abused teachers' rights. But this is definitely changing. There are many good, up-and-coming organisations which can be trusted. Teachers should ask around, be careful about contracts and conditions, and not agree to the first job they are offered without checking out the school, its size, reputation, etc.*
>
> **This may well apply to the established chains, but there are still many dodgy operators and swashbuckling and unscrupulous employers.**

Although one individual's personal experience is not always a good basis for generalising, there has been a lot of duplication in the litany of complaints made about language schools in Turkey which focus on contracts being ignored, late payment of wages, assigning inflated marks to students to keep or attract custom, and so on. So it is important to remember that some teachers have a marvellous time, as **Raza Griffiths** had at the first school he worked for, which was in the town of Ordu on the Black Sea coast:

> *It would be no exaggeration to say that as a native English person in a region of Turkey unused to foreigners, I enjoyed celebrity status, with lots of inquiring eyes and lots of invitations to dinner. Although the town did not exactly have a thriving cultural life as we would understand it, this was more than compensated for by the sociableness of the people and their deep desire for communication. Because it was a private school, money was not in short supply and the facilities were excellent with computers, etc. The free furnished flat I was given was large and very comfortable, and there was a free school minibus service that took teachers to the school. On either side of the school there were hazelnut gardens, behind there were mountains and in front the Black Sea, all quite idyllic, especially in summer. The other teachers (all Turkish) were very welcoming from day one, despite the fact that I was less experienced and was getting four times their salary. My salary was the equivalent of £400 per month*

but went down to about £325 due to spiralling inflation at the time; I could live very comfortably on this and still have a lot left over for spending on holidays and clothes.

Contracts are usually for 9, 10 or 11 months; some offer three-month summer contracts. If you want to stay longer than a year you are usually paid over the summer holidays. Do not put too much faith in your contract. **Rabindra Roy** described his as a '*worthless and contradictory piece of paper*'. Private language schools will expect you to work the usual unsocial hours and may chop and change your timetable at short notice, while *lises* offer daytime working hours plus (sometimes onerous) extracurricular duties such as marking tests, attending school ceremonies, etc.

The standard holiday allowance for teachers is four weeks. At inferior schools, national holidays must be taken out of this annual leave, including Muslim holidays such as Seker Bayrami, usually celebrated at the end of Ramadan and Kurban Bayrami. The former last three days, the latter four days, and it is customary to make the bridge to a full week. Christmas is not observed much and you may be offered very little time off, especially in smaller schools where the majority of the staff is Turkish. Big chains of schools, where native speakers are in the majority in the staff-room, tend to close for a week or a bit more. However, this is not always the case. **Olivene Aldridge-Tucker** from Sheffield worked for one of the big companies in Istanbul and her employer proposed giving the staff only one day off but she and her six colleagues stood their ground and got a week in the end. Most things can usually be negotiated in Turkey, be it the price of a carpet, or the terms of a contract. A further problem for Olivene was that she experienced racism due to her Afro-Caribbean origins but found a soul mate (and father of her child) in a Kurdish colleague.

One English teacher with extensive experience of teaching in Istanbul suggests shopping around carefully before accepting a job with a certain school. (Ideally before choosing you'd meet someone like him to give you the current lowdown):

I worked at four different schools in Istanbul. You'll want a school that's professional (with good resources, support and teacher development), offers a good package (salary, accommodation, holiday entitlement) and has a reasonable timetable (ie no split shifts and non-consecutive days off). Make sure your 24 contact hours are 24 50-minute lessons and not 32 45-minute lessons. Take a broad view of 'professionalism'. At one school I worked, the conditions were fine but some practices illegal. At another school they provided workshops and observations but one of the managers gossiped (truthfully or not) about former teachers. One school provided a teacher with a fake university degree (economics 1st class).

THE PUPILS

The major schools are well equipped with televisions, videos, language labs and course materials. But better than the back-up facilities is the enthusiasm of the pupils who are usually motivated, conscientious and well-behaved, and enjoy group discussions.

TEACHERS SHOULD NOT EXPECT TOO MUCH INTERACTION BETWEEN TEACHER AND PUPIL, AS TARA DERMOT, A TEACHER IN ISTANBUL DESCRIBES:
Walk into a classroom in Turkey and you are likely to find every kind of student that you would find all over the world: the eager, the shy, the lazy, the clever ones What sets Turkish students significantly apart in my

experience is their passivity. Turks grow up in an incredibly teacher-centred learning environment so that is what they are expecting. Having them participate in a far more student-centred, communicative course can therefore be frustrating, but given some time and some perseverance they will soon see the benefits and the fun to be had.

'Willing if unimaginative' was one teacher's description of her students. One undesirable aspect of Turkish education is that many *lises* (high schools) are too strongly oriented to exam preparation and university entrance. On the whole however, the friendly openness of young Turks may cause a foreign teacher to forget that Turkey is still an Islamic country where dress is conservative and where only a small percentage of women of university age actually attend (around 14%). Of course Turkey is in a process of constant change, and in the big cities such as Istanbul, Ankara and Izmir, it is increasingly common for women to go to university, and the constraints on appropriate dress are gradually dissolving. Teachers however, are still regarded as important figures in society and as such are expected to dress fairly conservatively.

Student behaviour differs radically depending on what kind of institution you teach in. Private secondary schools tend to be populated with spoiled and immature kids who do not always respect their teachers. **Joan Smith** found this hard to stomach at the private school in Kayseri where she taught:

Turkish parents indulge their children something rotten. Rich spoilt students abound in my classroom and discipline goes out the window. Foreign teachers are regarded as inferior and are given even less respect than the Turkish teachers.

Joan did not think that she should have to tolerate some of the innuendos her male students were getting away with, but had little hope of justice if they and their friends denied her allegations.

Others' experiences have been very different. **Dick Bird**, a veteran EFL teacher in Turkey and elsewhere, describes some of his female and other pupils:

I have found women students defer to a far higher level of male chauvinism than would be acceptable anywhere in the West. Turkish women also seem to have exceptionally quiet voices and I can't help feeling that this irritating characteristic is somehow related to their role in society – a case of being seen but not heard until you are very very close perhaps? Sometimes my students know too much grammar to be able to express themselves freely. As their own language is radically different to Indo-European languages they have a lot of difficulty adapting to the sentence structure of English: they regard relative clauses as a perversion and are baffled, if not mildly outraged, by the cavalier way English seems to use any tense it fancies to refer to future actions but is puritanically strict about how one may describe present and past events. Another difficulty Turks have is that we EFL teachers like to use a lot of words in our meta-language (ie language about language eg adjective, verb) which do not have cognates in Turkish as they do in other European languages, for example a teacher may inform their students that 'will' expresses probability, not intention; this will be readily understood by an elementary level Spaniard but is total gibberish to a Turk (as I suspect it is to a great many native speakers of English).

Dick's analysis of Turkish EFL students ends with a light-hearted description of their irrepressible energy and enthusiasm:

Whenever the class is asked a question they would fain prostrate themselves at their teacher's feet were it not that years of instilled discipline keep them penned by invisible bonds within the confines of their desks until the ringing of the bell, whereat pandemonium breaks loose as a thousand berserk adolescents fling themselves across the (highly polished) corridor floors and down the (marble) steps headlong into the playground. (This phenomenon may help to explain why fire drills are not a regular feature of Turkish school life.)

Paul Gallantry, at one time Director of Studies at Dilko English in Bakirköy, agrees that Turkish students are fun to teach but identifies a few of the problems he has encountered:

They have several major problems with English, especially mastering the definite article, the third person singular and the present perfect, none of which exist in Turkish. On the whole, their pronunciation is good, but they do have difficulty with words that have three consonants back to back. (My own surname Gallantry inevitably gets pronounced 'Galilantiree'.) If I have to be critical of my students, it is that they neither listen to, nor read, instructions; five minutes into an exercise there is always someone asking 'What am I supposed to do?' Also a recurring problem is that some students merely come to a language school in order to use it as a social club. They're more interested in meeting someone of the opposite sex than learning English, and this can have a demoralising effect in class.

ACCOMMODATION

If accommodation is provided as part of your contract, it may be located close to the school in a modern flat which you will have to share with another teacher or it may be some way away, possibly in an undesirable neighbourhood. Fortunately not many teachers are assigned accommodation as gruesome as **Philip Dray**'s in Izmir:

Cockroaches, centipedes, noisy neighbours, a filthy shower room and a fitted kitchen circa 1920, I was slowly adjusting to it all. But one day, while I was having a shower, I saw a rat looking at me from the ventilation shaft and I knew that my patience had run out. I asked for a new flat but they said they couldn't get a new one before May. So, reluctantly (as there were some very nice people at the school) I had to leave.

If the school doesn't provide a flat they will certainly help you find one and act as go-between with the landlord. Most provide some kind of rent subsidy, since rents in Turkey are high relative to the cost of living. The situation in over-crowded Istanbul is especially tight. It is usual to bargain over the rent as if you were buying a second-hand car. Flats are advertised through *Hurriyet* newspaper, or there are estate agencies called *emlak* but these tend to charge a month's rent. Rents often seem steep at the outset which may be because they are fixed for a 12-month period. Foreigners are usually considered an attractive proposition as they tend to be undemanding tenants.

In Istanbul, the nicest flats are along the Bosphorus where the air is clean, the views stunning and a lot of the buildings are older properties with a lot of character; this is why they have been snapped up by well-heeled diplomats and multi-nationals. The Asian side of the city has less charm (actually it has no charm at all), it has less pollution and many people prefer it.

Flats in Istanbul do not offer standards like those in Europe or Western countries, but things appear to have improved somewhat in recent years, and the horror stories of cockroaches, and freezing window-less rooms have been replaced with less drastic reports of leakages, small rooms, old facilities and untidy flatmates.

Ian McArthur's school was in a suburb on the Asian side, but he chose to stay in a cheap hotel in Sultanahmet, partly for the social life:

I had to commute (from Europe to Asia in fact) for an hour in the morning and evening, but the marvellous views of the sunrise over the domes and minarets from the Bosphorus ferry whilst sipping a much-needed glass of strong sweet tea, made the early rise worth it.

LEISURE

Even if you are earning a salary at the lower end of the scale, you should be able to afford quite a good life, especially if you eat a lot of bread, drink local wines and use public transport. Basic meals and food, transport, hotels and cinemas (most films are subtitled rather than dubbed) are still very reasonable, especially away from the seaside and Istanbul.

ONE FORMER TEACHER WHO WITH THE BENEFIT OF HINDSIGHT DECIDED THE HASSLES WEREN'T SO BAD AFTER ALL SAYS:
Recognise why you are in Turkey – for the experience – and try to enjoy that. You have a chance to live in a fascinating city for a year on the basis of a one-month certificate. You may live near Taksim and let's be honest, could you afford to live a stone's throw from the equivalent in London or New York? Don't fall into the trap of mixing only with EFL teachers. Broaden your horizons and don't spend all your time in ex-pat bars with a clique of English teachers. Socialising all the time with the same teachers can lead to a climate of moaning. Constructive criticism/advice is fine but too many teachers become bitter and vengeful. Most Turks are OK. If you want to make Turkish friends, get involved in sport or something that you'll see the same people regularly.

DICK BIRD POINTS OUT THE ADVANTAGES OF LIVING IN ANKARA:
It's safer than any European capital (except maybe Reykjavik) and although it may not hum at night, there are enough clubs etc. to keep you going for a year, plus very cheap classical concerts and cinemas. And the air pollution is not as bad as it was.

Travel in Turkey is wonderfully affordable. The efficiency, comfort and low cost of Turkish bus travel put the coach services of most other countries to shame (though not their safety record).

THERE IS VERY LITTLE CRIME IN TURKEY. WOMEN WILL HAVE TO LEARN TO HANDLE PESTERING, WHICH IS USUALLY BEST IGNORED. PAUL GALLANTRY TRIES TO PUT THE PROBLEM INTO PERSPECTIVE:
While Turkey is generally an exceptionally safe place, women teachers can expect a certain amount of harassment from a minority of Turkish men, who seem to believe that all foreign females are prostitutes. This attitude leaves a lot of teachers with a thoroughly negative attitude towards Turkey and Turkish people as a whole, which is unfair.

Turkey generally is a great place to live and work. It's a fascinating country, full of contradictions, as befits a land that is the bridge between East and West. Turkey is the ideal country for anyone starting their EFL career.

LIST OF EMPLOYERS

BEST ENGLISH

Bayindir (2) Sokak No. 53, 06650 Kizilay, Ankara

+312 417 1819/417 2536; fax 312 417 6808

best@bestenglish.com.tr

www.bestenglish.com.tr

NUMBER OF TEACHERS: 30 native speakers.

PREFERENCE OF NATIONALITY: none.

QUALIFICATIONS: first degree plus CELTA or equivalent plus minimum two years' experience.

CONDITIONS OF EMPLOYMENT: 1-year renewable contracts. Teaching load is 25 hours per week. Variable hours between 9am and 9pm, 7 days a week, with 2 days off a week. Students mostly young adults.

SALARY: varies according to qualifications and experience.

FACILITIES/SUPPORT: shared accommodation provided. Health insurance. One way airfare paid on completion of one year plus three weeks paid leave; return airfare and four weeks paid leave if teacher renews contract. In-house training.

RECRUITMENT: advertisements and direct application. Interviews held in UK and Ankara.

CAGDIL ENGLISH LANGUAGE CENTRE

Altiparmak Cd. 2, Otel Sk, I. Uluca Ismerkezi, 16050 Bursa

+224 222 22 52; fax 224 224 68 28

cagdil@cagdil.com

www.cagdil.com

NUMBER OF TEACHERS: 9.

PREFERENCE OF NATIONALITY: UK citizen.

QUALIFICATIONS: university degree plus TEFL Cert.

CONDITIONS OF EMPLOYMENT: 5, 8 or 12-month contracts commencing October to mid-June or at the end of September. Longer contracts by mutual agreement. 24 full hours per week, divided into 45- or 60-minute long teaching periods. 2 consecutive days off possible. Teachers are entitled to a 1-week paid holiday between the terms in February and two-week paid holiday in summer plus national holidays.

SALARY: a net income of YTL1,400–YTL1,600 according to experience and qualifications. End-of-contract bonus covering travel expenses.

FACILITIES/SUPPORT: rent-free centrally-heated furnished flat provided, to be shared between 2 teachers. Health insurance. In-service teacher training with regular programmes of workshops and mentoring system. Free Turkish classes.

Opportunity to work as oral examiner for Cambridge ESOL examinations.

RECRUITMENT: through advertising and direct.

DIALOGUE LANGUAGE SCHOOLS

Akdeniz Cad. no. 69, Fatih, Istanbul

+212 621 70 62; fax 212 621 70 62

faith@dialogueokul.com

Istayon Cad. Yakut Sk No. 8, Bakirkoy, Istanbul

+212 570 30 60; fax 212 570 30 60

bakirkoy@dialogueokul.com

Halitaga Cad. Vahapbey Sk. No. 18, Kadikoy, Istanbul

+216 550 13 17

kadikoy@dialogueokul.com

www.dialogueokul.com

NUMBER OF TEACHERS: 30 in 3 branches in Istanbul.

PREFERENCE OF NATIONALITY: British, American, Canadian, Australian, New Zealand.

QUALIFICATIONS: native English-speaking teachers without any regional accent, have completed university education, have good communication abilities and desire to teach, are available for at least a year and have a teaching certificate or experience.

CONDITIONS OF EMPLOYMENT: 12 months for full-time teachers; shorter periods for part-time teachers. Variable hours with classes 6 days a week in daytime and evenings.

FACILITIES/SUPPORT: full-time teachers are given rent allowance to find their own accommodation. No help with work permits.

RECRUITMENT: interviews essential.

DILKO ENGLISH

Cumhuriyet Meydani Hatboyu Caddesi No. 16, 34720 Bakirköy, Istanbul

+212 570 12 70; fax 212 543 61 23

bakirkoy@dilkoenglish.com

www.dilkoenglish.com

Franchise schools also in Kadiköy, Besiktas, Izmit, Canakkale, Adapazari and others

NUMBER OF TEACHERS: up to 30 in Bakirköy and 25–30 in other branches.

PREFERENCE OF NATIONALITY: native speakers.

QUALIFICATIONS: TEFL certificate or diploma and a 4-year university diploma.

CONDITIONS OF EMPLOYMENT: 9-month contracts (signing of agreement is compulsory). Minimum 24 hours per week, maximum 30, including weekend and evening classes. Minimum 1-day off per week. Mostly adults, including ESP groups, plus junior groups (ages 11–15) using the Open Doors series.

SALARY: US$750–US$1,000 per month according to qualifications and experience. Some paid in US dollars in first year, all paid in dollars if teacher renews contract.

RECRUITMENT: direct application mostly; sometimes use agents in England who can interview in London.

EF INSTITUTE – BAKIRKOY BRANCH
Zeytinlik Mah. Taevier Sok. No. 7, Bakirkoy, Istanbul
(phone) **+212 571 6424**

NUMBER OF TEACHERS: 15.

EF INSTITUTE – BEYOGLU BRANCH;
Istiklal cad. Beyoğlu Is
Merkezi No: 361–365 Kat: 5 Beyoğlu/;
Istanbul
(phone) **+212 245 9991**

NUMBER OF TEACHERS: 8.

EF INSTITUTE – BURSA BRANCH
Doğanbey Mah. Haşimiş
can cad. Tugsa Is Merkezi No: 9
Kat:2 D:35 Fomara / Bursa
(phone) **+224 225 1919**

NUMBER OF TEACHERS: 8.

EF INSTITUTE – LEVENT BRANCH
Aydin Sok. F Blok No. 12 1, Levent, Istanbul
(phone) **+212 282 90 64; fax 212 282 32 18**

NUMBER OF TEACHERS: 35

PREFERENCE OF NATIONALITY: must be native English speaker or Turk.

QUALIFICATIONS: degree plus CELTA/TESOL minimum. 1-year plus post-CELTA teaching experience desirable.

CONDITIONS OF EMPLOYMENT: 9- or 12-month contracts. Approx. 100 hours teaching a month. 1 week paid holiday plus national holidays (10 days).

SALARY: YTL2,250–YTL3,000 monthly (approx. US$2,000–US2,750), depending on experience, including

accommodation allowance of YTL500. Relocation allowance of up US$750. Full private health and life insurance.

FACILITIES/SUPPORT: assistance given in finding accommodation, usually shared with other teachers. Teachers pay their own rent. Active in-house teacher development programme, teachers required to attend 2 workshops per month. Free Turkish lessons. Financial and academic support for teachers taking DELTA. School has computer room, internet access and excellent resources/facilities. School organises work and residence permits. Registered centre for IBT TOEFL test.

RECRUITMENT: internet, direct application. Interviews essential but can be by telephone/Skype.

CONTACT: Michael Hardern, HR Manager (mhardern@efdilokulu.com or recruitment@efdilokulu.com).

EF INSTITUTE – OSMANBEY BRANCH (THE ENGLISH CENTRE)
Rumeli Cad. No: 92 80220 Osmanbey – ISTANBUL
(phone) **+212 225 91 72**

NUMBER OF TEACHERS: 10.

EF INSTITUTE – SUADIYE BRANCH
Kazim Ozalp Sok. 15/4 Saskinbakkal, Kadikoy 34740, Istanbul
(phone) **+216 385 84 31/302 72 50; fax 216 369 78 91**
(email) **dos@efdilokulu.com or zgunduzyeli @efdilokulu. com**

NUMBER OF TEACHERS: 25.

EF INSTITUTE – ZEKERIYAKOY BRANCH
Konaklar Mahallesi Manolya Sokak No:11 Zekeri yaköy, Sarıyer, Istanbul
(phone) **+212 202 8712**

NUMBER OF TEACHERS: 5.

ENGLISH CENTRE LANGUAGE SCHOOL – ISTANBUL
Rumeli Caddesi 92, Zeki Bey Apt. 4, Osmanbey, Istanbul
(phone) **+212 247 09 83; fax 212 240 77 17**
(email) **iletisim@englishcentre.com**
(web) **www.englishcentre.com**

NUMBER OF TEACHERS: 20.

PREFERENCE OF NATIONALITY: native speakers.

QUALIFICATIONS: university degree and CELTA or TESOL.

CONDITIONS OF EMPLOYMENT: 12 month contracts. 26 hours per week. 2 days off per week. 2-week paid holiday per contract. Mainly in-company teaching plus general English classes in school.

SALARY: Turkish lira salary.

FACILITIES/SUPPORT: school accommodation provided for first 4 months with subsidised rent; flight allowance; strong teacher development programme, including weekly workshops; well-stocked resource room, DVD cinema centre, computer lab with free internet access for teachers.

RECRUITMENT: www.tefl.com.

ENGLISH TIME
Buyukdere Cad, Matbuat Sok No. 2, Esentepe-Sisli, Istanbul 34950
- +212 273 2868; fax 212 273 2872
- esljob@englishtime.com
- www.englishtime.com

NUMBER OF TEACHERS: about 125 for 15 branches in Istanbul with branches in Izmit and Ankara.

PREFERENCE OF NATIONALITY: must be native English speakers.

QUALIFICATIONS: university diploma, TEFL certificate.

CONDITIONS OF EMPLOYMENT: teachers tend to be paid according to number of hours worked which can fluctuate.

SALARY: YTL20–YTL26 per hour plus end of contract bonus (equivalent of about US$100 per month) and some travel (US$400–US$800 depending on country of origin) and border run reimbursement.

FACILITIES/SUPPORT: 3 months in shared housing at a central location, rent allowance of YTL300 per month for full-time teachers in their own apartment. Help with work permits.

RECRUITMENT: internet (Daves ESL Café, tefl.com) and word of mouth.

CONTACT: Gulcin Kok Yucel, Educational Co-ordinator.

ENGLISH WEST
Cumhuriyet Bulvari, No 36 Kapani Ishani Kat 3, Konak, Izmir
- +232 425 9208; fax 232 441 8514
- info@englishwest.com or nihataksoy@english west.com
- www.englishwest.com

NUMBER OF TEACHERS: 3.

PREFERENCE OF NATIONALITY: British.

QUALIFICATIONS: BA degree; preferable English Literature degree (not essential). If not English Literature degree then TEFL/TESOL cert. Preferably 2–3 years' experience, but new teachers are welcome.

CONDITIONS OF EMPLOYMENT: 2-year contract. 20–25 hours per week.

SALARY: depending on qualifications and experience. Minimum YTL2,000 monthly.

FACILITIES/SUPPORT: free accommodation for a month. Once teacher finds own accommodation, YTL250 accommodation allowance is paid. Help with work permits and expense met.

RECRUITMENT: via eslcafe.com and others.

CONTACT: Nihat Aksoy, Principal.

EYUBOGLU SCHOOLS
Namik Kemal Mah, Eyuboglu Sok. 3, Umraniye, Istanbul
- +216 522 1212; fax 216 335 7198
- eyuboglu@eyuboglu.k12.tr
- www.eyuboglu.com

NUMBER OF TEACHERS: 250.

PREFERENCE OF NATIONALITY: British, Americans, Canadians, Australians etc.

QUALIFICATIONS: TEFL certificate and a minimum of 2 years' experience.

CONDITIONS OF EMPLOYMENT: 2-year contracts to work 24 hours per week.

SALARY: US$1,800–US$2,400 per month depending on credentials.

FACILITIES/SUPPORT: Fully furnished flats provided. The school takes care of all work permit requirements.

RECRUITMENT: locally and via direct application, recruitment fairs. Interviews are essential.

GENCTUR
Istiklal Cad. No.212, Aznavur Pasaji, Kat: 5, 80080 Galatasaray, Istanbul
- +212 244 62 30; fax 212 244 62 33
- workcamps@genctur.com or workcamps.in @genctur.com
- www.genctur.com

NUMBER OF TEACHERS: 10.

PREFERENCE OF NATIONALITY: native (or good) English speakers.

QUALIFICATIONS: experience with children, workcamp or teaching experience is preferred.

CONDITIONS OF EMPLOYMENT: volunteering for teaching English to children aged 12–17 at summer camps for 2 weeks, through outdoor activities, games and songs.

SALARY: free board and lodging.

RECRUITMENT: only through partner voluntary organisations abroad eg International Voluntary Service, Thorn House, 5 Rose Street, Edinburgh EH2 2PR (0131 2432745); scotland@irs-gb.org.uk also Concordia (01273 422218) and UNA Exchange (02920 223088). CV and 2 references needed; interviews not necessary.

INKUR ENGLISH LANGUAGE INSTITUTE
Ankara Cad. No: 8 Izmit, Kocaeli
+262 321 53 25; fax 262 322 53 91
inkur@inkur.com
www.inkur.com or www.inkur.org

NUMBER OF TEACHERS: 3–8.

PREFERENCE OF NATIONALITY: EU and OECD countries are preferred (easier visa procedure).

QUALIFICATIONS: minimum qualifications are a bachelor's degree and TEFL/TESOL certificate.

CONDITIONS OF EMPLOYMENT: 9-month contracts, 28 teaching hours per week.

SALARY: US$500–US$700.

FACILITIES/SUPPORT: free accommodation available. School applies for the work permit with teachers' academic document copies.

RECRUITMENT: face to face and/or telephone interviews, sometimes carried out in the UK or USA.

CONTACT: N.Gäkçiçek Doğan, Owner and Director.

ISTANBUL LANGUAGE CENTRE
Zeytinlik Mh., Yakut Sk, No.10, Bakirköy, Istanbul
+212 571 8284/8294; fax 212 571 8295
ilm@ilm.com.tr
www.ilm.com.tr

NUMBER OF TEACHERS: 40 in 4 branches (3 branches on European side, 1 on Asian).

PREFERENCE OF NATIONALITY: British, American.

QUALIFICATIONS: minimum university degree and CELTA/Trinity.

CONDITIONS OF EMPLOYMENT: 9–12 month contracts. 30 hours per week

SALARY: up to $1,500 per month.

FACILITIES/SUPPORT: rent-free furnished shared accommodation provided, within walking distance of school. Flights paid at end of contract.

RECRUITMENT: via advertisements in the *Guardian* and agency in the UK. Interviews can be held in UK.

KENT ENGLISH – ANKARA
Selanik Cad. 7, Hamiyet Ishani, Kat. 3 and 4, Kizilay 06430, Ankara
+312 433 60 10/434 38 33; fax 312 435 73 34
kentenglishankara@yahoo.com
www.kentenglish.org

Please note that the school of the same name in Istanbul is not related.

NUMBER OF TEACHERS: 15–18.

PREFERENCE OF NATIONALITY: none, but must be native English speaker.

QUALIFICATIONS: university degree plus CELTA or equivalent TEFL/TESOL certificate.

CONDITIONS OF EMPLOYMENT: 1-year contract (renewable) with loyalty increments for second and third years. Guaranteed salary for 80 contact hours per month; 5-day week with 2 consecutive days off. Approximately 4 weeks' paid holiday.

SALARY: for new teachers approximately £600/$1,300 for basic teaching hours. Overtime is always available and paid at a higher rate.

FACILITIES/SUPPORT: subsidised, fully-furnished accommodation. Residence and work permits paid for. Photocopier, pre-prepared testing materials, active programme of workshops, peer observation and support.

RECRUITMENT: email, fax, telephone or local interviews.

CONTACT: Carol Karadag, Director of Studies.

KENT SCHOOL OF ENGLISH – ISTANBUL
Kirtasiceyi Sokak No. 1, 34714 Kadiköy, Istanbul
+216 347 2791/347 2792; fax 216 348 9435
Email info@kentenglish.com. For job applications: dos@kentenglish.com
www.kentenglish.com

NUMBER OF TEACHERS: 15+.

PREFERENCE OF NATIONALITY: native speakers of English from the USA, the UK and Canada.

QUALIFICATIONS: BA and TEFL Cert. required. Priority given to teaching experience.

CONDITIONS OF EMPLOYMENT: 8, 10 or 12 month contracts. Weekend, weekday and evening classes in and away from school premises (in-company training programmes). Weekly teaching hours 25+.

SALARY: average US$1,400 per month.

FACILITIES/SUPPORT: work and residency permits arranged. Some training provided. Paid vacation. Health insurance. Intensive CTEFL course (Via Lingua) available.

RECRUITMENT: local interviews, telephone, fax, mail.

NUMBER OF TEACHERS: 20–30.

PREFERENCE OF NATIONALITY: British.

QUALIFICATIONS: degree plus EFL qualification. Experience desirable.

CONDITIONS OF EMPLOYMENT: 2 years (1-year negotiable). 24 contact hours per week (45 minutes each lesson) plus 3 hours on other ELT development activities.

FACILITIES/SUPPORT: shared, fully furnished accommodation, paid utilities, close proximity to school (about a 5-minute walk). Assistance with travel costs at the beginning and end of a 2-year contract. Residence and work permit procedures undertaken and costs met. 4 weeks paid annual leave, Christmas, national Turkish holidays. Settling-in bonus, private medical insurance, national social security covered.

RECRUITMENT: via the *Guardian*, *TES*, *EL Gazette*, internet and locally.

CONTACT: Ozlem Fraser, Administrative Co-ordinator.

AFRICA

Contradictions abound in a continent as complex as Africa, and one of them pertains to the attitude to the English language. On the one hand the emergent nations of Africa want to distance themselves from their colonial past. Hence the renaming of Leopoldville, Salisbury and Upper Volta to become Kinshasa, Harare and Burkina Faso. On the other hand, they are eager to develop and participate in the world economy and so need to communicate in English.

What makes much of Africa different from Latin America and Asia (vis-à-vis English teaching) is that English is the medium of instruction in state schools in many ex-colonies of Britain including Ghana, Nigeria, Kenya, Zambia, Zimbabwe and Malawi. As in the Indian subcontinent, the majority of English teachers in these countries are locals. But there is still some demand for native speakers in the secondary schools of those countries. The only countries in which there is any significant scope for working in a private language school or institute are the Mediterranean countries of Morocco, Tunisia and Egypt.

The drive towards English extends to most parts of the continent. Voluntary Services Overseas (VSO) supports ELT programmes in Rwanda, Mozambique, Tanzania, Eritrea, Ghana and Nigeria. More than a decade ago, newly independent Namibia decided to make English its official language to replace the unpopular Afrikaans. A demand for hundreds of native speakers, mainly at the advanced teacher-trainer level, was created overnight, which organisations such as the Overseas Development Agency (now the Department for International Development) and VSO attempted to supply. Across southern Africa, the dominant language of business and commerce and the language of university text books is English, leaving Portuguese-speaking Mozambique out in the cold (which is why there are so many EFL teachers posted there by Skillshare Africa and VSO).

To balance the picture, it must be said that in some countries (such as Zambia and Nigeria) the demand for English teachers has fallen off in favour of science, maths and technology teachers. And continuing unrest and hostility towards the west in the Sudan means that there are few opportunities for English teachers (in a country whose government once funded hundreds of native English speakers to teach in its schools). English teachers who do work in Sudan need to be aware of the sensibilities of certain sectors of the Muslim populace, as was shown by the case of English teacher Gillian Gibbons, who was at the centre of the 'teddy bear row'. She is now teaching English in China.

Even in ex-colonies of France (Morocco, Tunisia, Senegal, Mali etc.) and of Portugal (Mozambique), English is a sought-after commodity. World traveller **Bradwell Jackson** recently discovered paid on-the-spot teaching opportunities in Mali, Mauritania and Senegal. There are two British Council Teaching Centres in Francophone Cameroon (Yaoundé, the capital, and Douala). The only other British Council Teaching Centres in sub-Saharan Africa are in Nairobi and Johannesburg. But the British Council has an English Language Officer in most African countries who may be willing to advise on local opportunities (or the lack thereof). The Council is active in North Africa particularly in Tunisia where it has a large teaching centre (87 Avenue Mohamed V, 1002 Tunis Belvédère, Tunisia; ✆ +71 84 85 88; info@tn.britishcouncil.org; www.britishcouncil.org/tunisia.htm).

Political instability has beleaguered a few of the countries where English is in demand, such as Algeria (which is currently too dangerous for expat teachers to consider) and Liberia from which scores of American teachers had to be evacuated in the 1990s. The situation in Zimbabwe has deteriorated to such an extent that most foreign teaching and voluntary programmes have ceased operations. Indeed, in June 2008 Mugabe 'suspended' foreign aid agencies' work in Zimbabwe. The situation in Kenya has calmed down, although the 2008 violence was a salutary warning that even African countries that seem stable and desirable (at least to holidaymakers) can be politically volatile.

The situation is different in north Africa, where there is relatively more stability and prosperity. Libya is more like a Middle Eastern country and indeed some oil companies or recruitment companies working on their behalf employ highly qualified TEFL teachers on Saudi-style salaries.

PROSPECTS FOR TEACHERS

Few language schools exist in most African countries and even fewer can afford to employ expatriate teachers. The British Council maintains offices in most African countries and their assessment of the prospects for teachers tallies with that sent by the Information Manager of the British Council in Mbabane, Swaziland:

> *The English language is taught from a very early stage in Swaziland. As a result there are no institutes which specifically teach it. However, you may want to consider the university and colleges as institutions which teach English, even though it is at an advanced level.*

Because a high proportion of teaching opportunities in Africa is in secondary schools rather than private language institutes, a teaching certificate is often a prerequisite. Missionary societies have played a dominant role in Africa's modern history, so many teachers are recruited through religious organisations, asking for a Christian commitment even for secular jobs. Apart from work with aid or missionary agencies, there are quite a few opportunities for students and people in their gap year to teach in Africa. Students and other travellers have also stumbled upon chances to teach on an informal basis.

Bell operates a number of in-company language training programmes for clients in Libya. Under the supervision of in-country Project Managers, they are currently operating training programmes in various locations across the country. For further information on teaching opportunities visit www. bell-worldwide.com/jobs or email recruitment@bell-centres.com.

FINDING A JOB

Many organisations including a range of gap year agencies send people to Africa to teach English. These postings are normally regarded as 'voluntary' since if wages are paid at all they will be on a local scale though they often come with free housing. In some cases a substantial placement fee must be paid. See the chapter Finding a Job in part 1 for further details of the general agencies that send students such as **Sarah Johnson** from Cardiff to Zanzibar to teach English and geography at a rural secondary school. Once she started work Sarah discovered that:

> *The expectations which Zanzibari children have of school are worlds away from those of British school children. They expect to spend most of their lessons copying from the blackboard, so will at first be completely nonplussed if asked to think things through by themselves or to use their imagination. I found that the ongoing dilemma for me of teaching in Zanzibar was whether to teach at a low level which the majority of the class would be able to understand, or teach the syllabus to the top one or two students so that they would be able to attempt exam questions, but leaving the rest of the class behind. Teaching was a very interesting and eye-opening experience. I believe that both the Zanzibari teachers and I benefited from a cultural exchange of ideas and ways of life.*

Not everyone is so positive about being placed by an agency. The placement that was fixed up for **Till Bruckner** in the Sudan didn't live up to his expectations:

> *They'd told me at my interview in London that I'd be teaching international politics but when I arrived the local branch didn't know what I'd come for and wanted me to teach conversational English at a university in Khartoum. I figured that if I was going to teach English to kids from well-off families while living in a city of outstanding natural ugliness, I might as well go elsewhere and get paid for it. There'd be no problem finding work as an English teacher in Sudan. There's great demand and little supply as nobody (including most Sudanese) wants to live there. In a country with poverty on that scale, there's more useful things you can do with £500 than pay for a scheme to tutor English. If you want fun, go elsewhere; if you want to help, put the £500 in an Oxfam charity box.*

However, that is just one point of view and many people have felt that their contribution as a volunteer teacher has not been futile, either from the point of view of broadening their own horizons or helping others.

> NETWORKS SUCH AS COUCH SURFING (WWW.COUCHSURFING.COM) HAVE HOSTS REGISTERED ALL OVER AFRICA, WHO MIGHT BE INTERESTED IN EXCHANGING HOSPITALITY FOR ENGLISH LESSONS. BRADWELL JACKSON STAYED WITH A COUCH SURFING HOST IN BAMAKO, MALI, FOR TWO MONTHS:
>
> *He is a wealthy man who lives in a nice house, and I get all my meals, internet, my laundry, and a few other odds and ends done for free. I teach him two hours every day, which leaves me lots of time to explore Bamako and do whatever else I like.*

Just one word of caution about internet offers: if you see a job advertised that looks too good to be true: US$4,000 a month, say, for teaching in a relatively poor country such as Nigeria, then caution is advised. Although thankfully rare, scams aimed at 'greedy' foreigners can be sophisticated and seemingly plausible.

PLACEMENT ORGANISATIONS

Africa & Asia Venture: 10 Market Place, Devizes, Wiltshire SN10 1HT; ✆ 01380 729009; fax 01380 720060; av@aventure.co.uk; www.aventure.co.uk. Offers students and recent graduates (aged 18–24) the chance to spend 3–5 months teaching a wide variety of subjects, especially English and sports in Africa (Uganda, Kenya, Tanzania and Malawi).

Africatrust Networks: Africatrust Chambers, PO Box 551, Portsmouth PO5 1ZN; ✆ 01873 812453; info@africatrust.gi; www.africatrust.org.uk. 3–6 month placements in Cameroon, Ghana (for English speaking volunteers), and Morocco (for French/Arabic speaking volunteers). Programme includes (not exclusively) teaching English in schools, rural community centres, urban computer centres and in orphanages/institutions for the disabled. London interviews throughout the year for arrivals in country mainly in January and September.

BUNAC: 16 Bowling Green Lane, London EC1R 0BD; ✆ 020 7251 3472; fax 020 7251 0215; enquiries@bunac.org.uk; www.bunac.org.uk. Volunteer Ghana programme (see section on Ghana below). Also have Work South Africa and Volunteer South Africa programmes which allow participants to look for jobs after arrival, including as TEFL teachers.

i-to-i: 261 Low Lane, Leeds LS18 5NY; ✆ 0870 442 3043; www.i-to-i.com. Specialises in TEFL training and voluntary placements in many countries including Ghana, Kenya, Tanzania and South Africa.

Madventurer: The Old Casino, 1–4 Forth Lane, Newcastle upon Tyne NE1 5HX; ✆ 0845 121 1996; team@madventurer.com; www.madventurer.com. Arranges development projects in Ghana, Tanzania, and Kenya.

MondoChallenge: Town Hall Market place, Newbury RG14 5AA ✆ 01635 45556; www.mondochallenge.org. Projects in Tanzania, Kenya, Gambia and Senegal (though the latter involves teaching French). Volunteer teachers work in primary and secondary schools, as well as some adult education classes. Host-family accommodation. Placements cost £1,300 for three months.

Peace Corps: 1111 20th St NW, Washington DC 20526; ✆ 1 800 424 8580 (toll-free). Volunteers teach on 27-month assignments in more than 25 African countries, ranging from Morocco to South Africa. Must be US citizen, over 18 and in good health. All expenses, including airfare and health insurance, are covered.

Projects Abroad: Aldsworth Parade, Goring, Sussex BN12 4TX; ✆ 01903 708300; fax 01903 501026; info@projects-abroad.co.uk; www.projects-abroad.co.uk. Work placements in schools in Ethiopia, Ghana, Morocco, Senegal, South Africa, and Togo.

Project Trust: Hebridean Centre, Ballyhough, Isle of Coll, Argyll PA78 6TE; ✆ 01879 230444; fax 01879 230357; info@projecttrust.org.uk; www.projecttrust.org.uk. Sends school leavers (aged 17–19) to teach (often other subjects as well as English) in schools in across Africa including Namibia, Uganda, Botswana, Lesotho, Malawi, Mauritania and Swaziland. Participants must fund-raise to cover part of the cost of their 12 month placement, at present £4,660.

Skillshare International: 126 New Walk, Leicester LE1 7JA; ✆ 0116 254 1862; www.skillshare.org. Registered charity that recruits volunteer teachers to work for two years in southern Africa (Lesotho, Botswana, Mozambique, Swaziland, Namibia, Kenya, Tanzania, Uganda and South Africa). Pay approximately £500 per month plus flights, accommodation, insurance, etc. Its vision is a world without poverty, injustice and inequality where people, regardless of cultural, social and political divides come together for mutual benefit, living in a peaceful coexistence.

United Children's Fund: PO Box 20341, Boulder, CO 80308 3341; ✆ 1 800 615 5229; United@unchildren.org; www.unchildren.org. Volunteer programme in Uganda should resume in 2009 (check on website).

VAE Teachers Kenya: Bell Lane Cottage, Pudleston, Nr. Leominster, Herefordshire HR6 0RE; ✆ 01568 750329; vaekenya@hotmail.com; www.vaekenya.co.uk. 3-month or preferably 6-month gap year placements teaching in rural schools in the central highlands of Kenya. Inclusive fee of about £3,400.

Village Education Project Kilimanjaro: c/o Katy Allen, Mint Cottage, Prospect Road, Sevenoaks, Kent TN13 3UA; ✆ 01732 743000; project@kiliproject.org; www.kiliproject.org. 8-month attachments to village primary schools in the district of Marangu in Tanzania for about 8 participants a year, both gap year students and people taking career breaks. Training is given in the UK for 2 weeks before departure. The cost to the volunteers for participating in the project is about £2,900.

VSO: 317 Putney Bridge Road, London SW15 2PN; ✆ 020 8780 7500, www.vso.org.uk. Leading international development charity, sends teachers to countries across Africa and Asia and Rwanda. Placements are usually for 1–2 years, and all costs and accommodation are covered. Many placements involve training colleagues in student-centred approaches, as well as teaching, so at least 2 years' work experience is usually required plus degree and PGCE or TEFL qualification. There are also two options for 18–25-year-olds, who may have less experience, Global Xchange and Youth for Development. For teachers with 5 years' plus experience specialist short-term assignments are available which may involve working with ministries of education or with local and central government.

Worldteach: Center for International Development, Harvard University, 79 John F Kennedy Street, Cambridge, MA 02138, USA; ✆ 617 495 5527; www.worldteach.org. Non-profit organisation which recruits volunteers to teach English in Namibia among other countries around the world.

RELIGIOUS ORGANISATIONS

The following missionary societies place English teachers in Africa; in many cases a Christian commitment is a prerequisite:

Action Partners – Pioneers: Bawtry Hall, Bawtry, Doncaster DN10 6JH; ✆ 01302 710750; info@actionpartners.org.uk; www.actionpartners.org.uk. UK/Western Europe mobilisation office for Pioneers, enabling workers to join teams worldwide. At present there are over 1,700 members with Pioneers teams serving in over 80 countries.

Africa Inland Mission International: Halifax Place, Nottingham NG1 1QN; ✆ 0115 983 8120; Also: Box 178, Pearl River, NY 10965; ✆ 845 735 4014; personnel@aimeurope.net; www.aim-us.org; www.aimint.org. Have several opportunities for evangelical Christians to teach English in countries such as Mozambique, Chad, Namibia, Tanzania, Indian Ocean Islands, Kenya, Uganda, Tanzania and the Comoros Islands.

Christians Abroad: Room 233, Bon Marché Centre, 241 251 Ferndale Road, London SW9 8BJ; ✆ 0870 770 7900; fax 020 7346 5955; director@cabroad.org.uk; www.cabroad.org.uk. Send experienced primary school teachers to the Mwanza region of Tanzania.

ON THE SPOT

The best chances of picking up language teaching work on the spot are in north Africa, in Egypt, Morocco or Tunisia (treated separately below). Language schools are thriving in South Africa staffed in large measure by English-speaking South Africans but also by foreigners (see entry for Cape Studies). Tourists can enter South Africa on a tourist visa for three months, renewable for a further three at an office of the Department of Home Affairs. If teachers (British as well as American) are prepared to travel to an African capital for an interview with one of the US State Department-sponsored English teaching centres in Africa (often attached to American embassies), they may be given some freelance opportunities. Virtually all hiring of teachers in these government-run language programmes takes place locally, so speculative applications from overseas are seldom welcome. This is how one American got her foot in the door and went on to become the director:

> *Working in an American Cultural Center is a great way to start off. I myself did it five years ago and am now running a programme. It allows a person to work in Africa but also provides up-to-date material which teachers in the national programmes are often forced to go without. Classes are small and the hours are not too heavy but can usually be increased depending on the capabilities of the teacher. We also do outside programmes in specialised institutions and thus give teachers experience in ESP (hotels, oil companies, Ministries). People with degrees in EFL are very much in demand.*

At the opposite end of the spectrum, grass roots voluntary organisations may have teaching positions. For example the Save the Earth Network in Ghana (PO Box CT 3635, Cantonments-Accra, Ghana; ✆ 21 67791; ebensten@yahoo.com) claims to arrange voluntary placements as English and maths teachers in primary and junior secondary schools, among other projects. The Gibson Youth Academy in Addis Ababa, Ethiopia (✆ +251 11 662 8312; www.gyaschool.com) also advertises from time to time for volunteer teachers with experience of teaching children.

Till Bruckner is a veteran world traveller who shares this fondness for fixing up teaching and voluntary placements independently:

> *My advice to anyone who wants to volunteer in Africa (or anywhere else) is to go first and volunteer second. That way you can travel until you've found a place you genuinely like and where you think you might be able to make a difference. You can also check out the work and accommodation for yourself before you settle down. If you're willing to work for free, you don't need a nanny to tell you where to go. Just go.*

Opportunities crop up in very obscure corners of the continent. For example EU nationals are entitled to work in Réunion, a *département* of France between Madagascar and Mauritius. Apparently there is a market for freelance teachers; consider advertising in the papers *Quotidien* and *SIR*.

PROBLEMS AND REWARDS

If teachers in Finland and Chile suffer from culture shock, teachers in rural Africa often find themselves struggling to cope at all. Whether it is the hassle experienced by women teachers in Muslim north Africa or the loneliness of life in a rural west African village, problems proliferate. Anyone who has fixed up a contract should try to gather as much up-to-date information as possible before departure, preferably by attending some kind of orientation programme or briefing. Otherwise local customs can come as a shock. On a more basic level, you will need advice on how to cope with climatic extremes. Even Cairo can be unbearably hot in the summer (and surprisingly rainy and chilly in January/February).

ONE UNEXPECTED PROBLEM IN AFRICA IS BEING ACCORDED TOO MUCH RESPECT, AS MARY HALL DESCRIBES:

A white person is considered to be the be-all and end-all of everyone's problems for whatever reason. It's quite difficult to live with this image... Stare and stare again, never a moment to yourself. I'd like to say the novelty wore off but it never did. Obviously adaptability has to be one of the main qualities. We had no running water, intermittent electricity and a lack of such niceties as cheese and chocolate.

A certain amount of deprivation is almost inevitable; for example teachers, especially volunteers, can seldom afford to shop in the pricey expatriate stores and so will have to be content with the local diet, typically a staple cereal such as millet usually made into a kind of stodgy porridge, plus some cooked greens, tinned fish or meat and fruit. The cost of living in some African cities such as Libreville and Douala is in fact very high.

> **A TEACHING WAGE DOES NOT USUALLY PERMIT A LUXURIOUS LIFESTYLE. PETER KENT TAUGHT IN TANZANIA AND KEPT A JOURNAL THROUGHOUT HIS STAY:**
> *Bit worried about the food situation, only seems to be tomatoes, onions and potatoes at the market so a pretty boring diet. Sijaona is, if I understand her right, going to show us where you can buy more exotic veg … Taught standard one (ie year 1) today for the first time since they started this term. There are 105 kids, five or six to a bench which fits three normally. Quite a sight really, 105 bright-eyed kids staring expectantly at you. Mrs Msigwa, their teacher, seems really nice, keen and capable. We may get somewhere between us. You get the impression that if you stuck with them for years to come they'd be speaking English.*

But of course volunteer teachers can't stick around that long and after less than a year it was time for Peter Kent to bid farewell to his school amidst present-giving, choir singing and emotional speeches.

Health is obviously a major concern to anyone headed for Africa. The fear of HIV-contaminated blood or needles in much of central Africa prompts many teachers to outfit themselves with a complete expat medical kit before leaving home [see Introduction]. Malaria is rife and there is an alarming amount of mosquito resistance to the most common prophylactics, so this too must be sorted out with a tropical diseases expert before departure.

The visa situation differs from country to country of course but is often a headache. Whereas in Cameroon it is not really necessary to obtain a work permit, in Ethiopia it is much more problematic.

If all that Africa could offer was a contest with malaria and a diet of porridge, no one would consider teaching there. But anyone who has seen movies such as *Out of Africa, Gorillas in the Mist* or *The English Patient* can imagine how the continent holds people in thrall. A chance to see the African bush, to climb the famous peaks of Kilimanjaro or Kenya, to frequent the colourful markets, these are the pleasures of Africa which so many people who have worked there find addictive.

EGYPT

Despite past attacks on tourists by Islamic fundamentalists, there is anything but hostility to the English language in Egypt. Of Egyptians who want to learn English, a large percentage is from the business community, though there is also a demand among university students and school children. Many young Egyptians who aspire to work in their country's computing or tourist industry want to learn English. Students at computer training schools or at tourism training centres such as the one in Luxor might be looking for some private tuition from a native speaker.

At one end of the spectrum there are the two British Council Teaching Centres in Cairo and Alexandria and the International Language Institute in Cairo affiliated to International House. At the other there are plenty of dubious establishments. Whereas you will need a professional profile for the former, back street schools will be less fussy. The British Council in Cairo has a list of English-medium schools in Cairo plus a short list of TEFL establishments, several of which are in the suburb of Dokki. Check also the online Yellow Pages in English at www.egyptyellowpages.com.eg; a search for 'Schools – Language' reveals about 50.

The British Council at 192 El Nil Street, Agouza, Cairo is probably the first place to check for work. The minimum requirements are native English speaker status, UK passport, CELTA or equivalent and two years' post-qualification teaching experience. You can pick up an application form from the British Council reception or by email at teacherapplications@britishcouncil.org.eg. You will be invited for an interview and demonstration lesson (having sat in on another class beforehand). If they think you are suitable they'll take you on, which is more likely during the summer when the regular teachers tend to go away to escape the heat. During exam time there is also a need for paid invigilators. The British Council (as always) has a great library and is a good place to teach. There is another British Council in Heliopolis which is quite a way from the centre of town and therefore has its own social world. The El-Alsson School (PO Box 13, Embaba, 12411 Cairo; © +2 388 8510; info@alsson.com; www.alsson.com) out near the pyramids employs a number of expat teachers.

DAN BOOTHBY HAS SPENT TIME IN CAIRO AND FOUND IT ALMOST ALARMINGLY EASY TO FIND WORK:

I taught one-to-one lessons to several people and got about 5 hours a week work and charged £10 an hour. Frankly this was much more than I was worth but if you charge less than the market rate then it is felt that you are an amateur. I taught an isolated and lonely 5-year-old, son of the Georgian Consul, where I was more a babysitter than a tutor. I felt so guilty about charging E£50 an hour that I spent an hour trying to get him to learn something. I didn't feel so guilty charging E£55 to tutor the Georgian Ambassador since he probably passed the bill onto his government.

I got a lot of students through friends that I made who were teaching at the international schools. The kids at these schools are often in need of extra tuition towards exam times when their parents realise that they've been mucking about all year and are close to failing. The problem is that the kids tend to be very uninterested and so it is difficult to make them concentrate. But I enjoyed one-to-ones. One could build up a large group of students and earn a decent wage but equally teach less hours and have more time – one of the reasons for getting out of England.

Cairo seems to be a city where work seeks out the casual teacher rather than the other way round. Taxi drivers and hotel staff may ask you, unprompted, if you are available to teach. Most of these are genuine offers but it is best (especially for women) to be cautious. Most job-seekers find that potential bosses are not as interested in their educational background and experience as in how much confidence they can project. It is not unknown for an interview to take place over a game of chess and plenty of glasses of tea so that your general demeanour can be assessed. Jobs seem to be available year-round, so there is no right or wrong time to arrive.

Language schools are not only located in central Cairo but also in the leafy prosperous residential areas such as Heliopolis, Maadi or Zamalek. For example the Al Bashaer Language School is behind the bakery in District 9, New Maadi (© +2 516 8245; info@albashaerschools.com; www.albashaerschools.com). Teachers must have A levels and three years' teaching experience and are paid a monthly base salary of E£1,000 in addition to free accommodation and a food allowance. The school's mission is to '*apply Western methods of teaching with Islamic ideas and etiquette*'.

A simpler way of advertising your availability to teach might be to place an advert in the expatriate monthly *Egypt Today* (www.egypttoday.com) or the fortnightly *Maadi Messenger* (www.maadimessenger.info) published by the Maadi Women's Guild and distributed through expat haunts such as English-speaking churches. Another publication to look out for is the *Middle East Times* (www.metimes.com). The American University, centrally located at the eastern end of Tahrir Square, is a good place to find work contacts though teaching for the AUC itself is difficult; only five candidates a month are granted an interview so they can afford to be highly selective. Also try the notice boards at the Community Services Association (CSA No. 4, Road 21, Maadi, Cairo; ✆ +358 5284) where a range of adult education courses for expats is offered. In fact beginners and conversational English are taught on the premises. If you do decide to advertise your services as a freelance tutor, it might be a good idea to rent a post office box from a business centre (eg the IBA Center in Garden City).

According to **Dan Boothby**, the best places to meet other expats and find out about work opportunities are Deals Bar and Aubergine Restaurant in Zamalek and Deals 2 near the American University and the British Community Association (BCA) in Mohandiseen where you can only go as the guest of a member. Sunny Supermarket in Zamalek has a good notice board for jobs and flat shares.

STUDENTS

One former teacher describes his Egyptian pupils at the International Language Institute in the northwest suburb of Sahafeyeen (now the El-Alsson School; www.alsson.com) as 'rowdy and sometimes a little over-enthusiastic'. Having just obtained a Cambridge Certificate in London, he went to visit some friends in Cairo and was immediately offered a three-month summer contract where they were desperate for a teacher. He had to adapt his lessons to please both the ebullient Egyptian youths and a group of shy and industrious Somalis and describes his predicament with such a mixed class:

> *Different religions, different ways of thinking and (as I learnt in my first week at the school) different modes of dress must all be taken into consideration. One of the problems that English students in this area have difficulty with is hearing the difference between B and P. The exercise for this is to hold a piece of paper in front of the mouth and repeat the letters B and P. Since more air is exhaled during the sounding of the letter P than with B, the paper should fly up when P is said, and move only a little with B. The first time I made the students do this we went round the class, first Hamid the engineer from Alexandria, then Mona who was trying to get a job at the reception in the Hilton and then we came to Magda from Mogadishu (the capital of Somalia). All the Egyptians started to laugh – her whole face apart from her eyes was covered with a yashmak. I decided that this should not impede the exercise so if the yashmak moved it was a P, and not a B!*

Wages at the less prestigious schools will probably start at E£1,000 per month rising to E£3,500 (gross) at Heliopolis. Living expenses are cheap in Egypt and taxes low (5%–7%). This may account for the fact that the Cambridge Certificate course offered by the British Council is one of the cheapest in the world (£760 in 2008).

Most teachers enter Egypt on a tourist visa (multiple entry is £18 for UK/Canadians and £12 for USA citizens) and then ask their school to help them extend it. The tourist visa is valid for a maximum of three months. However, a business visa is issued for teachers to enter Egypt. This is valid for six months and schools will help to extend it. Work permits must be applied for from the Ministry of the Interior in Egypt, usually by your employer. UK citizens can find up-to-date visa information at www.egyptianconsulate.co.uk.

AMIDEAST AT THE AMERICAN CENTER ALEXANDRIA
3 El Pharana St, Alexandria
+219263; fax 3 487 9644
alexandria@amideast.org
www.amideast.org

NUMBER OF TEACHERS: 15–22.
PREFERENCE OF NATIONALITY: North American, but all native speakers are welcome to apply.
QUALIFICATIONS: minimum CELTA or TESOL certification.
CONDITIONS OF EMPLOYMENT: local term-to-term hire agreements according to student numbers. 20 hours per week. 9 5-week sessions per year. Students are working adults and university students.

SALARY: US$5.50–$8 an hour (paid in local currency).
FACILITIES/SUPPORT: good teachers' resources, internet access, friendly working environment. Operates out of two historic mansions on the Mediterranean. No financial assistance with accommodation given, but temporary housing can be arranged at no cost.
RECRUITMENT: enquiries accepted by email but on-site recruitment preferred. Online application via website.
CONTACT: Stephen Handey, Country Director.

GHANA

As one of the most stable countries in Africa, Ghana supports several organised schemes for volunteer teachers. BUNAC's Teach in Ghana is described in the entry below. BUNAC also runs a more general Work in Ghana programme for three to six months on which participants can arrange teaching placements in schools and universities. (Ghanaians all learn English at school.) Projects Abroad (see chapter Finding a Job in part 1) sends paying volunteers mainly to village primary schools for short-term attachments. The programme offers various starting dates and durations (three months costs £1,895 excluding flights to Accra).

A grass-roots Ghanaian organisation WWOOF/FIOH Ghana (c/o Ken Nortey-Mensah, PO Box 154, Trade Fair Centre, Accra, Ghana; +21 716091; kingzeeh@yahoo.co.uk) runs a varied working abroad programme which includes placing foreign students and teachers in kindergartens, primary schools and a technical school to teach English and other subjects. Volunteer placements last between one and six months and cost between $70 and $190 per month to cover food, accommodation and administration.

Ikando is a volunteer and intern recruitment agency based in Accra which deals with education positions lasting up to eight weeks, as well as many others (+233 21 222726; www.ikando.org). Volunteers stay in the Ikando house in the centre of Accra and cover their living expenses (£87 per week).

Ghana has a long tradition of welcoming foreign students to participate in its educational and commercial life. A short-term volunteer programme in Ghana is coordinated by Cross-Cultural Solutions (www.crossculturalsolutions.org); volunteers are placed in villages around the town of Ho in the eastern Plains of Ghana to teach English for a few weeks in village schools (among other projects). The programme fee of £1,400+ covers all expenses while in Ghana, but not airfares.

BUNAC VOLUNTEER GHANA

Volunteer Programmes Department, BUNAC,

16 B owling Green Lane, London EC1R OQH

020 7251 3472; fax 020 7251 0215

volunteer@bunac.org.uk

www.bunac.org

NUMBER OF TEACHERS: varies each year.

QUALIFICATIONS: applicants should be 18 or over. Previous classroom experience desirable.

CONDITIONS OF EMPLOYMENT: placements available for 3–6 months. Travel time available during and/or after placement.

SALARY: placements are unpaid and applicants are expected to take sufficient spending money with them (approx. £175 per month). Total programme cost is approx. £1,650, including return flight, comprehensive insurance, 5-day orientation, accommodation and meals, all programme literature plus full support services both during the application procedure and throughout your placement.

FACILITIES/SUPPORT: most stay in homestay accommodation which gives applicants a chance to become fully immersed in Ghanaian culture. Back up support and advice provided by BUNAC in the UK and the host organisation, Student & Youth Travel Organisation (SYTO) in Ghana. Applications are accepted year-round. Group flights depart every month.

RECRUITMENT: send a completed application form (downloadable from www.bunac.org), registration fee and any other documentation as specified to BUNAC's Volunteering Department. All applicants are invited to attend an interview as part of the application process.

KENYA

Kenya is another country which has a chronic shortage of secondary school teachers. The worst shortages are in Western Province. English is the language of instruction in Kenyan schools, so not knowing Swahili need not be an insuperable barrier. However, the Kenyan Ministry of Education restricts jobs in the state sector to those who have a university degree, teaching certification and at least one year of professional teaching experience. This was a major shift from the days when many teachers had no more advanced qualifications than a few A levels. Obviously each case is decided on its own merits and it seems that the Kenyan government does not always enforce this stipulation rigorously, especially in the case of science teachers. The few private language institutes that there are in Nairobi are not subject to this restriction. The British Council in Nairobi at Upperhill Road (© 20 283 6000; information@britishcouncil.or.ke; www.britishcouncil.or.ke) may be able to offer advice. Institutes of higher education may throw up possibilities, for example the ESL department at Alliant International University based in San Diego has a campus in Nairobi.

According to the Kenyan High Commission in London (45 Portland Place, London W1N 1AS; © 020 7636 2371), all non-Kenyan citizens who wish to work must be in possession of a work permit issued by the Principal Immigration Officer, Department of Immigration, PO Box 30191, Nairobi, before they can take up paid or unpaid work. The school should apply for work permits for the teachers even before they enter Kenya. Proof of professional qualifications are required. However, it is not certain that immigration regulations would be strictly enforced in the case of native English speakers looking for teaching work on the spot. Certainly in the past it was possible to fix up a teaching job by asking in the villages, preferably before terms begin in September, January and April. Be prepared to produce your CV and any diplomas and references on headed paper.

Also ascertain before accepting a post whether or not the school can afford to pay a salary, especially if it is a *Harrambee* school, ie non-government, self-help schools in rural areas. A cement or mud hut with a thatched or tin roof will normally be provided for the teacher's accommodation plus a local salary which would be just enough to live on provided you don't want to buy too much peanut butter or cornflakes in the city. Living conditions will be primitive with no running water or electricity in the majority of cases. The Kenyan version of maize porridge is called *ugali*. In Daisy Waugh's book *A Small Town in Africa* she describes how when she arrived at the village of Isiolo (a few miles from Nairobi) where she had arranged to teach, she was told that they didn't need any teachers and there were no pupils. She patiently waited and five weeks into term, her class arrived.

PEOPLE WHO CHOOSE TO TEACH IN KENYA DO IT FOR LOVE NOT MONEY. IN THE WORDS OF ERMON O KAMARA, PHD, FORMER DIRECTOR OF THE AMERICAN UNIVERSITIES PREPARATION & LEARNING CENTRE:
Candidates must view being in Kenya as a holiday with pay. The cost of living and corresponding local salaries sound quite low to foreigners. Consequently they must think of the opportunities to enjoy Kenya's beaches, mountains and game parks as well as experiencing a new and interesting culture. During weekends and holidays, one can travel the breadth of Kenya. Also the proximity to other countries in East and Southern Africa permits a traveller to see a good deal of our continent.

AVIF UK (Fair Mount, Hartwith Avenue, Summerbridge, North Yorkshire HG3 4HT; ✆ 0777 171 2012; volunteer@avif.org.uk; www.avif.org.uk) sends volunteers to teach English at children's summer schools in Kenya which will cost the volunteer only the price of the airfare plus subsistence costs of £25 per week. The deadline for applications is June so that online interviews can be arranged via email or Skype. At the end of each programme, AVIF organises an optional group safari from a base camp in Oropile, Maasai Mara or a climb of Kilimanjaro with an experienced guide.

AMERICAN UNIVERSITIES PREPARATION INSTITUTE
PO Box 14842, (Westlands Road, Chiromo Lane),
Nairobi
✆ +2 741764; fax 2 741690
 aupi@nbi.ispkenya.com

NUMBER OF TEACHERS: 16.
PREFERENCE OF NATIONALITY: American, Canadian, British, Australian.
QUALIFICATIONS: BA (English)/TEFL qualification; experience preferred. Must be native English speakers.

CONDITIONS OF EMPLOYMENT: 1-year renewable contracts. Daytime only. Students aged 16–40.
SALARY: stipend based on local rates.
FACILITIES/SUPPORT: accommodation (within a 5-minute walk of the school) provided and paid for by school. Training provided.
RECRUITMENT: local interviews if possible or telephone interview.

PEPONI SCHOOL
PO Box 236, Ruiru, Kenya
C +067 54007/54630; & +0733 615193 or 722 287248; fax 067 54479;
peponi@kenyaweb.com

Full-curriculum private boarding school.

NUMBER OF TEACHERS: 16.
PREFERENCE OF NATIONALITY: must be conversant with British exam system.
QUALIFICATIONS: full degree qualification plus teaching certificate and 4 years' experience.

CONDITIONS OF EMPLOYMENT: by law, 2-year contracts (renewable). 28 50-minute lessons per week and exams and curricular help.
SALARY: 125,000–180,000 Kenyan shillings per month (gross) less a third in tax and contributions.
FACILITIES/SUPPORT: on-site accommodation provided. School arranges work permits. Inset training meetings every term.
RECRUITMENT: adverts and interviews in Kenya and elsewhere.
CONTACT: DJ Marshall, Headmaster.

MOROCCO

Although Morocco is a Francophone country, English is increasingly a requirement for entrance to university or high ranking jobs, and there is increasing demand from the business communities of the main cities. Like so many African countries, Morocco has sought to improve the standards of education for its nationals so that almost all teaching jobs in schools and universities are now filled by Moroccans. But outside the state system there is a continuing demand for native speakers.

The Moroccan Ministry of Labour stipulates that the maximum number of foreign staff in any organisation cannot exceed 50%. It also insists that all foreign teachers have at least a university degree before they can be eligible for a work permit. Work permits are obtained after arrival by applying for authorisation from the Ministère de l'Emploi, Quartier des Ministères, Rabat. You will need copies of your diplomas, birth certificate and so on. Although a knowledge of French is not a formal requirement, it is a great asset for anyone planning to spend time in Morocco.

A number of commercial language schools employ native English speakers. The hourly rate of pay at most schools is between £5 and £7. American Language Centers are located in the main cities of Morocco; see their website www.aca.org.ma for details. They are private institutes but are affiliated to and partially funded by the US State Department. Two are included in the list of employers. The Casablanca branch recruits native speaker teachers from a number of courses including academic institutes in the USA, such as the University of North Texas which offers a graduate certificate in TESOL.

The work camps movement is active in Morocco and some of these summer volunteer projects take place on English language camps for Moroccan adolescents (see CSM entry below).

LIST OF EMPLOYERS

AMERICAN LANGUAGE CENTER
1 Place de la Fraternité, Casablanca 20000
C +22 277765; fax 22 207457
casa_dir@aca.org.ma
www.aca.org.ma or http://casablanca.aca.org.ma

NUMBER OF TEACHERS: 12–15 full-time teachers (mostly native speakers) plus about 20 part-time Moroccan teachers.
PREFERENCE OF NATIONALITY: North American, but British teachers are also welcome to apply.
QUALIFICATIONS: BA degree (or equivalent), some TEFL Certification and a minimum of 1-year EFL overseas teaching experience.

CONDITIONS OF EMPLOYMENT: a standard contract is for 12 months from 1 September to 31 August. 24 contact hours a week are standard for the adult programme; 18 contact hours per week are usual if classes are assigned in the children's/juniors' programme. However, some teachers have additional classes.

SALARY: based on qualifications and experience. For example a BA, certification and three years of TEFL experience would expect the equivalent of US$19 per hour. There is also a tax-free housing allowance of up to 3,000 Dhs per month plus a 5,000 Dhs settling in allowance which is also tax free. Taxes on salaries are relatively high (approximately 20% of the gross). Complete medical insurance (80% reimbursable) is provided for all full-time teachers. A ticket to New York (for North Americans) or London is provided if a teacher successfully completes 1 year at the centre.

RECRUITMENT: from CVs with photo, scanned copies of original diplomas and 2 letters of recommendation. All paperwork necessary for teachers to obtain work permits is done by administration staff. New teachers have to bring a copy of their birth certificate and university diplomas.

CONTACT: David Neuses (casa_dir@aca.org.ma).

AMERICAN LANGUAGE CENTER
4 Zankat Tanja, Rabat 10000
☎ **+37 767103; fax 37 766255**
🖱 **dir@alcrabat.org**

NUMBER OF TEACHERS: 20 full-time and 25 part-time teachers.

PREFERENCE OF NATIONALITY: none.

QUALIFICATIONS: BA in arts/letters mandatory; knowledge of French or Arabic highly desirable. MA (TEFL) or TEFL qualification required.

CONDITIONS OF EMPLOYMENT: 1-year renewable contracts. 20–25 hours per week full time. Hours of work generally between 11am and 9pm weekdays (Tues–Fri), 9am and 9pm Saturdays. Pupils aged from 7, mostly aged 14–35.

SALARY: US$16,000–US$20,000 per year (gross) for October to July school year. Possibility of paid overtime. Paid sick leave and medical insurance provided.

FACILITIES/SUPPORT: free housing/homestay provided for 2 weeks while permanent accommodation is sought. Pre- and in-service training fully supported. Free access to high-speed internet, free language classes (French and Arabic) and other perks.

RECRUITMENT: through TESOL convention and some walk-ins. Personal interviews essential. Video conference interviews also used.

CONTACT: Hal Ott, Director.

AMIDEAST
35 Rue Oukaimeden, Agdal, Rabat
☎ **+37 67 50 75/81/82**
Also: 3 Boulevard Al Massira Al Khadra, Maarif, Casablanca
☎ **+22 25 93 93**
🖱 **knorris@amideast.org**
🖥 **www.amideast.org/morocco**

NUMBER OF TEACHERS: approx. 35.

PREFERENCE OF NATIONALITY: must be native English speakers.

QUALIFICATIONS: TEFL qualification.

CONDITIONS OF EMPLOYMENT: 1-year contracts, preferably with a view to extending. To work around 70–100 hours per month.

FACILITIES/SUPPORT: free temporary accommodation until more permanent lodgings are found. Assistance with apartment search and work visas, which must be acquired within 3 months of arrival.

RECRUITMENT: via www.tefl.com or word of mouth. Telephone interview required. Information available at url www.amideast.org/offices/morocco/eltrecruitmentsheet.pdf.

CONTACT: Kenn Norris, Director of Studies for Morocco.

CHANTIERS SOCIAUX MAROCAINS (CSM – ICYE MOROCCO)
BP 456, Rabat
☎ **+37 262400; fax 37 262398**
🖱 **csm@wanadoo.net.ma or csm_morocco @yahoo.fr.**
ICYE UK address: Latin America House, Kingsgate Place, London NW6 4TA; ☎ **020 76810983**
🖥 **www.icye.org.uk**

NUMBER OF TEACHERS: 40 volunteers in Rabat, Marrakech, Fez, Sale, Kenitra and Casablanca.

QUALIFICATIONS: skills teaching children are required. French or Arabic an advantage. Independent attitude and the ability to work in difficult circumstances with little support.

CONDITIONS OF EMPLOYMENT: voluntary work teaching English to Moroccan youths aged 15–18 from modest or poor families. Programme runs for a month each year in the summer. Volunteers teach 25–30 students for 4 hours a day, Monday to Friday.

SALARY: voluntary work. Volunteers pay approx. £580, covering return flights, insurance, induction and administration.
FACILITIES/SUPPORT: Local host families provide board

and lodging. Pre-camp orientation at the beginning of July.
CONTACT: Raziq Abdeerazzak (Rabat) or Mr Rachad Izzat at the above emails.

AFRICA

TUNISIA

TUNISIA

Like its neighbour in the Maghreb, Tunisia is turning away from the language of its former colonial master. Although the young generation speak fluent French because they have been taught it in school, many teenagers prefer English as their second language. People may be interested in paying you for lessons, even though you plan to be in the country for a relatively short time, as **Roger Musker** was one winter:

> I decided to take a month off work as a kind of sabbatical and, if well planned, at no cost. I found all young people in Tunisia keen to practise and speak English whenever possible. I had one good contact in Sousse, who worked for the Tunisian Tourist Agency. I wrote to him from England and he replied that he could line up students on my arrival, which included himself and his 10-year-old daughter (who turned out to be my best student). At their house I was plied with extremely sweet tea and sticky cakes which you are obliged to eat. Altogether I had eight keen fee-paying students including a blind telephone operator, a teacher of English on a revision course and students from the Bourguiba Institute at Sousse University, which claims to be the second oldest university in the world. For the latter it was necessary to get permission from the Ministry of Education via the headmaster.
>
> Every day I tutored 8–10am and 5–7pm. The hourly rate was about £8, allowing me to cover basic costs while having a working holiday. Even without the contact and knowing Arabic, work is there for the asking. It just takes initiative. Go to any official institute, the tourism or municipal offices, demonstrate your availability and enthusiasm, give them your contact number and await replies.

The Bourguiba Institute in Tunis (47 Av. de la Liberté, 1002 Tunis; ✆ +71 832923; lblv@lblv.rnu.tn; www.iblv.rnu.tn) hire high-level teachers.

AMIDEAST TUNISIA
22 Rue Al Amine Al Abassi, B.P. 351, Cite Jardina 1002, Tunis, Tunisia
✆ +71 790 559/563, 841 488 or 842 488; fax 71 791 913
✉ tunisia@amideast.org
🖳 www.amideast.org

NUMBER OF TEACHERS: 25 full or part-time independent contract TEFL/TESL teachers.
PREFERENCE OF NATIONALITY: native speakers of English.
QUALIFICATIONS: ideally a degree or recognised international certificate in TEFL/TESL plus a minimum of 2 years' successful experience teaching English to non-native speakers.
CONDITIONS OF EMPLOYMENT: 1 year. Half of return

airfare from teacher's home reimbursed at end of contract. Classes for children, teenagers and adults held between 8.30am and 9pm. Courses also run for public and private sector organisations.
SALARY: US$12–US$13.50 per hour depending on qualifications and experience.
FACILITIES/SUPPORT: school will on request try to identify a Tunisian family willing to house the new teacher for an initial period until they find accommodation (with help of school). During the 4 months that American and Canadian citizens are allowed to stay as tourists, the school handles arrangements for getting a work permit and visa.
RECRUITMENT: via www.amideast.org plus regional and international TEFL conferences.
CONTACT: Lee Jennings, Country Director.

OTHER AFRICAN COUNTRIES

Mauritania

Mauritania is becoming a more popular overland route from Morocco to Senegal now that the tensions of the western Sahara seem to have cooled a bit. There's also a new paved road from Nouadibou to Nouakchott, which makes travel considerably easier. When **Bradwell Jackson** visited he was surprised by the number of Westerners he saw: '*It seems as though this country is up and coming as one of those unexplored gems that travellers haven't yet discovered.*'

Bradwell, who supplied all the information for this section, found a teaching job by a '*happy accident of fate*'. On striking up a conversation with a Westerner walking on the other side of the street, he asked her about English language schools, and was promptly taken to the front door of The English Language Centre.

> *I was lucky enough to speak with the owner right away. I was talking to her while she was busy doing some other things, so it was not a formal interview. I did not have to fill out an application, though she asked me to write a letter explaining why I wanted to work in Mauritania. She seemed very interested, and asked me to come back in a couple of days to do a mock class in front of her teachers. I was hired based on this.*

Bradwell's wages started at 50,000 ouguiyas (US$190) a month and increased to 68,000 (US$259) a month. He was told that a person hired from within the country is paid much less than a person hired from outside. Getting a work permit was refreshingly simple. The school simply took his passport to the employment office and paid for a 1-year work permit. Bradwell found the students to be a joy to work with, because they were 'serious' and hungry to learn.

Native English teachers could try Nouakchott English Center (B.P. 4473 ILOT P-29; ✆ +529 25 42; sagna@univ-nkc.mr). Mr Sagna, the Coordinator, hires six to eight teachers, one or two of whom he would like to be native English speakers, although this would depend on the school's income. Teachers work 4½ hours a week and are paid 1,500–2,500 ouguiyas per hour (about US$6–US$10/hr). British English is as popular as American English.

Senegal

The British Council has a brand new teaching centre in Dakar (Rue AAB-68, Amitie Zone A et B (BP 6232); ✆ 221 869 2700/869 2702; fax 221 864 0850; angus.bjarnason@britishcouncil.sn; www. britishcouncil.org/senegal) and hire well-qualified teachers. They will want to see your CV and certification, although Bradwell Jackson reports that they will consider hiring non-UK citizens and may leave you 'wriggle room' if you don't quite have the qualifications they officially require.

There are also three language assistant posts in Dakar every year, open to final year students or graduates with A level, higher grade or equivalent in French.

Teaching assistants work at the British-Senegalese Institute, teaching adults from beginners to advanced level. Assistants will have a full range of teaching duties, including producing teaching materials, arranging cultural activities and invigilating exams. The usual hours are 18 per week; the wage is CFA 170,000 per month net and accommodation is free.

The British Senegalese Institute (Rue du 18 Juin BP: 35 Dakar; ✆ +822 28 70, 822 40 23, 822 77 8; fax 822 77 74; yamarkhaya@hotmail.com) does not require teachers to have a specific certificate or experience, although these are certainly desirable. The average hours per week are 15, and the pay is around CFA 3,500 per hour.

Another possibility is the Centre Africain d'Etudes Superieres en Gestion (Boulevard du General De Gaulle, B.P. 3802–Dakar; ✆ 839 73 04 Direct 839 74 39; fax 839 75 66; moussa.dieng@cesag.sn). The school is located in a large, official complex and tends to cater for more affluent students. Bradwell Jackson spoke to Moussa Dieng, Chef du Departement Langues, who said that no specific certificate was required, just a good knowledge of the language. Moussa Dieng seemed to like the idea of hiring native English speakers. The American Language Program in Senegal continues to recruit.

Although Dakar is an interesting city of contrasts, Bradwell was not tempted to stay. He found the city sprawling and unwieldy, and a little too expensive.

Mali

Mali is one of west Africa's poorest countries, falling victim to droughts, dictatorship, rebellions and coups in the past 50 years. However, there are some opportunities, as **Bradwell Jackson** discovered. His first 'job' was courtesy of couch surfing (see earlier); however there are quite a few private language schools and one of the more prestigious is Gie Cours de Langues (see list of employers). General Director Ousmane Fofana would like to employ two native English speakers, paying 1,750 CFA (around US$4) per hour, extra if working off-site. He can assist with finding a reduced rate apartment and may be able to give experienced teachers extra paid work translating/marketing.

LIST OF EMPLOYERS

CAMEROON

CAMEROON VISION TRUST
PO Box 1075, Limbe
✆ 9 58 02 92
🖱 camvisiontrust@yahoo.co.uk

NUMBER OF TEACHERS: 15 per year.
PREFERENCE OF NATIONALITY: British or American.
QUALIFICATIONS: basic TEFL qualification or higher.
CONDITIONS OF EMPLOYMENT: 2-year maximum contract, to work 15 hours per week.
SALARY: voluntary work but hostel accommodation and a basic allowance are provided.
FACILITIES/SUPPORT: assistance provided with work permits and visas.
RECRUITMENT: interview required possibly in the UK and USA.
CONTACT: Ms Rosemary O M Enie.

LIBYA

BELL INTERNATIONAL – LIBYA
Hillscross, Red Cross Lane, Cambridge CB2 2QX
✆ 01223 275500; fax 01223 414080
🖱 info-overseas@bell-centres.com
🖳 www.bell-centres.com/jobs/list.asp

NUMBER OF TEACHERS: 25–35 for language training contracts in various locations across northern Libya.
PREFERENCE OF NATIONALITY: native English speakers.
QUALIFICATIONS: a university degree, CELTA/Trinity TESOL or recognised equivalent plus at least 5 years' EFL experience including 2 years' overseas. Experience of KET/PET and IELTS.
CONDITIONS OF EMPLOYMENT: 1-year temporary contracts. 24 contact hours per week over 6 days.
SALARY: gross annual salary range of between £25,000 and £27,000 per annum (pro-rata).

FACILITIES/SUPPORT: all posts are based on a 10-week rotation with 3–4 weeks paid leave and return flights to the UK for each 10-week block. Competitive salary, free accommodation and meals. Full medical insurance cover is provided.

RECRUITMENT: internet, newspapers, personal interview, telephone interview through Bell International in the UK.

MALI

COURS DE LANGUES PRODESCO
BPE 3461, Bamako
- /fax 221 74 22
- prodesco@arc.net.ml
- www.prodesco.org

NUMBER OF TEACHERS: would like to employ 2.

PREFERENCE OF NATIONALITY: already hired US teachers.

QUALIFICATIONS: TESL/TEFL experience with adults. Bachelor degree.

CONDITIONS OF EMPLOYMENT: around 12–15 hours per week, some teaching sessions scheduled on evenings and weekends if requested by participants. Experienced teachers may be able to take on paid administrative work (translation, marketing, interpreting).

SALARY: 1,750 CFA (around US$4) per hour, extra if working off-site.

FACILITIES/SUPPORT: assistance with finding a reduced rate apartment.

CONTACT: Ousmane Fofana, General Director.

MOZAMBIQUE

LYNDEN LANGUAGE SCHOOL
Av Zedequias Manganhela 267, JAT Building, 2nd Floor, Maputo
- +21 360494; fax 21 316065
- lynden@teledata.mz
- www.lynden.co.mz

NUMBER OF TEACHERS: 5.

PREFERENCE OF NATIONALITY: British, Australian, South African, etc.

QUALIFICATIONS: CELTA or Trinity plus 2 years' experience.

CONDITIONS OF EMPLOYMENT: 1 year. 25 hours per week.

SALARY: US$1,000; half paid in the local currency (meticals).

FACILITIES/SUPPORT: school finds and pays for accommodation. School applies to Ministry of Labour for work permit once teachers gather necessary documents.

RECRUITMENT: *EL Gazette* or internet. References checked by phone.

CONTACT: Denise Lord or Lynne Longley, Co-Directors.

SOUTH AFRICA

CAPE STUDIES LANGUAGE SCHOOL
PO Box 4425, Cape Town 8000 (or 2–17 Varney's Road, Green Point 8001)
- +21 439 0999; fax 21 439 3130
- info@capestudies.com
- www.capestudies.com

NUMBER OF TEACHERS: about 15.

PREFERENCE OF NATIONALITY: any but preferably those with permanent residency in South Africa.

QUALIFICATIONS: minimum TEFL experience, also CELTA. Teaching experience preferable.

CONDITIONS OF EMPLOYMENT: contracts can vary, although teachers are required to give 2 months' notice. Hours can be between 8am and 4.30pm.

SALARY: approx. R55 per lesson.

FACILITIES/SUPPORT: accommodation officer and host families.

RECRUITMENT: personal interview necessary.

INTERLINK SCHOOL OF LANGUAGES
28 Queens Road, Sea Point, Cape Town 8005
- +21 439 9834; fax 21 434 3267
- info@interlink.co.za
- www.interlink.co.za

NUMBER OF TEACHERS: 6.

PREFERENCE OF NATIONALITY: South Africans preferred.

QUALIFICATIONS: Minimum CELTA with experience.

CONDITIONS OF EMPLOYMENT: Full-time contracts last for 1 year. Part-time contracts reviewed weekly according to demand.

SALARY: varies according to experience and qualifications. Part-time salary R60 per hour.

RECRUITMENT: Interview required.

CONTACT: Luanne McCallum, Manager.

SUDAN

SUDAN VOLUNTEER PROGRAMME
34 Estelle Road, London NW3 2JY
☏ /fax 020 7485 8619
✉ davidsvp@blueyonder.com
🖥 www.svp-uk.com
UK registered charity which promotes English teaching among university students and other adults.

NUMBER OF TEACHERS: 10–20 at any time in and around Khartoum especially Omdurman.

PREFERENCE OF NATIONALITY: none, but should be native speakers of English.

QUALIFICATIONS: TEFL certificate, experience of travelling in developing countries and some knowledge of Arabic are helpful but not obligatory. Volunteers must be in good health and be native English speakers with some university education.

CONDITIONS OF EMPLOYMENT: preferred minimum 8 months to tie in with university semesters: September to January or January to April.

SALARY: SVP pays subsistence, accommodation and insurance beyond the initial 3 months. Volunteers must raise the cost of the airfare to Sudan (currently £485) plus £60 (cost of the first 3 months insurance).

FACILITIES/SUPPORT: accommodation with self-catering facilities is arranged, usually at the university where you are teaching.

RECRUITMENT: applications accepted year round. Two referees are also required. Prior to departure, medical check-up required plus selection interviews, orientation and briefings take place. Volunteers are required to write a report of their experiences and to advise new volunteers.

CONTACT: David Wolton.

TANZANIA

AANG SERIAN ('HOUSE OF PEACE')
PO Box 13732, Arusha, Tanzania
☏ +744 318548 or 743 009172
✉ aang_serian@hotmail.com
🖥 www.aangserian.org.uk or www.aangserian.org

NUMBER OF TEACHERS: 15–20 teaching assistants and qualified teachers in ESL and other subjects placed at Aang Serian Noonkondin Secondary School, in the rural Maasai village of Eluwai.

PREFERENCE OF NATIONALITY: all nationalities accepted. Non-native speakers of English should have IELTS 6.5 or above.

QUALIFICATIONS: classroom assistants who work alongside a qualified Tanzanian teacher should have the CELTA, TEFL or similar; a degree with education as a minor or supplementary subject, or previous teaching experience without a formal qualification in education.

CONDITIONS OF EMPLOYMENT: 2–3 months recommended for short-term volunteers though arrangements are flexible. Ideally 6–12 months from January or July for teachers.

SALARY: programme fee $420 includes donation to the school. Volunteers are also asked to cover their living costs, for which they should budget $40–$50 per week.

FACILITIES/SUPPORT: volunteers stay in a 3-bedroom staff house at the school (subject to availability) or in homestay. Some may camp during busy periods. Volunteers are also offered reduced rates for wildlife safaris, mountain-climbing expeditions, walking tours, short courses, academic lectures and visits to rural Chagga and Rangi communities, offered by a partner company in Arusha. Orientation given on arrival plus Swahili tuition and optional drum and dance classes.

RECRUITMENT: applications can be made online.

CONTACT: Gemma Enolengila, International Liaison.

MONDO CHALLENGE
Malsor House, Gayton Road, Milton Malsor, Northampton, NN7 3AB, UK;
☏ +01604 858225
✉ info@mondochallenge.org
🖥 www.mondochallenge.org

MondoChallenge sends volunteers (early retired, career break, post-university, gap year) to help with development programmes in Africa, Asia and South America. All programmes are community based, living alongside local people.

NUMBER OF PLACEMENTS: 12 teaching programmes, in primary and secondary schools, and additionally in adult education.

QUALIFICATIONS: ages 22+. Teaching experience and/or TEFL qualifications are desirable but not essential. Volunteers need a mature attitude and to be able to get stuck in with the many different aspects to teaching abroad.

CONDITIONS OF WORK: Programmes are generally 1-6 months, with an average of 3 months.

SALARY: None. There is a financial contribution from £900, depending on the length of stay. Accommodation is arranged locally with a host family.

FACILITIES/SUPPORT: managers oversee the volunteers' welfare. Extensive briefing pack, and lots of support from the UK staff prior to and during stay.

RECRUITMENT: Volunteers are recruited all year round. Interviews are done face to face when applicable, or alternatively over the phone.

CONTACT: Ben Szreider, Head of Recruitment.

UGANDA

SOFT POWER EDUCATION

55 Guildhall St, Bury St Edmunds, Suffolk, England IP33 1QF; in Uganda: PO Box 1493, Jinja, Uganda, East Africa

📞 +256 772 903344

🖱 info@softpowereducation.com

💻 www.softpowereducation.com

British registered non-religious charity to enhance the education facilities for hundreds of Ugandan children.

NUMBER OF TEACHERS: indeterminate number of volunteers to tutor mainly adults at the Omugezi Cultural Centre.

QUALIFICATIONS: creativity and initiative.

CONDITIONS OF EMPLOYMENT: 1 day to 3 months. Lessons take place in evenings and weekends since premises are used as a primary school during the day.

SALARY: none. Volunteers must cover their own living and travel expenses as well as a donation to the charity. Recommended amount is £75 a week.

FACILITIES/SUPPORT: Camping, dorms or living within the local community. Guest houses in Jinja are also an option, but they are located some distance away from the network of schools which means longer travelling times to site.

CONTACT: Hannah Small, Founder.

BY SEARCHING THE WEB, NEW ZEALAND ADVENTURER MARK TANNER FOUND OUT ABOUT THE BRITISH NGO SUDAN VOLUNTEER PROGRAMME (ENTRY ABOVE) AND WAS ACCEPTED ONTO THE SCHEME:

While some volunteers were required to use the syllabus as a guide, I had a free rein over what I taught and how. This prompted me to ask the students to suggest topics that were of interest to them and allowed me freedom to encourage discussion about parts of the Sudanese culture I was interested in. The main objective was to provide the students with a native English speaker and get them used to conversation. We were encouraged to do less formal sessions called the English Club. For example we themed the cooking class as our university was all-female and cooking was something they considered important. Some classes stand out in my memory such as the one where we tried to teach the students to juggle. The classrooms could be quite hot and were equipped with blackboard and chalk, although we used teaching aids based on our own initiative.

The lodgings provided were basic, but by Sudanese standards good. The stipend is $100 per month which is enough to subsist in Sudan, living like the Sudanese. As lovely as the Sudanese are, things are not as organised in the country as we would expect in the west. Yet it would be difficult to find more hospitable people than the Sudanese and there is never a shortage of offers for dinner or to visit a village, which provided a fantastic opportunity to experience the culture in a way many other NGO [non-governmental organisation] workers never saw.

There are many interesting things to see in Khartoum such as Nuba Wrestling, fish markets, Dervish dancing and museums. SVP has a deal with the Blue Nile Sailing Club which allows students to try their luck at sailing on the Nile. Many of the volunteers did other voluntary work for NGOs. I helped an NGO with marketing and to develop a website. My principal motivation for being in the Sudan was to paddle through Sudan on the Nile, and I spent a lot of my spare time trying to source permits for this.

One of the highlights for me was seeing the English of the students improve and the relationships develop from that. Teachers are greatly respected in the Sudan so volunteers are revered and treated with respect.

Although the English language is not a universal passport to employment, it can certainly be put to good use in many Asian countries where the demand for English teachers is substantial, even extraordinary as is the case with China, described as a 'black hole' for EFL teachers, by a European Director of Studies.

Conditions and remuneration will differ wildly between industrialised countries such as Japan, Korea and Taiwan with their Western-style economies, and developing countries such as Nepal and Cambodia, where both wages and the standard of living are lower. China combines rapidly industrialised cities with vast stretches of rural industry, although even in major cities wages are not usually as good as those to be found in Taiwan.

> **A CONCERTED JOB HUNT IN ASIA WILL ALMOST ALWAYS TURN UP POSSIBILITIES, AND SOMETIMES THE DIFFICULTY COMES IN CHOOSING AMONG THEM. ROSS MCKAY FROM GLASGOW WRITES OF HIS JOB HUNT:**
>
> *I was 50 and fed up for various reasons. So I wrote to about 500 institutions all over South East Asia. Whilst waiting for replies I did a distance TESOL course and College of Further Education teaching certificate. I got three offers, one in Hanoi, one in Bangkok, and I chose Jakarta as I knew nothing about Indonesia. My colleagues come from all over the English-speaking world and often become great pals. But there are some head-cases. I guess one has to be a little crazy to live this life, and a few people crack up. The great thing about life in Indonesia is that every morning you wake up and have no idea what the heck is going to happen next.*

It may not be necessary to organise a mass mail-out in order to arrange a teaching stay in Asia. For American students, both Princeton and Stanford Universities run voluntary programmes in various Asian countries including some TEFL teaching. VIA (Volunteers in Asia) has been providing international exchange opportunities since 1963. Each year VIA sends 30–40 volunteer English teachers to China, Vietnam, Indonesia, Myanmar, Cambodia and Laos on short (summer) and longer term (1-year or 2-year) assignments. All programmes are open to college students or graduates over 18. Occasional exceptions can be made for people without a college degree. Applications are due in mid-February and the participation fee is between US$1,500 and US$3,000. Further information is available online at www.viaprograms.org (℃ 650 723 3229; info@viaprograms.org).

For information about the Princeton programme, contact Princeton-in-Asia, Bobst Center for Peace and Justice, Room 202, 83 Prospect Avenue, Princeton University, Princeton, NJ 08544 (℃ 609 258 3657; fax: 609 275 1823; pia@princeton.edu; www.princeton.edu/~pia/). It currently places about 115 fellows in 15 Asian countries: China, East Timor, Hong Kong, Indonesia, Japan, Kazakhstan, Laos, Malaysia, Mongolia, Philippines, Singapore, South Korea, Taiwan, Thailand and Vietnam. Applications must be accompanied by a US$40 fee and be submitted by the beginning of December.

For UK teachers, recruitment organisations such as Saxoncourt (affiliated to Shane English Schools) and EF English First are active in the region. Saxoncourt recruits for Shane English Schools in Japan, China, Taiwan and Vietnam. There are more than 250 Shane schools in Asia. A couple of commercial recruitment agencies specialise in placing ELT-trained teachers in Asian countries. For example, the Anglo-Pacific (Asia) Consultancy (Suite 32, Nevilles Court, Dollis Hill Lane, London NW2 6HG; ℃ 020 8452 7836) is an educational consultancy which concentrates on recruiting teachers for schools, colleges and universities in Thailand, Taiwan and other South East Asian countries.

Teacharound ESL Recruitment based in Lancashire (www.teacharound.co.uk) recruits teachers with a degree and TEFL/PGCE for schools in Asia, mainly China, Taiwan and Japan, but also as unqualified volunteers in Vietnam, Cambodia and China.

REACH TO TEACH

21 Everett Rd. Extension, Albany, NY 12205, USA

✆ (USA)201 467 4612;

(Taiwan)+886 920 699 473;

fax(USA)480 247 5426

🖰 info@ReachToTeachRecruiting.com

🖳 www.ReachToTeachRecruiting.com

NUMBER OF TEACHERS: 300+ per year to work in Taiwan, Korea, Japan and China.

PREFERENCE OF NATIONALITY: applications accepted from USA, Canada, UK, South Africa, Australia, New Zealand and Ireland.

QUALIFICATIONS: teaching experience is a plus, but a positive, enthusiastic, dedicated and flexible attitude is much more important. Training for new teachers is provided.

CONDITIONS OF EMPLOYMENT: all contracts are for 1 year. Schedules vary but are generally either morning/af-ternoon or afternoon/evening.

SALARY: variable but enough to live on comfortably and usually to save some money.

FACILITIES/SUPPORT: all teachers receive assistance in finding accommodation. Depending on the country, accommodation might be provided for free (China, Korea). In other countries (Taiwan, Japan), the teacher is responsible for paying rent. All teachers are provided with full work permit, as part of the company promise to teachers. For teachers in Taiwan, Reach To Teach has monthly social gatherings and events for new teachers and year round support from the local offices.

RECRUITMENT: Phone interviews and on-campus visits/interviews (US only) and via website.

CONTACT: Richard Jones, Director of Recruiting (Richard@ReachToTeachRecruiting.com) and Mitch Gordon, Director of School Relations (Mitch@ReachToTeach Recruiting.com).

CHINA

Some commentators have predicted that the 21st century will belong to China. In order to fulfil this prediction, China wants to learn the language of the West in unprecedented numbers. Cyberspace is a-buzz with new companies and organisations offering English language training and looking for teachers.

In turn, native English speakers are heading to China in their thousands, barely bothering to look at teaching possibilities in Europe or even Japan. Western curiosity about this huge country, spurred on by a barrage of media stories, is rising exponentially.

Post 1978, one of China's first steps in its journey from collectivism to capitalism was to invite English language teachers to its institutes of higher education. Three decades later thousands of native speakers are teaching not only at schools and academic institutions around the country but in companies and (what would have been unthinkable not so long ago) private language institutes. Furthermore the emerging middle class aspires to send its children for private tuition just as in the capitalist countries of Taiwan, Korea and Japan.

One estimate has been made that there are 450 million English language learners in China, due in large measure to the fact that English is compulsory for school pupils from the age of 9. Although optional, English is now even taught from kindergarten. Many street and shop signs in the capital and other major cities are written in English as well as Chinese, though most Beijing citizens, especially the older generation, can speak very little English apart from 'McDonald's'. A great many students and teachers are very keen to improve their English to Cambridge Proficiency standard in the hope of being accepted to study overseas. Competition can be cut throat although children from the wealthiest families may be less inspired, knowing that they'll be going abroad eventually, whether their English is fluent or not. But most are eager to learn, even if the style of learning to which they have become accustomed can be difficult for foreign teachers to cope with.

It is easy to forget, amid the well-reported stories of sprawling urban metropolises rising almost in the night, that about 80% of China's population still lives in the countryside. **Sam Meekings** was surprised to discover that although he headed off to Beijing every other weekend to stock up on Western foods and see the sights, most of his students had never left the small city of Hengshui; only 15 years previously it had all been farmland.

The cumbersome bureaucracy with which teachers had to contend in the old days is much less of a problem. Even getting a work permit is now fairly straightforward and it is no longer necessary (in most schools in big cities) to fill out endless forms before being allowed to use the photocopier. Indeed the entire visa process is usually completed by the school and education authority, upon the teacher's arrival in China.

PROSPECTS FOR TEACHERS

'With just a university degree and a little determination anyone can find an opportunity to challenge themselves somewhere in twenty-first century China,' writes **Sam Meekings,** who taught in a state-run normal college before accepting an editing job with Oxford University Press in Shanghai. A degree is normally a minimum requirement these days and any teaching experience is useful, but not so much importance is attached to TEFL qualifications and quite often references are not taken up. However, the better schools have recently started to become more stringent in their recruiting methods and foreigners cannot simply walk into more lucrative jobs in the same way that they used to be able to. Nevertheless, there are still many schools so desperate that they will employ anyone simply to have a 'token foreigner' and hence enhance their status.

Theoretically, the Chinese government classifies teachers as either foreign experts (FEs) or foreign teachers (FTs). FEs are expected to have an MA in a relevant area (English, Linguistics, TEFL/TESOL, etc.) and some teaching experience at the tertiary level. FTs are usually under 25 and have only a university degree. In practice, most teachers are classified as 'FE's, even if they only have a degree.

It is almost impossible for a non-graduate to work in a university, including students on exchange schemes like those run by gap year organisations such as Lattitude (formerly GAP) and Project Trust. Instead these younger teachers are usually placed in middle schools (public secondary schools, often boarding schools). Non-graduates also often find work in schools that are not strictly legal, making it difficult for them to obtain the necessary working documents (schools must present copies of the passport, two references, the university degree, a CV and recent photographs in order to obtain work permits). Even some graduates work illegally, on various business and tourist visas. One teacher spent a year working 'under the table' before finally getting a work permit/visa, which required 'a whole bunch of paper work' and a trip to Hong Kong.

A large proportion of foreigners are employed in Beijing and Shanghai but there are many opportunities in the provinces as well, especially for FTs. The more remote the area or the more hostile the climate, the easier it will be to find a job. But there are also plenty of vacancies in comfortable cities such as Kunming and Dalian. Many vacancies for both FEs and FTs go unfilled. Specialist recruitment organisations are notified of more positions than they can find people to fill them.

DEMAND EXISTS IN THE HUNDREDS OF UNIVERSITIES, COLLEGES, FOREIGN LANGUAGE INSTITUTES, INSTITUTES OF TECHNOLOGY, TEACHER TRAINING COLLEGES (CALLED NORMAL UNIVERSITIES) AND SECONDARY SCHOOLS, ESPECIALLY IN THE PROVINCES IN CHINA. NORMAL UNIVERSITIES OFTEN SEEM TO BE OVERLOOKED WHEN FOREIGN TEACHERS ARE ASSIGNED CENTRALLY, SO THEY ARE A VERY PROMISING BET FOR PEOPLE APPLYING DIRECTLY OR ON-THE-SPOT. SAM MEEKINGS TAUGHT AT THE NORMAL UNIVERSITY IN HENGSHUI:

I lived on campus at the state-run normal college, sharing a kitchen and office with another foreign teacher. Though I was fresh out of university, I found myself teaching English literature to graduates who were often a couple of years older than me. This was initially challenging, only because, in common with teachers in most state schools, I was told that I must follow the syllabus. In practice, what this meant was not deviating from the textbook that all the students had been issued with.

Jessie Levene's first job was working for a company that hired teachers out to schools, which involved long hours (7am–5pm) and classes of 60 students. She prefers her second job, teaching at a university in Chengdu, '*I would highly recommend university teaching over working for a private company, even though the wages are much lower.*' She takes 14 classes a week of no more than 28 students. Classes are a manageable 40 minutes.

Applications can be made through the Chinese Embassy in your country, through various placement organisations, recruitment agencies (which don't charge teachers a fee) and voluntary bodies, or by applying directly to institutions advertised on the internet and elsewhere.

Even ordinary secondary schools employ native speakers; applications can be made through provincial education bureaux. Writing direct to the Foreign Affairs Office (*waiban*) of institutes of higher learning may lead to a job offer. Chinese institutes seem to attach more weight to the letter of application than to the curriculum vitae, but the CV should still be sent and should emphasise any work or experience in education. Also enclose a photo, a photocopy of the first page of your passport, a copy of any education certificates and two references. Jessie Levene notes that schools seem to prefer female teachers, particularly for younger students, and as a result, she was given more and more classes, despite an already full timetable.

Unfortunately, the mechanisms for placing teachers and communicating with them can be subject to the same tendency to bureaucratic ineptitude as plagues teachers in China. Once you have been promised a job, schools can be very remiss about keeping in touch, so keep pressing. Often this is because the person with whom you are in contact does not speak much English but doesn't want to lose face. You should also be aware of what one headteacher describes as the 'Chinglish factor'. For example, it is common for a Chinese person to reply to a job application with a 'welcome to our school'. This is not necessarily a positive reply and in fact often means simply 'I'm happy that you contacted me but.....'. If you are unsure of their meaning, it is always best to press further.

It is becoming increasingly common for schools to offer a job to an applicant but not guarantee employment until they arrive at the school. This is the result of foreigners having abused the system in the past, accepting numerous jobs in order to keep their options open. Many schools have also introduced a probationary period of between two and 10 weeks. While this may sound a bit daunting if you have already paid for flight tickets, it can work in the applicant's favour, as it allows time to ensure that the school is suitable for you. It is always best, wherever possible, to visit a school before signing a contract and talk to other foreign teachers, to make sure that the school is everything it says it is and to examine the accommodation.

Some schools and private language institutes that do offer contracts to unseen candidates rely on long-distance phone calls or competitively priced (or even free) innovations such as Skype.

Any university graduate travelling in China should be able to arrange a teaching contract just by asking around at the many colleges in the towns and cities on his or her itinerary. Even when foreign travellers have not been looking for work, they have been approached and invited to teach English. It has been suggested that standing in a railway station beside a notice advertising your availability to teach English would succeed, though probably more for private tuition than an institutional job. The going rate in the big cities for private English tuition is £10–£15 an hour.

If you fix up a job at FT level on the spot, it may not be for an entire academic year and your pay may be calculated on an hourly basis.

FINDING A JOB

With the explosion in opportunities, the job hunt is far more straightforward than it was a few years ago when most teacher applications were for institutes of higher education and had to go through the Chinese Education Association for International Exchange (CEAIE; www.ceaie.org) or one of its 37 provincial offices. Nowadays CEAIE recruits through www.chinajob.com (see below) and there are also many private recruiters, foundations or China-linked companies eager to sign up native speakers (with or without relevant experience) for an academic year.

Some of the tried and tested old schemes are still in place and still work. The British Council's Language Assistants Programme, in cooperation with the Chinese Education authorities places graduates in schools across China. TEFL training is provided on a two-week course in Shanghai which is paid for by the British Council. Participants receive free accommodation, and utilities and a flight back to the UK. Teaching experience and/or qualifications are not necessary. Details of the application procedure can be obtained from the Language Assistants Team at the British Council (10 Spring Gardens, London SW1A 2BN; ℂ 020 7389 4955; fax: 020 7389 4594; assistants@britishcouncil.org) or at www.languageassistant.co.uk. The British Council accepts applications up until the end of February (non-refundable placement fee £48). Applications are screened and then interviews conducted in April for positions starting in August. The minimum requirement is a university degree, though a TEFL certificate and/or teaching experience, preferably abroad, improve your chances of acceptance. Opportunities are available in a large variety of cities throughout mainland China, though initial training takes place for all participants in Shanghai in August.

The most common contract is for a minimum of 20 hours per week for a year starting at the beginning of term in early September. TEFL and Chinese language training will take place in August. Of course vacancies occur at other times of year, and another flurry of hiring takes place in March for five-month contracts to August. Most participants are paid the government-imposed minimum of RMB5,000 (Renminbi yuan) a month and all teachers are provided with free accommodation.

The www.chinajob.com job fair is now in its sixth year and offers a great (and free) opportunity for teachers to look for 'on the spot' opportunities in educational institutions, language training organisations, and private and national companies. Job fairs take place annually in late April in Beijing and Hangzhou. For more information visit www.chinajob.com or www.safea.gov.cn/english.

Some TEFL training courses offered in China also lead to jobs. The TEFL in China Certificate Training Program for foreign teachers, with job placement is run by China Connection Education Services (www.teachenglishinchina.com). Candidates complete an eight-day course at a cost of $570 for tuition and then start work. Another similar programme is run by China Services for Foreign Teachers (http://tefl.chinajob.com/Course_&_Certificate.htm).

PRIVATE LANGUAGE TRAINING

Ever since the legislation in China changed, allowing privatised companies to operate in the fields of media and education, a huge number of private language schools and training centres has opened. **Jane Pennington** who taught for four years in China carried out a little research and estimates that there are about 100 private language companies in Kunming, only about 15%–20% of which are officially licensed. These institutes are not allowed to invite foreign teachers without a lot of red tape, which is usually not worth their while. However they are very eager to hire native speakers on the spot, often people on a student visa at the university. Like private schools everywhere, a certain number of these are run by unscrupulous entrepreneurs interested only in profit. If considering working in the private sector, try to find out the degree of professionalism of the company that has expressed interest in hiring you, and talk to other foreigners working there, especially with regards to payment.

*International ELT organisations such as Wall Street Institute (WSI) may prove more reliable, although standards between franchise schools can vary substantially. **Yasmin Peiris** recounts My employment package included an airport transfer and a week in a hotel on arrival, so I felt pretty secure. The evening I arrived, a Wall Street Institute expat expert called me and was very supportive, in helping me find an apartment. I had a week of training, before starting my full time, 30 hour contract. We have training regularly which is helpful and refreshing and keeps you on your toes. Our class sizes range from 4 to 15 students and the working environment is very good, with modern classrooms and teaching resources readily available.*

The internet is a prolific source of possibilities and expanding all the time. According to a leading news agency, for the first time China now has more people online than the USA. Any web search or a trawl of the major ELT job sites is bound to turn up plenty of contacts. The China TEFL Network at www.chinatefl.net is excellent with long lists of jobs, all dated and described in a great deal of detail, some with photos. Another one to try is www.jobchina.net.

In the private sector, many large companies (such as hotel chains) have their own language training facilities for staff, especially if they are joint ventures with Western companies. Most recruitment of teachers by business and industry takes place locally, since they do not offer accommodation. If in Beijing, check classified adverts in the English language bimonthly magazine *Beijing Scene*.

PLACEMENT AGENCIES AND ORGANISATIONS

MANY ORGANISATIONS RECRUIT TEACHERS FOR CHINA FROM THE UK. NINA CAPEK CHOSE BUCKLAND INTERNATIONAL EDUCATION GROUP (SEE ENTRY BELOW) TO HELP ORGANISE HER TEACHING JOB IN CHINA, AND WAS FULL OF PRAISE FOR THEM:
Foreign teachers are not required to pay a fee to sign up with Buckland unlike some companies who charge a lot of money. They sorted out my work visa for me, they collected me from the airport and put all the new teachers up in a nice guest house for their first five days in the country. Pay was not as good as with some other companies, but the support and conditions made up for it and the wage was sufficient to live like a princess anyway. OK, some people lived like queens, but I wanted security.

Some of the organisations listed below are the UK office of Chinese companies. Others are ELT training centres or gap year placement agencies, charities or voluntary organisations. Several are businesses whose principal activity is to recruit foreign students to come to the UK to study and, through their links with foreign institutions, assist those institutes to find English teachers.

Buckland International Education Group: see entry on page 370.
Bunac: 16 Bowling Green Lane, London EC1R 0QH; ✆ 020 7251 3472; enquiries@bunac. org.uk; www.bunac.org/volunteer/teflchina/default.aspx. BUNAC runs a teach and travel programme which offers a four-week TEFL course, lessons in Mandarin, and placement as a trainee teacher intern. A 6-month programme costs £1,565, a 12-month programme, £1,665. Extra costs include flights, insurance, etc.
China Recruitment: 8 Florence Court, London, W9 1TB; ✆ 0207 289 1031/07869 211 336; mail@china-recruitment.co.uk; www.china-recruitment.co.uk. Sends English-speaking gap year students, university graduates and professionals on a career break to live and teach in China. The Gap Year Programme places an emphasis on learning Mandarin. The Graduate and Career Break Programmes consist primarily of teaching English to Chinese students of various ages. The fee of £600 includes free furnished accommodation, regular meals, utilities, internet, assistance with visas and membership in China Recruitment's networking

portal China Web (www.china-web.co.uk). China Recruitment also includes a free subscription to the Your Safe Planet programme (www.yoursafeplanet.com). On the career break and graduate programmes, candidates are reimbursed full airfare for one-year contracts and half of the airfare for 6-month contracts. They will also receive an average salary of RMB4,500 (£300).

EF English First: see entry.

i-to-i: (© 0870 442 3043; www.i-to-i.com) places volunteer teachers in China as well as Nepal, Sri Lanka, India, Vietnam and South Korea.

Language Link: 21 Harrington Road, London SW7 3EU; © 020 7225 1065; fax: 020 7584 3518; Email recruitment@languagelink.co.uk; www.languagelink.co.uk. International training and recruitment agency which has two schools in Beijing and affiliations with middle and primary schools for the training and upgrading of local teachers. It also runs CELTA courses in Beijing (celta@languagelink.com.cn) and offers many positions to teachers with TEFL Certificate, YL, DELTA or trainers.

Oaklands Educational Services: 121 Admirals Walk, West Cliff Road, Bournemouth, BH2 5HF; © 01202 297549; Email oaklands@dial.pipex.com. No placement charge; free board and accommodation together with a small salary. Contact: Dr Rod Cooper.

Projects Abroad: Aldsworth Parade, Goring, Sussex BN12 4TX; © 01903 708300; www.projects-abroad.co.uk. The teaching project is based in the country towns of Wu Jiang, about two and a half hours journey inland from Shanghai. In the summer months – from June to September – it moves to Language Schools in Shanghai; cost from £1,395 for 1 month excluding airfares.

Students International: 158 Dalby Road, Melton Mowbray, Leicestershire LE13 0BJ; © 01664 481997; fax: 01664 563332; www.studentsint.com. Trinity CertTESOL centre (see Training listings) that is cooperating with Chinese universities to supply English teachers for business, academic, teacher training and general English.

The Amity Foundation: 71 Han Kou Road, Nanjing, Jiangsu 210008, China; © 25 332 4607; fax: 25 663 1701. Every year this Chinese voluntary organisation sends 60–80 teachers to work mostly in Chinese teachers colleges where most of the middle school teachers are trained. Recruits are obtained through various church-related societies abroad, e.g. the China Forum of Churches Together in Britain & Ireland (35–41 Lower Marsh, London SE1 7RL), the Scottish Churches' China Group (121 St. George St, Edinburgh EH2 4YN; pjohnston@cofscotland.org.uk), Christians Abroad (recruitment@cabroad.org.uk), and the National Council of Churches of Christ in the US (475 Riverside Drive, Room 668, New York, NY 10115). These organisations recruit and select teachers of English for 2-year contracts beginning each August. Countries in which Amity operates through churches include Canada, Denmark, Finland, Germany, Japan, the Netherlands, Norway, the Philippines, Sweden and the US. Enquiries welcomed from graduates and others suitably qualified (e.g. BEd, CELTA) with Christian commitment to live and work in simple conditions. Applications are due between October and December with final selection in February for departures in July. All travel expenses are covered.

Travellers Worldwide: Caravelle House, 17–19 Goring Road, Worthing, West Sussex BN12 5HY; © 01903 502595; www.travellersworldwide.com. Many volunteers needed for teaching projects in Yantai and Shanghai. Guide cost for 3 months teaching in Shanghai £1,795 including food, accommodation and support.

A number of North American organisations involved in teacher placements in China have entries in the listings at the end of this chapter including the Colorado China Council, Appalachians Abroad,

US-China Educational Exchange and the AIEF Education Foundation. Forte International is a Chinese company with an office in Washington which aims to expand US-China business cooperation; as part of its work it recruits English teachers (National Press Building, 529 14th St. NW, Suite 270, Washington, DC 20045; ✆ 202 628 8180; www.forteintl.com).

WorldTeach at the Center for International Development at Harvard University (79 John F Kennedy Street, Cambridge, MA 02138; ✆ 617 495 5527; www.worldteach.org) is a non-profit organisation which sends volunteers to teach in secondary schools in Hunan Province for a full academic year or for the summer. Undergraduates and graduates can also participate in the Shanghai Summer Teaching programme. Volunteers teach small classes of high school students at a language camp in Shanghai. Volunteers pay about US$4,000 for the summer programme but only US$500 (US$1,000 deposit refunded on successful completion of the programme) for making a year long commitment, which includes airfares, orientation, health insurance, room and board and field support.

CONDITIONS OF WORK

With the rise of the free market the once rigid distinctions between FTs and FEs has become blurred since many reward packages are now open to negotiation. But there is still a strong tendency to heap more perks on anyone with a higher degree. They are more likely to have their airfares or shipping costs reimbursed and they usually earn more than FTs. The general monthly salary range for most ordinary native speaker teachers should start in the range RMB5,000 (£360) but can rise in the private sector (especially in sophisticated Shanghai and Beijing) to RMB9,000 or higher for qualified candidates. Note that the renminbi is a non-convertible currency and foreigners have to negotiate a clause in their contract to be able to convert a certain percentage (up to a maximum 70%). When **Bradwell Jackson** arrived in Tangshan, he assumed that since so many foreigners are working in China as English teachers, it must surely be straightforward to deposit earnings in a bank at home (in the USA in his case). After some research he discovered that the Bank of China will make deposits into US bank accounts, albeit for a significant fee, especially if you don't have an account with them.

Pounds are still very difficult to get from the bank, especially in the provinces, but there is no problem with US and Hong Kong dollars. Many people change their money on the black market, known as the 'real bank'. Outside the major eastern cities you can live on RMB1,500 a month so it is important to be able to convert your saved renminbi into a foreign currency. However, those living in the major eastern cities are more likely to spend RMB3,000–5,000 per month, depending on their lifestyle. (Of course a monk can get by on RMB1,000.) Inflation is high in China so hanging out in expat bars and taking taxis is becoming more expensive. In Beijing, the automatic charge for a taxi is 10 yuan, whereas in Tangshan (two hours east of the capital), it's only 5 yuan.

Virtually all teachers working for educational establishments have their accommodation provided by the host institution, either in on-site residences or in a foreigners' hotel. In a very few cases a housing allowance will be offered in lieu to those teachers who want to choose their own flat. **Jessie Levene's** first job provided a housing allowance; her current job at a university provides a free apartment, although she chooses not to live there, preferring somewhere that isn't full of 'foreign students'. Working and living conditions vary from one institute to the next and it is vital to negotiate as much as possible before arrival and to obtain all promises in writing.

The three or four week holiday over Chinese New Year should be paid as should vacation periods in state schools if you are contracted to continue teaching after it. Foreign teachers can sometimes arrange to have longer breaks depending on their exam commitments.

Many employers offer free internet access and some offer free Chinese lessons. **Michelle** from Ireland, who was employed by the Bond Institute in Guangdong (see entry), believes that the wages should be higher considering the amount of work she was asked to do. However, she appreciated being given the choice of an apartment in town or outside the city.

When you are first notified by your employer in China that you have a job, you should avoid the temptation to write back enthusiastically accepting it. Rather ask for more details such as your status, salary, timetable and other conditions. You could also ask for the names of any current foreign employees whom you can ask for inside information. What is agreed at this stage will set the terms of employment even though it is standard practice not to sign a contract until after two months' probation (if at all).

Although higher wages can be earned in the big cities of Beijing, Guangzhou and Shanghai, and also in any of the economic zones such as Hainan Island, life in Chinese cities has many drawbacks in terms of crowds and pollution. For quality of life, south-western China is probably better than much of the east. Yunnan province has a particularly congenial climate. This area is also reputed to be less money-oriented than the east coast cities, which may have the drawback that it may be more difficult to find paying private students.

While teaching in a suburb of Shanghai, **Marybeth Hao** noticed many Chinese parents were more than willing to pay native English speaker tutors high fees to tutor their children outside school hours. For her one of the main rewards of teaching in Shanghai was to experience a culture in the midst of such dramatic and hurried changes.

Foreign teachers can be expected to teach anything from 15 to 30+ hours a week. A load of 20 hours is typical though this sounds lighter than it actually is because there are bound to be extra duties. Often there is a heavy load of marking not to mention marketing. Teachers in the private sector are routinely asked to attend student recruitment events, for example to hand out flyers or to appear at drop-in evenings whose main purpose is to rope in new clients. Some teachers are expected to staff an 'English corner' or English club, or deliver a weekly lecture on Western culture.

JANE PENNINGTON WARNS THAT YOU SHOULD BE PREPARED TO BE THE TOKEN FOR-EIGNER AT THE MANY BANQUETS YOU WILL BE INVITED TO WHEN YOU FIRST ARRIVE AND ALSO BE PREPARED TO TURN SOME OF THEM DOWN. SAM MEEKINGS DESCRIBES HOW SUCH BANQUETS CAN LEAD TO A SUCCESSION OF NASTY HANGOVERS:

Every foreigner in China quickly becomes familiar with baijiu, a sharp clear liquor with a cloying aftertaste, which is measured out into shot glasses in front of you at the start of a meal. Though beer is increasingly popular, no large event is complete without baijiu. At any large banquet, especially with officials or high-ranking teachers at the school or college, you will be encouraged to drink with them. Your glass will be topped up throughout the meal, and often many people will wish to toast you, meaning you must once again down your drink as a sign of mutual respect. This is why, by eight or nine in the evening, restaurants begin to clear out – many diners are too wasted to do anything but go home and sleep. It should be noted, however, that women are usually exempted from this custom, and though I would have liked to have been spared the attention (and the subsequent hangovers), my female colleagues were not impressed that they were simply expected to sit and slowly sip beer or coca-cola while all the men went through the intricate tradition of getting each other as drunk as possible. Similarly, while almost all the male teachers in the college were heavy smokers (one of the best gifts to present to someone in a box of cigarettes), women smoking was frowned upon. Though these attitudes cannot be found in big cosmopolitan cities, I am certain that they persist throughout the smaller towns that make up the bulk of this vast country.

In cases where teachers are given a huge number of classes, the administration's main ambition is to maximise your exposure, which may have the effect of minimising your usefulness. On the whole **Michelle** really enjoyed her time in China, but she thinks that foreign teachers should be given more advice on what is required of them before they start teaching. It is not unusual for the school to leave it up to the foreign teachers to find out if any national exams are looming for which you should be helping the students to prepare. Hours of teaching are unpredictable and the teaching days can be very long. Students get up at 6am and work at night in supervised sessions. Michelle was asked to take classes at weekends, which left little time for travel. If you want to keep your weekends free for travel and relaxation, firmly decline teaching hours on Saturday and Sunday, and be aware that it is all too easy to over-commit yourself in the first few weeks.

On the other hand, you may find your colleagues and bosses bend over backwards to help and support you, as Bradwell Jackson reports:

> In March of 2008, I was offered a job with Aston in China on the basis of a telephone interview and I am very happy with this. Aston is good to me, and my co-workers scramble to help me whenever I have even a mild matter that needs attention. For example, when I told them I was looking for a kung-fu school, they took this as a very important issue and had many long discussions-cum-negotiations with each other in order to come up with the best option for me. I think it might be hard to convince a Westerner to come and stay in an out-of-the-way city like Tangshan.
>
> Really, I'm living the life of Reilly here. I've got nothing to complain about. The school has given me a free apartment complete with cable TV, washing machine, toaster oven, microwave, and refrigerator. Whenever I'm hungry, I just mosey on down to the street vendors and get some proper Chinese food for a friendly budget price. Who can ask for more?

THE PUPILS

'Big noses' (foreigners) are usually treated with respect. In the early years of Western contact with China, English teachers outside the big cities found themselves lionised, unable to complete the simplest task in public without an enormous audience. There are not many corners of China these days into which foreigners, whether teachers or travellers, have not penetrated, although in Hengshui, three hours south of Beijing, **Sam Meekings** was amazed at the reaction he received from people in the town, who would stop and gape at him, as though they has seen 'dinosaurs or dragons'.

Yasmin Peiris, based in Shenzhen, one of China's newest cities, agrees that the general attitude towards teachers is generally favourable, even though there is a language barrier. She chose to ask her students for advice on where to go at weekends and what to do (a foot massage, a little shopping and sampling tempting varieties of Chinese food were some of the suggestions).

AS (CENSORED) INTERNET USE CONTINUES TO RISE AND MORE CHINESE PEOPLE COME INTO CONTACT WITH WESTERNERS (IN THE ETHER OR IN PERSON), IT IS UNLIKELY THAT CHINA'S GENERALLY RESPECTFUL ATTITUDE TOWARDS FOREIGNERS WILL CONTINUE UNPERTURBED. BRADWELL JACKSON IDENTIFIED ANOTHER INTERESTING NEW TREND IN MODERN-DAY CHINA FROM HIS EXPERIENCES OF TEACHING IN A SMALL CITY IN 2008:

There is another interesting phenomenon in China, which is the syndrome of the 'Little Emperor'. Chinese children are well-behaved, but they were even better behaved 10 or 20 years ago. With the advent of the one-child policy, some interesting changes took place. It seems that with just one child in the house, and *especially if it's a boy, the child is much more likely to be spoiled and accommodated. Any English teacher here will probably get his/her small share of little brats who just can't understand why they can't do what they want.*

I agree with the premise that a teacher has to be a bossy boots in order to establish the discipline straight off the bat. I certainly did this, maybe even a bit too much, so that now the (naughty) kids are just a tad bit resistant sometimes. The parents, on the other hand, are deliriously happy with me. They specifically love the fact that I'm strict with the kids.

Slowly, newer pedagogical methods are being accepted by students and administrators alike. A strange phenomenon has swept the country called 'Crazy English' pioneered by a charismatic former radio disc jockey Li Yang who holds huge rallies at which language learners are encouraged to put aside their diffidence and shout out English phrases. But this new boldness hasn't penetrated into many classrooms yet.

WHERE IN ONE PLACE, TECHNIQUES THAT SMACK OF INNOVATION ARE GREETED WITH BLANK STARES, IN ANOTHER, THERE CAN BE LIVELY CLASS DISCUSSIONS. ADAM HARTLEY FOUND HIMSELF IN THE FORMER SITUATION:

Politics were a complete no-no in class and yet politics are so central to life that you find yourself always coming up against a brick wall of silent faces. Class participation of any kind was hard enough to achieve. I was given a class of 100 people (of vastly different standards) for listening comprehension. I was an absolute monkey, playing, rewinding and replaying a cassette with obnoxious voices and muddled questions. I'd play it twice or thrice, ask if they were ready. 'Yes.' Okay, who thinks the answer is A? No one. Who thinks B? 2 people. Who thinks C? 3 hands. And who thinks D? No one. 5 responses out of 100. I'd try it again and again, and only ever got 27 hands in the air for any one question.

I had another class of beginners, and spent two hours reading things very very slowly for them to repeat. Immensely dull, not stimulating and tiring work. Again a tape recorder could have done just as good a job as I did.

Jessie Levene, reaching for some colourful similes, agrees that the low point of her first teaching job was feeling like a 'robot' and a 'teaching monkey'. It seems that you may have to work fairly hard to introduce modern teaching techniques into the classroom, as from a very early age Chinese children are taught in a very traditional style, as Nina Capek found whilst teaching in a primary school:

The teaching style does take a bit of getting used to. The children are used to learning by rote and the general ethos is: whatever the teacher says, we copy. Teaching 'my name is. . . .' to 50 6-year old children proved very entertaining as they all copied me and said 'My name is Nina'.

Will Hawkes did not find the teaching such hard going:

I taught 12 hours a week, each class lasting a mammoth two hours. Chinese students are more familiar with American English and many prefer it. However, there is still a market for British English and thus British English is very much in demand to balance things out. The English level of my students, who were aged 17–23, was mostly fairly competent, but with extremes of good and dreadful. Getting into university in China is a great privilege, and most students were eager to grasp this opportunity as a route to greater things in life. I found teaching the Chinese a delight: the students were very eager to learn, ask questions, find out how life is in Britain, always looking to learn and not muck around. We discussed a wide variety of material in class and, although some political areas are best left untouched, general debate was enthusiastically devoured about, for instance, the existence of God, cloning, tradition versus modernity and aliens (a real favourite, with many believers).

TEACHERS HAVE FOUND THAT THERE IS A DEMAND FOR ANY ENGLISH, PROVIDED IT IS CLEARLY ENUNCIATED. IMAGINATIVE INTERACTIVE TEACHING METHODS CAN WORK AS SAM MEEKINGS FOUND WHEN HE HAD TO TEACH A 60-STRONG CLASS OF UNIVERSITY STUDENTS, WHOSE HOMEWORK LEFT SOMETHING TO BE DESIRED:

Each week I was supposed to go through the excerpts from Shakespeare or Dickens in the book, despite the fact that close to half of the class could barely communicate with me in English at all. Though the impulse was strong to follow the example of the Chinese teachers and teach only to the brighter students and hope the others kept quiet at the back, I soon found that it was much more enjoyable to try and work the material into games and activities that everyone could take part in. This took time, however, since some students were so used to either being ignored or simply learning by rote and repetition that they were too shy to speak up. This is a problem I have noticed even teaching in private school in bigger cities – students are often so heavily criticised for mistakes in their normal classes that they lack the confidence to risk answering a question or attempting to join a game or discussion in case they do something wrong. It sometimes feels as if you are not only in a different country but also in a different century. None of the students I taught had any real concept of exploring or questioning an idea. When I set some homework essays for my literature class or set debate topics for my English speaking class to try to engage with, I was invariably met with 60 identical responses. Students are taught to pass exams in China, to memorise the single correct response and then repeat it when instructed – there is no concept of coming up with your own ideas. My students were all adamant that there was always one right answer and that everything else could therefore be discounted as wrong. This meant most essays and debates were very, very short. Coupled with the fact that we were not allowed to fail any students (even if they could not write more than their name on the biannual exam papers we had to set), it quickly became clear that we would have to set aside most of our preconceptions about education. Yet when students do finally open up or try something new, there is no better feeling.

At university, students expect to pass, as it has been difficult for them to get in while some have paid to get in or used connections (*guanxi*), which means they expect to sail through. Don't be surprised if just before exam time your students ply you with gifts, expensive meals and even offer money. Teachers who accept these offers will find that their students expect high marks even if they do not turn up to the exam!

ACCOMMODATION

Every university has either a purpose-built hostel or similar. Foreign teachers are generally housed in the best accommodation the university can offer, often referred to as a 'Panda House' (on the analogy that pandas are pampered in zoos). These differ enormously from place to place, though on the whole the standard is more acceptable to people with Western tastes than it was a few years ago. In some places (such as Chengdu University of Science & Technology), the accommodation can be airy and comfortable. In other places it is decidedly spartan and in some cases downright depressing, especially if electricity and heat are rationed. Find out ahead of time whether you will have a phone and internet access. Note that with the gradual liberalisation of internet censorship, the ban on the BBC's online English language news service has recently been lifted.

REGULATIONS

Most institutes will issue teachers with an invitation or letter of appointment that can be taken to the Chinese Consulate or Embassy to apply for long-term work visa before leaving your country. The only problem with this is that having applied for a one-year work visa in the UK and then signed a year-long contract in China, your permit will run out before your contract does. Many people enter China on a tourist (L) visa (one to three months), and then the school issues (and often pays for) the work (Z) visa in China, also known as the Alien Residence permit. Make sure this happens before your visitor visa expires, which is calculated according to the date of entry to China rather than the expiry date of the visa. Otherwise you will be liable to a fine and will have to leave the country to change status. The government is getting more prickly about residence and related documentation for which the Olympics are partly responsible. An official health check and registration with the police are now compulsory in many places.

Once outside the country you must be prepared to wait up to a fortnight for the appropriate faxes to be sent from Beijing. The Z visa does not necessarily allow multiple entry so you should make sure it is if you intend to leave China during the year. Any employer who makes you pay for your visa is probably suspect, since the majority of respectable institutes cover the cost for their teachers. When you arrive, be sure that your host institution sorts out the various permits and teachers' cards to which you are entitled. It is now compulsory to undergo a medical check-up in China. Everything has to be officially stamped. If you are found without the appropriate documents you will be harshly fined. For example recently a teacher whose papers were mostly in order but hadn't got the resident's permit was fined RMB3,000 (several weeks' wages). State institutes of education usually do everything by the book but you shouldn't expect the same of private language schools.

LEISURE TIME

Foreigners who teach in Beijing can lead a standard expatriate life if they want to, socialising at expat bars and clubs. Life in the provinces will be very different. You may still be one of the very few foreigners that the local people have ever seen and are bound to be the object of curious stares (which will be even more persistent if you happen to be a person of colour).

The main way of socialising in China is going to restaurants, because a large banquet shared by many people is only marginally more expensive than cooking for yourself. However, as most people go out to eat around 6pm–7pm, restaurants do not usually stay open later than 10pm. Students in state institutions can be restricted by a strict curfew, but when everything closes at 10pm, native English teachers start to realise why the students are not so bothered.

In smaller settlements, there may be no restaurants even to rival the Chinese take-away in your home town; but the locals will be far more interested in you and perhaps even teach you to cook your own Chinese food. If there are several foreigners, communal dining facilities (often segregated) will normally be provided. Glutinous rice, soy beans and cabbage are staples and fresh produce may be in short supply in winter. In Tangshan, **Bradwell Jackson** reports that he can have a 'killer meal' of dumplings, quick and right off the street, for only 2 yuan. Learning Chinese is the ambition of many teachers and is a great asset especially outside cosmopolitan areas. Take a good teach-yourself book and CD/tapes, since these are difficult to obtain outside Beijing and Shanghai. Mastering Chinese characters is a daunting business, though the grammar is straightforward. Others prefer to study Tai Chi, Wushu or other exotic martial arts.

Be prepared for noise and air pollution even in small towns, though it is usually possible to escape into the countryside by bicycle or bus. Some universities with large contingents of foreign teachers organise excursions in the same way that Israeli kibbutzim do for their volunteers after a few months. School and college vacations take place over Spring Festival in or around February, when the trains are very crowded and the weather is cold. Often the holiday dates are not known until the very last minute which makes it difficult to plan vacation travels.

Some cities such as Kunming have a good expat community to which the Chinese cater with Western-style cafés and restaurants. There are plenty of films to watch (all pirated) and a couple of galleries to visit. Much of the time you will be responsible for your own amusement, so take plenty of reading matter, including *Wild Swans*, an astonishing account of life in the Cultural Revolution or perhaps the novel *The Drink and Dream Teahouse* by Justin Hill who taught English in China with Voluntary Service Overseas (VSO).

JESSIE LEVENE FOUND LOTS TO DO IN CHENGDU: *'LEARN CHINESE, TAKE PHOTOS, ENJOY THE AMAZING SICHUAN FOOD, HANG-OUT WITH FRIENDS, GO TO BARS. . .'* HOWEVER, ONE THING SHE DIDN'T COUNT ON WAS GETTING CAUGHT UP IN THE MASSIVE EARTHQUAKE THAT STRUCK SOUTH-WEST CHINA ON 12 MAY 2008.
I was teaching in a fourth floor classroom at my university when the big earthquake struck on Monday, at around 2.30pm. What started as a low rumble very quickly grew much louder and stronger, until the whole building was shaking violently. My students and I first crouched in doorways or under desks, but when it became apparent that it wasn't going to be over any time soon, we all ran outside, by which point the worst was over. It was an incredibly frightening experience, and many of my students were very upset, but thankfully where I was no one was hurt in the slightest.

Bradwell Jackson who arrived in the city of Tangshan in April 2008 would urge anybody to do TEFL in China:

My first impressions were that of a fascinating country with a splendid culture, and I wasn't even in a well-known city. The people are organised and respectful, and the food, of course, is a revelation. If you have just a little bit of travel experience to a non-Western country, you should be fine and have no worries at all. There is certainly no problem with safety. My school has been very good to me. You will find that most schools bend over backwards to get you here. All you need is a fair amount of teaching experience (and a college degree) and the whole new world of China awaits you.

LIST OF EMPLOYERS

AMERICAN INTERNATIONAL EDUCATION FOUNDATION (AIEF)

RM A202, No. 2633 Yan'an West Road, Shanghai, China 200336

- 21 6270 2768; fax: 21 6295 2742
- US office: 3350 E. Birch Street, Suite 210, Brea, CA 92821
- 714 985 1995; fax: 714 985 1996
- info@aief-usa.org; www.aief-usa.org

Non-profit international education organisation

NUMBER OF TEACHERS: varies, some summer positions available.

PREFERENCE OF NATIONALITY: native English speaking countries such as USA, UK, Canada and Australia.

QUALIFICATIONS: at least a bachelor's degree. Must have interest in promoting intercultural understanding. Experience in teaching ESL and/or TEFL certification preferred but not essential.

CONDITIONS OF EMPLOYMENT: varies.

SALARY: varies.

RECRUITMENT: please email info@aief-usa.org.

AMITY FOUNDATION

71 Han Kou Road, Nanjing, Jiangsu 210008

- 25 83260836; fax: 25 83260909
- amityed@amityfoundation.org.cn
- www.amityfoundation.org

NUMBER OF TEACHERS: 40–50.

PREFERENCE OF NATIONALITY: none, but must be native speaker or have a high level of proficiency in English and language teaching experience.

QUALIFICATIONS: minimum BA degree. Teaching experience, a knowledge of Chinese or of living in Asia are useful but not essential. A Christian faith commitment is generally required, however the 'mission' expected is to serve rather than to proselytise.

CONDITIONS OF EMPLOYMENT: initial 2-year contract with possible year by year extensions. Teaching 12–16 periods per week. Teaching in tertiary educational institutions in China, mostly small teacher training colleges in the west parts of China.

SALARY: $250 monthly plus RMB2,500. Expenses for travel, orientation, conferences and medical insurance are covered by the sponsoring agency.

FACILITIES/SUPPORT: accommodation is usually provided in the form of an apartment on the school campus.

RECRUITMENT: teachers are recruited primarily through church sending agencies (see earlier in chapter), ie mission agencies of various denominations in a range of countries including Canada, Finland, Germany, Sweden, Switzerland, Norway, the UK and the USA. See above website for contact details of these organisations. Interviews in person are expected and generally take place in the applicant's own country.

CONTACT: Ruhong Liu, Director, Education & Culture Exchange Division (amityed@amityfoundation.org.cn).

ANGLIA SCHOLARS EDUCATIONAL CONSULTANCY(ASEC) LTD

24 Hampshire Terrace, Portsmouth, Hampshire PO1 2QF, UK

- 02392 826636; fax: 02392 297101
- liuweidan@hotmail.com
- www.angliascholars.co.uk

NUMBER OF TEACHERS: 30.

PREFERENCE OF NATIONALITY: British, American, Canadian and Australian.

QUALIFICATIONS: BA, MA, TEFL.

CONDITIONS OF EMPLOYMENT: 1 academic year. 20 hours per week.

SALARY: RMB4,000–RMB6,000. The first RMB4,000 is tax-free.

FACILITIES/SUPPORT: free accommodation provided.

RECRUITMENT: newspaper advertisements. Interviews held in the UK.

CONTACT: Weidan Liu, Secretary.

APPALACHIANS ABROAD TEACH IN CHINA PROGRAM

Center for International Programs, Marshall University, One John Marshall Drive, Huntington, West Virginia 27555

- 304 696 6265; fax: 304 696 6353
- gochina@marshall.edu
- www.marshall.edu/gochina

NUMBER OF TEACHERS: 40–60 annually.

PREFERENCE OF NATIONALITY: American, Canadian and British.

QUALIFICATIONS: bachelor's degree is essential; accepted ages range from new college graduates to recent retirees.

CONDITIONS OF EMPLOYMENT: 10 months teaching contract from 1 September . Teaching 15–18 hours per week. at public and private primary and secondary schools and in institutes of higher education, mainly in Shanghai and Beijing but other areas as well.

SALARY: RMB4,800–RMB14,000+ per month, up to 1 month paid winter school break and full or partial international airfare paid on completion of teaching contract.

FACILITIES/SUPPORT: accommodation provided free by hosting school. 5-day orientation in Shanghai in late August before arriving at Chinese host school.

RECRUITMENT: internet advertisements and phone interviews. Application deadline 31 March/15 April. Application fee is $100; job placement and administrative fee is $1,150 which includes 9 weeks of online China TEFL training and 5-day orientation in Shanghai, visa service, and one-year travel accident insurance.

CONTACT: QingQing Zhao, Director of China Projects.

ASTON ENGLISH SCHOOLS

USA Recruiting Office, 80 Grand Avenue, Washington Boro, NJ 07882, USA or Dalian Head Office. Room 2003, Yue Xiu Mansion, No.82 Xin Kai Road, Xi Gang Dist. Dalian, Liaoning Province, China 116011

- (USA)1 908 835 8227; (China)+86 411 8376 9995; fax(USA)1 908 835-8149
- teachinchina@astonschool.com or teachinchina@aol.com
- www.astonschool.com

NUMBER OF TEACHERS: 200+ annually.

PREFERENCE OF NATIONALITY: UK, USA, Canada, Australia, New Zealand and South Africa.

QUALIFICATIONS: university degree (any subject) and a TEFL Certificate or TEFL experience. Candidates without a TEFL background can take a 1-week course in China which meets this requirement at a cost of $100, which is refunded after 3 months on the contract.

CONDITIONS OF EMPLOYMENT: contract lengths of 6–7 weeks in summer or winter, 6 months, 7.5 months, 12 months or 13.5 months. 15, 20 or 25 hours per week contracts.

SALARY: 6,200 RMB for 25 hours, 5,000 RMB for 20 hours and 4,000 RMB for 15 hours per week. Varying end-of-contract bonuses of up $1,150 based on hours and length of contract. Teachers pay for their own flights. Small tax deductions.

FACILITIES/SUPPORT: contracts provide teachers with private bedrooms in a 2- or 3-bedroom Chinese-style apartment. Teachers must pay for utilities. Proper documents provided for work visas before arrival and residence permit after.

RECRUITMENT: via all methods such as internet, phone and in-person interviews in China and the USA. Phone but not in-person interviews required. Teachers can meet recruitment team in offices in New Jersey as above, in Austin Texas or at schools in China.

CONTACT: Michael Wisner, Head Recruiter.

BELL PARTNER SCHOOLS

Hillscross, Red Cross Lane, Cambridge CB2 2QX

- 01223 275500; fax: 01223 41480
- info.overseas@bell-centres.com
- www.bell-centres.com

NUMBER OF TEACHERS: 20 for 2 language training centres in Shanghai, Beijing.

PREFERENCE OF NATIONALITY: none, but must have native-like fluency.

QUALIFICATIONS: BA and CELTA and 1 year's experience. Room for teachers of different levels of experience.

CONDITIONS OF EMPLOYMENT: 1 or 2-year renewable contracts. 20 contact hours per week over 5 days.

SALARY: gross annual salary range of between RMB72,000 and RMB120,000. Approx. 12% deductions.

FACILITIES/SUPPORT: flights for teachers recruited outside China. Accommodation or accommodation allowance provided. Work permit and visas arranged. End of contract payment. 6 weeks' paid holiday per year plus public holidays. Local medical insurance cover provided. Commitment to in-service training and continued professional development.

RECRUITMENT: internet, newspapers, personal interview, telephone interview through Bell International in the UK (jobs.china@bell-centres.com).

BERKELEY GLOBAL EMPLOYMENT & EDUCATION CENTER

3F No 29 Ganshui Road, Nangang Development District, Harbin Heilongjiang Province 150000

- 138 360 13072
- kenny@bklglobal.com
- www.bklglobal.com

NUMBER OF TEACHERS: 50.

PREFERENCE OF NATIONALITY: USA, Canada, Australia, New Zealand or Britain.

QUALIFICATIONS: TESOL/ESL experience.

CONDITIONS OF EMPLOYMENT: 1 year. 80–100 classes per month, 40–50 minutes each class.

SALARY: RMB5,000–RMB7,000 per month (net).

FACILITIES/SUPPORT: free furnished accommodation provided. Berkeley Global run 60-hour TESOL courses (tesol@bklglobal.com).

CONTACT: Kenny, International Department Manager.

BOND LANGUAGE INSTITUTE
Building No. 7, Song Mao Ge, Bai Yuan Xin Cun, Dong Qu, Shiqi, Zhongshan, Guangdong, 528403
℘ 760 8310963/8317181; fax: 760 3304286
🖱 bond_ Institute@hotmail.com/bond_Institute@ yahoo.com.cn/zongcheng007@hotmail.com
💻 www.tefl-bond.com /www.bond-Institute.com

NUMBER OF TEACHERS: 100+.

PREFERENCE OF NATIONALITY: all major English-speaking countries.

QUALIFICATIONS: preferably those with TEFL/TESOL certificates and college diploma and above.

CONDITIONS OF EMPLOYMENT: usually a six-month (five-month) or a one-year contract. The maximum weekly workload is about 20 hours.

SALARY: RMB6,000+ ($870) less RMB95 for tax.

FACILITIES/SUPPORT: complimentary accommodation; usually state-of-the-art fully-furnished apartment units equipped with major domestic and electric appliances. Nationally accredited and authorised to employ Western teachers and process work permits.

RECRUITMENT: by word of mouth and through partners throughout the world. Interviews are essential and are often carried out in the UK and in North America.

CONTACT: John Zhang or Maria Wang, Recruiting Officers.

BUCKLAND INTERNATIONAL EDUCATION GROUP
Dacunmen Villa District 555, Yangshuo, Guilin, P.R China 541900
℘ 773 882 7555; fax: 773 882 7111
🖱 bucklandgroup@gmail.com
💻 www.bucklandgroup.org

NUMBER OF TEACHERS: 80+.

PREFERENCE OF NATIONALITY: English native speakers from UK, USA, Canada, Australia, Ireland or New Zealand.

QUALIFICATIONS: BA/BS degree or TESOL certificate preferable.

CONDITIONS OF EMPLOYMENT: 5 or 11 month renewable contracts available. 15 teaching hours per week from Mon-Fri.

SALARY: RMB4,500–RMB6,500 after tax per month. Taxes paid by the school.

FACILITIES/SUPPORT: free accommodation provided for all teachers. Fully-furnished, private flats with at least one bedroom, living room, kitchen with full facilities, computer with internet access, air conditioning. Work visas provided for all teachers regardless of length of contract. Free training course which covers how to teach Chinese students.

RECRUITMENT: usually via the internet (Dave's ESL Café). Interviews not essential.

CONTACT: Owen Buckland.

COLORADO CHINA COUNCIL
4556 Apple Way, Boulder, CO 80301, USA
℘ 303 443 1108
🖱 alice@asiacouncil.org
💻 www.asiacouncil.org

NUMBER OF TEACHERS: 20–35 per year placed at universities throughout China.

PREFERENCE OF NATIONALITY: either native English speaker or a person with no discernible accent, preferably from North America.

QUALIFICATIONS: BA/BSc or higher degree (all majors considered, though English, TEFL, history, business, accounting, economics and engineering especially welcome). If recent college graduate, you need a good GPA (minimum 2.75) and two strong letters of recommendation. MA and PhDs are strongly encouraged to apply, as are couples. Teaching background especially desirable but not mandatory.

CONDITIONS OF EMPLOYMENT: full academic year programme runs from September to June. February to June also available for professional teachers. Summer programme placements also available for 1 month in Nanjing to teach oral English to high school and college age students – a great way to get beyond the tourist trap and see China from the inside. Year-long programme: teaching 14–20 hours per week. Three-week TESL and Mandarin Training Institute in Shanghai in August before classes start.

SALARY: monthly stipend approx. RMB3,000–RMB9,000 per month depending on academic background, free housing in foreign teachers' complex, medical benefits and 1–2 months paid vacation offered by Chinese institutions.

FACILITIES/SUPPORT: most schools reimburse round trip airfare or return fare at end of year depending on your academic background.

RECRUITMENT: deadline for applications is August/September. Start dates are 15 February and 1 May 1 for Nanjing Summer Program or until all positions are filled. Non-refundable application processing fee of $100. For fees, application and information please go directly to the website at www.asiacouncil.org.

CONTACT: Alice Renouf, Director.

DELTER INTERNATIONAL BUSINESS INSTITUTE
Delter/Railway Institute, 65 Jian Ning Road,
Nanjing, Jiangsu 210015
✆   25 8583 8653 or 772 369 0828
✉   sarah.hu@delter.com.cn
🖥   www.delter.com.cn

Joint venture between Delter Canada and the Chinese government.

NUMBER OF TEACHERS: 12 in Nanjing, 18 in other locations.

PREFERENCE OF NATIONALITY: must be native English speaker from Canada, USA, UK, Australia, New Zealand or South Africa.

QUALIFICATIONS: diploma.

CONDITIONS OF EMPLOYMENT: 12-month contracts for teaching adults. 20–23 hours per week.

SALARY: RMB4,000–RMB8,000. Personal allowance RMB4,800; 5% tax on RMB4,800–RMB5,300; 10% on RMB5,300–RMB6,800, 15% on RMB6,800–RMB9,800.

FACILITIES/SUPPORT: apartment and utilities supplied plus airfares and medical insurance provided.

RECRUITMENT: phone interviews.

CONTACT: Gary Williamson, Director of Education.

EF ENGLISH FIRST
Teacher Recruitment Department, 666 Fuzhou Road,
1F Jingling Hai Building, Shanghai 200001
✆   8621 6133 6047
✉   efrecruitment@ef.com
🖥   www.englishfirst.com/trt/

NUMBER OF TEACHERS: 1,000 a year for more than 100 EFL schools in China.

PREFERENCE OF NATIONALITY: native English speakers.

QUALIFICATIONS: university degree (preferred), internationally recognised TEFL certification and teaching experience (preferred).

CONDITIONS OF EMPLOYMENT: 12-month contracts. Teaching 21 (real) hours between 9am and 9pm five days a week.

SALARY: approx. RMB10,600 (US$1,514) per month, including an annual bonus at the end of each contract period.

FACILITIES/SUPPORT: Shanghai, Beijing, Guangzhou and Shenzhen schools will provide 2-weeks of free hotel accommodation for newly arrived teachers or a monthly housing allowance. School assigns staff member to new arrivals to help them find suitable apartment. International flight costs reimbursed. Comprehensive health insurance, orientation on arrival and ongoing training. Chinese lessons. Official Work Z-Visa, academic support, paid vacation in addition to public holidays, career promotion and transfer, professional development training.

RECRUITMENT: via EF's Online Recruitment Centre at www.englishfirst.com/trt/ or send resumé and qualification details to efrecruitment@ef.com

---

GOLDEN APPLE CHILD EDUCATION (GROUP) LTD
7 Xinguang Road, Gaoxin District, Chengdu,
Sichuan, 610041
✆   28 85133381/ 15902804305
✉   tranzchina@gmail.com or nigel@tranzchina.com
🖥   www.61bb.com/english/index.asp

NUMBER OF TEACHERS: 20–25.

PREFERENCE OF NATIONALITY: USA, UK, Canada, Australia, New Zealand, Ireland, South Africa.

QUALIFICATIONS: minimum bachelor's degree in any subject and two years post-graduation work experience in any field.

CONDITIONS OF EMPLOYMENT: standard 1-year contract. 15–25 hours per week.

SALARY: RMB4,000–RMB7,000 per month depending on hours and experience. Taxes are deducted from salaries over RMB4,800 per month.

FACILITIES/SUPPORT: school provides accommodation or a stipend towards housing, and a foreign expert's licence and working 'Z' visa. The procedure requires teachers to sign a contract with the school and the government, and get a medical in their own country on the official Chinese embassy paperwork. The school then applies for a government invitation letter using the paperwork, which takes about a month or so to receive. An invitation letter to the teacher is then posted and teachers apply for a Z visa from the Chinese embassy.

RECRUITMENT: through internet advertisements, word of mouth.

CONTACT: Nigel Jones, Director of English Education.

HAINAN YUDA FOREIGN LANGUAGE ACADEMY
Cheng Zhong Cheng, Bldg. A, Guo Mao, First Floor, Haikou, Hainan, CN 570125
- 898 6854 2687; fax: 898.6851 0632
- contact@yudafla.com
- http://yudafla.com/en

NUMBER OF TEACHERS: 7 for three branches in Haikou.

PREFERENCE OF NATIONALITY: United States, Canada, England, Australia.

QUALIFICATIONS: minimum – bachelor's degree, master's degree preferred. Considerable preference given to career educators with former relevant teaching experience in country of origin.

CONDITIONS OF EMPLOYMENT: 12-month renewable contract.

STARTING SALARY: RMB5,500–RMB8,000 per month net, contingent on education and experience with automatic annual increments, plus up to RMB15,000 per annum in bonuses paid semi-annually.

FACILITIES/SUPPORT: high standard single and married couple accommodation (close to the school) provided with furnishings and a Western, coiled-spring mattress. All teaching materials provided.

RECRUITMENT: email correspondence and telephone interview.

CONTACT: Gregory Mavrides, PhD, vice principal.

INTERLINGUA SCHOOL
Guiyang address: 149 Qianlingxilu, Guiyang, Guizhou, 550001
- 851 687 3852; fax: 851 685 9628

Zunyi address: 14 Yangliu Street Zunyi, Guizhou 563001
- 852 825 6850; fax: 852 825 6802
- job@doesl.com
- www.doesl.com

NUMBER OF TEACHERS: 6.

PREFERENCE OF NATIONALITY: UK, USA, Canada, Australia, New Zealand.

QUALIFICATIONS: BA/BSc degree necessary. ESL/EFL qualification required plus 1 year's experience.

CONDITIONS OF EMPLOYMENT: 1 year, 16–26 hours per week.

SALARY: RMB4,200–RMB8,000 net, depending on qualifications. Possibility of end-of-contract bonus (depending on terms).

FACILITIES/SUPPORT: accommodation offered free of charge. School applies for work permit from the provincial education administration on arrival. Mandarin lessons.

IST PLUS – TEACH IN CHINA PROGRAMME
Rosedale House, Rosedale Road, Richmond, Surrey TW9 2SZ
- 020 8939 9057
- info@istplus.com
- www.istplus.com

NUMBER OF TEACHERS: approximately 200 from UK, USA and Australia/New Zealand to teach in primary/secondary schools and colleges mainly in the developed eastern provinces of Jiangsu, Zheijangm, Shandong and Hubei.

PREFERENCE OF NATIONALITY: none, although non-native speakers of English must have near-native proficiency in English.

QUALIFICATIONS: university degree in any field essential, TEFL training or experience is not essential but preferred. Maximum age 65.

CONDITIONS OF EMPLOYMENT: 5- or 10-month renewable contracts starting in February or August, teaching Chinese students in schools, colleges or universities. 14–16 hours per week. Extra-curricular duties may involve running an English language club.

SALARY: minimum salary offered to teachers is RMB3,000 per month. Accommodation is provided free of charge by the host institution.

FACILITIES/SUPPORT: free accommodation (usually on campus), all-inclusive 7-day orientation in Shanghai on arrival including basic EFL training, accommodation, sight-seeing and airport transfer. IST Plus arrange school placement, visa and work permit, insurance and a 24-hour emergency hotline. Teachers who complete 10-month contracts starting in May will have their flight home paid for by the host school. All teachers who complete their contracts receive a TEFL Certificate.

RECRUITMENT: deadlines for applications are early May/June for an August departure, and November/September for February departure. IST Plus Teach in China Programme fee starts at £725.

JIANGXI AGRICULTURAL UNIVERSITY

Meilingxia, Nanchang 330045, Jiangxi

791 381 3351; fax: 791 3828053

Lanx1014@yahoo.com.cn and

ieojau@yahoo.com.cn

NUMBER OF TEACHERS: 4.

PREFERENCE OF NATIONALITY: British, American. Australian, Canadian; from English speaking countries. Must be native speaker.

QUALIFICATIONS: BA and TEFL Cert. Aged 21–65. Minimum 1 year teaching experience.

CONDITIONS OF EMPLOYMENT: to teach speaking, listening, reading, writing, business English and English Literature to students of English and Business Majors and postgraduates of various specialities. Some classes have 45 students. Some courses (speaking and writing) have about 25. Total teaching hours per week is 18 periods (45 minutes each). Minimum stay 6 months.

SALARY: RMB4,000–RMB4,900 per month. Monthly cost of food is about RMB400. Round-trip airfares paid.

FACILITIES/SUPPORT: 2-room apartments provided for each teacher, plus furniture, air conditioning, television, etc.

RECRUITMENT: via internet and exchange organisations.

CONTACT: Sharon Tsao, Official Clerk, International Affairs office.

LINDA YEE RECRUITING

No 59 f/F Percival Street,

Causeway Bay, Hong Kong

852 958 81 46 64; fax: 852 2575 8959

asiaconnections@gmail.com

NUMBER OF TEACHERS: 50–100 teachers placed per year. Also place teachers in Hong Kong and Taiwan.

PREFERENCE OF NATIONALITY: none.

QUALIFICATIONS: degree or diploma holder or non-degrees. Must be aged under 55.

CONDITIONS OF EMPLOYMENT: 1 year. 25 hours per week.

SALARY: RMB5,000–RMB8,000 per month.

RECRUITMENT: via partner recruiting offices.

CONTACT: Linda Yee.

REACH TO TEACH

21 Everett Road Ext., Albany, NY 12205

1 201 467 4612; fax: 1 480 247 5426

info@reachtoteachrecruiting.com

www.ReachToTeachRecruiting.com

NUMBER OF TEACHERS: 100 +.

PREFERENCE OF NATIONALITY: applicants must be from the USA, Canada, United Kingdom, Australia, New Zealand, Ireland or South Africa.

QUALIFICATIONS: teaching experience is an advantage but not a requirement. Enthusiasm and enjoyment around children are musts.

CONDITIONS OF EMPLOYMENT: 1 year. Schedules are generally either morning/afternoon (preschool) or afternoon/evening (elementary school).

SALARY: RMB6,000–RMB10,000 per month.

FACILITIES/SUPPORT: teachers are always assisted with finding housing. Most of the time this is fully paid for by the school. Teachers are also helped with work permits from beginning to end.

RECRUITMENT: telephone interviews are 100% essential. The company also carries out in-person interviews periodically in the US and UK.

CONTACT: Richard Jones, Director of Recruiting.

ROBERT'S EDUCATION CENTER (REC) BEIJING

8–2 Dong Dan San Tiao, #717,

Beijing, 100006

10 6526 1620

bobrec60@yahoo.com

NUMBER OF TEACHERS: 4–6.

PREFERENCE OF NATIONALITY: North American.

QUALIFICATIONS: college degree in English with a teaching credential.

CONDITIONS OF EMPLOYMENT: 1 year. Teaching hours 1pm–9pm.

SALARY: $1,000–$1,500 a month.

FACILITIES/SUPPORT: fully furnished studio apartment for one is provided. Teachers can arrive on tourist visa and REC can organise visa upgrade after arrival.

RECRUITMENT: TESOL Conventions in North America. Otherwise via internet/email.

CONTACT: Robert H Toomey, Director of Education.

SICHUAN INTERNATIONAL STUDIES UNIVERSITY (SISU)

Lieshimu, Shapingba District,

Chongqing 400031

23 653 85218; fax; 23 653 85875

mayuhuasisu@hotmail.com or

faosisu@sisu.edu.cn

www.sisu.edu.cn

NUMBER OF TEACHERS: varies.

PREFERENCE OF NATIONALITY: none, but should be native speaker.

QUALIFICATIONS: degree needed; teaching experience preferred.

CONDITIONS OF EMPLOYMENT: 6 months to 1 year.

SALARY: RMB3,500–RMB5,000 plus holiday bonus of RMB2,200 after a year (RMB1,100 for a half-year contract).

FACILITIES/SUPPORT: SISU will pay for the return airfare and provide free medical care. Also, free accommodation is provided.

RECRUITMENT: via internet and international contacts.

CONTACT: Yuhua Ma.

TOSIC INTERNATIONAL EDUCATION GROUP
206 555 The West Mall, Etobicoke, Ontario, Canada M9C 1G8

416 953 0218; fax: 416 626 1750

tosic@careerinchina.ca

www.careerinchina.ca

NUMBER OF TEACHERS: 500 recruited for various schools on TOSIC (Teach or Study in China) programme.

PREFERENCE OF NATIONALITY: Canada, USA, Britain, Australia.

QUALIFICATIONS: minimum bachelor's degree.

CONDITIONS OF EMPLOYMENT: standard length of contract is one year. 20 hours per week.

SALARY: RMB3,500+ net.

FACILITIES/SUPPORT: free accommodation provided.

RECRUITMENT: internet. Application can be made online.

CONTACT: Quartz Shi, Consultant.

US-CHINA EDUCATIONAL EXCHANGE
15 Locust St, Jersey City, NJ 07305, USA

646 831 8213

edexchange@gmail.com

www.US-ChinaEdExchange.org

NUMBER OF TEACHERS: 200 – 300.

PREFERENCE OF NATIONALITY: UK, US, Canada, New Zealand, Australia.

QUALIFICATIONS: native speaker. Minimum BA degree and commitment to teaching.

CONDITIONS OF EMPLOYMENT: 6 months or 1 year. 15 hours per week.

SALARY: varies.

FACILITIES/SUPPORT: schools provide free housing and send candidates visa approval documents.

RECRUITMENT: internet and newspaper advertisements. Interviews always conducted by phone.

VET (VOLUNTEER ENGLISH TEACHERS) PROGRAM
Dacunmen Villa 555, Yangshuo, Guilin, Guangxi, P.R. China 541900

+86 773 8811420

vetchina.yangshuo@gmail.com

www.vet-china.org or
www.guilin-yangshuo.com/VET/index.html

Licensed charity set up in 2004 by retired Canadian professor living in Yangshuo. Volunteers help students in village schools improve their oral English and give them an opportunity to meet foreigners, to improve their chances of getting out of poverty and finding employment in the tourist and service industry around Yangshuo.

NUMBER OF TEACHERS: VET works in 4–5 rural primary schools and one orphanage.

QUALIFICATIONS: Minimum age 18, no maximum. Anyone with a strong proficiency in English and an easily understood accent is acceptable. Previous work with children aged 9–12 is desirable. Volunteers should be imaginative and creative, energetic, motivated, patient, with the ability to work independently and as a member of a team.

CONDITIONS OF WORK: 3+ months; shorter stays by arrangement.

SALARY: none. Volunteers must cover return airfare from the country of origin; a three month tourist visa (if a volunteer stays longer VET will assist with a visa extension), spending money.

FACILITIES/SUPPORT: All volunteers have a 2-day orientation with a qualified teacher trainer and on-going support from the VET team. Free accommodation and meals for volunteers teaching one week or more. Free transportation to and from the village schools.

RECRUITMENT: Volunteers accepted throughout regular school year but not during exam or holiday periods; terms run September to mid-January and March to mid-June. Interviews are not required.

CONTACT: Laurie Mackenzie (Founder/Director) or Vivian Lau (Assistant Director).

WAN CHENG INTERNATIONAL EDUCATION CENTER
Plot 72, Kulim Industrial Estate, 09000 Kulim, Kedah, Malaysia

+60 4 489 2630; fax: +60 4 489 1360

wanchenginteducenter@gmail.com or
yeohjane@hotmail.com

skype janeyeoh; branch offices: Hengyang
(Hunan Province), Jiamusi (Heilongjiang Province),
Kunming & Qujing (Yunnan Province)

PREFERENCE OF NATIONALITY: British, American, Canadian, Australian, New Zealand, South African and French.
QUALIFICATIONS: Dedicated, outgoing and responsible candidates able to sign and complete at least a 4-month contract.
CONDITIONS OF EMPLOYMENT: minimum stay 1 semester lasting 4 months or 2 semesters, lasting 10 months. There are two intakes every year: in March and September. Lessons last 50 minutes. 80–100 hours per month. Teaching primary to high school level.
SALARY: RMB4,400 based on above teaching hours.
FACILITIES/SUPPORT: free fully furnished apartment, computer with internet access, television, fridge, air-conditioner, heater, washing machine, basic furniture, basic kitchen utensils etc. Partial assistance with airfare. Will work with local government to obtain work visa.
CONTACT: Jane Yeoh, Human Resources Officer.

MONGOLIA

NEW CHOICE MONGOLIAN VOLUNTEER ORGANIZATION
POB-159, Ulaanbaatar-210646 A, Mongolia
/fax+976 11 314577
info@volunteer.org.mn
www.volunteer.org.mn

NUMBER OF TEACHERS: 5.
PREFERENCE OF NATIONALITY: none.
QUALIFICATIONS: native speakers of English from UK, Ireland, USA or Australia with teaching skills.
CONDITIONS OF EMPLOYMENT: 12-week contracts. 4–6 hours per day; 20–30 hours per week.
SALARY: $100–$200 per month.
FACILITIES/SUPPORT: accommodation provided with host families or in apartment. New Choice will apply for teacher's work permission and long term visa.
CONTACT: Bayarjargal Damdindagva, Programme Director.

HONG KONG

Since the former British colony became the Hong Kong Special Administrative Region (HKSAR) of the People's Republic of China on 23 June 1997, 'everything has changed and nothing has changed', or so the saying goes. Only international schools and specialist 'ESF' (English Schools Foundation) primary schools offer a curriculum using English as the medium of instruction (EMI), although it's more common in secondary schools. Recently, there seems to be pressure to review the EMI/CMI situation and allow each school to decide for itself, according to its needs and students' abilities. So, all in all, it's debatable as to whether English has seen a decline in Hong Kong as interest in Putonghua (Mandarin Chinese) has increased, or vice versa. Certainly, many parents are still willing to spend vast sums on English tutors for their children and this high demand maintains a market for teachers at all levels.

To meet the demand for English teaching, the Hong Kong government employs hundreds of English speakers to teach in the state education system as part of the Native English Teacher (NET) scheme described below.

It is illegal to enter Hong Kong as a tourist and take up work so that those graduates who arrive on holiday and want to change their status are out of luck. However, it is possible to visit the city, fix up a teaching job and then apply for a work permit from a neighbouring country. The authorities will expect to see a university degree, relevant work experience and a corporate sponsor. Teachers who satisfy these requirements should have no difficulty obtaining a work permit. Anyone who manages to find an employer before arrival can seek sponsorship to obtain a work permit. This is a major undertaking for any employer so teachers should try to honour their commitments instead of flitting off to a better-paying school after a month or two.

FINDING A JOB

NET SCHEME

The NET scheme is administered by the Hong Kong Education Bureau (EDB), formerly the Education and Manpower Bureau (NET Administration Team, Room 1321, 13th Floor Wu Chung House, 213 Queen's Road East, Wan Chai, netrecruit@edb.gov.hk. www.edb.gov.hk/index.aspx?nodeID=262&langno=1). The website carries full details of the scheme and an application form. Acceptance is easier if you have had teacher training, though the programme is open to university graduates of language-related subjects with a TEFL certificate. Candidates who are considered for appointment but do not possess a TEFL/TESL qualification will be required to obtain this qualification at least to certificate level at their own expense and in their own time within the first contract. Foreign teachers known as 'Netters' are assigned randomly and singly to government schools (primary and secondary) across Hong Kong and working conditions can be tough especially in a Band 5 school with low-achieving pupils. On the other hand salaries and benefits are generous.

The salary range for primary NET is HK$21,830 to HK$38,265 per month and for secondary NET, HK$21,830 to HK$45,970. Exact salaries are dependent on experience and qualifications. However, every NET living abroad gets a 'housing allowance' of HK$12,950, which is straight cash: there's no obligation to spend it on rent. Also, there's a 15% gratuity on everything you earn, awarded at the end of the two-year contract, provided your conduct and performance have met with approval. Medical insurance and an allowance for excess baggage are also provided.

> **APPLICATIONS ARE USUALLY ACCEPTED UNTIL MID-JANUARY AND TERM BEGINS AROUND MID-AUGUST. AFTER WORKING IN THE PRIVATE SECTOR FOR THE CHATTERIS FOUNDATION (DESCRIBED BELOW), TOM GRUNDY BECAME A NETTER AND HAS POSTED LOTS OF USEFUL INFORMATION ABOUT LIVING AND WORKING IN HONG KONG ON HIS WEBSITE (WWW.GLOBALCITIZEN.CO.UK/TRAVELS/HONG%20KONG/INDEX.HTML) AND HAS PROVIDED INFORMATION FOR THIS CHAPTER. IN COMPARING THE TWO, TOM CONCLUDES:**
>
> *The government NET programme is more highbrow and demanding but offers a better package and wage. However, you don't get the 'instant social circle' you would with an employer like Chatteris. NET is ideal should you decide to remain in HK and great if you already have a TEFL or PGCE qualification.*

OTHER EMPLOYERS

> **THE CHATTERIS EDUCATIONAL FOUNDATION (33 SYCAMORE STREET, TAI KOK TSUI, KOWLOON; ✆ 2520 5736; INFO@CHATTERIS.ORG.HK; WWW.CHATTERIS.ORG.HK) OFFERS RECENT UNIVERSITY GRADUATES FROM ENGLISH-SPEAKING COUNTRIES THE OPPORTUNITY TO TEACH IN HONG KONG. TOM GRUNDY COMPLETED THE NINE-MONTH PROGRAMME BEFORE HE BECAME A NETTER:**
>
> *The wages were just enough to live on and save some for travel. I travelled for three months in total, bought two laptops and cameras and still was able to pay off my student overdraft, though I saved hard. Chatteris has its problems and its 'charitable' status is questionable, but they support and train you. You'll be placed with another British, Canadian, Australian or American in a primary or secondary school, there'll be several dozen others who you'll train with and so you'll immediately have a big social network. Chatteris have also started a 'college' programme, though the more traditional school programmes are a better option. With Chatteris, your emphasis will be on oral English with a 'non-formal' approach, ie games, crafts and other 'fun' activities.*

Ready to Learn (Administrative Office, G-1/F Nam Fung Court, Harbour Heights, No. 1 Fook Yum Road, North Point, Hong Kong; ℂ 2512 9338; fax: 2766 0414; headoffice@rtl.edu.hk; www. readytolearn.com.hk) employs about 30–40 teachers for a number of centres, although they are not interested in 'travellers seeing the world with a TEFL qualification or similar'. They are looking for teachers who will commit longer term and really take an interest in the company and its methods. Dramatic English (see list of employers) employs drama graduates on 10-month contracts who are able to use their performance skills to help children learn English.

Demand is very strong for native speakers to work in English-speaking kindergartens, for which a degree and a TEFL qualification are generally sufficient. Christians Abroad (www.cabroad.org.uk) are actively recruiting a considerable number of English teachers (who must have a Christian commitment) to various organisations in Hong Kong. English for Asia in Kowloon (see directory of Trinity CertTESOL courses in Part 1) is frequently contacted by local institutes when they are recruiting.

Both internet advertisements and the more traditional print-based means of advertising jobs are still going strong. For example the bumper Saturday edition of the *South China Morning Post* might contain some useful leads; its classifieds can be consulted online at www.classifiedpost.com. *HK Magazine* is a weekly listings paper aimed at the ex-pat community which is available every Thursday evening from branches of Pacific Coffee and other 'ex-pat friendly' outlets. BC magazine is a similar monthly publication.

Some companies specialise in recruiting and outsourcing teachers, saving schools the administrative burden of employing a foreigner. Elton Educational Services (3/F, 204 Prince Edward Road West, Kowloon; ℂ 2850 6967; fax: 2850 4493; www.eltoneducation.com) provides NETs to Hong Kong kindergartens and primary schools. Big English is a specialist HK recruitment site that is worth browsing for possible jobs: http://bigenglish.com/teaching.tutoring.php.

The *Yellow Pages* are an alternative source of institute addresses. Phone calls within the city limits are free, so by phoning around you can easily get an idea of the possibilities. Although hiring is continuous, the summer months bring even more openings, while the Chinese New Year in January/February is a bad time.

Freelance teaching can prove lucrative provided you are staying in Hong Kong legally. An attractive advertisement strategically placed in the letter boxes of the ritzy apartment estates in Mid Levels, Jardines, Lookout and Causeway Bay suburbs or in busy supermarkets might winkle out some private students. It is also possible to pick up tutoring work where you visit a family's home and help their child with homework/English games. The standard payment is £20–30 an hour. Summer schools, English drama organisations and language schools are also options in Hong Kong, but all foreign workers doing paid or voluntary work require a work visa, so make arrangements with an employer beforehand.

Although Hong Kong is famous for its big cities, smog and vivacity, there are quieter places and it is worth researching the exact place where you will be living and working. **J W Arble** worked at a secondary school in the New Territories in a suburban town 30 miles to the north of Hong Kong Island. '*I lived alone in a 12 by 16 ft flat, 17 floors above a colossal shopping centre of 600 stores, 30 restaurants and a single bookshop that mainly stocked self-help guides and comics. Everything shut at 10pm.*'

REGULATIONS

British citizens may visit the HKSAR without a visa for up to 180 days provided they can satisfy the immigration officer on arrival that they are entering as bona fide visitors with enough funds to cover the duration of their stay without working and, unless in transit to the Mainland of China or the region of Macau, hold onward or return tickets. USA citizens are given 90 days. The visa requirements are posted at www.immd.gov.hk/ehtml/hkvisas_4.htm. Visitors are not usually allowed to change their status (e.g. from visitor to employment) after arrival except in special circumstances.

Usually it will take about six weeks to process a visa application, assuming all accompanying documents are in order including the nomination of a local sponsor (usually the employer). Applicants should complete application form ID 990A (whereas the employer should complete ID 990B). The HKSAR Immigration Department is located on the 2nd Floor of Immigration Tower, 7 Gloucester Road, Wan Chai; ✆ 2824 6111; fax: 2824 1133; enquiry@immd.gov.hk.

CONDITIONS OF WORK

IF YOU DO NOT HAVE AN OFFICIAL CONTRACT AND ARE PICKING UP SOME TEACHING AT A PRIVATE INSTITUTE, YOU ARE LIKELY TO BE PAID ON AN HOURLY BASIS AND NOT VERY WELL. ERRATIC HOURS ARE ALSO A PROBLEM, AS LESLIE PLATT FOUND OUT:

My institute was very vague as to what hours I would be working. I would arrive in the afternoon as instructed only to be informed that no students had turned up but that I had better hang around for a few hours just in case one did. If none did, it meant I didn't get paid.

PUPILS

Hong Kong children are usually well behaved, eager and well mannered, even though so many are under huge pressure from exams, extra tuition, band practice, kung fu, lion dancing and extra sports. It can be just as important for teachers to help their pupils enjoy English and gain confidence, as to instil the finer points of English grammar. Hong Kong's British past can also lead to some interesting situations as **J W Arble** discovered:

It is traditional for Hong Kong students to adopt an English name alongside their Chinese ones. These too have, in fact, become family names, passed down with little variation and as a result I found myself surrounded by ghosts from the Edwardian era, Sibyls and Mabels and Ethels and Normans and even an Algernon. Other students chose their own English names: King Kong was the moniker of one 5 ft 14-year-old, School Bully was that of another, there was a Ferrari Vesper, an Omega – the student formerly known as Wong – and a Beckham, a 15-year-old covered in tattoos who literally slept through all my lessons undisturbed, who was rumoured to drive a minibus for the Triads. My favourite student name was Frozen Chicken Drumstick, belonging to a girl who had plucked it from a packet in the supermarket deep-freeze.

ACCOMMODATION

As of May 2008, Hong Kong has the highest rents in the world and rents have jumped by tens of percent in just the last couple of years. Serviced apartments, advertised in the *HK Magazine* and newspapers, are often a cheaper alternative. They're usually based in Jordan, Central, Wan Chai and Causeway Bay. The outlying islands such as Lamma and Lantau and the New Territories are still cheaper, often double the floor space for half the money. Even with Hong Kong's superb public transport system, the commute can be time-consuming, so living in Kowloon just north of

Hong Kong island might be a happy medium. **Tom Grundy** suggests that the best deals are in old buildings because local people are often not interested in them even though the floor space can be comparatively huge. He goes on to recommend looking up flat shares on Asia Expat (the main expat community online, www.asiaxpat.com), or Geo Expat (www.geoexpat.com) plus of course Facebook, Gumtree and similar.

Areas in Kowloon which are considered to be quite poor are becoming popular with foreigners, such as Sham Shui Po or Tai Kok Tsui, as they're cheaper and still on the MTR red line, which goes direct to Central on HK Island. A decent but very small two-bedroom flat would set you back about HK$6,000 per month.

LEISURE TIME

NOT SURPRISINGLY, CULTURE SHOCK IS KEPT TO A MINIMUM IN HONG KONG BY THE WESTERN AFFLUENCE AND THE LINGERING BRITISH BIAS. HONG KONG IS FAMED AS A SHOPPERS' PARADISE IN WHICH THE CHEAP FOOD, CLOTHING AND TRAVEL HELP TO ALLEVIATE THE PROBLEM OF EXPENSIVE ACCOMMODATION. TOM GRUNDY CONCLUDES THAT HONG KONG IS AN IDEAL PLACE TO LIVE:

In Hong Kong, tax is low to non-existent, it's super clean, has a huge ex-pat community with lots of English clubs, activities, sports, events and the public transport is the world's best. It's very compact and all of Asia is on the doorstep (cheap flights and trains to China, Indonesia, Philippines, Thailand, Cambodia, Vietnam, Laos, etc). The territory has dozens of tropical beaches, temples, a mind-blowing metropolis at its heart, fantastic hiking and outdoor activities, 248 idyllic outlying islands, huge country parks (80% of HK's area is actually green) and everything's a good deal cheaper than home, what with China next door. It's an ideal balance of East and West, English is widely spoken and Western food and luxuries are available everywhere. Though Hong Kong is an aggressively consumerist, capitalist society, it is 'tempered' with Chinese tradition and Buddhist beliefs.

LIST OF EMPLOYERS

CHATTERIS EDUCATIONAL FOUNDATION
33 Sycamore Street, Tai Kok Tsui, Kowloon
2520 5736; 2865 2815
hr@chatteris.org.hk
www.chatteris.org.hk

NUMBER OF TEACHERS: 50–60 per year.
PREFERENCE OF NATIONALITY: United Kingdom, Canada, USA, Australia, New Zealand.

QUALIFICATIONS: graduate bachelor's degree or higher qualification in any subject, no teaching experience necessary.
CONDITIONS OF EMPLOYMENT: 9-month contracts, 1 September–31 May (mandatory two week orientation begins mid August). 8 hours per day with 1 hour lunch break, weekends free.
SALARY: HK$13,000.
FACILITIES/SUPPORT: accommodation is provided free of charge by Chatteris during the first two week orienta-

tion period. During this time flat hunting workshops are provided to familiarise employees with the property system of Hong Kong. Chatteris office staff are also available for assistance with negotiation of rental agreements and any issues that may arise during this time. After acceptance into the programme comprehensive support is provided to applicants regarding the organisation and processing of work visas. Chatteris will request a number of documents such as original degree certificates, police clearance checks and references from accepted applicants in order for the visa to be processed.

RECRUITMENT: by word of mouth, seminars, online. Interviews are sometimes carried out in the UK/USA.

CONTACT: Grace Lee, Project Director.

CHILDREN'S ENGLISH CENTRE (CEC)
2nd Floor, Lee May Building, 788 790 Nathan Road, Kowloon, Hong Kong
+852 2728 1050; fax: +852 2728 5589
info@cec-edu.com
www.childrensenglishcentre.com

Provides local schools with teachers and courses as well as after-school classes held at CEC, which has been registered with the Hong Kong Education Department since 1995.

NUMBER OF TEACHERS: 12–16.

PREFERENCE OF NATIONALITY: must be native English speakers.

QUALIFICATIONS: Degree + TEFL (or equivalent). Training will be given to new teachers. Applicants without a degree but with relevant teaching experience may also be considered.

CONDITIONS OF EMPLOYMENT: 10-month contracts. 40 hours per week over 5.5 days.

SALARY: from HK$20,500 per month plus completion bonus (HK$8,000–HK$12,000) and medical insurance.

FACILITIES/SUPPORT: company apartments that teachers may opt to stay in. Sponsorship for work visa given.

RECRUITMENT: via internet and local newspapers. Initial interviews by telephone.

CONTACT: Miss Charlie Crow, Office Manager.

DEBORAH INTERNATIONAL PRE-SCHOOL AND PLAY SCHOOL
G/F Shop 5–5B Site 9, Whampoa Garden, Kowloon
2994 8998; fax: 2994 8812
deborah9admin@gmail.com

NUMBER OF TEACHERS: more than 60 for all schools; 8 kindergartens in Hong Kong and 2 in Shenzen, China.

PREFERENCE OF NATIONALITY: Canadian, Australian, British or American. Must be native speakers.

QUALIFICATIONS: any university degree or an early childhood certificate plus minimum 6 months' teaching experience.

CONDITIONS OF EMPLOYMENT: 2-year contract. School hours from 8.30am to 5pm Mon-Fri plus occasional Saturdays for special events. Must love children since teaching children aged 2–6.

SALARY: HK$16,000 approx., depending on experience. Airfare, medical cover and 8–9 weeks approx paid holiday provided.

FACILITIES/SUPPORT: free shared accommodation for 2–3 teachers or HK$2,000 accommodation allowance.

RECRUITMENT: via the internet, please send resumé/CV by email. Recruiting goes on year-round. Interviews not essential.

CONTACT: Miss Karina O'Carroll.

DRAMATIC ENGLISH
Room 601–02, Wing Kwok Centre, Jordan, Kowloon
28805080; fax: 2880 5055
de@dramaticenglish.com
www.dramaticenglish.org

NUMBER OF TEACHERS: around 40 full-time.

PREFERENCE OF NATIONALITY: none, as long as they are native English speakers.

QUALIFICATIONS: company largely deals with recent drama graduates. Candidates should have a degree in theatre/drama, or possibly some related field, backed up with performance experience. ESL qualification/experience is preferred, but not essential.

CONDITIONS OF EMPLOYMENT: contracts run for 10 months with the option to extend for a further month. Teachers may also continue for another contract term. 20 contact teaching hours/week, falling between 8:30am and 6pm, depending on school programmes and timetabling.

SALARY: $HK16,000 per month starting salary. Employees are required to pay their own taxes at the end of each financial year. There are tax-free thresholds, and due to the timing of contracts, first year employees end up paying little, if any tax.

FACILITIES/SUPPORT: a few company-owned flat options for teachers and also the option of temporary accommodation for new teachers. Local staff are happy to support teachers who experience communication problems with local real estate agents and/or property owners.

RECRUITMENT: via direct contact with universities and some websites. Phone interviews are essential. The company very occasionally carries out interviews abroad.

CONTACT: Sean Bilkey, Teacher Support Manager

NUMBER OF TEACHERS: 50–100 teachers placed per year. Also placed in China and Taiwan.

PREFERENCE OF NATIONALITY: none.

QUALIFICATIONS: degree or diploma holder or non-degrees. Must be aged under 55.

CONDITIONS OF EMPLOYMENT: 1 year. 25 hours per week.

SALARY: HK$15,000–HK$20,000 per month.

RECRUITMENT: via partner recruiting offices.

CONTACT: Linda Yee.

NUMBER OF TEACHERS: 4 full time, up to 10 part time.

PREFERENCE OF NATIONALITY: UK preferred, others considered.

QUALIFICATIONS: Degree holder, TEFL equivalent certification, at least 2 years teaching experience, proficiency in second language a plus.

CONDITIONS OF WORK: permanent contract with three months notice period. 5 days per week including Saturdays. Hours 9am–7pm, with 1.5-hour lunch breaks.

SALARY: commensurate with experience.

FACILITIES/SUPPORT: assistance offered in terms of advice and negotiations in renting accommodation. Sponsorship given for work permits which take around 6–8 weeks to be processed from date of application.

RECRUITMENT: via tefl.com or local newspapers. 2 rounds of interviews are always conducted, held in Hong Kong or by phone.

CONTACT: Agnes Tang, General Manager.

NUMBER OF TEACHERS/STAFF: 20.

PREFERENCE OF NATIONALITY: British, American, Australian and Canadian.

QUALIFICATIONS: 3- or 4-year full-time BA + TEFL/CELTA plus minimum 1-year teaching experience, preferably in Asia.

CONDITIONS OF EMPLOYMENT: 1-year contract. 110 contract hours per month.

SALARY: HK$20,000 per month (HK$240K per annum) subject to review after 3-month assessment. A gratuity of HK$10,000 paid on satisfactory completion of 1-year contract.

FACILITIES/SUPPORT: Help finding an apartment provided, soft set up loan available to employee, visa sponsorship.

RECRUITMENT: via internet with interviews in Hong Kong.

CONTACT: Clive Burns, Manager.

INDONESIA

Indonesia is the fourth most populous nation on earth. Since the president and vice-president were directly elected for the first time in 2004, the country has been reasonably stable and schools are attracting professional ELT teachers from abroad with benefits packages and reasonable salaries of 8–10 million rupiah (£450–£550). Extremist groups are still active, but any intrusion into internal politics is a 'no-no', and probably counter-productive, since the regime does not appreciate interfering outsiders.

The best jobs continue to crop up in the oil company cities. Although oil production has been declining, the industry is still important. The so-called 'native speaker schools' with multiple branches in Jakarta and the other cities continue to deliver English courses to the millions of Indonesians who still want to learn the language. These organisations can still afford to hire trained foreign teachers and pay them about ten times the local wage. EF English First is the biggest and most well-known chain of the franchised language schools, now with 24 schools in Jakarta and many others on Sumatra, Java, Sulawesi and Bali. The US-based international company ELS has language centres in Jakarta and Bandung (www.els-indonesia.com), whilst Wall Street Institute (WSI) has recently opened a plush branch on Jalan Sudirman, the capital's most prestigious thoroughfare. WSI and Direct English, also on Jalan Sudirman, capture market share by targeting office workers using a highly flexible schedule.

However, purely 'language' schools, as well as international schools, are feeling the heat from the burgeoning National Plus schools. According to the Sampoerna Foundation for improving education, there are now nearly 60 member schools of the Association of National Plus Schools (www.anpson-line.org). They tend to follow an international curriculum, often with some local content, and the instruction medium is English, or a mix of Indonesian and English. They are favoured by middle-class Indonesians and expats who are not on oil company salaries and/or who don't get their children's education funded by their employer. Many schools tend to follow a religious path (usually Catholic), perhaps as a marketing tool that appeals to parents, and they tend to pay a little better than the language schools. They also tend to start lessons at 7am.

Another source of work are the universities, although they don't always pay much more than small language schools.

FINDING A JOB

The CELTA is highly regarded in Indonesia and anyone who has acquired the Certificate has a good chance of pre-arranging a job in Jakarta, Surabaya, Bandung or Yogyakarta (arguably the most interesting city in Indonesia). While some schools clearly favour either British or North American teachers, others express no preference, and there are also quite a few Australian and New Zealand EFL teachers in Indonesia. The government stipulates that teachers must be native English speakers to be awarded a work permit.

IN ADVANCE

Private schools with overseas contacts advertise and recruit internationally, although this practice is less popular than it once was. Two or three of the main schools in Indonesia do reimburse airfares and visa costs at the end of a successful contract. A number offer medical insurance.

Even if you have missed an opportunity to be interviewed in your home country, it is still worth contacting the major schools by fax or email. Some hire their teachers on the basis of a telephone interview and, in some cases, a taped example of your voice.

A list of schools in Indonesia can be found at www.Eslbase.com/indonesia/schools including Real English in Yogyakarta whose webpage www.realenglish.or.id/be.php seems promising for prospective teachers. It is related to Real Language Training in Batam (eal_edu@telkom.net), which in the past has advertised for expat teachers on www.eslteachersboard.com.

ON THE SPOT

More and more teachers are being hired on the spot, which suits the major schools, who then don't have to pay for airfares. Local recruits can negotiate shorter contracts, for example six months, unlike teachers recruited abroad who usually have to commit for 12 months. Most teaching jobs start in July or September/October. Check advertisements in the English language *Jakarta Post*.

With a Cambridge or Trinity Certificate and university degree your chances of being offered a job are high. Unqualified applicants would have to be extremely well presented (since dress is very important in Jakarta), able to sell themselves in terms of experience and qualifications and prepared to commit themselves for a longish spell or to start with some part-time work in the hope of building it up. Caution is advised at the interview stage, because promises are not always kept or the full extent of deductions mentioned.

LOCAL SCHOOLS STAFFED BY INDONESIANS ABOUND, MANY WILLING TO HIRE A NATIVE ENGLISH SPEAKER AT LOCAL WAGES. SOME CAN EVEN ARRANGE A WORK PERMIT. HOWEVER, THERE IS NO 'EASY ANSWER' FOR HOW PROSPECTIVE TEACHERS SHOULD TRY AND SELL THEMSELVES, AS ROSS MCKAY, A LONG-TERM TEACHER IN JAKARTA, IS KEEN TO POINT OUT:

Each school has it own ethos. One place likes lots of chat but others are sober-sides who keep students' noses to the grindstone. I went to one interview and kept the class happy for an hour, only to be told that 'we're educators, not entertainers.' But another school didn't call me for interview because I'd stated that I took the job seriously and didn't go easy on students who habitually arrived late. Jam Karet, rubber-time, is a bad habit here, and you either adjust to it or get driven nuts.

TRAVELLERS HAVE STUMBLED ACROSS FRIENDLY LITTLE SCHOOLS UP RICKETY STAIRCASES THROUGHOUT THE ISLANDS OF INDONESIA, AS THE GERMAN ROUND-THE-WORLD TRAVELLER GERHARD FLAIG DESCRIBES:

In Yogyakarta you can find language schools listed in the telephone book or you just walk through streets to look for them. Most of them are interested in having new teachers. I got an offering to teach German and also English since my English was better than some of the language school managers. All of them didn't bother about work permits. The wages aren't very high but it is fairly easy to cover the costs of board and lodging since the cost of living is very low.

Opportunities exist not only in the large cities but in small towns too. **Tim Leffel** from New Jersey noticed a large number of English schools in the Javanese city of Solo, and others have recommended Bali. At local schools unused to employing native speaker teachers, teaching materials may be in short supply. One of the problems faced by those who undertake casual work of this kind is that there is usually little chance of obtaining a work permit (see below). It is also difficult for freelance teachers to become legal unless they have a contact who knows people in power.

IN INDONESIA, THE PROBLEM OF VISAS DOESN'T ARISE IF YOU TEACH ENGLISH ON A COMPLETELY INFORMAL BASIS AS STUART TAPPIN DID:

In Asia I managed to spend a lot of time living with people in return for teaching English. The more remote the towns are from tourist routes the better. I spent a week in Palembang Sumatra living with an English teacher and his family. You teach and they give their (very good) hospitality.

If you get stuck job hunting in Jakarta go to Jalan Jaksa, a small but lively street where many teachers hang out. They might be willing to pass on leads, and Romance Cafe-Bar is, according to **Ross Mckay**, a pleasant place on a Saturday afternoon.

REGULATIONS

The work permit regulations are rigidly adhered to in Indonesia and all of the established language schools will apply for a visa permit on your behalf. Some even employ a dedicated visa coordinator. The Embassy's 'General Information for Foreigners Wishing to Work in Indonesia' starts with the warning, '*Please be informed that it is not easy for foreigners to work and stay in Indonesia since Indonesia has very strict and complicated immigration/visa requirements and regulations, and the process can be very long*' (www.indonesianembassy.org.uk/consular_work_in_indonesia.html). The Indonesian government limits work permits to teachers holding passports from the USA, Canada, the UK, Australia and New Zealand.

If the job is arranged in plenty of time before you leave home, you may be sent a letter of sponsorship from your employer to take to the Indonesian embassy in London and, subject to current visa requirements, it will issue you with a visa valid for a maximum of 60 days, £35 non-refundable. Alternatively, it is possible to enter Indonesia on a tourist visa and have the school arrange the work permit by the time the tourist visa expires. Tourist visas are available on arrival, valid for 30 days, about £12, non-extendable. It is a good idea to explore the 60-day visa option despite the hassle, as 30 days probably isn't long enough to find a job and arrange the visa. Be careful – Indonesian authorities count both the first and last day of your stay as part of your entitlement. Work permit arrangements should be taken care of by your school on arrival, after you have provided your CV, TEFL course and university degree certificates, photocopies of your passport and application forms. Anyone without the necessary professional qualifications is unlikely to be granted the visa. The application is sent to the Indonesian Ministry of Education, the Cabinet Secretariat and the Immigration/Manpower Departments. If and when the application is approved, the work permit will be valid for one employer only and will be revoked and the offending teacher deported if work is undertaken outside the terms of the contract.

After your work permit and temporary stay permit have been granted (with a maximum validity of one year), the documentation will then be sent to the nearest Indonesian embassy (usually Singapore) where the teacher can have it stamped in his or her passport. These visa runs only take a couple of days and should be paid for by your employer, although some, such as Berlitz, consequently withhold 10% of your salary for the first six months, then reimburse the 10% monthly, starting in the seventh month, to ensure that teachers fulfil the year's visa.

It is possible to renew your tourist status by leaving the country every two months (e.g. flying to Singapore, or by ferry to Penang in Malaysia) but the authorities might become suspicious if you did this repeatedly. Anyone found working on a tourist visa will be deported and blacklisted from entering Indonesia in the future. Also, the employer would find himself in serious trouble.

CONDITIONS OF WORK

Salaries paid by the 'native speaker' schools can provide for a comfortable lifestyle including travel within Indonesia during the vacations. Most schools pay from Rp8 million per month, after Indonesian tax of 10% (on earnings of up to Rp25 million) has been subtracted. Since the cost of living is low, especially outside the cities, many teachers are able to enjoy a very comfortable lifestyle and travel in their free time. However, the government has removed much of the subsidy on fuel prices, and this combined with other factors has caused prices to rise sharply recently. You could probably save a little on a salary of Rp12 million per month in Jakarta, more outside of the major cities. If you plan to complete a one or two-year contract, enquire about reimbursement for airfares and a possible tax rebate. When **Bruce Clarke** started working for English First, he had no previous classroom experience, yet he was asked to become acting Director of Studies after only two months.

In addition to a decent starting salary, my school also agreed to reimburse me at the end of my contract for both the price of my plane ticket and my work visa. Basic living is relatively cheap. I spend about half my salary on Western luxuries like beer, CDs, movies, etc. I bank the rest so at the end of my year I expect to head home with a few thousand dollars saved. Most of the teachers I meet are in their early 20s, and are generally still at the 'let's party every night' stage of their lives. They complain about constantly being broke because they tend to nightclub two or three nights a week and waste a lot of money.

Many schools offer generous help with accommodation, ranging from an interest-free loan to cover initial rent payments or deposits, to free housing complete with free telephone, electricity and maid service. This perk may be at the expense of free choice though, and it is worth considering if you mind where you live/who you live with. It is customary in the Jakarta housing market to be asked to pay the annual rent in a lump sum at the beginning of your tenancy, and so access to a loan from your employer is often essential. **Ross McKay** warns that housing contracts should not be undertaken lightly since one of his ex-colleagues who refused to pay a year's rent on a house he had occupied for two months ended up behind bars and subject to a huge payment of Rp20 million.

If you happen to work for a school which takes on outside contracts, you may have the occasional chance to work outside the school premises, possibly in a remote oil drilling location in Sumatra, for up to double pay. The majority of teachers, however, conduct lessons at their school through the usual peak hours of 3.30pm to 8.30pm with some early morning starts as well. Many supplement their incomes with private pupils (provided their employer permits it). For example Ross McKay was paid by a doctor to teach him while they drove into Jakarta in the morning which boiled down to him being paid to be given a lift to work.

THE PUPILS

Outside the big cities, the standard of English is normally very low, with pupils having picked up a smattering from bad American television. Classes also tend to be large, with as many as 40 pupils, all expecting to learn grammar by the traditional rote methods. According to a VSO volunteer teaching in Western Java (as quoted in the TES), '*If I want to do something interesting, the students complain that it isn't in the exam*'. As is the case elsewhere in the world, the average age of English learners is getting younger, so anyone with experience of teaching children or teenagers will be appreciated.

STUDENTS IN JAKARTA PRESENT FEWER PROBLEMS THAN ELSEWHERE AS COLIN BOOTHROYD DESCRIBES:
The pupils are incredibly enthusiastic and are genuinely appreciative of the opportunity to learn from native speakers. I have never once had a discipline problem whilst I've been teaching here. My classes have varied from 2 to 20 in size. The students are generally unfamiliar with our communicative form of teaching, since kids aren't really expected to think for themselves in Indonesian schools. Students are reluctant to speak about controversial issues (the issues that should really provoke loads of communication) because they are afraid that big brother may overhear something that doesn't suit. Otherwise the students are brilliant.

ANDREW WHITMARSH, A TEACHER FOR WALL STREET INSTITUTE IN JAKARTA, ENJOYED BEING ABLE TO ENTICE HIS STUDENTS INTO UNIVERSITY-STYLE DISCUSSIONS:
As I look back over my experience, I would say that the best times have come during the classes when I almost forgot I was a teacher and they were my students, and instead felt like I was leading a discussion group back at university.

LEISURE TIME

Although Jakarta is a hot, dusty, overcrowded, polluted and poverty-stricken city, there is a great deal to see and do, and most teachers end up more than tolerating it. After quitting his job in information technology at age 37, **Bruce Clarke** obtained a TEFL Certificate from Winfield College in Vancouver and immediately landed a one-year teaching contract with EF in Indonesia and concluded that Indonesia is 'okay', though not quite as glamorous as he had hoped. He liked his school and staff, but found Jakarta just another big, crowded city.

On a happier note, **Simon Redman**, Director of Studies at Executive English Programs (EEP) writes:

> *Jakarta has moved on in leaps and bounds in many ways since I first arrived in 1994. The traffic may be viler than ever, but while it still certainly isn't Hong Kong or Singapore food-wise, the variety of good quality, reasonably-priced restaurants is very impressive these days. Once you know your way around!*

Indonesia is a fascinating country and most visitors, whether short-term or long, agree that the Indonesian people are fantastic. Travel is cheap and unrestricted, and excursions are very rewarding in terms of scenery and culture. Travel by public transport can be time-consuming and limiting for weekend trips, so you might consider getting a motorcycle, although Jakarta's traffic problems make this too dangerous and unhealthy for many. Internal flights are also within the range of most teachers. **Ross McKay** recommends using Bluebird or Express taxis in Jakarta as the most dependable and to use air-conditioned buses (but not after midnight). He also advises newcomers to arrive with crisp, new notes since banks are loath to handle creased or tatty foreign currency.

Predictably the community of expatriate teachers participates in lots of joint activities such as football and tennis matches, chess tournaments, beach excursions, diving trips and parties. Most teachers have DVDs but occasionally go out to see an undubbed American film. The pleasant city of Bandung might prove an attractive alternative to Jakarta and offers a good quality lifestyle to teachers, with a good mixture of rural and city life. Since the completion of the new toll road from Jakarta to Bandung a journey time of two hours is possible. It's choked at the weekends, but fine during the week.

SPEAKING OF WEEKENDS, ANDREW WHITMARSH HAS NO PROBLEM FINDING SOMETHING TO DO, OFTEN WITH THE HELP OF HIS STUDENTS:
This is one of the wildest and most wonderful countries I've worked in, so a lot of my time is spent getting out and seeing the city or jumping a train to check out the surrounding countryside. The traffic in Jakarta is tough to deal with and the air quality isn't great, but the opportunity for adventure and excitement is always just around the corner. Many of my students-turned-friends are great guides to the sights and always know the best nightclubs to visit, when the concerts are and where the best food is.

Bahasa Indonesian, almost identical to Malay, was imposed on the people of Indonesia after independence in 1949 and is one of the simplest languages to learn both in structure and pronunciation.

LIST OF EMPLOYERS

AIM FOR ENGLISH

Jalan Padang 5C, Manggarai, Jakarta

- 021 837 85 238
- ian@aimjakarta.com
- www.aimjakarta.com

NUMBER OF TEACHERS: 4.

PREFERENCE OF NATIONALITY: UK/Australia/NZ/Canada/ USA (currently all are from UK).

QUALIFICATIONS: at least CELTA, and at least 2 years' experience (teaching adults, business English nd academic English).

CONDITIONS OF EMPLOYMENT: 12-month contracts. 20 hours contact. 7 hours in the office, 5 days a week. Some evening work.

SALARY: Rp15 million.

FACILITIES/SUPPORT: return tickets home, end of contract bonus, full health insurance. Work permits taken care of: outsourced to a reliable agent.

RECRUITMENT: through online advertising, word of mouth. Interviews essential, and can be via web-meeting (via Skype/ yahoo messenger with webcam).

CONTACT: Ian Bishop, Managing Director.

BERLITZ LANGUAGE CENTRE

Hotel InterContinental MidPlaza Jakarta, Shopping Gallery R-26, Jl. Jendral Sudirman Kav. 10–11, Jakarta 10220

- 21 251 4589; fax: 21 251 4582
- lincoln@biz.net.id

NUMBER OF TEACHERS: approx. 10.

PREFERENCE OF NATIONALITY: none.

QUALIFICATIONS: degree minimum. TEFL Certificate and or experience preferred but not essential.

CONDITIONS OF EMPLOYMENT: 12-month contracts. School hours: 7.30am–9pm, Mon-Fri; 7.30am to 3pm Saturday. Lessons scheduled as available between these hours.

SALARY: approx. $1,000–$1,200 depending on qualifications and experience.

FACILITIES/SUPPORT: housing allowance. Berlitz instructor training free of charge.

RECRUITMENT: word-of-mouth, newspapers and via internet. Interviews by phone or held at nearby language centre.

CONTACT: Lincoln Taylor.

THE BRITISH INSTITUTE – see TBI below.

E-ACTIVE

Jalan Ulujami Raya No.12, Jakarta Selatan, Jakarta 12250

- 21 7388 9458; fax: 21 7088 3022
- e-active@e-active.org
- www.e-active.org

NUMBER OF TEACHERS: 3.

PREFERENCE OF NATIONALITY: none.

QUALIFICATIONS: TESOL, CELTA, DELTA, TESL, TEFL, MA, MSC (Teacher Training) plus HND or degree in any field. Must have 1 year's teaching experience.

CONDITIONS OF EMPLOYMENT: 1 year contract. 25 contact hours per week (maximum).

SALARY: Rp10,000,000 per month (net).

FACILITIES/SUPPORT: all visa requirements will be met by the school. Assistance given with accommodation.

RECRUITMENT: via local adverts and internet. Telephone interviews acceptable along with faxed copy of qualifications.

CONTACT: Nicholas Barooah, School Owner.

EF ENGLISH FIRST

Indonesian Head Office, Wisma Tamara Lt. 4, Suite 402, Jl. Jend. Sudirman Kav. 24, Jakarta 12920

- 21 520 6477; fax: 21 520 4719
- efrecruitment@ef.com
- www.englishfirst.com

NUMBER OF TEACHERS: more than 700 for 68 schools throughout Indonesia.

PREFERENCE OF NATIONALITY: British, Canadian, Australian, American or New Zealanders only (due to work visa restrictions).

QUALIFICATIONS: TEFL/TESL certificate indicating 120 hours of class work, observations and evaluated practice teaching. Experience, BA or MA degree and references may be submitted in lieu of the certificate.

CONDITIONS OF EMPLOYMENT: 12-month contracts. Usual hours are early afternoon until evening (1pm–9pm).

SALARY: varies significantly between cities: Rp6–9 million per month (no tax deduction).

FACILITIES/SUPPORT: most schools provide shared housing free or a monthly housing allowance. Teachers preferring to live alone are given advice and help but bear the contractual responsibilities themselves. Schools provide and pay for necessary working papers. Orientation on arrival, ongoing training and development, medical insurance, paid holidays and completion bonus provided. All schools are well equipped with a variety of resources.

RECRUITMENT: via EF's Online Recruitment Centre or approaching individual schools. Candidates are requested to register their details at www.englishfirst.com.

EF SWARA GROUP JAKARTA AND BOGOR-INDONESIA

The seven schools in this group are located in central Jakarta, the outskirts of Jakarta and the neighboring city of Bogor. For more details regarding the schools, please visit website (www.efjakarta.com)

NUMBER OF TEACHERS: more than 70.

PREFERENCE OF NATIONALITY: UK, Australia, Canada, USA, New Zealand.

RECRUITMENT: year-round, apart from in April and November.

CONTACT: send your CV by email to hrdswarajkt@pacific. net.id.

ENGLISH EDUCATION CENTER (EEC)
Jalan Let. Jend. S. Parman 68, Slipi, Jakarta 11410
- 21 532 3176/0044/0055; fax: 21 532 3178
- info@eec.co.id
- www.eec.co.id

OTHER BRANCHES IN JAKARTA: Jl. Raya Boulevard Barat Blok LC No. 56–57, Kelapa Gading Permai, Jakarta 14240; and Bintaro Jaya Sektor IX Blok B No. 4–7, Pondok Aren, Tangerang 15229.

NUMBER OF TEACHERS: 30 in three schools in Jakarta.

PREFERENCE OF NATIONALITY: American, British, Australian, New Zealand, Canadian.

QUALIFICATIONS: BA in relevant subject, CELTA and minimum 1 year's overseas TEFL experience.

CONDITIONS OF EMPLOYMENT: 1-year contracts. Maximum 24 hours per week, usually 2–9pm, but some 8.30am–12.30pm schedules. Students of all ages but many are teenagers and young adults.

SALARY: Rp8 million–Rp9 million per month.

FACILITIES/SUPPORT: assistance given with finding accommodation, including initial loan. Return air fare after completion of 1-year contract.

RECRUITMENT: teachers recruited locally.

EXECUTIVE ENGLISH PROGRAMS (EEP)
Jalan Wijaya VIII/4, Kebayoran Baru,
Jakarta Selatan 12160
- 21 722 0812/720 8864; fax: 21 720 1896
- simon-r@eep.web.id
- www.eep.web.id

Two additional branches in Bandung.

NUMBER OF TEACHERS: 40.

PREFERENCE OF NATIONALITY: UK, USA, Canadian, Australian, New Zealand.

QUALIFICATIONS: CELTA/Trinity Cert. plus university degree and at least a year's experience preferred. EEP specialises in in-company training projects, for which oil and gas industry experience is a definite asset.

CONDITIONS OF EMPLOYMENT: 1-year contracts to work a maximum of 28 hours per week.

SALARY: Minimum Rp 10 million per month for in-centre training. Increments for higher duties, in-company work and specialised training projects. Contract renewal bonus operates. Salary includes 20 days' paid holiday per year and limited medical coverage.

FACILITIES/SUPPORT: Will provide documentation and assist in finding accommodation.

RECRUITMENT: Through local newspapers (*The Jakarta Post*). Local interviews almost always necessary.

CONTACT: Simon Redman, Director of Studies.

IALF LANGUAGE CENTRES
Jl. Sumatera 49, Surabaya, East Java
- 31 502 6400; fax: 31 502 6408
- ialfsby@ialf.edu
- www.ialf.edu
Accredited IELTS Test Centre, East Java

NUMBER OF TEACHERS: 12.

PREFERENCE OF NATIONALITY: must be native English speaker.

QUALIFICATIONS: minimum Trinity Cert (TESOL) or CELTA plus 2 years' experience. IELTS Prep, EAP and Business English experience an advantage.

CONDITIONS OF EMPLOYMENT: 1 year. 8-hour-day. Average of 20 contact hours a week. School runs programmes for EAP, ESP, IELTS Prep & Testing, Business English and in-house training.

SALARY: depends on experience. Rp. 145,200,000 rupiah a year for teachers with minimum qualifications and experience. There is an additional Rp500,000 monthly transport allowance. Additional payment for IELTS testing. Teachers also get Expacare medical insurance. $1,500 bonus given on completion of each year of full-time employment. No deductions for tax or social security.

FACILITIES/SUPPORT: on-arrival housing allowance of Rp3 million and loan of 2 months' salary to assist with rental of accommodation deducted from monthly salary over first contract year. All work permits and visa provided. The IALF also has branches in Bali and Jakarta with different recruitment policies, terms and conditions, but they don't require staff at the moment.

RECRUITMENT: locally and via the internet.

IBLA (INDONESIA BRITAIN LANGUAGE ASSESSMENTS)

No. 42–44, Jl.Bogor sp Jl.Surabaya,
Medan 20212, North Sumatra
61 4150182/4150183; fax: 61 4557169
slg-bustaf@indosat.net.id

IBLA (formerly Logo Education Centre) is the official examination centre for the University of Cambridge Local Examinations Syndicate (UCLES) in Sumatra for English language and teaching.

NUMBER OF TEACHERS: 7.

PREFERENCE OF NATIONALITY: native English speakers.

QUALIFICATIONS: minimum bachelor's degree and TEFL qualifications, minimum 1 year general teaching experience, and experience in teaching preparatory for the Cambridge ESOL examinations (YLE/KET/PET/FCE/IELTS/BEC/TKT) and SAT I. Refer to www.cambridgeesol.org/index.html for detailed information. Also, candidates should have experience in teaching using an interactive whiteboard, should be able to recognise learners' needs and adapt teaching approaches accordingly, should be culturally sensitive and well groomed and able to promote an English-speaking environment.

CONDITIONS OF EMPLOYMENT: 1-year renewable contract, up to 27 contact hours with students per week. Classes are usually 1.5 hours in duration and conducted on weekdays at various times throughout the day and evening.

SALARY: beginning at Rp10 million monthly.

FACILITIES/SUPPORT: 25 working days' paid leave in addition to national holidays per contractual year, 5 working days' sick leave per contractual year, bonuses after completion of contract, work permit, housing allowance per contractual year, medical insurance.

RECRUITMENT: Interested applicants should email Chitra Bustaf at slg-bustaf@indosat.net.id with the following documents: a resumé/Curriculum Vitae, copies of certificates, copies of references, a copy of valid passport with photo and a cover letter stating the preferred choice of preparatory programmes to undertake.

CONTACT: Chitra Bustaf, Owner and Director.

INTERNATIONAL LANGUAGE STUDIES (ILS)

Jl. Ambengan 1-S, Surabaya 60272
31 534 2457; fax: 31 532 8369
felife@sby.dnet.net.id or
ils2000@mitra.net.id
Also: Simpang Darmo Permai Utara
No. 5, Surabaya 60226
31 731 7697

NUMBER OF TEACHERS: 3–5.

PREFERENCE OF NATIONALITY: British, American, Canadian and Australian.

QUALIFICATIONS: must have 4–5 week TEFL/TESOL certificate or equivalent preferably with at least 1 year's teaching experience. Able to teach English to all levels (children, teens and adults).

CONDITIONS OF EMPLOYMENT: 1- or 2-year contracts, renewable. Vacancies occur in January and July every year. 100 teaching hours per month. Freelance teaching is strictly prohibited. 2 weeks paid holidays during Christmas or Ramadan.

SALARY: Rp7,500,000–Rp9,500,000 per month (net).

FACILITIES/SUPPORT: private accommodation provided (with laundry). Occasional training workshops and seminars held. Bonus of a free trip to Bali at end of one-year contract plus school pays for round-trip airfare from home country and hospital cash plan during contract period and paid personal leave.

RECRUITMENT: advertisements in local papers and internet (Dave's Cafe). Interviews not necessary.

CONTACT: Felicia O Dien Koeswanto, Director.

KELT SURABAYA (formerly International Language Programs)

Jalan Jawa 34, Surabaya 60281, Jawa Timor
31 502 3333; fax: 31 503 0106
peter@k-elt.com
www.k-elt.com

NUMBER OF TEACHERS: 25 in 3 schools.

PREFERENCE OF NATIONALITY: must be classified native English speaker (to satisfy work permit requirements) ie from UK, USA, Canada, Australia or New Zealand.

QUALIFICATIONS: EFL qualification required, preferably CELTA or Trinity.

CONDITIONS OF EMPLOYMENT: 1-year contracts. 20 hours per week. teaching 5 days a week, between 2.30pm/ 3.45pm/5pm and 7pm/9.15pm. Pupils from age 4.

SALARY: starting salary is Rp10 million (net) per month.

FACILITIES/SUPPORT: accommodation provided including utilities and servants. Regular workshops held.

RECRUITMENT: advertisements on the internet (www.tefl. com). Recruitment drives 4 times a year.

CONTACT: Peter Mudd, Director of Studies (peter@k-elt. com) and Simon Bradshaw (simonb@k-elt.com)

LPTM (LEMBAGA PROFESI TEKNIK DAN MANAJEMEN)
Jalan Sunu Blok iX-20, Makassar 90152
lptm-mks@indo.net.id

NUMBER OF TEACHERS: volunteers exchange English conversation with young Indonesians in a cross-cultural exchange programme. LPTM Institute also places volunteers on its emergency education programme for children of urban poor families (LPTM, Jalan Tepi Kanal Baraya 9, Makassar 90153).

PREFERENCE OF NATIONALITY: any speaker of English (native and non-native).

QUALIFICATIONS: enthusiasm only. Minimum age 18, must be in good health, with travel and health insurance cover. More experienced candidates can become interns, who teach more structured programmes and even help with curriculum development.

CONDITIONS OF EMPLOYMENT: Volunteers become partners in classes and in extracurricular activities and excursions. Minimum 2-hour sessions twice a week.

SALARY: none. Programme fee is $75 for registration and $400 per month to cover 3-day orientation, accommodation, two meals a day if staying with a family, plus local back-up.

FACILITIES/SUPPORT: programme includes entitlement to 6-month visa rather than ordinary 1-month tourist visa. Many opportunities to visit local places of interest such as Toraja, Bantimurung, Malino and Tanjung Bira. After one month's stay, 1 week free time given for travel further afield, e.g. to Bali, Bunaken or Borobudur.

CONTACT: Baharuddin Abidin, Director.

THE BRITISH INSTITUTE (TBI) BANDUNG
Jl. Jawa 22, Bandung 40113
+62 22 421 1156; fax: +62 22 423 8421
tbibandung@tbi.co.id
Also: Jl. Dipati Ukur No. 46, Bandung 40132
22 253 4444; fax: 22 250 9584
Paskal Hyper Square B49–50 Bandung 40181
+62 22 8606 0940; fax: +62 22 8606 0773
Other branches
Bekasi: TBI SunCity Square
+62 21 8896 0328; fax: +62 021 8896 3004
Bogor: TBI Pajajaran
+62 251 385 5555; fax: +62 251 363031
Malang: TBI ABM Campus
+62 341 471 375; fax: +62 341 481 592
TBI Soekarno Hatta
+62 341 409 456; fax: +62 341 481 592
Surabaya: TBI Darmo Kali
+62 31 566 7773; fax: +62 31 566 5390
Medan: TBI Multatuli
+62 61 455 5123; fax: +62 61 457 6675

NUMBER OF TEACHERS: currently 60. TBI has 14 schools across Indonesia and has plans to expand further.

QUALIFICATIONS: CELTA or equivalent plus university degree minimum. Previous English language teaching experience preferred. Unqualified but experienced teachers may be considered for CELTA course sponsorship at TBI Jakarta (the only CELTA centre in Indonesia). TBI schools require teachers with a keen interest in teaching a wide variety of classes.

PREFERENCE OF NATIONALITY: UK, USA, Australia, New Zealand, Canada (only for visa reasons).

SALARY: base salary varies based on relative cost of living and number of teaching hours per week (22–25). Monthly salary after tax ranges from Rp8,400,000 to Rp14,000,000 approx.

FACILITIES/SUPPORT: Free health insurance coverage, settling-in loan, work permits and documentation paid. Six weeks paid leave per annum. Professional development programme of workshops and observed teaching with feedback. Possibility of training grants to undertake a further TEFL course, usually Young Learner Extension to CELTA, or DELTA. Good career development prospects, including management positions, as company expands.

RECRUITMENT: local hire or distance. Local applicants must teach a demonstration lesson. Distance applicants must complete tasks and have a telephone interview.

CONTACT: recruit@tbi.co.id or go to www.tbi.co.id.

JAPAN

The once unassailable Japanese economy experienced a sharp recession in the 1990s which saw the yen tumbling and unemployment a new fact of life. The impact for English teachers was that the market dipped, one or two major chains of language schools went bankrupt and the employment situation became generally much tighter with schools competing fiercely for a shrinking number of students. However, from 2003 to 2007 the economy entered a period of sustained recovery and prospects for hopeful language teachers were once again positive. The only major casualty of recent years is Nova, which went bust in October 2007, largely a victim of its own failings. Nearly 1,000 native English teachers were overnight left without jobs. It remains to be seen how the financial crisis of 2008 will affect the ELT market.

The basic monthly salary of 250,000 yen for full-time EFL teachers may not have risen in more than a decade, but it is worth nearly $2,800, considerably more than can be earned in most other countries. Wages are of course meaningless without balancing them against the local cost of living which is notoriously high. People used to say that you can't expect to break even and begin to save before you've been in Japan for about a year, but since the early 1990s there has been an incredible reduction in the cost of living. Developments such as the huge increase in the number of '100 yen shops' (the equivalent of 'pound shops') have made it far easier to outfit an apartment or buy teaching materials at reasonable prices.

The English language market is fairly mature: newcomers who could once count on finding a reasonably convenient job are now having to travel up to two hours to get to work. Schools which once accepted anyone with fluency have become more selective, and it is no longer a case of prospective teachers picking and choosing among employers. Yet there is still very little emphasis on TEFL qualifications. Image is of paramount importance to the Japanese and many employers are more concerned to find people who are lively and a touch glamorous than they are to find people with a background in teaching.

Many language training organisations operate on a huge scale, with many branches and large numbers of staff. For instance Aeon has five offices outside Japan: three in the USA, one in Canada and one in Australia. Companies such as Aeon and GEOS actively recruit in North America and Britain. These seem to be the employers most willing to consider teachers with no formal training, though all teachers in Japan must have a three-year bachelor's degree (which is an absolute requirement for work visas). Some chains have been described as factory English schools, where teachers are handed a course book and told not to deviate from the formula. They depend on a steady supply of fresh graduates who want the chance to spend a year or two in Japan. Often new recruits do not have much say in where they are sent and in their first year may be sent to the least desirable locations.

As long as your expectations are realistic, Japan should turn out to be an interesting choice of destination. Native speakers are hired in a surprising range of contexts: in-house language programmes in steel or electronics companies, state secondary schools, hot-house crammers, 'conversation lounges' where young people get together for an hour's guided conversation, vocational schools where English is a compulsory subject, 'ladies' classes' (quaintly so-called) where courses called 'English for Shopping' are actually offered, and also classes of children from as young as 2 years, since it has become a status symbol in Japan to send children of all ages to English classes. In fact, studying English for many Japanese is still more a social than an educational activity.

Culture shock grips most new arrivals to Japan. Incoming teachers are often so distracted by the mechanics of life in Japan and the cultural adjustments they have to make to survive that they devote too little energy to the business of teaching. On the other hand, anyone who has a genuine interest in Japan and who arrives reasonably well prepared may find that a year or two in Japan provides a highly rewarding experience.

PROSPECTS FOR TEACHERS

Jobs teaching English in Japan can be looked for in a variety of establishments including English conversation schools, trade schools, junior colleges, universities, high schools, and (increasingly popular) kindergartens. Most private language schools in Japan are looking for native speakers of any nationality with a four-year BA or BSc in any discipline and possibly some TEFL experience. Although only a minority are looking for professional qualifications in their teachers, there has been a noticeable increase in the number of qualified EFL teachers (especially from Australia) looking for work, and naturally schools prefer to take them over complete novices. Many schools have no set intake dates and serious applications are welcome at any time of the year, though most contracts begin in April and finish the following March (ie one year) which corresponds to the academic year.

A new development over the last few years, which may increase your prospects of finding work, has been the massive increase in demand for Business English and TOEIC courses. Japanese workers who have paid employment insurance for over three years are eligible to take courses with accredited learning institutions and claim a portion of the cost back from the government. The growth in the demand for business English is also due to companies expecting more of their existing workers and new recruits to be able to communicate in English in an increasingly global marketplace.

The favoured accent is certainly American and to a lesser extent Canadian. In fact, not many Japanese can distinguish a Scot from a Queenslander, or an Eastender from an Eastsider. What can be detected and is highly prized is clear speech. Slow precise diction together with a smart appearance and professional bearing are enough to impress some potential employers.

English teachers with proficiency in other languages will certainly increase their chances of finding gainful employment. There is currently a mini-boom in learning European languages, especially French, Italian and Spanish, and the bigger language schools are jumping on this bandwagon.

FINDING A JOB

With such a large selection of vacancies at a sub-professional level, it is often possible for university graduates to fix up a job before arrival. Most schools and companies which recruit abroad sort out visas and help with initial orientation and housing. The disadvantage is that their salary and working conditions will probably compare unfavourably with those of teachers who have negotiated their job after arrival; but most new recruits (*nama gaijin* or raw foreigners) conclude that the trade-off is a fair one. Of course the pool of foreign job-seekers already in Japan is large enough that the jobs offering good conditions tend to be snapped up quickly. Some organisations do not welcome speculative applications from outside Japan.

Before tackling the question of how to find a job after arriving in Japan, the possibilities of arranging a contract before leaving home need to be canvassed. The most prestigious programme of them all is the government-sponsored JET programme which offers what many consider to be a 'dream job' for new graduates.

THE JET PROGRAMME

The Japan Exchange and Teaching (JET) programme is an official Japanese government scheme aimed at improving foreign language teaching in schools and fostering good relations between the people of Japan and the 44 participating countries. The programme has been in existence since 1987 and is now responsible for placing about 2,500 native speakers of English for a minimum contract of one year in private and state junior and senior high schools throughout Japan, with an increasing emphasis on rural areas. Many consider the emphasis to be more on cultural exchange than on English teaching.

The majority of participants are from the USA (contact details below). Britain annually recruits about 200 graduates to the programme, making it the second largest employer of new graduates after the UK government. The prospects for people who wish to become Assistant Language Teachers (ALTs) in English on the JET Programme are excellent and the requirements few. Any UK national who is under 40 with a bachelor's degree and an interest in Japan is eligible to apply.

In the UK the scheme is administered by the JET Desk at the Embassy of Japan, 101–104 Piccadilly, London, W1J 7JT (✆ 020 7465 6668; fax: 020 7491 9347; info@jet-uk.org; www.jet-uk.org). Non-British applicants should contact the Japanese Embassy in their country of origin for information and application forms. US applicants can obtain details from any of the 16 Consulates in the US or from the JET Office, Japanese Embassy, 2520 Massachusetts Avenue NW, Washington, DC 20008 (✆ 202 238 6772/3 or 800-INFOJET; fax: 202 265 9484; eojjet@erols.com; www.embjapan.org).

The timetable for applicants from the UK is as follows: application forms are available online from late September; the deadline for applications is the last Friday in November; interviews are held between January and February; an intensive two-day orientation for successful candidates is held in London and Edinburgh at the start of July and departures for Japan take place in late July/August.

Robert Mizzi from Canada worked hard on his application, which paid off since he was called to an interview:

> *The interview was probably the most difficult interview I have ever had. It was only 20 minutes, but a painful 20 minutes. Besides the usual 'Why' and 'Tell us about yourself' questions, I was asked to teach a lesson on the spot using dramatic techniques I would use in class. Stunned, I managed to get out of my seat and draw some pictures of the stars and moon on the board, taught them the meaning of those words and then proceeded to ask the interview team to stand up and learn a little dance to the song 'Twinkle twinkle little star'. All I wanted to do was to create an impression and to stand out of the 300 people being interviewed. People remember you best when you are acting like a complete fool. When it is teaching English as a foreign language, the ability to act like a fool is one of the main requirements of the job. Getting Japanese men in suits up and dancing during a job interview with the prestigious JET programme was a half-crazed risk, but a successful one at that.*

Often government-run exchanges of this kind do not offer generous remuneration packages; however pay and conditions on the JET scheme are excellent. In addition to a free return flight, JET participants receive 3,600,000 yen a year. This is the salary after income and inhabitant taxes have been paid but there are further social and medical insurance fees of approximately 40,000 yen per month. The salary is standard for all JET participants. Contracts are with individual contracting organisations in Japan, so there can be discrepancies in working conditions. It is the luck of the draw that determines who goes where, although stated preferences will be taken into consideration. Pension regulations mean that JET teachers can reclaim money paid into the national insurance scheme as a lump sum equivalent to about one month's salary.

ALTS ARE THEORETICALLY EXPECTED TO WORK A SEVEN-HOUR DAY AND QUITE OFTEN TEACHERS ARE ASSIGNED AN AVERAGE OF THREE CLASSES A DAY, HOWEVER HOURS SPENT IN THE CLASSROOM WILL VARY BETWEEN PLACEMENTS. MARK ELLIOT FEELS THAT THE JET PROGRAMME IS 'PROBABLY THE BEST JOB IN THE WORLD' AND DESCRIBES HIS SITUATION:

I live on a wonderful island, three hours ferry ride from Nagasaki, nearer Shanghai than Tokyo. There is lots more to the job than teaching. After all, the programme is just as much about meeting people and participating in cultural exchange as it is about teaching.

All JET participants teach in partnership with a native Japanese teacher so those without significant teaching experience are not thrown in at the deep end. The degree of responsibility varies depending on the relationship built with the Japanese teacher with some ALTs effectively teaching the class in large part by themselves. JET teachers are often initially given a significant amount of free time to plan their lessons and settle into Japanese school life and to a large extent it is the hours put in outside the classroom that make the difference.

As **Rabindra Roy** wrote from Shizuoka prefecture, '*I can think of very few jobs where a freshly qualified graduate with an irrelevant degree and no experience can walk straight into such a big salary for this little work.*' He also describes the programme as 'desperately well organised'. But partly because of the variety in locations and schools and partly because Japan is such a weird and wonderful place, it is impossible to predict what life will be like, no matter how many orientations you attend. About two-thirds of JET participants renew for a second year, which indicates its success. A third of the second years stay for a third year, with five years now being the maximum a candidate can stay. The programme offers a tremendous amount of support and even those who are placed in remote or rural areas are usually within striking distance of other JET participants.

ZOE VAUGHAN ENJOYED HER EXPERIENCES WITH JET SO MUCH THAT SHE JOINED THE STAFF OF THE JET PROGRAMME AT THE EMBASSY OF JAPAN, LONDON AND WORKED AS ASSISTANT CO-ORDINATOR UPON HER RETURN:

I was placed in a rural town near Mount Fuji in central Honshu and although employed by the local Board of Education, spent my time teaching students from two kindergartens, two elementary schools and two junior high schools. I took part in club activities as well as being welcomed to join community events and festivals. JET provided me with an unforgettable, life-changing experience, giving me skills and confidence, along with memories that will last a lifetime.

In retrospect, **Susannah Kerr** was not too sorry to have been turned down by JET because their teachers have little control over where they are sent and end up in small towns (however, she wouldn't mind a JET salary).

IN ADVANCE

There are many other ways to fix up a job in Japan ahead of time, though these will usually require more initiative than signing on with JET. Many Japanese language schools have formed links with university careers departments, particularly in the US and Canada, so anyone with a university connection should exploit it. Another possibility for Americans is to explore the Japanese-American Sister City Program which assists some native English speakers to find teaching jobs in the city twinned with theirs.

As mentioned, GEOS and AEON carry out extensive recruitment campaigns in North America, Britain and Australia. Shane English Schools confine their recruitment to the UK through their partner, Saxoncourt. Try also Reach to Teach (see entry at the beginning of the Asia chapter). A steady trickle of advertisements appear in newspapers, *EL Prospects*, *TESOL Placement Bulletin*, etc. placed by individual schools in Japan and agents. Quite often schools and groups of schools will appoint a foreign recruiter. For example, the large language chain Kent School of English advertises in the *Guardian* for EFL teachers to send their CV and photo to a private address in London (see entry).

Many schools have no need to advertise abroad since they receive so many speculative résumés (the American term for CV is used in Japan). The internet has evolved into a valuable job search tool. Using any of the popular household search engines, type 'English Teaching in Japan' and dozens of job-related websites will appear. O-Hayo-Sensei (which means 'Good Morning Teacher') has pages of teaching positions across Japan at www.ohayosensei.com. Many of these are open only to candidates who are already in Japan. ELT Jobs in Japan (www.eltnews.com/jobs/jobsinjapan.shtml) lists ELT jobs throughout Japan and www.eltnews.com, is an online magazine for ELT teachers in Japan with news, jobs, classroom ideas, etc. It is a good idea to send your CV to the big schools before arrival, make some follow-up calls and hope to arrange some interviews in your first week.

Professional teachers can make contact with JALT, the Japan Association for Language Teaching (www.jalt.org). JALT categorically cannot help with employment but it does run professional development activities through its local branches.

ON THE SPOT

As has been mentioned, native speakers with a bachelor's degree certificate – and some without – have as good a chance of landing a job as an English teacher on arrival in Japan. The crucial question is how long will it take. The murderous cost of living means that job-hunters spend hundreds of dollars or pounds very quickly while engaged in the time-consuming business of answering advertisements, sending round CVs, and going for interviews.

IF YOU'RE STARTING COLD TRY TO ARRIVE ON A WEEKEND SO YOU CAN BUY THE MONDAY EDITION OF THE ENGLISH LANGUAGE *JAPAN TIMES* WHICH CARRIES ADVERTISEMENTS FOR ENGLISH TEACHERS. JOSEPH TAME FROM HEREFORDSHIRE ARRIVED IN TOKYO WITH TWO BIG ADVANTAGES, A WORKING HOLIDAY VISA AND A JAPANESE GIRLFRIEND WITH WHOM HE COULD STAY:

> *Having spent virtually all of my travel funds in my first 21 days in the city, I eventually decided to face the fact that I'd have to find a job, for a couple of months at least. What with all this talk of a global recession, I really didn't feel too positive. Furthermore I have virtually no experience teaching, have no teaching qualifications and indeed no university degree which all employers insist on. My first stop was the Japan Association for Working Holiday Makers. I was fortunate in that as I was being registered, a phone call came through from a private English school who were desperate for a teacher. Thirty minutes later I had a job paying £17 an hour. The catch was that it was only four hours per week, but that was my pocket money taken care of. I actually spent time surfing the web in an attempt to remember what pronouns and adjectives are; I only ever remember that a verb is a 'doing' word.*

Later he made good use of www.gaijinpot.com which remains a superb resource for jobs, accommodation and news for foreign residents in Japan. He also recommends www.findateacher.net for those wanting to teach English (or other languages). You simply enter the relevant information about what you teach, what area of Japan you teach in, how much you charge, etc. and the students will come to you. The free weekly English language magazine *Metropolis* (www.metropolis.co.jp) also has a good classifieds section which is worth checking for jobs.

Few things could be more intimidating for the EFL teacher than to arrive at Narita International Airport with no job and limited resources. The longer the job hunt takes, the faster the finances dwindle and the more nerve-racking and discouraging the situation becomes. One way to lessen the monumentality of the initial struggle would be to get out of Tokyo straightaway. Although there are more jobs in the capital, there is also more competition from other foreigners, to the point of saturation. Enterprising teachers who are willing to step off the conveyor belt which takes job-seekers from the airport to one of Tokyo's many '*gaijin* houses' (hostels for foreigners) may well encounter fewer setbacks. Osaka seems a good bet since it is within commuting distance of the whole Kansai area, including Kobe which is 20 minutes away by train. In Osaka the cost of living is as much as a quarter less than it is in Tokyo. Another promising destination is Sapporo in the north, the fifth largest city in the country. **Ken Foye** is a reader of this book who chose to teach on Hokkaido, the northern island on which Sapporo is located:

> *I have been teaching here for a year and a half now and I would recommend Hokkaido to anyone, especially those who don't find living in a large urban metropolis very appealing. Here the people seem much friendlier than in Tokyo, the cost of living isn't as high, there's fresh air and the scenery is magnificent. And I probably would not have ended up here if not for your book.*

Susannah Kerr was made redundant by Nova in late 2007 and swiftly began 'on the spot' job hunting in Tokyo courtesy of websites such as www.gaijinpot.com. She considered a large employer, Gaba (http://careers.gaba.co.jp), which specialises in one-to-one teaching. According to Susannah, the advantage of working for them is that you can choose your hours. The disadvantage is that earnings are dependent on your popularity as a teacher since students vote with their feet. Susannah was interviewed by a company called Balloon Kids, which employs up to 20 teachers and pays 250,000–300,000 yen per month. Instead of working from its own institute, the company hires rooms in (for example) suburban shopping malls, where 12–15 kids show up. The teacher would be expected to go to an office to pick up teaching materials and a key, and then let him/herself into the room, so there would be no contact with other teachers. They also withhold 10,000 yen per month to be paid at the end of the contract.

The six-month contract that Susannah eventually accepted was with MLS, a school that uses a proprietary drama method to teach English. With 36 branches in Tokyo and Yokohama, it is a small company by Japanese standards. Susannah was impressed with the efficacy of the method, and because the teachers were '*interesting, creative, often musical types, the children were often engaged and excited, and their spoken English really did improve. The teachers were always trying to use attention-grabbing games like charades.*'

Tokyo

One of the most often recommended places to start a job hunt in Tokyo is the Kimi Information Center (Oscar Building, 8th Floor, 2–42–3 Ikebukuro, Toshima-ku, Tokyo 171 0014; © 3 3986 1604; fax: 3 3986 3037; kimiinfo@kimiwillbe.com). Its website (www.kimiwillbe.com) carries teaching job advertisements. Like so many addresses in Japan, it is difficult to find without a map (print one off from their website) or follow the detailed directions provided by **Deborah Cordingley**: take the West Exit of Ikebukuro Station, walk straight past the McDonald's for one block and turn right when you see Marui Department Store. Go three blocks past Sumitomo Bank. Kimi is on the right across from the Post Office. The Kimi Center offers a range of useful services such as photocopying, computer time and a telephone answering service as well as advising on cheap accommodation (including at the Kimi Ryokan, their affiliated Japanese-style guest house), reasonable apartments in and around Tokyo and visa extensions. Free job opportunities booklets are available. World traveller **Joseph Tame** was impressed with one particular service they offer to people who register (which must be done in person): they will place an advert in Japanese in your local area newspapers advertising your availability to teach. Although they take a small cut, this is very worthwhile.

Joseph Tame was also impressed with the Japan Association for Working Holiday Makers (www.jawhm.or.jp) whose services are available to those with the appropriate visa (see section on Regulations below).

> *My first stop was the JAWHM, one of whose three offices is in the Nakano Sun Plaza in central Tokyo, 20 minutes by bicycle from where I was staying. They were very helpful. After registering (for free) I had access to their lists of jobs. Essentially it's a job centre for foreigners. They also have the latest copies of all the relevant magazines and newspapers with sits vacant columns. They will advise on housing, etc. etc.*

When looking for accommodation, try to pick up a list of *gaijin* houses from an information or tourist office and look for ones which charge a monthly rather than a nightly rent since these are the ones which attract long-term residents. Apple House (www.applehouse.ne.jp) is recommended for being affordable, friendly and in a good location. Because it is so difficult to rent flats, some teachers continue living in *gaijin* houses after they find work. Many foreigners live and work in the Roppongi district of Tokyo which might therefore be a sensible place to base yourself. One recommended agency is Fontana (© 3 3382 0151; www.fontana-apt.co.jp) which provides an excellent service.

Susannah Kerr rented a two-bedroom flat in the pleasant, traditional Japanese neighbourhood of Kagurazaka for 160,000 yen a month, but when her flatmates moved on and she had to pay the rent by herself, she decided to move. Even when accompanied by a local, using a local rental agency proved impossible so she used an English-speaking rental agency to find a one-bedroom apartment for 80,000 yen in Okubo, a bustling 24-hour-a-day area known as Koreatown, with a mildly sleazy reputation but gradually improving. Foreign letting agencies offer the advantage of not insisting that you provide a local guarantor. The Sakura House agency, which caters for non-Japanese accommodation-seekers (www.sakura-house.com), has become a prominent feature of the accommodation landscape in Tokyo, but there are many others.

A free advertisements paper called *Tokyo Classifieds* is distributed in the Roppongi district on Fridays carrying job and accommodation advertisements. Even tourist offices such as the one at

Hibuya station (exit A-3) have free notice boards where private lessons may be sought or offered, as well as accommodation.

Wherever you choose to conduct your job hunt, English language newspapers are the starting place for most. Jobs in secondary schools are advertised from September on. The Monday edition of the *Japan Times* carries fewer advertisements than it used to but it is still the best source. Note that advertisements often specify 'female' which usually indicates a job teaching young children. Male applicants for these posts may have to prove that they have prior experience of working with children. Jobs in the Kansai region around Osaka are listed at the end of the Tokyo classifieds.

Also pick up a copy of *Metropolis* (mentioned above) and *Tokyo Notice Board* available from expat bars and big downtown stores such as Tower Records. More mainstream papers such as the *Mainichi Daily News* and *Asahi Evening News* are also worth a look. As usual, the employers who advertise regularly tend to be the ones with the worst reputations and the highest staff turnover. The main publication in the Kansai area (Kobe, Kyoto, Osaka and Nara) is the monthly magazine *Kansai Time Out* whose classified advertisements can be consulted online at www.japanfile.com.

AMANDA SEARLE DESCRIBES WHAT SHE FOUND IN THE NEWSPAPERS WHEN SHE WAS JOB-HUNTING:

Most companies give little idea in their advertisements of the hours and salary, let alone the age and number of students or the textbooks used. They are not very willing to give that information over the phone, explaining that you will get the opportunity to ask questions if you are called for interview. I sent cover letters out with my resumé, explaining that I was looking only for full-time positions which offered visa sponsorship. I sent out about 20 applications and about ten companies contacted me and I went to eight interviews. I ended up being offered two full-time positions and three part-time ones.

The initial phone call is very important and should be considered as a preliminary interview. Since you may be competing with as many as 100 people answering the same advertisement, you have to try to stand out over the phone. Speak slowly, clearly, and be very *genki*, which means lively and fun. You may be asked to fax your CV to them; the cover letter should be short and intelligent, and the CV should be brief and interesting, emphasising any teaching experience. Always carry a supply of professional looking business cards (*meishi*).

Demonstration lessons now form an integral part of most job interviews in Japan, regardless of one's qualifications. Try to prepare yourself as much as possible if only because travelling to an interview in Tokyo is a major undertaking which can take up to three hours and cost a lot of money; it would be a shame to blow your chances because of a simple oversight. Dress as impeccably and conservatively as possible, and carry a respectable briefcase, since books are often judged by their covers in Japan. Inside you should have any education certificates you have earned, preferably the originals since schools have long since realised that a lot of forgeries are in circulation. Your resumé should not err on the side of modesty.

REGULATIONS

Britons, Canadians, Australians and New Zealanders are eligible to apply for a working holiday visa for Japan. Applicants must be aged 18–25 (or up to 30 in restricted circumstances). The working holiday visa allows 400 single young Britons to accept paid work in Japan for up to 12 months.

Applicants must show that they have sufficient financial backing, ie savings of £2,500. Note that applications are accepted from April and once the allocation of 400 has been filled, no more visas will be granted until April of the following year. Further details are available by ringing ✆ 020 7465 6565 or on the embassy website at www.uk.emb-japan.go.jp/en/visa/work_hol.html, which stipulates that the working holiday visa is not appropriate for those wishing to enter Japan to engage in full-time employment. The services of the Japan Association for Working-Holiday Makers mentioned above are now also available to Britons, and a large proportion of the jobs registered with the JAWHM in Tokyo, Osaka and Kyushu are as English teachers. For those ineligible for a working holiday visa, the key to obtaining a work visa for Japan is to have a Japanese sponsor. Documents which will help you to find a sponsor are the original or notarised copy of your BA or other degree and résumé. Most teachers are sponsored by their employers, although on rare occasions it is possible for the sponsor to be a private citizen. Not all schools by any means are willing to sponsor their teachers, unless they are persuaded that they are an ongoing proposition. Some schools rely on a stream of Canadians, Australians and New Zealanders on working holiday visas which they must obtain in their home countries through the SWAP Japan Programme. SWAP allows students aged 18–30 to work for six months in the first instance but is extendable to 18 months. To qualify you must prove that you have $3,000 at your disposal. Other nationalities will have to find a sponsor. If your visa is to be processed before arrival, you must have a definite job appointment in Japan. Your employer must apply to the Ministry of Justice in Tokyo for a Certificate of Eligibility which he or she then forwards to you. You must take this along with a photocopy of it, your passport, photograph and application form to any Consulate General of Japan. Usually a visa can be issued within three working days, though it can take longer. The regulations stipulate that anyone who works in Higher Education must have an MA in Education or TEFL.

The UK and USA have a visa exemption arrangement with Japan (www.uk.emb-japan.go.jp/en/visa/visa-exempt.html). British citizens can stay for up to six months without a visa, US citizens can stay for up to 90 days. It is possible to enter Japan, look for work and then apply for a work visa from outside Japan. Those found to be overstaying as tourists can be deported. Furthermore, employers who are caught employing illegal aliens as well as the foreign workers themselves are subject to huge fines, and both parties risk imprisonment.

Finding an employer to sponsor you for a work visa is very important. A number of schools advertising for teachers state in their advertisements that they are willing to consider only those who already have a work visa. Others are willing to act as sponsors. Sponsors obtain a Certificate of Eligibility inside Japan. Although immigration laws are being tightened, the government is making it easier for foreigners to get working visas. Whereas previously it was necessary for the teacher to leave the country, at great personal expense, to change their visa status (the Korean Visa Tour), these days the teacher need only take their Certificate of Eligibility into the local Immigration office, where the visa will be processed. However, those on a student visa still need to leave the country to complete the visa process. According to **Alan Suter** the cheapest way is to take a ferry from Kobe to Pusan, Korea.

The work visa is valid for six months, 12 months or 3 years. Renewal can be applied for in Japan. When renewing, one of the most important requirements is a tax statement showing your previous year's earnings. It is difficult to obtain a new visa unless you can show that you have earned at least 250,000 yen per month. Cash-in-hand and part-time jobs may be lucrative but they do nothing to help your visa application. If you break your contract with your employer, you will have to find another sponsor willing to act as sponsor the following year.

You are permitted to work up to 20 hours a week on a cultural or student visa. Cultural visas are granted to foreigners interested in studying some aspect of traditional Japanese culture on a full-time basis. In this case you must find a teacher willing to sponsor you. Cultural visas are often granted for *shodo* (calligraphy), *taiko* (drumming), karate, *aikido*, *ikebana* (flower arranging) and *ochakai* (tea ceremony). At one time these study visas were liberally handed out but nowadays you must produce concrete evidence that you actually are studying.

Teachers usually have the basic rate of national income tax in Japan (6%–7%) withdrawn at source. Although JET salaries were at one time tax-free, this is no longer the case. A further 3% is owing for local taxes, which are the teacher's responsibility only in their second and subsequent years in Japan. The Japanese government offers nationalised health insurance which covers about three-quarters of medical and dental care bills. The cost is about 40,000 yen per month. Many employers accustomed to hiring native English speaker teachers may offer more comprehensive private cover for less.

CONDITIONS OF WORK

DESPITE A WIDESPREAD FEELING THAT THE GLORY DAYS OF ELT IN JAPAN ARE OVER, ALL THINGS ARE RELATIVE AND MOST ESTABLISHED TEACHERS DO NOT FIND MUCH TO COMPLAIN ABOUT. AFTER A GRIM STINT OF TEACHING IN KOREA, TIM LEFFEL WAS ASTONISHED BY THE CONTRAST IN ATMOSPHERE WHEN HE ARRIVED IN JAPAN IN THE MIDST OF WHAT WAS PERCEIVED AS AN ECONOMIC CRISIS:
The big surprise to me was the attitude of teachers in Japan. The yen had dropped but nobody seemed too bothered. As one JET teacher said, 'We earned so much for doing so little work, it's hard to get upset about the exchange rate.' Those in private language schools may disagree but it's a far cry from the universal resentment, distrust and frustration you hear from those in Korea.

Despite the high cost of living, most teachers seem to be able to save money without having to lead too frugal an existence. Some even save half their salary in their first year by avoiding eating out and going to the cinema. **Amanda Moody** worked mostly from 10am to 7pm or 8pm in a small school in Nagoya and managed to save about $16,000. The longer you work in Japan the higher the salary and better working conditions you can command. Rank beginners outside Tokyo and Osaka can earn as little as 230,000 yen a month, but the steady average of 250,000 yen persists almost everywhere. Perks such as increments for higher qualifications, end-of-contract bonuses, free Japanese lessons and travel tickets, etc. are in fairly wide evidence, although it is always worth making sure that your contract mentions these perks. Amanda Moody discovered that her contract was 'illegal' and that she had been cheated out of an end-of-year bonus.

A tip for those who manage to save a significant sum was passed on by **Ted Travis**: buying an international postal money order (*yubin kawase*) from any post office is by far the cheapest way to transfer money out of the country.

Teaching schedules can be exhausting. Cost-cutting is a big part of the new Japanese economy, with some supermarkets charging customers for shopping bags, banks closing branches, companies hiring temps rather than full time employees to save on benefits, and rural municipalities merging for greater efficiency. Language schools are not exempt from this movement and the majority are filling teachers' schedules with bigger classes in an effort to reduce teacher numbers. Teachers are also increasingly asked to work 'outside their job description', helping out with advertising, student retention and the sale of study materials.

Timetables may be announced at the last minute, though it is more difficult to opt out in Japan than in other countries because of the dedication Japanese workers show to their firms. (At best a

Japanese worker gets 10 days of holiday a year and few take their full entitlement for fear of seeming lazy or disloyal to the company.) Some schools remain open all weekend and on public holidays too.

One of the advantages of working in state schools (as JET teachers do) is that they close for holidays, usually three weeks at Christmas and two weeks in August between semesters. Most schools offer one-week holidays (paid or unpaid or a combination of the two) at the beginning of May (the 'Golden Week') and in the middle of August ('*O-bon* vacation'). Holidays for those lucky enough to work in institutes of higher education are much more generous.

Private tutoring is still lucrative, paying between 3,000 and 6,000 yen an hour. **Susannah Kerr** managed to hold on to six hours of private teaching a week (teaching three children in one family) when Nova collapsed which netted her 18,000 yen, enough to eat. Occasionally you will meet someone who has been paid $100 just to have dinner with a language learner and converse in English, but these plums are few and far between.

THE PUPILS

The stereotype of the diligent Japanese pupil has becoming somewhat outmoded. The younger generation of Japanese is not always willing to play by the rules that their elders lay down, and there is increasing tension in schools which may manifest itself in (mildly) unruly behaviour. But mostly teachers find their students eager, attentive and willing to confer great respect on their teachers and in some out-of-the-way places even celebrity status. All teachers are expected to look the part and most schools will insist on proper dress (eg suits and dresses). But they do not want a formal approach to teaching.

JAPANESE ADULTS WILL HAVE STUDIED ENGLISH AT SCHOOL FOR AT LEAST SIX YEARS, AND THEIR KNOWLEDGE OF GRAMMAR IS USUALLY SOUND. THEY GO TO CONVERSATION SCHOOLS IN THE EXPECTATION OF MEETING NATIVE SPEAKER TEACHERS ABLE TO DELIVER CREATIVE AND ENTERTAINING LESSONS. YET SOME ARE CRIPPLED BY DIFFIDENCE OR EXCESSIVE ANXIETY ABOUT GRAMMATICAL CORRECTNESS. MICHAEL FROST IS ONE TEACHER WHO EXPERIENCED A CLASH OF CULTURES WHEN TRYING TO ENCOURAGE DISCUSSION IN HIS CLASSROOM:

It is very difficult for Japanese students to come out and express an individual opinion. The best tactic is to get them in pairs, so that together they can work something out. They are more productive and open in pairs, and it takes the pressure off them. Then get the pairs into fours, to express a mini-group opinion, then work for a total group agreement. The thing to avoid at all costs is to stroll into class, saying, 'OK, today we are going to discuss environmental issues. Tetsuya, you set the ball rolling: What do you think of pollution?' It will not work.

IT IS A POPULAR MYTH THAT JAPANESE STUDENTS HAVE GOOD READING ABILITIES IN ENGLISH AND REQUIRE ONLY CONVERSATION PRACTICE. THIS WAS NOT THE EXPERIENCE OF NATHAN EDWARDS, A DIPLOMA-QUALIFIED TEACHER FROM CANADA:

I am currently teaching at the Tokyo YMCA College of English, a pioneer in English teaching in Japan, established in 1880. The fact is that both reading and speaking in English present major challenges even to students with years of English instruction in the Japanese school system. It is highly advisable for teachers to bring a good supply of realia with them (various English brochures, used tickets, maps, coins, etc.) and old lesson plans.

Problems can arise in team teaching situations if your Japanese colleague has not attained a high enough level of English. While teaching in the JET programme, **Robert Mizzi** came to admire Japanese culture, but he did find some aspects of his job frustrating:

A lot of times I cannot introduce a game idea because, literally, it will take 20 minutes for the teacher to understand (never mind the students).

Amanda Moody worked in a small school in Nagoya, where she taught pre-school aged children using a mixture of the 'Gentle Revolution' and Rosetta Stone software:

My pupils were very smart and the children of successful Japanese. Some were the products of brain surgeons or music producers. Others were businessmen's kids. But most of them were reading and writing around the age of 3. Their parents expected the world of both us and their children.

Amanda loved her students, but hated her employer, who fined teachers for 'infringements' such as 'smelled strange and suspicious acting: 500 yen fine'. One aspect of Japanese culture which many foreigners find particularly disturbing is that any English native speaker who happens to have non-Caucasian features will almost certainly be discriminated against.

ACCOMMODATION

It is not uncommon for teachers who are hired overseas to be given help with accommodation, which is a tremendously useful perk, even if the flat provided is small and over-priced, with poor insulation and a badly equipped kitchen. If you are on your own, you will be forced to use a foreigners' rental agency. Rental costs are likely to range from 60,000 yen to 100,000 yen per person per month in Tokyo and perhaps 65,000 yen on average in Osaka. When you find a place through an agency, you will have to pay a commission of one month's rent and probably also a colossal deposit called 'key money' which can be as much as six months rent in advance. Unlike rent deposits in the West you can't expect to recoup it all. The system of paying huge deposits has been coming under increasing pressure and large rental agencies are starting to reduce the amount that has to be paid up front to a more manageable one month's rent. 'LeoPalace', which has apartments all over Japan, now advertises 'zero down payment' for monthly apartments (apartments rented on a rotating monthly contract, often furnished), and only requires one or two months' rent for yearly leases. Susannah Kerr was lucky enough not to have to pay any key money, although she did pay a deposit of one month's rent. Rents outside Tokyo and Osaka should be nearer 50,000 yen, with an additional monthly payment of at least 10,000 yen for utilities. Well-established schools may be prepared to lend you the key money or (exceptionally) pay it outright.

THERE ARE GREAT DISCREPANCIES IN THE ACCOMMODATION ASSIGNED TO JET TEACHERS. WHILE SOME GET BEAUTIFUL NO-RENT HOUSES, OTHERS GET ONE-ROOM APARTMENTS WITH HIGH RENT. ROBERT MIZZI HAD NO COMPLAINTS ABOUT THE RENT BUT HE DIDN'T GET MUCH FOR HIS MONEY:
I have no oven, dryer, hot water, shower or heating. A lot of things I had to buy for the apartment and a lot of things I had to give up. (The thrill of having running water certainly is a luxury where I am.)

A further problem is the near total absence of furnished apartments because Japanese people do not like to use belongings that have been used by other people, which means you may have to go shopping for curtains and cookers on top of all your other expenses. Again, schools which usually hire foreign teachers may keep a stock of basic furnishings which they can lend to teachers. If all this sounds too much hassle, perhaps staying in a *gaijin* house long term is not such a bad idea.

Obviously it is to your advantage to live as close to your place of work as possible but, as noted above, many teachers are forced to spend a sizeable chunk of their earnings and a lot of time commuting. Ask your employer to pay for your travel, preferably in the form of a monthly travel pass which can be used for your leisure travel as well. If you're in Tokyo, bear in mind that city buses charge a flat fare of 200 yen.

LEISURE TIME

According to some veteran teachers, leisure time and how to spend it will be the least of your worries. Depending on your circumstances, you may be expected to participate in extracurricular activities and social events which it would cause offence to decline – always a major concern in Japan. Although **Bryn Thomas** enjoyed the sushi which his school provided for teachers still at work at 9pm, he was less keen on the 'office parties when teachers were required to dress up in silly costumes and be nice to the students'. Most teachers are happy to accept occasional invitations to socialise with their Japanese colleagues or pupils, even if it does mean an evening of speaking very very slowly and drinking heavily. Many teachers find the socialising with students fun if expensive. Knowing a *gaijin* is a considerable status symbol for many Japanese, many of whom are willing to pay good money just for you to go to their houses once a week and eat their food. But it is not like that everywhere.

A GLUT OF WESTERNERS IN TOKYO MEANS THAT YOUR WELCOME MAY BE LESS THAN ENTHUSIASTIC. IN FACT NON-JAPANESE ARE REFUSED ENTRANCE TO SOME TOKYO BARS AND RESTAURANTS. MANY PEOPLE HEAD STRAIGHT OUT OF TOKYO FOR THE MORE APPEALING CITY OF OSAKA. JULIE FAST DESCRIBES THE CONTRAST:
I am still enamoured of Osaka; it is like a village after Tokyo. I am constantly amazed at the trees we see everywhere. I never realised in Tokyo how much I hated being constantly surrounded by people. I never had personal space in Tokyo. No one does – which explains the distant, sour looks on most people's faces. What a difference in Osaka. Osaka people have the roughest reputation in all of Japan. From a Western point of view, they are the friendliest. I have been invited to houses for lunch, children say hello and people in shops actually talk to you. Which proves you can't judge a country by its largest city.

All cities are expensive. Any entertainment which smacks of the West such as going out to a fashionable coffee house or a night club will be absurdly expensive. However, if you are content with more modest indigenous food and pastimes, you will be able to save money. A filling bowl of noodles and broth costs less than £3, though you may never take to the standard breakfast of boiled rice and a raw egg. Staying home to listen to Japanese language tapes or to read a good book (eg *Pictures from the Water Trade*, a personal account of life in Japan) costs nothing. Obviously the more settled you become, the more familiar you will be with the bargains and affordable amusements. For example while the Tokyo superclubs impose a cover charge of up to 4,000 yen, Susannah Kerr found much cheaper ones and in fact one where she got to know the DJs was free.

Finding your way around is nothing if not a challenge in a country where almost all road and public transport signs are incomprehensible. What use is an A–Z if you can't read the alphabet? Many feel that it is worth making an effort to master at least something of the written language. There are three alphabets in Japanese: *kanji* (ancient pictograms), *hiragana* and *katakana* (the characters used to spell loan words from English). Amanda Searle is just one teacher who feels that *kana* can be learned through independent study so that at least you will be able to read station names and menus. Learning some of the script not only impresses students and shows that you are making an effort to absorb some of the culture, it also helps you to survive. **Joseph Tame** signed up for Japanese lessons so he could get beyond 'large beer please' and 'I don't understand' to a variety of expressions to exclaim 'How much??' in disbelief.

Japanese addresses are mind-bogglingly complicated too: the numbers refer to land subdivisions: prefecture, district, ward, then building. When in doubt (inevitable) ask a friendly informant for a *chizu* (map). It is also a good idea to get a Japanese person to write your destination in both *kanji* and transliterated into *roma-ji* (our alphabet). Japanese people will sometimes go to embarrassing lengths to help foreigners. This desire to help wedded to a reluctance to lose face means that they may offer advice and instructions based on very little information, so keep checking. Young people in jeans are the best bets. Outside the big cities the people are even more cordial. Wherever you go, you don't have to worry about crime.

Travel is expensive. For example the bullet train from Tokyo to Sendai, a couple of hundred miles north, costs about £90 one way. Yet the pace of a teacher's life in Tokyo or another big city can become so stressful that it is essential to get on a local train and see some of the countryside. Tour operators do sometimes have special deals on train fares. For example, JR East (which operates in Kanto in Northern Japan) has an unlimited travel Saturday/Sunday ticket for around £100, which includes bullet trains. Shopping around for package tours is another good way to get to see Japan at the lowest possible price. For example, a two to three day hotel/transport package, will end up costing significantly less. Another option is hitch-hiking. In Japan this is safer, easier and more enjoyable than in most countries. The risk is not of being left by the roadside or of being mugged but of being taken unbidden to the nearest railway station (which might be a major detour for the hapless driver who feels obliged to do this out of courtesy). Others will buy meals and refreshments and are genuinely interested in foreigners.

The alienness of Japanese culture is one of the main fascinations of the place. It is foolish to become bogged down worrying about transgressing against mysterious customs. The JET literature, for example, may be unnecessarily intimidating in its pointing up of possible cultural faux pas. But in fact Japanese people are more tolerant of foreigners than many give them credit for. **Rabindra Roy** taught in a state school quite happily and no comment was ever passed on his long hair and beard, earrings and bangles. Similarly **Claire Wilkinson** felt quite overwhelmed after reading the JET literature. One of the many prohibitions mentioned is 'never blow your nose in public', and so the heavy cold with which she arrived made her even more miserable than it would have otherwise. But she soon discovered that the Japanese allow foreigners a great deal of latitude and that she could relax and be herself without causing grave offence. The price you pay for the tolerance extended to your alien ways is that you will always be treated as an outsider, no matter how adept you become with chopsticks or at using Japanese phrases.

The expat scene is also not to everyone's taste, as **Amanda Moody** discovered. She ended up writing short stories to express her frustration, one of which is called 'So You Think You're Hot? Try Dating in Japan!' She typecasts Western men as 'Gaijin Superstars' who are 'fluent in the language of computer science and Star Trek' and keen to secure an admiring Japanese girlfriend.

JAPAN IS A FASCINATING COUNTRY, BUT CLEARLY NOT SUITABLE FOR EVERYONE: YOU WILL NEVER BE ABLE TO BLEND IN OR GO INCOGNITO; IT IS VERY DIFFICULT TO BE 'ACCEPTED' BY THE JAPANESE. KRISTEN GHODSEE SUMS UP THE POTENTIAL HAZARDS:

I have seen many foreigners leave Japan angry and full of hatred towards the Japanese because they were unable or unwilling to understand Japanese ways. Outside the metropolises, being pointed at, stared at and laughed at is commonplace. Be prepared to sacrifice all vestiges of privacy. You are fair game in Japan because you are different. You can make and save an incredible amount of money, but you must have an incredible amount of patience and self-confidence. The Japanese are wonderful, friendly people if you can get past the surface differences. If you're coming only to make the quick buck (as many do), and are not willing to be open-minded to a radically different culture, you will make yourself miserable and worsen the ever-worsening opinion the Japanese have of foreigners working in their country.

LIST OF EMPLOYERS

ACC ENGLISH SCHOOL

252 Genjishinmei-Cho, Hekinan-Shi, Aichi-Ken 447 0872

- 81 566 422 332; fax: 81 566 422 332
- info@acc-english.co.jp
- www.acc-english.co.jp

PREFERENCE OF NATIONALITY: native speakers of English.
QUALIFICATIONS: university graduates. Teaching experience, basic Japanese language ability or TESOL training an advantage. Applicants must be prepared to teach all levels, from very young children to adults.
CONDITIONS OF EMPLOYMENT: 1-year full-time positions available. To teach approx. 25 hours per week. Approx. 4 weeks of paid vacation. Part-time positions sometimes available.
RECRUITMENT Speculative applications should be emailed/posted to the above addresses.

AEON CORPORATION

222 Sepulveda Blvd., Suite # 2000, El Segundo, CA 90245, USA

- 310 662 4706; fax: 310 662 4705
- aeonla@aeonet.com
- www.aeonet.com

One of the largest chains of English conversation schools in Japan with over 300 branches.

NUMBER OF TEACHERS 800.
QUALIFICATIONS: bachelor's degree in any subject and a perfect command of the English language.
CONDITIONS OF EMPLOYMENT: 12-month (renewable) contracts. 5-days a week. 36 hours/week work schedule.
SALARY: 270,000 yen per month.
FACILITIES/SUPPORT: single occupancy apartment furnished to Japanese standards. Subsidised monthly rent of 55,000 yen. Accident and sickness insurance provided under Japan's Socialised Health Insurance plan. 3 weeks of paid vacation and paid training.
RECRUITMENT: 5 full-time recruiting offices outside Japan including 3 in the USA (Los Angeles, New York, Chicago), 1 in Toronto, Canada and 1 in Sydney, Australia. Group and personal interviews held on a regular basis in the USA, Canada and Australia and 2–3 times a year in London, UK and Auckland, New Zealand. Positions start every month. Rolling deadlines. Initial applicants should send résumé and minimum 500-word essay entitled 'Why I want to live and work in Japan'. For up-to-date information regarding recruiting trips and application instructions see www.aeonet.com.

BERLITZ JAPAN

Shin Aoyama Bldg., East 16F, 1–1-1 Minami Aoyama, Minato-ku, Tokyo 107 0002

- /fax: 3 3479 3254
- http://teach.berlitz.co.jp

NUMBER OF TEACHERS: over 1,200.

PREFERENCE OF NATIONALITY: none.

QUALIFICATIONS: minimum university degree, business experience and/or teaching experience; non-native speakers of English must show proof of 12 years' education in an English-speaking environment and a degree in English literature or equivalent.

CONDITIONS OF EMPLOYMENT: 1-year contracts. Working hours vary but are usually around 27 hours per week.

SALARY: starting salary of 250,000 yen.

FACILITIES/SUPPORT: will act as guarantor on accommodation for qualified employees. Full visa assistance for qualified applicants. See website for details.

RECRUITMENT: via the above website. Interviews are essential and are conducted in Japan or overseas by telephone and internet.

CONTACT: Mark Richey, Manager.

BERNARD ENGLISH SCHOOL OF JAPAN

3-13-3 Matsushiro, Tsukuba City, Ibaraki-ken 305 0035

298 51 5049; fax: 298 56 2341

recruitment@bernard.co.jp

www.bernard.co.jp

NUMBER OF TEACHERS: 20+.

PREFERENCE OF NATIONALITY: American, Australian, British, Canadian.

QUALIFICATIONS: Must have a four-year university degree (any field), TESOL-type qualifications are a plus, must have a valid driver's licence (either a Japanese or an international licence).

CONDITIONS OF EMPLOYMENT: 1–2 year contracts. Renewable on mutual agreement. Both salaried and hourly positions available. Full-time teachers average about 110 hours per month, spread over 44 weeks per year, with 8 weeks of school holidays spread throughout the year.

SALARY: Starting at 250,000 yen per month, depending on qualifications and experience. Monthly incentives. Contract completion bonus of 100,000 yen. Special overtime rates.

FACILITIES/SUPPORT: Modern, fully equipped apartments are available through the company. Staff are free to choose other lodgings, if desired. Visa sponsorship can be provided. Company cars are available for lease. A vehicle is necessary for travel between schools. Weekly Japanese language classes available for all teachers free of charge.

RECRUITMENT: usually takes about 2 months from initial contact. Telephone interviews will be conducted. Checkable references are also required.

CONTACT: Frank Pridgen, Foreign Staff Manager.

CALIFORNIA LANGUAGE INSTITUTE

Yamaha Bldg 4F, Uomachi 1–1-1, Kokurakitaku, Kitakyushushi 802 0006

93 522 4141; fax: 93 522 1185

information@cli-kids.co.jp

www.cli-kids.co.jp

NUMBER OF TEACHERS: 50 for branches in various cities.

PREFERENCE OF NATIONALITY: none.

QUALIFICATIONS: none, but must like children.

CONDITIONS OF EMPLOYMENT: 1 year minimum. 32.5 hours per week.

SALARY: 250,000 yen per month less income tax (7%).

FACILITIES/SUPPORT: fully furnished single accommodation provided. Work visa applications carried out through Japanese immigration.

RECRUITMENT: interviews essential, available in UK. Advertisements appear in *Guardian* and *The Times Educational Supplement* about a month in advance or dates are posted on website.

DAVID ENGLISH HOUSE

Polesta Bldg, 7–5 Nakamachi, Naka-ku, Hiroshima City 730 0037

082 244 2633; fax: 082 244 2651

David@DavidEnglishHouse.com

www.DavidEnglishHouse.com

NUMBER OF TEACHERS: 35.

PREFERENCE OF NATIONALITY: native speakers of English.

QUALIFICATIONS: university degree, teaching certificate, experience and/or high grade on Cambridge course, comfortable with children. For positions that include teaching at university an MA is required.

CONDITIONS OF EMPLOYMENT: one-year renewable contract. Up to 22 classroom hours a week.

SALARY: starting salary 25,000 yen per month, less income tax and a little insurance.

FACILITIES/SUPPORT: assistance with finding accommodation and work permits.

RECRUITMENT: job announcements through the internet. Interviews not essential.

CONTACT: David Paul, President.

ECC FOREIGN LANGUAGE INSTITUTE

General Headquarters: 7th Floor, Sumisei Namba Minami Building, 2–3–19 Motomachi Naniwa-ku, Osaka 556 0016

- ℂ 6 6636 0122; fax: 6 6636 8875
- 🖳 www.japanbound.com (for job applicants)

KANTO MANAGEMENT CENTRE HEAD OFFICE:

5th Floor, San Yamate Building, 7–11–10 Nishi-Shinjuku, Shinjuku-ku, Tokyo 160 0023

- ℂ 3 5330 1585; fax: 3 5330 7084
- 🖰 eastjinj@ecc.co.jp

CHUBU MANAGEMENT CENTRE HEAD OFFICE:

Kanayama Building, 1–16–16 Kanayama, Naka-ku, Nagoya 460 0022

- ℂ 52 332 6165; fax: 52 332 6140
- 🖰 nhr@ecc.co.jp

KINKI MANAGEMENT CENTRE HEAD OFFICE:

8th Floor, Sumisei Namba Minami Building, 3–19 Motomachi 2 chome, Naniwa-ku, Osaka 556 0016

- ℂ 66 636 0334; fax: 66 636 7622
- 🖰 teaching@ecc.co.jp

NUMBER OF TEACHERS: 600 at 150 schools throughout Japan.

PREFERENCE OF NATIONALITY: citizens of countries in which English is the official language.

QUALIFICATIONS: BA required.

CONDITIONS OF EMPLOYMENT: 1-year contracts, ending yearly on 31 March. 29 total working hours per week mostly evenings. To work 5 days a week with variable days off. Teachers work some Saturday or Sunday shifts. Opportunities for paid overtime are plentiful.

SALARY: from 252,000 yen per month.

FACILITIES/SUPPORT: assistance with accommodation. Compulsory 50–70-hour pre-service training course over 2 weeks.

RECRUITMENT: visit the website www.japanbound.com for recruitment schedules. Main hiring period is January/February/March. UK Recruitment: c/o AIL International, Pardix House, Cadmore Lane, Cheshunt, Hertfordshire EN8 9LQ (01992 642677; fax: 01992 642675; ail@orbix.co.uk). Australia: AMAC Educational, PO Box 780, Stirling S.A. 5152 (08 8370 9293; fax: 08 8370 9102; email enquiries@amac.net.au). Canada: ECC Canada Office, Suite 1801, Toronto Star Building, 1 Yonge Street, Toronto, Ontario M5E 1W7 (416 703 3390; fax: 416 369 0515; email ecc@japanbound.com).

ENGLISH ACADEMY & HARVARD-KIDS ACADEMY

2–9-6 Ichibancho, Matsuyama 790 0001

- ℂ 89 931 8686; fax: 98 933 1210
- 🖰 marinbu@post.harvard.edu
- 🖳 www.islands.ne.jp/8686

NUMBER OF TEACHERS: 7–9.

PREFERENCE OF NATIONALITY: none.

QUALIFICATIONS: teachers with at least a 4-year degree. Some experience in teaching is also helpful although training is given. Native English speakers preferred.

CONDITIONS OF EMPLOYMENT: 18-month contracts. Hours noon–9pm Tues– Fri, 10am–6pm on Saturday.

SALARY: starting at 250,000 yen per month. Income tax is withheld and different arrangements are made for social security or health insurance depending on the circumstances of the teacher. Telephone interviews.

FACILITIES/SUPPORT: help in finding accommodation and loan in making initial deposit. Academy has two apartments which require only minimal deposits. Help to apply for Certificate of Prior Permission for a work visa and in visa renewal when the time comes.

RECRUITMENT: advertise in publications in Japan and sometimes at Ohayo-Sensei.

CONTACT: K Marin Burch Tanaka (marinbu@post.harvard.edu).

GEOS CORPORATION

Head Office: Shin-Osaki Kangyo Building 19F, 1–6-4 Osaki, Shinagawa-ku, Tokyo 141 0032

- ℂ 3 5434 0200; fax: 3 5434 0201
- 🖰 KYOUMU-002@email.geos.co.jp
- 🖳 www.geoscareer.com

One of Japan's three largest English language institutions.

NUMBER OF TEACHERS: approximately 2,000 teachers for over 500 schools throughout Japan.

PREFERENCE OF NATIONALITY: Canadian, American, British, Irish, South African, Australian, New Zealand.

QUALIFICATIONS: university bachelor's degree required (any discipline). Experience in education, social/customer services, coaching and/or sales highly desirable. CELTA/TESOL or equivalent would be an asset.

CONDITIONS OF EMPLOYMENT: 1 year renewable contracts. Long-term career commitment preferred. Part-time, 5 days a week, 29 hour working shift starting at 11am, noon or 1pm. 2 consecutive days off and 4 weeks' vacation in the first year.

SALARY: base salary is 250,000 yen per month less 5–10% tax. Extra payment available to teachers depending on student sign-up rates, student renewals, group lesson fees and overtime. Eligible for a bonus paid to teachers on completion of contract.

FACILITIES/SUPPORT: correspondence and preparatory courses and working visas provided prior to departure, and ongoing training in Japan including Japanese lessons. Single occupancy furnished apartment provided at a rental rate of about 60,000 yen per month plus 10,000 yen per month for utilities. Monthly commuting pass provided. Health and accident insurance provided. Career positions available such as teacher trainers/personnel manager, curriculum development, publishing staff, hiring officer, homestay co-ordinator, etc. After 2 years working with GEOS in Japan, teachers are eligible to apply for positions in one of GEOS's 50 schools outside Japan.

RECRUITMENT: all GEOS teachers are hired outside Japan. Positions commence 2–3 months after an offer of employment from GEOS Corporation in Japan is made. Contact GEOS Recruitment office in Vancouver on 1 877 584–4367.

INTERAC CO. LTD.
Fujibo Building 2F, 2–10–28 Fujimi, Chiyoda-ku, Tokyo 102 0071
- 3 3234 7840; fax: 3 3234 6055
- recruit@interac.co.jp
- www.interac.co.jp/recruit

Largest non-governmental provider of Assistant Language Teachers in Japan.

NUMBER OF TEACHERS: approx. 1,500 full-time employees throughout Japan.

PREFERENCE OF NATIONALITY: none, though majority are from Australia, New Zealand, Canada, US, UK and Ireland.

QUALIFICATIONS: minimum university degree, 12 years' education in the medium of English (all subjects taught in English at school for at least 12 years) plus a passion for teaching and a strong desire to live in Japan and work in Japanese public schools. Japanese language skills and teaching qualifications preferred but not a necessity.

CONDITIONS OF EMPLOYMENT: 12-month contracts from early April to late March. Approx. 40 hours per week: Mon-Fri 8am–5pm. 7 month contracts available from late August to late March.

SALARY: average monthly minimum of 250,000 yen. 7% deducted in tax. Paid vacations of approx. 6 weeks per year plus Japanese national holidays.

FACILITIES/SUPPORT: comprehensive training programme (3 to 4 days) is compulsory. Company acts as guarantor for

apartment contracts and visa sponsor. Subsidised health insurance cover. Free Japanese lessons available in some locations.

RECRUITMENT: overseas recruitment offices located in Melbourne, Oxford, Seattle, Provo and Toronto. Interviews conducted in other cities all year round.

CONTACT: Denis Cusack, Recruitment Manager.

JAMES ENGLISH SCHOOLS
Mitsui Sumitomo Bank Sendai Bldg. 9F, 2–2-6 Chuo, Aobaku-ku, Sendai, Miyagi
- 22 267 4911; fax: 22 267 4908
- Jesliaison@aol.com
- www.JesJapan.com

NUMBER OF TEACHERS: 80 for 16+ branches in the Tohoku region of northern Japan.

PREFERENCE OF NATIONALITY: none.

QUALIFICATIONS: bachelor's degree and TESOL.

CONDITIONS OF EMPLOYMENT: 1 year contract. Expect teachers to stay at least 2 years. 22 teaching hours per week (average).

SALARY: 250,000–290,000 yen per month.

FACILITIES/SUPPORT: loan provided for initial settling in costs. Visa sponsorship. Training and regular professional development offered.

RECRUITMENT: Application process completed through website. Telephone interviews.

CONTACT: Kathleen Sherba, Recruiting Manager.

JET PROGRAMME
JET Desk, Embassy of Japan, 101 104 Piccadilly, London W1J 7JT
- 020 7465 6668
- info@jet-uk.org
- www.jet-uk.org

NUMBER OF TEACHERS: 200+ each year from UK going to educational institutions all over Japan.

PREFERENCE OF NATIONALITY: UK passport holders only.

QUALIFICATIONS: must hold a bachelor's degree by the time of departure and be under 39 years of age. TEFL training or experience preferred but not essential.

CONDITIONS OF EMPLOYMENT: 12-month renewable contracts starting in August. Normal working hours are 35 hours per week although teaching hours are between 15 and 20.

SALARY: minimum salary is 3.6 million yen per annum.

FACILITIES/SUPPORT: JET finds placement, organises visa and insurance, hosts 2 day pre-departure orientation day in London or Edinburgh, beginners' TEFL training and basic Japanese language course, 2-day orientation in Tokyo, language books and return flights provided.

RECRUITMENT: deadline for application is the last week in November. Interviews in following January/February with decisions given in April.

CONTACT: JET Desk.

KENT SCHOOL OF ENGLISH

Shoppers' Plaza 706, 1–4-1 Irfune, Urayasu-shi, Chiba Ken 279 0012

 /fax: 47 353 8708

kentappli@aol.com

NUMBER OF TEACHERS: 8.

PREFERENCE OF NATIONALITY: none, but interviews held in London in early summer.

QUALIFICATIONS: minimum university degree plus Cert TEFL plus 2 years' TEFL experience.

CONDITIONS OF EMPLOYMENT: 1 year contract. 23 contact hours per week. 6 weeks' paid holiday.

SALARY: from 260,000 yen per month plus outward flight.

FACILITIES/SUPPORT: teachers' furnished flats available. Some shared, some single. All deposits/key money/gratuities paid, so teachers pay only the rent and utilities charges.

RECRUITMENT: advertisements in the *Guardian* and via the internet. Interviews held in the UK in June/July. Once contract is signed, permits are arranged and issued in mid-September.

CONTACT: Liz Fuse, Director of Studies.

MODEL LANGUAGE STUDIO (MLS)

Juken Building, 4F 1-38-13, Yoyogi, Shibuya-ku, Tokyo 151-0053.

(0)3-3320-1555; fax: (0)3-3320-3622

careers@mls-etd.co.jp

www.mls-etd.co.jp/recruiting_e.html

NUMBER OF TEACHERS: 150+ full and part-time instructors teaching English via the MLS Drama Method©, within 36 of its own schools all over Tokyo, including Central and Western Tokyo, Saitama, Chiba, Yokohama and Kanagawa.

PREFERENCE OF NATIONALITY: All native level English speakers are welcome.

QUALIFICATIONS: A minimum BA qualification is required for Visa sponsorship. Teaching experience is not necessary, as training is comprehensive/ongoing. An interest in drama and teaching is a plus, along with the following qualities - creative, responsible, energetic, enthusiastic, flexible and friendly.

CONDITIONS OF EMPLOYMENT: 12-month minimum contract (renewable) from April to March (Japanese school year) each year. Visa sponsorship is only available to full-time instructors working regular weekly schedules within the Junior Department. Vacancies within the Adult, Corporate and Actor Departments are on a part-time basis only and require previous experience.

SALARY: MLS offers an attractive package consisting of a highly competitive monthly salary, a healthy contract completion bonus and all transportation from home to work paid, in addition, there are 5 weeks vacation (Golden Week, Summer and Christmas) along with all National Holidays, all paid.

FACILITIES/SUPPORT: All teaching locations are owned by MLS, and are located within walking distance from mainline railway stations. Initial training lasts for two weeks and is coupled with regular weekly training/care and support sessions throughout employment (all training is paid). Housing and insurance assistance is also available.

Recruitment: Direct application by sending CV, cover letter and recent photo to the instructor for Human Resource section.

SHANE ENGLISH SCHOOL

c/o Saxoncourt, 59 South Molton Street, London W1K 5SN

 020 7491 1911; fax: 0207 499 9374

 recruit@saxoncourt.com

www.saxoncourt.com

NUMBER OF TEACHERS: 380 for 200 schools in the Greater Tokyo region.

PREFERENCE OF NATIONALITY: none, but native English speaker.

QUALIFICATIONS: University degree. CELTA or TESOL preferred but not essential. Training provided.

CONDITIONS OF EMPLOYMENT: 12 month renewable contracts. Average 25 contact hours per week. Pupils from age 2. 6 week paid holiday.

SALARY: from 250,000 yen per month plus quarterly bonuses and end of contract bonus.

FACILITIES/SUPPORT: accommodation provided, visas arranged, health insurance and in-house training given. Pre-service young learners training course available.

RECRUITMENT: via Saxoncourt in London. Interviews and starting dates year-round.

CONTACT: Ben Robinson, Recruitment Manager (ben.robinson@saxoncourt.com).

THE ENGLISH VILLAGE

3F Soa Building, 3–5–8 Kinshi, Sumida, Tokyo

✆ 3 3624 3300; fax: 3 3624 3700

✉ englishvillage@msg.biglobe.ne.jp

💻 www.englishvillage.gr.jp/jobs_e.html

NUMBER OF TEACHERS: 7.

PREFERENCE OF NATIONALITY: British.

QUALIFICATIONS: degree (any discipline) and CELTA qualification or qualification.

CONDITIONS OF EMPLOYMENT: 1-year contract, renewable. 30 50-minute lessons per week and sessions supervising free conversation room. School specialises in teaching British English to adult learners.

SALARY: 250,000 yen per month plus 200,000 yen completion bonus.

FACILITIES/SUPPORT: subsidised accommodation is arranged. New teachers are given a period of thorough training before they start teaching, followed by in-service training.

RECRUITMENT: British press advertisements. Interviews in the UK.

CONTACT: Neil Pearson, Principal.

UNIVERSE ACADEMY

3038 Miyamaru Miyakonojo, 885 0078 Miyazaki

✆ 986 261874; fax: 986 261878

✉ webmaster@uni.gr.jp

💻 www.uni.gr.jp

Combination English-medium, kindergarten teaching 2–6-year-olds, English conversation and cram school in sub-tropical southern Kyushu.

PREFERENCE OF NATIONALITY: native English speaker (British, American, Canadian).

QUALIFICATIONS: bachelor's degree. ESL certification and 2–3 years' teaching experience helpful (especially if with young children). Big heart needed to care for young children.

CONDITIONS OF EMPLOYMENT: 1 year renewable contract. Approx. 25 lessons per week. Must keep a journal of daily activities.

SALARY: competitive.

FACILITIES/SUPPORT: subsidised furnished housing (within 10 minutes walking distance of the school). Visa sponsorship. Return airfare to country of origin on completion of contract. Standard summer vacation, 2-weeks winter vacation.

RECRUITMENT: via internet. Candidates should submit by fax: downloaded application form, copy of diploma, transcript, reference and photo.

CONTACT: Masafumi Seguchi.

KOREA

Anyone who has witnessed the early morning scramble by students and businessmen to get to their English lessons before the working day begins in Seoul might be surprised to learn that the motto for South Korea is 'Land of the Morning Calm'. Because Korea's economy is so heavily dependent on export, English is a very useful accomplishment for people in business. An English proficiency test must be passed by all aspiring university students which is why so many students of secondary school age study the language so feverishly. Both these groups have probably studied English for many years at school but need to practise conversation with native speakers. School and university vacations (July and January) often see a surge in student enrolment at private language institutes. The teaching of children is booming more than ever and there is a huge demand for English teachers to teach in schools where English is compulsory.

The accomplished way in which Korea hosted the 2002 World Cup triumphantly demonstrated to the world that it has put firmly behind it the economic slump and unrest with which it was afflicted at the end of the 1990s. As in Japan at that time, some of the big language school chains closed and many foreign teachers who were there primarily to earn high wages to send home, fled what they perceived to be a sinking ship. This stigma has lingered and so has the language industry's bad reputation for shamelessly exploiting foreign teachers. Whatever the reasons, major language teaching organisations find themselves perennially short of native speaker staff and job-hunting for graduates is generally a cinch. (Note that in the case of Korea, 'schools' normally refer to the state sector whereas 'institutes' mean private language academies run as businesses.)

The bias is strongly in favour of North Americans, especially Canadians, and there are still relatively few British TEFLers in Korea, though this might be slowly changing with the arrival of UK-based recruiters dedicated to supplying teachers to Korean institutes (see entries for Flying Cows and HuntESL).

The number of small- to medium-sized *hagwans* (private language institutes) in all Korean cities interested in hiring a few native English speakers is massive. Hiring from abroad is complicated and expensive, so the vast majority enlist the help of recruitment agents based in Seoul or abroad (or both). Identifying the good ones who are interested in more than collecting their commission is tricky. The fact that recruiters come and go indicates that some are just out to make a fast buck. When dealing either with *hagwan* owners or recruiters, ask to be put in touch with foreigners whom they have employed/recruited in the past for an informal reference. And find out how long a recruitment agent has been in business.

PROSPECTS FOR TEACHERS

There are hundreds of *hagwans* in Seoul the capital, Pusan (Korea's second city, five hours south of Seoul) and in smaller cities. The majority of these are run as businesses, where profit is the primary or even sole reason. ELT training is superfluous in the majority of cases. Native-speaker status and a bachelor's degree are usually sufficient to persuade the owner of an institute to hire an English speaker. Education is greatly respected in Korea and degrees generally matter far more to most potential employers than specialist qualifications. For now, a BA is sufficient and an MA (no matter in what field) counts heavily in one's favour. The vast majority of students have a low level of English so that TEFL qualifications are not deemed necessary.

If you wait until you get to Korea, it is exceedingly easy to fix up a job, but the visa is more difficult to arrange, especially now that new regulations have come into force (see regulations). **Peter Burnside** offers three brief tips to people considering going to teach in Korea: '*follow your heart, trust your instincts and take insane risks*'.

FINDING A JOB

IN ADVANCE

The Korean government administers an official teacher placement programme in imitation of JET in Japan. EPIK (English Program in Korea) is run by the Ministry of Education and administered through Korean embassies and consulates in the US, Canada, Australia and the UK placing about 2,000 foreign graduates in schools and education offices throughout the country. The annual salary offered is 1.8 to 2.5 million won per month (depending on qualifications) plus accommodation, round trip airfare, visa sponsorship and medical insurance as an end-of-contract bonus. Teachers are also exempt from Korean income tax for their first two years. The deadline for applications in 2008 was June, but documents can be submitted all year round in case of openings.

Details of the programme are available from the EPIK website (http://epik.knue.ac.kr) or by contacting the local Korea government representative, eg in the UK the Education Director, Korean Embassy, 60 Buckingham Gate, London SW1E 6AJ (© 020 7227 5547; fax: 020 7227 5503;

education-uk@mofat.go.kr). Americans should contact any of the dozen Korean Consulates in the US. Other nationalities can contact the EPIK office in Korea (Center for In-Service Education, Korea National University of Education, Cheongwon, Chungbuk 363 791; ✆ 43 233 4516; epik@cc.knue. ac.kr). Note that EPIK does not attract the same high praise that the JET Programme does.

The internet is awash with job vacancies. Try for example www.eslpro.com.

RECRUITMENT AGENCIES

Most private recruiters offer one-year contracts to English speakers with a university or college diploma. Candidates with additional EFL/ESL qualifications and teaching experience can sometimes negotiate higher monthly salaries than the standard 1.9–2.1 million won. Recruited teachers are asked to commit themselves to teach 120 hours a month which is a heavy load. Return airfares, free accommodation, paid holidays, medical insurance and bonus on contract completion are all promised as a rule. Applicants who cannot be interviewed locally can do so by telephone or internet. Note that recruiters should not charge teachers any fee since they earn their commission from the schools and institutes. An agency in the UK called Flying Cows Consultancy formed in 2004 and now based at Nottingham Trent University aims to be as honest as possible about the rewards and drawbacks of teaching in South Korea (see entry). Try also Reach to Teach (see entry at the beginning of the Asia chapter).

Here is a list of Korea-based recruiters active at the time of writing. The list following directs North American readers to recruiting contacts on their continent, all of whom are located in Canada.

Rising English: Zest plaza 3F E-Dong 712–2 Ansan (risingenglish@yahoo.com; John@risin-genglish.com; www.risingenglish.com). Also has offices in Kang-nam, South Korea, New York, USA, Vancouver, Canada and soon in Sydney, Australia.

Seoul ESL Recruiting: 1014, LGSeochoECLAT, 1599–2 Seocho-dong, Seocho-gu, Seoul, S. Korea 137 070 (✆ 82 2–585 7871; fax: 82 2–585 7876; esl@seoulesl.com; www.seoulesl.com.

Think Outside: Woongjin Thinkbig Overseas Education Department 535–1, Moonbai-Ri, Gyoha-Eup, Paju-Shi, Gyeonggi-Do (✆ 31 9567326; apply@thinkoutsiderecruiting.com/ask@thinkoutsiderecruiting.com). Also has offices at 511 King Street West Street, 302 Toronto, Ontario, MSU 274 (✆ 416 9792300).

The following Canadian agencies are willing to place more than just Canadians provide they meet the requirements:

Asia-Pacific Connections: Jl. Yudistira 22, Br. Kalah, Peliatan, Ubud, Bali 80571, Indonesia (✆ 361 972731; fax: 866 352 8809; apply@asia-pacific-connections.com; www.asia-pacific-connections.com). Placed about 200 North American teachers in the past 2 years. Telephone interviews conducted globally and face-to-face if possible. Contact Kristopher Kinch, Director.

Canadian Connection Consulting Agency: 192 Spadina Avenue, Suite #416, Toronto, Ontario M5T 2C2 (✆ 416 203 2679; esl@canconx.com; www.canconx.com).

Canadian Education Centre (CEC) Network: 65 Queen St W, Suite 1100, Toronto, Ontario M5H 2M5 (✆ 416 869 0541; fax: 416 869 1696; www.cecnetwork.ca). Offices in Vancouver, Toronto, Montreal and 18 countries worldwide.

GMSC Recruiting: No. 207 10363 135st St, Surrey, BC V3T 4C3 (✆ 604 580 3481; 604 580 3462; gmsc@gmsc-recruiting.com; www.gmsc-recruiting.com).

International Language Institute: 7071 Bayers Road, Halifax, Nova Scotia BL3 2C2 (© 902 429 3636; fax: 902 429 2900; teach@ili.ca; www.ili.ca). Places teachers in one of a dozen cities where Korean partner organisation has institutes after they have completed the ILI Certificate in English Language Teaching to Children course.

JC Canada Recruitment: 394 Brown's Line, Toronto, Ontario M8N 3T8 (© 416 226 9787; fax: 416 226 6096; jccakr@yahoo.com; www.iloveesl.com). Korean ESL job placement agency. Offices in Toronto and Seoul. Opportunities to teach English at Korean schools available throughout the year.

Russell Recruiting: No. 207–35 East 16th Ave, Vancouver, BC V5T 2T1 (russell_recruiting@ yahoo.ca; www.russellrecruiting.com). Caters to ESL teachers wishing to work in Korea, Taiwan and China. Agency made up of former and current teachers so all services provided are safe, secure and free for job applicants. Schools are inspected and recommended by the current teachers working in Asia.

Scotia Personnel: 6045 Cherry St, Halifax, NS B3H 2K4 (© 902 422 1455; fax: 902 423 6840; scotiap@ns.sympatico.ca; www.scotia-personnel-ltd.com). Refers Canadians with university degree to teaching English in schools in South Korea. School provides airfare, accommodation, competitive salary and more.

Teach & Travel: resume@teachandtravel.net; www.teachandtravel.net.

Similar agencies are active in Australia and New Zealand. To identify just one: World English Service (47 Duke St, Dunedin, New Zealand; © 3 477 3790), website www.teachkoreanz.com contains 200 pages of hard information about working in Korea.

As mentioned above, it is usual to arrange a job without a face-to-face interview. One school suggests that would-be teachers send a cassette/CD of their voices or, even better, a video/DVD of them teaching a lesson, which would certainly be more memorable and impressive than simply sending a CV.

AFTER DOING A TWO-WEEK EVENING COURSE ON TESL-TEACHING IN HER FINAL TERM OF UNIVERSITY IN ONTARIO, CANADIAN JESSIE COX SCOURED THE JOB FORUMS AT WWW.DAVESESLCAFE.COM TO FIND SOME DECENT RECRUITERS FOR KOREA WHO WOULD NOT RENEGE ON THEIR AGREEMENTS. BEFORE LONG SHE WAS ON HER WAY TO PROVINCIAL KOREA:

I taught at the only middle school in a small farming town, and the biggest problem I encountered was the extremely low English level of most of the students. Even simple directions were hard for me to give, so we had to spend some time learning simple instructions like 'Open your book to page 22' or 'Repeat after me'. The language barrier also made discipline more of a challenge for me. If the Korean teacher wasn't in the room at the time, I was pretty much limited to 'Stop that' 'No!' and 'Be quiet please'. I was mostly responsible for leading pronunciation and speaking exercises, along with conducting memory tests in which the students had to recite a passage from the text book. The teaching was mostly textbook based. The best feature of working in a state school as the only non-Korean teacher was the chance to be completely immersed in Korean culture in a way that would never be possible as a tourist. The wages at public schools in Korea are quite good and the pay of 1.8 million won per month was more than enough to cover expenses. Although I travelled quite a bit, including to Thailand and Mongolia, I still managed to save about CAN$10,000 over the year. The biggest reward of my experience in Korea was seeing the world from a different perspective. I was able to climb mountains, visit Buddhist temples, visit the border between North and South Korea, explore ancient palaces, and even eat a live octopus!

Another possibility for anyone with an MA or advanced TEFL/TESL qualifications is to work for the language department of a Korean university (of which there are nearly 100). Universities probably offer the best paid and most stable employment. Serious teachers should enquire at their local Korean Consulate for addresses.

The internet is well equipped to keep track of the volatile English language market and many Korean employers rely exclusively on it. More than one web page lists good and bad employers along with lots of horror stories. Dave's www.eslcafe.com devotes an entire section to feedback from Korea; check out the Black List and Grey List before taking a job.

ON THE SPOT

Under new visa regulations (15 December 2007) any person who arrives in Korea to teach English must get their final visa processing completed in their own home country. This means that entering on a tourist visa in order to look for a job is simply not possible, at least this is the official line. There are all kinds of interesting conversations happening in Korea as to whether this regulation is really necessary.

Every day there are advertisements for teachers in the English language newspapers in Seoul, namely the *Korean Herald* and *Korea Times*. Often new arrivals stay in one of the popular *yogwons* (hostels) and hear on the grapevine about the English teaching scene.

REGULATIONS

For many years a number of Korean employers and agents have asked English teachers to arrive on a tourist visa and do a Japan visa run. This is no longer allowed. Teachers must get their final visa processing completed in their own home country if they are going to a *hagwan* job, although some exemptions exist for visa processing in a third country if you are going to a public school job.

Anyone working without a visa risks fines and possible deportation. Similarly, the schools which hire freelance foreigners without permits can be closed down by the government. So, if at all possible, obtain a work visa (E2) which is available only to people with a 3–4-year BA or BSc.

There are two formal stages of getting a visa for employment: you accept a contract and provide your required visa documents and signed contract to the employer, who files them into immigration to sponsor you. Immigration issues a visa issuance number, valid for 90 days, and during this time you cannot apply for any other job or have your documents filed for any other employer unless your employer cancels this letter at the immigration office. In the case of working in a public school a letter of employment is issued, not an issuance number.

Your employer informs you of the original visa issuance number (or posts your employment letter to you for public schools) and you take the number, your passport, your original degree, ID, money and the visa application form to your nearest Korean embassy in your home country. The embassy officer will give you a short interview and then stamp your passport with an E2 visa stamp. You then enter Korea and present your passport to an immigration officer: finally, your visa becomes valid and you may commence work immediately.

The E2 visa is valid only for employment with the sponsoring employer which means that freelance teaching is not permitted under the terms of your work permit and can (and does) lead to fines and deportation. However, the extremely high rates of pay available for private lessons (40,000 won per hour is not uncommon) prove too much a temptation for the majority of teachers, including the normally law-abiding ones. Koreans who inform the authorities about illegal workers are rewarded, so working illegally is more risky than ever.

Teachers are liable to income tax from their first day of work. The rate of tax should be 3.3%, so beware of unscrupulous employers who try to deduct more. Most teachers participate in the Korean National Medical Insurance Union; most employers pay half of the total (about 3% of earnings).

The law permits foreigners to send up to two-thirds of their salary out of the country. Transferring money from Korea to the UK has become much easier than it was.

CONDITIONS OF WORK

Discontentment seems to be chronic among English teachers in Korea. So many American teachers have run afoul of faulty contracts, that the US embassy in Seoul issues a handbook offering guidance called 'Teaching English in Korea: Opportunities and Pitfalls' (which can be requested from the American Citizens Services Branch, 32 Sejongno Road, Jongno-gu, Seoul, or viewed at http://usembassy.state.gov). The information provided by the Embassy about contracts is instructive:

> *Foreign instructors in Korea occasionally have contract disputes with their employers. Many have observed that in Korea, a contract appears simply to be a rough working agreement, subject to change depending on the circumstances. Many Koreans do not view deviations from a contract as a breach of contract, and few Koreans would consider taking an employer to court over a contract dispute. Instead, Koreans tend to view contracts as always being flexible and subject to further negotiation. Culturally, the written contract is not the real contract; the unwritten or oral agreement one has with one's employer is the real contract. However, many employers will view a contract violation by a foreign worker as serious, and will renege on verbal promises if they feel they can. Any contract should be signed with these factors in mind.*

Tim Leffel is one in a long line of American EFL teachers who came to the conclusion that '*nearly 100% of the* hagwan *owners are crooks or unbelievably inept – sometimes both and in Korea both oral and written contracts are a joke*'. He passes on the advice to carry a tape recorder to all interviews and meetings. By working for a big chain, he avoided most problems and was given a decent apartment, good wages and lots of support materials. He even got his post-contract $1,000 though he had to return to Korea six weeks after finishing work to insist on it. When there are conflicts over contracts, Tim advises teachers to choose their battles carefully and to remain civilised as long as possible.

The issue of severance pay is a sore point for many teachers. By law, anyone who completes a 52-week contract is entitled to one month's salary as severance pay. (Note that the length of contract offered by EPIK varies from 44–50 weeks.) Employers have been known to make life quite unpleasant for their teachers near the end of their contracts, so that they're tempted to leave and forego the bonus. The opening remark in **Peter McGuire**'s letter from Andong was '*You wouldn't believe how thrilled I am to be almost finished with a one-year contract here in Korea.*' He went on to say that he made it through to the end only because he is a very determined person and the stakes were high, since he was trying to clear debts at home in Wisconsin.

The quality of *hagwan* varies enormously. Some are run by sharks who may make promises at interview which they can't fulfil, and overfill classes to maximise profits. Many schools do not use recognised course books but rely on home-made materials of dubious usefulness. Despite Korea's reputation as a centre for high tech, some schools lack basic video and computer facilities. Few schools at this level offer any training.

It must be said that not all foreign teachers are disappointed. One of them was **Patrick Edgington** from California who answered a recruiter's advertisement in a US daily paper and was soon working for Ahil Foreign Language Institute in Ulsan (482 138 Seobudong Dong-Ku, Ulsan 682 036). While acknowledging that contracts in Korea guarantee nothing, he was lucky enough to find an honest employer who paid him on time and provided a 'cube' apartment above the institute building (which was acceptable, though cold in winter).

The financial gains are undeniably worthwhile, even if you have to work hard to earn them. Many graduates find themselves teaching in Korea primarily to pay off their student loans or other debts. The cost of living is very reasonable, and so it is possible to save a significant sum while also enjoying life. The average teaching schedule in Korea is five or six hours a day, five days a week. Only *hagwans* catering to adult workers require very early morning starts. The majority of first-time teachers will find that their first lessons are after 10am or sometimes not until 2pm. Weekend work is less commonplace than in many other countries and when a contract does include Saturday teaching, the financial rewards are significant. The teaching load in universities is often lighter. The problem seems to be that *hagwans* realise that teachers come to Korea for no more than a year and therefore milk them for every working minute. **Kathy Panton**'s assessment is that the teacher is there to exploit Korea for money, so Koreans turn around and exploit teachers for labour. She topped the record quoted in a previous edition of this book by working 181 hours in a month including privates and excluding preparation.

The majority of Korean language learners are serious (some attend two-hour classes three or four times a week) and want to be taught systematically and energetically, though even those who have been studying for years often show precious little confidence in conversing. They also expect their teachers to direct the action and are not happy with a laid-back 'let's have a chit-chat' approach. Whereas Judith Night (a certified teacher) found her pupils in the public school system 'eager to learn and a joy to teach', Mark Vetare, with no teaching background, found things very hard going, and concluded in the end that TEFL teaching was not for him:

> *The major drawback is teaching the sullen, bored, exhausted, precocious and* **Mok Dong** *spoiled children aged 14–16 – torture. (*Mok Dong *means upper mid class whatever that means.) They drain me of energy. What they want is a white monkey to entertain them and make them giggle. Trouble is they provide zero material to work from. No sports, no interests. Their stated hobbies are sleeping, TV and listening to music. Their parents want their kids to move up book by book as if that's a gauge of progress. 'Oh, you're in 10B, great.' Never mind that they still can't speak English.*

ACCOMMODATION

Most schools that recruit teachers from abroad will sort out accommodation for their teachers. If you are looking for accommodation independently, be prepared (as in Japan) to be required to pay a large deposit ('key money'). This should be returned to you at the end of your tenancy, though as in Japan, disagreements can arise. If you don't hear about available flats from your school or other foreigners, check the English language newspaper or find an English-speaking rental agent. Boarding house accommodation costs from 300,000 won per month.

LEISURE TIME

Visitors are often surprised to discover the richness and complexity of Korean history and culture, partly because Japanese culture is far better known. Despite being a bustling metropolis of more than 10 million, Seoul has preserved some of its cultural treasures. Assuming your teaching schedule permits, you should be able to explore the country and, if interested, study some aspect of Korean culture such as the martial art tae kwon do. The country's area is small, the public transport good, though traffic congestion at weekends is a problem.

TEACHERS OFTEN FIND THAT THEIR STUDENTS ARE FRIENDLY. ANYONE HOMESICK FOR THE WEST WILL GRAVITATE TO THE AREA OF SEOUL CALLED ITAEWON, WHERE FAST FOOD RESTAURANTS AND CLUBS ARE CONCENTRATED, NOT TO MENTION A JAZZ CLUB, A DECENT BOOKSTORE AND OTHER EXPATRIATE FORMS OF ENTERTAINMENT. TEACHERS IN THE PROVINCES WILL HAVE TO BECOME ACCUSTOMED TO A VERY QUIET LIFE AS JUDITH NIGHT DISCOVERED:

Anyone interested in coming here to have a social life will be very disappointed. In fact, they had better be ready to deal with isolation, because most likely they will be the only foreigner in the town, and the people may never even have met any foreigners before. If I stay in Korea another year, I will choose to live in Seoul, due to missing a social life.

Although William Naquin was also working a long way from the bright lights, he fared a little better:

Insofar as spare time goes, many weekends are spent recovering from 40+ hours in the classroom. During periods when we aren't quite as busy we watch movies, work out at the primitive health club, go to Seoul and drink. Mountain climbing is big here and when the weather is nice our students take us along with them. Portable hobbies such as music, writing and reading are indispensable.

LIST OF EMPLOYERS

BERLITZ KOREA
Kyoungam Building 3F, 157–27 Samseong-Dong, Kangnam-Gu, Seoul 135 526

 2 3453 3667; fax: 2 3453 4733
admin@berlitz.co.kr
www.berlitz.co.kr

NUMBER OF TEACHERS: 60.
Recruitment: mostly via internet. Applicants already in Korea are interviewed in person. Overseas applicants are interviewed over the phone.

CANADIAN CONNECTION CONSULTING AGENCY
192 Spadina Avenue, Suite #416, Toronto, Ontario M5T 2C2 Canada

 416 203 2679; fax: 416 203 7968
esl@canconx.com
www.canconx.com

NUMBER OF TEACHERS: 200 per year.
PREFERENCE OF NATIONALITY: Canada, USA, UK, Australia, New Zealand.
QUALIFICATIONS: BA in an English related field, EFL qualification and teaching experience minimum.

CONDITIONS OF EMPLOYMENT: 1-year contract. To teach 22–30 hours per week.
SALARY: 1.8–2.2 million won per month.
FACILITIES/SUPPORT: accommodation is supplied and paid for (teachers pay utilities). Agency handles all visa applications, teachers must supply a notarised copy of their degree, 4 passport photos, university transcript and passport.
RECRUITMENT: Interview required.
CONTACT: Shane Finnie, Director.

FLYING COWS
The Hive, Nottingham Trent University, Goldsmith St, Nottingham NG1 5JS
0115 848 2807 or 0845 055 3253 (local rate)
mail@flying-cows.com
www.flying-cows.com
Agency so-named because FC aims to provide a service 'without the bull'

NUMBER OF TEACHERS: up to 30 teachers placed per month in schools throughout South Korea.
PREFERENCE OF NATIONALITY: mostly British although can also be from Ireland, USA, Canada, New Zealand, South Africa or Australia.

QUALIFICATIONS: minimum degree in any discipline. Experience of teaching or working with kids is a bonus. TEFL not necessary.

CONDITIONS OF EMPLOYMENT: 12-month contracts. 6 hours per day, with varying hours. Positions available in after-school academies and public schools.

SALARY: from 2.1 million won per month. Deductions made for health insurance and income tax.

FACILITIES/SUPPORT: school arranges and pays for the accommodation and flights. Assistance given for obtaining the relevant E2 visa. Support in all aspects of placement – contract negotiation, location advice, etc.

RECRUITMENT: via ESL internet sites, university careers centres media advertising and careers fairs. Applicants will be interviewed by an FC representative over the phone then by the school also by phone. FC staff have personal experience of teaching in Korea. Applicants are free to visit FC for one-to-one consultations.

CONTACT: Amanda McGillivray, Director/Senior Consultant.

HUNT ESL

Apple Tree Cottage, Abbey Road, Old Buckenham, Attleborough, Norfolk NR17 1PU

0870 0669567

info@huntesl.com

www.huntesl.com

NUMBER OF TEACHERS: 12 per month.

PREFERENCE OF NATIONALITY: native English speakers.

QUALIFICATIONS: 3-year degree and TESOL/TEFL certificate required.

CONDITIONS OF EMPLOYMENT: 12-month contract, with completion bonus of 1 month's salary. Positions involve teaching children between the ages of 4–15. Up to 30 contact hours per week, usually Mon-Fri.

SALARY: Starting salary of 1.9 million won per month (around £1,000).

FACILITIES/SUPPORT: Return air fare provided, free accommodation. HuntESL process the visa and organise the flight.

RECRUITMENT: Apply via the website, email or post. All applicants must pass a telephone interview with HuntESL.

CONTACT: Adam Hunt, Placement Manager.

REACH TO TEACH

21 Everett Road Ext., Albany, NY 12205

1 201 467 4612; fax: 1 480 247 5426

info@reachtoteachrecruiting.com

www.ReachToTeachRecruiting.com

NUMBER OF TEACHERS: 200+.

PREFERENCE OF NATIONALITY: applicants must be from the United States, Canada, United Kingdom, Australia, New Zealand, Ireland or South Africa.

QUALIFICATIONS: teaching experience is great, but not a requirement. Enthusiasm and enjoying being around children are musts.

CONDITIONS OF EMPLOYMENT: 1 year. Schedules are generally either morning/afternoon (preschool) or afternoon/evening (elementary school).

SALARY: 2–3 million won per month.

FACILITIES/SUPPORT: free housing always given in a furnished one-bedroom apartment or a studio. Teachers are also helped with work permits from beginning to end.

RECRUITMENT: detailed telephone interviews are 100% essential. The company also carries out in person interviews periodically in the US and UK.

CONTACT: Richard Jones, Director of Recruiting.

THE ENGLISH FRIENDS ACADEMY

733, Banghak-3 Dong. DoBong-gu, Seoul 132 855

2 3493 6567; fax: 2 956 0125

tefaenglish@yahoo.co.kr

NUMBER OF TEACHERS: approx. 80 western teachers in 30 franchises throughout Korea.

PREFERENCE OF NATIONALITY: none, but should be native speaker of English.

QUALIFICATIONS: minimum 3- or 4-year bachelor's degree. Love of kids, mature interactive outlook.

CONDITIONS OF EMPLOYMENT: 12-month contract. Less than 30 hours teaching. Return airfare, medical insurance, 10 days vacation. End of contract bonus (1 month's salary).

SALARY: 2.2 million won per month (approx. US$2,300).

FACILITIES/SUPPORT: fully-furnished free single or shared accommodation. Well-resourced schools, supportive work environment, job security.

RECRUITMENT: via the internet and email.

YBM EDUCATION ECC (company owned branches)

YBM ECC Head Office, 56–16 Chongno 2ga, Chongno Gu, 8th Floor, Seoul 110 772

2267 0532; fax: 2267 6441

eccmain@ybmsisa.co.kr

www.ybmecc.co.kr

NUMBER OF TEACHERS: 200 at 31 company-owned ECC branches and about 450 at 74 franchise ECC schools that are not placed by YBM Head Office. YBM/ELS schools are for adults and offer slightly less advantageous terms of employment (www.ybmhr.co.kr).

PREFERENCE OF NATIONALITY: USA, Canada, UK, Australia, New Zealand, Ireland and South Africa.

QUALIFICATIONS: minimum requirement is BA/BSc in any field. No teaching experienced required but candidates must enjoy teaching young children using provided curriculum (training given).

CONDITIONS OF EMPLOYMENT: 12 month contracts. Schedule 1: 9:30am to 6pm. Schedule 2: 2pm to 9pm.

SALARY: 2 million to 2.4 million won per month.

FACILITIES/SUPPORT: YBM provides rent-free furnished accommodation near the school. Also, prepaid airfare, medical, severance pay and pension compliance, guaranteed contracts backed by the YBM Head Office, and assistance with visa: once applicant couriers off all the required documents to qualify for the teaching visa known as the E2 visa directly to the school, they will then apply for the E2 visa at the Korean Immigration Office. The school provides step-by-step instructions for applicant to complete the E2 visa at the Korean consulate. Documents needed for the E2 visa in Korea are a bachelor's degree, official transcripts, criminal background clearance and passport.

RECRUITMENT: job postings via internet, word of mouth referrals from previous teachers who recommend YBM ECC to people they know. Every applicant undergoes either a phone interview if they are not in Korea or a face-to-face interview if they are in Korea.

CONTACT: Danny J Kim, HR Manager YBM Education ECC Head Office.

YBM LANGUAGE INSTITUTES

7th Flr YBM Si/sa Annex Bldg, 48–1 Jongno 2-ga, Jongno-gu, Seoul, 110 722

℡ 2 2003 1686; fax: 2 2267 0854

✉ gregstapleton@ybmsisa.com,

✉ helenkim@ybmsisa.com

🖥 www.ybmhr.co.kr

NUMBER OF TEACHERS: between 200 and 250.

PREFERENCE OF NATIONALITY: America, Australia, Canada, New Zealand, South Africa, and the UK.

QUALIFICATIONS: minimum of a bachelor's degree plus 1 year formal teaching experience with adult learners. Candidates with graduate degrees in applied linguistics or CELTA/TESOL certification are preferred.

CONDITIONS OF EMPLOYMENT: 1 year renewable contract, 6 50-minute classes per day (30 hours per week).

SALARY: depending upon academic qualifications and teaching experience, salaries range from 2.1 million won to 2.5 million won per month.

FACILITIES/SUPPORT: Upon arrival teachers are provided with accommodation in a motel near their school. Within the first days the school's general affairs officer will show them several apartments from which the teacher can choose. The school then provides up to 10,000,000 won in key money (leasing) to secure the apartment.

RECRUITMENT: primarily through web-based job postings, followed by telephone/webcam interviews when candidates are outside South Korea. Candidates applying from within Korea must attend a face to face interview.

CONTACT: Helen Kim, National Recruiting Officer, YBM Language Institutes.

SOUTH ASIA AND SOUTH-EAST ASIA

In contrast to Thailand and Indonesia with their strong demand for native-speaker English teachers, other countries between Pakistan and the Philippines (with a few exceptions) are not easy places in which to find work as an English teacher. Poverty is the main reason why there is a very small market for expatriate teachers. Outside the relatively wealthy countries of Singapore, Malaysia and Brunei, there is no significant range of opportunities to earn money while teaching English. The largest growth area has been in those countries that were cut off from the West for many years, viz. Cambodia, Vietnam and Laos, where a number of joint-venture and locally owned language schools have been opened in recent years employing native English speaker teachers.

Elsewhere, the demand may exist but the resources do not. Very few ordinary citizens in much of South Asia can dream of affording the luxury of English conversation classes. Few Westerners could manage on the wages earned by ordinary teachers in India, Nepal, Sri Lanka, Pakistan, etc. However, those people prepared to finance themselves and volunteer their time can find eager students by asking around locally.

Mainstream voluntary organisations, especially VSO, are active in the region, especially Vietnam, Nepal, China and Cambodia where they recruit teachers to work in teachers colleges and vocational colleges. Travellers Worldwide send volunteers of all ages to India, Nepal, Sri Lanka, Brunei and Malaysia as do Lattitude (formerly GAP Activity Projects), Project Trust and other organisations for school-leavers. i-to-i sends people to India, Vietnam, Nepal, Sri Lanka, Malaysia, China, South Korea and Thailand for varying fees. Local voluntary organisations are also active, especially those concerned with improving literacy among women and children. Plenty of commercial language teaching also goes on.

India

Recent times have seen some trouble for the Indian subcontinent and tensions have been rising with Pakistan over Kashmir, as well as violence initiated by militant Islamic groups in unlikely places such as Jaipur. This has dissuaded many people from visiting or spending time there. However, the risk to any individual is infinitesimal and vast swathes of the region are unaffected by the problems.

Throughout the subcontinent, there are many private schools where English is the medium of instruction and a proportion of the educated classes speak English virtually as a first language. The small number of foreigners who do teach in this region do so in the private sector. Native English speakers have arranged to teach in the state sector, simply by entering a school and asking permission to sit in on an English class. Provided they do not expect a wage, some teaching role could probably be found for them. Recently, a volunteer from Derbyshire teaching in several village schools through VESL in Andhra Pradesh, India, wrote that she and her teaching partner were in such demand that a busload of volunteers would find work. But it can be very challenging and discouraging. Facilities can be brutal with no teaching materials and no space. The majority of local English teachers, who have not really mastered the language, are very badly paid and can be transferred without appeal at any time; it is not too surprising to find that most are demoralised. A number of organisations in the UK send volunteers to teach English in India in addition to VESL and Schoolhouse Volunteering (see entries below), including the main gap year placement organisations. For example Projects Abroad (℡ 01903 708300; www.projects-abroad.co.uk) arranges placements of up to six months in Kerala and Tamil Nadu, south India. Postings are mainly to English medium primary schools. i-to-i (℡ 0870 442 3043; www.i-to-i.com) has a range of teaching, community development, conservation and media placements available, as well as tours which combine sightseeing with voluntary work. Projects are available in Bangalore, Jaipur and Darjeeling (fees from £845 for two weeks, excluding flights). Africa & Asia Venture (℡ 01380 729009; www.aventure.co.uk) places school leavers as assistant teachers in primary and secondary schools in Nepal and the Indian Himalayas (as well as northern Thailand), usually for three months. Their programme includes in-country orientation course and organised travel including safari at end of period of teaching. The fee in 2008/9 is £2,975 plus air fares. Interserve (London office ℂ 020 7735 8227) can organise posts for self-funding Christian teachers in India and Pakistan.

Just before **Raymond George** (age 62) started his official retirement from his job as a university physics lecturer, he noticed an advertisement on a college notice board for volunteer teachers with Travellers Worldwide (ℂ 01903 502595; www.travellersworldwide.com). They were offering teaching placements in southern India, a region he was keen to see, so he enrolled for a two-month placement teaching spoken English in a primary school. This proved to be hugely rewarding, giving him a wonderful opportunity to experience life in a family and local community with enough spare time to travel to see the amazing temples of South India. Cross-Cultural Solutions with offices in the US and UK (www.crossculturalsolutions.org) organises volunteer vacations in India. Volunteers work alongside grassroots organisations doing a range of tasks including English teaching. The programme fee is from about $2,600 excluding airfares.

At age 66, **Gwen Dale Jones** went to Kalimpong in India for 3 months with MondoChallenge and recalls her time in the Himalayas: *'I taught in a small village school and loved the interaction with the children, even though I had never taught before. The little faces greeting me with a 'Namaste Miss' every morning was something I will never forget! At my age the best advice I could give anyone is - don't think about it, just do it!'*

LIST OF EMPLOYERS

BRITISH COUNCIL NEW DELHI

17 Kastuba Gandhi Marg, New Delhi, India

11 5149 7410/7411

www.britishcouncil.org/India

NUMBER OF TEACHERS: 10.

PREFERENCE OF NATIONALITY: British.

QUALIFICATIONS: minimum of the CELTA qualification and two years' post-CELTA experience.

CONDITIONS OF EMPLOYMENT: 2-year contracts standard for up to 24 hours per week.

SALARY: starts at approx. £1,260 net (paid in the local currency, plus a sterling component).

FACILITIES/SUPPORT: Visas and work permits are obtained by the school. Some assistance given with finding accommodation.

RECRUITMENT: Interview required. May be conducted over the telephone.

CONTACT: Andrew Carr, Teaching Centre Manager.

MANJOORANS GROUP

Corporate Office: Municipal Building, Kanjikkuzhi, Kottayam, Kerala

04812 571771/573071

Cochin Office: 3D, Metropalace, Cochin, Kerala

mobile+91 9446574292

manjuran@sify.com;

babu.manjuran@gmail.com

www.manjoorans.com/www.ieltslive.com

NUMBER OF TEACHERS: 50 at various centres in South India and East India.

PREFERENCE OF NATIONALITY: British, American, Australian.

QUALIFICATIONS: TEFL or degree.

CONDITIONS OF EMPLOYMENT: 6–12 months. Hours of teaching 9.30am–1pm and 2pm–4pm. To teach IELTS, TOEFL, conversational English.

SALARY: 8,000 rupees plus free food, accommodation and sponsored trips.

FACILITIES/SUPPORT: accommodation provided. Assistance given with sorting out visas.

RECRUITMENT: ELT websites. Interviews not essential.

CONTACT: Babu Manjooran, Director.

MUYAL LIANG TRUST

Denjong Padme Cheoling Academy, Pemayangtse, Sikkim, Northern India (UK contact address below)

PREFERENCE OF NATIONALITY: British, other.

CONDITIONS OF EMPLOYMENT: maximum stay 60 days because of Sikkim work permit restrictions. (Extensions are considered on a case-by-case basis.) School is in session between March and December. British volunteers set their own syllabus in teaching children aged 7–18 English or other subjects.

SALARY: none.

FACILITIES/SUPPORT: Indian instructors help volunteers.

RECRUITMENT: via members of the Trust in the UK.

CONTACT: Jules Stewart, 53 Blenheim Crescent, London W11 2EG, UK (fax: 020 7229 4774; Jjulesstewart@aol.com).

ROSE (Rural Organization for Social Elevation)

Social Awareness Centre, PO Kanda, Bageshwar, Uttarakhand 263631

 jlverma_rosekanda@hotmail.com

 www.rosekanda.org

PREFERENCE OF NATIONALITY: none.

QUALIFICATIONS: none required. Experience of teaching or living in a developing country useful. Flexibility, sense of humour and positive thinker.

CONDITIONS OF EMPLOYMENT: grassroots development project which organises range of activities to help this rural community in the Himalayan foothills includes teaching English in the KSS/ROSE office.

SALARY: none. Volunteers contribute to their living and food expenses (about £5 per day). Also registration fee Rs3500.

FACILITIES/SUPPORT: accommodation provided in local homes. Hindi instruction available.

RECRUITMENT: further details in UK from Bijon K Sinha and Richard Northridge, Cwm Harry Land Trust, Lower Cwm Harry, Tregynon, Powys SY16 3ES, Wales, UK; /fax: 01686 650231; Please send an SAE or 3 international reply coupons.

Nepal

After a decade long campaign against the constitutional monarchy, the Maoist rebels have secured its abolition and formed the government. In June 2008, King Gyanendra and his family quietly moved out of his palace (now to be turned into a museum). It is now to be hoped that Nepal's political problems will dissipate and the country can concentrate on improving the lives of its people, 100,000 of whom were displaced during the violence.

Nepali children must pass English exams in order to progress through the educational system in any subject, so the demand for effective tuition is strong. **Richard Davies** came away from Kathmandu with the impression that anyone could get a job teaching in Nepal. He had made the acquaintance of an Englishman who had simply walked into the first school and got a job teaching children and adults. He was finding the work very rewarding, but not financially.

The British Council in Kathmandu has an English teaching operation and Americans should make enquiries at the American Language Center (PO Box 58, Kathmandu; ℂ 1 419933; fax: 1 416746). By British Council standards, the plethora of locally run private language schools are poorly resourced and cannot pay a living wage to teachers. However, if they are an established school, they may be able to assist in getting foreign teachers long-stay visas. Tourist visas (which can be purchased on arrival for US$30 cash) are valid for 60 days and can be extended for up to 120 days from the Department of Immigration in Kathmandu and Pokhara Immigration Office on request (for US$30). An additional 30 days can be requested from the Department of Immigration, but that's the maximum. Note that a US$4,000 fine or up to a 10-year prison sentence can be imposed on foreigners found overstaying their visas.

A range of grassroots organisations makes it possible for people to teach in a voluntary capacity. No indigenous organisations can afford to bestow largesse on foreigners joining their projects, so Westerners who come to teach in a school or a village must be willing to fund themselves. Of course living expenses are very low by Western standards. Here are a few relevant organisations:

Cultural Destination Nepal: PO Box 11535, Dhapasi Height, Kathmandu (ℂ 1 437 7696/ 1 4377623; cdnnepal@wlink.com.np; www.volunteernepal.org.np). Operate Volunteer Nepal, a service work programme. €650 includes 2 weeks pre-service training, homestay (food and accommodation), lectures, cross-cultural orientation and many leisure activities such as jungle safari, hiking and white water rafting. €50 non-refundable application fee. Placements last 2–4 months starting February, April, June, August and October.

Gorkha District Health & Educational Development Scheme: c/o Joy Leighton, Chairwoman (fax: 01277 841224; info@nepal.co.uk; www.nepal.co.uk). Charity is always looking for volunteers to teach English to Nepalese school kids for a minimum of 3 weeks, among other projects.

Hope & Home: see entry.

Insight Nepal: see entry.

KEEP: (Kathmandu Environmental Education Project), PO Box 9178, Thamel, Jyatha, Kathmandu (ℂ 1 4216775; fax: 1 4216774; keep@info.com.np; www.keepnepal.org). KEEP provides opportunities for volunteers to teach English in different trekking villages, government schools and KEEP's annual English Language Courses (held during June–July and December–January). Volunteers must be totally self-funding and will stay with a host family to adjust to Nepali culture. The only fee charged is $20 membership fee and $30 for administrative support.

Mondo Challenge: see entry.

New International Friendship Club: see entry.

RCDP Nepal: Kathmandu Municipality, PO Box no-8957, Ward no.-14 Kathmandu (ℂ 1 4278305; fax: 1 413 2582; rcdpn@mail.com.np; www.rcdpnepal.com). Paying volunteers work on various programmes lasting 2 weeks to 5 months, including teaching English. Volunteers stay with families in villages.

Volunteer Service and Support Program Nepal (VSSP): Sinamangal, Kathmandu (© 977 9841 256906 or 1 6219343; vnepal@wlink.com.np; www.volunteer-nepal.org). Summer programme involves teaching two hours a day. Fee is €380 for 4 weeks, €38 for each extra week. (Contact Matrika Rijal.)

VSP: Birendramarg-397, Ghattekulo, KMC-32, Kathmandu (vsp2nepal@yahoo.com). Volunteer jobs and internship programme in remote and urban areas in Nepal, including school teaching. Qualification and experience are not essential. €100 per month towards their expenses plus €200 one-time registration fee to VSP-Nepal.

RACHEL SEDLEY SPENT SIX MONTHS BETWEEN SCHOOL AND UNIVERSITY AS A VOLUNTEER TEACHER AT THE SIDDARTHA SCHOOL IN KATHMANDU, ARRANGED THROUGH A UK GAP ORGANISATION AND CONVEYS SOME OF THE FLAVOUR OF THE EXPERIENCE:
The sun is shining and the kids are running riot. New Baneshwar is a suburb of Kathmandu, very busy and polluted, but of course so friendly. I do get tired of being a novelty, especially when I'm swathed in my five metres of bright turquoise silk (we wear saris for teaching) but I'm really loving it here. Already after one month, the thought of leaving the kids and my simple lifestyle is terrible. I find it funny that as a Westerner I'm seen to represent infinite stores of knowledge and yet the servant girl is having to patiently teach me to wash my own clothes. And the general knowledge people have of the fundamentals of life makes me feel helpless and incapable. The children are so gorgeous (most of the time) and the Principal's family with whom I am living are lovely. It seems to me unnecessary to come to Nepal through an organisation. Everyone here is so keen to help.

Rachel's main complaint about her situation was that she was teaching in a private school for privileged children when she had been led to believe that she would be contributing her time, labour and money to more needy children. While there, she met several people from various schools and orphanages who would love to have English volunteers.

LIST OF EMPLOYERS

HELP (HIMALAYAN EDUCATION LIFELINE PROGRAMME)

30 Kingsdown Park, Whitstable, Kent CT5 2DF, UK
© 01227 263055
help@help-education.org
www.help-education.org

HELP enables young people from poor communities in the Himalayas (Nepal and India) to improve their employment opportunities through education by providing financial and volunteer resources to their schools

NUMBER OF PLACEMENTS: volunteer teachers, as well as nurses and child-carers work in needy schools in the Kathmandu Valley, Pokhara and Chitwan (as well as Himalayan India).

QUALIFICATIONS: ages 19/20–60+. Teaching experience and/or TEFL qualifications are desirable but not essential. Volunteers should be mature, and resourceful people who can hit the ground running. Qualities needed include resilience and adaptability, an open mind and an interest in other cultures, good mental and physical health, plus tact and diplomacy. A love of and experience with children is vital.

CONDITIONS OF WORK: 2 months normally. Volunteers can stay for a maximum of 6 months (for visa reasons).

SALARY: none. Fee from £390 depending on volunteer's status and length of stay, including accommodation with host families or in school hostel.

FACILITIES/SUPPORT: volunteers receive a briefing pack. Advice is given by email and/or over the phone.

RECRUITMENT: applications accepted year round. Telephone interviews conducted after receipt of the online application form.
CONTACT: Jim Coleman, Executive Director.

HOPE AND HOME
Nepal Volunteer Program, Lazimpat, Kathmandu,
(PO Box 119, Kathmandu) Nepal
+977 1 441 5393; fax: +977 1 4415176
info@hopenhome.org
hopenhome@gmail.com
www.hopenhome.org

Community-oriented volunteer opportunities for international volunteers with homestay and cultural exchange.
NUMBER OF PLACEMENTS PER YEAR: 55–60 in the Kathmandu Valley, Pokhara, Chitwan and Nawalparasi areas of Nepal.
QUALIFICATIONS: Ages 18–35. All that is needed is a genuine desire to help people.
CONDITIONS OF WORK: Volunteer opportunities lasting 2 weeks to 3 months are in the fields of teaching English, as well as community, health and environmental programme.
SALARY: none. Volunteer fees entirely fund programme and include homestay accommodation and food. From $250 for 2 weeks to $600 for 6 weeks to $800 for 3 months.
RECRUITMENT: Online applications accepted year round.
FACILITIES/SUPPORT: Language class, cultural information and project information provided.
CONTACT: Rabyn Aryal, Director.

INSIGHT NEPAL
PO Box 489, Pokhara, Kaski, Nepal
977 61 30266
insight@fewanet.com.np
www.insightnepal.org.np

NUMBER OF TEACHERS: 60 volunteers accepted each year for development projects mainly in the Pokhara Valley.
PREFERENCE OF NATIONALITY: all.
QUALIFICATIONS: minimum 'A' levels for UK volunteers, high school diploma for Americans. Age limits 18–65. Teaching or volunteering experience desirable but not necessary.
CONDITIONS OF EMPLOYMENT: placements last 7 weeks or 3 months starting year round.
SALARY: none. Programme participation fee is $990 for 3 months, $650 for 7 weeks.
FACILITIES/SUPPORT: accommodation and two meals a day provided, usually as homestay. 3-month programme

includes pre-orientation training, placement in a primary or secondary school in Nepal to teach mainly English or in community development projects, a 1-week village or trekking excursion and 3 days in Chitwan National Park.
RECRUITMENT: application forms, 3 photos and introductory letter should be sent 3 months in advance of proposed starting date.

MondoChallenge
Malsor House, Gayton Road,
Milton Malsor, Northampton, NN7 3AB, UK;
01604 858225
info@mondochallenge.org
www.mondochallenge.org

MondoChallenge sends volunteers (early retired, career break, post-university, gap year) to help with development programmes in Africa, Asia and South America. All programmes are community based, alongside local people.
NUMBER OF PLACEMENTS: 6 teaching programmes in primary schools.
QUALIFICATIONS: ages 18+. Teaching experience and/or TEFL qualifications are desirable but not essential. Volunteers need a mature attitude and to be able to get stuck in with the many different aspects to teaching abroad.
CONDITIONS OF WORK: Programmes are generally 1–6 months, with an average of 3 months.
SALARY: None. There is a financial contribution from £900, depending on the length of stay. Accommodation is arranged locally with a host family.
FACILITIES/SUPPORT: managers oversee the volunteers' welfare. Volunteers receive an extensive briefing pack and lots of support from the UK staff prior to and during stay.
RECRUITMENT: Volunteers are recruited all year round. Interviews are done face to face when applicable, or alternatively over the phone.
CONTACT: Ben Szreider, Head of Recruitment.

NEW INTERNATIONAL FRIENDSHIP CLUB (NIFC) NEPAL
Post Box 11276, Maharajgunj, Kathmandu, Nepal
+977 1 442 7406
nifc@mos.com.np
www.geocities.com/nifcnepal

NUMBER OF TEACHERS: 40.
PREFERENCE OF NATIONALITY: native speakers.
QUALIFICATIONS: minimum university degree.

CONDITIONS OF EMPLOYMENT: 3–5 hours a day teaching English in schools or colleges. Saturday is a day off. In Kathmandu, Sunday is also a day off.

SALARY: none. Volunteer teachers should pay a fee of US$150 and then contribute US$100 per month for their keep (unless they become a project expert). Basic Nepalese standard accommodation is provided and Nepali (rice-based) meals.

RECRUITMENT: direct application preferred by email. Postal enquiries should include 2 international reply coupons.

CONTACT: Prakash Babu Paudel, President.

VOLUNTEER NEPAL NATIONAL GROUP
Jhaukhel 4, Bhaktapur, Nepal
1 661 3724
info@volnepal.np.org or
volunteer_nepal2002@yahoo.com
www.volnepal.np.org

Community-based non-profit organisation that coordinates local and international work camps to empower community self-help initiatives

NUMBER OF PLACEMENTS PER YEAR: 100 in Kathmandu Valley near the historic city of Bhaktapur.

QUALIFICATIONS: Minimum age 18.

CONDITIONS OF WORK: Placements for volunteers in schools, colleges and universities, lasting 2 weeks to 5 months, starting January, April, August and November. Volunteers help with sports, music, extracurricular activities as well as English teaching and other administrative and social welfare work.

RECRUITMENT: Application form, CV and references needed.

SALARY: none. US$500 fee includes pre-service training, language instruction, homestay and meals, trekking, rafting, jungle safari and volunteering. Sample costs are US$150 for school and orphanage volunteers. Second and third months cost US$100.

CONTACT: Anish Neupane, Director.

Bangladesh and Pakistan

The need for English in Bangladesh is frequently replaced by the desperate need for more basic aid, as the country is regularly devastated by floods, water contamination and other natural disasters. But no doubt, schools will be rebuilt and the Bangladeshi people will carry on as they have had to do so many times before. Many schools are willing to take on native-speaker teachers of English, but the usual problems pertain: lack of remuneration and difficulty with visas. Most opportunities are available only to teachers willing to finance themselves and to work on a three-month tourist visa. Security clearance and visa processing can take months, and is very difficult unless you have someone to push for you. The British Council employs eight qualified teachers at its own Teaching Centre in Dhaka, who are recruited in London. The Centre also employs a number of hourly paid teachers who are recruited locally but the demand for courses fluctuates so much that steady employment cannot be guaranteed. People who are established in Dhaka (such as spouses of expat managers, etc.) manage to earn reasonable part-time wages teaching private classes.

Far fewer gap placement agencies and other educational charities send volunteers to Bangladesh than to Nepal. The Daneford Trust includes Bangladesh among its destinations but that scheme is open only to students and school leavers resident in London; details from the Daneford Trust (020 7729 1928; www.danefordtrust.org).

Few private language schools exist in Pakistan. The British Council organises exams, but does not run teaching courses. The US counterpart is the Pakistan American Cultural Center (PACC) with four branches throughout the country; there are three centres in Karachi; the main one is at 11 Fatima Jinnah Road. There is one centre in Hyderabad.

However, despite Pakistan's colonial hangover and understandable wish to prioritise its national language, Urdu, many of its citizens acknowledge that English is a global language, an increasingly necessary tool in the global marketplace. It can also be profitable, something likely to motivate youngsters who are already using the word 'cool' or 'kool' as a linguistic fashion statement. Also, sad to say, working in a Western call centre probably still pays better than an engineering job.

Opportunities for native English teachers are probably there for the taking, tutoring businessmen, university students and children, if teachers are respectful and resourceful. While loitering in a secondhand bookshop in Scotland, **Hannah Adcock** fell into conversation with a Pakistani university professor who promptly offered food and board in exchange for working at his wife's private school for children near Karachi. Having a native speaker is apparently a real status symbol for a school (something you wouldn't guess from reading the British/American press).

Government policy also seems to favour teaching children English right from grade 1 (as opposed to grade 6) and this can only have a knock on effect in terms of demand for ELT.

BANGLADESH WORK CAMPS ASSOCIATION (BWCA)
289/2 Workcamp Road, North Shajahanpur,
Dhaka-1217, Bangladesh
© 2 935 8206/6814; fax: 2 956 5506/5483
bwca@bangla.net
www.mybwca.org

BWCA organises work camps for volunteers in rural and urban areas of Bangladesh.

NUMBER OF TEACHERS: 5 per year (2 male and 3 female).

QUALIFICATIONS: native English speakers.
CONDITIONS OF EMPLOYMENT: volunteers work 30 hours per week on placements which last 2–6 months. Work includes teaching and developing English speaking and writing to primary and secondary school teachers, as well as to students.
SALARY: voluntary work. Volunteers bear all expenses at a cost of equivalent to $250 per month for the first three months and then $50 per month plus $2 a day for food.

Sri Lanka

In Sri Lanka, the government has recently introduced an English-medium stream in schools to raise the profile of English in order to find some neutral ground between bitterly opposed Tamil and Sinhala language speakers. This is only one example of the increasing importance attached to the English language, whose profile increased during the relative calm of recent years. Since then violence has been escalating and the government has withdrawn from the ceasefire agreement. It remains to be seen how the political situation will develop, but teachers are advised to monitor the situation closely if they would like to teach or volunteer in Sri Lanka.

The British Council (49 Alfred House Gardens, Colombo 3; © 11 258 1171; fax: 11 258 7079) has offices with libraries and teaching centres in both Colombo and Kandy. The teaching centres offer classes to adults and young learners. Teachers need a minimum of two years' post-certificate experience to be considered. The Council runs occasional CELTA courses in Colombo. For details on current programmes, check www.britishcouncil.org/srilanka.

FOR A NUMBER OF YEARS, THE VOLUNTEER AGENCY VESL HAS BEEN SENDING TEACHERS TO SRI LANKA AND MORE RECENTLY HAS BRANCHED OUT TO ANDHRA PRADESH IN INDIA WITH HOPES TO EXPAND TO TAMIL NADU AND NORTHERN INDIA. FIONA PASSEY FROM DERBYSHIRE HAD A BACKGROUND IN BANKING RATHER THAN TEACHING BUT DECIDED THAT SHE WANTED TO DO SOME VOLUNTEER TEACHING:
I found VESL on the web and liked what I read about them. The VESL selection day in London helped me make up my mind as Tom and Ian, VESL's co-founders, strike the right balance between the serious issues that volunteer teachers face (poverty, Aids, disease) with an acknowledgement that you are a volunteer who wants a great experience.

For the first month, my volunteer partner Avni and I ran a summer school for local children teaching spoken English and arts and crafts. For the next three months we taught English in local primary and secondary schools. We teach at four schools in the village, all of which are desperately poor and short of teachers so we are much in demand. There have been so many great moments but if I had to pick one it would be seeing the children's faces light up as they grasp something new for the first time and the knowledge that in a small way you helped with their transformation. Teaching was a revelation in many ways. Firstly, it was a shock how long it takes to prepare a good hour's lesson of spoken English when you have no props or blackboard. Secondly, I rediscovered my love for English literature, particularly creative writing and poetry. I think this came through in my teaching. Also I have come to understand how tiring teaching is, since to teach a good lesson demands a lot of you every minute. My respect for UK teachers has increased immensely, given they have the additional challenges of dealing with unmotivated and unruly children.

A new venture run by experienced English teachers is Schoolhouse Volunteering (www.school housevolunteering.com), which will be placing volunteer teachers and teaching assistants in government schools in Sri Lanka and India (see entry).

ELLA MCFARLANE AND HER HUSBAND ED MALLARD (BOTH AGED 30) WERE TEACHING AT A PRIVATE SCHOOL IN HORSHAM WHEN THEY DECIDED TO TRAVEL AND TEACH ABROAD. THEY APPROACHED MONDOCHALLENGE (WWW.MONDOCHALLENGE.ORG) WHO ARRANGED FOR THEM TO WORK AT A SCHOOL IN SRI LANKA:
We wanted to visit a country where we thought that we could make a difference, and where we hoped that our teaching skills would be beneficial. This placement was certainly valuable in seeing the outcome of our teaching, be it an increased confidence in English conversation, their first English words, or merely a smile. We really don't think that it was the academic value of our teaching that was of most use, but just being there and the fun that we had with them day to day. The staff were also very interested in the ways we teach in UK. We feel so grateful to have lived with the people of our period in Kandy. They were always so generous with their time and were truly 'adopted' family.

SCHOOLHOUSE VOLUNTEERING
Schoolhouse, Anderson Road, Ballater,
Aberdeenshire, Scotland AB35 5QW
 01339 756333
info@schoolhouse-english.com
www.schoolhousevolunteering.com

New supported volunteering programme in Sri Lanka and India that has grown out of Schoolhouse English, a family-run language school in Scotland, plus a longstanding connection of the owners with Sri Lanka and India.
NUMBER OF TEACHERS: New programme so numbers not known.
PREFERENCE OF NATIONALITY: Must be native English speaker (or equivalent). Ideally candidates can attend pre-placement training in Scotland.
QUALIFICATIONS: Must be good communicator with enthusiastic personality, an open mind and a desire to contribute to and learn from a different culture whilst developing skills and taking a professional approach. Teaching experience is not essential but these placements may be of particular interest to newly qualified teachers seeking teaching experi-

ence, those wishing to explore the world of teaching with a view to training in the future, practising teachers seeking a fulfilling and refreshing sabbatical, retired teachers or anyone who feels that they might benefit from a memorable and potentially life-changing teaching experience.
CONDITIONS OF EMPLOYMENT: Volunteer English teaching and teaching assistant placements in government schools through the Ministry of Education in Colombo and a partner organisation in Tamil Nadu. Placements last 1 month to 1 year. Preferred minimum one term, starting in October or January (when directors will be on hand to oversee settling-in period).
FACILITIES/SUPPORT: A 6-day residential EFL training course is given at language school in Scotland with much of the teaching method being demonstrated in a hands-on way as volunteers are introduced to the language of their placement country using the methods they will use to teach English. Schoolhouse places much emphasis on pre-placement training and cultural orientation. For those who cannot attend the training in Scotland, pre-placement training will be on offer in the host country. Schoolhouse staff will be on hand during the first month of placement to provide

on-going teaching and lesson planning support and to ensure volunteers settle down well into their host community. Assistance will be given with difficult-to-obtain visas. Volunteers will stay with selected host families or in a serviced house with a group of other volunteers. On-going support for learning the local language (Sinhala or Tamil) throughout.

RECRUITMENT: Applications welcomed year round including at the last minute. After submitting a CV, applicants can be interviewed by Skype. Wherever possible, applicants attend a half-day selection session in Scotland, where free overnight accommodation is offered.

COST: first month £1,025–£1,060 plus £426–£465 for each additional month including training and orientation as above.

CONTACT: Alan and Cathy Low, Partners.

VESL (VOLUNTEERS FOR EDUCATIONAL SUPPORT & LEARNING)

19 Bryson Road, Polworth, Edinburgh EH11 1ED

℡ 0845 094 3727

🖱 info@vesl.org

🖳 www.vesl.org

Formerly Volunteers for English in Sri Lanka, VESL is a charity registered in the UK and is a non-governmental organisation (NGO) in Sri Lanka that sends volunteers to work on projects in Asia.

NUMBER OF TEACHERS: Up to 40.

QUALIFICATIONS: Minimum age 18, though most volunteers are older. Volunteers should be enthusiastic, motivated and up for a challenge. TEFL experience and some experience overseas are helpful but not a requirement.

CONDITIONS OF EMPLOYMENT: 3–6 month projects throughout the year and also 4/5 week summer programmes in July and August. Volunteers and qualified teachers are sent to run English language summer schools in remote communities in the southern, central and north-eastern provinces of Sri Lanka. Work is being done in response to the tsunami.

RECRUITMENT: Applications accepted throughout the year. All candidates are invited to information and selection days that take place throughout the UK.

SALARY: voluntary work. All applicants pay a programme fee ranging from £500 to £950, which covers costs of setting up the projects, training, orientation, insurance, visas, accommodation, food, in-country travel and comprehensive back up and support. VESL is run mainly by volunteers so costs are kept to a minimum.

CONTACT: Tom Harrison, Programme Director.

Malaysia

For the many Malaysian students who aspire to go to university in the US, Britain or Australia, intensive English language tuition is an essential part of their training. The government has now decided to increase the profile of English as a medium of instruction in the state education system so the demand is set to increase. CfBT has been in Malaysia for over 20 years assisting the Malaysian Ministry of Education to improve the standard of English in schools; details from Chris Frankland, Project Manager, Suite B-306, Block B, Phileo Damansara 1, No.9 Jalan 16/11, Off Jalan Damansara, 46350 Petaling Jaya, Selangor Darul Ehsan, ℡ 3 7958 18782/7958 8896; fax: 3 7958 1736; cfrankland@cfbt.com.my; www.cfbt.com.my.

Positions include 32 district English language co-ordinators (DELCs) and 10 project English teachers (PETs). DELCs will help encourage and develop ELT in all aspects in target districts. DELCs work out of medium-sized provincial towns in Sabah, Sarawak and West Malaysia and liaise at district and schools levels, working closely with heads, heads of departments and teachers. Applicants must have a degree, postgraduate qualification in ELT, a minimum of five years in ELT and a driving licence, since they will have the use of a project car. PETs teach in Government residential schools for gifted students and provide native speaker inputs for teachers and students, new ideas and approaches in the language classroom and encourage the use of English outside the language classroom. Applicants must have a degree, certificate in ELT and a minimum of two years' ELT. Benefits of a two-year package include a good local salary, return airfares, housing allowance, medical expenses and an end-of-contract bonus. The government issues work permits only to highly qualified applicants. People caught working on tourist visas can expect to be fined and deported.

The British Council has English Teaching Centres in Kuala Lumpur and Penang; the former offers the CELTA course throughout the year and the CELTYL once a year. According to the British Council in Kuching, apart from CfBT, institutions in Sabah and Sarawak recruiting teachers from overseas are almost non-existent, apart from Sarawak University in Kuching and Curtin University in Miri. If interested obtain the lists of tuition centres in Sarawak and Kota Kinabalu (Sabah) from the British Council.

Some demand may persist in the business market. Check advertisements in the *Malay Mail* though the best way to learn of possible openings is to get to know Kuala Lumpur's expatriate community. The Bangsar English Language Centre in KL has employed foreign teachers to teach Business English in the past (60–1 Jalan Ma'arof Bangsar Baru, 59100 Kuala Lumpur; ℗ 3 282 3166 8; fax: 3 282 5578).

One aspect of life in Malaysia which can be difficult to accept is that racial Malays are accorded special privileges over other citizens of Chinese, Indian or tribal origins. For example, places at the universities mentioned above are available exclusively to bumiputeras or 'bumis', which means literally 'sons of the soil', ie ethnic Malays. Otherwise Malaysia offers a pleasant multi-cultural environment and teachers usually suffer less from culture shock than they do in Thailand and Indonesia. Kuala Lumpur (KL) is a model of modernity and efficiency when compared to the neighbouring capitals of Jakarta and Bangkok.

Singapore

Malaysia's tiny neighbour clinging to the tip of the Malay peninsula is a wealthy and Westernised city-state in which there is a considerable demand for qualified English teachers on minimum 1-year contracts. Once a teacher does get established in a school, freelance teaching is widely available paying from S$30 an hour.

The Ministry of Education in Singapore (1 North Buona Vista Drive, Singapore 138675; Customer Services ℗ 6872 2220; contact@moe.edu.sg) recruits foreign teachers in English Language/English Literature, as well as Geography, History and Economics, on one- to three-year contracts in secondary schools and junior colleges (Grades 7 to 12). Candidates should possess a relevant and very good degree preferably with teaching/higher qualifications and experience. Details and application form can be found at www.moe.gov.sg/careers/teach. Salaries are in the range of S$2,472-S$4,200 plus an end-of-year bonus and airfares into/out of Singapore. The British Council at 30 Napier Road has a teaching operation which hires qualified teachers locally and can provide a list of language schools. Many are located in the ubiquitous shopping centres, especially along Orchard Road, for example Berlitz (501), Brandt (442), Bunka Private Language School (402), Geos (400), Linguarama (220), Children's Language School (218), Goro (268) and Tien Hsia (277). Note that these are not complete postal addresses. Try also the Harriet Educational Group (www.harrietgroup.com) which hires native English speaker teachers and also offers an ELT training course. The vast majority of these language centres are Chinese-owned with a high proportion of teachers from Australia.

Singapore is not a recommended destination for the so-called 'teacher-traveller' who, without qualifications but with a smart pair of trousers, hopes to be able to impress a language school owner. Even people who have qualifications cannot count on walking into a job. However, there are exceptions, and persistent enquiries have resulted in the offer of hourly work.

If you would like to go to Singapore to look for work you can apply online (free; www.mom.gov.sg) for the Employment Pass Eligibility Certificate (EPEC), which allows foreigners who are holders of selected university qualifications (their list includes most respectable universities) to stay in Singapore for up to one year to facilitate their job search. Generally, if you have been granted an EPEC by the Ministry of Manpower (MOM), you are likely to qualify for an Employment Pass upon securing employment.

Once you have a sponsoring employer, the prospective employer must contact the Singapore Immigration and Checkpoints Authority (10 Kallang Road, ICA Building, Singapore 208718; ℰ 6391 6100; fax: 6298 0843; www.ica.gov.sg) for an application form and approval letter, or simply apply online. The process usually takes between six and eight weeks, and it is necessary to wait for the approval letter before travelling as you will be required to present it at Immigration Control in Changi Airport.

Some teachers have reported that they have quickly tired of Singapore, coming to see it as one giant shopping mall. So if shopping malls and a repressive regime (for example, there are signs threatening to fine you if you fail to flush the loo) leave you cold, Singapore is perhaps best avoided.

Brunei

Few people can locate Brunei Darussalam (Brunei, the Abode of Peace) on a map of the world, let alone anticipate that there is a steady demand for qualified English teachers there. This wealthy oil state on the north shore of Borneo can afford universal education for its population of just 360,000. The Ministry of Education has been implementing a bilingual educational system which 'ensures the sovereignty of the Malay language while at the same time recognising the importance of the English language'.

Brunei, mostly covered in luxuriant tropical rainforest, has a pollution free, healthy environment, few traffic jams and one of the lowest crime rates in the world. It provides a very pleasant place to live and work for those who like the outdoor lifestyle and don't crave a wide variety of nightlife. For watersports enthusiasts, the warm calm waters of the South China Sea provide an ideal environment for diving, sailing and power boating. Most expatriates join one of the many sports and social clubs which provide excellent facilities.

Brunei has a rich cultural heritage and still boasts the largest water village in the world in the capital, Bandar Seri Begawan. There are many opportunities to participate in colourful, cultural extravaganzas to mark national events such as the Sultan's birthday on 15 July and National Day on 23 February. In the rural areas there is an opportunity to see how the other indigenous groups celebrate their traditional harvest festivals. Although Brunei is a Malay Islamic monarchy, other religions are allowed to practise freely and Chinese New Year and Christmas day are also national holidays, in addition to the numerous Islamic public holidays.

There are currently around 200 expatriate primary and secondary EFL teachers working in Brunei in state sector schools. CfBT Education Services (Locked Bag 50, MPC, Old Airport Road, Berakas BE3577, Brunei; hr@cfbt.org; www.cfbt.org) recruits suitably qualified and experienced individuals along guidelines set by the Brunei Ministry of Education. All teachers must have Qualified Teacher Status, eg PGCE or equivalent, plus a degree and minimum three years' experience including EFL/ESL. The package currently includes tax-free salary, end-of-contract bonus, accommodation, flights, baggage allowance and other benefits. Contracts are usually for two years initially. A car driving licence is advisable. CfBT also runs a range of courses for teachers and the public including Cambridge ICELT, general English and ESP, ICT and Malay. CfBT also administers IELTS. Borneo Outdoors is a division of CfBT in Brunei and runs youth enrichment and environmental courses, GAP programmes and professional development programmes. They also cater to the corporate sector by providing management training/team building courses for clients in Brunei and Malaysia.

ASIA

BRUNEI

LIST OF EMPLOYERS

INLINGUA SCHOOL OF LANGUAGES
41 Sunset Way, No. 02–01/04 Clementi Arcade,
Singapore 597071
ℰ 6463 0966; fax: 6467 5483
jobs@inlinguaSingapore.com
www.inlinguaSingapore.com

NUMBER OF TEACHERS: 9 English teachers (50 teachers in total in 16 departments).
PREFERENCE OF NATIONALITY: multinational team from UK, USA, and Australia. Teachers from UK preferred.
QUALIFICATIONS: degree and teaching qualification required (TEFL, CELTA or TESOL). Experience is not essential

but candidates must be effective teachers who can work well in a team.

CONDITIONS OF EMPLOYMENT: standard 18-month contract. 40 hours per week including up to 25 hours of teaching (30 lessons lasting 50 minutes each). Lessons blocked for teachers between 9am and 9pm Mon–Fri. Private tuition between 8am and 1pm on Saturdays possible.

SALARY: starting at S$2,600 a month. After 3-month probationary period and satisfactory performance, monthly salary rises to S$2,700. Terminal bonus of 1–3 months' salary given on successful completion of contract. 18-month contracts taxed at 3%. Teachers do not need to pay CPF contributions (Central Provident Fund).

FACILITIES/SUPPORT: temporary homestay accommodation can be arranged for first month (and S$600 deducted). Teachers welcome to use staffroom telephone and newspapers to secure their own accommodation.

RECRUITMENT: via homepage online teacher application form and through other inlingua schools worldwide. Interview and demonstration lesson in Singapore preferred but not essential.

CONTACT: Nicky Sage.

MORRIS ALLEN STUDY CENTRES

03–02 51 Bishan Street 13, Bishan Community Club, Singapore 579799

☎ 6253 5737; fax: 6253 2698

🖱 bishan@morris-allen.com.sg

💻 www.morris-allen.com.sg

NUMBER OF TEACHERS: 40+.

PREFERENCE OF NATIONALITY: British, Australian, New Zealand, Canadian, American, South African.

QUALIFICATIONS: minimum 3 years' experience + degree in education; or BA + teacher training specialising in English, primary or early childhood education. Most teachers have classroom experience with native speaking children before starting at the school.

CONDITIONS OF EMPLOYMENT: 2 years (1 year is available, extensions welcome). 26 teaching hours per week out of total working week of 35 hours. To teach Singapore children from 3 to 16 years, in an English medium education system.

SALARY: S$3,500 per month, tax free.

FACILITIES/SUPPORT: S$500 per month per person provided for accommodation expenses. Assistance given in finding an apartment. Employer will submit visa applications.

RECRUITMENT: advertisements in foreign teachers' journals. Face-to-face interviews are organised in UK every year, in USA on demand. Telephone interviews also possible.

CONTACT: Morris Allen, Principal.

NYU LANGUAGE CENTRE

The Adelphi 04–35, 1 Coleman St, Singapore 179803

☎ 338 3533; fax: 338 4680

🖱 admin@nyu-online.com

NUMBER OF TEACHERS: 5.

PREFERENCE OF NATIONALITY: American, British.

QUALIFICATIONS: degree with teaching experience in English.

CONDITIONS OF EMPLOYMENT: 1 year contracts. Hours 9.30am–5.30pm Mon-Fri.

SALARY: S$2,500–S$3,000 per month.

FACILITIES/SUPPORT: help given with work permits.

RECRUITMENT: via advertisements or recommendation.

CONTACT: Nance Teo, Principal.

SHINES EDUCATION CENTRE SINGAPORE

1208 Upper Boon Keng Road, Singapore 387312

☎ 6235 8289; fax: 6879 3989

🖱 shinesac@shineseducation.com

💻 www.shineseducation.com

NUMBER OF TEACHERS: 14.

PREFERENCE OF NATIONALITY: native English speaking.

QUALIFICATIONS: degree and ESL qualifications.

CONDITIONS OF EMPLOYMENT: 1 year (shorter summer contracts are offered). Classes are scheduled between 9am–6pm, teaching two, 3-hour classes a day.

SALARY: S3,500+ depending on experience.

FACILITIES/SUPPORT: the centre can contact agents with information based on teachers' individual needs. Teachers must be registered with the Ministry of Education before applying for the work visa with the Ministry of Manpower. The whole process and costs are taken care of by the school.

RECRUITMENT: via internet sites dedicated to ESL. Phone interviews are necessary

CONTACT: Sean Maguire, Academic Director.

Vietnam

The demand for English in Vietnam, Cambodia and Laos is phenomenal. In the beginning, opportunities were mainly voluntary and in refugee camps. Government agencies (both local and foreign), international aid organisations and religious groups all remain active in the region, offering extensive development and relief assistance including English language programmes.

Although Vietnam is still a one party communist state, it bears all the trappings (complete with garish advertising hoardings and American pop music) of a capitalist society. The lifting of the US trade embargo a few years ago made it possible for foreign firms to move in to Hanoi and to a lesser extent Ho Chi Minh City, all looking for staff with some knowledge of English. So ELT is a huge growth market and the number of schools in Ho Chi Minh City (the business capital) has grown more than eightfold in as many years. The booming oil industry operates largely in English and there is a growing young middle class investing actively in electronic goods, luxury items and English. Often these things can go together: At Intel's new one billion dollar plant in Ho Chi Minh City all employees are required to communicate in English. The British Council offers many different types of English courses, from 'corporate training solutions' to 'English for study success'. VSO carries out an energetic campaign to recruit TEFL teachers for the region but still can't fulfil all the requests it receives. (VSO requires a degree plus TEFL certificate and minimum 6 months' experience.) Language Link Vietnam is rapidly expanding and has just opened a new campus in Hanoi. These developments have meant that from Ho Chi Minh City in the south to Hanoi in the north, opportunities abound both for trained professionals and freshly certified CELTA/TESOL graduates.

The increasing demand for English and a short supply of suitably qualified teachers have forced wages up to around US$21 per hour for well qualified staff. Even at the lower end of the scale wages are between US$10 and US$15 per hour, yet the cost of living remains very low (for example, Ho Chi Minh City is much cheaper to live in than Bangkok), so Vietnam is a good country for those trying to save some money.

Prospective teachers in Vietnam should be aware that the country is becoming increasingly qualifications conscious. A degree is often no longer seen as sufficient and EFL teaching qualifications are very desirable. This attitude is reflected in the fact that there are now at least four CELTA course providers in Vietnam; Language Link in Hanoi (24 Dai Co Vet; ✆ 4 974 4999; www.languagelink.edu.vn), the University of Danang (✆ 84 511 849 123; elidanang.edu.vn), Apollo Education and Training (✆ 844 943 2053; www.apolloedutrain.com) and ILA Vietnam (see list of employers).

Stephanie Fuccio had no trouble getting work in Hanoi with Language Link at the beginning of 2007 after doing the CELTA course. Outside Hanoi and Ho Chi Minh City opportunities to earn a decent living are drastically reduced. Vacancies at private language schools such as ILA, Apollo, and Language Link are regularly advertised at Dave's ESL Café and the TEFL Professional Network. VUS English Training Centre (72bis Vo Thi Sau, District 1, Ho Chi Minh City (Head Office); ✆ 8 820 7076; stevebaker@vus-etsc.edu.vn; www.vus-etsc.edu.vn) has seven training centres in Vietnam and was looking to recruit native English speakers with a degree and certificate in 2008. Newly certified ESL teachers were welcome to apply. VSO is always recruiting and it will give you a subsistence allowance although most placements are in the countryside where basic amenities are often lacking.

Often the best way to find work is to simply arrive in Hanoi or Ho Chi Minh City and look around. The British Council has offices in both Hanoi and HCMC and the latter office (25 Le Duan Street, District 1; ✆ 8 823 2862; fax: 8 823 2861; bchcmc@britishcouncil.org.vn; www.britishcouncil.org/Vietnam) can provide a recently updated list of language schools in the city. Some of the better schools on this list include ILA, ACET, RMIT, Apollo, AUSP and the British Council schools. RMIT (702 Nguyen Van Linh Boulevard, Tan Phong Ward, District 7 Ho Chi Minh City; ✆ 8 776 1369; employment@rmit.edu.vn; www.rmit.edu.vn) the Asian hub of the Royal Melbourne Institute of Technology has been seen advertising for qualified and experienced English language tutors to fill positions in Ho

Chi Minh City and Hanoi. Universities recruit native speakers and some give a small salary, accommodation and help with visa arrangements. There is a burgeoning ex-pat population and Korean, Japanese, Taiwanese and affluent Vietnamese parents are always on the look-out for private tutors. Opportunities also exist for consultancy work for those with Masters qualifications or higher and relevant experience.

Bell Vietnam, located in Ho Chi Minh City provides high quality English language training. The school focuses exclusively on language training for adults, particularly those who need to achieve a high level of English language competence. Classes offered range from pre-intermediate through to advanced with each language level delivered in 135 hours, divided into three 45-hour modules. All courses incorporate the latest materials which are both Council of Europe compliant and geared towards the needs of the Cambridge ESOL suite of exams. For a list of current vacancies visit http://www.bell-worldwide.com/jobs/list.asp or email recruitment@bell-centres.com.

Ho Chi Minh City is a little more expensive than Hanoi. As a rough guide, US$200–US$300 a month should find a pleasant flat while a decent sized house goes for between US$300 and US$500+. There is a two-tier system for utilities and travel in Vietnam, which means foreigners pay substantially more than locals for almost everything.

If you don't like cooking, the cities are wonderfully packed with good, cheap restaurants serving excellent healthy food and it is quite easy to get by on US$5 a day eating at Com Binh Dan or Bia Hoi, the Vietnamese street side restaurants. Some of the very best food can be found at the smallest street stalls at ridiculously cheap prices. International restaurants and cafés are more expensive but still affordable for the average teacher.

As with other Asian countries there is a thirst to learn English which can make teaching a very satisfying and rewarding way to earn a living. The private language schools are well stocked with materials. Oxford University Press has an office in Ho Chi Minh City and textbooks such as Headway, Reward and Lifelines are widely available. Teachers are generally held in high regard and students will constantly be inviting you out especially on teachers' day. Exams are taking off in Vietnam and many students strive to obtain a good TOEFL score in the hope of going to America, while the Cambridge suite of exams and IELTS are popular with those wanting to take up scholarships to Australia and the UK.

Hanoi is smaller and more beautiful yet bustling and noisy whereas Ho Chi Minh City is a Bangkok in the making. This sophisticated, sprawling commercial centre boasts a skyline already dotted with fledgling skyscrapers. A teacher's salary can afford you a comfortable lifestyle combined with an exotic location in which to enjoy it. The three main complaints are traffic, noise and street hassle. Vietnam is a developing country and although the wealth of the nouveau riche classes in the cities is very visible, the countryside is still desperately poor. Countryside and cities alike experience frequent power cuts and things in general don't always work as they're supposed to.

Travelling round the region is very affordable, and has become more so with the introduction of the low-cost airline Pacific Airlines serving Hanoi and also HCMC's new airport. It is possible to get a bus from HCMC to Phnom Penh for the unbelievable price of $6 (US$14 for a more comfortable one). The Reunification Express is a train that runs the full-length of the country (over 1,300km). The Vietnamese people are often very friendly.

BETH BUFFAM FROM THE USA HAS SPENT TWO PERIODS OF TIME TEACHING IN VIETNAM AND HAS MADE INROADS INTO LEARNING THE LANGUAGE. ON THE RECENT OCCASION SHE WAS GIVEN FREE ACCOMMODATION AND LIVED SO FRUGALLY THAT SHE WAS ABLE TO SAVE US$800 A MONTH TO COVER HER BILLS AT HOME. SHE DESCRIBES HOW SHE FELT THAT HER LIFE HAD BEEN TAKEN OVER BY HER MINDER:

My main problem during the six months I was in Hanoi with the Ministry of Trade was communication. Very few people spoke any English. I had a delightful liaison person, Hue, who unfortunately didn't speak much English. Since I knew quite a bit of Vietnamese and wanted to learn more, at first this was a plus. But eventually it became a huge problem. Most requests I made to Hue were answered with a smile and a sigh. Although Hue couldn't or didn't solve my problems, she loved to spend time with me, hand in hand, arm tightly in arm, walking around. It felt controlling and uncomfortable, and unpleasant given the fact that eventually I didn't feel very close to her.

People were VERY respectful, but almost too much so. For meals, it was extremely difficult for me ever to pay for my own or everyone's food. I really wanted to be 'one of the guys', but it was always: 'It's our custom, we pay for our guests'. Even after six months? And I got tired of the fact that although I'm strong and carried a lot of heavy books most of the time, when Hue and I had some work to do (like moving tables), she rushed to make sure I didn't lift a finger.

I also felt like a puppet, pushed and pulled. People were always telling me what to do, never asking, and inviting me to their homes on minimal notice ('but my wife is cooking right now. . .'). So many invitations which all assumed a Yes answer. Finally, after four months there, I realised the existence and value of the word 'No'. Another irritant was invariably being introduced as: 'This is Beth. She is 59 years old. She has one son but no husband. Her son is 36 years old.' So much for keeping personal matters personal!

However, what you see is not always what you get. Behind that charming Vietnamese smile is more often than not the intent to extract money. Of particular note are the numerous women in search of a foreign husband, a foreign passport and an airline ticket. Single men should beware. Internet access is widely available and improving although it is still unreliable, slow and censored. Government firewalls prohibit prying eyes from seeing anything they don't want you to see.

In order to get a work permit in Vietnam teachers need to bring the original copies of their university degree, TEFL certification and police clearance or criminal history certificate, all properly certified. Teachers must also undergo a medical exam after arriving in Vietnam and provide information on their accommodation. Alternatively your employer may be able to arrange a business visa (usually for 6 months) before you arrive. Once in the country visa renewals cost as little as US$60 for six months.

APOLLO EDUCATION & TRAINING (INTERNATIONAL HOUSE)

Hanoi: 91 Pho Hue, Hai Ba Trung District, Hanoi

℡ 4 943 2051; fax: 4 943 2052

Also: 176 Thai Ha Street, Dong Da District, Hanoi

℡ 4 537 3251; fax: 4 537 3247

67 Le Van Huu Street, Hai Ba Trung District, Hanoi

℡ 4 943 2051; fax: 4 944 5309

and 36 Phan Van Truong, Dich Vong Hau ward, Cau Giay District, Hanoi

℡ 4 755 4733

Ho Chi Minh City: 26 Phung Khac Khoan, District 1, Ho Chi Minh City

℡ 8 823 3597; fax: 8 823 3596

Danang: 81 Quang Trung, Hai Chau District, Danang

℡ 5 11 840 665; fax: 5 11 840 661

Hai Phong: 484 Lach Tray St., Ngo Quyen District

℡ 3 13 736 997

✉ recruitment@apolloedutrain.com

🖳 www.apolloedutrain.com

Established in 1994; Apollo is affiliated to International House World Organisation and offers training in English, Professional Development and overseas study consultancy as well as teacher training from May 2008 (Cambridge CELTA). Apollo also has an increasing number of younger learner and corporate classes in addition to partnership contracts with local schools.

NUMBER OF TEACHERS: Approximately 100 nationwide, more in the summer months.

PREFERENCE OF NATIONALITY: none, but must be native English speaker.

QUALIFICATIONS: teachers must have a CELTA or equivalent (ie 100 hours minimum with at least 6–8 hours of observed classroom teaching practice). Vietnamese Work Permit regulations (for contracts longer than 3 months) stipulate that teachers must also have a degree.

CONDITIONS OF EMPLOYMENT: 1-year contract (some 3-month short-term contracts are available, particularly for the summer programme). Teaching hours are between 7.30am–9.45 pm, Mon–Fri; 7.45am–8.15 pm Sat; 7.45am–6pm Sun.

SALARY: a highly competitive package including 20 days holiday, 9 days public holidays, contract completion bonus and re-signing bonus.

FACILITIES/SUPPORT: medical insurance, flights and DELTA sponsorship plus visa and internal work permit costs. For short term contracts, accommodation is provided. For one-year contracts teachers are placed in Apollo-rented accommodation or given agents' names and/or a Vietnamese member of staff can visit accommodation with the teacher to assist with translation and negotiation.

RECRUITMENT: through local advertisements and internationally using posters, websites etc. Interviews are essential, and are occasionally carried out in the UK/USA.

ASIAN INSTITUTE OF TECHNOLOGY CENTER IN VIETNAM

Education Management Section, 21 Le Thanh Tong, GPO Box 136, Hanoi

☏ 4 825 3493 ext. 131; fax: 4 824 5490

🖱 hang@aitcv.ac.vn

NUMBER OF TEACHERS: 2.

PREFERENCE OF NATIONALITY: none.

QUALIFICATIONS: at least 5 years' experience and preferably a Masters degree.

CONDITIONS OF EMPLOYMENT: up to course availability.

SALARY: US$20 per hour (Grad. Dip in TEFL/TESOL or TESOL certificate), US$25 per hour (Master in TEFL or TESOL).

FACILITIES/SUPPORT: some assistance with finding accommodation. No assistance with work permit.

RECRUITMENT: word-of-mouth. Interviews.

CONTACT: Nguyen Thu Le Hang.

ILA VIETNAM

Head Office, 51 Nguyen Cu Trinh, District 1, Ho Chi Minh City

☏ +848 838 6788

    fax: +848 838 6790

🖱 recruitment@ilavietnam.com

🖥 www.discovereltvietnam.com

NUMBER OF TEACHERS: 200+ with centres in Ho Chi Minh City, Danang, Vung Tau and Hanoi.

PREFERENCE OF NATIONALITY: native speakers of English.

QUALIFICATIONS: minimum requirements are university degree (any discipline), CELTA or equivalent TEFL certification and native English speaker.

CONDITIONS OF EMPLOYMENT: 9–12 months contracts available, relocation and contract completion allowances, visa and work permit provided by ILA, free Vietnamese lessons, regular social events, teacher training courses, CELTA, DELTA and CELTYL offered in-house.

SALARY: US$1,530–$1,880 (gross) per month depending on qualifications and experience.

FACILITIES/SUPPORT: school pays for the first week's accommodation at a guesthouse and Teacher Welfare Coordinator assists with housing and other issues. Academic Coordinators assist with lesson planning and hold monthly professional development workshops.

RECRUITMENT: via the internet. Telephone interviews for overseas hires; in-person interviews for applicants in Vietnam. Applicants must send CV with covering letter, supporting documents and passport details. Local applicants must also provide visa details.

Cambodia

Cambodia is a relatively stable country, emerging from the shadow of its past and of its neighbours. Political stability means that it is safe and people can feel settled there. Incidents involving firearms are now quite rare, although armed robberies do still take place in Phnom Penh after dark.

The ELT market has been wide open to private enterprise in Cambodia ever since the UN ceased to be in charge in the 1990s. Although the major aid agencies such as VSO still supply English teachers to Cambodia at a supervisory level, the private sector is now flourishing. Foreign ministries and government offices are all keen to sign up for private lessons as are the diplomatic corps and their families as well as the military. The British Council does not maintain an office in Phnom Penh.

Mark Vetare was impressed by the demand for English teachers on a visit to Phnom Penh:

Just rent yourself a moto *for the day and have a spin around Phnom Penh. There's virtually a school on every corner. Not all schools employ native speakers since many poor Khmer can't afford them. Pay and hours are the main problems for teachers. Time was when you could get four hours a day. Now you've got to stick around for the better times and more hours. Things are becoming more stringent in the 'real' schools. That being said, it's backpacker heaven: young men with long hair, good (but not necessarily native) English and no high level education still get jobs.*

Wages for casual teachers are about US$8 an hour in a country where you can live comfortably on US$20 a day. Qualified EFL teachers can earn double or even treble that amount. Cambodia still operates on a dollar economy, so few wages are quoted in riels. Visa extensions are relatively easy to get and schools usually organise them for their teachers. Tourists are given one-month visas which are extendable. Those who want to work should get a business visa at the airport, for US$25 rather than US$20 for a tourist visa, as business visas are renewable indefinitely.

One of the longest established schools is the Australian Centre for Education or ACE which employs upwards of 75 teachers with at least a degree and the CELTA or Trinity TESOL. In addition there are many other commercial institutes like ELT (www.elt.edu.kh), New World Institute (www.nwi.edu.kh) and Home of English in Phnom Penh. Opportunities can also be created in Kampong Som, Siem Reap and Batambang.

Volunteers can offer to teach at Savong's School, near Siem Reap, which was set up by Svay Savong to give children who can't afford tuition fees the chance to learn a language and improve their job prospects. The school's website (www.savong.com) advises: '*take around a few goodies (there's an informal tradition of taking the school such things as soccer balls, volleyballs or Frisbees), as well as stationery – just ask Savong to see what he needs from the book store in Siem Reap) and, if you're up to it, try a spot of teaching. Savong and the others won't leave you stranded*'. On her gap year Pascale Hunter from Cambridge noticed a flyer up in her hostel and spent a short time teaching teenagers and younger children. Although she found the experience interesting, she felt it was '*fairly commercial, with the kids clamouring for Western souvenirs*'. However plenty of other volunteers have enjoyed their visit and are impressed by the dedication of the students.

Another organisation to try is Volunteer in Cambodia with an office in Phnom Penh (No 85, St. 155, Corner St. 478 and St. 155, Toul Tumpung; www.volunteerincambodia.org) which recruits volunteers to teach at Conversation With Foreigners (CWF), a local conversational English school in Phnom Penh. Money raised by the programme goes towards the Cambodian Rural Development Team, a local organisation working to improve livelihoods in rural communities. Volunteers stay three months (there are specific group starting dates) and contribute to their living costs. Teaching qualifications/experience is an advantage, but not required. A sister organisation, CamTEFL, runs industry standard 120 hour TEFL courses in Phnom Penh (www.camtefl.org).

Experienced teachers and education managers can work as VSO volunteers, who are placed at all levels within education, ranging from Provincial Teacher Training Colleges to District Offices of Education. Placements at the Ministry of Education enable volunteers to influence policy and work on national agendas, such as updating the curriculum (www.vso.org.uk/about/cprofiles/cambodia.asp).

AUSTRALIAN CENTRE FOR EDUCATION
PO Box 860, Phnom Penh, Cambodia
23 724204; fax: 23 426608
info@acecambodia.org
www.cambodia.idp.com/ace.aspx

NUMBER OF TEACHERS: 62 in Phnom Penh and 14 in Siem Reap.

PREFERENCE OF NATIONALITY: none; any native speaker is acceptable.

QUALIFICATIONS: undergraduate degree plus CELTA or equivalent.

CONDITIONS OF EMPLOYMENT: standard contracts from 10 weeks to 1 year. Hours vary: the school is open 6am–8pm and on Saturday mornings.

SALARY: US$16 per hour casual, US$1,700–US$2,100 contract.

FACILITIES/SUPPORT: advice given on affordable accommodation which is not hard to find in Phnom Penh. Assistance given before arrival on obtaining a business visa. The school is well equipped and resourced and a variety of professional development sessions are held at least once a month.

RECRUITMENT: web advertisements, word-of-mouth. Interviews are required, but can be done over the phone and are carried out in Australia from time to time. Professional referees are checked.

CONTACT: Paul Cooke (Assistant Director of Studies) or Louise FitzGerald (Director).

Laos and Myanmar

Laos was the last country in South East Asia region to open its doors to foreigners. Over the past few years an amazing number of English schools have opened in the Laotian capital of Vientiane, ranging from well-established institutions to small, shop-front institutions staffed with locals or expats passing through on tourist visas. When English institutes first started opening in Vientiane, most were fly-by-night operations. But there are some respectable schools now (in addition to the college whose entry appears below) such as the Lao-American College (232 Phonsath Road, PO Box 327, Vientiane; ℃ 21 900453 5; lac@etllao.com/thelaoamericancollege@yahoo.com; www.lac.edu.la). These schools can help their teachers to obtain a long-stay visa.

The visa procedures are constantly changing in Laos. If possible, obtain a letter of invitation from your employer before arrival which entitles the holder to enter Laos on a B2 visa (non-immigrant, business visa) instead of a tourist visa. The B2 visa costs around $400 for a year, although 6 month and 3 month visas are available at a reduced rate. To extend the B2 visa if you are working at the same school costs about US$200 a year. Prices change now and then. A number of schools will cover the cost of the visa, although some will subtract it from your first month's pay packet.

In order to obtain the invitation, your sponsor needs a copy of the passport and probably copies of the educational credentials. Otherwise it is possible to apply for a tourist visa outside of the country (Bangkok is the closest and easiest place) for around $40/£20 and enter the country on a one-month tourist visa. Once they are in the country then the employer will have to make the invitation for a B2 visa for them and they will have to go out of the country again (usually across the border to Thailand) and enter again on the B2 visa for a further fee.

Salaries and conditions of work can vary as much as the schools themselves do. The Vientiane International School (PO Box 3180, Vientiane; ℃ 21 313606; fax: 21 315008; stevea@ourvis.com (director); www.vislao.com) and Vientiane College (see entry below) provide by far the best working conditions, staff development programmes and benefit packages. The majority of language schools pay by the hour, from as little as US$5 up to US$15 at the higher end of the range.

Demand for native speakers also occasionally comes from schools: Vientiane Pattana School, a small primary school in Laos was recently seen advertising on Dave's ESL Café for someone who could teach all the usual primary subjects and commit for at least nine months (jackieintha @gmail.com).

Teaching opportunities also exist in larger companies and ministries for in-house teachers. Again, conditions vary greatly and there are often delays with payments and payments may be made in the local currency (kip). It is possible to advertise on notice boards around the town, or in the English language newspaper, the *Vientiane Times* (www.vientianetimes.org.la) in order to pick up one or two private students.

Some volunteer opportunities exist in Laos, for example with the Thai organisation Openmind Projects (mentioned below in the chapter on Thailand) and with the Sunshine School (see entry).

Surprisingly, the new regime in Myanmar (formerly Burma) has retained English as a major language and theoretically there might be scope for teaching the military rulers and businessmen (albeit for negligible wages), although their minds will, presumably, be focused on the devastation wreaked by Cyclone Nargis for some time to come. But as **Mark Vetare** says of the country, *'it is truly a place to champion the poor not cater to the murderers and thieves who run the country.'* Many organisations recommend boycotting Myanmar completely to avoid bringing any wealth or comfort to the leaders. Interested teachers should find out more from Amnesty International or Tourism Concern in London (Stapleton House, 277 281 Holloway Road, London N7 8HN; ℂ 020 7133 3330; www.tourismconcern.org.uk). For information about a teaching programme for Burmese refugees in northern Thailand, see entry for Burma Volunteer Program in Thailand directory.

Horizon International Education Centre, established in June 2000 in Yangon, is a private institution that offers an English-medium education to students of all nationalities (25 Po Sein Rd Bahan Township/Yangon; ℂ 728016/543926; www.horizon.com.mm).

SUNSHINE SCHOOL

PO BOX 7411, Vientiane, LAO PDR

 +856 21 214522

 sunshinelaos@gmail.com

NUMBER OF TEACHERS: volunteers only.

PREFERENCE OF NATIONALITY: English-speaking countries.

QUALIFICATIONS: creative approach to working with the kids is important; experience in teaching or experience with young kids are both good assets.

CONDITIONS OF EMPLOYMENT: 1 week to 11 months. School hours include 7 teaching periods from 8am to 4pm weekdays. Volunteers usually have 4–5 teaching periods a day (may be less depending on the volunteer's needs), and may also be involved in lunchtime creative or teachers' classes activities.

SALARY: voluntary basis only. Long-term volunteers staying 6–12 months may get a small living allowance (max. US$100 a month) or help with housing depending on the financial condition of the school at the time.

FACILITIES/SUPPORT: long-term volunteers will be supported with working visas (which cost US$250–US$450). All volunteers get a vegetarian lunch provided on school days.

RECRUITMENT: via www.go-mad.com and via www.gurukul.com.

CONTACT: Cathy Lee, Director.

VIENTIANE COLLEGE

PO Box 4144, Vientiane, Lao PDR

 21 414873/414052/412598; fax: 21 414346

vtcollege@laopdr.com

www.vientianecollege.com

NUMBER OF TEACHERS: 25.

PREFERENCE OF NATIONALITY: native English speakers from any region.

QUALIFICATIONS: minimum bachelor's degree and CELTA. ESP/EAP experience preferred.

CONDITIONS OF EMPLOYMENT: sessional and contract.

SALARY: from US$1,200–US$2,000 per month less 10% income tax.

FACILITIES/SUPPORT: assistance with finding accommodation. School arranges and pays for work permit and residence visa. In-house training programme.

RECRUITMENT: personal interview necessary.

CONTACT: Catherine M Wood, Registrar; Denley Pike, Director.

YANGON INTERNATIONAL EDUCARE CENTRE

No. W-22, Mya Kan Thar Main Road, Mya Kan Thar Housing, 5th Quarter, Hlaing Township, Yangon, Myanmar

 1 6822231/682672/724483; fax: 1 665904

 yiec.ygn@mptmail.net.mm or

yiec@mec.com.mm

NUMBER OF TEACHERS: 72.

PREFERENCE OF NATIONALITY: none; native speakers preferred.

QUALIFICATIONS: bachelor's degree at least. Experience in primary or middle schools would be useful.

CONDITIONS OF EMPLOYMENT: 1–2 year contracts at this international school. Hours of teaching 8.30am–3.30pm.

SALARY: negotiable (more than enough to live well and save).

FACILITIES/SUPPORT: assistance with locating housing, maintenance. Assistance with complicated procedures in obtaining work permit.

RECRUITMENT: locally, advertisements in Bangkok newspapers, recruitment fairs in Asia, recruitment through Search Associates. Interviews necessary.

CONTACT: Christopher Nefstead.

TAIWAN

Taiwan remains a magnet for English teachers of all backgrounds and the ELT industry is booming. Part of the appeal of teaching in Taiwan is that the wages compare favourably with countries such as Japan, yet the cost of living is significantly lower. Equally important is that finding a job here is fairly easy. It used to be the case that schools were looking for only three things: a passport from an English-speaking country, a BA and a pulse. These days however, the better schools are becoming choosier, it is more difficult to get a working visa and many schools and local education departments are looking for an ELT qualification and prior experience. Nevertheless, the opportunities for teaching English in Taiwan are endless. For example, hundreds of private cramming institutes or *bushibans* continue to teach young children and high school students for university entrance examinations.

English language schools in Taiwan are becoming increasingly regulated. Only the reputable language schools, those who are fully licensed as foreign language schools, are permitted to employ English-speaking foreigners and sponsor them for visas, provided that they are willing to sign a one-year contract. Only native speaker teachers with a university degree (in any subject) are eligible. Taiwanese consumers of English have a clear preference for the North American accent because of strong trading and cultural links between Taiwan and the USA. However, many schools will hire presentable native speakers whatever their accent. Few want their staff to be able to speak Chinese; in fact one teacher reported seeing a sign in a *bushiban* window boasting 'Teachers Not Speak Chinese'. Language teachers and tutors working in Taipei are predominantly American; native speakers of other nationalities tend to gravitate to southern Taiwan. **Amanda Searle** from the UK felt only slightly discriminated against:

My employer claimed that they did not discriminate between people of different nationalities, but this is not what I have found. North Americans are the first choice when hours are allocated. I have had students complain that they wanted an American teacher because they wanted to learn 'real' English, though I have never had a student complain to me or the secretaries that my accent was difficult to understand.

This has not been everybody's experience however, and some schools even boast 'English comes from England and so do our teachers'. Many non-Caucasians have experienced prejudice in Taiwan.

The market for teaching children from about age 3 seems boundless at the moment, so anyone who enjoys working with primary age children, ie likes to sing songs, play games and comfort little ones who miss their mums, may be able to find a job. However, recent government regulations require all kindergarten teachers to be fully qualified kindergarten specialists. While many CELTA trained teachers can no longer legally work in kindergartens, many still do so. English immersion kindergartens are all the rage and tend to pay their teachers very well. Women are often considered to have an advantage in this regard, and also tend to be preferred by the mothers of female pupils. Employers in this field generally provide detailed lesson plans which means that little time needs to be spent on lesson preparation.

FINDING A JOB

Many websites contain a wealth of detail about Taiwan and what it's like to teach there. The site www.taiwan-teachers.com belongs to a teacher placement agency based in Kaohsiung but which can conduct interviews in Canada and Boston. Jobs and lots of information about teaching in Taiwan can be found at www.tealit.com and the chat forums in www.taiwanho.com are good places to get sensible answers to any queries you may have about living and teaching in Taiwan. The US-based recruiter for Asia Reach to Teach (see entry) is very active in Taiwan where its main centre is located. Another possibility is Dewey Educational Consultants (Tung Chien Building, 3F.-1, No.668, Sec. 2, Wucyuan W. Rd., Nantun District, Taichung City 408; ✆ 4 2381 3698; fax: 4 2381 3705; service_de-wey. com.tw; mickeyhou1978@yahoo.com.tw; skype 1.houmickey; www.elsdewey.com.tw).

If you would like to teach English while studying Mandarin, it might be worth investigating ESL House (32 Ta Sheng St, Taichung City 408; ✆ 4 2319 4845; fax: 4 2319 2548; ittasia@mars. seed.net.tw), the university Mandarin education centre which also introduces students of Chinese to local English language institutes. For a full placement service, which means you could walk into a job as soon as you arrive, it is necessary to pay a mediation fee of US$150. (Given the abundance of work and of recruitment agencies which charge nothing, you may decide that this is superfluous.)

A number of indigenous recruiters in Taiwan are in the business of matching teachers with employers. For example the Taiwan TEFL Network works with schools throughout the country (No. 49, Lane 140, Sec. 1, Dungshan Rd, Beituen Chiu, Taichung; ✆ 925 106697; fax: 4 2437 5449). See also entries for Linda Yee Recruiting and International Avenue Consulting below.

When using a recruitment agency in Taiwan, it is best to proceed with caution. In recent years there have been a number of reports of teachers accepting jobs before arriving in Taiwan, only to find that they have been placed not in Taipei as they agreed, but in some three-goat mountain village. Discrepancies also sometimes occur between the contracts agents have given to teachers in English, and those given to employers in Chinese. Many people arrive on spec to look for work. Finding a *bushiban* willing to hire you is not as difficult as finding a good one willing to hire you. If possible, try to sit in on one or two classes or talk to another teacher before signing a contract. (If a school is unwilling to permit this, it doesn't bode well.) Read the fine print of the contract to find out what the penalties are for breaking a contract.

ON THE STRENGTH OF THE ALI TEFL COURSE SHE HAD COMPLETED IN SAN DIEGO (SEE TRAINING DIRECTORY) AND A YEAR SPENT TEACHING IN POLAND WITH ECSC, FREELANCE PHOTOGRAPHER ALICIA WSZELAKI WANTED A TASTE OF TEACHING IN THE FAR EAST. SHE JOINED A SHORT SUMMER TEACHING PROJECT IN TAIWAN FOR ADOLESCENT GIRLS, RUN BY THE AMERICAN LANGUAGE VILLAGE (WWW .KIDSCAMP.COM.TW) THAT SHE HAD NOTICED ON DAVE'S ESL CAFÉ. TEACHERS WERE HOUSED IN A HOTEL NOT FAR FROM THE CAMP AND SHE FOUND WORKING CONDITIONS TO BE VERY GOOD ALTHOUGH THE HOURS WERE LONG OVER 10 STRAIGHT DAYS.

I realised a few days into the camp that this was indeed a summer camp and the kids were there not only to learn English but also to have fun. We played games, had lessons on pizza and hamburgers and other subjects that were more real world. The students really enjoyed these. There was lots of songs and dancing. If you choose to do a camp of this nature, bring lots of energy, smiles, optimism, an open mind, and water. It was a wonderful and rewarding experience. The students were great and the teachers were some of the most incredible people I have met – a truly great blend of personalities and experiences.

The best time to arrive is at the beginning of summer (the end of the school year), when Chinese parents enrol their offspring in English language summer schools. Late August is another peak time for hiring, though there are openings year-round. Always check the positions vacant column of the English language *China Post* and the *China News* though work tends to result from personal referrals more than from advertising. Word-of-mouth is even more important in Taiwan than elsewhere because there is no association of recognised language schools.

If you want to meet foreigners who are clued up about the current teaching situation, try visiting well-known Taipei hostels or pubs. A good notice board is located in the student lounge on the sixth floor of the Mandarin Training Center of National Taiwan Normal University at 129 Hoping East Road. You might also make useful expat contacts in Taipei at the Community Services Centre, 25 Lane 290 Chung Shan North Rd, Sec. 6, Tien Mu (2 2836 8134; www.community.com.tw) or at the Gateway Community Centre, 7Fl, 248 Chung Shan North Rd, Sec. 6, Tien Mu (2 2833 7444).

Once you have decided to approach some schools for work, make contact by email or telephone in the first place, possibly from the Taipei Railway Station or the Northgate GPO Telegraph Office where there are private cubicles or simply buy a mobile phone. Next you must present yourself in person to the schools. Many schools in Taiwan are used to and expect cold-callers. In order to get around Taipei you should invest in the invaluable English language Taipei Bus Guide available from Caves Books (corner of Chung Shan Road and Minsheng E. Road) or Lucky Book Store in the university. Take along your university certificate and any other qualifications, and take the trouble to look presentable. **Peter McGuire** was told point blank that your appearance and how you conduct yourself at interview count for everything, and concluded that '*all your experience in life or teaching in other countries really doesn't mean a thing here.*' **David Hughes** specifically recommends paying attention to your feet:

> *Bring plenty of socks/tights. You have to leave your shoes at the door of Chinese homes, and it's difficult to appear serious and composed with a toe poking through.*

Anyone with a high level of education (ie MA or PhD) might find work attached to one of the scores of universities and colleges, where working conditions are very good. Foreigners are also allowed to work in public high schools, though it is difficult to function without a knowledge of the language.

FREELANCE TEACHING

Work visas are valid only for employment with the sponsoring employer. However many teachers teach private students, which pays handsomely, from NT$700 to NT$1,000 per hour.

IN A COUNTRY WHERE FOREIGNERS ARE SOMETIMES APPROACHED IN BARS OR ON TRAINS AND ASKED TO GIVE ENGLISH LESSONS, IT IS NOT HARD TO SET UP INDEPENDENTLY AS AN ENGLISH TUTOR. PETER MCGUIRE FOUND THE DREAM JOB OF TUTORING A TRAVEL AGENT THREE TO SIX HOURS A DAY, SEVEN DAYS A WEEK AND THEN WAS INVITED TO ACCOMPANY HIS CLIENT ON A TRIP TO HAWAII:
Some of my lessons are given at private clubs, saunas, in taxicabs and fine restaurants. Actually, it's kind of unbelievable.

Although it would be possible to make a good living by teaching privately, you will need to work for a school in order to obtain the visa. A helpful hint is to have business cards printed up, calling yourself 'English consultant'. It is even more lucrative if you can muster a small group of students and charge them, say, NT$300 per person. Women normally find this easier to set up than men. The main problem is finding appropriate premises.

Cancelled hours are a perennial problem. Freelancers will find it prudent to explain to students gently but forcefully that they will be liable to pay if they cancel without giving sufficient notice; most will not object. You can even request one month's fees in advance. Once you are established, other jobs in the English field may come your way such as correcting business faxes, transcribing lyrics from pop tapes or writing CVs and letters of application for Taiwanese students hoping to study overseas.

REGULATIONS

Tourists who arrive without any visa are allowed to stay in Taiwan no more than 14 days. People who intend to look for work can apply for the resident visa after arrival; however they will need to enter the country on a visitor visa valid for 60 days (an extension may be granted, but this isn't easy). To apply for this visa you need proof of a return air ticket and a document verifying the purpose of your visit, or a recent bank statement. During those 60 days, you must find a job and organise all the paperwork described in this section. If time runs out you will have to leave the country.

Information on visas should be requested from the Taiwan overseas office in your country of origin which is also where you apply for the visitor visa. Do not reveal on any form that you are considering looking for work. You will have a choice of a single-entry visa (£25) and a multiple entry visa (£50), although to apply for the 6-month multiple entry visa you need a letter of confirmation from your UK employer stating the purpose of your visit. The Taipei Representative Office in the UK is at 50 Grosvenor Gardens, London SW1W 0EB (✆ 020 7881 2650; fax: 020 7259 9394; www.tro-taiwan. roc.org.uk). Details may be obtained in the US from the Co-ordination Council for North American Affairs (CCNAA, 4201 Wisconsin Avenue NW, Washington, DC 20016 2137; ✆ 202 895 1800) and in western Canada from the Taipei Economic & Cultural Office in Vancouver (20th Floor, 2008 Cathedral Place, 925 W Georgia St, Vancouver V6C 3L2; ✆ 604 689 4119).

To stay legally in the country, teachers need to obtain an Alien Resident Certificate (ARC). Once you arrive and find a school offering a one-year contract, your school applies to the local education authority for a working permit for which they will need a copy and translation of your degree diploma, contract, medical certificate (requiring various tests) and passport. Once that is processed you can apply for a resident visa at the Ministry of Foreign Affairs; the fee will be about £45. Up to two weeks later your resident visa will be stamped in your passport. You are then obliged to apply to the Foreign Affairs police within two weeks for an ARC and a multiple entry permit (which will involve another fee of about £20). Some schools may make a contribution towards permit costs when the contract is renewed for a further year. For instance, the Taipei Language Institute pays for the medical and translation costs.

If your tourist visa is due to expire before you have arranged a resident visa, you will also have to leave Taiwan to renew your tourist visa, and have a plausible reason why you want to remain in the country. If you claim to need an extension because you are studying Chinese, you can expect a spot test in Mandarin. (It is not clear if the same applies if you're a student of Kung Fu.)

TAX

After the work visa has been issued, tax will be withheld from your pay. The tax rate for foreigners who stay in Taiwan for less than 183 days in one calendar year (category A) is 20%. After six months, the rate of tax drops to between 6% and 13% but only on income beyond the standard exemption of NT$72,000. Most teachers earn between NT$370,001 and NT$990,000 so will pay 13% on their taxable income. Once residency is established, it is possible to apply for a substantial rebate of about 70% of taxes paid. All teachers must file their tax return in May (the tax year runs from 1 January to 31 December) and refunds are issued by the end of August. There is a small levy (equivalent to about an hour's wages) for health insurance (Lao Bao).

CONDITIONS OF WORK

Most jobs are paid by the hour, and for the past three or four years, the minimum hourly rate a teacher should expect is around NT$500 (approx. US$15). For a monthly salary you should expect to receive around NT$55,000 (approx. US$1,600) for 25 hours per week. Occasionally the rate for cushy morning classes drops lower and unsociable hours are rewarded (if you're lucky) with a premium rate of NT$600–NT$700. Rates outside Taipei (where the cost of living is lower) tend to be slightly higher due to the relative scarcity of teachers.

As usual some schools are shambolic when it comes to timetabling their teachers' hours. In a profit-driven atmosphere, classes start and finish on demand and can be cancelled at short notice if the owner decides that there are too few pupils to make it economic. When you are starting a new job, ask your employer to be specific about the actual number of hours you will be given. It is not uncommon for teachers who have been promised a full timetable at the point of hiring to find themselves with fewer hours than promised and a considerably lower pay packet.

ALTHOUGH EXPLOITATION OF TEACHERS (AND PUPILS) IN TAIWAN IS NOT AS RIFE AS IN KOREA, YOU SHOULD BE PREPARED FOR ANYTHING, AS RUSTY HOLMES HAD TO BE:
The real reason there was such a high turnover rate of staff at one school was because of the supervisor's habit of barging into class at unpredictable moments and accusing the teacher (especially my Scottish colleague) of mispronouncing words, when she herself could barely speak English. The worst incidents occurred when she beat her own children in the face for getting poor grades, when she engaged a parent in a fistfight over a tuition dispute, and when she physically ran her husband out of the school, all right in front of our students.

Having discovered the joys of world travel at age 30, **Stephanie Fuccio** from the USA took the plunge and fixed up a teaching job with Todd's English School in Tainan via the internet. She found that good money could be earned and the cost of living was really low, which had the disadvantage that many of the foreigners there were focused on money to the exclusion of everything else. Her low overheads included $200 a month for a small apartment all to herself and a used scooter bought for $250. Meanwhile she was earning $17 an hour despite having no teaching certificate or experience. She stayed for most of an academic year but left a little early having tired of teaching only young children. She concludes that '*the whole country is simply gone mad with learning English*'.

The usual problems which bedevil TEFL teachers occur in Taiwan, such as split shifts, often ending at 10pm, and compulsory weekend work, especially if you are teaching children. Few schools provide much creative training or incentives to do a good job. Like the educational system of China and so many other countries, Taiwanese state schools rely heavily on rote learning, making it difficult to introduce a more communicative approach, especially at the beginner level.

Whereas some schools offer no guidance whatsoever, others leave almost nothing to the teacher. What is termed a 'training programme' often consists of a paint-by-number teaching manual. Here is an extract from the Teacher's Book of one major chain of schools:

> *How to teach ABCs (eg the letter K): Review A-J... Using the flash cards, say 'A – apple, B – boy, C – cat... J – jacket'. The whole class repeats after the teacher. Then say, 'A-B-C-D-E-F-G-H-I-J' and have the whole class repeat. Show the letter K flashcard. Say 'K' having the whole class repeat it each time you say it. Say 'K' 4 or 5 times.*

And so on. This certainly makes the inexperienced teacher's job easier but possibly also very boring. Not everyone can be comfortable with such a regimented curriculum.

LEISURE TIME

Flats are predictably expensive in central Taipei so many teachers choose to commute from the suburbs, where living conditions are more pleasant in any case. Rents in the moderate-sized town of Chiayi are NT$7,000–NT$12,000 for a three-bedroom apartment, so a flat share would be quite affordable plus about NT$1,500 for utilities. There are so many foreigners coming and going, and the locals are so friendly and helpful, that it is not too difficult to learn of flats becoming vacant. You will have to pay a month's rent in advance plus a further month's rent as a deposit; this bond or 'key money' usually amounts to £300–£400. Several schools will appoint a Chinese member of staff to chaperone new arrivals and translate on house-hunting trips.

Taipei has a rapid transit system which is far more enjoyable (and cheaper) than running a motorbike. Some teachers stay in hostels near the central station and commute to work in a satellite city where wages are higher than in Taipei (eg Tao Yuan and Chung Li). Without doubt, the biggest inconvenience and danger in Taiwan is on the roads. Taiwanese drivers often commit driving manoeuvres that would result in lynching in other countries. Red lights and traffic laws are more often than not ignored and foreigners compound the problem by riding too fast on scooters, with little experience, and often under the influence.

Not a single visitor to Taipei, which is one of the most densely populated cities in the world, fails to complain of the pollution, second only to that of Mexico City. Not only is the air choked with the fumes and noise of a million motorised vehicles, but apparently chemicals have infiltrated the water table, contaminating locally grown vegetables. It is really horrific. The weather is another serious drawback. The typhoon season lasts from July to October, bringing stormy wet weather and mouldy clothes. The heat and humidity at this time also verge on the unbearable.

Taipei is not the only city to suffer from pollution; Taichung and Kaohsiung are also bad. Even Tainan with two-thirds of a million people has some pollution; 100 new cars are registered here every day adding to the problem. (This is a statistic which rather detracts from Tainan's appeal as the most historic city on the island with many old temples, etc.) Kaohsiung on the south-west coast is a large industrial city with a high crime rate but has the advantage of being near the popular resort of Kenting Beach and within reach of mountain campsites such as Maolin. The geographical advantage of

Taichung further north is proximity to the mountains as well as a good climate and cultural activities. The east coast is more tranquil, though some find it dull.

Wherever you decide to teach, one of the highlights of living in Taiwan is the hospitality of the locals. In fact some people report being smothered by kindness, since the Taiwanese will not accept a refusal of any food or drink offered, and even paying for meals or drinks can be a struggle.

In general, apart from some petty crime, corrupt politicians and fairly well hidden gang activity, Taiwan is virtually crime free, so you are free to pursue your leisure pursuits without worry. Taipei has a 24-hour social scene which can seriously cut into savings. Heavy drinking is commonplace. Films (which are usually in English with Chinese subtitles) cost about US$10. The serious saver will follow **David Hughes'** example and join the local library. For the truly homesick there are some English-style pubs with pool tables and darts boards. For **Rusty Holmes,** the food was a highlight:

Eating out is just as much a pastime in Taiwan as it is in Hong Kong. There are countless little mom-and-pop restaurants which offer delicious and inexpensive food. My favourite is the US$4 black pepper steak. Considering the high price of food in supermarkets, it would be cheaper to eat out than to cook at home. Taiwan is also a fruit-lover's paradise, though most are expensive by American standards. My favourite is the outstanding sugarcane Taiwan produces.

LIST OF EMPLOYERS

AAC
14 Coventry Road, Strathfield, NSW 2135, Australia
4 1432 5870; fax: 4 2376 0496
www.aacircle.com.au

NUMBER OF TEACHERS: 25.
PREFERENCE OF NATIONALITY: from an English-speaking country.
QUALIFICATIONS: bachelor's degree or minimum 2-year diploma with a TEFL certificate.
CONDITIONS OF EMPLOYMENT: 1 year contract. 25 teaching hours per week.
SALARY: NT$50,000–NT$60,000 per month.
FACILITIES/SUPPORT: free accommodation or a housing subsidy is available from the school. This depends on the position. If no accommodation is provided, the school will help teachers to find something suitable and possibly act as guarantor. Upon taking up a position, the school begins the process of applying for the teacher's work permit, which takes around 45 days to process.
RECRUITMENT: online advertising, word of mouth, industry fairs.
CONTACT: Peter Allen, Human Resources.

BERLITZ INTERNATIONAL (TAIWAN) CO LTD
6th Fl, No.563, Zhong Xiao East Road, Sec. 4, Taipei
2 7719 9999; fax: 2 7719 9998
teach@berlitz.com.tw

NUMBER OF TEACHERS: 20.
PREFERENCE OF NATIONALITY: must be native English speakers from a country where English is an official language.
QUALIFICATIONS: university degree essential. Teachers preferred with at least 2 years' business teaching related experience. Business experience important. Looking for friendly, energetic teachers who work well in small groups or private classes.
CONDITIONS OF EMPLOYMENT: 1 year. Part-time evening work: 5pm–10pm Mon–Fri and 9am–3pm on Saturdays. Classes made up of two 40-minute units. Full-time contract available for those part-time instructors who prove themselves to be excellent Berlitz instructors.
SALARY: NT$450 per 40 minute unit.
FACILITIES/SUPPORT: no formal assistance with accommodation.
RECRUITMENT: refer to the Berlitz Career Services homepage: http://careers.berlitz.com.
CONTACT: Regina Hsu, Manager of Instruction.

NUMBER OF TEACHERS: 4.

PREFERENCE OF NATIONALITY: North America, UK, South Africa.

QUALIFICATIONS: degree needed; experience preferred but not essential.

CONDITIONS OF EMPLOYMENT: 1+ years. 20 to 24 teaching hours.

SALARY: NT$50,000–NT$65,000 per month depending on qualifications.

FACILITIES/SUPPORT: help given with finding accommodation and obtaining visa. Good range of teaching materials available.

RECRUITMENT: via agents. Interview essential.

CONTACT: Joseph Gao, Director.

NUMBER OF TEACHERS: 100.

PREFERENCE OF NATIONALITY: USA, Canada, UK.

QUALIFICATIONS: bachelor's degree or college diploma and TESOL certificate, Must be native English speaker and citizen of an official English-speaking country.

CONDITIONS OF EMPLOYMENT: 6 or 12 months. Most classes are between 4pm and 9pm on weekdays and all day Saturday.

SALARY: NT$600 per hour for teachers without previous teaching experience (approx. US$18.50). Deductions vary from 0% to 10% depending on length of employment.

FACILITIES/SUPPORT: rent-free accommodation at one of the school's dormitories provided for 15 months. School will provide assistance with all related visa paperwork, but teachers are responsible for paying for their work permits.

RECRUITMENT: online job postings, newspaper job postings, referrals by current or previous employees. Phone interviews are mandatory. If the applicant is already in Taiwan, in-person interviews are preferable.

CONTACT: Penny Chang, Director of Teaching Administration.

NUMBER OF TEACHERS: 500 native speaking teachers in more than 150 language schools and 70 kindergartens throughout Taiwan. About 200 new teachers hired each year.

PREFERENCE OF NATIONALITY: must have passport from officially recognised English speaking country, ie USA, Canada, UK, Ireland, Australia, New Zealand and South Africa.

QUALIFICATIONS: bachelor's degree (in any subject) plus desire to work with varied age groups and to experience Chinese culture.

CONDITIONS OF EMPLOYMENT: 1 year renewable contracts. 3 contract options are available to suit each teacher's preference. Contract A: Hess Language School (for 6–14 year olds) are held Mon-Fri, with Saturday classes as well from 4:30pm -8:30pm. Contract B: Hess Language School + Kindergarten (ages 2–6) in the morning and Contract C: Full-time kindergarten work for those interested in Early Childhood Education.

SALARY: NT$560 per hour (gross), with some variation between locations. Tax rate is 20% for first six months then drops to 10%. A raise and bonus system is also part of the pay structure.

FACILITIES/SUPPORT: airport pick-up and free hotel accommodation during initial 9-day training period. Hess provide full TEFL and curriculum training plus four follow-up training sessions at 1, 3, 6 and 9 months. Upon completion of full training programme and one-year contract, teachers are issued a Hess TEFL Certificate. Every branch assists NSTs to find housing. Actively assist NSTs to obtain resident visas and work permits. Application process should be started 3 months in advance to allow time to collect visa and work permit documents. However, applications are welcomed sooner.

RECRUITMENT: Apply online through Hess website at www.hess.com.tw, which has application instructions, or contact Meagan Solomon at meagan.solomon@hess.com.tw. 4 major new teacher intakes per year. Applications accepted all year round.

CONTACT: meagan.solomon@hess.com.tw.

NUMBER OF TEACHERS: 39 in Tainan County, Taichung City, Pingtung County and Keelung City.

PREFERENCE OF NATIONALITY: USA, Canada, UK, Australia, New Zealand.

QUALIFICATIONS: native English speakers, bachelor's degree. Government recognised Provincial/State Teaching Certificate.

CONDITIONS OF EMPLOYMENT: 1-year contract. 25 teaching hours per week (approx. 40 working hours per week). 14 days paid leave per year. IACC collects a service charge of NT$24,000, paid in instalments. This is refunded upon successful completion of the contract.

SALARY: NT$60,890–NT$70,895 per month. Performance bonus.

FACILITIES/SUPPORT: airport pick up and temporary accommodation for the first days. Assistance in finding an apartment and signing the contract with the landlord. Assistance in processing the work permit, ARC and NHI cards. Help in opening a bank account. Online Teacher Management System.

RECRUITMENT: all interviews carried out in Taiwan.

CONTACT: apply online or email CV.

NUMBER OF TEACHERS: dozens for 600 schools in Taiwan plus some in China, 32 starting July, August or September.

PREFERENCE OF NATIONALITY: British (southern English accent preferred) and Canadian.

QUALIFICATIONS: Must be native speaker with a BA degree and TESOL certificate. Applicants should love working with children and have lots of energy to teach children aged 3–12.

CONDITIONS OF EMPLOYMENT: about 1 year. Basic 16 hours per week.

SALARY: NT$40,000–NT$60,000 per month less deductions (6%–20% tax depending on length of stay and NT$500 for health insurance).

FACILITIES/SUPPORT: help in search for affordable accommodation. Assistance with work permit application which takes about a month.

RECRUITMENT: newspaper advertisements, via TEFL training centres and word of mouth.

QUALIFICATIONS: Teaching experience required but it doesn't have to be with children.

CONDITIONS OF EMPLOYMENT: to start from 1 July or 1 September or other dates. Guaranteed hours with extra hours available. Teaching children aged 3–12 in classes of 16 students from planned curriculum with complete teaching materials. Teachers should arrive a week in advance in order to receive a 2–3 day induction.

SALARY: depends on qualification and experience.

FACILITIES/SUPPORT: work visa and health insurance provided. Airport pickup. Accommodation provided on arrival.

CONTACT: Lydia Lee, Human Resources Representative.

NUMBER OF TEACHERS: 10 (7 for the language department and 3 kindergarten teachers).

PREFERENCE OF NATIONALITY: British, American, Canadian, Australian, South African.

QUALIFICATIONS: minimum BA and at least 1 year's experience.

CONDITIONS OF EMPLOYMENT: 1-year contract. Working hours in the language department 1pm–9.20pm. Working hours in the kindergarten 8am–5pm.

SALARY: NT$64,000–NT$70,000 per month (less 6% for taxes and social security) for the first year, depending on qualifications and experience. Contract fulfilment bonus of NT$36,000 (minimum).

FACILITIES/SUPPORT: free accommodation for the first month during compulsory training and assistance to find suitable housing thereafter. KNES will also help teachers to obtain a working visa.

RECRUITMENT: via website. Interview required. May be possible to have an interview in the USA.

CONTACT: Serena Wen, Principal.

KNS LANGUAGE INSTITUTE
24 Chiuchang Rd, Niaosung Hsiang, Kaohsiung Hsein
7 370 6565; fax: 7 370 6555
knschris@yahoo.ca
www.kns.com.tw

NUMBER OF TEACHERS: 45.
PREFERENCE OF NATIONALITY: North American.
QUALIFICATIONS: at least a B.A. Teaching experience, TESOL certification or B.Ed. preferred.
CONDITIONS OF EMPLOYMENT: 1 year. Hours 2pm–9.10pm Mon–Fri.
SALARY: $NT585/hour plus bonus.
FACILITIES/SUPPORT: assistance with accommodation, no interest loans, paid training, paid work permit fees.
RECRUITMENT: via internet, university placement offices. Interviews in Taiwan or at KNS office in Canada. Telephone interviews also possible.
CONTACT: Chris Aitken, Director of Teacher Recruitment.

KOJEN ELS
10F-2, No. 200, Roosevelt Road, Sec. 4, Taipei
2 8663 8287; fax: 2 2930 0006
luisarecruit@hibox.hinet.net
www.kojenenglish.com

NUMBER OF TEACHERS: around 300 (16 locations in Taipei plus 5 in Kaohsiung and 2 in Taichung).
PREFERENCE OF NATIONALITY: passport holders of USA, Canada, UK, Australia, South Africa, Ireland or New Zealand.
QUALIFICATIONS: BA/BSc minimum. ESL experience and/or TESOL/TEFL certificate will increase chance of employment.
CONDITIONS OF EMPLOYMENT: 1-year contracts. Afternoon, evening and Saturday work. Pupils range in age from 13 to 60.
SALARY: starting wage NT$580–NT$590 per hour. Bonuses paid at end of contract, calculated according to number of hours taught for hourly teachers.
FACILITIES/SUPPORT: 1–2 weeks of free accommodation in shared apartments. Training provided.
RECRUITMENT: direct application/walk-ins. Local interviews compulsory for some applicants. Applicants may be asked

to teach a sample lesson. A photocopy of bachelor's degree must be brought to Taiwan.

CONTACT: Luisa Sia, Recruiter/Consultant.

LINDA YEE RECRUITING
No 59 5/F Percival Street, Causeway Bay, Hong Kong
852 9588 14664; fax: 852 2575 8959
asiaconnections@gmail.com

NUMBER OF TEACHERS: 50–100 teachers placed per year. Now also place teachers in Hong Kong and China.
PREFERENCE OF NATIONALITY: none.
QUALIFICATIONS: degree or diploma holder or non-degrees. Must be aged under 55.
CONDITIONS OF EMPLOYMENT: 1 year. 25 hours per week.
SALARY: NT$45,000–NT$50,000 per month.
RECRUITMENT: via partner recruiting offices.
CONTACT: Linda Yee.

MICHAEL ENGLISH SCHOOL
261 Tong-Nan Street, Hsin-Chu 300
michaelenglishschool@hotmail.com
A privately owned school managed by a Brit and his Taiwanese wife since 1985.

NUMBER OF TEACHERS: 3.
QUALIFICATIONS: native English speakers with recognised university degree. Teaching/coaching experience/EFL qualifications. References required. A genuine interest in teaching is essential. The school provides a more family approach to education.
CONDITIONS OF EMPLOYMENT: minimum 1-year contract. Afternoon and evening work only. 80/115 hours per month.
SALARY: NT$600 per teaching hour.
FACILITIES/SUPPORT: one month (paid) induction course. 15 days paid holidays, 5 days unpaid. Gratuity fund. Free airport pick up. Assistance finding accommodation. Work visa, national healthcare, alien resident certificate, all available through school.
RECRUITMENT: via UK education newspapers and the internet. Interview (in Taiwan or by telephone).
CONTACT: Michael Weatherley, Proprietor.

MODERN LANGUAGE SCHOOL
113–2 Wen-chou 1 St., Chiayi
5 286 9816; fax: 5 286 9893
tinahugo@ms22.hinet.net

NUMBER OF TEACHERS: 4–5.

PREFERENCE OF NATIONALITY: Canada or USA.

QUALIFICATIONS: BA preferably in English or education.

CONDITIONS OF EMPLOYMENT: 1 year, 20–30 hours per week Mon–Fri. Mainly afternoons and evenings.

SALARY: NT$60,000 per month.

FACILITIES/SUPPORT: accommodation provided for first week and assistance given in finding a place to live, acting as translator between teacher and prospective landlord and as co-signer on lease.

RECRUITMENT: via the net. Telephone interviews.

CONTACT: Hugo McGlinchey, Managing Director.

REACH TO TEACH

21 Everett Road Ext., Albany, NY 12205 USA

info@reachtoteachrecruiting.com
1 201 467 4612; fax: 1 480 247 5426
www.ReachToTeachRecruiting.com

NUMBER OF TEACHERS: 100 +.

PREFERENCE OF NATIONALITY: applicants must be from the USA, Canada, UK, Australia, New Zealand, Ireland or South Africa.

QUALIFICATIONS: teaching experience is great, but not a requirement. Enthusiasm and enjoying being around children are musts.

CONDITIONS OF EMPLOYMENT: 1 year. Schedules are generally either morning/afternoon (preschool) or afternoon/evening (elementary school).

SALARY: Between NT$55,000 and NT$70,000 per month (approximately US$1,800–US$2,300).

FACILITIES/SUPPORT: teachers are always assisted with finding housing. Generally, newly arrived teachers

take over the apartment from the teacher who is finishing their contract, so it's usually at least partially furnished. Teachers are also helped with work permits from beginning to end.

RECRUITMENT: telephone interviews are 100% essential. The company also carries out in person interviews periodically in the US and UK

CONTACT: Richard Jones, Director of Recruiting.

SHANE ENGLISH SCHOOL

6F-1, 41 Roosevelt Road, Section 2, Taipei

2 2351 7755; fax: 2 2397 2642
dave.roberts@shane.com.tw
www.shane.come.tw/en

NUMBER OF TEACHERS: 150 in about 50 language schools and 3 English immersion kindergartens.

PREFERENCE OF NATIONALITY: must be citizen of English-speaking country.

QUALIFICATIONS: TEFL/CELTA/PGCE (dependent on position applied for).

CONDITIONS OF EMPLOYMENT: 1-year renewable contracts. Guaranteed salaries. 5 days per week schedule.

SALARY: NT$42,400–NT$60,000 per month depending on position, location and experience. Outward flights also paid.

FACILITIES/SUPPORT: up-to-date facilities including interactive CD-ROMs. Work permits, assistance with accommodation, and comprehensive initial and ongoing training provided.

RECRUITMENT: applicants should contact the Principal directly and telephone or face-to-face interviews will be arranged.

CONTACT: Dave Roberts, Principal.

THAILAND

Although progress has been made on restoring democratic rule after the September 2006 coup by the army, Thailand's political scene remains unpredictable. The confidence of the Thai people is understandably muted, particularly because the country's economy is again suffering as it did during the Asia credit crisis of the late 1990s.

Against expectations, however, there are still plenty of opportunities for teachers, especially in schools that teach English to children and (to a lesser extent) executives. The British Council stipulates that it will only consider candidates who have a degree and at least 200 hours post CELTA experience teaching EFL to kids (7–11) and/or teens (12–16). The downside is that since the recent change of government, stricter regulations have been enforced with regard to the recruitment of foreign teachers. If you have a degree you should be able to find work, particularly as schools have had difficulty attracting foreign teachers because of the low wages and red tape issues. Certified teachers will fare even better. However, all teachers are meant to have a teaching licence, something that may involve a (compulsory) investment of time and money on a 'Foreign Teacher Thai Culture Training Program', designed by The Teachers Council of Thailand (see regulations).

Certain schools have already noticed a drop in applicants (from 800 for 12 positions to only 400!) since the new regulations came into force, although Thailand remains a popular EFL (and holiday) destination. The new regulations are hard to pin down and possibly prone to alteration, but their basic aim is to improve the quality of English teaching in Thailand and, according to the Ministry of Education, to ensure that 'fake' teachers (possibly criminals) cannot be so easily accepted into the expat community.

A knowledge of English is eagerly sought by almost all urban young people and, in the context of Thailand, 'urban' is almost synonymous with 'Bangkok', which is five times larger than its nearest rival Chiang Mai. The *Bangkok Post* is as full as ever of advertisements for native English speaker teachers and the Thai-specific website www.ajarn.com described below is a treasure trove of information, contact details and job advertisements.

PROSPECTS FOR TEACHERS

Only a small percentage of recruitment takes place outside Thailand. The major schools use foreign recruitment agencies and the internet to make contact with potential teachers, but most organisations depend on finding native-speaker teachers locally, including Thai universities and teachers' colleges, as well as private business colleges which all have EFL departments. Originally set up as teacher training colleges, there are now 36 Rajabhat Institutes around Thailand which are autonomous and hire their own English teachers (though you can obtain more information from the central office in Bangkok; ℰ 2 628 5281 90).

Thailand also appeals to English speakers who would like a career break and find that teaching is the best job going. **Ed Reinert** worked as a salesman for 25 years before becoming a teacher in Thailand; **Carlos Vega** was a computer technician who thinks that his teaching job is the best he can get in Thailand, '*there is nothing else you can do here but be a teacher, even if you are not a teacher.*'

Thais are exuberant and fun-loving people and their ideas about education reflect this. They seem to value fun and games (*senuk*) above grammar, and an outgoing personality above a teaching certificate, although this attitude may be changing. Of course, there is already a nucleus of professional EFL teachers working at the most prestigious institutes in Bangkok. Many international and Thai bilingual schools look for individuals who can teach art, maths and science through the medium of English. Many of these advertise on Dave's ESL Café.

Some schools and language institutes may be more keen to hire women on the assumption that they are less likely to become engrossed by the seamier side of Thailand's night life. However, all teachers now have to pay for a criminal background check, so this gender bias may be less relevant.

One thing to consider is that Thai salaries have not really increased in the last few years, even though the government wants to attract more professional teachers. This is something of a sticking point, and teachers who want to make a good living in Asia would be better off looking at Korea or Taiwan. However, living costs are still fairly low in Thailand (Bangkok and tourist resorts excepted) and many teachers have such an exciting time that they don't give a thought to savings, or indeed to coming home.

FINDING A JOB

IN ADVANCE

The Anglo-Pacific (Asia) Consultancy (Suite 32, Nevilles Court, Dollis Hill Lane, London NW2 6HG; ✆ 020 8452 7836) is an educational consultancy which concentrates on recruiting teachers for schools, colleges and universities in Thailand, Taiwan and other South East Asian countries. Teachers are placed every month by APA, which not only welcomes graduates with a CELTA or Trinity Certificate but also tries to place people with any TEFL background and/or appropriate personalities as long as they have a university degree. Their recruits are given briefing notes on their country of destination and a follow-up visit in their school if possible. Recruits are guaranteed a salary, regardless of timetable fluctuations, something which can be incredibly valuable when schools and institutes promise to pay 35,000 baht for 28 teachings hours, which then fails to materialise.

The Bell network of Partner Schools in Thailand is an association of independent language centres and language programmes established by Bell in partnership with three of the most prestigious private schools and colleges in Thailand. In collaboration with these long-established institutions, Bell Partner Schools and Programmes in Thailand share a commitment to academic excellence, and the highest standards of management and staff development. Bell language programmes provide primary and secondary level English to students of the host colleges as part of the Thai English language curriculum, and offer in-service teacher development programmes to Thai teachers of English and other subjects such as Maths and science. For a list of current vacancies visit http://www.bell-worldwide.com/jobs/list.asp or email recruitment@bell-centres.com.

One of the best all-round sources of information about teaching in Thailand with an emphasis on Bangkok and on inside information about the main hiring companies is the website www.ajarn.com with stories and tips as well as many job vacancies. The site is run and constantly updated by a teacher, **Philip Williams**, who has been in Thailand for many years. Other places to look include www.teflasia.com and Craig's List Bangkok which was how **Felix Poon** found a job that paid an excellent 50,000 baht a month (58,000 for a master's) plus reimbursed airfares; see http://bangkok.craigslist.org/edu for leads (although there was nothing that well paid at the time of writing).

The webpage http://phuketdelight.com/teach.htm has background information for teaching in Phuket.

LAST YEAR BARRY O'LEARY TAUGHT FROM OCTOBER TO MAY AT OUR LADY OF PERPETUAL HELP SCHOOL IN BANGKOK (NAWAMIN 48, KLONGCHAN BANGKAPI, BANGKOK; ✆ 2 733 4060 9; SCHOOL@PRAMANDA.AC.TH) WHICH HE FOUND ON WWW.TEFL.COM. THE MEDIATING AGENCY WAS CALLED A2Z INTERNATIONAL, WHOSE DIRECTOR SIRILUCK BURAPAVICHIT IS ALWAYS LOOKING FOR TEACHERS IN BANGKOK:
The application was straightforward. I applied online, my references were checked and then I received an email with details of the job, school and general information about Bangkok. When I was greeted at Bangkok by the agency director, I was shocked because I had been expecting a man and found a tiny Thai lady. I was even more shocked when I was led out to meet two small nuns who were to become my bosses. During my interview with the Head Sister the following day, she asked me about my social habits including drinking and smoking and what I thought about Thai women. She then warned me of the dangers of Thai women. I was provided with a flat just outside the school which was great but I wasn't allowed any guests, not even colleagues. This was because a former teacher had abused the rules by taking 'ladies' back to his

room. I was also asked to get my hair cut in order to be seen as a respected teacher (I didn't have much choice on that one).

There were many good features about the job: I loved the students, they were so much fun and interested in the lessons. There were a few discipline problems, which was why there was always a Thai teacher standing by with a cane, which I didn't agree with at all. At times it was difficult to get them to talk in English. I found that they responded much better to a game or competition to get them talking. Over seven months teaching the same class, I really got to know the students and their English improved immensely.

Although Barry had previously been just a TEFL teacher, in this job he was expected to teach English, science, art, maths and swimming to a class of 9-and 10-year-olds. He had to follow lesson plans and a set syllabus, preparing and marking exams at the end of term. Extracurricular activities were great fun and involved organising performances for the parents including his triumph, a Spanish salsa event. One of the daily duties (not recommended with a hangover apparently) was to get the children ready for assembly and for singing the national anthem outside in the playground, a task which became more difficult as the summer temperatures hit 40 degrees. The monthly wage of 35,000 baht (rent-free) allowed him to live very well – always eating out, doing things at weekends – as well as saving £1,500 for a brilliant trip home to England at the end via Laos, Vietnam, Cambodia, China and the Trans-Siberian Express.

VOLUNTEERING

Various organisations enlist the help of volunteer teachers in Thailand. For example Gap Year Thailand (✆ 07899 887276; david@gapyearthailand.org.uk; www.gapyearthailand.org.uk) offers a comprehensive volunteer placement programme for a fee of £980. The giant commercial volunteer agency i-to-i (www.i-to-i.com) offers packaged opportunities as paid or volunteer teachers in Thailand.

Starfish Ventures (www.starfishventures.co.uk) is a British company that places volunteers of all nationalities in development projects in Surin, northeast of Bangkok, including teaching. Fees are from about £900 for a month to £1,400 for three months which include homestay accommodation and in-country supervision. **Peter and Debra Hardy** from Devon, aged 46 and 51, decided to take time out to do some voluntary teaching in Thailand through Starfish Ventures. Pete had to negotiate unpaid leave from his job as a veterinary practice manager, which was the major limiting factor on their time:

We can both honestly say that it was one of the great experiences of our lives, and if anybody is debating whether to embark on a Starfish project, then do it. I have never taught before, but the intensive weekend TEFL course set me up well for the job. I was a bit apprehensive on my first day teaching, but I needn't have been. The Thai kids are wonderful – very keen to learn, very respectful, and a total joy! After a busy but hugely enjoyable English Camp at one school, we even taught the kids to play rounders and cricket! ...We are now trying to persuade all our friends to get off their backsides and be volunteers!

Another Thai-based organisation is Travel to Teach which provides volunteer teaching opportunities (among others) in various locations. Fees start at €550 for a month and full details are available from T2T, 1161/2 Soi Chitta Panya, 43000 Nong Khai (✆ /fax: 42 460 351; www.travel-to-teach.org/thai/english_teaching.html).

The flourishing Thai-based TEFL training organisation TEFL International (see Directory of Training Courses Abroad) offers a voluntary opportunity in conjunction with the local department of education. Graduates of its 4-week certificate course in Ban Phe (about 120 miles from the capital) can be placed in rural Thailand for four months, working in government schools and deprived communities who would not normally have access to native English speakers. A wage is paid but it is very low (15,000 baht a month). The programme fee is $1,690. Details appear on their website www. teflcourse.com/specials/ruralthai.

The Thailand Experience (www.thailandexperience.com) affiliated to the London-based World TEFL School (see entry in Training Directory) offers a package that includes a four-week accredited TEFL course in Phuket, and various job placement or volunteer options around the country. This 'premium plus' package costs £2,196. Another volunteer teacher programme is run by Openmind Projects (1039/3 Keawworawut Road, Tumbol Naimuang Amphor Muang, 43000 Nong Khai; ℂ 42 413 578; www.openmindprojects.org). The fee range is from €495 for a fortnight to €1,955 for 24 weeks.

The Karen Hill Tribes Trust (Midgley House, Heslington, York YO10 5DX; ℂ 01904 415124; www. karenhilltribes.org.uk) sends self-funding volunteers (including gap year students) to northern Thailand to work in communities of Karen tribespeople, sometimes as language teachers. The Global Service Corps (300 Broadway, Suite 28, San Francisco, CA 94133; ℂ 415 788 3666 ext 128; gsc@globalservicecorps.org; www.globalservicecorps.org) sends young volunteers for two, four or six weeks or longer as interns (for a fee of $2,705-$4,427). Students who are interested in Buddhism can teach English to Thai monks.

ON THE SPOT IN BANGKOK

Any new arrival in Bangkok would be well advised to spend a week getting his or her bearings and asking foreigners living in the city for inside information about possible employers. Many people say that the teaching scene has become so exploitative and life in the city so unpleasant that it is better to leave Bangkok as quickly as you can.

For those who feel strong enough to survive in Bangkok, language schools are very easy to locate, to approach on spec. The best place to start is around Siam Square where numerous schools and the British Council are located. For example you could try the Siam Square branch of EF English First which is often hiring (noppadol@ef.com). The Council has a list of private and public universities, institutes, teachers' colleges and international schools throughout the country which have English departments and therefore possible openings for a native speaker, but most people rely on the *Yellow Pages*, which include dozens of language school addresses. Note that the Thai school year ends in mid-March and restarts the second week of May.

Another excellent source of job vacancies is the English language press, viz. the *Bangkok Post* (with at least five advertisements every day) and to a lesser extent the *Nation*. A favourite teachers' hangout is the Hole-in-the-Wall pub on Khao San Road. Or try the Hard Rock Café in Siam Square.

If the Siam Square schools are not short of teachers, which may be the case in the slack season, you will have to try schools further afield. Travelling around this city of eight million is so time-consuming and unpleasant that it is important to plot your interview strategy on a city map before making appointments. Also be sure to pick up a map of the air-conditioned bus routes, particularly if you are contemplating a job which involves travelling to different premises. (Another handy acquisition is a smog mask which costs a few baht.)

It may not be necessary to do much research to discover the schools with vacancies. Many of the so-called back street language schools (more likely to be on a main street, above a shop or restaurant) look to the cheap hotels of Banglamphu, the favourite haunt of Western travellers in the northwest of Bangkok. There is such a high turnover of staff at many schools that there are bound to be vacancies somewhere for a new arrival who takes the trouble to present a professional image and can show a convincing CV. As usual, it may be necessary to start with part-time and occasional work with several employers, aiming to build up 20–30 hours in the same area to minimise travelling in the appalling traffic.

The teaching of children is an expanding area; if you don't want to teach the alphabet, don't accept pupils under the age of five. On the strength of her claim that she had experience of 'working with children', **Alison Eglinton** was soon earning a reasonable wage (and she suggests that anyone teaching young children should master at least one word of Thai: *hong nam* which means toilet).

When visiting a school, wear your posh clothes and carry CVs and passport photos to clip onto the application forms, otherwise you'll be asked to come back when you have obtained some on the Khao San Road. Don't be surprised if the application form asks some weird questions, such as asking you to give the name, age and profession of every member of your family. You won't be hired on the spot but may well be contacted within a day or two; contact is made by telephone so make sure you are staying in a guesthouse with a phone or have your own phone.

EVERYONE WHO HAS EVER HAD ANYTHING TO DO WITH TEACHING ENGLISH IN THAILAND EMPHASISES THE NEED TO DRESS SMARTLY, AS BRUCE LAWSON DESCRIBES

The Thais like their pet farangs (ie foreign teachers) to look as much like currency dealers as possible. I bought a suit in Bangkok for £50 especially for the job hunt. Men should take out all earrings and wear a tie, thus risking asphyxiation in the heat and humidity of the hot season. Women should wear a decent skirt, not trousers.

Appropriate dress was also a problem for **Susannah Kerr** who had been told by her sending agency (i-to-i) that T-shirts and flip flops would be appropriate. But this was not the case at her school in Nakhon Nayok (pop 250,000), and she was promptly taken on a compulsory shopping expedition and was obliged to spend money on smarter clothes which she didn't care for.

Ajarn – the Thai word for teachers – are particularly respected in Thailand and are expected to look respectable. As well as dressing smartly for an interview, try to maintain a reserve in your manner while still projecting a relaxed and easy-going image. Too many gesticulations and guffawing are considered impolite and immature and will not earn you the respect of Thai people.

The busiest season for English schools is mid-March to mid-May during the school holidays, when many secondary school and university students take extra tuition in English. This coincides with the hot season. Vacancies continue to be advertised through June, July and August. The next best time to look for teaching work in private schools is October, while the quietest time is January/February.

ON THE SPOT IN CHIANG MAI

According to **Annette Kunigagon** who has made her home in Chiang Mai and is something of a resident expert in teaching in her adopted town, far more people have been coming to Chiang Mai to look for work than was the case a few years ago, since no one wants to live in Bangkok. She co-owns the Eagle Guesthouse at 16 Chang Moi Gao Road, Soi 3 (© 53 874126/235387; mail@eaglehouse.com; www.eaglehouse.com). She even organises unpaid teaching work as part of her Helping Hands Social Projects scheme (see her website).

Teaching opportunities crop up in branches of the big companies such as ECC and AUA and in academic institutes. There are lots of so-called bilingual programmes sometimes called 'English Programme' or just 'EP' at Thai schools favoured by parents who want their children to have more exposure to English than in the standard school and cannot afford the prices of an international school. Schools included are Anubaan Chiang Mai School, Wattano Payap School, Waree School and Fatih School. When approaching the bilingual schools, seek out the English teacher (who will be teaching in the normal Thai programme).

THERE ARE FIVE INTERNATIONAL SCHOOLS WHICH EMPLOY ENGLISH TEACHERS, THOUGH MOST ARE RECRUITED ABROAD, EG AT INTERNATIONAL TEACHERS' FAIRS LIKE THOSE SPONSORED BY SEARCH ASSOCIATES (WWW.SEARCH-ASSOCIATES.COM) RATHER THAN LOCALLY. MURRAY TURNER IS ONE TEACHER WHO SUCCEEDED IN FINDING WORK, PARTLY WITH ANNETTE'S HELP:

I am working seven hours a week in Chiang Mai after arriving one week ago. I'm staying at Eagle Guest House which is run by Annette who knows everything about language schools (and everything else). I found the job by hiring a bicycle and dutifully doing the rounds of the language schools, colleges and kids' schools. I took plenty of passport photos, photocopies of my passport and of my certificate from the one-week TEFL course I'd done.

Annette requests that anyone who contacts her should include their CV, qualifications and proof of a genuine interest, to avoid the time-wasters.

Other jobs are available in the school holidays at summer and weekend camps held at resort hotels and attended by rich children from Bangkok. Getting in to these and the summer camps run by the British Council and YMCA is by word of mouth, friends or advertisements. Annette's advice is to be brazen, knock on doors, try hotels, shops catering to tourists, companies which export or have to deal with foreigners, pubs, restaurants, computer shops, large shops in the Night Bazaar area, etc.

ON THE SPOT IN THE PROVINCES

Teaching opportunities outside Bangkok have almost doubled, however not many foreigners show an interest since the pay is much less than in Bangkok. The estimated four-fifths of teachers who are single men enjoying the nightlife in Bangkok are unwilling to move to a less exciting country town.

Competition for work is almost non-existent in lesser known cities such as Nakhon Sawan, Khon Kaen, Udon Thani, Ubon Ratchathani and Pathumthani. For a job in a university you will probably have to show a higher degree or teaching certificate. The best places are Hat Yai and Songkhla. Hotels are always worth asking, since many hotel workers are very keen to improve their English. If you find a place which suits and you decide to stay for a while, ask the family who run your guesthouse about local teaching opportunities.

SOMETIMES THE HAPPIEST AND MOST MEMORABLE EXPERIENCES OF TEACHING ENGLISH IN THAILAND TAKE PLACE AWAY FROM THE CITIES AND THE TOURIST RESORTS. BRIAN SAVAGE RETURNED TO ENGLAND AFTER A SECOND LONG STINT OF TEACHING IN THAILAND AND DESCRIBES ONE OF THE HIGHLIGHTS FOR HIM:

My most rewarding experience was my week teaching English conversation in a rural high school in Loei province in northeast Thailand. These children had rarely seen and had certainly never spoken to a farang (foreigner in Thai) before. My work during that week and a subsequent second visit was really appreciated by the pupils. The first visit came about after I was introduced to a teacher at the Chiang Mai school where I was teaching. If travellers get away from Bangkok and the resorts, they too can have experiences such as this, especially in the friendly towns of the north and northeast. A little voluntary teaching can really boost the confidence of students who are usually too poor to pay to study with native speakers.

REGULATIONS

In the past few years Thailand has tightened up regulations with regard to the recruitment of foreign teachers. No teacher, whether paid or a volunteer, is meant to be employed without a non-immigrant B visa and a work permit. You also must pay the requisite taxes, which are (on average) 3%–5% of your gross monthly salary. It seems that the halcyon days of informal or ignored regulations are gone, at least for now. Paid teachers should apply for non-immigrant visa, type 'B' at the Royal Thai Embassy. According to the embassy, they are expected to submit: a copy of their education certificate; an official recommendation letter from the education institution in Thailand to the Embassy; a copy of school licence/principal; a copy of licence of school manager; information of the employment terms of the applicant in Thailand; verification stating that the applicant has no criminal record issued from the country of his/her nationality or residence (valid for not more than three months and officially notarised). If the applicant has 'appropriate qualification' (presumably a degree), the Embassy will issue a non-immigrant visa, type 'B', single entry with three months validity to the applicant within three working days. With this kind of visa, the applicant can stay in Thailand for no longer than 90 days. Once the teacher arrives in Thailand, their school/institution should apply for a teacher's licence at the Ministry of Education or the Ministry of University Affairs (see later) and also apply for a work permit at the Ministry of Labour. Note that requirements for obtaining the non-immigrant B visa vary among countries so you should find out from the embassy exactly what is required. After being granted a teacher's licence and work permit, the teacher is required to submit the teacher's licence, work permit, employment contract and employment certificate to the Immigration Bureau in order to apply for a visa extension to cover the term of employment. Voluntary teachers must apply for a non-immigrant visa, type 'O', at the Royal Thai embassy, where they should submit: an official recommendation letter from the volunteer organisation in Thailand to the embassy and information on the term of voluntary work. If the teacher has 'appropriate qualifications', the embassy will issue a non-immigrant visa, type 'O', single entry with three month validity. The teacher can stay in Thailand no longer than 90 days; to extend the visa they are required to submit an application to the Immigration Bureau by enclosing 'an official introduction letter of the Organization in Thailand'.

The wording of some of these demands is loose to say the least. A teacher is probably best advised to find out as much as they can from their prospective school/institute or voluntary organisation, who may well be prepared to help with the paperwork/interpretation of the paperwork. The ajarn forum of www.ajarn.com is a very good place to read about the evolving red tape situation and its practical (rather than theoretical) implications. Once a work permit is granted, tax will be withdrawn at a very modest rate, sometimes as low as 2%. Thailand's national health scheme applies to visitors and so not all teachers worry about private insurance.

Current Thai Labor Law demands that '*all people who work in The Kingdom of Thailand must be covered by The National Health Care Program, no exceptions, and regardless of nationality.*' Many employers may not even know this or keep it to themselves, in order to not have to pay any insurance fees. The maximum *any* employer can charge you, per month, is 750 baht. Your employer then pays the same amount per month, to the government, for your health coverage. The number you receive is permanent and it rolls over to your next employer, after you have stopped working at your original employer. It is based on your salary level and, if you or someone from your employing organisation wishes to know the details, you can go to the local Social Security office.

TEACHER'S LICENCE

There still seems to be some debate as to whether teachers 'need' a licence or not. All the Thai Ministry of Education could say in a recent interview was that licences are 'only an individual school's requirement' and not compulsory. However, some schools report being asked to apply for a teacher's licence under the new regulations. These regulations appear to stipulate that almost everyone has to take a 'foreign teacher Thai Culture Program', which is 20 hours and costs anywhere between 3,000 and 8,000 baht. If you don't have a degree in education, you might also need to attend a year long 'teacher professional licensing course', at a cost of 60,000 baht or pass a four part written exam, which costs 4,000 baht in total. Failing that (or with no degree) your school needs to send a very persuasive letter to the relevant authority (The Teachers' Council of Thailand) basically begging them to issue you a teacher's licence, because they can't find anyone else. The Teachers' Council may or may not issue one.

Schools can also apply for 'an extension of permission to work without a teacher's licence' which can cover up to two years, or perhaps one if you are listening to the Teachers' Council. For up-to-date information browse **Jason Alavi**'s incredibly detailed column on Ajarn: http://ajarn.com/Contris/jasonalavimay2008.htm.

CONDITIONS OF WORK

In Thailand, the wages for *farang* teachers tend to be low. The basic hourly rate has risen only slightly over the past six years from 150–200 baht an hour with some schools paying 250+ baht. Company work can pay as much as 400–600 baht depending on location, but in-company contract work has greatly diminished. The norm is for schools to keep their staff on as part-time freelancers while giving them full-time hours; this is primarily to avoid taxes. Most language institutes pay weekly in cash, but beware of schools which turn pay day into a moveable feast.

The best remuneration is available from international schools such as the Bangkok Patana School (2/38 Soi Lasalle, Sukhumvit 105, Bangkok 10260; ✆ 2 398 0200; fax: 2 399 3179; reception@patana.ac.th; www.patana.ac.th). Note that the pay at international schools in Bangkok is as much as twice that paid by international schools elsewhere in the country. For a list of international schools in Thailand go to the website of the International Schools Association of Thailand (www.isat.or.th).

Carlos Vega works at Sathit Rangsit Bilingual School, in an inner suburb of Bangkok, just over the north-eastern city line. It has all the modern facilities of a Western school and he is able to save about 50% of his income (although he does own outright his own car and house). Few employers help with accommodation, which does not matter much since vacant apartments are not hard to locate and rental deposits not crippling as they are in Japan. According to **Helen Welch**, teachers in Bangkok are increasingly likely to want to live in foreigners' compounds, patrolled by armed guards. Things are more relaxed in Chiang Mai where a group of people can rent a house or live Thai-style in a studio room with attached bathroom for very affordable rents.

Remember never to touch a student on the head, which is difficult if you are teaching children. In class a show of anger will soon lose the students' respect since the Thais value a 'cool heart' (*jai yen*) and go to great lengths to avoid displays of negative emotion. Calm, smiling and enthusiastic personalities make all the difference.

Carlos Vega thinks that there are two types of pupils, '*Primary are nice and ready to learn every day. Secondary students mostly don't care and don't want to learn anything in a system that makes it impossible for any student to fail. No one really has to do any work in order to pass the grade, so why bother? Usually if the parents are involved with the school the student tends to do well.*' **Ed Reinert** also teaches in a private school, and although he's sometimes struck by the poor standard of his pupils' English, even after years of teaching, he has also taught students '*who loved to learn and at the end of the day made it worth while*'.

LEISURE TIME

It has to be said that Bangkok may be an exciting and lively city but it is not beautiful. It has very few parks, bad traffic congestion and polluted air. **Bruce Lawson** describes one way of travelling between Banglamphu and Siam Square:

> You can travel to work on the cesspool that they call a canal (**klong**). It's about a five-minute walk from Banglamphu on the other side of the Democracy Monument. Get on a boat picking up on the right of the bridge. It costs a few baht and takes just over 10 minutes compared to the 45-minute ride on the non-air con bus. But you swap traffic fumes for the stench of stagnant water full of decomposing rubbish, animals and hideous eight-inch swimming millipedes. So don't fall in.

There is also a great deal of what some might consider moral pollution, and there is a certain element of the teaching fraternity in Bangkok who are there primarily for the easy availability of sex in the notorious Patpong district (despite the fact that there is a veritable Aids crisis in Thailand). **Helen Welch** reports that at least one school has banned all its staff from going into Patpong, for fear of being spotted by a client or their parents. Also, Thai Labor Law stipulates that '*any employees who comport themselves in a manner which would embarrass or cause serious damage to employers' reputation may be terminated immediately, by employer, with no legal recourse available to employee.*' This applies on *and* off the clock. Many a *farang* man has been spotted in a 'night-time establishment' and been fired the next day.

With the ratio of foreign men to women teachers atleast six to one, many women (although in great demand as teachers) do not enjoy the atmosphere in the city and leave as quickly as they can. Although there are plenty of night clubs and restaurants in Bangkok, there is a dearth of dance and film, and also of sports clubs. Fortunately for teachers earning a low wage, the more innocent pleasures of Thailand come cheap. **Felix Poon** wrote from Bangkok to say that the extremely low cost of living makes even a low salary enough for a very comfortable lifestyle. You can eat a good meal for about 40 baht and a beer is only 60 baht in a bar.

Apparently there is a national shortage of Marmite, so homesick Britons will embrace any new arrival with a supply. Even part-time teachers should be able to afford to travel round the country, visiting jungle attractions such as Kanchanaburi, where you can ride an elephant along the banks of the River Kwai, and islands like Koh Samet, Koh Samui and Koh Phangan where life is slow and the beaches are wonderful. Bangkok is also an important hub for travellers and cheap tickets are available to India, etc.

Try to learn a little Thai as **Bruce Lawson** did after getting fried battered banana when he thought he had ordered garlic chicken. He recommends organising word-swaps with students, which will also illustrate to them that they are not the only ones who have to struggle with alien sounds.

> **ALTHOUGH CARLOS VEGA HAS A FEW WORDS OF WARNING ABOUT CULTURAL DIFFERENCES, HE IS ENTHUSIASTIC ABOUT THE REWARDS OF LIVING AND TEACHING IN THAILAND:**
>
> *Generally, if a foreign teacher is calm, cool and collected under pressure and has a very open mind, they'll do well here. Thais don't handle criticism or dissent well. Sometimes this can be very frustrating or restricting to a Westerner 'just off the boat'. I love it here and I don't want to go back. I have a Thai wife, who is also a teacher, and a good life. Just don't 'rock the boat' here and you'll do just fine. After all, this is their country and we shouldn't (I think) try to change them, too much. I recommend teaching here wholeheartedly. There's no way to know if you'll like it but to do it!*

LIST OF EMPLOYERS

THE AMERICAN ENGLISH LANGUAGE SCHOOL
79/29 Warabodin Village, Tambol Bang Pood,
Amphoe Muang, Pathumthani, Thailand, 12000

 924 3163

teacherfinder@hotmail.com

NUMBER OF TEACHERS: 178.

PREFERENCE OF NATIONALITY: American.

QUALIFICATIONS: at least a bachelor's degree (in anything) from an internationally accredited academic institution. Bachelor's (or higher) in Education will receive preference.

CONDITIONS OF EMPLOYMENT: 1-year contract, Mon–Fri, 8am to 4pm.

SALARY: starts at 35,000 baht per month with a ceiling of 45,000–90,000 baht. The AELS sends teachers to many levels of schools. Taxes are anywhere from 1,000 to 1,750 baht per month and 750 baht per month for Social Security.

FACILITIES/SUPPORT: company helps teachers find a place that has a good location, for a good rent, with good amenities, and takes them to all the necessary offices, every step of the way, to get the necessary papers (but doesn't pay for them).

RECRUITMENT: by personal interviews and teaching demonstrations, followed by credential checks. Company rarely hires directly from overseas: three videoconferencing interviews have led to only one hire so far.

CONTACT: Jason Alavi, Owner.

NUMBER OF TEACHERS: about 200 in total: 50–60 at main branch, up to 20 at other branches. Offers SIT TEFL Certificate Course.

PREFERENCE OF NATIONALITY: American, Canadian, British, Australian and New Zealand.

QUALIFICATIONS: BA in any field and CELTA (or equivalent) and completion of high school.

CONDITIONS OF EMPLOYMENT: 1 year commitment preferred. 4–6 hours teaching daily (considered to be full-time). Teaching year consists of 7 6-week terms separated by 1 free week (unpaid). Courses aimed at professionals aged 18–35.

SALARY: starting rate is 300+ baht per hour depending on experience/qualifications. Annual bonus paid after completion of Professional Development Program, free health insurance, work permit obtained but paid for by the teacher for first 2 years.

FACILITIES/SUPPORT: participation in pre-service training session (32 hours) is preferred before teaching hours are assigned. Mentoring programme for new teachers, 15,000 titles in resource library.

RECRUITMENT: advertisements in the *Bangkok Post*, the internet and word of mouth. Apply online.

Academic-oriented summer camp for Thai secondary school students March to May or longer.

NUMBER OF TEACHERS: 10–15 temporary positions.

PREFERENCE OF NATIONALITY: native English speakers only.

QUALIFICATIONS: minimum first degree plus CELTA or other TESOL certificate; 2+ years experience preferred. Teaching assistant positions available for those without TESOL background.

CONDITIONS OF EMPLOYMENT: 8 week contracts March to May; may be extended to August (18 weeks maximum). 18–20 teaching hours plus class preparation and other duties bring total to 40 hours per week.

SALARY: minimum 30,000 baht plus room and board.

FACILITIES/SUPPORT: accommodation provided and up to 21 meals a week. School provides all necessary documentation for legal employment.

RECRUITMENT: candidates must be interviewed.

NUMBER OF TEACHERS: 80+ for 7 independent language centres mainly in Bangkok.

PREFERENCE OF NATIONALITY: none, but must be native speaker.

QUALIFICATIONS: BA and CELTA (better still PGCE and/or DELTA). Experience of and/or interest in teaching English to young learners preferred. Candidates should be dependable and culturally sensitive team players.

CONDITIONS OF EMPLOYMENT: 1- or 2-year renewable contracts. Up to 21 contact hours per week (Mon–Fri or Tues–Sat). Much of the work is with young learners.

SALARY: gross salary 42,000–54,000 baht per month (for degree and CELTA) or 55,000–62,000 baht (DELTA).

FACILITIES/SUPPORT: flight for teachers recruited outside Thailand. Hotel accommodation on arrival. Assistance in finding suitable accommodation. A loan for accommodation is made available, repayable over initial 3 months of employment. Work permit arranged. End of contract gratuity. 8 weeks' paid holiday per year plus public holidays. Health and medical insurance cover provided. Commitment to in-service training and professional development.

RECRUITMENT: internet, newspapers, personal interview or through Bell International in the UK.

BRITISH AMERICAN

Two schools: Rangsit (Future Park)

02 958 0351 5; fax: 02 958 0356

Ramintra (Fashion Island)

2 947 5104/5; fax: 2 947 5114

New school in Lart Prow opening October 2008

www.british-american.ac.th

NUMBER OF TEACHERS: about 40.

PREFERENCE OF NATIONALITY: native speakers.

QUALIFICATIONS: enthusiasm and positive attitude are essential.

CONDITIONS OF EMPLOYMENT: usually part-time, 4–6 teaching hours per day.

SALARY: earnings usually approx. 30,000+ baht per month. Local rent for an apartment is approximately 3,000 baht monthly.

FACILITIES/SUPPORT: provide details of recommended apartments. All the visa paperwork is done by the school, but the teacher pays for visa and out of pocket expenses.

RECRUITMENT: advertising in national newspapers.

BURMA VOLUNTEER PROGRAM (BVP)

PO Box 114, Mae Sot, Tak, 63110 Thailand

n/a; fax: n/a

maesotel@gmail.com

www.burmavolunteer.com

NUMBER OF TEACHERS: volunteers accepted on a rolling basis as needed.

PREFERENCE OF NATIONALITY: none.

QUALIFICATIONS: teaching experience, interest In the Burma issue, creativity, and comfort with ambiguity. Minimum age 21 years.

CONDITIONS OF EMPLOYMENT: 3-month stays. Teaching 3 hours per day, 5 days per week.

SALARY: accommodation and food are generally provided.

RECRUITMENT: interviews not necessary.

CONTACT: Aryca Myers, Volunteer Co-ordinator.

CHIANG MAI UNIVERSITY

Department of English, Faculty of Humanities, 239 Huay Kaew Road, Muang District, Chiang Mai 50200

53 943231/943251; fax: 53 943258

headengl@chiangmai.ac.th

NUMBER OF TEACHERS: 40.

PREFERENCE OF NATIONALITY: none.

QUALIFICATIONS: university degree relevant to teaching English as a second language, native speakers, teaching experience in ESL.

CONDITIONS OF EMPLOYMENT: 1-year contract. 9–15 teaching hours per week.

SALARY: 20,000 baht per month and 8,000 baht for monthly rent (full-time positions), 300–350 baht per hour (part-time positions).

FACILITIES/SUPPORT: no assistance with accommodation. Help given with work permits, visa extension fee and insurance.

RECRUITMENT: direct applications. Interview required.

CONTACT: Head of English Department.

DRAGONFLY

1719 Mookamontri Soi 13, A. Meuang Nakhon Ratchasima, 30000 Songpon

/fax: +66 4428 1073

dan@thai-dragonfly.com

www.thai-dragonfly.com

NUMBER OF VOLUNTEER PLACEMENTS PER YEAR: 100.

QUALIFICATIONS: Good working knowledge of English (or Thai!), flexibility and an open mind.

CONDITIONS OF WORK: 4–52 weeks. Usual hours 8am to 4pm with 15–20 hpw actual teaching.

SALARY: none. Volunteers pay a participation fee of 16,000 baht for 4 weeks, and 2,500 baht per week thereafter. TEFL training courses extra.

RECRUITMENT: Online.

FACILITIES/SUPPORT: Meals and accommodation provided as home stay with Thai family. TEFL courses available through local providers; choice of online option and courses based in beach towns in Thailand. 3-day intensive courses (£395), 120-hour TEFL course (£1,100) baht including 4-week volunteer placement.

CONTACT: Dan Lockwood, Project Manager.

ECC (Thailand)

5th Floor, Big C Rajdamri, Rajdamri Road, Lumpini, Pathumwan, Bangkok Thailand 10330

66 02 253 3312 or 66 02 6551236; fax: 66 02 655 1238

jobs@ecc.ac.th or tesol@ecc.ac.th

www.eccthai.com

50 schools in Bangkok and in most major centres outside Bangkok (including Chiang Mai and Phuket). Largest private language school in Thailand.

NUMBER OF TEACHERS: around 500 native speakers (usually recruit 10–15 new teachers each month).

PREFERENCE OF NATIONALITY: none.

QUALIFICATIONS: preferably bachelor's degree + TEFL certificate (CELTA, Trinity or equivalent).

CONDITIONS OF EMPLOYMENT: 100 hours per month (average 25 hours per week), 6-day week, BUPA medical insurance, end of contract bonus (12,000 baht), location allowance in Bangkok (3,000–5,000 baht per month).

SALARY: Depending on qualifications and experience 30,000–38,000 baht per month.

FACILITIES/SUPPORT: work permit and 1-year visa applied for once in country. Assistance (non-financial) given with finding accommodation. Professional development with regular workshops, including a number of short courses which are free to ECC teachers: Teaching English to Young Learners and Teaching Business English. For those who are not qualified and wish to get qualified ECC offer the Cambridge CELTA course and a locally recognised Introduction to TESOL course.

RECRUITMENT: advertisements in the *Guardian*, *Times Educational Supplement*, *EL Gazette*, internet and qualified walk-ins.

CONTACT: Teacher Recruitment Manager (jobs@ecc.ac.th)

E.S.C.D. ENGLISH CENTRE
8/36 Sukhumvit Road Siracha Chonburi 20110
- 38 328203; fax: 38 321792
- wnschool@cscoms.com
- http://eec.escd.or.th/vacancies.htm

NUMBER OF TEACHERS: 20 per year.

PREFERENCE OF NATIONALITY: Australian, European, American, Canadian.

QUALIFICATIONS: degree plus TEFL. Aged 20–40.

CONDITIONS OF EMPLOYMENT: 12-month contracts to teach in local Catholic schools. 16–25 hours per week.

SALARY: 25,000 baht per month. Free flight at end of contract.

FACILITIES/SUPPORT: accommodation 2,500 baht per month. Help with visas given; teachers must bring original of their degree certificate.

RECRUITMENT: interviews essential.

CONTACT: Peter Srisook, Manager.

INLINGUA INTERNATIONAL SCHOOL OF LANGUAGES
7th Floor, Central Chidlom Tower, 22 Ploenchit Road, Pathumwan, Bangkok 10330
- 2 254 7028 30; fax: 2 254 7098
- chidlom@inlinguabangkok.com
- www.Inlinguabangkok.com

NUMBER OF TEACHERS: 100 full-time, 60 part-time.

PREFERENCE OF NATIONALITY: native speakers from Britain, Canada, USA, Australia, New Zealand, South Africa.

QUALIFICATIONS: candidates must have at least 2 of the following: bachelor's degree, TESOL/TEFL/CELTA, experience.

CONDITIONS OF EMPLOYMENT: 1 year. Children's classes are on Saturday/Sunday 9am–6pm. Teachers work a 6-day week or 5 for corporate work.

SALARY: guaranteed 35,000 baht. Possibly more, depending on workload.

FACILITIES/SUPPORT: try to point staff in the direction of suitable accommodation. Full support given in work permit/visa applications. BUPA medical insurance.

RECRUITMENT: internet advertisements on www.ajarn.com. Applications welcomed on above email address. Mostly local hires.

CONTACT: Fraser Morrell, Director of Studies (fraserm@inlinguabangkok.com)

IST PLUS – TEACH IN THAILAND PROGRAMME
Rosedale House, Rosedale Road, Richmond, Surrey TW9 2SZ
- 020 8939 9057
- info@istplus.com
- www.istplus.com; www.widenyourworld.org

NUMBER OF TEACHERS: 20–30 each year.

PREFERENCE OF NATIONALITY: none, although non-native speakers of English must have near-native proficiency in English.

QUALIFICATIONS: university degree in any field essential. TEFL training or experience is not essential but preferred.

CONDITIONS OF EMPLOYMENT: 5 or 10-month renewable contracts starting in either May or October, teaching 16–22 hours per week.

SALARY: minimum salary 14,000 baht per month.

FACILITIES/SUPPORT: free accommodation (usually on-campus), all-inclusive 7-day orientation in Bangkok on arrival including basic EFL training, accommodation, sight-seeing and airport transfer. IST Plus arrange school placement, visa and work permit, insurance and 24-hour emergency hotline.

RECRUITMENT: deadlines for application are early February/March for May departure and August/September for October departure. Teach in Thailand Programme fee starts at £725. Teachers who complete 10-month contracts starting in May will have their one-way flight home paid for by the host school. All teachers who complete their contracts will receive a TEFL Certificate.

CONTACT: rallemano@istplus.com.

KING'S COLLEGE OF ENGLISH

SCB Park Plaza, Bangkok, plus several other offices

☎ 2 937 9300; fax: 2 937 9295

✆ recruitkings@yahoo.co.uk

🖳 www.kingsthailand.com

Part of group of King's English Language Schools based in Bournemouth, UK.

NUMBER OF TEACHERS: 45 for 3 schools in Bangkok and 1 in Chiang Mai.

PREFERENCE OF NATIONALITY: British (majority), Canadian, American, Australian, New Zealand.

QUALIFICATIONS: university degree (any subject) plus CELTA or equivalent. Preference given to applicants with qualifications or experience teaching young learners.

CONDITIONS OF EMPLOYMENT: 1-year contracts. Contractual arrangement is 112 contact hours per month; preparation time is extra. Saturday and Sunday are working days. 2 consecutive days off a week.

SALARY: approx. 34,000–35,000 baht per month depending on qualifications and experience. Yearly increment, paid holidays. End-of-contract bonus. Overtime, company work and specialist teaching (eg IGCSE) paid at a higher rate. Less 5%–10% deducted for tax.

FACILITIES/SUPPORT: assistance with accommodation; loan can be given for deposit and deducted from monthly salary. Help teachers arrange temporary visa before arrival and then to process work permit and teacher certification. B6,000 will be deducted over 3 months for this process, which will be returned (with interest) at the end of contract. Basic private health insurance (BUPA) provided by school.

RECRUITMENT: local and web advertisements and UK recruitment agency. UK applicants should contact John Hudson (hudson.111@virgin.net) in the first instance.

CONTACT: Academic Director.

KITTIVIT BILINGUAL SCHOOL

118 Kanjanavanitch Road, Banpru, HatYai, Songkhla 90250

☎ 74 210826/210945

🖳 www.kittivit.th.edu

NUMBER OF TEACHERS: 10–15.

PREFERENCE OF NATIONALITY: none.

QUALIFICATIONS: university degree plus some teaching experience. Teaching degree/TESOL preferred.

CONDITIONS OF EMPLOYMENT: 1–2 years. Applicants accepted on a rolling basis throughout the year, though most posts commence in May. Hours 7.50am–4pm.

SALARY: approx. 30,000 baht.

FACILITIES/SUPPORT: accommodation provided. Full assistance with work permits.

RECRUITMENT: via newspaper and internet advertisements, recruitment agency. Interviews in person or by phone.

CONTACT: Programme Director.

NES-BAAN PASA

Nimmarnhemin: 10 Nimmarnhemin 17 Road, T. Suthep, A. Muang, Chiangmai 50200

☎ 53 221362/894807; fax: 53 222361

✆ baanpasa@loxinfo.co.th

Somphet: Chaiyapoom Road, T. Changmoi A. Muang, Chiang Mai 50300

☎ 53 233050/233550

Chiangrai: 162 Banpaprakarn Rd., T. Wiang A. Muang, Chiangrai 57000

☎ 53 712244; fax: 53 52447

Nes-Baan Pasa is a well-known, independent language school in the north of Thailand, with three schools in Chiangmai. Also in Chiangrai, Lamphun and Tak Province; registered with the Thai Ministry of Education. NES (New Zealand Education Services) provides counselling and placement for students who would like to study in New Zealand.

NUMBER OF TEACHERS: 20 for 3 sites with 30 classrooms.

PREFERENCE OF NATIONALITY: none, but must be native speaker.

QUALIFICATIONS: degree, diploma or certificate with some teaching experience.

CONDITIONS OF EMPLOYMENT: minimum stay 6 months, renewable. Contracted to teach minimum of 20 hours. Part-time teachers also needed.

SALARY: negotiable depending on qualifications and experience.

FACILITIES/SUPPORT: help in finding accommodation.

RECRUITMENT: via local interview only.

CONTACT: Khun Tan Worapant, Assistant Director, or apply in person to Head Office in Nimmarnhemin.

PATHOMPAT SCHOOL

518/22 Soi Sahakarnpramoon, Prachautid Road, Wangthonglang, Bangkok 10310

☎ 2 957 5550 3

🖳 www.pathompat.ac.th

NUMBER OF TEACHERS: 5.

PREFERENCE OF NATIONALITY: USA, Canada, UK.

QUALIFICATIONS: bachelor's degree, prior teaching experience and/or living abroad is a definite plus.

CONDITIONS OF EMPLOYMENT: 1 school year. Hours of lessons 7.40am–4.00pm.

SALARY: starts at 40,000 baht (net) per month.

FACILITIES/SUPPORT: teachers are provided with a monthly living allowance of 10,000 baht and advice given on finding accommodation locally. Teachers must provide the school with the proper documents to obtain a teaching licence. School then applies for a work permit which must be renewed annually.

RECRUITMENT: job postings on local websites such as www.ajarn.com. Face-to-face interviews where possible, otherwise by phone. Occasionally interviews possible in USA.

CONTACT: Khun Jumrean Prakob (Principal) or Naerisa Koletschka (Head of Curriculum Development).

SIAM COMPUTER & LANGUAGE INSTITUTE

471/19 Ratchawithi Road, Bangkok 10400

2 247 2345 ext. 370 373; fax: 2 644 6974

teach@siamcom.co.th

www.siamcom.co.th

NUMBER OF TEACHERS: 37 at 35 school locations in the greater Bangkok area and 49 at 38 external Thai school locations in the greater Bangkok area.

PREFERENCE OF NATIONALITY: native speaker of English.

QUALIFICATIONS: college degree required; CELTA or equivalent and experience preferred.

CONDITIONS OF EMPLOYMENT: 1-year contracts. Full-time internal teachers 6 days per week in air-conditioned facilities; 15 or fewer students per class. All ages. Full-time external teachers 5 days per week in Thai classrooms. 50 students per class from kindergarten to high school level.

SALARY: 30,000 baht and up per month based on experience. Bonus plans for external teachers. Hourly rates for part-time internal and external teachers.

FACILITIES/SUPPORT: assistance with finding local accommodation. 15 paid Thai vacation days per year, assistance in obtaining a teacher's licence, work permit and 1-year visa. Complete teacher orientation and teacher training before entering the classroom and bimonthly teachers' meetings.

RECRUITMENT: advertisements in the *Bangkok Post* and on the worldwide web, and contacts with schools in Australia and the USA. Interviews in Bangkok required.

CONTACT: Mr Ben.

SIAM COMPUTER AND LANGUAGE SCHOOL PETCHABURI

73,75 Old Petchakaseam Road, Klongkrachang, Muang, Petchaburi 76000

/fax: 32 401219

noavaratt@hotmail.com or

noraa111@hotmail.com

NUMBER OF TEACHERS: 14.

PREFERENCE OF NATIONALITY: none.

QUALIFICATIONS: experience preferred though training can be provided.

CONDITIONS OF EMPLOYMENT: 6 or 12 months. 100 hours per month.

SALARY: 20,000–30,000 baht a month for full-time teacher.

FACILITIES/SUPPORT: Free accommodation provided 5-minute walk from beach. Internet access also provided at school.

RECRUITMENT: interviews not always necessary or can be conducted by phone.

CONTACT: Noavarat Tosuwan, Manager.

NUMBER OF TEACHERS: 50.

PREFERENCE OF NATIONALITY: Native English Speakers.

QUALIFICATIONS: TESOL certified with degree or diploma preferred. Inexperienced individuals have opportunities to undergo formal or in-house training through a staff development programme.

CONDITIONS OF EMPLOYMENT: 10-month renewable contract. 20–25 hours per week. Monday–Friday, Evening, weekend and summer holiday work are offered as overtime.

SALARY: starting salary 32,000–45,000 Baht per month.

FACILITIES/SUPPORT: Training in ESL is provided on-site. Assistance given with finding accommodation in the school vicinity to suit teacher's lifestyle. School takes care of all work permit requirements for teachers who wish to transfer their visa status.

RECRUITMENT: Most staff are recruited directly from the teacher training course that Spencer International provides (TESOL/TEFL, accredited by Chichester College, UK).

NUMBER OF TEACHERS: 5.

PREFERENCE OF NATIONALITY: none, but must be a native speaker of English.

QUALIFICATIONS: university degree essential. Must have the right attitude: a willingness to learn, be flexible about living in an Eastern culture, to think creatively and be patient. Must enjoy working with children and have a sincere desire to teach them English and to have an impact on their lives.

CONDITIONS OF EMPLOYMENT: standard 1-year contract. Schedules vary greatly but no more than 25 hours per week. Some teachers work in the morning and have their afternoons off; others prefer late mornings and continuing through the early evening. Classes finish at 7.30pm.

SALARY: 250 baht per hour. Current average salary is around 27,500 baht per month less tax deductions of 196 baht per month.

FACILITIES/SUPPORT: shared, furnished house (private bedroom) in an ideal location of Surat Thani is provided for each teacher with a living-room, bedroom, bathroom and storage space. Paperwork provided pre-arrival for a 3-month non-immigrant B visa. School will process that visa into a 1-year non-immigrant visa and will obtain a 1-year labour permit and 3-year teacher's licence for the teacher.

RECRUITMENT: advertisements on www.eslcafe.com. Interviews are essential.

CONTACT: Peter C Meltzer, Owner and Director.

PROGRAMME DESCRIPTION: teaching English, computer skills to disadvantaged children and/or adults in Thailand. Maintaining computers.

NUMBER OF PLACEMENTS PER YEAR: 100.

DESTINATIONS: mainly north-eastern Thailand (Isan province).

PREREQUISITES: minimum age 18. Good command of English language. Computer trainers need computer skills, open mind and patience to deal with the different environment. No TEFL certificate needed as volunteers do not replace teachers but assist them, encouraging students to practise their English language skills and motivating them to learn more.

DURATION AND TIME OF PLACEMENTS: 1 week–1 year; typically 2–3 months.

SELECTION PROCEDURES AND ORIENTATION: application can be made online. Volunteers can be placed at short notice but 2–3 months advance warning preferred.

COST: €200 for 1 week, €500 for 1 month, €250 per month if staying 6 months or more. Fees include orientation, pre-arranged accommodation, travel within the project and support before and during the stay.

CONTACT: Sabine Lindemann, Project Manager.

TIBET

Tibet (known as Xizang province in Mandarin) in the far west of China, has fascinated people in the West for centuries and until 1986 was inaccessible to the outside world. On the highest plateau in the world and encompassing a large section of the Himalayan mountains, Tibet offers something quite different from the rest of China, especially in terms of teaching English. Tibet's former isolation has created a population hungry to communicate with the outside world for the first time and there is a huge demand to learn English, also fuelled by increasing numbers of visitors to the area, something that is set to increase thanks to the controversial Lhasa Express, an ambitious rail link between Tibet and mainland China.

The EFL industry in Tibet, currently in its infancy, can only expand in the future, if given the chance. However, the recent fatal clash between Chinese protestors and the authorities in China suggests that political instability may continue to affect the region.

Currently, there are very few official positions for teachers in the Tibet autonomous region, due at least in part to the labyrinthine red tape involved in obtaining a work permit, and paranoia in official Chinese circles that foreigners will fill the heads of Tibetans with Western ideology. Most EFL teachers therefore enter Tibet as volunteers. Tibet covers a vast area of land, larger than Germany, France and Italy combined, yet it is still one of the poorest areas in the world. China has invested heavily in Tibet over the past six years, and its economy has apparently maintained 12% growth year-on year since 2001 (Chinese figures), but basic problems such as providing access to water and a shortage of doctors and qualified teachers takes time to remedy, as well as the political will to make sure that aid reaches Tibetans who need it most.

VOLUNTEERING AS AN ENGLISH TEACHER IN TIBET CAN THEREFORE BE A VERY REWARDING EXPERIENCE AS DARIN WAHL, AN INTREPID TRAVELLER WHO SPENT SOME MONTHS VOLUNTEERING AS AN ENGLISH TEACHER IN TIBET DISCOVERED:
I worked with Tibetan children in an orphanage/special school. There were about 12–25 students in each class, many of whom had varying disabilities, but their attitudes and those of the other children made the hardships of Tibet (the cold, altitude sickness, the poverty) all worthwhile. Tibetans are not crippled by the stigmas that the western world imposes on those with mental or physical disabilities, nor are they ashamed or made to feel so by society. The attitude was 'If you can talk you can sing; if you can walk you can dance', and they did. On top of this, the children were incredibly self-disciplined, they were interested and they were interesting.

It is possible to enquire about voluntary positions once in Lhasa. Darin Wahl was pointed in the direction of the Lhasa Jatson Chumig Welfare Special School (Bariku Road, PO Box 101, Lhasa, Tibet, PR China; ✆ 916 851043; contact Tenzin Choedrun, Academic Co-ordinator). Alternatively, you can do some online research before arriving. The website www.volunteertibet.org has an EFL bulletin board advertising a range of voluntary English teaching positions in the autonomous province. The majority of people, however, organise their placement with an organisation prior to arrival. Many volunteer organisations are active in Tibet and they are able to place teachers in an appropriate school or orphanage and arrange a visa for the desired length of stay (visa extensions in Tibet are notoriously difficult to obtain and many applicants are lucky to get 10 days). Some organisations require TEFL qualifications, but the majority are happy to take on any native English speakers.

One organisation worth approaching is Global Crossroad (11822 Justice Avenue, Suite A-5, Baton Rouge, LA 70816, USA; ✆ 225 295 4950; fax: 225 295 4954; info@globalcrossroad.com; www.globalcrossroad.com), which offers placements teaching English to poor, destitute and disabled children aged from 6–13 years. Placements last from 2–10 weeks and involve 20–30 hours of teaching per week. Room and board with a host family are provided.

VOLUNTEER TEACHING POSITIONS IN TIBET OFTEN INVOLVE ONLY 18–25 HOURS A WEEK, LEAVING TEACHERS FREE TO EARN A LITTLE SPENDING MONEY BY OFFERING PRIVATE LESSONS, AS DARIN WAHL DISCOVERED:

There is no lack of opportunity for those interested in private tutoring. Even just putting up a sign will generate more than sufficient interest. The only problem is that few Tibetans have enough money to spend on luxuries such as schooling and it would be difficult to generate enough income to cover your living costs in Lhasa.

Those looking for paid teaching work in a school will find that salaries are low (local Tibetan teachers receive just US$2–US$3 per day) and will have trouble staying on the right side of the law. Work permits are very hard to get, especially for American citizens. It seems that while foreigners can teach in Tibet, they can only do so in Lhasa and currently there are only two institutions in the city where people can teach officially: Tibet University (Foreign Affairs Office, Tibet University, Lhasa, Tibet 850000, PR China; ✆ 891 6331024/6321247; fax: 891 6334489; fsd@utibet.edu.cn; www.utibet.edu.cn) and the Tibet Academy of Social Sciences.

There are, however, a number of schools in Lhasa where foreigners teach without a work permit, but they generally do not advertise and tend to be slightly suspicious when approached. Public schools can be crowded, and the teaching difficult, with up to 50 students to a class. Generally, the schools are clean and well-run, but they struggle to provide the necessary resources.

Teaching in Tibet promises to be an exciting and rewarding experience, as Darin Wahl puts it: '*Only a lucky few get to spend as much time here, to meet as many smiling faces and to be shown such kindness as teachers do*'.

LATIN AMERICA

Spanning 75 degrees of latitude, the mammoth continent of South America together with the Caribbean islands and the eight countries of Central America, offer an eclectic range of teaching opportunities. With the important exception of Brazil where Portuguese is spoken, most South American countries have a majority of Spanish speakers and, as in Spain itself, there is a great demand for English teaching, from dusty Mexican towns near the American border to Punta Arenas at the southern extremity of the continent, south of the Falkland Islands.

The countries of most interest to the travelling teacher are Chile, Argentina, Colombia, Ecuador, Venezuela, Brazil and Mexico. Certain patterns emerged during the research for this book, though sweeping generalisations are of limited value and will not apply to all countries and all situations. Inflation is still a problem for many of the nations of Latin America, which means that salaries quickly lose their value unless there are frequent adjustments. Although pay scales are often quoted in US dollars, wages are almost always paid in the local currency, which in many cases is worth little outside the country.

Urban life in the big cities of Brazil and Chile is more like that of Europe than of developing countries. In such cities, the greatest demand for English comes from big business, and because of the strong commercial links between the two American continents, the demand tends to be for American English, though an increasing number of British and Australian teachers are finding work in these countries.

Among the most important providers of the English language are Bi-National Centers and Cultural Centers, the American counterpart of the British Council. There are scores of these centres in Latin America, including over 60 in Brazil including the sub-network, plus about 16 in Argentina and seven in Mexico. A complete list (under the rather worrying heading 'American Republics' instead of 'Latin America') is available from the US Department of State, Cultural and Binational Centers, English Teaching Fellow Program. Contact information for the individual binational centres can be obtained from the website http://exchanges.state.gov/education/engteaching. These centres are all engaged in the teaching of English, some on such a large scale that they employ more than 20 teachers. While some want a commitment from teachers to stay for two years, others are happy to take someone on for shorter periods or part-time. While some require teachers with a BA/MA in TESL from a US university, others are looking for no more than a good command of English (whatever the accent).

Britain also has cultural representatives in nine Latin American nations. The longest established Culturas Inglesas are in Argentina, Brazil, Chile, Mexico, Peru and Uruguay, with Costa Rica, Paraguay and Guatemala having joined the list more recently. These Cultural Associations aim to teach English within the framework of British culture and work closely with the British Council and represent the elite end of the market. Usually they require their teachers to have specialised ELT training and experience. Only a few recruit abroad so it is worth making local enquiries on arrival.

Several South American nations have a number of British or American-style bilingual schools and *colegios*. Although this book is not centrally concerned with English-medium schools, which are usually looking for teachers with a PGCE or full teacher accreditation, international schools in South America are mainly for local nationals (rather than expatriates) who want a bilingual Spanish-English education and have a very strong emphasis on English language teaching. Despite the prestige of these schools, some are willing to consider EFL teachers who have not done teacher training. For example, many of them accept school leavers participating in gap year projects.

Finally, there are private and commercial language institutes from International House (Argentina, Chile, Colombia, Costa Rica, Mexico) through Berlitz (which is strongly represented in Latin America) to the cowboy operations where standards and wages will be extremely low. **David Hewitt**, a computer programmer from Yorkshire with no TEFL training or experience, was surprised not only to walk into a teaching job in Brazil but also to find himself giving lessons to the director of the school.

In whatever kind of school you teach, or if you just give occasional private lessons to contacts, you will probably find the local people extremely friendly and eager to help. The ethnic diversity and Latin warmth encountered by foreign teachers and travellers throughout the continent usually more than compensate for low wages and (in the big cities) a high crime rate.

PROSPECTS FOR TEACHERS

In a land where baseball is a passion and US television enormously popular, American (and also Canadian) job-seekers have an advantage. The whole continent is culturally and economically oriented towards the States. There is a decided preference among language learners for the American accent and for American teaching materials and course books, which explains why so many language institutes are called Lincoln and Jefferson. Business English is gaining ground throughout the region, particularly in Argentina, Chile, Venezuela, Colombia, Brazil and Mexico, and anyone with a business background will have an edge over the competition.

The academic year begins in February or early March and lasts until November/December. In the southernmost nations of Chile and Argentina, January and February are very slack months for language schools; while further north in Bolivia, for example, the summer holiday consists of December/January. The best time to arrive to look for work is a few weeks before the end of the summer holidays. But many institutes run eight to 12 week courses year round and will be eager for the services of a native speaker whatever the time of year.

> **VERY SELDOM IN LATIN AMERICA WILL YOU FIND THE GLUT OF TEACHERS YOU FIND ELSEWHERE IN THE WORLD, AS NICK BRANCH FOUND:**
> *English teachers are still much in demand in South America, probably because fewer native speakers visit this region than other parts of the world, due to the perception by many that it is the world's most dangerous/corrupt continent – partly true, but hugely exaggerated in the minds of many. I had no problems at all in South America. One just has to be a little more vigilant than usual.*

FINDING A JOB

Speculative enquiries from EFL teachers are much less likely to work if sent before arrival than after, although sending a 'warm-up' CV may help your job search. What the principal of a girls' school in Lima wrote to us is echoed by many other institutes. '*Anyone interested in a job is welcome to write to me at any time. If they happen to be in Lima they are equally welcome to come into school.*' Unless you are very well qualified or have met your prospective employer before, you are unlikely to be offered a contract while out of the country. This is unfortunate since work visas are best applied for in the country of origin of the teacher (see below).

IN ADVANCE

Very few Latin American language schools advertise in the UK press. Even the most prestigious schools complain of the difficulties they encounter recruiting teachers abroad, mainly due to the low salaries they can offer and the very bureaucratic procedures for obtaining a work permit. Some British Council offices in South America keep lists of schools, as do some embassies and consulates in London and Washington. When 20-year-old **James Gratton** was making plans for his first trip to South America, he wrote to all the embassies in London and received quite a lot of literature, including a number of lists of language schools, for Paraguay, Uruguay, Peru, etc. He claims that the Argentinian Embassy was particularly helpful and friendly. Serious candidates might ask the Cultural Attaché for advice.

Language school chains and organisations which might be of assistance to qualified British TEFL teachers are International House, Berlitz and Wall Street Institutes. Saxoncourt Recruitment is occasionally active in several countries of South America (see chapter Finding a Job in part 1) and sometimes recruits on behalf of Culturas Inglesas and international schools. i-to-i (www.i-to-i.com) sends paying volunteers to teach in Argentina, Brazil, Costa Rica, Ecuador and Peru, while Travellers Worldwide (www.travellersworldwide.com) offers the opportunity for unpaid volunteers to teach in Argentina, Brazil, Bolivia, Peru and Guatemala.

TEFL training colleges in the USA often have close ties with Latin American language schools. The training centres in the USA such as Transworld Schools send large numbers of their graduates to posts in South America.

The British Council arranges for language assistants to work in a number of Latin American countries for an academic year. Applicants must be aged 20–30 with at least A Level Portuguese or Spanish. The level of placements and the nature of the duties are more suited to graduates than undergraduates. Application forms are available from October; the deadline is 1 December of the academic year preceding placement.

The Association of American Schools in South America (AASSA, 12333 NW 18th Street, Suite 5, Pembroke Pines, FL 33026; ✆ 954 436 4034; info@aassa.com; www.aassa.com) coordinates teacher recruitment for its 40 members, all American-international schools in 14 Latin American countries. Candidates who attend a recruiting fair in December must be state-certified teachers. There is a US$100 registration fee and if you are hired your school pays a US$250–US500 placement fee.

The TESOL Placement Bulletin carries occasional notices of vacancies in South American schools. A few schools, including some of the biggest Bi-National Centers, attend TESOL Conventions. South American Explorers (formerly the South American Explorers' Club) keeps lists of schools which employ English teachers. They have a volunteer database for members to access with information about volunteering opportunities throughout South America. Many of the organisations listed will take on English teachers without TEFL certification. Membership costs US$50 per year and residents outside the USA pay an additional US$10 for postage. Contact SAE for further details (26 Indian Creek Road, Ithaca, NY 14850; ✆ 607 277 0488; fax 607 277 6122; explorer@saexplorers.org/ don@saexplorers.org; www.saexplorers.org).

Africa & Asia Venture Ltd. (10 Market Place, Devizes, Wiltshire SN10 1HT, UK; ✆ 01380 729009; fax 01380 720060; av@aventure.co.uk; www.aventure.co.uk) runs a voluntary scheme in Mexico. The scheme runs for four months and involves assisting teachers at primary and secondary schools. The cost of this scheme at the time of writing is £2,975, which includes orientation, accommodation and food except during independent group travel, insurance and back-up support but not flights, visas or drinks.

MondoChallenge sends volunteer teachers to projects in the Elqui Valley of Chile and in the Andes or on the coast of Ecuador. The work is mainly in primary schools for a minimum of 8 weeks (Ecuador) or ten weeks (Chile). Knowledge of Spanish is essential and the company arranges host-family accommodation.

Other voluntary and international exchange organisations involved in arranging for young people to do some English tutoring include WorldTeach with programmes in Costa Rica, Chile, Ecuador and AmeriSpan in Philadelphia (215 751 1100; www.amerispan.com) which is primarily a language training organisation but which arranges internships in education and other fields, lasting two weeks to six months, in many Spanish-speaking countries.

ON THE SPOT

The concept of 'job vacancy' is very fluid in many Latin American language institutes and, provided you are willing to work for local teaching wages, you should be able to create your own job almost anywhere. As throughout the world, local applicants often break into the world of language teaching gradually by teaching a few classes a week. Non-contractual work is almost always offered on an unofficial part-time basis. So if you are trying to earn a living you will have to patch together enough hours from various sources. Finding the work is simply a matter of asking around and knocking on enough doors. For those who speak no Spanish, the first hurdle is to communicate your request to the secretaries at language schools since they invariably speak no English. Try to memorise a polite request in Spanish to pass your CV (*hoja de vida*) and letter (in Spanish if possible) to the school director who will know at least some English. Try to charm the receptionist, librarian or English language officer at the British Council, Bi-National Center or any other institute (such as South American Explorers in Peru and Ecuador) which might have relevant contacts or a useful notice board. Check advertisements in the English language press such as *The News* in Mexico City or the *Buenos Aires Herald*. English language bookshops are another possible source of teaching leads.

Ask in expatriate bars and restaurants, check out any building claiming to be an 'English School', however dubious looking, and in larger cities try deciphering the telephone directory for schools or agencies which might be able to use your services. There is more competition as well as more opportunities in the major cities (for example it is said that up to half a million Americans live in Mexico City), so if you are having difficulties rounding up work, you could try smaller towns and cities off the beaten track.

The crucial factor in becoming accepted as an English teacher at a locally run language school may not be your qualifications or your accent as much as your appearance. You must look as neat and well-dressed as teachers are expected to look, at least when you're job-hunting. Later your standards might slip a little; **Nick Wilson** who taught for two years in Mexico says that it is easy to spot the English teachers in banks and office buildings; they're the ones wearing jeans, T-shirts and carrying cassettes.

FREELANCE TEACHING

In most Latin American cities, there is a thriving market in private English lessons, which usually pay at least half as much again as working for an institute. It is not uncommon for teachers to consider the language school which hires them as a stepping stone to setting up as a private tutor. After they have familiarised themselves with some teaching materials and made enough contacts among local language learners, they strike out on their own, though this is far from easy unless you can get by in the local language and also have a telephone and suitable premises. Clients can be found by advertising in the quality press, by placing notices on strategic notice boards or by handing out business cards. If the latter, use the local method of address and omit confusing initials such as BA after your name: teachers often call themselves *Profesor* or *Profesora*.

REGULATIONS

Of course requirements vary from country to country but the prospects are dismal for teachers who insist on doing everything by the book. It is standard for work visas to be available only to fully qualified and experienced teachers on long-term contracts. Often you will have to present an array of documents, from university certificates and transcripts to FBI clearance, which have been authenticated by your consulate abroad or by the consulate of the host country. Although many schools will not offer a contract before interview and then will make it contingent on a work permit, the procedures should be started in the teacher's country of origin, which makes the whole business very difficult. All of this can take as long as six months or even a year and involve a great deal of hassle and expense, not least for the employer.

The upshot is that a high percentage of teachers work unofficially throughout Latin America. It is hardly an issue in some countries, for example virtually no one gets a work permit in Brazil, not even long-resident language school teachers and no one seems to worry about it. Teaching on a tourist visa or as a 'tourist' in countries where you don't need a visa, is a widespread practice in Mexico and Peru. Brazil is much stricter: all exchanges of money are supposed to be accompanied by receipts, which is likely to make life more difficult for casual teachers. Even if you have all the documentation, it can cost US$4,000 and take five months. There are ways round the regulations, for example to work on a student/trainee/cultural exchange visa (as in Ecuador or Venezuela).

CONDITIONS OF WORK

The problem of low wages has already been emphasised, and is even worse when inflation is rising. It is customary to be quoted a wage in American dollars (often in the range US$3–US$5 per hour) and to be paid the equivalent in the local currency. Assuming you are able to save any of your earnings, you will be unable to convert it into a hard currency except on the black market.

Some schools offer perks such as 14-month salaries or return flights to teachers who stay for a two-year contract. Contracts are fairly hard to come by and almost always require a minimum commitment of a year. The advantages are that you are guaranteed a certain income and you have a chance of applying for a work permit.

Teachers without the CELTA or Trinity Certificate are not greatly disadvantaged, partly because this qualification is not as widely known in Latin America as it is in Europe. One exception might be in Uruguay where two institutes offer the Trinity Certificate in TESOL, including the Dickens Institute Montevideo. Many institutes offer their own compulsory pre-job training (to be taken at the teacher's own expense), which provides a useful orientation for new arrivals.

One of the seldom-mentioned perks of teaching in Latin America is the liveliness and enthusiasm of the pupils. Brazilian students have been described as the 'world's most communicative students' and classrooms around the continent often take on the atmosphere of a party. You may also be dazzled by the level of knowledge of Western pop culture, and should be prepared to have your ignorance shown up. Also be prepared to lose their attention if a lesson coincides with a major sporting event.

LEISURE

Whether you are a serious student of Spanish or a frivolous seeker after the excitement generated by Latin carnivals, South America is a wonderful place to live in and travel. Women teachers may find the machismo a little hard to take, but will soon learn how to put it in its place. If you want to travel around, the annually revised *South American Handbook* definitely justifies the initial outlay of £20.

ARGENTINA

The teaching market in Argentina is ticking over without being really buoyant. Hundreds of institutes operate at varying standards. The economy is recovering well, with average growth forecast at between 4% and 5%. The exchange rate is quite convenient for both European and American citizens with roughly 3 pesos to the US dollar and 5 pesos to the euro. However, getting paid in pesos can be a problem, because inflation is still high at more than 10%. Economists predict that if the government doesn't act, it could go higher.

Although language schools, many of which specialise in the business market, have not really made a full recovery from the last deep recession (1999–2002) there is cause for some optimism. Teachers are most likely to secure a job once they are in Argentina.

Several companies accept untrained teachers as interns, who are given free board and lodging with a family, free Spanish tuition, a small stipend and plenty of opportunities to travel and see the country. For example Road2Argentina in Buenos Aires (✆ 11 48213271; www.road2argentina.com) offers cultural exchange and language immersion programmes in which international interns of any nationality undertake various placements in and around the capital, including some as ESL teachers (for which no knowledge of Spanish is required). Participants stay with families for between one and six months and take up various extracurricular activities such as tango lessons, cookery and photography. ESL programme fees start at US$975. Road2Argentina also offers a four-week TEFL training course costing from US$1,975, including accommodation in a student residence or other options.

Another company that offers TEFL training is TEFLocal (www.teflocal.net) which also offers cultural immersion, local advice, tours and Spanish courses (see entry in Training Directory). EBC in Buenos Aires (www.teflgap.org or www.ebc-tefl-course.com) also offers a month-long course followed by a job placement programme.

Many companies are located in the outskirts of Buenos Aires, a city whose area is larger than London's. It can sometimes take more than an hour to reach some companies from downtown (where teachers might live) by bus, so make sure you negotiate a block of three hours minimum in one place, or it may not be worth your while. Language schools are linked from www.inglesnet.com, which also has a decent community section. Courses in Argentina tend to start in March and finish in December. The hourly wage for starting teachers is usually between 20 and 24 Argentine pesos, currently equivalent to US$6.50–US$7.50. Job seekers can try the *Buenos Aires Herald*, which accepts advertisements for English teachers and there is a useful notice board in El Ateneo, the English language bookshop at 340 Calle Florida (the main shopping street). For information on other English language bookshops, often good places to meet native speakers and to discover informal opportunities, download Buenos Aires' Brilliant Bookshops (http://argentinastravel.com/downloads/bookstore-guide.pdf). Another contact point is the Instituto de Lengua Espanola para Extranjeros or ILEE where many foreign residents take Spanish classes.

Bi-national Centers (Instituto de Intercambio Cultural Argentino-Americano) offer English courses, as do the two International House schools in the capital (located in Recoleta and Belgrano). To work at one of these, you normally have to have worked for IH before. A large number of full-curriculum private schools prepare students for Cambridge and other exams, such as the Belgrano Day School (Juramento 3035, (c1428doa) Ciudad de Buenos Aires; ✆ 11 4781 6011/11 4781 0011; www.bds.edu.ar), which has pupils from kindergarten to school leaving age.

IT IS COMMONPLACE FOR AMERICANS AND BRITONS TO MOVE FROM LEARNING SPANISH TO TEACHING ENGLISH ACCORDING TO RICHARD FERGUSON, A NEW ZEALANDER WHO TRAVELLED EXTENSIVELY IN SOUTH AMERICA IN 2008:

Right now I'm in Buenos Aires. There are heaps of English schools and everyone wants to learn English. I made a few basic signs in Spanish advertising conversational classes, stuck them around Palermo (a wealthier suburb) and sometimes I'll stand on a busy corner and hand out leaflets. I'm charging about 30 pesos an hour and have a few students already so it's a good bet. I think any native speaker can teach here, better with experience and better still with qualifications. Either do as I did, approach some schools or look in the papers in the jobs section. I saw at least 15 in one edition of the Buenos Aires Herald.

LUKE MCELDERRY FROM TEXAS AND HIS GIRLFRIEND JENNY JACOBI SPENT HOURS RESEARCHING POTENTIAL TEACHING EMPLOYERS IN BUENOS AIRES ON THE INTERNET. AFTER COMPLETING A TRAINING COURSE WITH TEFLOCAL, HE SENT A MASS EMAIL WITH CV ATTACHED TO AT LEAST 40 ADDRESSES AND WAITED FOR RESPONSES TO TRICKLE IN, AND ENDED UP HEARING FROM ABOUT A QUARTER. HE DESCRIBES HIS JOB HUNT:

The first interviews were varied, some in English, one in Spanish, but all fairly casual. Most take 30 minutes and they seem to care more about your availability than your experience. I was asked a couple of times if I had any visa/permit and said no, and the employers didn't seem to care at all. I have heard the biggest institutes are the ones who care, and ironically pay the least!

Before long, they were both working for an institute (Speak Spanish which also teaches English; www.speakspanish.com.ar) which sent them out to teach classes in businesses. Sometimes they were assigned to comfortable conference rooms with whiteboards, free photocopies, faxes and coffee.

LUKE MCELDERRY AND JENNY JACOBI FOUND THAT ALL WENT SMOOTHLY, APART FROM FINDING ACCOMMODATION:

It is a real hassle finding an apartment as they want to charge you tourist rates and it is nearly impossible to get a lease as an ex-pat. Accommodation prices depend on your ability to find a rental agency that doesn't require a garantía from an Argentine property owner saying that you will pay the entire rental term in full; some places will let you pay everything up front, usually six months or more, but these places are very few and far between.

> **ALICIA META OF ACM BUSINESS ENGLISH, BUENOS AIRES, EXPLAINS HOW THE LETTING MARKET WORKS:**
>
> *A one-bedroom apartment in a decent neighbourhood might now cost U$S 1,000 if it is furnished, if not, around US$600. If it is a short contract, the agents will ask you to pay in full. For a short-term contract you also have to pay a commission to the real estate agency of about 8% of the total amount. For a one-year contract the commission is the equivalent of one and a half months of the rent to be paid. The deposit for a long-term contract (one year) is equal to two months rent. It is always returned once the deal is over.*
>
> *It is difficult for tourists to rent an apartment and unfortunately I believe that there is no other way out. My advice would be to get some feedback before coming to Argentina, go to a hostel and then calmly try to look for the best option. Usually, apartments in the outskirts of Buenos Aires can be cheaper but the payment method might not differ.*

RED TAPE

Working papers can be obtained from the National Direction of Migrations by employers, though a school will be willing only for long-term propositions. It will be necessary for the applicant to provide a contract of employment for a minimum of a year, and birth certificate (notarised by a notary public in Argentina), as well as passport. Non-British passport holders must also provide a certificate of good conduct from the police authorities in his or her country or countries of residence in the five years prior to applying.

The Argentine Embassy in London states on their website that British nationals (and also US nationals) do not need a tourist visa to enter Argentina for up to 90 days, which can be extended for another 90 days at the Dirección Nacional de Migraciones.

Most teachers are paid hourly by the language institutes employing them. Self-employed people are obliged to register with the DGI (tax office) and pay approximately 15% of their full-time earnings in tax.

LIST OF EMPLOYERS

ACM BUSINESS ENGLISH
Viamonte 2660, Buenos Aires
11 155 025 4752 (mobile); fax 11 4961 3421
info@acmbusinessenglish.com.ar
www.acmbusinessenglish.com.ar

NUMBER OF TEACHERS: 3–4.
PREFERENCE OF NATIONALITY: USA, UK, Canada. A strong Australian accent is usually difficult for Latin Americans to understand.
QUALIFICATIONS: TEFL, ESL or equivalent. Experience teaching ESL to adults in companies needed. Candidates with a teaching degree are the most sought after. General knowledge and high intellectual level needed for training executives who will be dealing with native speakers at headquarters.
CONDITIONS OF EMPLOYMENT: no contracts. Part-time work so people are self-employed. Most teachers intend to stay in the country for at least one year, starting in March. Courses in Argentina start in March and finish in December. Usually 2–3 hours twice a week teaching in different companies. Usually a block of 3 hours minimum in one place is offered.
SALARY: between 20 and 24 pesos per hour, paid at the beginning of the following month.
FACILITIES/SUPPORT: no training given. No assistance with accommodation.

RECRUITMENT: word of mouth/posting on international websites, and in the *Buenos Aires Herald* (local English newspaper). Interviews in Buenos Aires.

CONTACT: Alicia Meta, Director.

THE AMERICAN TRAINING CO

Av. Santa Fe 3192 Piso 10º 'B' (1425) Buenos Aires

☎ 11 5290 5202/3; fax ext 6

✉ contactenos@americantrainingco.com.ar

🖥 www.americantrainingco.com.ar

NUMBER OF TEACHERS: 20 +.

PREFERENCE OF NATIONALITY: none.

QUALIFICATIONS: TESL Certificate or similar, university degree (preferably in humanities, eg English, literature), experience in personal teaching of foreigners, at least for a number of hours in the teacher training school.

CONDITIONS OF EMPLOYMENT: no contract, as it is all part-time work in businesses. However, most teachers work at least 25 hours a week. The usual hours are early mornings, lunchtimes and evenings. All students are adults in businesses.

SALARY: 22 pesos per hour.

RECRUITMENT: through teacher training schools. Interview are essential and take place in Buenos Aires, after arrival.

CONTACT: Evelina Fleischer, Director.

COLONIAS DE INMERSION AL IDIOMA (CII)

Casilla de Correo 044, Sucursal Plaza Italia, 1425 Buenos Aires

☎ +/fax 11 4831 8152

✉ info@coloniasdeinmersionalidioma.com or exchange@ecolonias.com

🖥 www.coloniasdeinmersionalidioma.com

NUMBER OF TEACHERS: 25–35 per semester.

PREFERENCE OF NATIONALITY: any English-speaking country.

QUALIFICATIONS: university students and graduates aged 20–26, no specific qualifications or experience required.

CONDITIONS OF EMPLOYMENT: 3–12 months, preferably starting 10 March or 25 July. Most schools prefer applicants who can commit to at least 4 months. Schedules vary from school to school. Total of 25 hours a week.

SALARY: small stipend. The programme provides homestay accommodation with full board, Spanish coaching, opportuni-

ties to travel around Argentina and Chile making use of CII's network of schools and families.

FACILITIES/SUPPORT: TEFL training given on arrival as well as Spanish Immersion Programme. Spanish coaching throughout placement. Exchange students enter the country on a 3-month tourist visa which is automatically renewed when leaving the country on a day trip.

RECRUITMENT: through cooperating universities and the internet. Interviews sometimes carried out in the UK and Ireland.

CONTACT: Fernando Damian Carro or Silvia von Lurzer, Programme Coordinators.

CONNECTING SCHOOLS TO THE WORLD

Luis Maria Campos 545 1 D

✉ connectingschools@gmail.com

🖥 www.connectingschools.com.ar

NUMBER OF TEACHERS: 16 teachers per year. All placed in different towns.

PREFERENCE OF NATIONALITY: any English-speaking country.

QUALIFICATIONS: university graduates.

CONDITIONS OF EMPLOYMENT: teaching periods of 1–2 semesters. 25 hours of work per week. First semester starts in March and second in July.

SALARY: Homestay in Argentine family, private Spanish tutoring, round trip bus ticket from Buenos Aires to location, US$100 monthly stipend.

FACILITIES/SUPPORT: 1 week of intensive ESL training on arrival. Supervision and help with lesson planning throughout.

RECRUITMENT: via internet. Resumé, list of references and a telephone interview with director required.

CONTACT: Cristina Rapela, Director.

GIC ARGENTINA

Lavalle 397 – 1 – 1, Buenos Aires, C1047AAG

☎ /fax 11 4902 5153

✉ info@gicarg.org

🖥 www.gicarg.org

NUMBER OF TEACHERS: 10.

PREFERENCE OF NATIONALITY: none.

QUALIFICATIONS: none.

CONDITIONS OF EMPLOYMENT: 3 month contracts offered. To work 20 hours per week.

SALARY: Unpaid (internships).

FACILITIES/SUPPORT: Accommodation provided in a student dorm or with host families.

RECRUITMENT: Interview required.

CONTACT: Graciela Cerquatti, Director.

INTERACTION LANGUAGE STUDIO
Av. L. N. Alem 428 6 I, Buenos Aires 1003
- +11 4311 7220; fax 11 4312 1376
- info@interactionls.com
- www.interactionls.com

NUMBER OF TEACHERS: 5–8.

PREFERENCE OF NATIONALITY: USA or UK.

QUALIFICATIONS: TEFL certificate and some teaching experience.

CONDITIONS OF EMPLOYMENT: contracts from March to December. Usual hours 3–20 a week.

SALARY: 16 pesos per hour (around US$5).

RECRUITMENT: CV by mail, interview and mock or admission lesson. Interviews essential.

CONTACT: Professor Virginia López Grisolia, Director of Studies and Owner.

INTERCHANGE LANGUAGE SERVICE
Perú 84 – 5to. Piso – Of. 74, 1084 Capital Federal, Buenos Aires
- /fax 11 4345 3132/7979
- andresf@interchangels.com.ar
- www.interchangels.com.ar

NUMBER OF TEACHERS: up to 5.

PREFERENCE OF NATIONALITY: none; diversity of accent appreciated.

QUALIFICATIONS: experience of business and business English would be helpful.

FACILITIES/SUPPORT: can sometimes offer accommodation at low prices (40–50 minutes travelling from downtown). Pleasant accommodation available near the school for US$300 a month.

RECRUITMENT: spontaneous CVs and local interviews (or via video-cam and/or phone).

CONTACT: Andrés Figueroa, Executive Director.

BOLIVIA

Even the poorest of Latin American nations offers reasonable possibilities to EFL teachers, provided you are prepared to accept a low wage. In contrast to the standard hourly wage of US$15–US$20 per hour in Santiago or Brasilia, the wages paid by language schools in Bolivia are about 14 bolivianos (US$2 at the time of writing). However, a lot of businesses choose to pay their employees in dollars, so how much you earn can depend a lot on the current exchange rate.

Many teachers touring South America prefer Bolivia for cultural reasons. La Paz is a city with a low cost of living and a colourful social mix. The class structure is immediately apparent with the upper class consisting of people of Spanish descent, the middle class or *mestizos* of mixed Spanish/Bolivian ancestry and the underclass of Indians still wearing their traditional costume. Bolivia may have preserved its traditional culture more successfully than other Latin American countries, but the inequality of wealth distribution has led socialist president Evo Morales to implement stringent wealth distribution measures, including nationalising much of the energy industry. Four of the country's wealthiest regions, including Santa Cruz, have been threatening (or declaring) autonomy in protest. It is an interesting political situation.

Only a handful of language schools and a couple of *colegios* (private schools) are listed in the La Paz *Yellow Pages* (www.guia-amarilla.com) and they are unlikely to commit themselves to hiring a teacher without meeting them first. Terms normally last from early February to early September, resuming at the end of September to the beginning of December. The biggest language school in the country is the ultra respectable Centro Boliviano Americano or CBA (Parque Iturralde Zenón 121, La Paz; +2 243 0107; http://cba.edu.bo) with three other locations in La Paz plus schools in other cities such as Sucre, Cochabamba (www.cbacoch.org) and Santa Cruz (see entry below). Despite its name it hires British and Irish native speakers as well.

Colegios employ native speakers for their English departments and tend to pay as much as twice as much as the private language schools. Also, the hours of 8.30am–1.30pm are more convenient. Jonathan Alderman was happy to put up with low pay in exchange for the excellent quality of life he found in Bolivia, which he says '*can feel like an idyllic paradise sometimes, because of the climate*'. He did things that would be unimaginable at home such as swimming in a pool (in Oruro) whose waters were heated underground by a volcano, attending one of the many carnivals in February and throwing water balloons at the locals.

> *I first went to Cochabamba as a volunteer to give conversation classes in the city's public university, San Simon. This was through Projects Abroad (www.projects-abroad.co.uk). Everything was organised for me before I arrived, including accommodation and Spanish lessons. This was a great gentle introduction for someone new to the city and to teaching. In the university it is easy to settle in and make friends very quickly.*
>
> *That only lasted for a few months, but I was sufficiently taken with Cochabamba to want to go back the following January. Before arriving, I had already fixed myself up with a job teaching at the Pan American English Center, which was a genuinely enjoyable place to work because of the relaxed atmosphere. But I became fed up with being paid late and left after only a couple of months to travel a bit. I wasn't breaking any contract, as there was none.*
>
> *I came back to Cochabamba after a little while exploring South America and took a job in another institute, El Britanico Boliviano de Cultura (BBC, Calle España 171, Cochabamba; ℅ +422 0936; britanicoboliviano@hotmail.com). This was much better paid, at US$3.50 an hour. The lessons were mostly in the evening, but I was lucky to get some one-to-one classes through the school to teach during the day as well. This school was professionally run and the director paid me on the last day of the month without any hassle. In this school I also taught mostly adults rather than kids. One thing that makes this school stand out from the many others in Cochabamba is the strong emphasis on British rather than American English (as the name would suggest). This is the only institute in Cochabamba where students can take Cambridge exams. BBC often finds it quite hard recruiting teachers, simply because it is difficult to attract teachers to Bolivia due to the low salaries.*
>
> *I would highly recommend staying and working in Bolivia – and if you are staying in Bolivia, it just has to be Cochabamba, because of the perfect spring-like climate. Teaching Bolivian students can be very fun, though the kids can be boisterous (I especially found teenage boys to be a pain . . .). When teaching adults, it was nice to be able to establish friendships with the students. I obviously made a very positive impression with one class of students I taught for four months at the BBC, because when I left they presented me with a most ornate chess set (with many of the pieces in the shape of native Americans or llamas) – it was the best present I think I have ever received!*

Last year Jonathan went back to Cochabamba to concentrate on teaching private classes and doing some translation work, while still teaching an hour and a half a day in the Britanico. He concluded, '*if someone wants to earn a decent wage teaching English in Bolivia, one has to turn to private classes.*' When he first arrived, he advertised in the local newspaper for private classes charging 30–35 Bolivianos an hour. He says you can expect to be approached in shops and restaurants as well as by your pupils and asked about private classes, but these will generally come from people who would find it a hardship to pay even US$2 an hour. The best place to advertise private English lessons is the Sunday edition of the newspaper *El Diario* (www.eldiario.net).

Most teachers arrive on a tourist visa (US$100 for Americans) and should in theory apply for a work visa. As Jonathan admits, most simply continue to work on a tourist visa:

This is illegal, of course, but there doesn't tend to be a great problem with it, as you are allowed four 90-day stamps in a year. In fact, schools tend to encourage their teachers to work this way, from my experience. One simply has to leave the country and return to get another tourist stamp. If I were asked questions at immigration I would say that I was working on a voluntary project in Bolivia and they would accept it. Of the people I knew who did get a long-stay visa they did it off their own bat with no help from their school as far as I know.

This year he will be going back to Bolivia to get married to his Bolivian girlfriend.

Mike Martin is another teacher who has fallen under the spell of Bolivia:

I love it here and get on very well with Bolivians. It's only fair to point out, though, that unrest is always here, and there are periodic protests and outbreaks of violence. I should also mention that I now teach free. I am in the fortunate position of being able to do this as I took early retirement and receive a pension, which goes a lot further here than at home. I reckon that you could live reasonably comfortably here for about US$600 a month, allowing US$150 for an apartment. And be prepared for lots of hassles with the immigration paperwork. When I was charging my students, I charged US$3 an hour if they could afford it. A young woman joined and wanted four hours a week tuition. A few weeks later I asked her what she was earning and she was paying me about 70 percent of her salary as a part-time professional, so I halved her fees and later halved them again. It's because of stories like this that I eventually decided to teach free. I do think that if you advertised in the local press, you would have a plentiful supply of students as most want to learn English.

LIST OF EMPLOYERS

CENTRO BOLIVIANO AMERICANO

Calle Cochabamba No. 66, Santa Cruz

- /fax 3 334 2299
- marrazola@cba.com.bo or miguelar
  razola@yahoo.com
- www.cba.com.bo

NUMBER OF TEACHERS: depends on vacancies available.

PREFERENCE OF NATIONALITY: none.

QUALIFICATIONS: must be willing and interested in teaching in Bolivia. Minimum age 21.

CONDITIONS OF EMPLOYMENT: 1 year. Candidate selects hours between 7.30am and 7.30pm.

SALARY: from US$2 an hour, with possible deductions of 12% for tax.

FACILITIES/SUPPORT: advice given on finding accommodation. Work contract supplied which can be used to apply for work visa. All teachers are required to do a 70-hour pre-teacher training course.

RECRUITMENT: personal interview required.

CONTACT: Miguel Arrazola, Academic Director.

SPEAKEASY INSTITUTE

Av. Arce 2047, La Paz

- +2 244 1779
- speakeasyinstitute@yahoo.com
- www.speakeasyinstitute.com

NUMBER OF TEACHERS: 8.

PREFERENCE OF NATIONALITY: none.

QUALIFICATIONS: minimum CELTA qualification or equivalent plus 1 year experience.

CONDITIONS OF EMPLOYMENT: 6 month to 1 year contracts available. Minimum 20 teaching hours per week. School open from 7.30am to 9pm Monday to Friday.

SALARY: 3,200 bolivianos (£225) per month.

FACILITIES/SUPPORT: Help provided with finding accommodation and getting visa.

RECRUITMENT: via internet. No interview required.

CONTACT: Robert Finestone, Academic Director, or Alix Shand, Coordinator.

BRAZIL

The stabilisation of Brazil's currency over the past few years has encouraged the market for English teaching, which is not confined to the major cities of São Paulo and Rio de Janeiro. There are about 40 SBCIs (Sociedades Brasileiras de Cultura Inglesa) and 23 ICBEUs (Instituto Cultural Brasil-Estadios Unidos) scattered all over the fifth largest country in the world. Schools in smaller places often notify cooperating institutes in the big cities of any job vacancies for native speakers. But speculative visits to towns of any size would probably be successful eventually. Any of the four British Council offices in Brazil (Brasilia, Recife, Rio and São Paulo) may be able to supply a list of Cultura Inglesas and other established schools to people who call on them. The distinguishing feature of Brazilian EFL is the high proportion of well-qualified Brazilian English teachers. Recruiting teachers from overseas is seen to be unjustifiably costly and also very difficult from the visa point of view. Only individuals with very specialised expertise are invited to work in very senior posts.

Visas are a major headache. You are permitted to stay no more than six months on a tourist visa after which you will have to leave the country (usually across the Paraguayan border) or get an extension from the Federal Police.

The Administrative Director of one of Rio de Janeiro's upmarket schools describes the difficulties:

> *Unfortunately, teaching English is not an area the government considers a priority in issuing visas. There are only two situations in which foreigners can teach in Brazil. Illegally, since there are numerous small schools who can afford to run the risk of hiring illegal foreigners. As a result, pay is usually bad and employment unstable. The alternative is available only to specialists, and is extremely rare. Because we have a webpage, I get requests from foreigners all the time. I basically tell them that it is an adventure here, only for the strong of stomach, and you have to be willing to subject yourself to the unsavoury experiences that go along with working without proper papers. I have come across dozens of foreigners who have been promised work-related visas. In 27 years of living in Brazil, I have never, not once, seen this happen. The only cases I know of where a person has taught legally, it has been when they enter the country with visas issued at the Brazilian consulate in their country of residence.*

At the prestigious end of the market, schools like the Culturas Inglesas, bi-national cultural centres do recruit outside Brazil and enable their contracted teachers to obtain permits, though it can take up to six months.

Otherwise it will be a case of looking around after you arrive, by using the *Yellow Pages*, expatriate networks or informative websites such as www.gringoes.com, run by expats. In São Paulo a good source of teaching jobs is the newspaper, *Folha de São* Paulo, on a Sunday. **Richard Jenkins**, a New Zealander who has learned Portuguese, spent time in Brazil in early 2008 but didn't pursue his idea of looking for teaching work since he decided to move on to Argentina. However he did meet an American who gave private English lessons in São Paulo charging 50 reais an hour (more than US$30). But he bemoaned the fact that the city was hard to get around (the Metro area has a population of just under 20 million) and he insisted that you need to have the students pay in advance for a few lessons. This is because Brazilians are notorious for no shows, being late or last minute cancellations (and don't see the problem) so you need to take some precautions so as not to waste your time. When job-hunting, expect to go through quite a rigorous interview procedure, as **Jon Cotterill** discovered:

> *When you drop your CV in, the school may ask you to take a written English test on the spot. This can consist of anything up to 100 questions plus a composition section. If you pass the test, you may get*

invited to a group interview, a 'dinamica de grupo'. This consists of a group of potential teachers (usually Brazilians) and you have to perform various tasks in small teams or pairs. If you are successful then you may be asked to do a two-week training course (usually unpaid). Only after all of this will you be offered work.

If you want to study Portuguese, you can apply for a student visa which would make it easier to stay on. For example, many foreigners register at the Pontificia Universidade Católica in Rio de Janeiro (Extension Department, Casa 15, Rua Marques São Vincente 225, Gávea, ✆ +22453 900 Rio; 21 529 9212). This is an excellent place to link up with students and advertise classes if you want to offer private lessons (which pay much better than working for an institute).

The best time to start work is following Carnaval which takes place during the week over Ash Wednesday every February. The well-travelled TEFLer Barry O'Leary arrived in Salvador (northern Brazil) just before Carnaval. He bought a map, borrowed a telephone directory from his hostel and walked round all the 25 language academies with his CV. His luck wasn't as quick as it had been in Ecuador (described later) because most academies couldn't tell how many students they would have until after Carnaval. But Barry managed to find an evening job at an academy outside Salvador and later found two other jobs:

I taught in three Institutes, PEC (www.pec.com.br), Okey Dokey and AEC Idiomas. The business academy sent me to various offices which were all fully equipped and well organised. Generally working conditions were excellent and so was the pay; I received about US$8 an hour which was a good rate for Brazil. The pupils were a mixed bag, yet they all had a great sense of humour and participated in the lessons, though some students were there only because their boss wanted them to be and had little interest.

I worked at another academy one afternoon a week. The approach here was to teach English through music, followed by group conversation lessons. Each week the director would translate two or three songs for the students to sing along in English. The students enjoyed this immensely, and I thought it was a very original way to learn. Most students seemed to be more interested in asking me questions about England and my life rather than pay attention to the lessons, but it was a good way for them to improve their fluency. I found Brazilian students very happy go-lucky people, they were always smiling and interested in learning English.

I was lucky enough to live in the old quarter of Salvador called Pelourino which was the hub of the nightlife, but also the hub of any trouble. I lived in a house with 15 people including Brazilians, Nigerians, French and Irish, for which I paid US$20 a month and had a brilliant three months.

AFTER 20 YEARS OF CORRESPONDING WITH A PEN FRIEND IN BRAZIL, LEE STEWART FROM NORTHAMPTONSHIRE FINALLY MADE THE JOURNEY TO SOUTHERN BRAZIL TO MEET HER:
I had no intention of working, as everyone had told me that it would not be possible to find work without speaking Portuguese. My friend works as a part-time teacher in Curitiba so I had an advantage. I approached CCLA, a very popular school in the city, and after only a five-minute chat I was offered part-time work for one or two evenings a week. The lessons comprised listening to adults having conversations in English while I waited for them to make mistakes and correct them. Teaching like this at least pays your youth hostel bills and gives you enough to eat, but you can't expect more than a few hours.

FOR CASUAL TEACHING, EXPERIENCE AND QUALIFICATIONS ARE NOT REQUIRED. JOHN BUCKLEY, OWNER OF A PRINTING BUSINESS IN BLACKPOOL, IS JUST ONE TRAVELLER WHO WAS SURPRISED AT HOW WELCOME HE WAS MADE TO FEEL BY A LANGUAGE SCHOOL WHEN HE HAD NO TEFL TRAINING OR EXPERIENCE:

When I was in Brazil for Christmas and New Year, I thought I would go to the local English school to see what went on, armed with a bunch of roses for the teacher (luckily female) and a little knowledge of Portuguese. Before I knew it, I was teaching English, words, pronunciation, slang and English life in general. This carried on for a few days with the class getting bigger and bigger. I felt like an alien landed from Mars, but what a buzz. I have found my vocation in life and am now looking for a good TEFL training course.

LIST OF EMPLOYERS

BRITANNIA SCHOOLS
Central Department, Rua General Rabelo 36,
Gávea, Rio de Janeiro, RJ-22451 010
+21 2511 0143; fax 21 2512 4707
www.britannia.com.br

Group of four high quality schools in Rio.
NUMBER OF TEACHERS: 30 native English-speaking teachers.
PREFERENCE OF NATIONALITY: British, American, Canadian.
QUALIFICATIONS: Cambridge CELTA (B Pass) or DELTA, BA and 3 years' experience required.
CONDITIONS OF EMPLOYMENT: minimum stay 10–12 months, August to June or February to December. Full-time: 25 hours per week teaching plus overall support. Students grouped according to age starting at 14–15 up to adults and executives. Schools are centres for Cambridge exams, TOEIC and London Chamber of Commerce.
SALARY: varies according to teachers' qualifications/scale.
FACILITIES/SUPPORT: subsidised assistance with accommodation provided. Orientation and teacher development provided: CELTA, DELTA and COTE courses offered.

IICA (INSTITUTO DE INTERCAMBIOS E CULTURA AMERICANA)
Avenida 29, 12541 Ituiutaba, MG 38300–114
+34 3269 6099; fax 34 3269 3505
icbeu@mgt.com.br
www.mgt.com.br/icbeu

ETP/ESL is a semi-volunteer Program to Brazil for a living/teaching/learning experience and ETP/ESL Certificate.
NUMBER OF TEACHERS: 30 openings in several host schools throughout Brazil for the ETP/ESL Certificate Program.
PREFERENCE OF NATIONALITY: USA, UK, Canada. Applicants from other English speaking countries are also considered.
CONDITIONS OF EMPLOYMENT: 6 or 12 months. 36 hours per week for English teaching or other cultural activities.
SALARY: allowance of 660 reals (US$300) per month plus room and board with family.
FACILITIES/SUPPORT: programme eligible for special trainee visa status so participants are issued with an ICL (Invitation Cultural Letter) to present to Brazilian consulate in their country.
RECRUITMENT: deadlines fall on 30 April (for August start) and 30 October for February start. Interviews not required. Application must include university transcripts.
CONTACT: Professor Jacy Pimenta, Programme Director (ETP/ESL).

NEW START COMUNICACOES Ltda.
Rua Uruguiana 10/1211, Centro, 20050 090 Rio de Janeiro, RJ
+21 2508 6917
newstart@newstart.com.br
www.newstart.com.br

NUMBER OF TEACHERS: 10–20.

PREFERENCE OF NATIONALITY: must be a native speaker of English.

QUALIFICATIONS: preferably CELTA or Trinity TESOL certificate and some classroom experience.

CONDITIONS OF EMPLOYMENT: minimum 5 months work.

Salary: 29 reals (US£9) per hour.

FACILITIES/SUPPORT: training in business English.

RECRUITMENT: direct application by CV via email and telephone.

CONTACT: Stephanie Crockett, Director of Studies.

SCHUTZ & KANOMATA ESL & PSL
Rua Galvao Costa 85, Santa Cruz do Sul 96810–170
- +51 3715 3366
- sk@sk.com.br
- www.sk.com.br/guests/sk-lcb

NUMBER OF TEACHERS: 3 every semester on Brazilian Language and Culture Program.

PREFERENCE OF NATIONALITY: Canadian, American, British.

QUALIFICATIONS: main qualification is personality; must be communicative, considerate and interested in making friends. ESL teaching experience desirable.

CONDITIONS OF EMPLOYMENT: 5 or 10 month contracts. 20 hours per week, mostly in the evenings.

SALARY: average net income above the cost of living.

FACILITIES/SUPPORT: programme provides accommodation, meals and occasional weekend tours. Advice given on appropriate visas, eg visitor visa acceptable for 5-month programme and trainee visa for 10-month one.

RECRUITMENT: strong internet exposure. Also former teacher in Canada acts as agent.

CONTACT: Ricardo Schütz, Principal.

SPEAKING–CENTRO DE CULTURA AMERICANA LTDA.
R. Cel. Renno, 321 Centro, Itajuba, Minas Gerais 37500–050
- +35 3621 3354
- speakingidiomas@walla.com
- www.speaking.com.br

NUMBER OF ESL TEACHERS: 2 per year.

PREFERENCE OF NATIONALITY: USA or Canada.

QUALIFICATIONS: TESL or similar.

CONDITIONS OF EMPLOYMENT: standard commitment February to December. 32 hours per week Monday-Friday.

SALARY: 13 reals (US$7.43) per hour net. Wage is enough for living in a small town in Brazil.

FACILITIES/SUPPORT: school provides a small furnished studio flat with utilities, housekeeper, laundry and internet connection.

RECRUITMENT: via ESL websites.

Contact: Dagmar Andrade, Director.

CHILE

Chile has an economy which is flourishing and is still attracting foreign (mainly American) investment. As commercial, touristic and cultural contacts with the outside world have increased, so has the demand for the English language. The most booming market is for business English, though there is also demand for teachers of children, created largely by the Chilean government lowering the age at which English is taught in state schools from 7th grade to 5th grade.

Several years ago there was a further push to raise the level of English language teaching in Chile, when the Ministry of Education launched a major initiative, the Programa Inglés Abre Puertas ('English Opens Doors'). This 10-year plan has four main strands: the introduction of standards of English for 8th grade and 12th grade students, and for English teachers; a massive in-service programme, including courses both in English and ELT methodology; increased support for state schools where English is taught; and the provision of English courses for small business employees. This programme is having a dramatic effect on the demand for English.

Of course most of the opportunities are in the capital Santiago where there are more than 30 major language schools, though there are some relevant institutes in the Valparaiso-Viña del Mar area. There will be less competition for teaching vacancies and a lower cost of living in smaller places like the aptly named La Serena in the dry north of the country, or other towns such as Arica, Iquique, Antofagasta, Talca, Concepció, Valdivia, Osorno and Punta Arenas, all of which have possibilities for teachers, albeit on a smaller scale. Some course providers in Santiago serve clients in Valparaiso and their teachers either commute to 'Valpo' twice a week or live there.

The prestigious Instituto Chileno-Británico de Cultura at Santa Lucía 124 in Santiago recruits only highly qualified teachers, and has a good library which incorporates the British Council's resource library for teachers; anyone prepared to pay the membership fee can borrow materials, though many schools in Santiago have good libraries themselves. Native speaker teachers are also hired by the Institutos Chileno-Britanico de Cultura in Concepcion, Arica, Viña del Mar and in a few other branches.

SOUTH AMERICAN LANGUAGE SCHOOLS TEND TO PREFER FACE-TO-FACE MEET-INGS RATHER THAN EMAILS AND PHONE CALLS. HEIDI RESETARITS TYPED 'ENGLISH SCHOOLS IN SANTIAGO' INTO A SEARCH ENGINE, CAME UP WITH A HUGE LIST OF LANGUAGE SCHOOLS IN AREAS SHE WANTED TO APPLY TO AND THEN DROPPED OFF RESUMÉS IN PERSON:

I actually got an interview on the spot at the second school I applied to ... and I happened to just walk by it – it wasn't even on my list! Santiago is a very modern city and new schools are popping up all the time. It's worth it just to walk around town and see what's there. I know that South Americans appreciate face-to-face meetings rather than emails and phone calls, so I walked in and asked to meet with a director. I decided to stay and chat a bit with the receptionist, and he made me an appointment for the next day.

The interview was a face-to-face with the director of the school (Communicorp, mentioned below). After we talked about my resumé and a bit about my teaching experience, we set up a teaching practice (he chose a topic and a student) for the next day. I got the job within 3 days.

Doug Burgess went job hunting in Santiago in 2007/8, armed with a CELTA he had acquired at home in Cambridge and some experience. He had an interview with both Burford and English First (see entry). Burford works exclusively from their own site, whereas about 60% of English First's classes are in offices. English First offered Doug a contract for 12 months with work visa and a rate of 5,500 pesos an hour, more if he had to travel more than two metro stations or worked at their other campus. Burford did not offer a contract: their rate of pay was 4,000 pesos an hour which would have gone up to 6,000 after a three-month probationary period. In the end, Doug accepted another offer from the prestigious Instituto Chileno-Británico de Cultura at Santa Lucía 124, paying 5,400 pesos an hour, more if he teaches high level classes, on Saturdays or in another branch of the British Institute. His contract is for 15 hours which is enough to secure a work visa, although he has the option of working up to 30 hours or more.

Before Doug secured a full-time teaching job, he participated in an exchange programme run by Woodward School, Providencia. For every Spanish lesson he received, he gave an English lesson, and went from being a complete beginner in the language to fairly competent. Another school, which operates an exchange programme, is the Chileno Swiss Institute.

A further possibility is to teach at English-medium *colegios*, where a longer commitment will be necessary and a reasonable salary paid. Although they employ mainly certified teachers, often hired at recruitment fairs and through international advertising, they do need some native speak-ers for their English departments. For example, **Eleanor Padfield** also from Cambridge was de-termined to work abroad after finishing her A levels but did not want to go through an agency where she would be with lots of other British students. After spending the first half of her year in Salamanca, Spain, she sent emails in Spanish all over the world to fix up something to do, preferably in Latin America. Of the many schools and language schools she contacted, one of the few to reply was the Redland School in Chile (Camino El Alba 11357, Las Condes, Santiago), an upmarket private school. Although the school told her that it didn't usually accept gap year students (since so many previous gappers had left prematurely to travel), it made an exception for Eleanor when she promised to stick it out till the end of the term beginning in March and ending in August. When June rolled round, she was tempted to leave early but her conscience (or her mother's exhortations) persuaded her to keep her promise, trying to see as much of the country as she could in her days off.

Heidi Resetarits was an English teacher for Universidad de Las Americas (August 2006 to March 2008) and Comunicorp, Santiago (July 2006 to March 2008). She found her pupils to be very different:

> *I had two sets of students. My students from the institute were mainly businessmen who needed to learn English for work. These men were preoccupied with work but took their lunch breaks to take classes. They do want to learn, but more often than not, work took priority. I had a few women who were very dedicated and learned rather quickly.*
>
> *I also taught 4th year college students how to write essays and give public speeches. They were at a different level than my business students (they were majoring in Teaching English) and they had a better grasp of the language. They were about 50–50 with effort and participation, but I could also have higher expectations for them. I really enjoyed working with these students.*

The commercial institutes in Santiago vary greatly in size, reliability in their treatment of employees and teaching methods. Newcomers to the city quickly learn which are the better schools and gradually acquire more hours with them. In-company teaching usually takes place early in the morning; middle-ranking staff tend to be taught before the official working day begins while directors and higher-ranking executives take their classes at a more civilised mid-morning hour. Most teachers enjoy the variety of off-site teaching rather than classroom teaching which tends to be more textbook-based.

AFTER COMPLETING THE TEFL CERTIFICATE COURSE AT THE AMERICAN LANGUAGE INSTITUTE IN SAN DIEGO, BRIANNA ANTMAN HEARD ABOUT VACANCIES TEACHING BUSINESS PEOPLE AT COMUNICORP IN SANTIAGO, CHILE. SHE SENT HER CV TO THE DIRECTOR AND AFTER A PHONE INTERVIEW WAS GIVEN A CONTRACT TO WORK FOR THE STANDARD ACADEMIC YEAR.

Most of my classes were one-on-one with managers, CEOs and other employees of large companies held in their offices. We were given a course summary sheet for each level which described the grammar points and functions that we were supposed to cover. Since we worked in a business atmosphere we were required to dress formally and adapt to the professional/business world.

I found accommodation in the local newspaper El Mercurio. However, most teachers found their accommodations through word of mouth and/or friends that were already here. Because the school is one of the higher paying institutes in Santiago, the wages of 6,000 pesos an hour were quite decent, enough to live off and travel. The school had a teachers' room filled with a plethora of resources, books, shared lessons on the computer, CDs, and incredibly experienced people in the field. All of the books were scanned onto the computer, thus making it quite easy to find/plan lessons.

The academic year runs from March to December with a two-week winter holiday in July and one week recess in mid-September, so the best time to apply for a contract is the end of February. There are 19 British curriculum schools listed on the website of the Association of British Schools in Chile (www.absch.cl). The Santiago *Yellow Pages* are a useful source; look up Instituto de Idiomas or check online www.chilnet.cl/rc/port_select_companies.asp?acti_code=779.

Non-contractual work is usually paid by the hour, starting at less than 5,000 pesos per hour and rising to 6,000 pesos. Established teachers working for universities such as UNIACC in Providencia can top 15,000 pesos but this is rare. The cost of living is higher than in many other places on the continent but teachers can still support themselves. Heidi Resetarits says that '*you won't be able to do much saving in South America in general*,' and recommends that you don't move to Chile without savings, if you want to have fun and money to travel. Normally 10% of earnings must be paid in tax, which in some cases can be reclaimed the following year.

Usually the CELTA certificate or equivalent is a minimum requirement for anyone considering working in the private sector. However, those looking to work within the state system of education will find that CELTA qualifications will not be accepted. In Chile a teaching degree takes five years, and school directors tend to look quite disparagingly upon one month/120 hour courses.

Details of a placement scheme can be found at www.teflinstitute.com/chile_summer_program. php, which is geared to college students and graduates, mainly but not exclusively from the USA, who volunteer as English teachers in small villages and towns throughout Chile for the summer.

RED TAPE

If you are offered a job before arrival, there are two ways to obtain the appropriate visa permit. Either your employer submits the application at the Ministry of Foreign Affairs in Chile (Direccion de Asuntos Consulares y de Imigracion, Bandera 46, Santiago) or you apply at the Chilean Consulate in your country of origin. You will need a signed and notarised work contract and a full medical report. If granted, the visa will be valid for one year. After that you may be eligible for a visacion de residencia which allows an unlimited stay.

If you are from New Zealand or Australia you can apply for a working holiday visa which allows you to work anywhere and to live and work without a contract for one year.

If you arrive to look for work, you will need to apply for a Temporary Residents Visa (cost varies according to nationality), for which you will need a written, notarised contract. Applicants will be given a card allowing them to work legally while they are waiting for their documents to be processed. This usually takes around 2–3 months. If you are able to commit yourself for a year, your employer may be willing to help. Many teachers who enter the country on a 90-day tourist visa, simply get a new tourist visa every three months from over the border in Mendoza, Argentina, knowing that the immigration authorities are much less likely to raid language institutes than they are hotels and restaurants where migrant Peruvians work.

ADVERTISING FOR PRIVATE CLIENTS

The average rate for private lessons is about 10,000–12,000 pesos per hour. There are many ways to meet the expatriate community from playing cricket at the Prince of Wales Club to frequenting the English language bookshop Books and Bits (Av. Apoquindo 6856, Las Condes-Santiago; ✆ 2 210 9100; fax 2 210 9191; booksbit@booksandbits.cl; www.booksandbits.cl).

You can advertise for private clients in *El Mercurio*, the leading quality daily. Other newspapers such as *La Epoca* and *La Tercera* have classified advertisements sections which will cost slightly less than *El Mercurio*. There is a magazine called *El Rastro* consisting of nothing but advertisements, to which you can phone in a small advertisements free of charge (though the response may be less than spectacular).

Advertising at your embassy has helped some teachers. A useful option is to find a supermarket which has a notice board for small advertisements in its entrance hall. For example the Almac and Jumbo chains of stores have such notice boards. Almac is located on the corner of Avenida Pedro de Valdivia and Bilbao, while Jumbo is on the corner of Portugal and Diagonal Paraguay. If you can translate between English and Spanish, it will be worth advertising yourself as a translator as well. The best way to find private clients however, is by word of mouth.

LEISURE TIME

Although Santiago is cosmopolitan and modern, there are pockets of poverty and the men can be aggressive, shouting across the street at women. The quality of life, however, is enviable. **Brianna Antman** points out that, '*Chile has a lot of beautiful places to visit and enjoy nature. Since the Andes are so close, there are a lot of activities to do in the mountains (horseback riding, trekking, white water rafting, etc)*'. **Heidi Resetarits** managed to keep herself pleasantly busy in her spare time:

> *I planned trips all over Chile at least once a week. I wrote for a magazine. I joined a gym and a swim team. I bought a bike and rode around town. I also spent a lot of time drinking coffee, pisco sours and/or wine on patios, reading or just enjoying the day. Santiago is a great city to spend time in, and it is very easy to get around in and relatively safe. The people are friendly and want to know who you are and where you are from. My favourite days were spent walking to a random café, meeting a friend and letting that meeting go into a warm summer Santiago night.*

LIST OF EMPLOYERS

AMERICAN BUSINESS ENGLISH LANGUAGE SERVICES
Barros Errázuriz 1954, of 501, Providencia, Santiago
(phone) +2 946 2629; fax 2 046 2657
(email) dday@netexpress.cl

NUMBER OF TEACHERS: 54.
PREFERENCE OF NATIONALITY: none, but must be native speaker of English.
QUALIFICATIONS: ESL certification, followed by amount of experience, followed by length of time candidate commits to stay in Chile and age of candidate.
CONDITIONS OF EMPLOYMENT: teachers are helped to get contracts. Teaching hours between 8am and 9.30am, noon and 3pm, 6pm and 9pm.

SALARY: higher than 95% of other institutes. Actual pay depends on geographic location of classes. Deductions of 10% for taxes and social security unless teacher has appropriate visa and pays their own contributions.
FACILITIES/SUPPORT: advice given on finding accommodation. Teachers are given a guide to explain visa procedures.
RECRUITMENT: *Yellow Pages*, referrals, Dave's ESL Café, newspaper advertisements, TEFL training institutes, local associations, small advertisements in places frequented by teachers, other teachers. Interviews essential.
CONTACT: Dennis Parish (Teacher Coordinator) or Douglas Day (Director).

BERLITZ LANGUAGE CENTRES

San Martin 524, Concepcion, VIII Region

✆ +41 239936; fax 41 235007

✉ berlitz-biobio@entelchile.net

🖥 www.berlitz.com

NUMBER OF TEACHERS: 15.

PREFERENCE OF NATIONALITY: Canada, USA, UK, Australia, South Africa.

QUALIFICATIONS: young native English speakers with CELTA qualification required.

CONDITIONS OF EMPLOYMENT: 6-month to 1-year contracts, to work 30 hours a week.

SALARY: approx. US$700 per month, less 10% income tax deductions.

FACILITIES/SUPPORT: school provides training, help with visa and generally with getting teachers settled in Chile.

RECRUITMENT: interview required, but may be carried out via MSN Messenger, phone or email.

COMUNICORP

Hernando de Aguirre 129, Providencia, Santiago

✆ +2 234 1010; fax 2 2330744

✉ dgreenst@comunicorp.cl

🖥 www.comunicorp.cl

NUMBER OF TEACHERS: approximately 25.

PREFERENCE OF NATIONALITY: none. Company prefers to have a wide variety of cultures and accents represented on the staff.

QUALIFICATIONS: at least one of the following: CELTA, TEFL certificate, MA in TESOL, MA in Education, MA in Communicative Disorders with CCC, and at least 1 year of classroom EFL experience, preferably with adult business English students.

CONDITIONS OF EMPLOYMENT: standard contract is 6–9 months. Hours are usually spread out during the day. Most business students prefer to have classes at the peak hours which are: 8:30–10am, 1–2:30pm, 6–7:30pm. Other students, who are more flexible, take classes during the off-peak hours from 10–11:30am and from 3–4:30pm.

SALARY: varies according to classroom experience, degree held, and time with the company. The lowest salary would be 444,000 Chilean pesos per month up to 580,000 Chilean pesos per month. There are additional benefits such as a travel bonus at the end of the contract for those hired from abroad and a monthly transportation budget. Taxes are less than 5% and social security is not an issue if the teacher has a home pension plan.

FACILITIES/SUPPORT: assistance with finding accommodation. School processes the work visa, except for the steps requiring the teacher to be present.

RECRUITMENT: internet and word of mouth.

CONTACT: Diane Greenstein, Academic Director.

EES EXECUTIVE ENGLISH SOLUTIONS

Luis Thayer Ojeda 0130 Providencia-Santiago

✆ +2 3357781; fax 2 2323571

✉ hspencer@ees.cl

🖥 www.ees.cl

NUMBER OF TEACHERS: 20–30.

PREFERENCE OF NATIONALITY: none.

QUALIFICATIONS: 4 + year degree, TESOL, CELTA or TEFL and 1+ years experience preferred.

CONDITIONS OF EMPLOYMENT: standard contracts are 6 to 12 months. The usual hours are mornings, lunch time and evenings Monday-Friday.

SALARY: 6,000 to 8,000 Chilean pesos per hour, 25–30 hours per week. Deductions of 10% refundable with filing of tax return.

FACILITIES/SUPPORT: company assists in contacting landlords and will provide proof of employment for lease and rental agreement. All foreign employees receive a Chilean work visa.

RECRUITMENT: in person interviews, sometimes carried out in the UK/USA.

CONTACT: Howard H. Spencer, Director of Studies.

EF ENGLISH FIRST

Hernando de Aguirre 215, Providencia, Santiago

✆ +2 374 2180

Av del Condor 844, Ciudad Empresarial, Huechuraba, Santiago

✆ 2 242 8380

✉ chile@ef.com

🖥 www.ef-chile.cl and
www.englishfirst.com

NUMBER OF TEACHERS: 35–40.

PREFERENCE OF NATIONALITY: none (native English preferred).

QUALIFICATIONS: TEFL/TESOL/CELTA (preferably not online). At least 1 year's EFL experience preferred.

CONDITIONS OF EMPLOYMENT: 9, 12 months or unlimited contracts. Full-time 20–30 hours per week or part-time flexible hours.

SALARY: 500,000 Chilean pesos a month. Part-time 5,500–10,000 pesos per hour, depending on location. Minimum 10% tax deducted.

FACILITIES/SUPPORT: advice given on accommodation and help with visa procurement from Extranjeria for full-time teachers. Free unlimited internet access and Spanish lessons at a minimum cost.

RECRUITMENT: locally only (no advance contracts).

CONTACT: Erik Petko, School Director (erik.petko@ef.com).

ENGLISH FOR LIFE
Av. Tobalaba 1829, Santiago
2 415 0416; fax 2 415 0417
info@englishforlife.cl
www.englishforlife.cl

An Associate Member of International House.

NUMBER OF TEACHERS: around 20.

PREFERENCE OF NATIONALITY: none.

QUALIFICATIONS: CELTA, Trinity Tesol or IH Certificate are essential, and preferably at least 1 year's experience teaching adults.

CONDITIONS OF EMPLOYMENT: contract is initially for 1 academic year (9 months). A full-time teacher works 40 hours a week including meetings/preparation/travel with a maximum of 27 teaching hours a week.

SALARY: US$640–US$700 (Chilean pesos) depending on experience. 7% deduction for health insurance.

FACILITIES/SUPPORT: accommodation is found and paid for, for the first two weeks. After that, help is given in looking for accommodation (eg with phone calls, talking to landlords). Teachers enter on a tourist visa, when they have signed a contract the organisation applies for a work permit/visa.

RECRUITMENT: through IHWO website or www.tefl.com. Interviews are essential and usually done by SKYPE or in IH in London.

CONTACT: Helen Ray, Director of Studies.

FISCHER ENGLISH INSTITUTE
Cirujano Guzmán 49 Providencia, Santiago de Chile
2 235 6667/2 235 9812; fax 235 9810
contacto@fischerinstitute.cl
www.fischerinstitute.cl

NUMBER OF TEACHERS: 15

PREFERENCE OF NATIONALITY: USA.

Qualifications: university degree and TEFL certificate or similar and 1 year experience teaching.

CONDITIONS OF EMPLOYMENT: minimum 1-year contract, 20–25 hours a week.

FACILITIES/SUPPORT: none.

RECRUITMENT: references, school abroad. Interviews essential, carried out in Santiago.

CONTACT: Celsa Contreras, Academic Secretary.

HOLISTIC LEARNING CENTRE
Merced 629, Quillota
/fax 33 358417
julia@chilebilingue.cl
www.chilebilingue.cl

NUMBER OF TEACHERS: 6.

PREFERENCE OF NATIONALITY: teachers welcomed from Canada, USA, UK, Australia and anyone whose first language is English.

QUALIFICATIONS: HLC is looking for personality, experience with travel and other cultures and professional experience. All ages.

CONDITIONS OF EMPLOYMENT: 6 or 12 months, though some teachers have been accepted for 3 months. 20 hours of student contact (usually 5 hours, 4 days a week) plus some hours for planning and travelling.

SALARY: US$250 per month (paid in cash) plus housing, all meals and full programme of Spanish lessons (10 hours a week).

FACILITIES/SUPPORT: return ticket provided for teachers who complete 12 months. Health insurance also paid. School completes paperwork for work permit.

RECRUITMENT: via websites, some universities and personal recommendation by former staff. Personal interviews not essential but all references and criminal records are checked. Interviews conducted by phone. Recruitment takes place year round.

CONTACT: Julia Silva, Director.

INSTITUTO CHILENO-BRITANICO DE CULTURA
Santa Lucia 124, Santiago
2 638 2156; fax 2 632 6637
www.britanico.cl

Other branches in Las Condes, La Florida, Nuñoa and Providencia.

NUMBER OF TEACHERS: 10.

PREFERENCE OF NATIONALITY: none, but should be native speaker.

QUALIFICATIONS: a degree in English or Modern Languages, plus a TEFL qualification. However, experience is valued more than TEFL qualification.

CONDITIONS OF EMPLOYMENT: 1 year, March to February. 30 teaching hours per week mostly evenings.

SALARY: £700 per month.

FACILITIES/SUPPORT: help with finding accommodation is provided. Teachers are provided with a settling in grant towards their accommodation.

RECRUITMENT: usually on the spot.

INSTITUTO CHILENO-NORTEAMERICANO DE CULTURA

Moneda No. 1467, Santiago

2 696 3215; fax 2 697 0365

info@norteamericano.cl

www.norteamericano.cl

NUMBER OF TEACHERS: 15–20.

PREFERENCE OF NATIONALITY: American, Canadian.

QUALIFICATIONS: BA in Education or TESL/TEFL and 6 months' teaching experience, or BA in related field with Certificate in TESL/TEFL and 2 years' teaching experience.

CONDITIONS OF EMPLOYMENT: 1-year contracts starting in March. 30 hours per week. Peak hours of work early morning and early evening, and some Saturdays. Classes for adults, children, teens, business and academic English.

SALARY: equivalent of US$1,100 per month in Chilean pesos.

FACILITIES/SUPPORT: assistance given in obtaining visas. Training provided. Teachers' room with computers, email access and cafeteria privileges.

RECRUITMENT: direct application by mail, email, phone or fax. Applicants should send cover letter, resumé, recent photo, copy of diplomas/certificates and letters of reference from recent employers.

REDLAND SCHOOL

Camino el Alba 11357, Las Condes, Santiago

2 247 5410; fax 2 247 5407

secretaria_rector@redland.cl

www.redland.cl

NUMBER OF TEACHERS: 16.

PREFERENCE OF NATIONALITY: British.

QUALIFICATIONS: university degree and teaching qualification (although in some cases a short TEFL course is sufficient).

CONDITIONS OF EMPLOYMENT: 1–3 year contract. Classes run from 8am to 3.30pm or 5pm. Pupils aged 4–18.

SALARY: on application.

FACILITIES/SUPPORT: free accommodation and utilities provided.

RECRUITMENT: direct contact with British universities and recruiting agencies. Interviews normally take place in the UK.

THE SAM MARSALLI ENGLISH LANGUAGE INSTITUTE

Av. Los Leones 1095, Santiago

2 328 9114; fax 2 328 9120

consulta@sammarsalli.cl

www.sammarsalli.cl/sammarsalli/welcome/work.html

NUMBER OF TEACHERS: 60.

PREFERENCE OF NATIONALITY: from USA and Canada only.

QUALIFICATIONS: college education, communication skills, leadership skills, intercultural relations and skills; experience living in a non-English speaking country for an extended period of time.

CONDITIONS OF EMPLOYMENT: 12 continuous months. Split shifts (8am–12pm and 6pm-9pm) plus 2 Saturday mornings per month.

SALARY: average take home pay is approximately 300,000 Chilean pesos. Teachers are paid on a per class taught basis.

FACILITIES/SUPPORT: database of affordable housing provided. Accommodation arranged for new arrivals. 1-year renewable work contract given to full-time teachers and work permits to cover them while their visa is being processed. Teachers must cover work permit and visa fees. After 90 days of employment, school provides free private health care plan.

RECRUITMENT: internet, newspapers, word of mouth. Interviews are essential and are conducted on-site in Santiago, or by telephone.

CONTACT: Teacher Selection Committee.

TEACHING CHILE

Av. Vitacura 3355, Dept 113, Santiago

720 221 3831 (US phone number routes calls to Santiago office)

020 8150 6981 (UK phone number routes calls to Santiago office); fax 720 221 3831 or 775 206 1089 (US)

info@teachingchile.com

www.teachingchile.com

NUMBER OF TEACHERS: approximately 40 native English-speaking teachers per year.

PREFERENCE OF NATIONALITY: none. To date, TeachingChile have placed teachers from Australia, Canada, England, Ireland, New Zealand, Scotland and the United States.

QUALIFICATIONS: varies among schools. Overall, applicants should be a graduate of a university or in their final year of undergraduate studies, ESL/TEFL/TESOL certification and teaching experience are desired but not required. Spanish language skills are not required for classroom instruction but elementary conversational language skills are recommended for the teacher's cultural enjoyment.

CONDITIONS OF EMPLOYMENT: minimum contract 6 months. A majority of teachers choose a 1-year contract. All contracts are renewable directly with the teaching institution assuming the school has positions available and the teacher has a good rapport with the employer and students.

SALARY: minimum 300,000 Chilean pesos per month for a base of 15 hours of classroom time per week. For longer hours teachers can earn up to 450,000 pesos. Some schools deduct 13% for tax and an optional 7% for medical insurance, but salaries are adjusted accordingly and teachers make about the same net salary.

FACILITIES/SUPPORT: guaranteed work contract, visa processing assistance, and accommodation arrangements are in place before the teacher leaves home. TeachingChile provides assistance with accommodation and a pre-paid transfer from Santiago airport to the first night's accommodation.

RECRUITMENT: via the internet, universities and ESL/TEFL/TESOL job placement websites. Applicants submit an application package available from TeachingChile's website. And are interviewed by telephone.

Contact: Bruce Thompson, Managing Director.

TRONWELL S.A.Apoquindo 4499, Piso 3, Las Condes, Santiago
+2 2461040; fax 2 2289739
www.tronwell.com/jobs.php

NUMBER OF TEACHERS: 40–50.
PREFERENCE OF NATIONALITY: none.
QUALIFICATIONS: native speakers. Preferably with degree in English or CELTA or equivalent.
CONDITIONS OF EMPLOYMENT: minimum one year. Hours for full-time staff include 7.35am–4.45pm or 1.15pm–8.15pm. Part-time positions also available.
FACILITIES/SUPPORT: no assistance with accommodation. Advice on work permit procedure.
RECRUITMENT: Interview followed by a 5-day training programme to learn the Tronwell methodology and instructional system. After the training period teachers are asked to prepare and teach a demonstration class on which depends the job offer. Apply online at the above website.

COLOMBIA

Since most people's only associations with Colombia are with crime and violence, it is not surprising to learn that teaching institutes in that country sometimes have trouble attracting qualified foreign teachers. Foreign teachers are extremely unlikely to become involved in any drug-inspired tensions but are guaranteed to be welcomed by the locals. Memories will be of a local carnival rather than of a neighbourhood shoot-out.

DAVE CROWDER TAKES STRONG EXCEPTION TO KNEE-JERK NEGATIVE REACTIONS TO HIS ADOPTED COUNTRY AND TO THE WARNING CONTAINED IN US AND UK EMBASSY LITERATURE:

I have found the people of Colombia to be universally friendly and helpful to strangers. Unlike the USA, the welcome here is genuine, open and amicable, and the people are genuinely interested in the novelty of a stranger among them. There is no more drug trafficking in Medellín where I live than in any other major city anywhere in the world (I used to live in Miami where there is much more drug gang activity). As a matter of fact, I will extend my comments about Medellín to every part of the nation that I have visited, which is everywhere but the few FARC/ELN-controlled areas in the boondocks.

With the expansion of trade (called Apertura), interest in English has increased, as evidenced employers by the popularity of English language media like newspapers and radio stations. However, a local law prohibits more than a 30% participation of foreign nationals in a school, so jobs for native English speakers are fewer than demand would seem to suggest. First Class English (see list of employers) about 24 teachers, but can only offer 6 jobs to native English speakers without dual citizenship.

Colombia is even more strongly oriented towards the USA than elsewhere in South America with an extensive network of Colombian-American Cultural Centers around the country. However, **Charles Seville** from Oxford, who spent a year as an English language assistant at the University de Los Llanos in Villavicencio, was struck by how keen Colombians were to learn British English. There is a British Council Teaching Centre in Bogotá whose market is primarily university students and young learners (www.britishcouncil.org.co).

It is possible to access the Colombian *Yellow Pages* on the internet (www.quehubo.com) which might provide a starting place for finding school addresses. The website www.poorbuthappy.com contains a very long list of language schools in Medellín, compiled by **Peter Van Dyck**, who got to know the teaching scene very well, and who maintains a forum for people to share information about Colombia.

Some global EFL companies have a strong presence in Colombia. EF Education First is based at the World Trade Center, Calle 100 # 8a-55, Torre C–Oficina 801, Bogotá; ✆ 1616 1130; www.ef.com.co and Berlitz runs 12 centres, including six in Bogota.

The main newspaper *El Tiempo* carries numerous advertisements for language schools in the capital. There are plenty of local language schools where untrained native speakers can find work, but there are two main disadvantages. Wages and conditions can be very poor; many schools offer a few thousand pesos an hour (possibly about US$3.50), though the schools listed below offer more attractive salaries, with an upper limit of 18,500 Colombian pesos per hour (US$8). The second problem is the red tape. As usual, temporary working visas must be applied for in your country of residence. The Colombian Consulate in London has information about the requirements on their website (www.colombianconsulate.co.uk), which includes an undertaking by the employer to bear the cost of repatriation if the visa is cancelled and a letter from the Ministry of Work & Social Security testifying that the Colombian employer is not exceeding the legal limit on foreign employees. The visa fee is £130. If a teacher intends to stay in Colombia longer than six months, he or she must register in person at DAS, the Colombian equivalent of the FBI, within 30 days of arrival. Approval will mean that you are entitled to acquire a *Cédula de Extranjería* (foreigners' ID).

LIST OF EMPLOYERS

CENTRO COLOMBO AMERICANO – MEDELLIN

Cra. 45 No. 53–24, 8743 Medellín

✆ +4 513 4444 ext 239; fax 4 513 2666

🖳 www.colomboworld.com

US Binational Center

NUMBER OF TEACHERS: 110 in programme.

PREFERENCE OF NATIONALITY: US or Canadian. Other countries welcome.

QUALIFICATIONS: BA or MA (Education, Language Teaching, TESOL, Linguistics).

CONDITIONS OF EMPLOYMENT: 1-year contract (renewable). Vacancies year round. 6 contact hours per day. English for children, teenagers and adults.

SALARY: starting at 1.5–1.8 million pesos per month (for 6–8 hours of work a day, Saturday shifts mandatory). Salaries adjusted for inflation every January. Bonuses paid every 6 months.

FACILITIES/SUPPORT: round trip ticket and visa expenses paid from USA or Canada. Housing assistance. Pre-service and in-service training. Medical benefits and Spanish lessons provided.

RECRUITMENT: extensive recruitment information on website. Direct application with CV and 3 references. Selection made through references and phone interview. The best time to apply is November to start January, and May for the July session.

CONTACT: Angela Cardona, Director, Human Resources (amardona@colomboworld.com).

COLEGIO JEFFERSON AA 6621 Cali
℡ +2 658 2700; fax 2 658 2701
🖥 www.jefferson.edu.co
Private mixed bilingual school for all ages.

NUMBER OF TEACHERS: maximum 12.

PREFERENCE OF NATIONALITY: UK, Canada, USA.

QUALIFICATIONS: university preferred. At least 1 year in a school situation (not just TEFL language institute).

CONDITIONS OF EMPLOYMENT: 2-year contract, renewable. Hours 7.30am–2.30pm.

SALARY: 2.63 million pesos per month plus annual bonuses. Salary review yearly.

FACILITIES/SUPPORT: suitable accommodation can be found for teacher and rent subsidy paid. Can assist with work permit if teacher arrives with relevant diplomas certified by Colombian consulate in originating country.

FIRST CLASS ENGLISH (FCE)
Carrera 12 # 93–78 Oficina 407 Bogotá
℡ +1 6232380; fax 1 6232381
🖱 gerencia@fcecolombia.com
🖥 www.fcecolombia.com

NUMBER OF TEACHERS: 24+ native English speakers (a proportion grant is required due to the local laws that prohibit a 30% participation of foreign nationals in the school. On average the school has space for at least 6 foreign national teachers that do not have dual citizenship).

PREFERENCE OF NATIONALITY: US and UK.

QUALIFICATIONS: at least 1 year's teaching experience, preferably with executives/professionals, CELTA, ICELT certification is a plus. But the bottom line is that the candidate must have 3+ year college/university degree, preferably in business or related areas.

CONDITIONS OF EMPLOYMENT: minimum 1 year, if volunteering a minimum of 4 months. Up to 8 hours of teaching within the hours of 6am to 9pm.

SALARY: contracted hourly pay oscillates from 15,000 to 18,500 Colombian pesos per hour, disbursed every 15 days. The *retencion* (tax) deduction, specific to this type of contract, is about 7% of income.

FACILITIES/SUPPORT: can assist with accommodation if necessary on a case-by-case basis. School provides paperwork for working visa, however the teacher is required to activate the visa by travelling to a neighbouring country and going to the local consulate. This process can take up to 60 days in total from the time the visa is requested.

RECRUITMENT: email requests and walk-ins. Interviews followed by a 20-hour mandatory selection process that includes training, simulated class, teaching crash course, administrative instruction (use of teaching and admin tools) and certification.

CONTACT: Andrew Diaz, Director.

INSTITUTO DE IDIOMAS (UNIVERSIDAD DEL NORTE)
Km 5 Via Pto Colombia, Barranquilla
℡ +5 3509736; fax 5 3598852
🖱 arey@uninorte.edu.co
🖥 www.uninorte.edu.co/extensiones/idiomas/

NUMBER OF TEACHERS: around 20 a year.

PREFERENCE OF NATIONALITY: none.

QUALIFICATIONS: Master's degree in TESOL, Linguistics, Psychology, English, Elementary/Bilingual Education, or related areas. Must have certified experience teaching EFL, preferably outside the USA. Must be a native English speaker; be able to teach and evaluate students effectively; and have experience using language lab equipment.

CONDITIONS OF EMPLOYMENT: minimum 1 year. 8 hours a day depending on classes assigned. Most likely 9am to 5pm.

SALARY: depends on qualifications. If the teacher has a master's degree, the salary will be around US$2,500 a month plus a living allowance of around US$300 for rent. The university pays in Colombian pesos.

FACILITIES/SUPPORT: university provides an agency for teachers to rent an apartment or house through and the university serves as a guarantor. When teachers arrive, the university pays for a hotel for two weeks. The university also provides transportation and assistance in visiting places and all documentation teachers need for the working visa, plus the university pays the issuing costs.

RECRUITMENT: via websites such as www.studyabroad.com, newspaper advertisements, plus the university website contains information for teachers who wish to apply. Face-to-face interviews are not essential. The university uses Skype or other types of videoconferencing.

CONTACT: Lourdes Rey, Academic Coordinator.

ECUADOR

Compared to its neighbours, Peru and Colombia, Ecuador represents an oasis of political stability. The economy has pretty much stabilised after the turn of the century recession when the country was forced to adopt the US dollar as the national currency. Teaching wages are still low, but obviously EFL teachers do not go to Ecuador to save money and it is still possible to live on the wages paid. For example a night in a budget hotel costs from US$8 and a three-course meal costs US$4.

Demand for English continues to thrive, particularly for American English, in the capital Quito, the second city Guayaquil and in the picturesque city and cultural centre of Cuenca in the southern Sierra. The majority of teaching is of university students and the business community whose classes are normally scheduled early in the morning (starting at 7am) to avoid the equatorial heat of the day and again in the late afternoon and evening. Many schools are owned and run by expatriates since there are few legal restrictions on foreigners running businesses.

WHEN BARRY O'LEARY ARRIVED IN QUITO, HE VISITED A TOURIST AGENCY WHICH HAD THE ADDRESSES OF ALL THE POSSIBLE ACADEMIES AND INSTITUTES. HE STARTED HIS FIRST TEFL JOB HUNT ARMED ONLY WITH A BASIC TEFL CERTIFICATE AND SPEAKING VERY LITTLE SPANISH. AS LUCK WOULD HAVE IT HE FOUND TWO JOBS IN 24 HOURS JUST BY WALKING ROUND THE CITY WITH COPIES OF HIS CV:

I can still remember the buzz I felt when José, my first employer, said 'Yeah we're looking for someone to start next week.' I couldn't quite believe it. With this institute there wasn't really a formal interview or application process. With another school I had a basic interview to make sure I could speak and wasn't a monster, they didn't even ask for my TEFL certificate. In Ecuador everyone I knew was working without a work visa. I remember being worried about telling them I was only staying for three months but they were just happy to have a native speaker teaching their students.

The teaching varied. In one school I was responsible for conversation classes. I had no guidance with the type of lessons they wanted so had to use resources from my course, the internet and my imagination. In every lesson a local teacher was there to help with any language barriers. The working conditions were very relaxed, no lesson plans or meetings'. I was just given a timetable and left to get on with it. As long as the students were smiling I was seen to be a good teacher.

I was lucky enough to find an apartment with an Ecuadorian family through an advertisement in an internet café. I made enough money to pay for my rent, food and some social activities and even managed to travel a bit with my last pay packet – and the dollars went much further in Peru.

The students were all great, the teenagers tending to be cheeky, a few times they changed the theme of the lessons to 'Make the teacher dance like a fool' before they did any work, but this was all part of the fun. It was a very relaxed atmosphere most of the time. I really enjoyed working with local teachers and they were all very open and friendly and interested in my life in England since many of them had never left Ecuador.

The highlight of Ecuador was helping my first students to prepare a presentation for the directors on their chosen topics of hooliganism, pollution and anorexia. The looks on their faces when they received

Wages are not as high as in Chile but higher than in Colombia, and usually allow teachers to enjoy a comfortable lifestyle since the cost of living is low. A qualified teacher can expect to earn over US$600 a month, or US$7,200 a year. Accommodation is harder to find in Quito than in Cuenca. Qualified TEFLers should not accept less than US$6 an hour though the private institutes which accept unqualified teachers pay accordingly less. All teachers (both contract and freelance) have taxes withdrawn at source of between 3% and 8%, with the majority deducting a flat rate of 7%, although tax regulations have been prone to change in recent years.

Quito is not as large and daunting a city as some other South American capitals and it should be easy to meet longer term expats who can help with advice on teaching. The helpful British Council will give you a list of ELT schools throughout the country and will (unofficially) indicate which offer the best teacher support and modern teaching methods and resources. One possible source of information is the South American Explorers clubhouse (membership costs US$50). In Quito the Club is at Jorge Washington 311 y Leonidas Plaza (Apartado 17–21 431; ✆ +/fax 2 225228). The club includes language schools in Ecuador on its database and has a useful notice board.

As throughout the continent, charitable schools for children can always use voluntary help. Nick Branch worked in Quito at Guarderia Maria-Ausiliadora (Don Bosco y Paraiso; 2–51034), a pre-school for disadvantaged children where he did some teaching from the front as well as painting, physical education activities and games with the children.

Another programme is Children of Ecuador based in Bahía de Caráquez. It is part of the Genesis of Ecuador Foundation, a non-profit organisation created to raise the level of education of Ecuadorian children. Volunteers receive a week of supervised in-class training, and are expected to teach 7.20am–1.20pm, Monday to Thursday (Friday optional), helped by the class instructor. The cost of a minimum four-week homestay is US$1,290, a third of which aids the programme. Spanish classes and other extras are provided (✆ +593 269 2400; www.childrenecuador.org).

The London-based gap year company Greenforce (✆ 020 7470 8888; www.greenforce.org) offers paying jobs in South America from three months or longer. The £900 programme fee covers airport collection and briefing, a city tour of Quito old town, two weeks accommodation, school placement, three meals per day and country support.

Genevieve Coombe decided to teach in Ecuador with MondoChallenge and was placed in Penaherrera on the slopes of the Western Andes: *I lived in the community with a local family. It was basic but comfortable and ideally located. I helped in the preparation of the local fiestas, made decorations for the election of the school queen and assisted the head with preparation for the sports day. I also worked at the nursery school and did a radio show with the president's wife, during which we taught basic English vocabulary. It has been fairly tough coming down to earth since returning to London but I'm already planning my next trip to South America!*

RED TAPE

Technically you shouldn't work on a tourist visa but there is little control. Britons and Americans can stay 90 days. If possible, teachers should get a 12-IX document in their country of origin, which can be extended by visiting a neighbouring country (usually Colombia). Most employers will help teachers who commit themselves for a reasonable stay to obtain a cultural exchange visa, normally valid for a year. The requirements are as follows: two letters attesting to good character, a notarised copy of a police report, health certificate (including HIV test) and birth certificate, letter of invitation from an Ecuadorian employer, letter of financial support from a backer and a return airline ticket.

LIST OF EMPLOYERS

CENTRO DE EDUCACIÓN CONTINUA DE LA ESCUELA POLITÉCNICA NACIONAL

Edificio Araucaria, Baquedano 222 y Reina Victoria, Quito

 22 500068; fax 22 553605

henryguygooch@yahoo.com

www.cec-epn.edu.ec

NUMBER OF TEACHERS: 100+.

PREFERENCE OF NATIONALITY: USA and UK.

QUALIFICATIONS: BA in English, Applied Linguistics, TEFL, Drama, International Studies or a related field. TEFL certificate, one-year experience.

CONDITIONS OF EMPLOYMENT: 1 year minimum (40 weeks of teaching). 6 hours per day.

SALARY: volunteers are not paid a salary, but are provided with a monthly subsistence allowance of from US$580 to US$696 net as required by law and written agreement.

FACILITIES/SUPPORT: teachers must find their own accommodation. Instructors are contracted as Cultural Exchange Volunteers under the agreement the University maintains with the Ecuadorian Ministerio de Relaciones Exteriores.

RECRUITMENT: word of mouth. Telephone interviews are conducted.

CONTACT: Henry Guy Gooch, Director of Linguistics and Cultural Exchanges.

CENTRO DE ESTUDIOS INTERAMERICANOS/CEDEI

Casilla 597, Cuenca

 7 2839003; fax 7 2833593

English@cedei.org

www.cedei.org

A non-profit institution dedicated to the study of American languages and cultures.

NUMBER OF TEACHERS: 50

PREFERENCE OF NATIONALITY: native English speakers.

QUALIFICATIONS: minimum university degree in related field and TEFL/CELTA/TESOL Certificate or university degree in TESL/TEFL. Experience in teaching EFL/ESL.

CONDITIONS OF EMPLOYMENT: minimum 6-month stay, preference given to year-long commitments. Courses run from January to mid-March, early April to early June, mid-June to mid-August and early October to mid-December. Teachers teach on average 20 hours per week. Most classes meet Monday to Thursday and there are also Saturday Intensives. To teach both classroom courses and individuals. In addition to classroom classes, teachers may elect to give tutorials and conversation classes to supplement their income.

SALARY: approximately US$275 per teenage/adult course, US$220 per children's course, and US$234 per Saturday class. Courses are 40–50 hours long and teachers are given 3–4 courses per term (10 weeks). This is a high salary by Ecuadorian standards.

FACILITIES/SUPPORT: apartments are very reasonably priced. Cost of living is low. Average rent for a shared apartment/house is between US$80 and US$120 per month. Free Spanish classes, dance classes and Internet access for teachers. Beautiful school building. Very charming city in an Andean setting.

RECRUITMENT: via www.tefl.com or www.eslemployment.com. Use the website www.cedei.org.

CONTACT: Elisabeth Rodas, Academic Director of English Programs.

EF SCHOOL OF ENGLISH – QUITO

Catalina Aldaz No. 363 y Portugal, Quito

+2 224 8651/245 7289/246 5335 ext 116; fax 2 246 6833

steve.tomkins@ef.com

www.ef.com

NUMBER OF TEACHERS: 20.

PREFERENCE OF NATIONALITY: none; school aims to have a mixture of nationalities and accents.

QUALIFICATIONS: CELTA or equivalent teaching qualification.

CONDITIONS OF EMPLOYMENT: 6 months to 2 years. 35 hours per week.

SALARY: average US$700+ per month after deductions of 12% for tax.

FACILITIES/SUPPORT: accommodation arranged in local hostel, EF residence or with host family. Pre-arrival pack contains detailed information about the options. Free transfers on arrival.

RECRUITMENT: via internet or worldwide network of EF schools. Telephone interviews. Teachers also recruited locally. For senior positions and long-term posts, applicants may be asked to present themselves at a local EF centre.

CONTACT: Steven Tomkins, English School Director.

INLINGUA

Sebastian Quintero N37–12 y Jose Correa (behind the Atahualpa Olympic Stadium), Quito

+2 245 8763; fax 2 276 921

inlinguaquito@inlingua.com

www.inlingua.com

NUMBER OF TEACHERS: 30-40.

PREFERENCE OF NATIONALITY: none (but native speakers preferred).

QUALIFICATIONS: preferably recognised TEFL and/or teaching experience (particularly Business English).

CONDITIONS OF EMPLOYMENT: minimum 6 months part-time/full time contracts. Hours vary.

SALARY: US$6–US$7.20 per hour depending on experience and/or qualifications.

FACILITIES/SUPPORT: Full training on Inlingua's international programme and teaching resources provided. Spanish classes offered.

RECRUITMENT: applications by email, interview and induction in Quito on arrival.

CONTACT: Danni Walters, Academic Coordinator (academic@inlingua.com).

KEY LANGUAGE SERVICES

Alpallana E6–114 y Whymper, Quito (Casilla 17–07–9770)

+2 222 0956

kls@andinanet.net

NUMBER OF TEACHERS: 10–15.

Preference of nationality: any native speaker welcome.

QUALIFICATIONS: TEFL qualification a must. Experience preferred. Tidy appearance and professional manner essential.

CONDITIONS OF EMPLOYMENT: 3 months absolute minimum, 6 months or longer preferred. Mainly off-site business classes offered 7am–9am, 12pm–2pm and 4pm–8pm.

SALARY: US$7.50 per hour.

FACILITIES/SUPPORT: notice board in office carries details of rental accommodation. Advice given on visas. Monthly professional development sessions. Teachers are allocated a pedagogical mentor.

RECRUITMENT: local interview and observation. Longer-term preferred. Any time of year.

NEXUS: LENGUAS Y CULTURAS

PO Box 01011013, Cuenca;

+593 7 409 0062; fax 593 7 409 0060

mcarrasco@nexus.edu.ec

www.nexus.edu.ec

NUMBER OF TEACHERS: 3 or 4 teachers per term.

PREFERENCE OF NATIONALITY: none.

QUALIFICATIONS: teaching certification (CELTA or similar at least). Teaching experience of at least one year.

CONDITIONS OF EMPLOYMENT: 6 month contracts. 3 regular terms per year plus a summer session. 18 hours per week.

SALARY: US$288 per month.

FACILITIES/SUPPORT: assistance given to teachers in getting Cultural Visas by sending them the necessary invitations and certificates. Spanish classes at special price.

RECRUITMENT: on-site interview or via email.

CONTACT: Marcela Carrasco, Director.

MEXICO

The lure of the USA and its language is very strong in Mexico. The frenzy of American investment in Mexico after the North American Free Trade Agreement (NAFTA) saw a huge upswing in both the demand for English by businesses and the resources to pay for it. That boom is now over, but the market for English is still enormous in universities, in business, almost everywhere. Proximity to the USA and a tendency towards what Australians call the cultural cringe (in Mexico called Malinchism after the lover of Cortès who betrayed her people) means that there will always be an unquenchable thirst for English taught by native English speakers in Mexico. Foreign teachers are automatically respected and are often promoted almost immediately.

Companies of all descriptions provide language classes for their employees especially in the early mornings and evenings (but seldom on weekends or even Fridays). **Roberta Wedge** even managed to persuade a 'sleek head honcho in the state ferry service' that he needed private tuition during the sacred siesta and that busy executives and other interested employees of a local company needed English lessons at the same time of day.

It is not surprising that enrolment in English courses is booming when some employees have been threatened with dismissal unless they master some English. A vet going to Dubai, a stockbroker doing deals with the New York Stock Exchange, housewives who have to go to parties with their executive husbands, teenagers with exam worries, all are keen to improve their English. After each six-year presidential term of office, the top layers of management in companies (especially oil and banking) are replaced by new staff who need new training, especially English. Elections always boost the demand for English not only in Mexico City and the border cities to which US industries looking for cheap labour have relocated, but throughout the country, including the Yucatan Peninsula and other unlikely places, at least one of which must remain nameless in order to preserve **Roberta Wedge**'s dreams:

> *After doing a 'taster' ESL course in Vancouver, I set out for Nicaragua with a bus ticket to San Diego and US$500 – no guide book, no travelling companion, no Spanish. On the way I fell in love with a town in Mexico (not for worlds would I reveal its name – I want to keep it in a pristine timewarp so I can hope to return) and decided to stay. I found a job by looking up all the language schools in the phonebook and walking around the city to find them. The problem was that many small businesses were not on the phone. So I kept my eye out for English school signs. I had semi-memorised a little speech in Spanish, 'I am a Canadian teacher of English. I love your town very much and want to work here. This is my CV . . .' Within two days I had a job at a one-man school.*

The British Council in Mexico City can provide the addresses of the 25 or so language centres attached to state universities and also keeps the *Yellow Pages* which has a few pages of language schools. Also check the website of the Unión Nacional de Escuelas de Idiomas A.C. www.unei. org.mx. The British Council runs English teaching centres in Mexico. For more information visit www. britishcouncil.org/mexico. The Council also works closely with the Cultura (Instituto Anglo-Mexicano de Cultura) which has 12 branches in four cities. Mexican-American bi-national centres employ scores of native speakers, mostly on a local basis. The school year starts in early August and lasts for 11 months.

Canadian Bruce Clarke is currently teaching English at a state university in Oaxaca. With a TEFL qualification and a year's experience in Indonesia, he was in a good position to make use of the Mexico forum on eslcafe.com, where he learned of his current employer. He reports that his students are pleasant and fun-loving, though not particularly energetic or keen to complete homework. He loves his current position, although the high price of flying home to visit family and friends is a drawback.

A further possibility is to work at English medium schools modelled either on the American or British system. Many of these advertise internationally for certified teachers or recruit through recruiting fairs but, as in Chile, Peru and elsewhere, some are willing to interview native speakers locally to work in the EFL department. Without a TEFL background or at least a solid university education you are unlikely to break into any of these more upmarket institutes.

THE PRIVATE SECTOR

A host of private institutes supplies language training to business either on their own premises or in-company. The norm is for teachers to freelance and work for a combination of companies. There are also full-time school-based jobs with teaching companies such as Harmon Hall and Interlingua which have a national network of branches. Wages are higher (as much as four times higher) at the former, but hours are fewer and less predictable and a lot of time is taken up travelling from office to office. Getting three hours of work a day (early morning and early evening) is easy. Anything above that is much trickier. Freelance teachers must be prepared for frequent holidays cutting into earnings. Normally institutes do not pay for public holidays, sickness or annual leave. For example, attendance goes into a sharp decline after Independence Day on 20 November in the month leading up to Christmas and there are no classes over Easter. Most courses run for three months and there may be a lapse of one or two weeks before another starts. Usually freelancers are paid cash-in-hand with no deductions for tax. Few have working papers (see Regulations).

The spectrum of institutes varies enormously. At one extreme there is the employer who pays the equivalent of US$4 an hour, never pays on time, and who employs only Mexicans with poor English or native English speakers who have just arrived with their backpacks and no interest in or knowledge of teaching. The top of the range pays US$14–US$18 an hour, offers free training and gives contracts that aren't cancelled. These institutes are of course a lot more choosy about their teachers. Whereas a few companies want to control their teachers completely and send inspectors into classes, most leave teachers alone as long as the clients are happy. The typical institute consists only of four people: the owner who gets the contracts, a teacher coordinator, a secretary and an office boy. According to **Nick Wilson** from Cumbria, who spent several years teaching freelance in Mexico City, there is a lot of jealousy between the training institutes with mutual accusations of spying, so discretion is advised. He was working for the wife of his director in her own school along with three other teachers she had poached from her unwitting husband. Some institutes try to poach teachers from rival institutes by offering more money.

On arrival in Mexico City, a good place to meet foreigners is the famed Casa de los Amigos, the Quaker-run guest house at Ignacio Mariscal 132 (✆ 5 705 0521/705 0646; amigos@avantel.net; www.casadelosamigos.org), centrally located near Metro Revolucíon. This guesthouse is firm about who it will receive as guests and does not regard itself as a casual guest house. They are, however, always happy to put people in touch with volunteer organisations. Check advertisements in the major Spanish-language daily *El Universal* as well as the English language newspaper *The News*. Rupert Baker answered an advertisement in *The News* and was invited to attend a disconcertingly informal interview at a restaurant (to which he still wore his tie). He ended up working for six months.

Obviously a TEFL qualification is an advantage though few employers are concerned about whether it is from a 130-hour or a 30-hour course. Business and financial experience is also beneficial, possibly more than a university degree. An ability to make a class interesting and patience are the two key qualities that many employers are looking for. As one of Nick Wilson's bosses said, '*The most important thing is that the students enjoy their classes and think that they are learning English; don't just teach or we'll lose customers.*' Word-of-mouth recommendations are very important in Mexican culture, and jobs are seldom filled by postal applications.

Michael Tunison contacted half a dozen major teaching organisations from the *Yellow Pages* and was interviewed by Berlitz and Harmon Hall. Both offered tentative positions based more on his native speaking than his American university degree and journalism background. The starting wage at both schools was the peso equivalent of US$400 per month which seemed typical of the large chains. One problem here is that these organisations do not pay cash-in-hand and therefore they want to hire only teachers with working papers. Another international chain of language schools represented in Mexico is Wall Street Institute (www.wallstreetinstitute.com.mx) with 18 schools.

Guadalajara and resorts such as Puerto Vallarta, Cancun, Acapulco and Mazatlan are places where a great many locals need to master English before they can be employed in the booming tourist industry, though wages tend to be lower than in the capital. Several independent US training organisations have set up TEFL training centres in Mexico.

AMERICAN BRADWELL JACKSON IS FUNDING HIS ROUND-THE-WORLD TRAVELS BY TEACHING ENGLISH:

After reading **Work Your Way Around the World**, *I made the decision to quit my job, leave my home, give most of my belongings to charity and sell my car, so that I could wander the earth freely. I wondered if it was really possible to get a job teaching English so easily. Well I found out that it is. I was sitting at a metro stop in Mexico City, trying to figure out what school to go to for my first planned job enquiry. After I decided that the particular school I had in mind was too far away, I looked up and saw an English school right across the street. Providence, I thought. I was right. I sauntered on upstairs, cheerfully asked if they needed an English teacher, and about an hour and a half later, I was told when to start my training. It really was that easy.*

I teach a range of students including some teenage girls. For them I came up with the idea of asking them to talk about a television programme Rebelde, which is very popular among teens here. I also got them to pull out a teen magazine and tell me about the stars in it. I have also asked my students about popular Spanish songs and asked them to translate them into English for me.

Mexico is the first country I have visited on my world wanderings and I can't believe how lucky I've been. The people are top-notch and I certainly must count my blessings.

FREELANCE TEACHING

Private lessons are in great demand, and may be given informally in exchange for board and lodging. But it is also possible to teach on a more business-like footing. With so many clients seeking one-to-one tuition through institutes, it is worth considering setting up as an independent tutor and offering private lessons at a rate which undercuts the institutes. Teachers who are tempted to poach students from the organisation they work for should bear in mind that employers who find out have been known to set the immigration department on errant teachers. However, it is legitimate to advertise yourself in the press and distribute printed business cards. Elizabeth Reid based some of the material in her book *Native Speaker: Teach English & See the World* on her experiences of teaching in a small Mexican city. She started by developing her own private classes in borrowed premises (a disused shop). She recommends approaching the local community centre (*casa de cultura*), chamber of commerce or public library and offering one free sample class before signing up paying students. To increase goodwill she offered 'scholarships' to a limited number of students who really couldn't afford to pay.

Teaching in companies sometimes produces lucrative spin-offs in the field of translation and editing documents in English. Clients may offer other kinds of work too; for example **Nick Wilson** was asked to set up a Mexican-British arts foundation through a bank trust by someone he tutored in English.

Anyone willing to pay a fee to have a job arranged for them should investigate the website www. teach-english-mexico.com. The programme fee is US$950.

REGULATIONS

The red tape situation in Mexico is a difficult one. Visitors are not allowed to work or engage in any remunerative activity during a temporary visit. The Free Trade Agreement makes it somewhat easier for Americans and Canadians but still not straightforward. British citizens can stay in Mexico for 180 days without a visa as a tourist, according to the consulate website (http://mexico.embassy-uk.co. uk). As has been mentioned, established schools are not usually willing to contract people without an employment visa, unlike private institutes. The most respectable schools may be willing to help full-time contracted teachers with the paperwork but won't pay the cost (estimates vary between US$100 and US$700). Among the required documents are a CV in Spanish, notarised TEFL and university certificates which have been certified by a Mexican consulate.

LIST OF EMPLOYERS

AHPLA INSTITUTE
Juan Escutia No. 97, Colonia Condesa, C.P. 06140, Mexico, D.F
+5 286 9016 (ext. 113); fax 5 286 2515
www.ahpla.com

NUMBER OF TEACHERS: 35.
PREFERENCE OF NATIONALITY: none.
QUALIFICATIONS: educated, flexible, willing to work with a team and travel. People skills and personality a must.
CONDITIONS OF EMPLOYMENT: expect minimum 6 months. Hours mainly 7–9am and 5–7pm.
SALARY: 122 pesos per hour.
FACILITIES/SUPPORT: no help with accommodation or flights. Help given with working papers when teacher has shown a commitment to AHPLA.
RECRUITMENT: word of mouth, internet, local paper.

BERLITZ (CENTRO INTEGRAL DE IDIOMAS)
Av. Benito Juarez No. 2005, Local Sub Ancla M Plaza Sendero, Colonia Estrella de Oriente, C.P. 78396
+444 166 35 70
anja.woitke@berlitzslp.com.mx

NUMBER OF TEACHERS: 20.
PREFERENCE OF NATIONALITY: none.
QUALIFICATIONS: TESOL, TEFL, CELTA certification or a university degree in education.
CONDITIONS OF EMPLOYMENT: standard 1 year contract. Hours mainly 7am to 9am and 6pm to 9pm, Mon–Fri, Sat 8am to 2pm.
SALARY: 60 pesos per 45 minutes of class.
FACILITIES/SUPPORT: school makes sure that the applicant has a place to stay after arrival.
RECRUITMENT: by email and telephone interview.
CONTACT: Anja Woitke, Language Instructor Supervisor.

DUNHAM INSTITUTE
Avenida Zaragoza 23, Chiapa de Corzo, Chiapas 29160
+961 61 61498
academic-coordinator@dunhaminstitute.com
www.dunhaminstitute.com

NUMBER OF TEACHERS: 3.
PREFERENCE OF NATIONALITY: native English speaker.
QUALIFICATIONS: ESL certified.
CONDITIONS OF EMPLOYMENT: minimum 5 months. 3–4 hours in the afternoon and study Spanish in the mornings.

SALARY: none. Exchange of English teaching for free accommodation with a local family and 2 hours of Spanish tuition a day.
FACILITIES/SUPPORT: work permits not required.
RECRUITMENT: interviews not necessary.

EF EDUCATION FIRST – MEXICO

México D.F. Jaime Balmes, Local 6, Col.
Polanco, D. F. 11550
- +55 5282 2150; fax 55 5282 2155
- www.ef.com.mx

NUMBER OF TEACHERS: 10.
PREFERENCE OF NATIONALITY: British, Irish, North American, Australian, New Zealand.
QUALIFICATIONS: minimum RELSA TEFL Cert (Irish) or equivalent. Experience and university degree preferable but not essential.
CONDITIONS OF EMPLOYMENT: 12-month contract (renewable). 30 contact teaching hours plus 10 hours preparation and extra activities (eg training) per week.
SALARY: 7000–10,000 Mexican pesos a month depending on experience and qualifications, plus bonus scheme, medical insurance and 3 weeks paid vacation.
RECRUITMENT: primarily local hires but also via internet and EF Recruitment Brighton/Boston.

ENGLISH UNLIMITED

Cuauhtemoc 1205, Colonia Jardin, San Luis Potosi,
SLP 78270
- 52 444 833 1277/833 5018; fax 52 444 833 5015
- teaching@englishunlimited.org
- www.englishunlimited.org

NUMBER OF TEACHERS: 18–25 throughout the year.
PREFERENCE OF NATIONALITY: none.
QUALIFICATIONS: TESL/TEFL/TESOL certified (or equivalent), experience is a plus but not necessary.
CONDITIONS OF EMPLOYMENT: 1-year contract preferred but not a requirement; short-term teaching positions also available. Hours from 7am–10.30am; 4pm-9.30pm, Monday to Friday and 9am–2pm Saturday.
SALARY: Full-time teachers earn US$60 Mexican pesos per hour plus incentives. 10% tax deduction. 15 hours guaranteed per week.
FACILITIES/SUPPORT: help with finding accommodation; translate if necessary. Assistance with immigration forms and procedures.

RECRUITMENT: internet or through schools where teachers complete their ESL course.
CONTACT: Michael Tan, General Director.

EXPERIENCE MEXECO LTD

38 Award Road, Fleet, Hampshire, GU52 6HG
- /fax 01252 629411
- info@experiencemexeco.com
- www.experiencemexeco.com

English teaching projects, among other volunteer opportunities, on Pacific coast of Mexico.
QUALIFICATIONS: all nationalities and ages (average 19–26). All backgrounds welcomed as any necessary training is provided. Spanish is not a necessity as local staff speak English and Spanish.
CONDITIONS OF PARTICIPATION: 1–3 months.
SALARY: none. Programme fee £799–£899 for 1 month, £1,899–£1,999 for 3 months which covers accommodation (homestay or private) and food throughout placement plus insurance and 24-hour in-country support, but excludes flights.
CONTACT: Daniel Patman, Director.

FAST ENGLISH INSTITUTE

Tlalpan 1525, Col. Portales, Mexico City 03300
- /fax 55–1251 5974; Mob: 3094 9508
- fastamericanenglish@yahoo.com.mx or fast1@att.net.mx

NUMBER OF TEACHERS: 7.
PREFERENCE OF NATIONALITY: none.
QUALIFICATIONS: ability to communicate effectively in English, spoken and written.
CONDITIONS OF EMPLOYMENT: teachers may sign a contract after 3 months (no contract required at the beginning). Hours can fall any time between 7am and 10pm.
SALARY: from US$7 an hour. Maximum US$14 per hour.
FACILITIES/SUPPORT: some teachers stay at school's residential facilities.
RECRUITMENT: interview and written exam.
CONTACT: R Alaiyo Moreno T, Academic Director.

HARMON HALL PACHUCA

Blvd. Valle de San Javier 225, Fracc. Valle de San
Javier, Pachuca Hidalgo, CP 42086
- /fax 7 71 780900/781910
- www.harmonhall.com

95 branches across Mexico but all hire teachers individually.

NUMBER OF TEACHERS: 8+.

PREFERENCE OF NATIONALITY: British or Canadian.

QUALIFICATIONS: must be responsible, interested in Mexican culture and have a desire to teach. BA degree or university undergraduate.

CONDITIONS OF EMPLOYMENT: standard length of stay is 1 year. Minimum of 3 hours per day. Usual schedule 7am–11am and 5pm–8.30pm.

SALARY: from 42 pesos per hour.

FACILITIES/SUPPORT: school has a house for teachers. If full, help is given in finding alternative accommodation. Help given with work permits. Teachers have to bring University Certificate and Diploma and ESL certificate stamped by the Mexican Consulate.

RECRUITMENT: telephone and internet interviews acceptable.

UNIVERSIDAD DEL MAR

Bahias de Huatulco, Oaxaca 70989

 +958 587 2559

 umarmxjob@yahoo.com

www.umar.mx

NUMBER OF TEACHERS: 16

PREFERENCE OF NATIONALITY: none but must be native speaker.

QUALIFICATIONS: degree level education, TEFL teaching qualification, at least 1 year's experience working in a foreign country.

CONDITIONS OF EMPLOYMENT: 1 year commitment. Teaching hours are 8am–1pm and 4pm–7pm Mon–Fri.

SALARY: 14,881 pesos gross (more for candidates with a master's in TEFL or education plus 2 years' experience), plus free medical service, Christmas and vacation bonuses, savings scheme and monthly shopping vouchers. Monthly deduction of about 2,000 pesos for tax and social security.

FACILITIES/SUPPORT: teachers must arrange their own accommodation. University files paperwork for work permit on arrival; processing can take up to 3 weeks and teachers cannot start work without work visa.

RECRUITMENT: most via internet advertisements and emailed CVs. Telephone interviews essential; short-listed candidates are telephoned.

CONTACT: Director of Languages.

PERU

Lima has in the past been considered one of the most stressful and dangerous South American cities in which to live, however, threats from guerrilla groups have largely passed and Peru is returning to the mainstream of destinations for English language teachers. Continuing low wages and the difficulty of obtaining working papers mean that few professional teachers can be attracted to the private EFL sector. For those who are, it is worth sending a CV to the English Language Officer at the British Council, which will send a list of British schools and language teaching institutes to anyone sufficiently well qualified or alternatively pass the CV to potentially interested institutions such as the five branches of the British-Peruvian Cultural Association (known familiarly as Britanica).

Yet the range of opportunities in Lima is enormous. The stampede to learn English is unstoppable. Many company employees have been told by their bosses to learn English within three months or risk demotion. Some employers organise a course at their place of work, but most expect their staff to fix up private lessons making the freelance market very promising at the moment. In-company training courses in all industries are often offered in English, so knowledge of the language is becoming essential for all ambitious Peruvians. The Peruvian economy is not in dire straits at present, as evidenced by the stability of its currency, the new sol.

Many temporary visitors to Peru who lack a TEFL background end up doing some English teaching once they have established a base in the capital, usually earning about US$5 an hour at an institute. Some employers offer a free or subsidised training course to new potential recruits, at which native English speakers usually excel over the locals whose knowledge of English is often very weak.

James Gratton arrived in Lima to take up what had sounded like a dream job. He had contacted the institutes included on the list sent by the Peruvian Embassy in London and was contacted enthusiastically by one. (On the strength of a certificate earned from a one-week intensive TEFL training course in London and nine months of living and teaching in Venezuela the year before.) High wages and many perks were offered, including a promise to meet him at the airport. His new employers' non-appearance at the airport was just the first promise they broke, and the lesson he learned over the next few months was that in Peru (and probably more widely in the continent), you must confirm and reconfirm any arrangements. He lasted only six weeks with this company (and was told that this was a record stay for an expat teacher) but concluded that such bad employers can be used as stepping stones to better opportunities.

For those who prefer to organise in advance, a safer bet might be to join a work placement scheme organised by Projects Abroad (✆ +01903 708300; www.volunteer-teaching-peru.org), which has a programme in Peru for volunteer teachers supervision and back-up from local staff. The minimum stay is a month and the cost for up to three months is about £1,695 which includes food and lodging.

Eco Trek Peru does not sound like a volunteer teaching programme but this ecotourism travel agency based in Cusco sends volunteers to remote Peruvian community schools for up to six months. Participants must be over 25, know Spanish and be adventurous (✆ + 51 84 247286; www.ecotrekperu.com).

A list of bilingual and English medium schools plus a few private schools and universities is available from the Cultural Office of the Peruvian Embassy in London.

FREELANCE TEACHING

Setting up as a freelance tutor is potentially very lucrative. A standard fee is US$10 a lesson, though this can be reduced for clients who want to book a whole course. With wages like that and assuming you have found enough clients, it is possible to earn over US$1,000 a month (in a country where the minimum wage is US$70). James Gratton put a cheap advertisement (written in English) in the main daily *El Comercio* and signed up two clients. This was possible in his case since he was staying at his girlfriend's house where he had free access to a telephone. His new students were both employees of Petro-Peru, and soon other clients contacted James for lessons. He admits that freelancers do lose out to cancellations, though some of his students willingly paid for missed lessons. Freelancing is a continual process of advertising and getting new students to replace the ones that fall by the wayside. James continued giving private lessons for six months and now wonders about the possibility of returning from Northampton to Lima to set up his own small institute.

REGULATIONS

Peruvian work visas are very rare and most people teach as tourists. British and Irish nationals, as well as US citizens, do not require a tourist visa when travelling as tourists to Peru; neither do nationals from EU countries. They are allowed to stay in Peru for up to 90 days, although they are required to possess an onward/return ticket. After that it is necessary to cross the Peruvian border. One reason which many people use to extend their stay is that they have formed a romantic attachment to a local woman/man. James Gratton felt that the authorities were not interested in rooting out illegal workers.

When he approached the immigration office about the requirements for a work visa, they knew he was working but took no steps to stop him.

In his quest for a work visa, James gathered together all the necessary documents, including contract (the duration does not matter particularly), notarised certificates and documents translated into Spanish. All of this cost him a lot of money and time, and he still didn't succeed. He concluded that it would be possible only if you knew someone in the Immigration Department who could give your application a safe passage without having to pay fines (bribes) at every stage. Making key contacts is more important than gathering documentation.

Care must be taken to keep on the right side of the tax office (SUNAT) to which about 15% of earnings are supposed to be paid. James Gratton obtained a tax number even though his passport clearly indicated his status as tourist, but ended up paying virtually no tax.

LIST OF EMPLOYERS

INSTITUTO CULTURAL PERUANO NORTEAMERICANO
M.M.Izaga No. 807, Chiclayo
+74 231241/233331; fax 74 227166
www.icpna.edu.pe

Bi-national Centre.
NUMBER OF TEACHERS: 6 native speakers at present; would like to increase to 10 or 12.
PREFERENCE OF NATIONALITY: US preferred; others considered.
QUALIFICATIONS: university degree that qualifies candidate for teaching EFL/ESL. Experience not a necessity.
CONDITIONS OF EMPLOYMENT: minimum 3 months and maximum 1 year, renewable. Teachers work 6–8 hours a day between 7am and 10.30pm. Classes are 2 hours long.
SALARY: minimum of 9 sol an hour and maximum 20 sol.
FACILITIES/SUPPORT: can find apartments for teachers or arrange homestays. Help given with work permits for long-stay teachers.
RECRUITMENT: via TESOL conferences and internet. Interviews not essential.

SEPA DEL PERU (Servicios Educativos Peruanos Americanos del Peru)
Puente Bolognesi 114–116, Arequipa
54 222390
educationalexcellence@gmail.com or sepa @perupass.com
www.perupass.com (click on logo of SEPA del Peru)

NUMBER OF TEACHERS: 5 foreign teachers at a time; participants are considered volunteers.
PREFERENCE OF NATIONALITY: native-speaking English countries although fluent speakers from Germany, Malta, China and Japan have also been accepted.
QUALIFICATIONS: most come from in-house TEFL/TESOL training course (see Directory of Training Courses). Normal minimum age is 22. Personality is key and most have completed at least 2 years of university, taken Spanish courses and volunteered elsewhere in Peru (eg on SEPA's Volunteers for Educational Victory programme) by the end of the course.
CONDITIONS OF EMPLOYMENT: minimum commitment 13 weeks up to 1 year. Volunteers stay 1–13 weeks. Maximum 30 hours per week.
SALARY: monthly stipend (no deductions) for classes taught based on an hourly rate of US$3–US$5.
FACILITIES/SUPPORT: offers the 'World's Toughest TEFL/TESOL Program'. Teachers are provided with homestay accommodation or alternative accommodation if requested after arrival.
RECRUITMENT: normally through personal recommendation and graduates of SEPA's own TEFL/TESOL training course; sight-unseen candidates and backpackers are not the programme's focus. Interviews compulsory, including for acceptance onto training course. Interviews are carried out via telephone or video conferencing. Application procedure requires submission of an essay.
CONTACT: Mark J Lipski, Founder and International Programs Director.

VENEZUELA

Proximity to the USA and the volume of business which is done with El Norte mean a strong preference for American accents and teaching materials in Venezuela. Oil wealth abounds in the business community and many corporations hire in-company language trainers through Caracas-based agencies. But work is not exclusively for Americans, as **Nick Branch** from St Albans discovered, nor is it confined to the capital:

> *Merida is very beautiful and a considerably more pleasant place to be than Caracas. The atmosphere and organisation of the institute where I worked were very good. But alas, as with all the English teaching institutes in Merida, the pay is very low. Merida is three times cheaper to live in than Caracas, but the salaries are five to six times lower.*

Nick Branch investigated most of the schools and agencies in Venezuela and worked for several of them including one based in the Oriente coastal resort of Puerto la Cruz. Once again the pay was less than in Caracas but advantages like easy access to the Mochima National Marine Park compensated. Opportunities for English teachers even exist on the popular resort island of Margarita.

Check advertisements in Caracas' main English language organ, the *Daily Journal*. Most give only a phone number. A typical advertisements might read:

> *We need English teachers and offer remuneration according to the market, stable incomes, paid training, organization in the work, more earnings according to commissions. Excellent working condition. Work with best team. Punctual payment.*

The last item is worth noting, since many institutes do not pay as much or as often as they promise at the outset. In fact, Caracas has more than its fair share of shady characters running language schools, so that newcomers should take their time about signing any contracts.

REGULATIONS

Most people work on a tourist card which is valid for 90 days non-extendable. It is also at least possible to apply for a multiple entry visa (about US$30) if you can provide proof of employment, sufficient funds and a return ticket. A combined work/study contract (internship in American parlance) is the solution which the Centro Venezolano Americano and Venusa have come up with (see entries) but this is available only to US citizens.

Most long-stay foreigners take brief trips to Curacao or Trinidad and Tobago and get an extension of their tourist card when returning to Venezuela. Work permits are available only if the employer has obtained approval from the Ministry of Internal Affairs (DEX) and sent the necessary papers to a Venezuelan consulate in the teacher's country of residence. Even with a backer as well established as the British Council, the visa problem looms large.

NICK BRANCH DESCRIBES THE PROCESS OF GETTING A WORK PERMIT IN CARACAS AS A NIGHTMARE:
On no account attempt to get one on your own, since this involves dealing with the DEX, a truly horrific organisation housed in what resembles a prison and with appalling disorganisation. Two years ago they lost 3,000 passports of people who were applying for work permits. It was later discovered that they had been sold on the black market.

James Gratton obtained a definite job offer from a university extension department on Margarita Island and presented the letter to the Venezuelan Embassy in London. His application was turned down. His main complaint was that you hear a different story from every official. Even renewing his tourist card at the immigration office took a week and involved his having to present a typed letter in Spanish (and why would a bone fide tourist be expected to do that?). Yet he managed to stay legally in Venezuela for nine months, leaving the country when necessary and returning without once being asked to show a ticket home as proof of his intention to leave the country. His most serious problem occurred when one of his employers threatened to report his tourist status to the police if he quit to look for a better job. (James did quit and the police were not called.)

LIST OF EMPLOYERS

CANADIAN EDUCATIONAL SERVICES
Urb. El Parral, Calle Río Cabriales no.U-483, Caracas
- +241 825 2686/416 449 5767
- guevaraangel@yahoo.com
- www.cesca.biz

NUMBER OF TEACHERS: 2–3.
PREFERENCE OF NATIONALITY: Canada and USA.
QUALIFICATIONS: university degree, with ESL studies. Experience not essential.
CONDITIONS OF EMPLOYMENT: minimum stay 4–6 months. Usual hours: 3 in the morning (7am–10am) and 3 in the evening between 3pm and 7pm.
SALARY: about US$320 a month (no airfare or medical Insurance).
FACILITIES/SUPPORT: room with private bathroom provided in a large house in a very good area of the city.
RECRUITMENT: via advertisements on internet and interviews via email.
CONTACT: Angel Guevara, Director.

CENTRO VENEZOLANO AMERICANO DEL CARACAS
Av Principal José Marti, Edf. CVA, Urbanización Las Mercedes, Caracas 1060-A
- 2 993 7911/8422; fax 2 993 6812
- academ@cva.org.ve
- www.cva.org.ve

NUMBER OF TEACHERS: 110 teachers for approx. 4,000 students.
PREFERENCE OF NATIONALITY: American, Canadian, Venezuelan.
QUALIFICATIONS: BA or teachers with EFL/ESL experience.

A written and oral test is given to all non-native English speaking applicants.
CONDITIONS OF EMPLOYMENT: minimum 6 months with renewals up to 2 years. Choice of children's courses (for ages 9–11), teens (12–15) and regular and Saturday courses for adults. Minimum 30 academic hours per week.
SALARY: 9,000 bolivars per 90 minute class plus a 300,000 bolivars housing bonus.
FACILITIES/SUPPORT: assistance with obtaining accommodation, health insurance and visas. 2-week pre-service training course for interns is paid. Free Spanish course. Computer lab and access to cultural centre activities.
RECRUITMENT: mail, fax, email.

CENTRO VENEZOLANO AMERICANO DEL ZULIA (CEVAZ)
Calle 63, No. 3E-60, Apartado 419, Maracaibo, Estado Zulia
- +261 718 0842/0843/0844/0845; fax 261 792 1098
- cjwong@cevaz.org
- www.cevaz.org

Non-profit organisation sponsoring mutual cooperation between Venezuela and the USA founded in 1973.

INLINGUA VENEZUELA
Av. Principal de El Bosque, Torre Cricard, Piso 1, Ofc. 131, Chacaíto, Caracas
- +212 952 1645/7542/9251; fax 212 952 3873
- vzla@inlingua.com
- www.inlingua.com

NUMBER OF TEACHERS: 50 (around half are native English speakers).

PREFERENCE OF NATIONALITY: native English speakers.

QUALIFICATIONS: TESOL, TEFL, CELTA qualification plus teaching experience. International living and working experience a bonus. Candidates should be flexible, responsible and professional with a positive attitude.

CONDITIONS OF EMPLOYMENT: 12-month contract. To work irregular hours (three primary shifts, starting 7am, noon, 6pm). However, teachers must be available from 7am to 7pm Monday to Friday.

SALARY: US$520 gross per month – paid in the local currency (bolivares).

FACILITIES/SUPPORT: initial hotel accommodation first 14 days to allow the teacher to become acclimatised and find accommodation. Visa sponsorship (teachers enter the country on a student visa as they participate in a scholarship programme, studying Spanish and teaching English as part of an internship).

RECRUITMENT: via internet and direct applications. Email interview required.

IOWA INSTITUTE

Avenida 4 con Calle 18, Mérida Edo. Mérida 5101

✆ +58 274 2526404; fax 58 274 2449064

🖱 cathy@iowainstitute.com or cesar @iowainstitute.com

🖥 www.iowainstitute.com

NUMBER OF TEACHERS: 7 native speakers.

PREFERENCE OF NATIONALITY: none.

QUALIFICATIONS: university degree in Education, Linguistics, Modern Languages or some related field. If degree not in TEFL related field then a TEFL Cert. or teaching experience is essential. All teachers must attend a 4-day seminar on school teaching methods held during September and again in January. Jobs for less qualified (ie native speakers who have not yet completed their degree) also possible. Those with experience working in children's camps for example, have been ideal for helping in the children's programme.

CONDITIONS OF EMPLOYMENT: 10 months minimum. Full-time posts 6–8 hours a day. Part-time can be as few as 2 hours a day.

SALARY: by the hour, always a bit above the standard rate.

FACILITIES/SUPPORT: no accommodation assistance. Group Spanish lessons are free, private classes at cost price.

CONTACT: Cathy Jensen de Sánchez.

VENUSA COLLEGE

International Studies and Modern Languages, 49–49 Avenida Urdaneta, Merida Venezuela

US contact address: 6586 Hypoluxo Rd 324, Lake Worth, FL 33467

✆ +561 357 8802; fax 561 357 9199

🖱 venusa@earthlink.net

🖥 www.venusacollege.org

NUMBER OF TEACHERS: 25–40 a year.

PREFERENCE OF NATIONALITY: US, Canada, UK.

QUALIFICATIONS: TESL certification and experience preferred but not required.

CONDITIONS OF EMPLOYMENT: 3-month to 1-year contracts. Hours vary.

SALARY: varies.

FACILITIES/SUPPORT: homestay or room option offered (some meals included). Visa application and information provided.

RECRUITMENT: internet, alumni. Interviews not essential. Apply electronically.

CONTACT: Rosa Corley, Programme Director.

WALL STREET INSTITUTE (WSI)

Av. Francisco de Miranda, Edif. Easo, Piso14, Officina 14A, El Rosal, Caracas

✆ +212 953 7659/952 7026; fax 212 952 3228

🖱 wsiven@cantv.net

🖥 www.wsi.com.ve

NUMBER OF TEACHERS: as many as possible.

PREFERENCE OF NATIONALITY: none.

QUALIFICATIONS: teaching degree not necessary but some experience teaching English as a second language is helpful. WSI trains all teachers in-house.

CONDITIONS OF EMPLOYMENT: no contract but minimum of 6 months. 8 teaching hours.

SALARY: local average.

FACILITIES/SUPPORT: assistance with work permits.

RECRUITMENT: word of mouth, advertising in local papers and group called Aisec. Telephone interviews.

CENTRAL AMERICA AND THE CARIBBEAN

If you keep your ears open as you travel through this enormous isthmus squeezed between two great oceans, you may come across opportunities to teach English, especially if you are prepared to do so as a volunteer. Salaries on offer may be pitiful but if you find a congenial spot on the 'gringo trail' (for example the lovely old colonial town of Antigua in Guatemala), you may decide to prolong your stay by helping the people you will inevitably meet who want to learn English.

COSTA RICA

As the wealthiest country in Central America, Costa Rica is a good starting (and perhaps finishing) point for many native English teachers. In March 2008 the Education Ministry presented a national plan to improve English instruction and produce a bilingual workforce for the nation's growing economy. Although such rhetoric can never be completely relied upon, it does at least suggest that English is seen as an important economic asset. The English language newspaper *Tico Times* (www. ticotimes.net) corroborates this, and has recently run a series of articles headlined 'Learning English is a good investment' and 'Tourism will grow thanks to English speaking cops'. It is also government policy to teach English in primary schools which has greatly increased the demand for English teachers. Although state schools can't usually afford to import expat teachers, they are often willing to accept an offer of voluntary assistance. The school year runs from 1 March to 1 December.

There are plenty of private language academies in the capital San José. Temporary six-month renewable working visas are issued to teachers working for established employers like the Instituto Britanico (now International House) where **Jane Roberts** worked. After deciding that she needed a complete change from Hounslow and an office job, Jane signed up for a CELTA course and had to decide where she wanted to job-hunt. Her course tutors at International House (IH) London had told her group that they would probably have to work in Eastern Europe to start with:

> *No thank you I thought, I want to work in a hot Latin country. IH had said don't expect to get a job straightaway in your dream destination, but I have proved this wrong. I got the address of Instituto Britanico (from your book!), emailed them my CV and a covering letter, within two weeks was offered a job and a couple of weeks later I was here in Costa Rica.*
>
> *The working conditions are fine with a very well-equipped library, cassettes, all necessary equipment for the classroom, and free email and internet access (when it works). My students are very motivated, lovely to work with, keen to learn, really want to speak a lot. I have the greatest admiration for them as they often come after a hard day at work to a 3-hour lesson and put a lot into it. I have to ensure that it is as interesting as possible for them. My advice is to smile, relax, be nice to people. I have not found any problems with Latin Machismo, no hassles with men. They love my accent but have not been pushy or offensive. Costa Rican people are so friendly and helpful. It's a very chilled country.*

If teachers wish to stay longer, the red tape becomes a little more painful. International House in San José advises: '*Candidates must have copies of their birth certificate and a police report certified by their foreign ministry or state department and the Costa Rican consulate in their country of birth. This involves some expense on the part of the candidate. After arrival, IH completes all necessary paperwork and applies for permission at their expense.*'

BRYSON PATTERSON MADE USE OF CONTACTS FROM THE TEFL COURSE HE DID AT ALI SAN DIEGO TO GET HIS FIRST JOB IN COSTA RICA AT PRO-LANGUAGE (ENTRY BELOW).

During my first job, I spent a lot of time on the bus going from class to class. This was a drawback. On the plus side, San José is right in the middle of Costa Rica and for a US$4 bus ride of two hours you can be on either the Pacific or Caribbean coast. Shorter bus rides and less money get you to great mountain and volcano locations. Pro-Language was really cool about giving teachers time off to travel as well. Most of the other people working down here as English teachers are young people travelling around or older people doing the same thing. It is kind of a nice mix. As far as the students go, Costa Ricans are great. In an economy so closely linked to the US many people realise that it is imperative that they learn English.

Afterwards I moved to a town called Jaco on the Pacific Coast where I worked at a high school and then at the Marriott Hotel. I was teaching English first to high school students (that was hell) then to the hotel staff which was cool. A lot of people will tell you that there are no ESL jobs on the coast but they are wrong.

NICARAGUA

Nicaragua is the second poorest country in Central America. The average per capita income is US$60 per month, and most EFL jobs outside Managua pay US$1 to US$3 an hour. In Granada, US$4 an hour is reputed to be the maximum anyone can get for tutoring. It is possible to find a few EFL teaching jobs paying US$6–US$12 per hour in the capital city, Managua. However, Managua is not a city most foreigners want to live and work in. The city is spread out like Los Angeles, taxi fares can add up quickly and the bus system has pickpockets and it is not safe after dark.

So, teachers interested in earning good money (or even earning a living) should steer clear of Nicaragua. However, those with a genuine desire to help thousands of intelligent and motivated people become bilingual may care to read on. There are many reasons why Nicaraguans may wish to learn English: at least 40% of Nicaragua's trade is with the USA and Canada, and there are over one million family members living in the USA, Canada and Costa Rica. North American English is the language of choice, but many schools employ British English speakers.

Scott Banks, director of Granada English College, kindly provided most of the information for this section. He has lived and worked in Granada for 2.5 years:

I enjoy living and working in Nicaragua because I have directly helped hundreds of motivated adults and young adults improve their economic futures and broaden their education. I have been fortunate to work with many generous teachers who were willing to earn less than it costs to live here.

Less than 5% of the country's families are wealthy and send their children to high-quality private schools. There are also many very low-quality, private schools with low tuition costs, although you will need to speak basic Spanish in order to explain the grammar and manage everyday living. Immersion learning would only occur in a handful of very expensive schools, although those schools have a very low turnover of teaching staff.

Teachers with a Christian commitment may like to make contact with the Association of Christian Schools International (http://missionteach.com) which recruits native English teachers with experience and certification. Some of their Nicaraguan schools need missionary teachers who are willing to raise their own support; others provide some sort of stipend and/or benefits to their teachers, reducing the amount of support that a teacher needs to raise. Still others offer competitive salaries and benefit packages.

For teachers dedicated and indeed fortunate enough to secure a teaching job, Nicaragua can be a wonderful place to live. It has many beautiful ecologies rich in diversity: Ometepe Island (100 sq miles) in the middle of Lake Nicaragua (40 miles by 100 miles) is as beautiful as Kauai (Hawaii). There are beautiful rain and cloud forests, world-class surfing, hundreds of miles of beautiful beaches and indigenous tribes preserving their culture on the Atlantic Coast.

DOMINICAN REPUBLIC

A major tourist destination, the Dominican Republic provides plenty of opportunities for native English teachers, although these may well be low paid (or volunteer positions) because the country is still one of the poorest countries in the Caribbean. A useful resource is the Dominican Republic One news and information service (www.dr1.com) in English, which has a classified section (including vacancies for English speakers at the time of writing), a blog, and a message board where you can ask the online community for information. The *Listín Diario* (www.listin.com.do), in Spanish, is a large circulation newspaper with a strong classified section, online and in print.

Possible leads include the Instituto Cultural Dominico-Americano (© +5350665 ext 287 for the human resource manager; www.icda.edu.do) and Universidad APEC's English Department, (© 686 0021; http://unapec.edu.do). There are also plenty of English speaking or bilingual schools that you can try. The Blogspot 'Dominican Republic Live' has a reasonably up-to-date list (http://dr-live.blogspot.com/2007/06/educacin.html).

Another option is to take part in the TESOL Exchange Program of the American Language Partnership International (Calle San Luis #83, Santiago, 971 1422; fax 583 0553; info@alpinternational.com; www.alpinternational.com). Teachers are able to exchange ideas and activities through workshops, seminars and in the classroom, and work with ALPI's Dominican students of English. Those with little experience can 'cut their teeth' on lessons with the guidance and full support of the faculty. EFL teachers willing to participate in seminars, workshops and classes may qualify for paid housing and a stipend during their stay.

LIST OF EMPLOYERS

COSTA RICA

BUTLER ACADEMY
25 Meters South of Casa Blanca, Heredia
© 237 9733/4
✍ esl@butleracad.com
🖥 www.butleracad.com

NO OF TEACHERS: 25+.

PREFERENCE OF NATIONALITY: native speakers preferred but not required.

QUALIFICATIONS: ESL teachers but also positions for volunteers, aides and support staff. Experience in Fluency development, Latin accent management, Placement and Achievement test development for applied English skill sets.

CONDITIONS OF EMPLOYMENT: contracts 'At Will' due to labour regulations in Costa Rica. Hours from 9am to 9pm. Class times vary from 1–4 hours.

SALARY: varies with experience. Entry level teachers find they can live comfortably on the salary they receive.

FACILITIES/SUPPORT: provide some assistance in finding accommodation. Work permits are not needed if a teacher is a contracted consultant.

RECRUITMENT: word of mouth and internet agents.

CONTACT: Bill Oswald, Academic Coordinator.

CANADIAN ACADEMY OF LANGUAGE

Detrás del Hipermas, 200 mts. este Heredia

237 1397

john@inglesencostarica.com

www.inglesencostarica.com

NO OF TEACHERS: 8.

PREFERENCE OF NATIONALITY: North American preferred.

QUALIFICATIONS: mature, responsible, professional, business experience helpful, teaching experience preferred.

CONDITIONS OF EMPLOYMENT: no contract, hours vary.

SALARY: US$9–US$16 per hour.

FACILITIES/SUPPORT: none.

RECRUITMENT: through internet advertisements and other teachers. Face-to-face interviews essential.

CONTACT: John Lalonde, President.

CENTRO CULTURAL COSTARRICENSE NORTEAMERICANO

Apartado Postal 1489–1000, San José

+506 207 7500; fax 506 224 1480

ecolton@cccncr.com or work4us@cccncr.com

www.cccncr.com

NUMBER OF TEACHERS: varies. Teachers also needed for centres in San Pedro, La Sabana and Cartago.

PREFERENCE OF NATIONALITY: none, but must be native speaker of English.

QUALIFICATIONS: experience in ESL and/or EFL is indispensable.

CONDITIONS OF EMPLOYMENT: standard length of contract is 4 months. Minimum 10 hours per week.

SALARY: US$5 an hour paid in local currency (colones). Deduction of about US$15 a month for voluntary insurance.

FACILITIES/SUPPORT: no assistance with accommodation or work permits.

RECRUITMENT: via newspaper advertisements, work fairs and internal recommendations. Interviews carried out at CCCNCR sites in Costa Rica after applications have been processed centrally.

CONTACT: Eloisa Quesada Colton, Recruitment and Professional Development Coordinator.

ENGLISH LEARNING CENTERS

Universidad Interamericana de Costa Rica, Apdo 6495 1000, San José

+506 2277 8054; fax 506 2261 3212

elccr@uinteramericana.edu

www.uinteramericana.edu

NUMBER OF TEACHERS: 20.

PREFERENCE OF NATIONALITY: none, but must be native speaker of English.

QUALIFICATIONS: CELTA certificate and a recognised undergraduate degree or Costa Rican residency.

CONDITIONS OF EMPLOYMENT: 12-month contract. Hours from 7.30am–9pm, split shifts Mon–Thurs, 8am–2.30pm Saturday.

SALARY: US$500 per month with 24 contact hours a week.

FACILITIES/SUPPORT: Housing assistance provided if requested in advance. Help with work permits.

RECRUITMENT: local newspapers and via email contacts.

CONTACT: Jay Terwilliger, Academic Director of Languages.

INTERCULTURA LANGUAGE AND CULTURAL CENTER

Apdo. 1952–3000, Heredia

+506 2260 8480; fax 506 2260 9243

info@interculturacostarica.com

www.interculturacostarica.com

NUMBER OF TEACHERS: 24.

PREFERENCE OF NATIONALITY: USA, Canada, Australia and Great Britain.

QUALIFICATIONS: at least 1 year teaching experience plus TEFL/CELTA certification.

CONDITIONS OF EMPLOYMENT: 1 year. Average 20 hours teaching per week. Hours of teaching Mon–Thurs 4pm–9pm plus some Saturday mornings. Students aged 13–50 years.

SALARY: US$600–US$800 per month net.

FACILITIES/SUPPORT: local housing arrangements to help teachers find accommodation. Free Spanish lessons. Monthly TEFL training courses offered with Costa Rica TEFL (www.costaricatefl.com).

RECRUITMENT: TEFL websites, local advertisements and phone interviews. cm@prolanguage.org

CONTACT: Barbara Miller, Executive Sub-Director, English Department Director.

NUMBER OF TEACHERS: 28.

PREFERENCE OF NATIONALITY: none.

QUALIFICATIONS: minimum qualifications are CELTA, Cert. TESOL Trinity College London, IHCTL, BEd with TEFL component, PGCE with TEFL. Global TESOL, TEFL International or online qualifications are not accepted. Minimum 12 months' experience.

CONDITIONS OF EMPLOYMENT: 12 or 24 months. 24 contact hours per week.

SALARY: minimum at 1/1/08 CRC 321,000, more for teachers with longer than minimum experience and higher qualifications.

FACILITIES/SUPPORT: first 2 weeks' free accommodation, then secretarial and logistical help in finding somewhere suitable. Foreign hire teachers are also paid an overseas allowance of CRC 92,000 (at the time of writing). Candidates must have copies of their birth certificate and a police report certified by their foreign ministry or state department and the Costa Rican consulate in their country of birth. This involves some expense on the part of the candidate.

After arrival, IH completes all necessary paperwork and applies for permission at their expense. Country specific details are made available to candidates during the recruitment process.

RECRUITMENT: through IHWO recruitment, occasionally TEFL.com. Interviews essential, usually by phone, although sometimes IH affiliates interview in the country where the candidate is living.

CONTACT: Mark Budworth, Gerente Programa de Inglés para Adultos.

NUMBER OF TEACHERS: 40.

PREFERENCE OF NATIONALITY: none, but native English speaker fluency.

QUALIFICATIONS: TEFL certification or equivalent and a minimum of 6 months experience.

CONDITIONS OF EMPLOYMENT: 6-month to 1-year contracts.

SALARY: US$7 per hour.

FACILITIES/SUPPORT: Assistance with accommodation and work permits. Free Spanish lessons and free training.

RECRUITMENT: newspaper advertisements, internet, alliances with teacher training organisations.

CONTACT: Christian Moraga, Administrative Coordinator.

NUMBER OF TEACHERS: 12–18.

PREFERENCE OF NATIONALITY: North American/British.

MANDATORY: Mother tongue English.

QUALIFICATIONS: TESL/TESOL/CELTA certified. Prefer 2 years experience teaching English as a second language. Prefer minimum age 30.

CONDITIONS OF EMPLOYMENT: 6-month stay.

SALARY: US$8 per hour (net).

FACILITIES/SUPPORT: initial hotel booking arranged and advice on locating suitable apartment.

RECRUITMENT: via internet. Interviews essential.

CONTACT: Michael J Whittemore, General Manager.

EL SALVADOR

NUMBER OF TEACHERS: 4–10 volunteer teachers at any one time.

PREFERENCE OF NATIONALITY: none.

QUALIFICATIONS: no teaching experience or certification needed. Must be committed to social justice and reciprocal learning between students and teacher.

CONDITIONS OF EMPLOYMENT: minimum stay 9 weeks for complete English cycle. Time commitment includes teaching English 3 days a week (Monday, Tuesday and Thursday) 5.15pm–7pm, weekly 2 hour teachers meeting, plus time spent on lesson planning. Please contact for more details about rural volunteer placements and longer-term placements.

SALARY: none.

FACILITIES/SUPPORT: help given in finding but not paying for accommodation. The CIS has a host family network with whom volunteers can live. Training for teachers provided. Tourist visa ($10 at border) is sufficient (check with your country's consulate with regard to travelling document requirements).

RECRUITMENT: word of mouth, internet, travel publications.

CONTACT: Rachel Burrage, English School Co-ordinator.

NICARAGUA

ABC SCHOOL
519 Calle Consulado, Granada
© +55 552 0812
🖰 abc@cablenet.com.ni or marlonabc@hotmail
.com.

NUMBER OF TEACHERS: 5 volunteers.

PREFERENCE OF NATIONALITY: North America.

QUALIFICATIONS: TEFL or equivalent, minimum 2 months' EFL teaching experience, some Spanish, some travel outside country of origin, interest in Nicaragua.

CONDITIONS OF EMPLOYMENT: minimum stay 3 months. 20 hours per week on week days between 3pm and 8pm and on Saturday mornings and afternoons.

SALARY: contribution of US$160–US$240 per month for housing.

FACILITIES/SUPPORT: teachers are helped to find rooms to rent, or homestays.

RECRUITMENT: Internet and word of mouth. Phone interviews.

CONTACT: Marlon Gutierrez, Owner/Director.

GRANADA ENGLISH COLLEGE
Parque Xalteva, Calle Xalteva, Granada
© 505 552 1314
🖰 scottbanks@cablenet.com.ni
💻 www.granada-english-college.com

NUMBER OF TEACHERS: 8 paid teachers currently.

PREFERENCE OF NATIONALITY: native US and Canadian English speakers only.

PREFERRED QUALIFICATIONS: TEFL or equivalent, minimum 2 months EFL teaching experience, basic Spanish necessary.

CONDITIONS OF EMPLOYMENT: minimum stay 2 months.

SALARY: Basically a volunteer position but US$3 an hour is paid at the end of the month towards living costs. Living costs will be US$400–US$600 per month depending on standard of living.

FACILITIES/SUPPORT: assistance with finding rooms to rent, or homestays.

RECRUITMENT: Internet and word of mouth. Most teachers are hired only after they demonstrate teaching ability in Granada though occasionally exceptional teachers are offered positions after communicating electronically.

CONTACT: Scott Banks, Owner & Recruiter.

Countless programmes in English as a Second Language (ESL) in the USA are subsumed under several distinct programme types, in contrast to the heavy emphasis on 'academy' type EFL or 'workplace' ESP in Europe. Just about every university and college in the major cities has an ESL programme, as do a range of government and charitable organisations. Commercial schools offer a wide variety of classes but tend to focus on survival ESL and EAP (English for Academic Purposes) with writing as a major component. Berlitz and Inlingua are represented throughout the USA and are a completely different type of commercial school, concentrating on conversational skills and foreign languages for business people. Embassy CES (330 Seventh Avenue, New York NY 10001; ✆ 212 629 7300; www.embassyces.com) has adult English schools in Boston, New York, Fort Lauderdale, San Diego, Los Angeles and Seattle, plus one in Vancouver. These are hardly worth applying to because they recruit locally.

Bilingual/bicultural classes are run in thousands of high schools across the country. Many require staff who are not only state-certified teachers but also bilingual in exotic languages such as Hmong or Gujarati. Most larger cities have at least one free or low-cost workplace literacy/vocational ESL programme which caters for immigrants needing assistance with the basics of English. Some of these programmes operate in outposts (eg churches, libraries) and many depend on local volunteers as tutors. Volunteer positions can conceivably lead to better things. Another way of getting your foot in the door is to make yourself available as a substitute (for which you will need a telephone and preferably an answering machine).

Although the demand for ESL teachers is enormous, it is very difficult for foreigners who do not have a 'green card' to obtain the necessary working visa. The J-1 visa is available to university students participating in an approved Exchange Visitor Programme (which are only for the summer) and to researchers and teachers whose applications are supported by their employing institution in the USA. Similarly it is extremely difficult to obtain the H-1B 'Temporary Worker' visa which is available for prearranged professional or highly skilled jobs for which there are no suitably qualified Americans, an increasingly unlikely circumstance as more and more Americans are becoming qualified to teach ESL/EFL. Although more US organisations now recognise the Cambridge Certificate than before, the MA in TESOL still dominates the American EFL scene. The *EL Gazette* carries some advertisements for openings in the USA, though most of those are academic posts in universities where it might be possible for the employer to overcome the visa problem in the case of highly qualified candidates.

Even for qualified American teachers, part-time work is the norm, often referred to as being hired as an 'adjunct'. Many contracts are not renewed, creating a transient English teaching population. Pay is hourly and varies according to region, e.g US$20–US$30 in Chicago, US$25–US$40 in San Francisco. Part-timers almost never get benefits which means no health insurance or vacation pay. Even full-time teaching openings may be for just nine months with pay as little as US$20,000 in the Midwest.

One possibility might be to teach at summer courses or work on summer camps attended by young people from overseas. For example the Council on International Educational Exchange recruits ESL instructors for language camps on the east and west coasts, responsible for teaching English language classes to high school age international students in July and August. Even for such short appointments they look for an MA in TESOL or at least a strong background in ESL.

Canada has a flourishing ELT industry, however, the difficulty of getting a visa is a major stumbling block for foreign teachers. People with experience might have expected to be able to do some casual one-to-one tutoring of new immigrants, but stiff competition makes this difficult. When **David Hughes** arrived in Vancouver after a lengthy stint of teaching English in Taiwan, he felt fairly confident that with his experience he would be able to acquire a few fee-paying students from among the huge Chinese population in the area. But he didn't get a single reply to his advertisement.

Two sources of possible contacts are the Canadian Association of Private Language Schools (www.capls.com) and TESL Canada (www.tesl.ca). Institutes such as the YMCA International College, (200–1166 Alberni Street, Vancouver, BC; ✆ 604 681 9622; www.vanymca.org) and Pacific Gateway International College which employs 100 teachers in four locations (3rd Floor, 1155 Robson St, Vancouver, BC V6E 1B5; ✆ +604 687 3595; info@pacificgateway.net; www.pacificgateway.net) will usually consider only Canadian citizens or those with work permits or landed immigrant status. The hourly wage is about Can$25 per hour.

AUSTRALASIA

While Europeans tend to have a somewhat Eurocentric view of the world, the Antipodean English language industry has built itself into a giant. Teaching English as a Foreign Language has a very high profile in both Australia and New Zealand. There are no fewer than 20 Cambridge CELTA training centres in Australia and nine in New Zealand, most of them attached to flourishing English language colleges. There are a further eight Trinity TESOL centres in New Zealand, despite its tiny population of about four million.

Gareth Lewis of International House Sydney's Teacher Training Centre has generously provided an assessment of the ELT scene in Australia.

AUSTRALIA

The growth in student numbers and ELT schools has resulted in strong job prospects for TESOL qualified teachers. In 2007, approximately 80,000 students studied English in Australia on student visas and the Australian immigration department estimate that another 60,000 students studied on other visas, such as working holiday and tourist visas. This is an increase of 80% on the year 2000 figures, proving that the industry has made a full recovery following the Asian economic downturn of the late 1990s. For obvious reasons of geography, the majority of Australia's international students are from Asia, although there are a growing number of students coming from elsewhere including Europe.

Australia is a strong and growing market for longer-term students, eg academic English students (20+ weeks) and English for high school students (20–30 weeks) who need to improve their English skills for entry into an Australian university or high school. This longer term student market has resulted in relatively steady student numbers year round. While Australia does experience a peak in student numbers over summer (September to May) due to an influx of study tours, there is not the same dramatic seasonal fluctuation as in Europe.

There are approximately 100 English language colleges in Sydney alone, around 70% of which are NEAS-accredited National ELT Accreditation Scheme. The profession is strictly regulated in Australia and standards are high in both the private and public sector. The minimum acceptable qualification to teach at an Australian NEAS-accredited language school is a degree in any discipline (or 3-year full-time diploma) plus a recognised TESOL qualification and 800 hours of teaching experience (or a higher than pass grade in the TESOL qualification or if you can show references from your TESOL course director about your performance).

An acceptable TESOL qualification must have a practical component including at least six hours supervised and assessed practice teaching in TESOL and involve no less than 100 contact hours in total (or the equivalent in Distance Education programmes). To check the current requirements and a list of accredited language schools see the NEAS website (www.neas.org.au).

Most non-accredited schools in Sydney employ TESOL trained teachers who do not hold a degree or diploma. It is interesting to note that due to the strong demand for TEFL qualified teachers in Sydney, job-seekers with the CELTA but without a degree have still been offered positions by accredited schools.

Candidates (whether Australians or foreigners on working visas) are regularly offered employment in Sydney and in other Australian cities within a week or two of completing the Cambridge CELTA course. Generally teaching contracts are short-term and renewable. Once a relationship has been built between school and teacher the teacher can opt to work long term with one school or short-term with a number of schools.

Annual salaries range from around AUS$40,000 for a newly qualified graduate teacher without experience to AUS$60,000 for a head teacher.

Many foreigners teach English on a working holiday visa. Australia now has reciprocal working holiday maker arrangements with 23 countries. Travellers aged between 18 and 30 years can apply for working holiday visas for up to 12 months. For further information visit www.immi.gov.au.

When Barry O'Leary arrived in Sydney with a working holiday visa, he had very little money left so needed a job fast. He had emailed a number of language institutes in Sydney in advance and fixed up an interview the day after he arrived. In addition to walking round all the schools he could find, he used Australian search engines such as www.seek.com.au, www.jobsearch.gov.au and www.mycareer.com.au. Soon he found a job with Maewill English College in Brookvale, an outer suburb of Sydney (www.mec.edu.au):

This was my first full-time job and I was thrown in at the deep end. Initially I was doing maternity cover and working 15 hours a week, but this later increased to 45 including preparation time. The wages were fantastic, I wasn't paying any tax because I set myself up as a contractor and I was paid AUS$30 an hour (the going rate then) and AUS$300 every two weeks for the evening business course I taught. I managed to save about AUS$8,000 in three months which paid for a brilliant trip up the east coast of Australia. There was always a laugh in the staff room and a lot of banter between England and Australia. I really enjoyed the mixed classes because there was such a range of opinions although they were challenging at times because each nationality would have different weaknesses.

LIST OF EMPLOYERS

ACCESS LANGUAGE CENTRE
72 Mary Street, Surry Hills, Sydney NSW 2010
 +2 9281 6455; fax 2 9281 7455
english@access.nsw.edu.au
www.access.nsw.edu.au

NUMBER OF TEACHERS: 16.
PREFERENCE OF NATIONALITY: none.
QUALIFICATIONS: BA or BSc plus TESOL Cert. Some experience essential.
CONDITIONS OF EMPLOYMENT: 4 weeks renewable to start.
SALARY: depends on qualifications and experience.
FACILITIES/SUPPORT: no assistance with accommodation.
RECRUITMENT: advertising and direct enquiries.
CONTACT: Blake Compton, Director of Studies.

EMBASSY CES
Level 1, 63 Oxford Street, Sydney,
New South Wales 2010
 2 9291 9300; fax 2 9283 3302
enquiries@embassyces.com

Schools also in Brisbane, Gold Coast, Perth and Melbourne.
NUMBER OF TEACHERS: 15 in Sydney, 20 Brisbane and Melbourne, 14 Gold Coast, 10 Perth.
PREFERENCE OF NATIONALITY: none.
QUALIFICATIONS: NEAS minimum qualifications.
CONDITIONS OF EMPLOYMENT: permanent, sessional (yearly or 3-monthly) casual depending on area.
SALARY: depends on experience and qualifications. Current average hourly rate is around AUS$35.
FACILITIES/SUPPORT: excellent academic environments. Computer labs, wireless internet and email access, student

common room. Homestay and lodge accommodation available.

RECRUITMENT: local advertising.

INTERNATIONAL HOUSE QUEENSLAND

130 McLeod St, Cairns, Queensland 4870

7 4031 3466; fax 7 4031 3464

admin@ihqld.com

Brisbane campus: Levels 1 & 2, 379 Queen Street, Brisbane Queensland 4000

7 3220 1011; fax 7 3220 1113

adminbrisbane@ihqld.com

www.ihqld.com

NUMBER OF TEACHERS: approx. 20.

PREFERENCE OF NATIONALITY: none.

QUALIFICATIONS: CELTA or equivalent and minimum 1 year experience.

CONDITIONS OF EMPLOYMENT: 2 year contract. 25 hours per week.

SALARY: Australian award rates.

FACILITIES/SUPPORT: accommodation department provides assistance.

RECRUITMENT: CV and interview. Interviews occasionally conducted overseas.

MILNER INTERNATIONAL COLLEGE OF ENGLISH

379 Hay Street, Perth, Western Australia 6000

+8 9325 5444; fax 8 9221 2392

info@milner.wa.edu.au

www.milner.wa.edu.au

NUMBER OF TEACHERS: 25–35.

PREFERENCE OF NATIONALITY: none. Teachers from the UK and Canada can come on a Working Holiday visa if they are under 30.

QUALIFICATIONS: Degree plus CELTA (or equivalent).

CONDITIONS OF EMPLOYMENT: no contracts for casual teachers. School hours 9am–3pm.

SALARY: there is an award scale for EL teachers ranging from AUS$27 to AUS$35 per hour.

FACILITIES/SUPPORT: teachers find their own accommodation.

RECRUITMENT: CV and interview.

CONTACT: Deborah Pinder, Director of Studies.

NEW ZEALAND

The English language teaching market in New Zealand is fairly similar to Australia; highly developed, although subject to demand fluctuation. Several years ago Chinese students, attracted by the favourable exchange rate and a liberalisation of the immigration regulations governing foreign students, swamped the market and with a CELTA and several years experience, **Mr Roy** found himself in a very strong position:

When I came here a year ago, I've never felt so popular. I was amazed how many jobs I got offered cold-calling with a CV. I entered the country on a visitor visa which, as a British passport holder, gave me six months in the country. Before coming here I had looked on the internet for the addresses of English language schools and I brought a stack of CVs with me too. I just typed 'English language schools New Zealand' into the Google search engine and clicked on the second link www.english-schools.co.nz/ which gave me some useful information. I didn't jump at the first three jobs I was offered in Auckland because I wanted to check out Christchurch, the other main centre for EFL schools. There I was offered a few more jobs and decided to take up a post at Aspect ILA at 116 Worcester Street in the city centre. The students are mainly Chinese, Korean and Japanese but there are notable groups from Taiwan, Switzerland and South America too. My school was helpfully willing to aid me with the visa bureaucracy and now I have residency. My school has a core of staff with open-ended contracts and a larger number of casual/part-time staff including some British people with working holiday visas who work for some months and then continue travelling. The hourly rate is about NZ $26.

Today, demand is not quite so high, as the number of Chinese students has decreased. However there are plenty of Saudis/South Americans etc who cans see the appeal of learning a foreign language in this beautiful country.

Private language schools are regulated by the government agency NZQA (http://www.nzqa.govt.nz/providers/index.do). Their website lists all the educational establishments in New Zealand, but is worth looking through for leads (or search for 'language' to narrow it down). The national organisation of English language teachers, TESOLANZ (www.tesolanz.org.nz/), has a useful links page on their website, whilst English New Zealand (www.englishnewzealand.co.nz) is a group of schools which has its own accreditation process.

British citizens aged between 18 and 30 can work in New Zealand through the working holiday visa scheme (www.immigration.govt.nz/migrant/stream/work/workingholiday).

LIST OF EMPLOYERS

BUCKSWOOD ST NOVA INSTITUTE

7 Auburn Street, PO Box 333–47, Takapuna, Auckland

9 488 7777; fax 9 488 7778

info@novanz.com

www.novanz.com

NUMBER OF TEACHERS: 12.

PREFERENCE OF NATIONALITY: none.

QUALIFICATIONS: TEFL/CELTA minimum. Summer School experience an advantage.

CONDITIONS OF EMPLOYMENT: renewal of contract done term by term. 25 hours per week

SALARY: NZ$27 per hour + 6% holiday pay + meeting allowances.

FACILITIES/SUPPORT: help with finding accommodation given occasionally. Job offer provided for teacher to take to NZ Immigration Service to apply for work visa.

RECRUITMENT: via newspaper and internet. Telephone interviews acceptable if backed up with references. Some UK interviews possible at partner school.

DOMINION ENGLISH SCHOOLS

PO Box 4217, Auckland

+9 377 3280; fax 9 377 3473

dos@dominion.school.nz

Christchurch address: PO Box 3908, Christchurch

dos@dominion.school.nz

www.dominion.school.nz

NUMBER OF TEACHERS: up to 20.

PREFERENCE OF NATIONALITY: none but must be native English speakers.

QUALIFICATIONS: minimum Cambridge/RSA CELTA or Trinity Cert. TESOL or recognised equivalent. Preferably also university degree and experience.

CONDITIONS OF EMPLOYMENT: Flexible contracts. Part time hours 12.5 per week from 9am to 12pm. Full-time hours 25 per week, 9am–4pm.

SALARY: Starting wage approx. NZ$27 per hour.

FACILITIES/SUPPORT: Applicants must hold a valid work visa/permit.

RECRUITMENT: Local interviews essential.

CONTACT: Andrew Hart, Director of Studies.

SELECT EDUCATION AGENCY

Level 4, 48 Greys Avenue, Auckland

+9 300 7408; fax 9 300 7409

EAlly@selecteducation.co.nz

www.selecteducation.com.

NUMBER OF TEACHERS: 60.

PREFERENCE OF NATIONALITY: UK, Ireland, Australia.

QUALIFICATIONS: CELTA or Trinity with one year experience.

CONDITIONS OF EMPLOYMENT: day-to-day employment. Hours 9am–3.30pm.

SALARY: NZ$24 an hour for relief; NZ$35,000–NZ$50,000 per year.

FACILITIES/SUPPORT: teachers must have valid work permit.

CONTACT: Shaun Pulman, International Co-ordinator.

PART 3
APPENDICES

APPENDIX 1 –
CURRENCY CONVERSION CHART
APPENDIX 2 –
EMBASSIES/CONSULATES IN
LONDON AND WASHINGTON
APPENDIX 3 –
BRITISH COUNCIL OFFICES

APPENDIX 1

CURRENCY CONVERSION CHART

COUNTRY	£1	US$1
Argentina	4.9 peso	3.3 peso
Australia	A45$2.40	AUS$1.62
Eurozone	1.18 euro	.80 euro
Bolivia	10.4 boliviano	7 boliviano
Brazil	3.5 real	2.4 real
Brunei	2.2 Brunei dollar	1.53 Brunei dollar
Bulgaria	2.3 lev	1.52 lev
Canada	CAN$1.80	CAN$1.18
Chile	981 peso	664 peso
China	10 renminbi	6.8 renminbi
Colombia	3,482 peso	457 peso
Czech Republic	30.3 koruna	20.5 koruna
Denmark	8.8 kroner	5.9 kroner
Ecuador	US$1.48	1
Egypt	8.2 Egyptian pound	8.5 Egyptian pound
Hong Kong	11.5 HK dollar	7.7 HK dollar
Hungary	319 forint	214 forint
India	74 rupee	50 rupee
Indonesia	17,950 rupiah	12,150 rupiah
Japan	140 yen	95 yen
Kenya	116 shilling	78 shilling
Korea	2,213 won	1,500 won
Malaysia	5.3 ringgit	3.6 ringgit
Mexico	20.6 peso	13.5 peso
Morocco	13 dirham	8.8 dirham
Nepal	118 rupee	80 rupee
New Zealand	NZ$280	NZ$1.90
Norway	10.5 krone	7.1 krone
Peru	4.6 new sol	3.1 new sol
Poland	4.5 zloty	3.0 zloty
Russia	40.7 rouble	27.5 rouble
Saudi Arabia	5.5 riyal	3.75 riyal
Singapore	2.26 Singapore dollar	1.53 Singapore dollar
Slovakia	36 koruna	24 koruna
Sweden	12.2 krona	8.3 krona
Switzerland	1.8 franc	1.2 franc
Taiwan	49 Taiwan dollar	33 Taiwan dollar
Thailand	52 baht	35 baht
Turkey	2,5 lira	1,7 lira
USA	1.48 dollar	
Venezuela	3.2 bolivar	2.1 bolivar

Current exchange rates are printed every Monday in the *Financial Times* and are available on the internet, for example the Universal Currency Converter can be found at www.xe.com/ucc.

APPENDIX 2

EMBASSIES/CONSULATES IN LONDON AND WASHINGTON

Austria: 18 Belgrave Mews West, London SW1X 8HU; ✆ 020-7344 3250; www.bmeia.gv.at/en/embassy/london.html. 3524 International Court NW, Washington DC 20008; ✆ 202-895 6767; www.austria.org.

Belgium: 17 Grosvenor Crescent, London SW1X 7EE; ✆ 020-7470 3700; www.diplomatie.be/london. 3330 Garfield St NW, Washington DC 20008; ✆ 202-333 6900; www.diplobel.us.

Brazil: Consular Section, 6 St. Alban's Street, Haymarket, London SW1Y 4SQ; ✆ 020-7930 9055; www.brazil.org.uk. 3006 Massachusetts Ave NW, Washington, DC 20008; ✆ 202-238 2700; www.brasilemb.org.

Bulgaria: 186-188 Queen's Gate, London SW7 5HL; ✆ 020-7584 9400; www.bulgarianembassy.org.uk. 1621 22nd St NW, Washington, DC 20008; ✆ 202-387 0174; www.bulgaria-embassy.org.

Chile: 12 Devonshire St, London W1G 7DS; ✆ 020-7580 1023. 1732 Massachusetts Ave NW, Washington DC 20036; ✆ 202-785 1746; www.chile-usa.org.

China: Visa Section, 31 Portland Place, London W1B 1QD; ✆ 020-7631 1430; www.chinese-embassy.org.uk. 2300 Connecticut Ave NW, Washington DC 20008; ✆ 202-328 2500; www.china-embassy.org.

Colombia: Consulate General, Wescott House, 3rd Floor, 35 Portland Place, London W1B 1AE; ✆ 020-7637 9893; www.colombianembassy.co.uk. 2118 Leroy Place NW, Washington, DC 20008; ✆ 202-387 8338; www.colombiaemb.org.

Croatia: 21 Conway Street, London W1T 6BN; ✆ 020-7387 2022/1144; http://uk.mvp.hr. 2343 Massachusetts Ave NW, Washington DC 20008; ✆ 202-588 5899; www.croatiaemb.org.

Czech Republic: 26 Kensington Palace Gardens, London W8 4QY; ✆ 020-7243 1115; www.czechembassy.org.uk. 3900 Spring of Freedom St NW, Washington DC 20008; ✆ 202-274 9123; www.mzv.cz/washington.

Ecuador: Flat 3b, 3 Hans Crescent, Knightsbridge, London SW1X 0LS; ✆ 020-7584 2648. 2535 15th St NW, Washington, DC 20009; ✆ 202-234 7166; www.ecuador.org.

Egypt: 2 Lowndes St, London SW1X 9ET; ✆ 020-7235 9719. 3521 International Court NW, Washington DC 20008; ✆ 202-895 5400; www.egyptembassy.net.

Finland: 38 Chesham Place, London SW1X 8HW; ✆ 020-7838 6200; www.finemb.org.uk. 3301 Massachusetts Ave NW, Washington DC 20008; ✆ 202-298 5800; www.finland.org.

France: 21 Cromwell Road, London SW7 2EN; ✆ 020-7073 1200; www.ambafrance-uk.org. 4101 Reservoir Road NW, Washington DC 20007; ✆ 202-944 6200; www.info-france-usa.org.

Germany: 23 Belgrave Square, London SW1X 8PZ; ✆ 020-7824 1300; www.london.diplo.de. 4645 Reservoir Road NW, Washington DC 20007-1998; ✆ 202-298 4000; www.germany-info.org.

Greece: 1A Holland Park, London W11 3TP; ✆ 020-7229 3850; www.greekembassy.org.uk. 2221 Massachusetts Ave NW, Washington DC 20008; ✆ 202-939 1300; www.greekembassy.org.

Hungary: 35 Eaton Place, London SW1X 8BY; ✆ 020-7235 2664; www.mfa.gov.hu/emb/london. 3910 Shoemaker St NW, Washington DC 20008; ✆ 202-362 6730; www.huembwas.org.

India: India House, Aldwych, London WC2B 4NA; ✆ 020-7836 8484; www.hcilondon.net. 2107 Massachusetts Avenue NW, Washington, DC 20008; ✆ 202-939 7000; www.indianembassy.org.

Indonesia: 38 Grosvenor Square, London W1K 2HW; ✆ 020-7499 7661; www.indonesianembassy.org.uk. 2020 Massachusetts Ave NW, Washington DC 20036; ✆ 202-775 5200; www.embassyofindonesia.org.

Italy: 38 Eaton Place, London SW1X 8AN; ✆ 020-7235 9371; www.amblondra.esteri.it. 3000 Whitehaven St NW, Washington DC 20008; ✆ 202-612 4400; www.ambwashingtondc.esteri.it.

Japan: 101-104 Piccadilly, London W1J 7JT; ✆ 020-7465 6500; www.uk.emb-japan.go.jp. 2520 Massachusetts Ave NW, Washington DC 20008; ✆ 202-238 6700/6800; www.us.emb-japan.go.jp.

Korea: 60 Buckingham Gate, London SW1E 6AJ; ✆ 020-7227 5505; www.koreanembassy.org.uk. 2450 Massachusetts Ave NW, Washington, DC 20008; ✆ 202-939 5600;www.dynamic-korea.com.

Laos: 74 Avenue Raymond Poincaré, 75116 Paris, France; ✆ +33 1-45 53 02 98. 2222 S St NW, Washington, DC 20008; ✆ 202-332 6416; www.laoembassy.com.

Latvia: 45 Nottingham Place, London W1U 5LY; ✆ 020-7312 0040; www.london.mfa.gov.lv/en. 4325 17th St NW, 20011 2306 Massachusetts Ave NW, Washington, DC 20008; ✆ 202-328 2840; www.latvia-usa.org.

Lithuania: 84 Gloucester Place, London W1U 6AU; ✆ 020-7486 6401; www.lithuanianembassy.co.uk. 2622 16th St NW, Washington, DC 20009-4202; ✆ 202-234 5860; www.ltembassyus.org.

Malaysia: 45 Belgrave Square, London SW1X 8QT; ✆ 020-7235 8033. 3516 International Court NW, Washington DC 20008; ✆ 202-572 9700.

Malta: Malta House, 36-38 Piccadilly, London W1J 0LE; ✆ 020-7292 4800; www.foreign.gov.mt/london/. 2017 Connecticut Ave NW, Washington, DC 20008; ✆ 202-462 3611.

Mexico: 8 Halkin St, London SW1X 7DW; ✆ 020-7235 6393; www.embamex.co.uk. 1911 Pennsylvania Ave NW, Washington, DC 20006; ✆ 202-728 1600; www.embassyofmexico.org.

Morocco: 49 Queen's Gate Gardens, London SW7 5NE; ✆ 020-7581 5001. 1601 21st St NW, Washington DC 20009; ✆ 202-462 7979.

Netherlands: 38 Hyde Park Gate, London SW7 5DP; ✆ 020-7590 3200; www.netherlands-embassy.org.uk. 4200 Linnean Ave NW, Washington DC 20008; ✆ 2877-388 2443; www.netherlands-embassy.org.

Oman: 167 Queen's Gate, London SW7 5HE; ✆ 020-7225 0001. 2535 Belmont Road NW, Washington DC 20008; ✆ 202-387 1980; www.omani.info.

Peru: 52 Sloane St, London SW1X 9SP; ✆ 020-7838 9223; www.peruembassy-uk.com. 1700 Massachusetts Ave NW, Washington DC 20036; ✆ 202-833 9860; www.peruvianembassy.us.

Poland: 47 Portland Place, London W1B 1JH; ✆ 0870-774 2700; www.polishembassy.org.uk. 2640 16th St NW, Washington, DC 20009; ✆ 202-234 3800; www.polandembassy.org.

Portugal: 3 Portland Place, London W1B 1HR; ✆ 020-7291 3770. 2125 Kalorama Road NW, Washington DC 20008; ✆ 202-328 8610.

Romania: Arundel House, 4 Palace Green, London W8 4QD; ✆ 020-7602 9777; www.londra. mae.ro. 1607 23rd St NW, Washington, DC 20008; ✆ 202-332 4846; www.roembus.org.

Russian Federation: 13 Kensington Palace Gardens, London W8 4QX; ✆ 020-7229 8027. 2650 Wisconsin Ave NW, Washington, DC 20007; ✆ 202-298 5700; www.russian embassy.org.

Saudi Arabia: 30 Charles Street, Mayfair, London W1J 5DZ; ✆ 020-7917 3000; www.mofa. gov.sa. 601 New Hampshire Ave NW, Washington DC 20037; 202-337 4076; www.saudi embassy.net.

Singapore: 9 Wilton Crescent, London SW1X 8SP; ✆ 020-7235 8315; www.mfa.gov.sg/ london. 3501 International Place NW, Washington, DC 20008; ✆ 202-537 3100; www. mfa.gov.sg/washington.

Slovak Republic: 25 Kensington Palace Gardens, London W8 4QY; ✆ 020-7243 0803; www.slovakembassy.co.uk. 3523 International Court NW, Washington, DC 20008; ✆ 202-237 1054; www.slovakembassy-us.org.

Slovenia: 10 Little College Street, London SW1P 3SH; ✆ 020-7222 5700. 2410 California St NW, Washington, DC 20008; ✆ 202-386 6601; www.washington.embassy.si.

Spain: 20 Draycott Place, London SW3 2RZ; ✆ 020-7589 8989. 2375 Pennsylvania Ave NW, Washington, DC 20037; ✆ 202-452 0100; www.spainemb.org.

Sudan: 3 Cleveland Row, St. James's, London SW1A 1DD; ✆ 020-7839 8080; www.sudan-embassy.co.uk. 2210 Massachusetts Ave NW, Washington DC 20008; ✆ 202-338 8565; www.sudanembassy.org.

Sweden: 11 Montagu Place, London W1H 2AL; ✆ 020-7917 6400; www.swedishabroad. com/london. 2900 K St NW, Washington, DC 20007; ✆ 202-467 2600; www.sweden abroad.com.

Switzerland: 16/18 Montagu Place, London W1H 2BQ; ✆ 020-7616 6000; www.swiss embassy.org.uk. 2900 Cathedral Ave NW, Washington DC 20008; ✆ 202-745 7900; www. swissemb.org.

Taiwan: Taipei Representative Office in the UK, 50 Grosvenor Gardens, London SW1W 0EB; ✆ 020-7881 2650; www.taiwanembassy.org/uk. 4201 Wisconsin Ave NW, Washington, DC 20016; ✆ 202-895 1800; www.roc-taiwan.org/us.

Thailand: 29-30 Queen's Gate, London SW7 5JB; ✆ 020-7589 2944; www.thaiembassyuk. org.uk. 1024 Wisconsin Ave NW, Suite 401, Washington DC 20007; ✆ 202-944 3600; www.thaiembdc.org.

Turkey: 43 Belgrave Square, London SW1X 8PA; ✆ 020-7393 0202; www.turkishconsulate. org.uk. 2525 Massachusetts Ave NW, Washington DC 20008; ✆ 202-612 6700; www. turkishembassy.org.

Ukraine: 60 Holland Park, London W11 3SJ; ✆ 020-7727 6312; www.ukremb.org.uk. 3350 M St NW, Washington, DC 20007; ✆ 202-333 7507;www.mfa.gov.ua/usa/en.

Venezuela: Consular Section, 56 Grafton Way, London W1T 5DL; ✆ 020-7387 6727; www. venezlon.co.uk. 1099 30th St NW, Washington, DC 20007; ✆ 202-342 2214; www. embavenez-us.org.

Vietnam: 12-14 Victoria Road, London W8 5RD; ✆ 020-7937 1912; www.vietnamembassy. org.uk. 1233 20th St NW, Suite 400, Washington DC 20037; ✆ 202-861 0737; www. vietnamembassy-usa.org.

For the names of the relevant personnel in the UK, e.g. the Education Attaché, see *The London Diplomatic List* either on the website of the Foreign & Commonwealth Office (www.fco.gov.uk) or in print in a library. For Washington embassies check www.embassy.org.

APPENDIX 3

BRITISH COUNCIL OFFICES

Afghanistan: House 15-17, Kart-e-Parwan, Behind Nadirya High School, Kabul; ✆ 79-0000 102; info.afghanistan britishcouncil.org; www.britishcouncil.org/afghanistan.htm

Albania: Rr. Perlat Rexhepi P197 Ana, Tirana ✆ 4-2240856/7; info@britishcouncil.org.al; www.britishcouncil.org/albania

Argentina: Marcelo T de Alvear 590, 4th Floor, C1058AAF Buenos Aires; ✆ 11-4 114 8600; info@britishcouncil.org.ar; www. britishcouncil.org/argentina.htm

Armenia: Baghramian Avenue 24, Yerevan 0019; ✆ 10-56 99 23; info@britishcouncil.am; www.britishcouncil.org/armenia

Austria: Siebensterngasse 21, 1070 Vienna; ✆ 1-533 2616 70; office@britishcouncil.at; www. brigithcouncil.org/austria

Azerbaijan: 1 Vali Mammadov Street, Icheri Sheher, Baku AZ1000; ✆ 12-497 2013; enquiries@britishcouncil.az; www.britishcouncil.org/azerbaijan

Bahrain: AMA Centre (PO Box 452), 146 Shaikh Salman Highway, Manama 356; ✆ 17-261555; bc.enquiries@britishcouncil.org.bh; www.britishcouncil.org/me-bahrain.htm

Bangladesh: 5 Fuller Road, Dhaka 1000; ✆ 2-861 8905; Dhaka.Enquiries@bd.britishcouncil.org; www.britishcouncil.org/bangladesh. Offices also in Chittagong and Sylhet.

Belgium/Luxembourg: Leopold Plaza, Rue du Trône 108/Troonstraat 108, 1050 Brussels; ✆ 2-227 08 40; englishcourses@britishcouncil.be; www.britishcouncil.org/brussels.htm

Bosnia and Herzegovina: Ljubljanska 9, 71000 Sarajevo; ✆ 33-250220; British.Council@britishcouncil.ba; www.britishcouncil.org/bih.htm

Botswana: British High Commission Building, Queen's Road, The Mall, PO Box 439, Gaborone; ✆ 3953602; general.enquiries@britishcouncil.org.bw

Brazil: Ed. Centro Empresarial Varig, SCN, Quadra 04, Bloco B, Torre Oeste Conjunto 202, 70714-900 Brasilia; ✆ 61-2106 7500; brasilia@britishcouncil.org.br; www.britishcouncil.org/brasil.htm

Bulgaria: 7 Krakra Street, 1504 Sofia; ✆ 2-942 4344; bc.sofia@britishcouncil.bg; www.britishcouncil.org/bulgaria

Burma (Myanmar): 78 Kanna Road, (PO Box 638), Rangoon (Yangon), Union of Myanmar; ✆ 1-254 658/256 290; enquiries@mm.britishcouncil.org; www.britishcouncil.org/burma. Office also in Mandalay.CAMEROON: Avenue Charles de Gaulle, BP 818, Yaoundé; ✆ 22 20 31 72/22 21 16 96; bc-yaounde@britishcouncil.cm

Chile: Eliodoro Yáñez 832, 750-0651 Providencia, Santiago; ✆ 2-410 6900; info@britishcouncil.cl; www.britishcouncil.cl

China: British Embassy, Cultural & Educational Section, 4/f Landmark Building, 8 North Dongsanhuan Road, Chaoyang District, Beijing 100004; ✆ 10-6590 6903; bj@britishcouncil.org.cn; www.britishcouncil.org/china. Offices also in Shanghai, Guangzhou, Chonqqing and Hong Kong (see below).

Colombia: Carrera 9, No 76-49 Piso 5, Bogotá; ✆ 1-325 9090; customer.services@britishcouncil.org.co; www.britishcouncil.org/colombia

Croatia: Illica 12, 10001 Zagreb; ✆ 1-4899 500; zagreb.info@britishcouncil.hr; www.britishcouncil.org/croatia

Cuba: c/o British Embassy, Calle 34 No.702, esq. A 7ma. Ave, Miramar, Havana; ✆ 7-214 2266; information@cu.britishcouncil.org; www.britishcouncil.org/cuba

Cyprus: 1-3 Aristotelous St, CY 1011 Nicosia; ✆ 22-585000; enquiries@cy.britishcouncil.org; www.britishcouncil.org/cyprus

Czech Republic: Bredovsky dvur, Politickych veznu 13, 110 00 Prague 1; ✆ 221 99 1111; info. praha@britishcouncil.cz; www.britishcouncil.org/czechrepublic

Denmark: Gammel Mønt 12.3, 1117 Copenhagen K; ✆ 33-369 400; british.council@british council.dk; www.britishcouncil.org/denmark

Egypt: 192 El Nil Street, Agouza, Cairo; ✆ 2-19789; information@britishcouncil.org.eg; www. britishcouncil.org/egypt

Estonia: Vana-Posti 7, Tallinn 10146. ✆ 0 625 7788; british.council@britishcouncil.ee; www. britishcouncil.org/estonia

Ethiopia: (PO Box 1043), Artistic Building, Adwa Avenue, Addis Ababa; ✆ 11-1550 022; information@et.britishcouncil.org; www.britishcouncil.org/ethiopia

Finland: Urho Kekkosen katu 2 C, 00100 Helsinki; ✆ 9-774 3330; info@britishcouncil.fi; www. britishcouncil.fi

France: 9 rue de Constantine, 75340 Paris Cedex 07; ✆ 1-4955 7300; information@british council.fr; www.britishcouncil.org/france

Georgia: 34 Rustaveli Avenue, Tbilisi; ✆ 32-250407 office@ge.britishcouncil.org

Germany: Alexanderplatz 1, 10178 Berlin; ✆ 30-311 0990; info@britishcouncil.de; www. britishcouncil.de

Ghana: 11 Liberia Road (PO Box GP 771), Accra; ✆ 21-683068; infoaccra@gh.britishcouncil. org; www.britishcouncil.org/ghana

Greece: 17 Kolonaki Square (Plateia Philikis Etairas), 10673 Athens; ✆ 210-369 2333; customerservices@britishcouncil.gr; www.britishcouncil.org/greece

Hong Kong: 3 Supreme Court Road, Admiralty, Hong Kong; ✆ 2913 5100; enquiries@british council.org.hk; www.britishcouncil.org/hongkong

Hungary: Benczúr Utca 26, 1068 Budapest; ✆ 1-483 42020; information@britishcouncil.hu; www.britishcouncil.org/hungary

India: British High Commission, 17 Kasturba Gandhi Marg, New Delhi 110 001; ✆ 11-23711401; delhi.enquiry@in.britishcouncil.org; www.britishcouncil.org/india. Offices also in many other Indian cities.

Indonesia: Gedung Bursa Efek Jakarta, Tower 2, 16th Floor, Jalan Jenderal Sudirman Kav 52-53, Jakarta 12190; ✆ 21-515 5561; information@britishcouncil.or.id; www.britishcouncil. org/indonesia

Iran: North Entrance, British Embassy Compound, Shariati Street, Qholhak, Tehran 193 96; ✆ 21-2200 1222; info@ir.britishcouncil.org; www.britishcouncil.org/iran

Israel: Crystal House, 12 Hahilazon Street, Ramat Gan 52136; ✆ 3-611 3600; info@british council.org.il; www.britishcouncil.org/israel

Italy: Palazzo de Drago, Via delle Quattro Fontane 20, 00184 Rome; ✆ 06-478 141; studyand cultureuk@britishcouncil.it; www.britishcouncil.org/italy. Offices also in Milan and Naples.

Japan: 1-2 Kagurazaka, Shinjuku-ku, Tokyo 162-0825; ✆ 3-3235 8031; enquiries@british council.or.jp; www.britishcouncil.org/japan. Office also in Osaka.

Jordan: Rainbow St, Off First Circle, Jabal Amman, PO Box 634, Amman 11118; ✆ 6-4636147/8; Info@britishcouncil.org.jo; www.britishcouncil.org/jordan

Kazakhstan-Kyrgyzstan: Republic Square 13, 050013 Almaty; ✆ 327-272 01 11; general@ kz.britishcouncil.org; www.britishcouncil.org/kazakhstan. Office also in Astana.

Kenya: Upperhill Road, PO Box 40751, 00100 Nairobi; ✆ 20-283 6000; information@british council.or.ke; www.britishcouncil.org/kenya. Office also in Mombasa.

Korea: 4F, Hungkuk Life Insurance Building, 226 Shinmunro 1-ga, Jongro-gu, Seoul 110-786; ✆ 2-3702 0600; info@britishcouncil.or.kr; www.britishcouncil.org/korea

Kosovo: Perandori Justinian 6, Qyteza Pejton, 10000 Prishtina; ✆ 38-243292; info@ ks.britishcouncil.org; www.britishcouncil.org/kosovo

Kuwait: 2 Al Arabi St, Mansouriya, PO Box 345, Safat 13004; ✆ 252 0067; info@ kw.britishcouncil.org; www.britishcouncil.org/me-kuwait.htm

Latvia: Blaumana iela 5a-2, Riga LV-1011 ✆ 6-728 1730; mail@britishcouncil.lv.; www. britishcouncil.org/latviaLEBANON: Berytech Technology & Health, Mathaf/Sodeco Street, Damascus Road, Beirut; ✆ 1-428900; general.enquiries@lb.britishcouncil.org; www. britishcouncil.org/lebanon

Lithuania: Jogailos 4, LT - 01116 Vilnius, Lithuania; ✆ 5-264 4890; mail@britishcouncil.lt; www.britishcouncil.lt

Macedonia: Bulevar Goce Delcev 6, PO Box 562, 1000 Skopje; ✆ 2-313 5035; info@british council.org.mk; www.britishcouncil.org/macedonia

Malawi: PO Box 30222, Lilongwe 3; ✆ 1-773244; info@britishcouncil.org.mw

Malaysia: Ground Floor, West Block, Wisma Selangor Dredging, 142 C Jalan Ampang, 50450 Kuala Lumpur; ✆ 3-2723 7900; kualalumpur@britishcouncil.org.my; www.britishcouncil. org/malaysia

Malta: Exchange Buildings, Republic Street, Valetta VLT 05, Malta; ✆ 2122 6377; info@british council.org.mt; www.britishcouncil.org/malta

Mauritius: Royal Road, Rose Hill; ✆ 403 0200; general.enquiries@mu.britishcouncil.org

Mexico: Lope de Vega 316, Col. Chapultepec Morales, , 11570 Mexico City DF; ✆ 55-5263 1900; info@britishcouncil.org.mx; www.britishcouncil.org/mexico

Montenegro: Bulevar Svetog Petra Cetinjskog 149/3, 81000 Podgorica; ✆ 20-205 440; pginfo@britishcouncil.org.yu; www.britishcouncil.org/montenegro

Morocco: 36 rue de Tanger, BP 427, Rabat; ✆ 37-760836; rabat.info@britishcouncil.org.ma; www.britishcouncil.org/morocco. Office also in Casablanca

Mozambique: Rua John Issa 226, Maputo; ✆ 1-355000; general.enquiries@britishcouncil. org.mz

Namibia: 1-5 Fidel Castro Street, Windhoek; ✆ 61-226 776; infona@britishcouncil.org

Nepal: PO Box 640, Lainchaur, Kathmandu; ✆ 1-4410 798; general.enquiry@britishcouncil. org.np; www.britishcouncil.org/nepal

Netherlands: Weteringschans 85a, 1017 RZ Amsterdam; ✆ 20-550 6060; information@ britishcouncil.nl; www.britishcouncil.org/netherlands

Norway: Storgaten 10B, 0155 Oslo; ✆ 22-396 190; british.council@britishcouncil.no; www. britishcouncil.org/norway

Oman: Road 1, Medinat al Sultan, Qaboos West, Muscat, PO Box 73, Postal Code 115; ✆ 24681000; bc.muscat@om.britishcouncil.org; www.britishcouncil.org/me-oman. htmPAKISTAN: PO Box 1135, Islamabad; ✆ 51-111 424 424; info@britishcouncil.org.pk; www.britishcouncil.org/pakistan.

Palestinian Territories: 31 Nablus Road, PO Box 19136, Jerusalem 97200; ✆ 2-626 7111; british.council@ps.britishcouncil.org; www.britishcouncil.org/ps

Philippines: 10th Floor, Taipan Place, F Ortigas Jr Avenue, Ortigas Centre, Pasig City 1605; ✆ 2-914 1011-14; britishcouncil@britishcouncil.org.ph; www.britishcouncil.org/philippines

Poland: Al Jerozolimskie 59, 00-697 Warsaw; ✆ 22-695 5900; bc.warsaw@britishcouncil.pl; www.britishcouncil.org/poland

Portugal: Rua Luis Fernandes, 1-3, 1249-062 Lisbon; ☏ 21-321 4500; lisbon.enquiries@pt.britishcouncil.org; www.britishcouncil.org/portugal

Qatar: 93 Al Sadd Street, PO Box 2992, Doha; ☏ 425 1888; general.enquiries@qa.britishcouncil.org; www.britishcouncil.org/me-qatar.htm

Romania: Calea Dorobantilor 14, 010572 Bucharest; ☏ 21-307 9600; contact@britishcouncil.ro; www.britishcouncil.org/romania

Russia: Ulitsa Nikoloyamskaya 1, Moscow 109189; ☏ 495-287 1800; moscow@britishcouncil.ru; www.britishcouncil.org/russia.htm

Saudi Arabia: Office No. C-14, 3rd Floor, Al Fazary Square, Diplomatic Quarter, (PO Box 58012), Riyadh 11594; ☏ 1-483 1818; enquiry.riyadh@sa.britishcouncil.org; www.britishcouncil.org/me-saudiarabia.htm. Offices also in Jeddah and Khobar.SENEGAL: Rue AAB-68, Amitié Zone A et B, CB 6232, Dakar; ☏ 869 2700; information@britishcouncil.sn; www.britishcouncil.org/senegal

Serbia and Montenegro: Terazije 8/1, 11000 Belgrade; ☏ 11 3023 817; info@britishcouncil.org.yu.

Serbia: Terazije 8/1, 11000 Belgrade; ☏ 11-3023 800/817; info@britishcouncil.org.yu; www.britishcouncil.org/serbia

Sierra Leone: Tower Hill, PO Box 124, Freetown; ☏ 22 222 223; enquiry@sl.britishcouncil.org.

Singapore: 30 Napier Road, Singapore 258509; ☏ 6473 1111; contact@britishcouncil.org.sg; www.britishcouncil.org/singapore

Slovakia: Panská 17, PO Box 68, 81499 Bratislava; ☏ 2-5443 1074; info@britishcouncil.sk; www.britishcouncil.org/slovakia

Slovenia: Tivoli Center, Tivolska 30, 1000 Ljubljana; ☏ 1-300 2030; info@britishcouncil.si; www.britishcouncil.org/slovenia

South Africa: Ground Floor, Forum 1, Braampark, 33 Hoofd Street, Braamfontein 2017; ☏ 11 718 4300; information@britishcouncil.org.za.

Spain: Paseo del General Martínez, Campos 31, 28010 Madrid; ☏ 91-337 3500; madrid@britishcouncil.es; www.britishcouncil.org/spain

Sri Lanka: 49 Alfred House Gardens, PO Box 753, Colombo 3; ☏ 11-452 1500/1521; enquiries.cmb@britishcouncil.org; www.britishcouncil.org/srilanka

Sudan: 14 Abu Sinn Street, PO Box 1253, Khartoum; ☏ 183-777310; info@sd.britishcouncil.org; www.britishcouncil.org/sudan

Sweden: c/o British Embassy, Skarpogatan 6-8, PO Box 27819, S- 11593 Stockholm; ☏ 8-671 3110; info@britishcouncil.se; www.britishcouncil.org/sweden

Switzerland: Sennweg 2, PO Box 532, CH 3000 Bern 9; ☏ 31-301 1473; britishcouncil@britishcouncil.ch; www.britishcouncil.org/switzerland

Syria: Maysaloun Street, Shaalan, PO Box 33105, Damascus; ☏ 11-3310631; info@sy.britishcouncil.org; www.britishcouncil.org/syria

Taiwan: 2F-1, 106 Xin Yi Rd., Sec. 5, Taipei 110; ☏ 2-8722 1000; enquiries@britishcouncil.org.tw; www.britishcouncil.org/taiwan

Tanzania: Samora Avenue/Ohio Street, PO Box 9100, Dar Es Salaam; ☏ 22-211 6574; info@britishcouncil.or.tz; www.britishcouncil.org/tanzania

Thailand: 254 Chulalongkorn Soi 64, Siam Square, Phayathai Road, Pathumwan, Bangkok 10330; ☏ 2-652 5480; info@britishcouncil.or.th; www.britishcouncil.org/thailand

Tunisia: 87 Avenue Mohamed V, 1002 Tunis; ☏ 71-848588; info@tn.britishcouncil.org; www.britishcouncil.org/tunisia

Turkey: PO Box 16, Besiktas, Istanbul; ☏ 212-355 5657; customer.services@britishcouncil.org.tr; www.britishcouncil.org/turkey

Uganda: Rwenzori Courts, Plot 2 and 4a, Nakasero Road, PO Box 7070, Kampala; ✆ 41 234 737; emailinfo@britishcouncil.or.ug.

Ukraine: 4/12 Hryhoriya Skovorody, Kyiv 04070; ✆ 44-490 5600; enquiry@britishcouncil.org.ua; www.britishcouncil.org/ukraine

United Arab Emirates: Villa no 7, Al Nasr Street, Al Khaldiay District, (PO Box 46523), Abu Dhabi; ✆ 4 313 5300; information@ae.britishcouncil.org.

United States of America: British Embassy, 3100 Massachusetts Avenue, NW Washington DC 20008; ✆ 1 800 488 2235.

Uzbekistan: University of World Languages Building, 11 Mirobod Street, Tashkent 700031; ✆ 71-140 0660; bc-tashkent@britishcouncil.uz; www.britishcouncil.org/uzbekistan

Venezuela: Torre Credicard, Piso 3, Av. Principal de El Bosque, Chacaito 1050, Caracas; ✆ 212-952 9965; information@britishcouncil.org.ve; www.britishcouncil.org/venezuela

Vietnam: 40 Cat Linh St, Hanoi; ✆ 4-843 6780; bchanoi@britishcouncil.org.vn; www.britishcouncil.org/vietnam

Yemen: 3rd Floor, Administrative Tower, Sana'a Trade Center, Algiers St, PO Box 2157, Sana'a; ✆ 1-448 356; information@ye.britishcouncil.org; www.britishcouncil.org/me-yemen.htm

Zambia: Heroes Place, Cairo Road, Lusaka; ✆ 1 228332; info@britishcouncil.org.zm.

www.crimsonpublishing.co.uk